Computer Netwo...

A Top-Down Approach Featuring the Internet

preliminary edition

Computer Networking

A Top-Down Approach Featuring the Internet

preliminary edition

James F. Kurose University of Massachusetts, Amherst

Keith W. Ross Institute Eurécom

 **ADDISON-WESLEY**

An imprint of Addison Wesley Longman, Inc.

Reading, Massachusetts • Menlo Park, California
New York • Harlow, England • Don Mills, Ontario
Sydney • Mexico City • Madrid • Amsterdam

Senior Acquisitions Editor	Susan Hartman
Assistant Editor	Lisa Kalner
Project Managers	The Publisher's Group
	Trillium Project Management
Executive Marketing Manager	Michael Hirsch
Compositor	Michael and Sigrid Wile
Technical Artist	The Aardvark Group
Copyeditor	Roberta Lewis/Donald Lafferty
Proofreading	Trillium Project Management
Cover Designer	Joyce Cosentino

Library of Congress Cataloging-in-Publication Data

Ross, Keith W., 1956–
    Computer networking : a top-down approach featuring the Internet / Keith W. Ross,
James F. Kurose.—Preliminary ed.
        p.   cm.
    Includes bibliographical references and index.
    ISBN 0-201-61274-7
    1. Computer networks.   2. Internet (Computer network)   I. Kurose, James F.   II. Title.
TK5105.5.R722 2000
004.6—dc21   99-048057
                                                                              CIP

Many of the designations used by manufacturers and sellers to distinguish their products are claimed as trademarks. Where those designations appear in this book, and Addison-Wesley was aware of a trademark claim, the designations have been printed in initial caps or all caps.

The programs and applications presented in this book have been included for their instructional value. They have been tested with care but are not guaranteed for any purpose. The publisher and author do not offer any warranties or representations, nor do they accept any liabilities with respect to the programs or applications.

Cover image © 1999 PhotoDisc, Inc.

Access the latest information about Addison-Wesley titles from our World Wide Web site: http://www.awlonline.com

This book was typeset in FrameMaker 5.5 on a Macintosh G3. The font families used were Utopia and Franklin Gothic. It was printed on New Era Matte.

1 2 3 4 5 6 7 8 9 10–CRS–030201009

To MOTL, and our three precious
ones—Chris, Charlie, and Nina

JK

To my wife, Véronique, and our
trois petits pois, Cécile, Claire, and Katie

KWR

Preface

Welcome to the preliminary edition of the textbook, Computer Networking: A Top-Down Approach Featuring the Internet. We (Jim Kurose, Keith Ross, and Addison Wesley Longman) like to believe that this textbook offers a fresh approach to the teaching of computer networking. Why is a fresh approach needed, you ask? In recent years we have witnessed two revolutionary changes in the field of networking, changes that are not reflected in the networking texts published in the 1980s and 1990s. First, the Internet has taken over the universe of computer networking. Any serious discussion about computer networking today has to be done with the Internet in mind. Second, over the past ten years the biggest growth area has been in networking services and applications, which can be seen with the emergence of the Web, ubiquitous use of e-mail services, audio and video streaming, Internet phone, and Internet commerce. These revolutionary changes in the field of computer networking call for a rethinking of the topics that should be covered in a networking text, and a rethinking of how these topics should be organized.

WHAT IS UNIQUE ABOUT THIS TEXTBOOK?

As indicated by the title, this textbook has an Internet focus. Most of the existing textbooks give significant weight to a variety of telecommunications networks, and treat the Internet as just one of many networking technologies. We instead put Internet protocols in the spotlight, and use the Internet protocols as a primary vehicle for studying some of the more fundamental computer networking concepts. But why put the Internet in the spotlight, why not some other networking technology such as ATM? First, computer networking is now synonymous with the Internet. This wasn't the case five-to-ten years ago, when there was a lot of talk about ATM LANs and applications directly interfacing with ATM (without passing through TCP/IP). But now we have reached the point where just about all data traffic is carried over the Internet (or intranets). There is only one other class of networks that competes with the Internet, namely, circuit-switched telephone networks. Although the majority of voice traffic is carried over the telephone networks, networking equipment manufacturers and telephone company operators are currently preparing for a major migration of the telephone traffic to the Internet.

The second reason for spotlighting the Internet is that most networking students have already had significant "hands on" experience with the Internet (at the very least, surfing the Web and sending e-mail). We have found that modern-day students in computer science and electrical engineering, being intensive users of the Internet, are enormously curious about what is under the hood of the Internet. Thus, it is easy for an instructor to get students excited about the subject when using the Internet as the guiding vehicle.

Because our book has an Internet focus, it is organized around a five-layer Internet architecture rather than around the more traditional seven-layer OSI architecture. These five layers consist of the application, transport, network, link, and physical layers.

Another unique feature of this book is that the subject matter is organized top-down. As just indicated, this text—as almost all computer networking textbooks do—uses a layered architectural model to organize the subject matter. However, unlike other texts, this text begins at the application layer and works its way down the protocol stack. The rationale behind this top-down organization is that once one understands the applications, one can then understand the network services needed to support these applications. One can then, in turn, examine the various ways in which such services might be provided and implemented by a network architecture. Covering applications early thus provides motivation for the remainder of the text.

An early emphasis on application-layer issues differs from the approaches taken in most other texts, which have only a small (or nonexistent) amount of material on network applications, their requirements, application-layer paradigms (e.g., client/server), and the application programming interfaces. Studying application-layer protocols first allows students to develop an intuitive feel for protocols in the context of the network applications which they use daily (e.g., the Web, e-mail, and FTP). Furthermore, the inclusion of a significant amount of material at the application layer reflects our own belief that there has been, and will continue to be, a significant growth in emphasis (in the research community and in industry) in the higher levels of network architecture. These higher layers—as exemplified by the Web as an application layer protocol—is the true "growth area" in computer networking.

This textbook also contains material on application programming development—material not covered in depth by any other introductory computer networking textbook. (While there are books devoted to network programming, they are not introductory networking textbooks.) There are several compelling reasons for including this material. First, anyone wanting to write a network application must know about socket programming—the material is thus of great practical interest. Second, early exposure to socket programming is valuable for pedagogical reasons as well—it allows students to write actual network application-level programs and gain first-hand experience with many of the issues involved in having multiple geographically distributed processes communicate. We present the material on application programming in Java rather than in C, because socket programming in Java is simpler, and allows students to quickly "see the forest for the trees."

ADDRESSING THE PRINCIPLES

The field of networking is now mature enough that a number of fundamentally important issues can be identified. For example, in the transport layer, the fundamental issues include reliable communication over an unreliable channel, connection establishment/teardown and handshaking, congestion and flow control, and multiplexing. In the network layer, two fundamentally important issues are how to find "good" paths between two routers, and how to deal with large, heterogeneous systems. In the data link layer, a fundamental problem is how to share a multiple access channel. This text identifies fundamental networking issues as well as approaches towards addressing these issues. We believe that the combination of using the Internet to get the student's foot in door and then emphasizing the issues and solution approaches will allow the student to quickly understand just about any networking technology. For example, reliable data transfer is a fundamental issue in both the transport and data link layer. Various mechanisms (e.g., error detection, use of timeouts and retransmit, positive and negative acknowledgments, and forward error correction) have been designed to provide reliable data transfer service. Once one understands these approaches, the data transfer aspects of protocols like TCP and various reliable multicast protocols can been seen as case studies illustrating these mechanisms.

ONLINE VERSION: www.awlonline.com/kurose-ross

Log into the online version of the text as:

User name: networking

Password: jupiter

Perhaps the most unique and innovative feature of this textbook is that it is also available online (accessible through a Web browser). We believe that our online format has several things going for it. First, an online text can be accessed from any browser in the world, so a student (or any other reader) can gain access to the book at any time from any place. Second, as all of us Internet enthusiasts know, much of the best material describing the intricacies of the Internet is in the Internet itself. The hyperlinks of the online version, embedded in a coherent context, provide the reader direct access to some of the best sites relating to computer networks and Internet protocols. The links do not only point to RFCs but also to sites that are more pedagogic in nature, including home-brewed pages on particular aspects of Internet technology and articles appearing in online trade magazines. The online version also includes many interactive features, including direct access to the Traceroute program, direct access to search engines for Internet Drafts, Java applets that animate difficult concepts, a newsgroup in which the topics of this book are discussed, and (in the near future) direct access to streaming audio. Being online enables us to use more fonts and colors (both within the text and in diagrams), making the text both perky and cheerful. Finally, an online format will allow us to frequently release new editions, which will enable the text to keep pace with this rapidly changing field.

The online version is ideally suited for asynchronous online courses. Such courses are particularly appealing to students who commute to school or have difficulty scheduling classes due to course time conflicts. The authors already have significant experience in leading asynchronous online courses, using an earlier draft of this online text. They have found that one successful asynchronous format is to have students do weekly asynchronous readings (and listenings!) and to have students participate in weekly newsgroup discussions about the readings. Students can have a virtual presence by sharing the URLs of their personal Web pages with the rest of the class. Students can even collaborative on joint projects, such as research papers and network application development, asynchronously over the Internet. If you are interested in learning more about asynchronous online learning, please visit the Asynchronous Learning Network site at http://www.aln.org.

THE TARGET AUDIENCE

This textbook is for a first course on computer networking. It can be used in both computer science and electrical engineering departments. In terms of programming languages, the book only assumes that the student has experience with C, C++, or Java. A student who has programmed only in C or C++ and not Java should not have any difficulty following the application programming material, even though this material is presented in a Java context. Although this book is more analytical than many of the other computer networking texts, it rarely uses any mathematical concepts that are not taught in high school. In a few subsections we make use of some very elementary probability. We have made a deliberate effort to avoid using any advanced calculus, probability, or stochastic process concepts. The book is therefore appropriate for undergraduate courses and for first-year graduate courses. This book should also be useful to practitioners in the telecommunications industry.

PRELIMINARY EDITION AND ACCOMPANYING MATERIALS

The current version of the book is a preliminary edition. Much of the material in this preliminary version has been tested with University of Pennsylvania, Eurecom, and University of Massachusetts students. Nevertheless, the current preliminary edition should be viewed as a draft edition that is being made available for the Spring 2000 semester use. A fully polished hardback first edition of the textbook (with multicolor graphics, and a slightly different layout) will be available internationally in the summer of 2000.

In addition to the Web the site, the authors will make available PowerPoint presentations for each of the chapters. Instructors will be able to download the presentations directly from the book's Web site. By making the presentations of all of the chapters available, instructors should be able to easily switch to this new textbook. A solutions manual will also be available for the homework problems. All materials can be found at http://www.awlonline.com/kurose-ross. The solutions manual is for instructors only. It is available through your Addison-Wesley sales representative or by sending an email message to aw.cse@awl.com.

We are very interested in feedback about the preliminary edition of the textbook, about the online version, and about the accompanying materials. If you have comments, send e-mail to kurose@cs.umass.edu, ross@eurecom.fr, or to susan.hartman@awl.com.

ACKNOWLEDGEMENTS

Lots of people have given us invaluable help on this project since it began in 1996, and/or have been influential in shaping our thoughts on how to best organize and teach a networking course. For now, we simply say "Thanks!" and list some of the names alphabetically:

Paul Amer, Daniel Brushteyn, John Daigle, Wu-chi Feng, Albert Huang, Sugih Jamin, Jussi Kangasharju, Hyojin Kim, Roberta Lewis, William Liang, Willis Marti, Deep Medhi, Erich Nahum, Jitendra Padhye, George Polyzos, Martin Reisslein, Despina Saparilla, Henning Schulzrinne, Mischa Schwartz, Subin Shrestra, Don Towsley, David Turner, Raj Yavatkar, Yechiam Yemini, Ellen Zegura, Lixia Zhang, Shuchun Zhang.

We would also like to thank all of the UPenn, UMass, and Eurecom students who have given us their feedback about earlier drafts.

Contents

Chapter 1 | Computer Networks and the Internet

1.1 WHAT IS THE INTERNET?

In this book we use the public Internet, a specific computer network (and one which probably most readers have used), as our principle vehicle for discussing computer networking protocols. But what is the Internet? We would like to give you a one-sentence definition of the Internet, a definition that you can take home and share with your family and friends. Alas, the Internet is very complex, both in terms of its hardware and software components, as well as the services it provides.

1.1.1 A Nuts and Bolts Description

Instead of giving a one-sentence definition, let's try a more descriptive approach. There are a couple of ways to do this. One way is to describe the nuts and bolts of the Internet, that is, the basic hardware and software components that make up the Internet. Another way is to describe the Internet in terms of a networking infrastructure that provides services to distributed applications. Let's begin with the nuts-and-bolts description, using Figure 1.1 to illustrate our discussion.

The public Internet is a world-wide **computer network,** that is, a network that interconnects millions of computing devices throughout the world. Most of these computing devices are traditional desktop PCs, Unix-based workstations, and so called "servers" that store and transmit information such as Web (WWW) pages and e-mail messages. Increasingly, nontraditional computing devices such as Web TVs, mobile computers, pagers, and toasters are being connected to the Internet. (Toasters are not the only rather unusual devices to have been hooked up to the Internet; see the The Future of the Living Room [Greenberg 1997].) In the Internet jargon, all of these devices are called **hosts** or **end systems.** The Internet applications with which many of us are familiar, such as the Web and e-mail, are **network application programs** that run on such end systems. We will look into Internet end systems in more detail in Section 1.3 and then delve deeply into the study of network applications in Chapter 2.

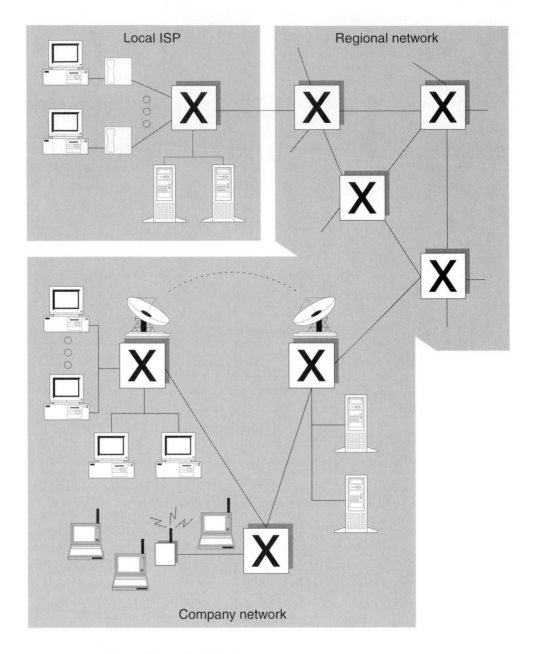

FIGURE 1.1 Some "pieces" of the Internet

End systems, as well as most other "pieces" of the Internet, run **protocols** that control the sending and receiving of information within the Internet. **TCP** (the Transmission Control Protocol) and **IP** (the Internet Protocol) are two of the most important protocols in the Internet. The Internet's principle protocols are collectively known as **TCP/IP protocols.** We begin looking into protocols in Section 1.2. But that's just a start—much of this entire book is concerned with computer network protocols!

End systems are connected together by **communication links.** We'll see in Section 1.5 that there are many types of communication links. Links are made up of different types of **physical media,** including coaxial cable, copper wire, fiber optics, and radio spectrum. Different links can transmit data at different rates. The link transmission rate is often called the **link bandwidth,** and is typically measured in bits/second.

Usually, end systems are not directly attached to each other via a single communication link. Instead, they are indirectly connected to each other through intermediate switching devices known as **routers.** A router takes information arriving on one of its incoming communication links and then forwards that information on one of its outgoing communication links. The **IP protocol** specifies the format of the information that is sent and received among routers and end systems. The path that transmitted information takes from the sending end system, through a series of communications links and routers, to the receiving end system is known as a **route** or **path** through the network. We introduce routing in more detail in Section 1.4, and study the algorithms used to determine routes, as well as the internal structure of a router itself, in Chapter 4.

Rather than provide a *dedicated* path between communicating end systems, the Internet uses a technique known as **packet switching** that allows multiple communicating end systems to share a path, or parts of a path, at the same time. We will see that packet switching can often use a link more "efficiently" than circuit switching (where each pair of communicating end systems gets a dedicated path). The earliest ancestors of the Internet were the first packet-switched networks; today's public Internet is the *grande dame* of all existing packet-switched networks.

The Internet is really a **network of networks.** That is, the Internet is an interconnected set of privately and publicly owned and managed networks. Any network connected to the Internet must run the IP protocol and conform to certain naming and addressing conventions. Other than these few constraints, however, a network operator can configure and run its network (that is, its little "piece" of the Internet) however it chooses. Because of the universal use of the IP protocol in the Internet, the IP protocol is sometimes referred to as the **Internet dial tone.**

The topology of the Internet, that is, the structure of the interconnection among the various pieces of the Internet, is **loosely hierarchical.** Roughly speaking, from bottom-to-top, the hierarchy consists of end systems connected to local **Internet service providers (ISPs)** though **access networks.** An access network may be a so-called local area network within a company or university, a dial telephone line with a modem, or a high-speed cable-based or phone-based access network. Local ISPs are in turn connected to regional ISPs, which are in turn connected to national and international ISPs. The national and international ISPs are connected together at the highest tier in the hierarchy. New tiers and branches (that is, new networks, and new networks of networks) can be added just as a new piece of Lego can be attached to an existing Lego construction. In the first half of 1996, approximately 40,000 *new* networks were added to the Internet [Network 1996]—an astounding growth rate.

At the technical and developmental level, the Internet is made possible through creation, testing, and implementation of **Internet standards.** These standards are developed by the Internet Engineering Task Force (IETF). The IETF standards documents are called **RFCs** (request for comments). RFCs started out as general request for comments (hence the name) to resolve architecture problems that faced the precursor to the Internet. RFCs, though not formally standards, have evolved to the point where they are cited as such. RFCs tend to be quite technical and detailed. They define protocols such as TCP, IP, HTTP (for the Web) and SMTP (for open-standards e-mail). There are more than 2,000 different RFCs.

The public Internet (that is, the global network of networks discussed above) is the network that one typically refers to as *the* Internet. There are also many private networks, such as certain corporate and government networks, whose hosts are not accessible from (that is, they can not exchange messages with) hosts outside of that private network. These private networks are often referred to as **intranets,** as they often use the same "internet technology" (for example, the same types of host, routers, links, protocols, and standards) as the public Internet.

1.1.2   A Service Description

The discussion above has identified many of the pieces that make up the Internet. Let's now leave the nuts-and-bolts description and take a more abstract, service-oriented view:

- The Internet allows **distributed applications** running on its end systems to exchange data with each other. These applications include remote login, file transfer, electronic mail, audio and video streaming, real-time audio and video conferencing, distributed games, the World Wide Web, and much much more [AT&T Apps 1998]. It is worth emphasizing that the Web is not a separate network but rather just one of many distributed applications that use the communication services provided by the Internet. The Web *could* also run over a network besides the Internet. One reason that the Internet is the communication medium of choice for the Web, however, is that no other existing packet-switched network connects more than 43 million [Network 1999] computers together and has 100 million or so users [Almanac 1998]. (By the way, determining the number of computers hooked up to the Internet is a very difficult task, as no one is responsible for maintaining a list of who's connected. When a new network is added to the Internet, its administrators do not need to report which end systems are connected to that network. Similarly, an exiting network does not report its changes in connected end systems to any central authority.)

- The Internet provides two services to its distributed applications: a **connection-oriented service** and a **connectionless service.** Loosely speaking, connection-oriented service guarantees that data transmitted from a sender to a receiver will eventually be delivered to the receiver in-order and in its entirety. Connectionless service does not make any guarantees about eventual delivery. Typically, a distributed application makes use of one or the other of these two services and not both. We examine these two different services in Section 1.3 and in great detail in Chapter 3.

- Currently the Internet does not provide a service that makes promises about *how long* it will take to deliver the data from sender to receiver. And except for increasing your access bit rate to your Internet service provider, you currently cannot obtain better service (for example, shorter delays) by paying more—a state of affairs that some (particularly Americans!) find odd. We'll take a look at state-of-the art Internet research that is aimed at changing this situation in Chapter 6.

Our second description of the Internet—in terms of the services it provides to distributed applications—is a nontraditional, but important, one. Increasingly, advances in the "nuts-and-bolts" components of the Internet are being driven by the needs of new applications. So it's important to keep in mind that the Internet is an *infrastructure* in which new applications are being constantly invented and deployed.

We have given two descriptions of the Internet, one in terms of the hardware and software components that make up the Internet, the other in terms of the services it provides to distributed applications. But perhaps you are even more confused as to what the Internet is. What is packet switching, TCP/IP, and connection-oriented service? What are routers? What kinds of communication links are present in the Internet? What is a distributed application? What does the Internet have to do with children's toys? If you feel a bit overwhelmed by all of this now, don't worry—the purpose of this book is to introduce you to both the nuts and bolts of the Internet, as well as the principles that govern how and why it works. We will explain these important terms and questions in the subsequent sections and chapters.

1.1.3 Some Good Hyperlinks

As every Internet researcher knows, some of the best and most accurate information about the Internet and its protocols is not in hard-copy books, journals, or magazines. The best stuff about the Internet is in the Internet itself! Of course, there's really too much material to sift through, and sometimes the gems are few and far between. Below, we list a few generally excellent Websites for network- and Internet-related material. Throughout the book, we will also present links to relevant, high quality URL's that provide background, original, or advanced material related to the particular topic under study. Here is a set of key links that you will want to consult while you proceed through this book:

- Internet Engineering Task Force (IETF) http://www.ietf.org/: The IETF is an open international community concerned with the development and operation of the Internet and its architecture. The IETF was formally established by the Internet Architecture Board (IAB) http://www.isi.edu/iab in 1986. The IETF meets three times a year; much of its ongoing work is conducted via mailing lists by working groups. Typically, based upon previous IETF proceedings, working groups will convene at meetings of the IETF to discuss the work of the IETF working groups. The IETF is administered by the Internet Society, http://www.isoc.org, whose Website contains lots of high-quality, Internet-related material.

- The World Wide Web Consortium (W3C) http://www.w3.org/Consortium/: The W3C was founded in 1994 to develop common protocols for the evolution of the World Wide Web. This an outstanding site with fascinating information on emerging Web technologies, protocols and standards.

- The Association for Computing Machinery (ACM) http://www.acm.org and the Institute of Electrical and Electronics Engineers (IEEE) http://www.ieee.org: These are the two main international professional societies that have technical conferences, magazines, and journals in the networking area. The ACM Special Interest Group in Data Communications (SIGCOMM), http://www.acm.org/sigcomm, the IEEE Communications Society http://www.comsoc.org, and the IEEE Computer Society http://www.computer.org/ are the groups within these bodies whose efforts are most closely related to networking.

- Connected: An Internet Encyclopedia http://www.FreeSoft.org/CIE/index.htm: An attempt to take the Internet tradition of open, free protocol specifications, merge it with a 1990s Web presentation, and produce a readable and useful reference to the technical operation of the Internet. The site contains material on over 100 Internet topics.

- Data communications tutorials from the online magazine Data Communications http://www.data.com: One of the better magazines for data communications technology. The site includes many excellent tutorials.

- Media History Project http://www.mediahistory.com/: You may be wondering how the Internet got started. Or you may wonder how electrical communications got started in the first place. And you may even wonder about what preceded electrical communications! Fortunately, the Web contains an abundance of excellent resources available on these subjects. This site promotes the study of media history from petroglyths to pixels. It covers the history of digital media, mass media, electrical media, print media, and even oral and scribal culture.

1.2   WHAT IS A PROTOCOL?

Now that we've got a bit of a feel for what the Internet is, let's consider another important buzzword in computer networking: "protocol." What *is* a protocol? What does a protocol *do*? How would you recognize a protocol if you met one?

1.2.1   A Human Analogy

It is probably easiest to understand the notion of a computer network protocol by first considering some human analogies, since we humans execute protocols all of the time. Consider what you do when you want to ask someone for the time of day. A typical exchange is shown in Figure 1.2. Human protocol (or good manners, at least) dictates that one first offers a greeting (the first "Hi" in Figure 1.2)

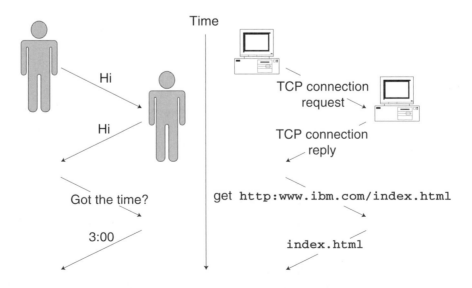

FIGURE 1.2   A human protocol and a computer network protocol

to initiate communication with someone else. The typical response to a "Hi" message (at least outside of New York City) is a returned "Hi" message. Implicitly, one then takes a cordial "Hi" response as an indication that one can proceed ahead and ask for the time of day. A different response to the initial "Hi" (such as "Don't bother me!" or "I don't speak English," or an unprintable reply that one might receive in New York City) might indicate an unwillingness or inability to communicate. In this case, the human protocol would be to not ask for the time of day. Sometimes one gets no response at all to a question, in which case one typically gives up asking that person for the time. Note that in our human protocol, *there are specific messages we send, and specific actions we take in response to the received reply messages or other events (such as no reply within some given amount of time).* Clearly, transmitted and received messages, and actions taken when these message are sent or received or other events occur, play a central role in a human protocol. If people run different protocols (for example, if one person has manners but the other does not, or if one understands the concept of time and the other does not) the protocols do not interoperate and no useful work can be accomplished. The same is true in networking—it takes two (or more) communicating entities running the same protocol in order to accomplish a task.

Let's consider a second human analogy. Suppose you're in a college class (a computer networking class, for example!). The teacher is droning on about protocols and you're confused. The teacher stops to ask, "Are there any questions?" (a message that is transmitted to, and received by, all students who are not sleeping). You raise your hand (transmitting an implicit message to the teacher). Your teacher acknowledges you with a smile, saying "Yes . . ." (a transmitted message encouraging you to ask your question—teachers *love* to be asked questions) and you then ask your question (that is, transmit your message to your teacher). Your teacher hears your question (receives your question message) and answers (transmits a reply to you). Once again, we see that the transmission and receipt of messages, and a set of conventional actions taken when these messages are sent and received, are at the heart of this question-and-answer protocol.

1.2.2   Network Protocols

A network protocol is similar to a human protocol, except that the entities exchanging messages and taking actions are hardware or software components of a computer network, components that we will study shortly in the following sections. All activity in the Internet that involves two or more communicating remote entities is governed by a protocol. Protocols in routers determine a packet's path from source to destination; hardware-implemented protocols in the network interface cards of two physically connected computers control the flow of bits on the "wire" between the two computers; a congestion control protocol controls the rate at which packets are transmitted between sender and receiver. Protocols are running everywhere in the Internet, and consequently much of this book is about computer network protocols.

As an example of a computer network protocol with which you are probably familiar, consider what happens when you make a request to a Web server, that is, when you type in the URL of a Web page into your Web browser. The scenario is illustrated in the right half of Figure 1.2. First, your computer will send a "connection request" message to the Web server and wait for a reply. The Web server will eventually receive your connection request message and return a "connection reply" message. Knowing that it is now OK to request the Web document, your computer then sends the name of the Web page it wants to fetch from that Web server in a "get" message. Finally, the Web server returns the contents of the Web document to your computer.

Given the human and networking examples above, the exchange of messages and the actions taken when these messages are sent and received are the key defining elements of a protocol:

> A **protocol** *defines the format and the order of messages exchanged between two or more communicating entities, as well as the actions taken on the transmission and/or receipt of a message or other event.*

The Internet, and computer networks in general, make extensive use of protocols. Different protocols are used to accomplish different communication tasks. As you read through this book, you will learn that some protocols are simple and straightforward, while others are complex and intellectually deep. Mastering the field of computer networking is equivalent to understanding the what, why, and how of networking protocols.

1.3 THE NETWORK EDGE

In the previous sections we presented a high-level description of the Internet and networking protocols. We are now going to delve a bit more deeply into the components of the Internet. We begin in this section at the edge of network and look at the components with which we are most familiar—the computers (for example, PCs and workstations) that we use on a daily basis. In the next section we will move from the network edge to the network core and examine switching and routing in computer networks. Then in Section 1.5 we will discuss the actual physical links that carry the signals sent between the computers and the switches.

1.3.1 End Systems, Clients, and Servers

In computer networking jargon, the computers that we use on a daily basis are often referred to as **hosts** or **end systems.** They are referred to as "hosts" because they host (run) application-level programs such as a Web browser or server program, or an e-mail program. They are also referred to as "end systems" because they sit at the "edge" of the Internet, as shown in Figure 1.3. Throughout this book we will use the terms hosts and end systems interchangeably, that is, *host = end system.*

Hosts are sometimes further divided into two categories: **clients** and **servers.** Informally, clients often tend to be desktop PCs or workstations, while servers are more powerful machines. But there is a more precise meaning of a client and a server in computer networking. In the so-called **client-server model,** a client program running on one end system requests and receives information from a server running on another end system. This client-server model is undoubtedly the most prevalent structure for Internet applications. We will study the client-server model in detail in Chapter 2. The Web, e-mail, file transfer, remote login (for example,

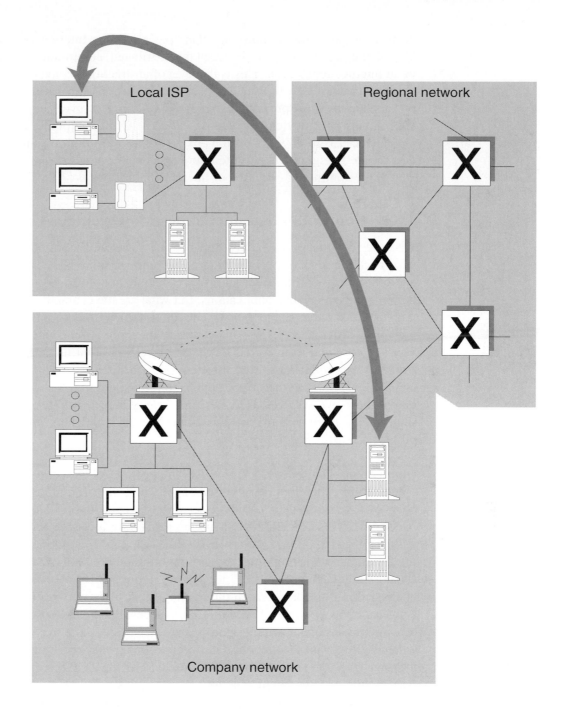

FIGURE 1.3   End system interaction

Telnet), newgroups, and many other popular applications adopt the client-server model. Since a client typically runs on one computer and the server runs on another computer, client-server Internet applications are, by definition, **distributed applications.** The client and the server interact with each other by communicating (that is, sending each other messages) over the Internet. At this level of abstraction, the routers, links and other "pieces" of the Internet serve as a "black box" that transfers messages between the distributed, communicating components of an Internet application. This is the level of abstraction depicted in Figure 1.3.

Computers (for example, a PC or a workstation), operating as clients and servers, are the most prevalent type of end system. However, an increasing number of alternative devices, such as so-called network computers and thin clients [Thinplanet], Web TVs and set top boxes [Mills 1998], digital cameras, and other devices are being attached to the Internet as end systems. An interesting discussion of the continuing evolution of Internet applications is [AT&T Apps 1998].

1.3.2   Connectionless and Connection-Oriented Services

We have seen that end systems exchange messages with each other according to an application-level protocol in order to accomplish some task. The links, routers, and other pieces of the Internet provide the means to transport these messages between the end system applications. But what are the characteristics of the communication services that are provided? The Internet, and more generally TCP/IP networks, provide two types of services to its applications: **connectionless service** and **connection-oriented service.** A developer creating an Internet application (for example, an e-mail application, a file transfer application, a Web application, or an Internet phone application) must program the application to use one of these two services. Here, we only briefly describe these two services; we shall discuss them in much more detail in Chapter 3, which covers transport layer protocols.

Connection-oriented service.   When an application uses the connection-oriented service, the client and the server (residing in different end systems) send control packets to each other before sending packets with real data (such as e-mail messages). This so-called handshaking procedure alerts the client and server, allowing them to prepare for an onslaught of packets. It is interesting to note that this initial hand-shaking procedure is similar to the protocol used in human interaction. The exchange of "hi's" we saw in Figure 1.2 is an example of a human "handshaking protocol" (even though handshaking is not literally taking place between the two people). The two TCP messages that are exchanged as part of the WWW interaction shown in Figure 1.2 are two of the three messages exchanged when TCP sets up a connection between a sender and receiver. The third TCP message (not shown) that forms the final part of the TCP three-way handshake (see Section 3.7) is contained in the `get` message shown in Figure 1.2.

Once the handshaking procedure is finished, a "connection" is said to be established between the two end systems. But the two end systems are connected in a very loose manner, hence the terminology "connection-oriented." In particular, only the end systems themselves are aware of this connection; the packet switches (that is, routers) within the Internet are completely oblivious to the connection. This is because a TCP connection is nothing more than allocated resources (buffers) and state variables in the end systems. The packet switches do not maintain any connection state information.

The Internet's connection-oriented service comes bundled with several other services, including reliable data transfer, flow control, and congestion control. By **reliable data transfer,** we mean that an application can rely on the connection to deliver all of its data without error and in the proper order. Reliability in the Internet is achieved through the use of *acknowledgments* and *retransmissions.* To get a preliminary idea about how the Internet implements the reliable transport service, consider an application that has established a connection between end systems A and B. When end system B receives a packet from A, it sends an acknowledgment; when end system A receives the acknowledgment, it knows that the corresponding packet has definitely been received. When end system A doesn't receive an acknowledgment, it assumes that the packet it sent was not received by B; it therefore retransmits the packet. **Flow control** makes sure that neither side of a connection overwhelms the other side by sending too many packets too fast. Indeed, the application at one side of the connection may not be able to process information as quickly as it receives the information. Therefore, there is a risk of overwhelming either side of an application. The flow-control service forces the sending end system to reduce its rate whenever there is such a risk. We shall see in Chapter 3 that the Internet implements the flow control service by using sender and receiver buffers in the communicating end systems. The Internet's **congestion-control** service helps prevent the Internet from entering a state of gridlock. When a router becomes congested, its buffers can overflow and packet loss can occur. In such circumstances, if every pair of communicating end systems continues to pump packets into the network as fast as they can, gridlock sets in and few packets are delivered to their destinations. The Internet avoids this problem by forcing end systems to diminish the rate at which they send packets into the network during periods of congestion. End systems are alerted to the existence of severe congestion when they stop receiving acknowledgments for the packets they have sent.

We emphasize here that although the Internet's connection-oriented service comes bundled with reliable data transfer, flow control, and congestion control, these three features are by no means essential components of a connection-oriented service. A different type of computer network may provide a connection-oriented service to its applications without bundling in one or more of these features. Indeed, any protocol that performs handshaking between the communicating entities before transferring data is a connection-oriented service [Iren 1999].

The Internet's connection-oriented service has a name—**TCP** (Transmission Control Protocol); the initial version of the TCP protocol is defined in the Internet Request for Comments RFC 793 [RFC 793]. The *services* that TCP provides to an application include reliable transport, flow control, and congestion control. It is important to note that an application need only care about the services that are provided; it need not to worry about *how* TCP actually implements reliability, flow control, or congestion control. *We,* of course, are *very* interested in how TCP implements these services and we shall cover these topics in detail in Chapter 3.

Connectionless service.   There is no handshaking with the Internet's connectionless service. When one side of an application wants to send packets to another side of an application, the sending application simply sends the packets. Since there is no handshaking procedure prior to the transmission of the packets, data can be delivered faster. But there are no acknowledgments either, so a source never knows for sure which packets arrive at the destination. Moreover, the service makes no provision for flow control or congestion control. The Internet's connectionless service is provided by **UDP** (User Datagram Protocol); UDP is defined in the Internet Request for Comments RFC 768 [RFC 768].

Most of the more familiar Internet applications use TCP, the Internet's connection-oriented service. These applications include Telnet (remote login), SMTP (for electronic mail), FTP (for file transfer), and HTTP (for the Web). Nevertheless, UDP, the Internet's connectionless service, is used by many applications, including many of the emerging multimedia applications, such as Internet phone, audio-on-demand, and video conferencing.

1.4 THE NETWORK CORE

Having examined the end systems and end-end transport service model of the Internet in Section 1.3, let us now delve more deeply into the "inside" of the network. In this section we study the network core—the mesh of routers that interconnect the Internet's end systems. Figure 1.4 highlights the network core in the thick, shaded lines.

1.4.1 Circuit Switching, Packet Switching, and Message Switching

There are two fundamental approaches towards building a network core: **circuit switching** and **packet switching.** In circuit-switched networks, the resources needed along a path (buffers, link bandwidth) to provide for communication between the end systems are *reserved* for the duration of the session. In packet-switched networks, these resources are *not* reserved; a session's messages use the resource on demand, and as a consequence, may have to wait (that is, queue) for access to a communication link. As a simple analogy, consider two restaurants—one that requires reservations and another that neither requires reservations nor accepts them. For the restaurant that requires reservations, we have to go through the hassle of first calling (or sending an e-mail!) before we leave home. But when we arrive at the restaurant we can, in principle, immediately communicate with the waiter and order our meal. For the restaurant that does not require reservations, we don't need to bother to reserve a table. But when we arrive at the restaurant, we may have to wait for a table before we can communicate with the waiter.

The ubiquitous telephone networks are examples of circuit-switched networks. Consider what happens when one person wants to send information (voice or facsimile) to another over a telephone network. Before the sender can send the information, the network must first establish a connection between the sender and the receiver. In contrast with the TCP connection that we discussed in the previous section, this is a bona fide connection for which the switches on the path between the sender and receiver maintain connection state for that connection. In the jargon of telephony, this connection is called a **circuit.** When the network establishes the circuit, it also reserves a constant transmission rate in the network's links for the duration of the connection. This reservation allows the sender to transfer the data to the receiver at the *guaranteed* constant rate.

Today's Internet is a quintessential packet-switched network. Consider what happens when one host wants to send a packet to another host over a packet-switched network. As with circuit-switching, the packet is transmitted over a

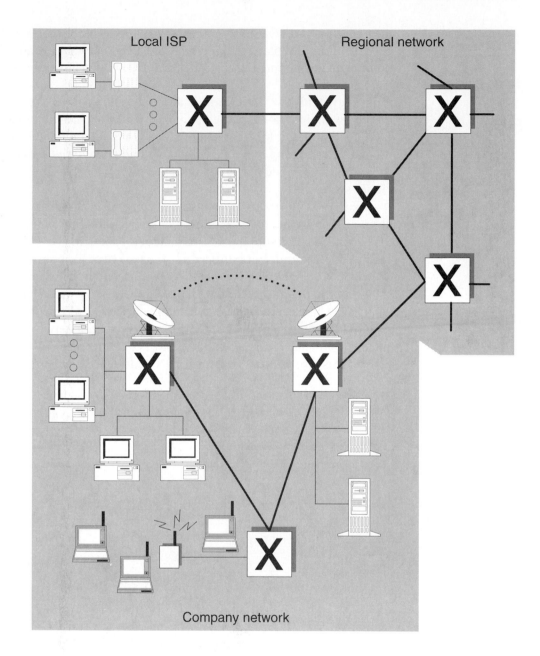

FIGURE 1.4   The network core

series of communication links. But with packet-switching, the packet is sent into the network without reserving any bandwidth whatsoever. If one of the links is congested because other packets need to be transmitted over the link at the same time, then our packet will have to wait in a buffer at the sending side of the transmission line, and suffer a delay. The Internet makes its *best effort* to deliver the data in a timely manner, but it does not make any guarantees.

Not all telecommunication networks can be neatly classified as pure circuit-switched networks or pure packet-switched networks. For example, for networks based on the ATM technology, a connection can make a reservation and yet its messages may still wait for congested resources! Nevertheless, this fundamental classification into packet- and circuit-switched networks is an excellent starting point in understanding telecommunication network technology.

Circuit switching. This book is about computer networks, the Internet, and packet switching, not about telephone networks and circuit switching. Nevertheless, it is important to understand why the Internet and other computer networks use packet switching rather than the more traditional circuit-switching technology used in the telephone networks. For this reason, we now give a brief overview of circuit switching.

Figure 1.5 illustrates a circuit-switched network. In this network, the three circuit switches are interconnected by two links; each of these links has n circuits, so that each link can support n simultaneous connections. The end systems (for example, PCs and workstations) are each directly connected to one of the switches. (Ordinary telephones are also connected to the switches, but they are not shown in the diagram.) Notice that some of the hosts have analog access to the switches, whereas others have direct digital access. For analog access, a modem is required. When two hosts desire to communicate, the network establishes a dedicated *end-to-end circuit* between two hosts. (Conference calls between more than two devices are, of course, also possible. But to keep things simple, let's suppose

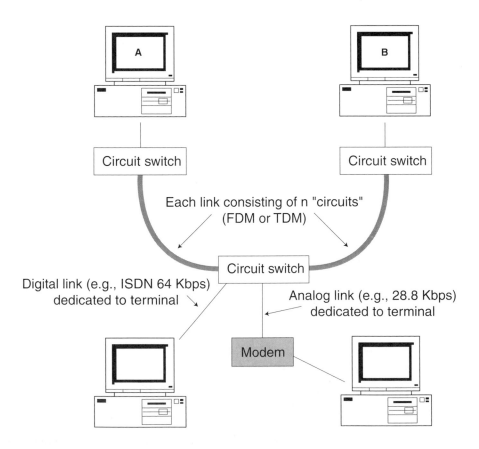

FIGURE 1.5 A simple circuit-switched network consisting of three circuit switches interconnected with two links

for now that there are only two hosts for each connection.) Thus, in order for host A to send messages to host B, the network must first reserve one circuit on each of two links. Each link has *n* circuits; each end-to-end circuit over a link gets the fraction 1/*n* of the link's bandwidth for the duration of the circuit. The *n* circuits in a link can be either TDM or FDM circuits.

Multiplexing. A circuit in a link is implemented with either **frequency-division multiplexing (FDM)** or **time-division multiplexing (TDM).** With FDM, the frequency spectrum of a link is shared among the connections established across the link. Specifically, the link dedicates a frequency band to each connection for the duration of the connection. In telephone networks, this frequency band typically has a width of 4 kHz. The width of the band is called, not surprisingly, the **bandwidth.** FM radio stations also use FDM to share microwave frequency spectrum.

The trend in modern telephony is to replace FDM with TDM. The majority of the links in most telephone systems in the United States and in other developed countries currently employ TDM. For a TDM link, time is divided into frames of fixed duration and each frame is divided into a fixed number of time slots. When the network establishes a connection across a link, the network dedicates one time slot in every frame to the connection. These slots are dedicated for the sole use of that connection, with a time slot available for use (in every frame) to transmit the connection's data.

Figure 1.6 illustrates FDM and TDM for a specific network link. For FDM, the frequency domain is segmented into a number of circuits, each of bandwidth 4

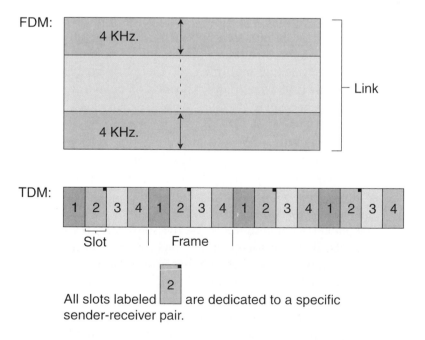

FIGURE 1.6 With FDM, each circuit continuously gets a fraction of the bandwidth. With TDM, each circuit gets all of the bandwidth periodically during brief intervals of time (that is, during slots)

kHz (that is, 4,000 Hertz or 4,000 cycles per second). For TDM, the time domain is segmented into four circuits; each circuit is assigned the same dedicated slot in the revolving TDM frames. The transmission rate of the frame is equal to the frame rate multiplied by the number of bits in a slot. For example, if the link transmits 8,000 frames per second and each slot consists of 8 bits, then the transmission rate is 64 Kbps.

Proponents of packet switching have always argued that circuit switching is wasteful because the dedicated circuits are idle during **silent periods.** For example, when one of the conversants in a telephone call stops talking, the idle network resources (frequency bands or slots in the links along the connection's route) cannot be used by other ongoing connections. As another example of how these resources can be underutilized, consider a radiologist who uses a circuit-switched network to remotely access a series of x-rays. The radiologist sets up a connection, requests an image, contemplates the image, and then requests a new image. Network resources are wasted during the radiologist's contemplation periods. Proponents of packet switching also enjoy pointing out that establishing end-to-end circuits and reserving end-to-end bandwidth is complicated and requires complex signaling software to coordinate the operation of the switches along the end-to-end path.

Before we finish our discussion of circuit switching, let's work through a numerical example that should shed further insight on the matter. Let us consider how long it takes to send a file of 640 Kbits from host A to host B over a circuit-switched network. Suppose that all links in the network use TDM with 24 slots and have a bit rate of 1.536 Mbps. Also suppose that it takes 500 msec to establish an end-to-end circuit before A can begin to transmit the file. How long does it take to send the file? Each circuit has a transmission rate of (1.536 Mbps)/24 = 64 Kbps, so it takes (640 Kbits)/(64 Kbps) = 10 seconds to transmit the file. To this 10 seconds we add the circuit establishment time, giving 10.5 seconds to send the file. Note that the transmission time is independent of the number of links. The transmission time would be 10 seconds if the end-to-end circuit passes through one link or one hundred links. AT&T Labs provides an interactive site [AT&T Bandwidth 1998] to explore transmission delay for various file types and transmission technologies.

Packet switching. We saw in Sections 1.2 and 1.3 that application-level protocols exchange **messages** in accomplishing their task. Messages can contain anything the protocol designer desires. Messages may perform a control function (for example, the "hi" messages in our handshaking example) or can contain data, such as an ASCII file, a Postscript file, a Web page, or a digital audio file. In modern packet-switched networks, the source breaks long messages into smaller **packets.** Between source and destination, each of these packets traverse communication links and **packet switches** (also known as **routers**). Packets are transmitted over each communication link at a rate equal to the *full* transmission rate of the link. Most packet switches use **store-and-forward transmission** at the inputs to the links. Store-and-forward transmission means that the switch must receive the entire packet before it can begin to transmit the first bit of the packet onto the outbound link. Thus store-and-forward packet-switches introduce a **store-and-forward delay** at the input to each link along the packet's route. This delay is proportional to the packet's length in bits. In particular, if a packet consists of L bits, and the packet is to be forwarded onto an outbound link of R bps, then the store-and-forward delay at the switch is L/R seconds.

Within each router there are multiple buffers (also called queues), with each link having an **input buffer** (to store packets that have just arrived to that link) and an **output buffer.** The output buffers play a key role in packet switching. If an arriving packet needs to be transmitted across a link but finds the link busy with the transmission of another packet, the arriving packet must wait in the output buffer. Thus, in addition to the store-and-forward delays, packets suffer output buffer **queuing delays.** These delays are variable and depend on the level of congestion in the network. Since the amount of buffer space is finite, an arriving packet may find that the buffer is completely filled with other packets waiting for transmission. In this case, **packet loss** will occur—either the arriving packet or one of the already-queued packets will be dropped. Returning to our restaurant analogy from earlier in this section, the queuing delay is analogous to the amount of time one spends waiting for a table. Packet loss is analogous to being told by the waiter that you must leave the premises because there are already too many other people waiting at the bar for a table.

Figure 1.7 illustrates a simple packet-switched network. Suppose Hosts A and B are sending packets to Host E. Hosts A and B first send their packets along 28.8 Kbps links to the first packet switch. The packet switch directs these packets to the 1.544 Mbps link. If there is congestion at this link, the packets queue in the link's output buffer before they can be transmitted onto the link. Consider now how Host A and Host B packets are transmitted onto this link. As shown in Figure 1.7, the

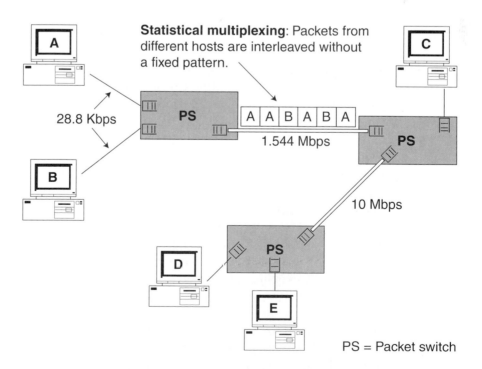

FIGURE 1.7   Packet switching

sequence of A and B packets does not follow any periodic ordering; the ordering is random or statistical because packets are sent whenever they happen to be present at the link. For this reason, we often say that packet switching employs **statistical multiplexing.** Statistical multiplexing sharply contrasts with time-division multiplexing (TDM), for which each host gets the same slot in a revolving TDM frame.

Let us now consider how long it takes to send a packet of L bits from host A to another host across a packet-switched network. Let us suppose that there are Q links between A and E, each of rate R bps. Assume that queuing delays and end-to-end propagation delays are negligible and that there is no connection establishment. The packet must first be transmitted onto the first link emanating from host A; this takes L/R seconds. It must then be transmitted on each of the $Q - 1$ remaining links, that is, it must be stored and forwarded $Q - 1$ times. Thus the total delay is QL/R.

Packet switching versus circuit switching. Having described circuit switching and packet switching, let us compare the two. Opponents of packet switching have often argued that packet switching is not suitable for real-time services (for example, telephone calls and video conference calls) because of its variable and unpredictable delays. Proponents of packet switching argue that (1) it offers better sharing of bandwidth than circuit switching and (2) it is simpler, more efficient, and less costly to implement than circuit switching. Generally speaking, people who do not like to hassle with restaurant reservations prefer packet switching to circuit switching.

Why is packet switching more efficient? Let us look at a simple example. Suppose users share a 1 Mbps link. Also suppose that each user alternates between periods of activity (when it generates data at a constant rate of 100 Kbits/sec) and periods of inactivity (when it generates no data). Suppose further that a user is active only 10% of the time (and is idle drinking coffee during the remaining 90% of the time). With circuit switching, 100 Kbps must be *reserved* for *each* user at all times. Thus, the link can support only 10 simultaneous users. With packet switching, if there are 35 users, the probability that there are 10 or more simultaneously active users is less than 0.0017. If there are 10 or fewer simultaneously active users (which happens with probability 0.9983), the aggregate arrival rate of data is less than 1 Mbps (the output rate of the link). Thus, users' packets flow through the link essentially without delay, as is the case with circuit switching. When there are more than 10 simultaneously active users, then the aggregate arrival rate of packets will exceed the output capacity of the link, and the output queue will begin to grow (until the aggregate input rate falls back below 1 Mbps, at which point the queue will begin to diminish in length). Because the probability of having 10 or more simultaneously active users is very very small, packet-switching almost always has the same delay performance as circuit switching, *but does so while allowing for more than three times the number of users.*

Although packet switching and circuit switching are both very prevalent in today's telecommunication networks, the trend is certainly in the direction of packet switching. Even many of today's circuit-switched telephone networks are slowly migrating towards packet switching. In particular, telephone networks

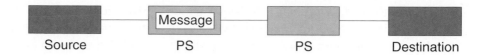

FIGURE 1.8 A simple message-switched network

often convert to packet switching for the expensive overseas portion of a telephone call.

Message switching. In a modern packet-switched network, the source host segments long messages into smaller packets and sends the smaller packets into the network; the receiver reassembles the packets back into the original message. But why bother to segment the messages into packets in the first place, only to have to reassemble packets into messages? Doesn't this place an additional and unnecessary burden on the source and destination? Although the segmentation and reassembly do complicate the design of the source and receiver, researchers and network designers concluded in the early days of packet switching that the advantages of segmentation greatly compensate for its complexity. Before discussing some of these advantages, we need to introduce some terminology. We say that a packet-switched network performs **message switching** if the sources do not segment messages (that is, they send a message into the network as a whole). Thus message switching is a specific kind of packet switching, whereby the packets traversing the network are themselves entire messages.

Figure 1.8 illustrates message switching in a route consisting of two packet switches (PSs) and three links. With message switching, the message stays intact as it traverses the network. Because the switches are store-and-forward packet switches, a packet switch must receive the entire message before it can begin to forward the message on an outbound link.

Figure 1.9 illustrates packet switching for the same network. In this example, the original message has been divided into five distinct packets. In Figure 1.9, the first packet has arrived at the destination, the second and third packets are in transit in the network, and the last two packets are still in the source. Again, because the switches are store-and-forward packet switches, a packet switch must receive an entire packet before it can begin to forward the packet on an outbound link.

One major advantage of packet switching (with segmented messages) is that it achieves end-to-end delays that are typically much smaller than the delays associated with message switching. We illustrate this point with the following simple

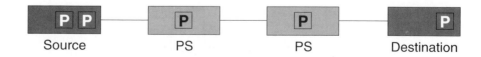

FIGURE 1.9 A simple packet-switched network

example. Consider a message that is 7.5 Mbits long. Suppose that between source and destination there are two packet switches and three links, and that each link has a transmission rate of 1.5 Mbps. Assuming there is no congestion in the network, how much time is required to move the message from source to destination with message switching? It takes the source 5 seconds to move the message from the source to the first switch. Because the switches use store-and-forward transmission, the first switch cannot begin to transmit any bits in the message onto the link until this first switch has received the entire message. Once the first switch has received the entire message, it takes 5 seconds to move the message from the first switch to the second switch. Thus it takes 10 seconds to move the message from the source to the second switch. Following this logic we see that a total of 15 seconds is needed to move the message from source to destination. These delays are illustrated in Figure 1.10.

Continuing with the same example, now suppose that the source breaks the message into 5,000 packets, with each packet being 1.5 Kbits long. Again assuming that there is no congestion in the network, how long does it take to move the 5,000 packets from source to destination? It takes the source 1 msec to move the first packet from the source to the first switch. And it takes the first switch 1 msec to move this first packet from the first to the second switch. But while the first packet is being moved from the first switch to the second switch, the second packet is *simultaneously* moved from the source to the first switch. Thus the second packet reaches the first switch at time = 2 msec. Following this logic we see that the last packet is completely received at the first switch at time = 5,000 msec = 5 seconds. Since this last packet has to be transmitted on two more links, the last packet is received by the destination at 5.002 seconds (see Figure 1.11).

Amazingly enough, packet switching has reduced the message-switching delay by a factor of three! But why is this so? What is packet switching doing that is different from message switching? The key difference is that message switching

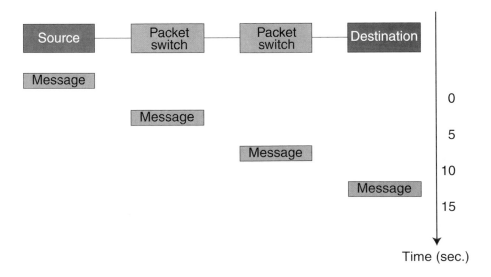

FIGURE 1.10   Timing of message transfer of a 7.5 Mbit message in a message-switched network

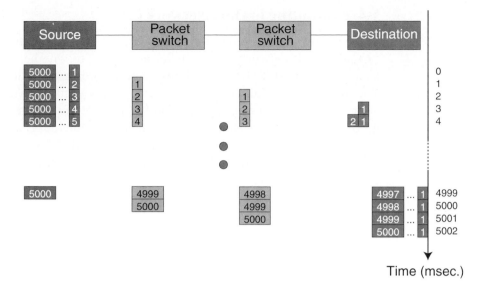

Time (msec.)

FIGURE 1.11 Timing of packet transfer of a 7.5 Mbit message, divided into 5,000 packets, in a packet-switched network

is performing sequential transmission whereas packet switching is performing parallel transmission. Observe that with message switching, while one node (the source or one of the switches) is transmitting, the remaining nodes are idle. With packet switching, once the first packet reaches the last switch, three nodes transmit at the same time.

Packet switching has yet another important advantage over message switching. As we will discuss later in this book, bit errors can be introduced into packets as they transit the network. When a switch detects an error in a packet, it typically discards the entire packet. So, if the entire message is a packet and one bit in the message gets corrupted, the entire message is discarded. If, on the other hand, the message is segmented into many packets and one bit in one of the packets is corrupted, then only that one packet is discarded.

Packet switching is not without its disadvantages, however, with respect to message switching. We will see that each packet or message must carry, in addition to the data being sent from the sending application to the receiving application, an amount of control information. This information, which is carried in the packet or message **header,** might include the identity of the sender and receiver and a packet or message identifier (for example, number). Since the amount of header information would be approximately the same for a message or a packet, the amount of header overhead per byte of data is higher for packet switching than for message switching.

Before moving on to the next subsection, you are highly encouraged to explore the Message-Switching Java Applet (http://www.seas.upenn.edu/~ross/book/overview/MessageSwitching.html) that is available on the WWW site for this book. This applet will allow you to experiment with different message and packet sizes, and will allow you to examine the effect of additional propagation delays.

1.4.2 Routing in Data Networks

There are two broad classes of packet-switched networks: datagram networks and virtual circuit networks. They differ according to whether they route packets according to host destination addresses or according to virtual circuit numbers. We shall call any network that routes packets according to host destination addresses a **datagram network.** The IP protocol of the Internet routes packets according to the destination addresses; hence the Internet is a datagram network. We shall call any network that routes packets according to virtual circuit numbers a **virtual circuit network.** Examples of packet-switching technologies that use virtual circuits include X.25, frame relay, and ATM.

Virtual circuit networks.   A virtual circuit (VC) consists of (1) a path (that is, a series of links and packet switches) between the source and destination hosts, (2) virtual circuit numbers, one number for each link along the path, and (3) entries in VC-number translation tables in each packet switch along the path. Once a VC is established between source and destination, packets can be sent with the appropriate VC numbers. Because a VC has a different VC number on each link, an intermediate packet switch must replace the VC number of each traversing packet with a new one. The new VC number is obtained from the VC-number translation table.

To illustrate the concept, consider the network shown in Figure 1.12. Suppose host A requests that the network establish a VC between itself and host B. Suppose that the network chooses the path A–PS1–PS2–B and assigns VC numbers 12, 22, 32 to the three links in this path. Then, when a packet as part of this VC leaves host A, the value in the VC-number field is 12; when it leaves PS1, the value is 22; and when it leaves PS2, the value is 32. The numbers next to the links of PS1 are the **interface numbers.**

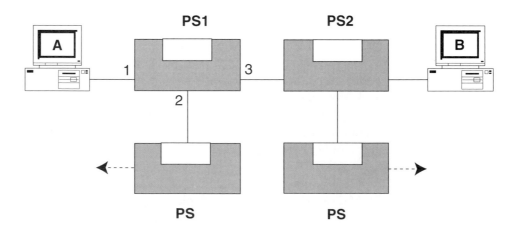

FIGURE 1.12   A simple virtual circuit network

How does the switch determine the replacement VC number for a packet traversing the switch? Each switch has a VC-number translation table; for example, the VC-number translation table in PS1 might look something like this:

Incoming interface	Incoming VC #	Outgoing Interface	Outgoing VC #
1	12	3	22
2	63	1	18
3	7	2	17
1	97	3	87
...	...	...	...

Whenever a new VC is established across a switch, an entry is added to the VC-number table. Similarly, whenever a VC terminates, the entries in each table along its path are removed.

You might be wondering why a packet doesn't just keep the same VC number on each of the links along its route? The answer to this question is twofold. First, by replacing the number from link to link, the length of the VC field is reduced. Second, and more importantly, by permitting a different VC number for each link along the path of the VC, a network management function is simplified. Specifically, with multiple VC numbers, each link in the path can choose a VC number independently of what the other links in the path chose. If a common number were required for all links along the path, the switches would have to exchange and process a substantial number of messages to agree on the VC number to be used for a connection.

If a network employs virtual circuits, then the network's switches must maintain **state information** for the ongoing connections. Specifically, each time a new connection is established across a switch, a new connection entry must be added to the switch's VC-number translation table; and each time a connection is released, an entry must be removed from the table. Note that even if there is no VC-number translation, it is still necessary to maintain state information that associates VC numbers to interface numbers. The issue of whether or not a switch or router maintains state information for each ongoing connection is a crucial one—one that we return to shortly below.

Datagram networks.   Datagram networks are analogous in many respects to the postal services. When a sender sends a letter to a destination, the sender wraps the letter in an envelope and writes the destination address on the envelope. This destination address has a hierarchical structure. For example, letters sent to a location in the United States include the country (the USA), the state (for example, Pennsylvania), the city (for example, Philadelphia), the street (for example, Walnut Street) and the number of the house on the street (for example, 421). The postal services use the address on the envelope to route the letter to its destination. For example, if the letter is sent from France, then a postal office in France will first direct the letter to a postal center in the USA. This postal center in the USA will then send the letter to a postal center in Philadelphia. Finally a mail person working in Philadelphia will deliver the letter to its ultimate destination.

In a datagram network, each packet that traverses the network contains in its header the address of the destination. As with postal addresses, this address has a hierarchical structure. When a packet arrives at a packet switch in the network, the packet switch examines a portion of the packet's destination address and forwards the packet to an adjacent switch. More specifically, each packet switch has a routing table that maps destination addresses (or portions of the destination addresses) to an outbound link. When a packet arrives at a switch, the switch examines the address and indexes its table with this address to find the appropriate outbound link. The switch then sends the packet into this outbound link.

The whole routing process is also analogous to the car driver who does not use maps but instead prefers to ask for directions. For example, suppose Joe is driving from Philadelphia to 156 Lakeside Drive in Orlando, Florida. Joe first drives to his neighborhood gas station and asks how to get to 156 Lakeside Drive in Orlando, Florida. The gas station attendant extracts the Florida portion of the address and tells Joe that he needs to get onto the interstate highway I-95 South, which has an entrance just next to the gas station. He also tells Joe that once he enters Florida he should ask someone else there. Joe then takes I-95 South until he gets to Jacksonville, Florida, at which point he asks another gas station attendant for directions. The attendant extracts the Orlando portion of the address and tells Joe that he should continue on I-95 to Daytona Beach and then ask someone else. In Daytona Beach another gas station attendant also extracts the Orlando portion of the address and tells Joe that he should take I-4 directly to Orlando. Joe takes I-4 and gets off at the Orlando exit. Joe goes to another gas station attendant, and this time the attendant extracts the Lakeside Drive portion of the address, and tells Joe the road he must follow to get to Lakeside Drive. Once Joe reaches Lakeside Drive he asks a kid on a bicycle how to get to his destination. The kid extracts the 156 portion of the address and points to the house. Joe finally reaches his ultimate destination.

We will be discussing routing in datagram networks in great detail in this book. But for now we mention that, in contrast with VC networks, *datagram networks do not maintain connection-state information in their switches*. In fact, a switch in a pure datagram network is completely oblivious to any flows of traffic that may be passing through it—it makes routing decisions for each individual packet. Because VC networks must maintain connection-state information in their switches, opponents of VC networks argue that VC networks are overly complex. These opponents include most researchers and engineers in the Internet community. Proponents of VC networks feel that VCs can offer applications a wider variety of networking services. Many researchers and engineers in the ATM community are outspoken advocates for VCs.

How would you like to actually see the route that packets take in the Internet? We now invite you to get your hands dirty by interacting with the Traceroute program, using the interface (http://www.seas.upenn.edu/~ross/book/overview/traceroute.htm) provided on the Web site for this book.

Network taxonomy. We have now introduced several important networking concepts: circuit switching, packet switching, message switching, virtual circuits,

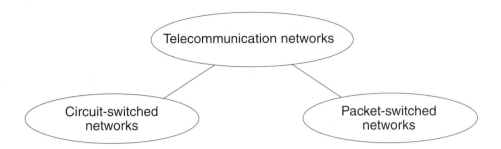

FIGURE 1.13   Highest-level distinction among telecommunication networks: Circuit-switched or packet-switched?

connectionless service, and connection-oriented service. How does it all fit together?

First, in our simple view of the world, a telecommunications network either employs circuit switching or packet switching (see Figure 1.13). A link in a circuit-switched network can employ either FDM or TDM (see Figure 1.14). Packet-switched networks are either virtual circuit networks or datagram networks. Switches in virtual circuit networks route packets according to the packets' VC numbers and maintain connection state. Switches in datagram networks route packets according to the packets' destination addresses and do not maintain connection state (see Figure 1.15).

Examples of packet-switched networks that use VCs include X.25, frame relay, and ATM. A packet-switched network either (1) uses VCs for all of its message routing, or (2) uses destination addresses for all of its message routing. It doesn't employ both routing techniques. (This last statement is a bit of a white lie, as there are networks that use datagram routing "on top of" VC routing. This is the case for "IP over ATM," as we shall cover later in the book.)

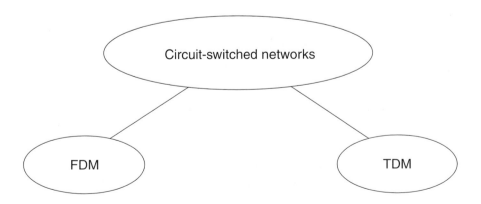

FIGURE 1.14   Circuit switching implementation: FDM or TDM?

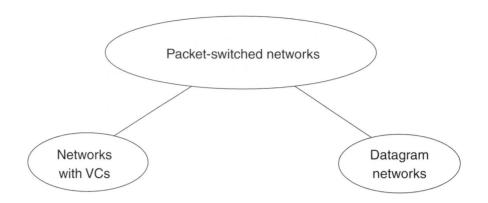

FIGURE 1.15 Packet-switching implementation: Virtual circuits or datagrams?

A datagram network is *not,* however, either a connectionless or a connection-oriented network. Indeed, a datagram network can provide the connectionless service to some of its applications and the connection-oriented service to other applications. For example, the Internet, which is a datagram network, provides both connectionless and connection-oriented service to its applications. We saw in Section 1.3 that these services are provided in the Internet by the UDP and TCP protocols, respectively. Networks with VCs—such as X.25, Frame Relay, and ATM—are always, however, connection-oriented.

1.5 ACCESS NETWORKS AND PHYSICAL MEDIA

In Sections 1.3 and 1.4 we have examined the roles of end systems and routers in a network architecture. In this section we consider the **access network**—the physical link(s) that connect an end system to its **edge router**—that is, to the first router on a path from the end system to any other distant end system. Since access network technology is closely tied to physical media technology (fiber, coaxial pair, twisted pair telephone wire, radio spectrum), we consider these two topics together in this section.

1.5.1 Access Networks

Figure 1.16 shows the access networks' links highlighted in thick, shaded lines. Access networks can be loosely divided into three categories:

- **Residential access networks,** connecting a home end system into the network
- **Institutional access networks,** connecting an end system in a business or educational institution into the network
- **Mobile access networks,** connecting a mobile end system into the network

These categories are not hard and fast; some corporate end systems may well use the access network technology that we ascribe to residential access networks, and

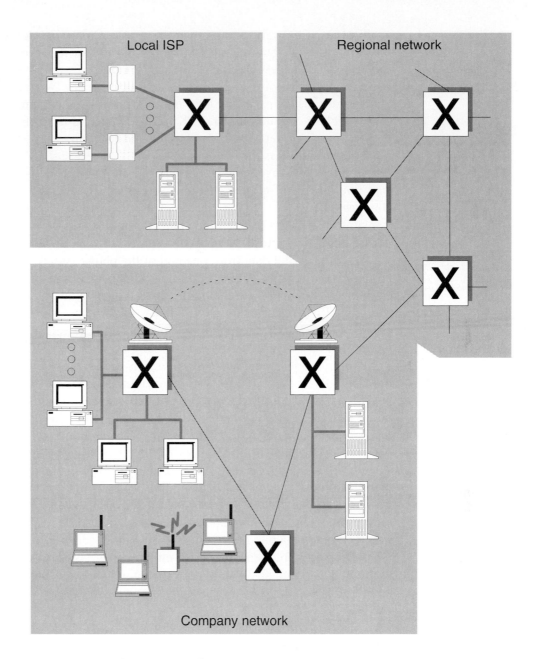

FIGURE 1.16 Access networks

vice versa. The following descriptions are meant to hold for the common (if not every) case.

Residential access networks. A residential access network connects a home end system (typically a PC, but perhaps a Web TV or other residential system) to an edge router. Probably the most common form of home access is by use of a **modem** over a POTS (plain old telephone system) dialup line to an Internet service provider (ISP). The home modem converts the digital output of the PC into analog format for transmission over the analog phone line. A modem in the ISP converts the analog signal back into digital form for input to the ISP router. In this case, the "access network" is simply a point-to-point dialup link into an edge router. The point-to-point link is your ordinary twisted-pair phone line. (We will discuss twisted-pair later in this section.) Today's modem speeds allow dialup access at rates up to 56 Kbps. However, due to the poor quality of twisted-pair line between many homes and ISPs, many users get an effective rate significantly less than 56 Kbps.

Whereas dialup modems require conversion of the end system's digital data into analog form for transmission, so-called narrowband **ISDN** technology (Integrated Services Digital Network) [Pacific Bell 1998] allows for all-digital transmission of data from a home end system over ISDN "telephone" lines to a phone company central office. Although ISDN was originally conceived as a way to carry digital data from one end of the phone system to another, it is also an important network access technology that provides higher speed access (for example, 128 Kbps) from the home into a data network such as the Internet. In this case, ISDN can be thought of simply as a "better modem" [NAS 1995]. A good source for additional Web information on ISDN is Dan Kegel's ISDN page [Kegel 1999].

Dialup modems and narrowband ISDN are already widely deployed technologies. Two new technologies, **asymmetric digital subscriber line (ADSL)** [ADSL 1998] and **hybrid fiber coaxial cable (HFC)** [Cable 1998] are currently being deployed. ADSL is conceptually similar to dialup modems: It is a new modem technology again running over existing twisted-pair telephone lines, but can transmit at rates of up to about 8 Mbps from the ISP router to a home end system. The data rate in the reverse direction, from the home end system to the central office router, is less than 1 Mbps. The asymmetry in the access speeds gives rise to the term "asymmetric" in ADSL. The asymmetry in the data rates reflects the belief that home users are more likely to be a consumer of information (bringing data into their homes) than a producer of information.

ADSL uses frequency division multiplexing, as described in the previous section. In particular, ADSL divides the communication link between the home and the ISP into three nonoverlapping frequency bands:

- A high-speed downstream channel, in the 50 kHz to 1 MHz band
- A medium-speed upstream channel, in the 4 kHz to 50 kHz band
- An ordinary POTS two-way telephone channel, in the 0 to 4 KHz band

One of the features of ADSL is that the service allows the user to make an ordinary telephone call, using the POTS channel, while simultaneously surfing the Web. This feature is not available with standard dialup modems. The actual amount of downstream and upstream bandwidth available to the user is a function of the distance between the home modem and the ISP modem, the gauge of the twisted-pair line, and the degree of electrical interference. For a high-quality line with negligible electrical interference, an 8 Mbps downstream transmission rate is possible if the distance between the home and the ISP is less than 3,000 meters; the downstream transmission rate drops to about 2 Mbps for a distance of 6,000 meters. The upstream rate ranges from 16 Kbps to 1 Mbps.

ADSL, ISDN, and dialup modems all use ordinary phone lines, but HFC access networks are extensions of the current cable network used for broadcasting cable television. In a traditional cable system, a cable head end station broadcasts through a distribution of coaxial cable and amplifiers to residences. (We discuss coaxial cable later in this chapter.) As illustrated in Figure 1.17, fiber optics (also to be discussed soon) connect the cable head end to neighborhood-level junctions, from which traditional coaxial cable is then used to reach individual houses and apartments. Each neighborhood juncture typically supports 500 to 5,000 homes.

As with ADSL, HFC requires special modems, called cable modems. Companies that provide cable Internet access require their customers to either purchase or lease a modem. One such company is Cyber Cable, which uses Motorola's Cyber Surfer Cable Modem and provides high-speed Internet access to most of the neighborhoods in Paris. Typically, the cable modem is an external device and connects to the home PC through a 10-BaseT Ethernet port. (We will discuss Ethernet in great detail in Chapter 5.) Cable modems divide the HFC network into two channels, a downstream and an upstream channel. As with ADSL, the downstream channel is typically allocated more bandwidth and hence a larger transmission rate. For example, the downstream rate of the Cyber Cable system is 10 Mbps and the upstream rate is 768 Kbps. However, with HFC (and not with ADSL), these rates are shared among the homes, as we discuss next.

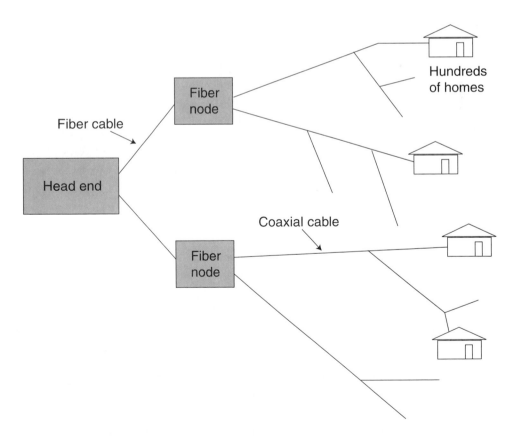

FIGURE 1.17　A hybrid fiber–coax access network

One important characteristic of HFC is that it is a shared broadcast medium. In particular, every packet sent by the head end travels downstream on every link to every home; and every packet sent by a home travels on the upstream channel to the head end. For this reason, if several users are receiving different Internet videos on the downstream channel, the actual rate at which each user receives its video will be significantly less than the downstream rate. On the other hand, if all the active users are Web surfing, then each of the users may actually receive Web pages at the full downstream rate, as a small collection of users will rarely receive a Web page at exactly the same time. Because the upstream channel is also shared, packets sent by two different homes at the same time will collide, which further decreases the effective upstream bandwidth. (We will discuss this collision issue in some detail when we discuss Ethernet in Chapter 5.) Advocates of ADSL are quick to point out that ADSL is a point-to-point connection between the home and ISP, and therefore all the ADSL bandwidth is dedicated rather than shared. Cable advocates, however, argue that a reasonably dimensioned HFC network provides higher bandwidths than ADSL [@Home 1998]. The battle between ADSL and HFC for high speed residential access has clearly begun; see for example, [@Home 1998].

Company access networks. In company access networks, a local area network (LAN) is used to connect an end system to an edge router. As we will see in Chapter 5, there are many different types of LAN technology. However, Ethernet technology is currently by far the most prevalent access technology in company networks. Ethernet operates 10 Mbps or 100 Mbps (and now even at 1 Gbps). It uses either twisted-pair copper wire or coaxial cable to connect a number of end systems with each other and with an edge router. The edge router is responsible for routing packets that have destinations outside of that LAN. Like HFC, Ethernet uses a shared medium, so that end users share the transmission rate of the LAN. More recently, shared Ethernet technology has been migrating towards switched Ethernet technology. Switched Ethernet uses multiple coaxial cable or twisted-pair Ethernet segments connected at a "switch" to allow the full bandwidth of an Ethernet to be delivered to different users on the same LAN simultaneously [Cisco LAN 1998]. We will explore shared and switched Ethernet in some detail in Chapter 5.

Mobile access networks. Mobile access networks use the radio spectrum to connect a mobile end system (for example, a laptop PC or a PDA with a wireless modem) to a base station. This base station, in turn, is connected to an edge router of a data network.

An emerging standard for wireless data networking is **cellular digital packet data (CDPD)** [Wireless 1998]. As the name suggests, a CDPD network operates as an overlay network (that is, as a separate, smaller "virtual" network, as a piece of the larger network) within the cellular telephone network. A CDPD network thus uses the same radio spectrum as the cellular phone system, and operates at speeds in the tens of Kbits per second. As with cable-based access networks and shared Ethernet, CDPD end systems must share the transmission media with other CDPD end systems within the cell covered by a base station. A media access control (MAC) protocol is used to arbitrate channel sharing among the CDPD end systems; we will cover MAC protocols in detail in Chapter 5.

The CDPD system supports the IP protocol, and thus allows an IP end system to exchange IP packets over the wireless channel with an IP base station. A CDPD network can actually support multiple network layer protocols; in addition to IP, the ISO CNLP protocol is also supported. CDPD does not provide for any protocols above the network layer. From an Internet perspective, CDPD can be viewed as extending the Internet dialtone (that is, the ability to transfer IP packets) across a wireless link between a mobile end system and an Internet router. An excellent introduction to CDPD is [Waung 98].

1.5.2   Physical Media

In the previous subsection, we gave an overview of some of the most important access network technologies in the Internet. While describing these technologies, we also indicated the physical media used. For example, we said that HFC uses a combination of fiber cable and coaxial cable. We said that ordinary modems, ISDN, and ADSL use twisted-pair copper wire. And we said that mobile access networks use the radio spectrum. In this subsection we provide a brief overview of these and other transmission media that are commonly employed in the Internet.

In order to define what is meant by a "physical medium," let us reflect on the brief life of a bit. Consider a bit traveling from one end system, through a series of links and routers, to another end system. This poor bit gets transmitted many, many times! The source end system first transmits the bit, and shortly thereafter the first router in the series receives the bit; the first router then transmits the bit, and shortly afterwards the second router receives the bit, and so on. Thus our bit, when traveling from source to destination, passes through a series of transmitter-receiver pairs. For each transmitter-receiver pair, the bit is sent by propagating electromagnetic waves across a **physical medium.** The physical medium can take many shapes and forms, and does not have to be of the same type for each transmitter-receiver pair along the path. Examples of physical media include twisted-pair copper wire, coaxial cable, multimode fiber-optic cable, terrestrial radio spectrum, and satellite radio spectrum. Physical media fall into two categories: **guided media** and **unguided media.** With guided media, the waves are guided along a solid medium, such as a fiber-optic cable, a twisted-pair copper wire, or a coaxial cable. With unguided media, the waves propagate in the atmosphere and in outer space, such as in a digital satellite channel or in a CDPD system.

Some popular physical media.   Suppose you want to wire a building to allow computers to access the Internet or an intranet. Should you use twisted-pair copper wire, coaxial cable, or fiber optics? Which of these media gives the highest bit rates over the longest distances? We shall address these questions below.

But before we get into the characteristics of the various guided medium types, let us say a few words about their costs. The actual cost of the physical link (copper wire, fiber-optic cable, and so on) is often relatively minor compared with the other networking costs. In particular, the labor cost associated with the installation of the physical link can be orders of magnitude higher than the cost of the material. For this reason, many builders install twisted pair, optical fiber, and coaxial cable to every room in a building. Even if only one medium is initially used, there is a good chance that another medium could be used in the near future, and so money is saved by not having to lay additional wires.

Twisted-pair copper wire.   The least-expensive and most commonly used transmission medium is twisted-pair copper wire. For over one-hundred years it has been used by telephone networks. In fact, more than 99% of the wired connections from the telephone handset to the local telephone switch use twisted-pair copper wire. Most of us have seen twisted-pair in our homes and work environments. Twisted-pair consists of two insulated copper wires, each about 1 mm thick, arranged in a regular spiral pattern (see Figure 1.18). The wires are twisted together to reduce the electrical interference from similar pairs close by. Typically, a number of pairs are bundled together in a cable by wrapping the pairs in a protective shield. A wire pair constitutes a single communication link.

Unshielded twisted pair (UTP) is commonly used for computer networks within a building, that is, for local area networks (LANs). Data rates for LANs using twisted-pair today range from 10 Mbps to 100 Mbps. The data rates that can be achieved depend on the thickness of the wire and the distance between transmitter and receiver. Two types of UTP are common in LANs: category 3 and category 5. Category 3 corresponds to voice-grade twisted-pair, commonly found in office buildings. Office buildings are often prewired with two or more parallel pairs of category 3 twisted-pair; one pair is used for telephone communication, and the additional pairs can be used for additional telephone lines or for LAN networking. 10 Mbps Ethernet, one of the most prevalent LAN types, can use category 3 UTP. Category 5, with its more twists per centimeter and Teflon insulation, can handle higher bit rates. 100 Mbps Ethernet running on category 5 UTP has become very popular in recent years. In recent years, category 5 UTP has become common for preinstallation in new office buildings.

When fiber-optic technology emerged in the 1980s, many people disparaged twisted-pair because of its relatively low bit rates. Some people even felt that fiber-optic technology would completely replace twisted-pair. But twisted-pair did not give up so easily. Modern twisted-pair technology, such as category 5 UTP, can achieve data rates of 100 Mbps for distances up to a few hundred meters. Even higher rates are possible over shorter distances. In the end, twisted-pair has emerged as the dominant solution for high-speed LAN networking.

As discussed in the section on access networks, twisted-pair is also commonly used for residential Internet access. We saw that dialup modem technology enables access at rates of up to 56 Kbps over twisted-pair. We also saw that ISDN is available in many communities, providing access rates of about 128 Kbps over twisted pair. We also saw that ADSL (asymmetric digital subscriber loop) technology has enabled residential users to access the Web at rates in excess of 6 Mbps over twisted-pair.

Coaxial cable.   Like twisted-pair, coaxial cable consists of two copper conductors, but the two conductors are concentric rather than parallel. With this construc-

FIGURE 1.18   Twisted-pair

tion and a special insulation and shielding, coaxial cable can have higher bit rates than twisted-pair. Coaxial cable comes in two varieties: **baseband coaxial cable** and **broadband coaxial cable.**

Baseband coaxial cable, also called 50-ohm cable, is about a centimeter thick, lightweight, and easy to bend. It is commonly used in LANs; in fact, the computer you use at work or at school is probably connected to a LAN with either baseband coaxial cable or with UTP. Take a look at the connection to your computer's interface card. If you see a telephone-like jack and some wire that resembles telephone wire, you are using UTP; if you see a T-connector and a cable running out of both sides of the T-connector, you are using baseband coaxial cable. The terminology "baseband" comes from the fact that the stream of bits is dumped directly into the cable, without shifting the signal to a different frequency band. 10 Mbps Ethernets can use either UTP or baseband coaxial cable. As we will discuss in Chapter 5, it is a little more expensive to use UTP for 10 Mbps Ethernet, as UTP requires an additional networking device, called a **hub.**

Broadband coaxial cable, also called 75-ohm cable, is quite a bit thicker, heavier, and stiffer than the baseband variety. It was once commonly used in LANs and can still be found in some older installations. For LANs, baseband cable is now preferable since it is less expensive, easier to physically handle, and does not require attachment cables. Broadband cable, however, is quite common in cable television systems. As we saw earlier, cable television systems have recently been coupled with cable modems to provide residential users with Web access at rates of 10 Mbps or higher. With broadband coaxial cable, the transmitter shifts the digital signal to a specific frequency band, and the resulting analog signal is sent from the transmitter to one or more receivers. Both baseband and broadband coaxial cable can be used as a guided **shared medium.** Specifically, a number of end systems can be connected directly to the cable, and all the end systems receive whatever any one of the computers transmits. We will look at this issue in more detail in Chapter 5.

Fiber optics.   An optical fiber is a thin, flexible medium that conducts pulses of light, with each pulse representing a bit. A single optical fiber can support tremendous bit rates, up to tens or even hundreds of gigabits per second. They are immune to electromagnetic interference, have very low signal attenuation up to 100 kilometers, and are very hard to tap. These characteristics have made fiber optics the preferred long-haul guided transmission media, particularly for overseas links. Many of the long-distance telephone networks in the United States and elsewhere now use fiber optics exclusively. Fiber optics is also prevalent in the backbone of the Internet. However, the high cost of optical devices—such as transmitters, receivers, and switches—has hindered their deployment for short-haul transport, such as in a LAN or into the home in a residential access network. AT&T Labs provides an excellent site [AT&T Optics 1999] on fiber optics, including several nice animations.

Terrestrial and satellite radio channels.   Radio channels carry signals in the electromagnetic spectrum. They are an attractive media because they require no physical "wire" to be installed, can penetrate walls, provide connectivity to a mobile user, and can potentially carry a signal for long distances. The characteristics of a radio channel depend significantly on the propagation environment and the distance over which a signal is to be carried. Environmental considerations determine path loss and shadow fading (which decrease in signal strength as the signal travels over a distance and around/through obstructing objects), multipath fading (due to signal reflection off of interfering objects), and interference (due to other radio channels or electromagnetic signals).

Terrestrial radio channels can be broadly classified into two groups: those that operate as local area networks (typically spanning from ten to a few hundred meters) and wide-area radio channels that are used for mobile data services (typically operating within a metropolitan region). A number of wireless LAN products are on the market, operating in the range of from one to tens of Mbps. Mobile data services (such as the CDPD standard we touched on in Section 1.5), typically provide channels that operate at tens of Kbps. See [Goodman 97] for a survey and discussion of the technology and products.

A communication satellite links two or more Earth-based microwave transmitter/receivers, known as ground stations. The satellite receives transmissions on one frequency band, regenerates the signal using a repeater (discussed below), and transmits the signal on another frequency. Satellites can provide bandwidths in the gigabit per second range. Two types of satellites are used in communications: geostationary satellites and low-altitude satellites.

Geostationary satellites permanently remain above the same spot on Earth. This stationary presence is achieved by placing the satellite in orbit at 36,000 kilometers above Earth's surface. This huge distance from ground station through satellite back to ground station introduces a substantial signal propagation delay of 250 milliseconds. Nevertheless, satellite links are often used in telephone networks and in the backbone of the Internet.

Low-altitude satellites are placed much closer to Earth and do not remain permanently above one spot on Earth. They rotate around Earth just as the Moon does. To provide continuous coverage to an area, many satellites need to be placed in orbit. There are currently many low-altitude communication systems in development. The Iridium system, for example, consists of 66 low-altitude satellites. Lloyd's satellite constellation systems Web page [Wood 1999] provides and collects information on Iridium as well as other satellite constellation systems. The low-altitude satellite technology may be used for Internet access sometime in the future.

1.6 DELAY AND LOSS IN PACKET-SWITCHED NETWORKS

Having now briefly considered the major "pieces" of the Internet architecture—the applications, end systems, end-to-end transport protocols, routers, and links—let us now consider what can happen to a packet as it travels from its source to its destination. Recall that a packet starts in a host (the source), passes through a series of routers, and ends its journey in another host (the destination). As a packet travels from one node (host or router) to the subsequent node (host or router) along this path, the packet suffers from several different types of delays at *each* node along the path. The most important of these delays are the **nodal processing delay, queuing delay, transmission delay,** and **propagation delay;** together, these delays accumulate to give a **total nodal delay.** In order to acquire a deep understanding of packet switching and computer networks, we must understand the nature and importance of these delays.

1.6.1   Types of Delay

Let us explore these delays in the context of Figure 1.19. As part of its end-to-end route between source and destination, a packet is sent from the upstream node through router A to router B. Our goal is to characterize the nodal delay at router A. Note that router A has three outbound links, one leading to router B, another leading to router C, and yet another leading to router D. Each link is preceded by a queue (also known as a buffer). When the packet arrives at router A (from the upstream node), router A examines the packet's header to determine the appropriate outbound link for the packet, and then directs the packet to the link. In this example, the outbound link for the packet is the one that leads to router B. A packet can only be transmitted on a link if there is no other packet currently being transmitted on the link and if there are no other packets preceding it in the queue; if the link is currently busy or if there are other packets already queued for the link, the newly arriving packet will then join the queue.

Processing delay.   The time required to examine the packet's header and determine where to direct the packet is part of the **processing delay.** The processing delay can also include other factors, such as the time needed to check for bit-level errors in the packet that occurred in transmitting the packet's bits from the upstream router to router A. After this nodal processing, the router directs the packet to the queue that precedes the link to router B. (In Section 4.7 we will study the details of how a router operates.)

Queuing delay.   At the queue, the packet experiences a **queuing delay** as it waits to be transmitted onto the link. The queuing delay of a specific packet will depend on the number of other, earlier-arriving packets that are queued and waiting for transmission across the link; the delay of a given packet can vary significantly from packet to packet. If the queue is empty and no other packet is currently being transmitted, then our packet's queuing delay is zero. On the other

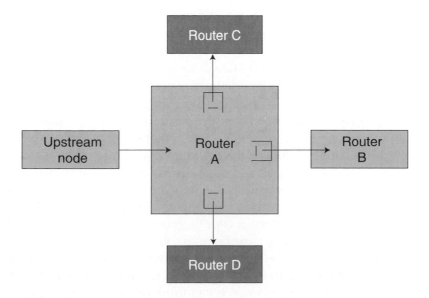

FIGURE 1.19   The delay through router A

hand, if the traffic is heavy and many other packets are also waiting to be transmitted, the queuing delay will be long. We will see shortly that the number of packets that an arriving packet might expect to find on arrival (informally, the average number of queued packets, which is proportional to the average delay experienced by packets) is a function of the intensity and nature of the traffic arriving to the queue.

Transmission delay.   Assuming that packets are transmitted in first-come-first-serve manner, as is common in the Internet, our packet can be transmitted once all the packets that have arrived before it have been transmitted. Denote the length of the packet by L bits and denote the transmission rate of the link (from router A to router B) by R bits/sec. The rate R is determined by transmission rate of the link to router B. For example, for a 10 Mbps Ethernet link, the rate is $R = 10$ Mbps; for a 100 Mbps Ethernet link, the rate is $R = 100$ Mbps. The **transmission delay** (also called the store-and-forward delay, as discussed in Section 1.4) is L/R. This is the amount of time required to transmit all of the packet's bits into the link.

Propagation delay.   Once a bit is pushed onto the link, it needs to propagate to router B. The time required to propagate from the beginning of the link to router B is the **propagation delay.** The bit propagates at the propagation speed of the link. The propagation speed depends on the physical medium of the link (that is, multi-mode fiber, twisted-pair copper wire, and so on) and is in the range of

$$2 \cdot 10^8 \text{ meters/sec to } 3 \cdot 10^8 \text{ meters/sec}$$

which is equal to, or a little less than, the speed of light. The propagation delay is the distance between two routers divided by the propagation speed. That is, the propagation delay is d/s, where d is the distance between router A and router B and s is the propagation speed of the link. Once the last bit of the packet propagates to node B, it and all the preceding bits of the packet are stored in router B. The whole process then continues with router B now performing the forwarding.

Comparing transmission and propagation delay.   Newcomers to the field of computer networking sometimes have difficulty understanding the difference between transmission delay and propagation delay. The difference is subtle but important. The transmission delay is the amount of time required for the router to push out the packet; it is a function of the packet's length and the transmission rate of the link, but has nothing to do with the distance between the two routers. The propagation delay, on the other hand, is the time it takes a bit to propagate from one router to the next; it is a function of the distance between the two routers, but has nothing to do with the packet's length or the transmission rate of the link.

An analogy might clarify the notions of transmission and propagation delay. Consider a highway which has a toll booth every 100 kilometers. You can think of the highway segments between toll booths as links and the toll booths as routers. Suppose that cars travel (that is, propagate) on the highway at a rate of 100 km/hour (that is, when a car leaves a toll booth it instantaneously accelerates to 100 km/hour and maintains that speed between toll booths). Suppose that there is a caravan of 10 cars that are traveling together, and that these 10 cars follow each other in a fixed order. You can think of each car as a bit and the caravan as a packet. Also suppose that each toll booth services (that is, transmits) a car at a rate of one car per 12 seconds, and that it is late at night so that the caravan's cars are the only cars on the highway. Finally, suppose that whenever the first car of the caravan arrives at a toll booth, it waits at the entrance until the nine other cars have arrived and lined up behind it. (Thus the entire caravan must be "stored" at the toll booth before it can begin to be "forwarded.") The time required for the toll booth to push the entire caravan onto the highway is 10/(5 cars/minute) = 2 minutes. This time is analogous to the transmission delay in a router. The time required for a car to travel from the exit of one toll booth to the next toll booth is 100 km/(100 km/hour) = 1 hour. This time is analogous to propagation delay. Therefore, the time from when the caravan is "stored" in front of a toll booth until the caravan is "stored" in front of the next toll booth is the sum of "transmission delay" and "the propagation delay"—in this example, 62 minutes.

Let's explore this analogy a bit more. What would happen if the toll-booth service time for a caravan were greater than the time for a car to travel between toll booths? For example, suppose cars travel at rate 1000 km/hr and the toll booth services cars at rate one car per minute. Then the traveling delay between toll booths is 6 minutes and the time to serve a caravan is 10 minutes. In this case, the first few cars in the caravan will arrive at the second toll booth before the last cars in caravan leave the first toll booth. This situation also arises in packet-switched networks—the first bits in a packet can arrive at a router while many of the remaining bits in the packet are still waiting to be transmitted by the preceding router.

If we let d_{proc}, d_{queue}, d_{trans}, and d_{prop} denote the processing, queuing, transmission and propagation delays, then the total nodal delay is given by

$$d_{nodal} = d_{proc} + d_{queue} + d_{trans} + d_{prop}$$

The contribution of these delay components can vary significantly. For example, d_{prop} can be negligible (for example, a couple of microseconds) for a link connecting two routers on the same university campus; however, d_{prop} is hundreds of milliseconds for two routers interconnected by a geostationary satellite link, and can be the dominant term in d_{nodal}. Similarly, d_{trans} can range from negligible to significant. Its contribution is typically negligible for transmission rates of 10 Mbps and higher (for example, for LANs); however, it can be hundreds of milliseconds for large Internet packets sent over 28.8 Kbps modem links. The processing delay, d_{proc}, is often negligible; however, it strongly influences a router's maximum throughput, which is the maximum rate at which a router can forward packets.

Queuing delay.   The most complicated and interesting component of nodal delay is the queuing delay, d_{queue}. In fact, queuing delay is so important and interesting in computer networking that thousands of papers and numerous books have been written about it [Bertsekas 1992], [Daigle 1991], [Kleinrock 1975], [Kleinrock 1976], [Ross 1995]! We only give a high-level, intuitive discussion of queuing delay here; the more curious reader may want to browse through some of the books (or even eventually write a Ph.D. thesis on the subject!). Unlike the other three delays (namely, d_{proc}, d_{trans}, and d_{prop}), the queuing delay can vary from packet to packet. For example, if 10 packets arrive at an empty queue at the same time, the first packet transmitted will suffer no queuing delay, while the last packet transmitted will suffer a relatively large queuing delay (while it waits for the other nine packets to be transmitted). Therefore, when characterizing queuing delay, one typically uses statistical measures, such as average queuing delay, variance of queuing delay, and the probability that the queuing delay exceeds some specified value.

When is the queuing delay large and when is it insignificant? The answer to this question depends largely on the rate at which traffic arrives to the queue, the transmission rate of the link, and the nature of the arriving traffic, that is, whether the traffic arrives periodically or whether it arrives in bursts. To gain some insight here, let a denote the average rate at which packets arrive to the queue (a is in units of packets/sec). Recall that R is the transmission rate, that is, it is the rate (in bits/sec) at which bits are pushed out of the queue. Also suppose, for simplicity, that all packets consist of L bits. Then the average rate at which bits arrive to the queue is La bits/sec. Finally, assume that the queue is very big, so that it can hold essentially an infinite number of bits. The ratio La/R, called the **traffic intensity,** often plays an important role in estimating the extent of the queuing delay. If $La/R > 1$, then the average rate at which bits arrive to the queue exceeds the rate at which the bits can be transmitted from the queue. In this unfortunate situation, the queue will tend to increase without bound and the queuing delay will approach infinity! Therefore, one of the golden rules in traffic engineering is: *Design your system so that the traffic intensity is no greater than 1.*

Now consider the case $La/R =< 1$. Here, the nature of the arriving traffic impacts the queuing delay. For example, if packets arrive periodically, that is, one packet arrives every L/R seconds, then every packet will arrive to an empty queue and there will be no queuing delay. On the other hand, if packets arrive in bursts but periodically, there can be a significant average queuing delay. For example, suppose N packets arrive at the same time every $(L/R)N$ seconds. Then the first packet transmitted has no queuing delay; the second packet transmitted has a queuing delay of L/R seconds; and more generally, the nth packet transmitted has a queuing delay of $(n - 1)L/R$ seconds. We leave it as an exercise for the reader to calculate the average queuing delay in this example.

The two examples described above of periodic arrivals are a bit academic. Typically, the arrival process to a queue is *random,* that is, the arrivals do not follow any pattern; packets are spaced apart by random amounts of time. In this more realistic case, the quantity La/R is not usually sufficient to fully characterize the delay statistics. Nonetheless, it is useful in gaining an intuitive understanding of the extent of the queuing delay. In particular, if traffic intensity is close to zero, then packets are pushed out at a rate much higher than the packet arrival rate; therefore, the average queuing delay will be close to zero. On the other hand, when the traffic intensity is close to 1, there will be intervals of time when the arrival rate exceeds the transmission capacity (due to the burstiness of arrivals), and a queue will form. As the traffic intensity approaches 1, the average queue length gets larger and larger. The qualitative dependence of average queuing delay on the traffic intensity is shown in Figure 1.20.

One important aspect of Figure 1.20 is the fact that as the traffic intensity approaches 1, the average queuing delay increases rapidly. A small percentage increase in the intensity will result in a much larger percentage-wise increase in

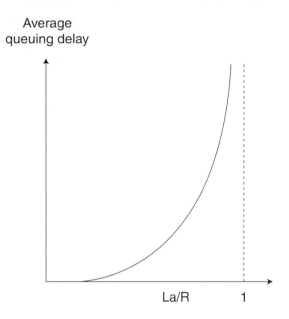

Average
queuing delay

La/R   1

FIGURE 1.20 Dependence of average queuing delay on traffic intensity

delay. Perhaps you have experienced this phenomenon on the highway. If you regularly drive on a road that is typically congested, the fact that the road is typically congested means that its traffic intensity is close to 1. If some event causes an even slightly-larger-than-usual amount of traffic, the delays you experience can be huge.

Packet loss.   In our discussions above, we have assumed that the queue is capable of holding an infinite number of packets. In reality a queue preceding a link has finite capacity, although the queuing capacity greatly depends on the switch design and cost. Because the queue capacity is finite, packet delays do not really approach infinity as the traffic intensity approaches 1. Instead, a packet can arrive to find a full queue. With no place to store such a packet, a router will **drop** that packet; that is, the packet will be **lost.** From an end-system viewpoint, this will look like a packet having been transmitted into the network core, but never emerging from the network at the destination. The fraction of lost packets increases as the traffic intensity increases. Therefore, performance at a node is often measured not only in terms of delay, but also in terms of the probability of packet loss. As we shall discuss in the subsequent chapters, a lost packet may be retransmitted on an end-to-end basis, by either the application or by the transport layer protocol.

End-to-end delay.   Our discussion up to this point has been focused on the nodal delay, that is, the delay at a single router. Let us conclude our discussion by briefly considering the delay from source to destination. To get a handle on this concept, suppose there are $Q - 1$ routers between the source host and the destination host. Let us also suppose that the network is uncongested (so that queuing delays are negligible), the processing delay at each router and at the source host is d_{proc}, the transmission rate out of each router and out of the source host is R bits/sec, and the propagation delay between each pair or routers and between the source host and the first router is d_{prop}. The nodal delays accumulate and give an end-to-end delay,

$$d_{end-end} = Q\,(d_{proc} + d_{trans} + d_{prop})$$

where, once again, $d_{trans} = L/R$, where L is the packet size. We leave it to the reader to generalize this formula to the case of heterogeneous delays at the nodes and to the presence of an average queuing delay at each node.

1.7 PROTOCOL LAYERS AND THEIR SERVICE MODELS

From our discussion thus far, it is apparent that the Internet is an *extremely* complicated system. We have seen that there are many "pieces" to the Internet: numerous applications and protocols, various types of end systems and connections between end systems, routers, and various types of link-level media. Given this enormous complexity, is there any hope of *organizing* network architecture, or at least our discussion of network architecture? Fortunately, the answers to both questions is yes.

1.7.1 Layered Architecture

Before attempting to organize our thoughts on Internet architecture, let's look for a human analogy. Actually, we deal with complex systems all the time in our everyday life. Imagine if someone asked *you* to describe, for example, the airline system. How would you find the structure to describe this complex system that has ticketing agents, baggage checkers, gate personnel, pilots and airplanes, air traffic control, and a worldwide system for routing airplanes? One way to describe this system might be to describe the series of actions you take (or others take for you) when you fly on an airline. You purchase your ticket, check your bags, go to the gate, and eventually get loaded onto the plane. The plane takes off and is routed to its destination. After your plane lands, you de-plane at the gate and claim your bags. If the trip was bad, you complain about the flight to the ticket agent (getting nothing for your effort). This scenario is shown in Figure 1.21.

Already, we can see some analogies here with computer networking: You are being shipped from source to destination by the airline; a packet is shipped from source host to destination host in the Internet. But this is not quite the analogy we are after. We are looking for some *structure* in Figure 1.21. Looking at Figure 1.21, we note that there is a ticketing function at each end; there is also a baggage function for already ticketed passengers, and a gate function for already-ticketed and already-baggage-checked passengers. For passengers who have made it through the gate (that is, passengers who are already ticketed, baggage-checked, and through the gate), there is a takeoff and landing function, and while in flight, there is an airplane routing function. This suggests that we can look at the functionality in Figure 1.21 in a *horizontal* manner, as shown in Figure 1.22.

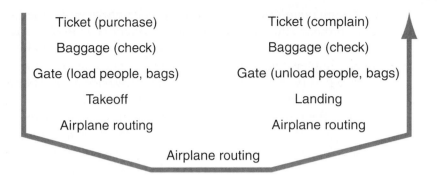

FIGURE 1.21 Taking an airplane trip: Actions

Figure 1.22 has divided the airline functionality into *layers,* providing a framework in which we can discuss airline travel. Now, when we want to describe a part of airline travel, we can talk about a specific, well-defined component of airline travel. For example, when we discuss gate functionality, we know we are discussing functionality that sits "below" baggage handling, and "above" takeoff and landing. We note that each layer, combined with the layers below it, implement some functionality, some *service*. At the ticketing layer and below, airline-counter-to-airline-counter transfer of a person is accomplished. At the baggage layer and below, baggage-check-to-baggage-claim transfer of a person and their bags is accomplished. Note that the baggage layer provides this service only to an already ticketed person. At the gate layer, departure-gate-to-arrival-gate transfer of a person and bags is accomplished. At the takeoff/landing layer, runway-to-runway transfer of a person (actually, many people) and their bags, is accomplished. Each layer provides its functionality (service) by (1) performing certain actions within that layer (for example, at the gate layer, loading and unloading people from an airplane) and by (2) using the services of the layer directly below it (for example, in the gate layer, using the runway-to-runway passenger transfer service of the takeoff/landing layer).

As noted above, a layered architecture allows us to discuss a well-defined, specific part of a large and complex system. This simplification itself is of considerable value. When a system has a layered structure it is also much easier to

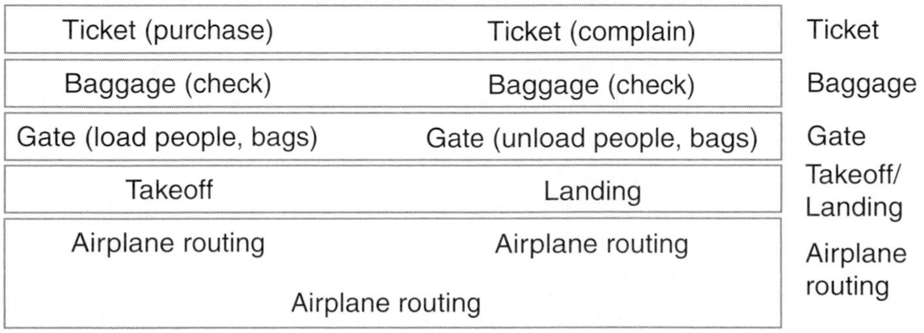

Ticket (purchase)	Ticket (complain)	Ticket
Baggage (check)	Baggage (check)	Baggage
Gate (load people, bags)	Gate (unload people, bags)	Gate
Takeoff	Landing	Takeoff/ Landing
Airplane routing	Airplane routing	Airplane routing
Airplane routing		

FIGURE 1.22 Horizontal "layering" of airline functionality

change the *implementation* of the service provided by the layer. As long as the layer provides the same service to the layer above it, and uses the same services from the layer below it, the remainder of the system remains unchanged when a layer's implementation is changed. (Note that changing the implementation of a service is very different from changing the service itself!) For example, if the gate functions were changed (for example, to have people board and disembark by height), the remainder of the airline system would remain unchanged since the gate layer still provides the same function (loading and unloading people); it simply implements that function in a different manner after the change. For large and complex systems that are constantly being updated, the ability to change the implementation of a service without affecting other components of the system is another important advantage of layering.

But enough with airlines. Let's now turn our attention to network protocols. To reduce design complexity, network designers organize protocols—and the network hardware and software that implements the protocols—in **layers.** With a layered protocol architecture, each protocol belongs to one of the layers. It's important to realize that a protocol in layer n is *distributed* among the network entities (including end systems and packet switches) that implement that protocol, just as the functions in our layered airline architecture were distributed between the departing and arriving airports. In other words, there's a "piece" of layer n in each of the network entities. These "pieces" communicate with each other by exchanging layer-n messages. These messages are called layer-n protocol data units, or more commonly n-**PDUs.** The contents and format of an n-PDU, as well as the manner in which the n-PDUs are exchanged among the network elements, are defined by a layer-n protocol. When taken together, the protocols of the various layers are called the **protocol stack.**

When layer n of Host A sends an n-PDU to layer n of Host B, layer n of Host A *passes* the n-PDU to layer $n - 1$ and then lets layer $n - 1$ deliver the n-PDU to layer n of B; thus layer n is said to *rely* on layer $n - 1$ to deliver its n-PDU to the destination. A key concept is that of the **service model** of a layer. Layer $n - 1$ is said to offer **services** to layer n. For example, layer $n - 1$ might guarantee that the n-PDU will arrive without error at layer n in the destination within one second, or it might only guarantee that the n-PDU will eventually arrive at the destination without any assurances about error.

Protocol layering. The concept of protocol layering is fairly abstract and is sometimes difficult to grasp at first. This concept will become clear as we study the Internet layers and their constituent protocols in greater detail. But let us now try to shed some insight on protocol layering and protocol stacks with an example. Consider a network that organizes its communication protocols in four layers. Because there are four layers, there are four types of PDUs: 1-PDUs, 2-PDUs, 3-PDUs, and 4-PDUs. As shown in Figure 1.23, the application, operating at the highest layer, layer 4, creates a message, M. Any message created at this highest layer is a 4-PDU. The message M itself may consist of many different fields (in much the same way as a structure or record in a programming language may contain different fields); it is up to the application to define and interpret the fields in the message. The fields might contain the name of the sender, a code indicating the type of the message, and some additional data.

Within the source host, the contents of the entire message M is then "passed" down the protocol stack to layer 3. In the example in Figure 1.23, layer 3 in the source host divides a 4-PDU, M, into two parts, M_1 and M_2. The layer 3 in the source host then adds to M_1 and M_2, so-called **headers,** to create two layer-3 PDUs. Headers contain the additional information needed by the sending and receiving sides of layer 3 to implement the service that layer 3 provides to layer 4. The procedure continues in the source, adding more header at each layer, until the 1-PDUs are created. The 1-PDUs are sent out of the source host onto a physical link. At the other end, the destination host receives 1-PDUs and directs them up the protocol stack. At each layer, the corresponding header is removed. Finally, M is reassembled from M_1 and M_2 and then passed on to the application.

Note that in Figure 1.23, layer n uses the services of layer $n - 1$. For example, once layer 4 creates the message M, it passes the message down to layer 3 and relies on layer 3 to deliver the message to layer 4 at the destination.

Interestingly enough, this notion of relying on lower-layer services is prevalent in many other forms of communication. For example, consider ordinary postal mail. When you write a letter, you include envelope information such as the destination address and the return address with the letter. The letter, along with the address information, can be considered a PDU at the highest layer of the protocol stack. You then drop the PDU in a mailbox. At this point, the letter is out of your hands. The postal service may then add some of its own internal information onto your letter, essentially adding a header to your letter. For example, in the United States a barcode is often printed on your letter.

Once you drop your envelope into a mailbox, you *rely* on the services of the postal service to deliver the letter to the correct destination in a timely manner. For example, you don't worry about whether a postal truck will break down while carrying the letter. Instead the postal service takes care of this, presumably with well-defined plans to recover from such failures. Furthermore, within the postal service itself there are layers, and the protocols at one layer rely on and use the services of the layer below.

In order for one layer to interoperate with the layer below it, the interfaces between the two layers must be precisely defined. Standards bodies define precisely

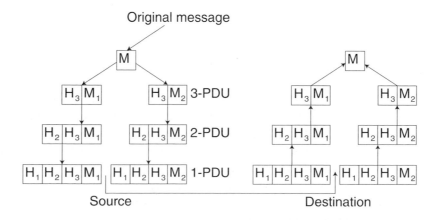

FIGURE 1.23   Different PDUs at different layers in the protocol architecture

the interfaces between adjacent layers (for example, the format of the PDUs passed between the layers) and permit the developers of networking software and hardware to implement the interior of the layers as they please. Therefore, if a new and improved implementation of a layer is released, the new implementation can replace the old implementation and, in theory, the layers will continue to interoperate.

Layer functions. In a computer network, each layer may perform one or more of the following generic set of tasks:

- **Error control,** which makes the logical channel between the layers in two peer network elements more reliable
- **Flow control,** which avoids overwhelming a slower peer with PDUs
- **Segmentation and reassembly,** which at the transmitting side divides large data chunks into smaller pieces and at the receiving side reassembles the smaller pieces into the original large chunk
- **Multiplexing,** which allows several higher-level sessions to share a single lower-level connection
- **Connection setup,** which provides the handshaking with a peer

Protocol layering has conceptual and structural advantages. We mention, however, that some researchers and networking engineers are vehemently opposed to layering [Wakeman 1992]. One potential drawback of layering is that one layer may duplicate lower-layer functionality. For example, many protocol stacks provide error recovery on both a link basis and an end-to-end basis. A second potential drawback is that functionality at one layer may need information (for example, a timestamp value) that is present only in another layer; this violates the goal of separation of layers.

1.7.2 The Internet Protocol Stack

The Internet stack consists of five layers: the physical, data link, network, transport, and application layers. Rather than use the cumbersome terminology n-PDU for each of the five layers, we instead give special names to the PDUs in four of the five layers: frame, datagram, segment, and message. We avoid naming a data unit for the physical layer, as no name is commonly used at this layer. The Internet stack and the corresponding PDU names are illustrated in Figure 1.24.

A protocol layer can be implemented in software, in hardware, or using a combination of the two. Application-layer protocols—such as HTTP and SMTP—are almost always implemented in software in the end systems; so are transport-layer protocols. Because the physical layer and data link layers are responsible for handling communication over a specific link, they are typically implemented in a network interface card (for example, Ethernet or ATM interface cards) associated with a given link. The network layer is often a mixed implementation of hardware and software.

We now summarize the Internet layers and the services they provide:

Application layer. The application layer is responsible for supporting network applications. The application layer includes many protocols, including HTTP to support the Web, SMTP to support electronic mail, and FTP to support file trans-

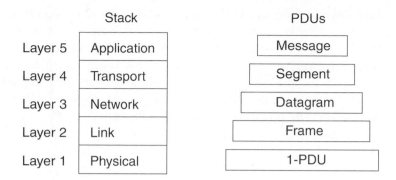

FIGURE 1.24 The Internet protocol stack, and protocol data units

fer. We shall see in Chapter 2 that it is very easy to create our own new application-layer protocols.

Transport layer.   The transport layer is responsible for transporting application-layer messages between the client and server sides of an application. In the Internet there are two transport protocols, TCP and UDP, either of which can transport application-layer messages. TCP provides a connection-oriented service to its applications. This service includes guaranteed delivery of application-layer messages to the destination and flow control (that is, sender/receiver speed matching). TCP also segments long messages into shorter segments and provides a congestion control mechanism, so that a source throttles its transmission rate when the network is congested. The UDP protocol provides its applications a connectionless service, which (as we saw in Section 1.3) is very much a no-frills service.

Network layer.   The network layer is responsible for routing datagrams from one host to another. The Internet's network layer has two principle components. It has a protocol that defines the fields in the IP datagram as well as how the end systems and routers act on these fields. This protocol is the celebrated IP protocol. There is only one IP protocol, and all Internet components that have a network layer must run the IP protocol. The Internet's network layer also contains routing protocols that determine the routes that datagrams take between sources and destinations. The Internet has many routing protocols. As we saw in Section 1.4, the Internet is a network of networks and within a network, the network administrator can run any routing protocol desired. Although the network layer contains both the IP protocol and numerous routing protocols, it is often simply referred to as the IP layer, reflecting the fact that IP is the glue that binds the Internet together.

The Internet transport layer protocols (TCP and UDP) in a source host passes a transport-layer segment and a destination address to the IP layer, just as you give the postal service a letter with a destination address. The IP layer then provides the service of routing the segment to its destination. When the packet arrives at the destination, IP passes the segment to the transport layer within the destination.

Link layer. The network layer routes a packet through a series of packet switches (that is, routers) between the source and destination. To move a packet from one node (host or packet switch) to the next node in the route, the network layer must rely on the services of the link layer. In particular, at each node IP passes the datagram to the link layer, which delivers the datagram to the next node along the route. At this next node, the link layer passes the IP datagram to the network layer. The process is analogous to the postal worker at a mailing center who puts a letter into a plane that will deliver the letter to the next postal center along the route. The services provided at the link layer depend on the specific link-layer protocol that is employed over the link. For example, some protocols provide reliable delivery on a link basis, that is, from transmitting node, over one link, to receiving node. Note that this reliable delivery service is different from the reliable delivery service of TCP, which provides reliable delivery from one end system to another. Examples of link layers include Ethernet and PPP; in some contexts, ATM and frame relay can be considered link layers. As datagrams typically need to traverse several links to travel from source to destination, a datagram may be handled by different link-layer protocols at different links along its route. For example, a datagram may be handled by Ethernet on one link and then PPP on the next link. IP will receive a different service from each of the different link-layer protocols.

Physical layer. While the job of the link layer is to move entire frames from one network element to an adjacent network element, the job of the physical layer is to move the *individual bits* within the frame from one node to the next. The protocols in this layer are again link dependent, and further depend on the actual transmission medium of the link (for example, twisted-pair copper wire, single mode fiber optics). For example, Ethernet has many physical layer protocols: one for twisted-pair copper wire, another for coaxial cable, another for fiber, and so on. In each case, a bit is moved across the link in a different way.

If you examine the Table of Contents, you will see that we have roughly organized this book using the layers of the Internet protocol stack. We take a **top-down approach,** first covering the application layer and then preceding downwards.

1.7.3   Network Entities and Layers

The most important network entities are end systems and packet switches. As we shall discuss later in this book, there are two types of packet switches: routers and bridges. We presented an overview of routers in the earlier sections. Bridges will be discussed in detail in Chapter 5 whereas routers will be covered in more detail in Chapter 4. Similar to end systems, routers and bridges organize the networking hardware and software into layers. But routers and bridges do not implement *all* of the layers in the protocol stack; they typically implement only the bottom layers. As shown in Figure 1.25, bridges implement layers 1 and 2; routers implement layers 1 through 3. This means, for example, that Internet routers are capable of implementing the IP protocol (a layer 3 protocol), while bridges are not. We will see later that while bridges do not recognize IP addresses, they are capable of recognizing layer 2 addresses, such as Ethernet addresses. Note that

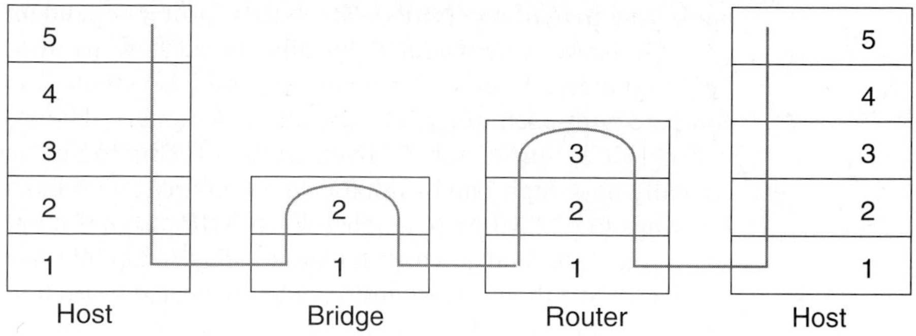

FIGURE 1.25   Hosts, routers and bridges; each contain a different set of layers, reflecting their differences in functionality

hosts implement all five layers; this is consistent with the view that the Internet architecture puts much of its complexity at the "edges" of the network. Repeaters, yet another kind of network entity to be discussed in Chapter 5, implement only layer-1 functionality.

1.8   INTERNET BACKBONES, NAPS, AND ISPS

Our discussion of layering in the previous section has perhaps given the impression that the Internet is a carefully organized and highly intertwined structure. This is certainly true in the sense that all of the network entities (end systems, routers and bridges) use a common set of protocols, enabling the entities to communicate with each other. If one wanted to change, remove, or add a protocol, one would have to follow a long and arduous procedure to get approval from the IETF, which will (among other things) make sure that the changes are consistent with the highly intertwined structure. However, from a topological perspective, to many people the Internet seems to be growing in a chaotic manner, with new sections, branches, and wings popping up in random places on a daily basis. Indeed, unlike the protocols, the Internet's topology can grow and evolve without approval from a central authority. Let us now try to get a grip on the seemingly nebulous Internet topology.

As we mentioned at the beginning of this chapter, the topology of the Internet is loosely hierarchical. Roughly speaking, from bottom-to-top the hierarchy consists of end systems (PCs, workstations, and so on) connected to local Internet service providers (ISPs). The local ISPs are in turn connected to regional ISPs, which are in turn connected to national and international ISPs. The national and international ISPs are connected together at the highest tier in the hierarchy. New tiers and branches can be added just as a new piece of Lego can be attached to an existing Lego construction.

In this section we describe the topology of the Internet in the United States as of 1999. Let's begin at the top of the hierarchy and work our way down. Residing at the very top of the hierarchy are the national ISPs, which are called **national**

backbone providers (NBPs). The NBPs form independent backbone networks that span North America (and typically abroad as well). Just as there are multiple long-distance telephone companies in the USA, there are multiple NBPs that compete with each other for traffic and customers. The existing NBPs include internetMCI, SprintLink, PSINet, UUNet Technologies, and AGIS. The NBPs typically have high-bandwidth transmission links, with bandwidths ranging from 1.5 Mbps to 622 Mbps and higher. Each **NBP** also has numerous hubs that interconnect its links and at which **regional ISPs** can tap into the NBP.

The NBPs themselves must be interconnected to each other. To see this, suppose one regional ISP, say MidWestnet, is connected to the MCI NBP and another regional ISP, say EastCoastnet, is connected to Sprint's NBP. How can traffic be sent from MidWestnet to EastCoastnet? The solution is to introduce switching centers, called **network access points (NAPs),** which interconnect the NBPs, thereby allowing each regional ISP to pass traffic to any other regional ISP. To keep us all confused, some of the NAPs are not referred to as NAPs but instead as MAEs (metropolitan area exchanges). In the United States, many of the NAPs are run by RBOCs (regional Bell operating companies); for example, PacBell has a NAP in San Francisco and Ameritech has a NAP in Chicago. For a list of major NBPs (those connected into at least three MAPs/MAE's), see [Haynal 99].

Because the NAPs relay and switch tremendous volumes of Internet traffic, they are typically in themselves complex high-speed switching networks concentrated in a small geographical area (for example, a single building). Often the NAPs use high-speed ATM switching technology in the heart of the NAP, with IP riding on top of ATM. (We provide a brief introduction to ATM at the end of this chapter, and discuss IP-over-ATM in Chapter 5.) Figure 1.26 illustrates PacBell's San Francisco NAP. The details of Figure 1.26 are unimportant for us now; it is worthwhile to note, however, that the NBP hubs can themselves be complex data networks.

The astute reader may have noticed that ATM technology, which uses virtual circuits, can be found at certain places within the Internet. But earlier we said that the "Internet is a datagram network and does not use virtual circuits." We admit now that this statement stretches the truth a little bit. We made this statement because it helps the reader to see the forest through the trees by not having the main issues obscured. The truth is that there are virtual circuits in the Internet, but they are in localized pockets of the Internet and they are buried deep down in the protocol stack, typically at layer 2. If you find this confusing, just pretend for now that the Internet does not employ any technology that uses virtual circuits. This is not too far from the truth.

Running an NBP is not cheap. In June 1996, the cost of leasing 45 Mbps fiber optics from coast-to-coast, as well as the additional hardware required, was approximately $150,000 per month. And the fees that an NBP pays the NAPs to connect to the NAPs can exceed $300,000 annually. NBPs and NAPs also have significant capital costs in equipment for high-speed networking. An NBP earns money by charging a monthly fee to the regional ISPs that connect to it. The fee that an NBP charges to a regional ISP typically depends on the bandwidth of the connection between the regional ISP and the NBP; clearly a 1.5 Mbps connection would be charged less than a 45 Mbps connection. Once the fixed-bandwidth connection is in place, the regional ISP can pump and receive as much data as it pleases, up to the bandwidth of the connection, at no additional cost. If an NBP

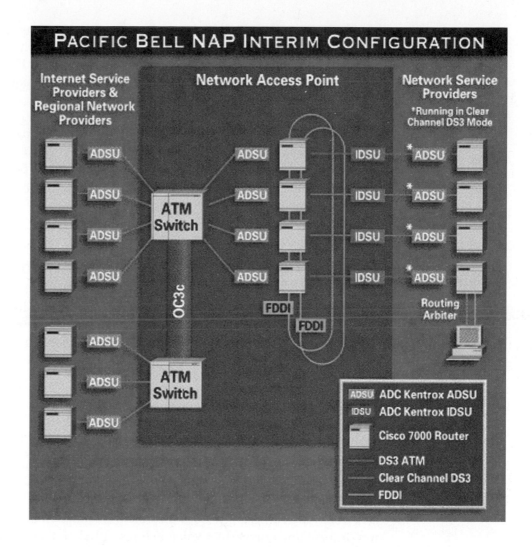

FIGURE 1.26   The PacBell NAP architecture (courtesy of the Pacific Bell Web site)

has significant revenues from the regional ISPs that connect to it, it may be able to cover the high capital and monthly costs of setting up and maintaining an NBP.

A regional ISP is also a complex network, consisting of routers and transmission links with rates ranging from 64 Kbps upward. A regional ISP typically taps into an NBP (at an NBP hub), but it can also tap directly into an NAP, in which case the regional ISP pays a monthly fee to a NAP instead of to an NBP. A regional ISP can also tap into the Internet backbone at two or more distinct points (for example, at an NBP hub or at a NAP). How does a regional ISP cover its costs? To answer this question, let's jump to the bottom of the hierarchy.

End systems gain access to the Internet by connecting to a local ISP. Universities and corporations can act as local ISPs, but backbone service providers can also serve as a local ISP. Many local ISPs are small "mom and pop" companies, however. A popular Web site known simply as "The List" contains links to nearly 8,000 local, regional, and backbone ISPs [List 1999]. The local ISPs tap into one of the regional ISPs in its region. Analogous to the fee structure between the regional ISP and the NBP, the local ISP pays a monthly fee to its regional ISP that depends on the bandwidth of the connection. Finally, the local ISP charges its customers (typically) a flat, monthly fee for Internet access: the higher the transmission rate of the connection, the higher the monthly fee.

We conclude this section by mentioning that anyone of us can become a local ISP as soon as we have an Internet connection. All we need to do is purchase the necessary equipment (for example, router and modem pool) that is needed to allow other users to connect to our so-called "point of presence." Thus, new tiers and branches can be added to the Internet topology just as a new piece of Lego can be attached to an existing Lego construction.

1.9 A BRIEF HISTORY OF COMPUTER NETWORKING AND THE INTERNET

Sections 1.1–1.8 presented an overview of technology of computer networking and the Internet. You should know enough now to impress your family and friends. However, if you really want to be a big hit at the next cocktail party, you should sprinkle your discourse with tidbits about the fascinating history of the Internet.

1.9.1 Development and Demonstration of Early Packet Switching Principles: 1961–1972

The field of computer networking and today's Internet trace their beginnings back to the early 1960s, a time at which the telephone network was the world's dominant communication network. Recall from Section 1.4 that the telephone network uses circuit switching to transmit information from a sender to receiver—an appropriate choice given that voice is transmitted at a constant rate between sender and receiver. Given the increasing importance (and great expense) of computers in the early 1960s and the advent of timeshared computers, it was perhaps natural (at least with perfect hindsight!) to consider the question of how to hook computers together so that they could be shared among geographically distributed users. The traffic generated by such users was likely to be "bursty"—intervals of activity, such as the sending of a command to a remote computer, followed by periods of inactivity while waiting for a reply or while contemplating the received response.

Three research groups around the world, all unaware of the others' work [Leiner 98], began inventing the notion of packet switching as an efficient and robust alternative to circuit switching. The first published work on packet-switching techniques was the work by Leonard Kleinrock [Kleinrock 1961, Kleinrock 1964], at that time a graduate student at MIT. Using queuing theory, Kleinrock's work elegantly demonstrated the effectiveness of the packet-switching approach for bursty traffic sources. In 1964, Paul Baran [Baran 1964] at the Rand Institute had begun investigating the use of packet switching for secure voice over military networks, while at the National Physical Laboratory in England, Donald Davies and Roger Scantlebury were also developing their ideas on packet switching.

The work at MIT, Rand, and NPL laid the foundations for today's Internet. But the Internet also has a long history of a let's-build-it-and-demonstrate-it attitude that also dates back to the early 1960s. J.C.R. Licklider [DEC 1990] and Lawrence Roberts, both colleagues of Kleinrock's at MIT, went on to lead the computer science program at the Advanced Research Projects Agency (ARPA) in the United States. Roberts [Roberts 1967] published an overall plan for the so-called ARPAnet [Roberts 1967], the first packet-switched computer network and a direct ancestor of today's public Internet. The early packet switches were known as interface message processors (IMPs) and the contract to build these switches was awarded to the BBN company. On Labor Day in 1969, the first IMP was installed at UCLA under Kleinrock's supervision, with three additional IMPs being installed shortly thereafter at the Stanford Research Institute (SRI), UC Santa Barbara, and the University of Utah (Figure 1.27). The fledgling precursor to the Internet was four nodes large by the end of 1969. Kleinrock recalls the very first use of the network to perform a remote login from UCLA to SRI, crashing the system [Kleinrock 1998].

By 1972, ARPAnet had grown to approximately 15 nodes, and was given its first public demonstration by Robert Kahn at the 1972 International Conference on Computer Communications. The first host-to-host protocol between ARPAnet end systems known as the network control protocol (NCP) was completed [RFC 001]. With an end-to-end protocol available, applications could now be written. The first e-mail program was written by Ray Tomlinson at BBN in 1972.

1.9.2   Internetworking, and New and Proprietary Networks: 1972–1980

The initial ARPAnet was a single, closed network. In order to communicate with an ARPAnet host, one had to actually be attached to another ARPAnet IMP. In the early to mid 1970s, additional packet-switching networks besides ARPAnet came into being; ALOHAnet, a satellite network linking together universities on the Hawaiian islands [Abramson 1970]; Telenet, a BBN commercial packet-switching network based on ARPAnet technology; Tymnet; and Transpac, a French packet-switching network. The number of networks was beginning to grow. In 1973, Robert Metcalfe's Ph.D. thesis laid out the principle of Ethernet, which would later lead to a huge growth in so-called local area networks (LANs) that operated over a small distance based on the Ethernet protocol.

Once again, with perfect hindsight one might now see that the time was ripe for developing an encompassing architecture for connecting networks together. Pioneering work on interconnecting networks (once again under the sponsorship of DARPA—Defense Advanced Research Projects Agency), in essence creating a *network of networks*, was done by Vinton Cerf and Robert Kahn [Cerf 1974]; the term "internetting" was coined to describe this work. The architectural principles that Kahn articulated for creating a so-called "open network architecture" are the foundation on which today's Internet is built [Leiner 98]. These principles include:

- *Minimalism, autonomy.* A network should be able to operate on its own, with no internal changes required for it to be internetworked with other networks.
- *Best effort service.* Internetworked networks should provide best effort, end-to-end service. If reliable communication was required, this could be accomplished by retransmitting lost messages from the sending host.

FIGURE 1.27   The first internet message processor (IMP), with L. Kleinrock

- *Stateless routers.* The routers in the internetworked networks would not maintain any per-flow state about any ongoing connection.
- *Decentralized control.* There would be no global control over the internetworked networks.

These principles continue to serve as the architectural foundation for today's Internet, even 25 years later—a testament to the insight of the early Internet designers.

These architectural principles were embodied in the TCP protocol. The early versions of TCP, however, were quite different from today's TCPs. The early versions of TCP combined a reliable in-sequence delivery of data via end-system retransmission (still part of today's TCP) with forwarding functions (which today are performed by IP). Early experimentation with TCP, combined with the recognition of the importance of an unreliable, non-flow-controlled end-end transport service for applications such as packetized voice, led to the separation of IP out of TCP and the development of the UDP protocol. The three key Internet protocols that we see today—TCP, UDP, and IP—were conceptually in place by the end of the 1970s.

In addition to the DARPA Internet-related research, many other important networking activities were underway. In Hawaii, Norman Abramson was developing ALOHAnet, a packet-based radio network that allowed multiple remote sites on the Hawaiian islands to communicate with each other. The ALOHA protocol [Abramson 1970] was the first so-called multiple-access protocol, allowing geographically distributed users to share a single broadcast communication medium (a radio frequency). Abramson's work on multiple-access protocols was built upon by Robert Metcalfe in the development of the Ethernet protocol [Metcalfe 1976] for wire-based shared broadcast networks. Interestingly, Metcalfe's Ethernet protocol was motivated by the need to connect multiple PCs, printers, and shared disks together [Perkins 1994]. Twenty-five years ago, well before the PC revolution and the explosion of networks, Metcalfe and his colleagues were laying the foundation for today's PC LANs. Ethernet technology represented an important step for internetworking as well. Each Ethernet local area network was itself a network, and as the number of LANs proliferated, the need to internetwork these LANs together became increasingly important. An excellent source for information on Ethernet is Spurgeon's Ethernet Web Site, which includes Metcalfe's drawing of his Ethernet concept, as shown below in Figure 1.28. We discuss Ethernet, Aloha, and other LAN technologies in detail in Chapter 5.

In addition to the DARPA internetworking efforts and the Aloha/Ethernet multiple-access networks, a number of companies were developing their own proprietary network architectures. Digital Equipment Corporation (Digital) released

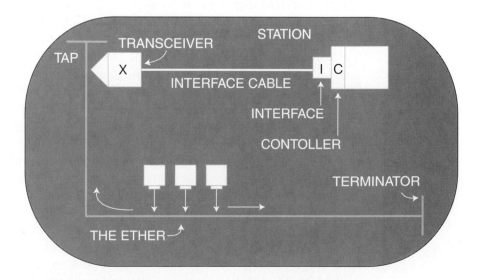

FIGURE 1.28 Metcalf's original conception of the Ethernet.

the first version of the DECnet in 1975, allowing two PDP-11 minicomputers to communicate with each other. DECnet has continued to evolve since then, with significant portions of the OSI protocol suite being based on ideas pioneered in DECnet. Other important players during the 1970s were Xerox (with the XNS architecture) and IBM (with the SNA architecture). Each of these early networking efforts would contribute to the knowledge base that would drive networking in the 80s and 90s.

It is important to note here that in the 1980s (and even before), researchers (such as [Fraser 1983, Turner 1986, Fraser 1993]) were also developing a "competitor" technology to the Internet architecture. These efforts have contributed to the development of the ATM (asynchronous transfer mode) architecture, a connection-oriented approach based on the use of fixed-size packets, known as cells. We will examine portions of the ATM architecture throughout this book.

1.9.3 A Proliferation of Networks: 1980–1990

By the end of the 1970s, approximately 200 hosts were connected to the ARPAnet. By the end of the 1980s the number of hosts connected to the public Internet, a confederation of networks looking much like today's Internet, would reach 100,000. The 1980s would be a time of tremendous growth.

Much of the growth in the early 1980s resulted from several distinct efforts to create computer networks linking universities together. BITnet (because it's there network) provided e-mail and file transfers among several universities in the Northeast. CSNET (computer science network) was formed to link together university researchers without access to ARPAnet. In 1986, NSFNET was created to provide access to NSF-sponsored supercomputing centers. Starting with an initial backbone speed of 56 Kbps, NSFNET's backbone would be running at 1.5 Mbps by the end of the decade, and would be serving as a primary backbone linking together regional networks.

In the ARPAnet community, many of the final pieces of today's Internet architecture were falling into place. January 1, 1983 saw the official deployment of TCP/IP as the new standard host protocol for ARPAnet (replacing the NCP protocol). The transition [RFC 801] from NCP to TCP/IP was a "flag day" type event—all host were required to transfer over to TCP/IP as of that day. In the late 1980s, important extensions were made to TCP to implement host-based congestion control [Jacobson 1988]. The Domain Name System, used to map between a human-readable Internet name (for example, `gaia.cs.umass.edu`) and its 32-bit IP address, was also developed [RFC 833, RFC 1034].

Paralleling this development of the ARPAnet (which was for the most part a U.S. effort), in the early 1980s the French launched the Minitel project, an ambitious plan to bring data networking into everyone's home. Sponsored by the French government, the Minitel system consisted of a public packet-switched network (based on the X.25 protocol suite, which uses virtual circuits), Minitel servers, and inexpensive terminals with built-in low speed modems. The Minitel became a huge success in 1984 when the French government gave away a free Minitel terminal to each French household that wanted one. Minitel sites included free sites—such as a telephone directory site—as well as private sites, which collected a usage-based fee from each user. At its peak in the mid 1990s, it offered more than 20,000 different services, ranging from home banking to specialized research databases. It was used by over 20% of France's population, generated more than $1 billion each year, and created 10,000 jobs. The Minitel was in a large proportion of French homes 10 years before most Americans had ever heard of the Internet. It still enjoys widespread use in France, but is increasingly facing stiff competition from the Internet.

1.9.4 Commercialization and the Web: The 1990s

The 1990s were ushered in with two events that symbolized the continued evolution and the soon-to-arrive commercialization of the Internet. First, ARPAnet, the progenitor of the Internet ceased to exist. MILNET and the Defense Data Network had grown in the 1980s to carry most of the U.S. Department of Defense related traffic and NSFnet had begun to serve as a backbone network connecting regional networks in the United States and national networks overseas. In 1991, NSFNET lifted its restrictions on use of NSFNET for commercial purposes. NSFNET itself would be decommissioned in 1995, with Internet backbone traffic being carried by commercial Internet service providers.

The main event of the 1990s, however, was to be the release of the World Wide Web, which brought the Internet into the homes and businesses of millions and millions of people worldwide. The Web also served as a platform for enabling and deploying hundreds of new applications, including online stock trading and banking, streamed multimedia services, and information retrieval services. For a brief history of the early days of the Web, see [W3C 1995].

The Web was invented at CERN by Tim Berners-Lee in 1989–1991 [Berners-Lee 1989], based on ideas originating in earlier work on hypertext from the 1940s by Bush [Bush 1945] and since the 1960s by Ted Nelson [Ziff-Davis 1998]. Berners-Lee and his associates developed initial versions of HTML, HTTP, a Web server and a browser—the four key components of the Web. The original CERN browsers only provided a line-mode interface. Around the end of 1992 there were about 200 Web servers in operation, this collection of servers being the tip of the iceberg for what was about to come. At about this time several researchers were developing Web browsers with GUI interfaces, including Marc Andreesen, who led the development of the popular GUI browser Mosaic for X. He released an alpha version of his browser in 1993, and in 1994 formed Mosaic Communications, which later became Netscape Communications Corporation. By 1995, university students were using Mosaic and Netscape browsers to surf the Web on a daily basis. At about this time the U.S. government began to transfer the control of the Internet backbone to private carriers. Companies—big and small—began to operate Web servers and transact commerce over the Web. In 1996, Microsoft got into the Web business in a big way.

During the 1990s, networking research and development also made significant advances in the areas of high-speed routers and routing (see Chapter 4) and local area networks (see Chapter 5). The technical community struggled with the problems of defining and implementing an Internet service model for traffic requiring real-time constraints, such as continuous media applications (see Chapter 6). The need to secure and manage Internet infrastructure (see Chapters 7 and 8) also became of paramount importance as e-commerce applications proliferated and the Internet became a central component of the world's telecommunications infrastructure.

1.10 ASYNCHRONOUS TRANSFER MODE (ATM) NETWORKS

Thus far, our focus has been on the Internet and its protocols. But many other existing packet-switching technologies can also provide end-to-end networking solutions. Among these alternatives to the Internet, so called **asynchronous transfer mode (ATM) networks** are perhaps the most well-known. ATM arrived on the scene in the early 1990s. It is useful to discuss ATM for two reasons. First, it provides an interesting contrast to the Internet, and by exploring its differences, we will gain more insight into the Internet. Second, ATM is often used as a link-layer technology in the backbone of the Internet. Since we will refer to ATM throughout this book, we end this chapter with a brief overview of ATM.

1.10.1 The Original Goals of ATM

The standards for ATM were first developed in the mid 1980s. For those too young to remember, at this time there were predominately two types of networks: telephone networks, that were (and still are) primarily used to carry real-time voice; and data networks, that were primarily used to transfer text files, support remote login, and provide e-mail. There were also dedicated private networks available for video conferencing. The Internet existed at this time, but few people were thinking about using it to transport phone calls, and the WWW was as yet unheard of. It was therefore natural to design a networking technology that would be appropriate for transporting real-time audio and video as well as text, e-mail, and image files.

ATM achieved this goal. Two standards committees, the ATM Forum [ATM Forum] and the International Telecommunications Union [ITU] have developed ATM standards for broadband integrated services digital networks (BISDNs). The ATM standards call for packet switching with virtual circuits (called virtual channels in ATM jargon); the standards define how applications directly interface with ATM, so that ATM provides complete networking solution for distributed applications. Paralleling the development of the ATM standards, major companies throughout the world made significant investments in ATM research and development. These investments have led to a myriad of high-performing ATM technologies, including ATM switches that can switch terabits per second. In recent years, ATM technology has been deployed very aggressively within both telephone networks and the Internet backbones.

Although ATM has been deployed within networks, it has been unsuccessful in extending itself all the way to desktop PCs and workstations. And it is now questionable whether ATM will ever have a significant presence at the desktop. Indeed, while ATM was brewing in the standards committees and research labs in the late 1980s and early 1990s, the Internet and its TCP/IP protocols were already operational and making significant headway:

- The TCP/IP protocol suite was integrated into all of the most popular operating systems.
- Companies began to transact commerce (e-commerce) over the Internet.
- Residential Internet access became very inexpensive.

Many wonderful desktop applications were developed for TCP/IP networks, including the World Wide Web, Internet phone, and interactive streaming video.

Thousands of companies are currently developing new applications and services for the Internet.

Furthermore, throughout the 1990s, several low-cost high-speed LAN technologies were developed, including 100 Mbps Ethernet and more recently Gigabit Ethernet, mitigating the need for ATM use in high-speed LAN applications. Today, we live in a world where almost all networking application products interface directly with TCP/IP. Nevertheless, ATM switches can switch packets at very high rates, and consequently they have been deployed in Internet backbone networks, where the need to transport traffic at high rates is most acute. We will discuss the topic of IP over ATM in Section 5.8.

1.10.2 Principle Characteristics of ATM

We shall discuss ATM in some detail in subsequent chapters. For now we briefly outline its principle characteristics:

- The ATM standard defines a full suite of communication protocols, roughly from the transport layer all the way down through the physical layer.
- ATM uses packet switching with fixed-length packets of 53 bytes. In ATM jargon, these packets are called **cells.** Each cell has 5 bytes of header and 48 bytes of "payload." The fixed-length cells and simple headers have facilitated high-speed switching.
- ATM uses virtual circuits (VCs). In ATM jargon, virtual circuits are called **virtual channels.** The ATM header includes a field for the virtual channel number, which is called the **virtual channel identifier (VCI)** in ATM jargon. As discussed in Section 1.3, packet switches use the VCI to route cells towards their destinations; ATM switches also perform VCI translation.
- ATM provides no retransmissions on a link-by-link basis. If a switch detects an error in an ATM cell, it attempts to correct the error using error correcting codes. If it cannot correct the error, it drops the cell and does not ask the preceding switch to retransmit the cell.
- ATM provides congestion control on an end-to-end basis. That is, the transmission of ATM cells is not directly regulated by the switches in times of congestion. However, the network switches themselves do provide feedback to a sending end system to help it regulate its transmission rate when the network becomes congested.
- ATM can run over just about any physical layer. It often runs over fiber optics using the SONET standard at speeds of 155.52 Mbps, 622 Mbps, and higher.

1.10.3 Overview of the ATM Layers

As shown in Figure 1.29, the ATM protocol stack consists of three layers: the ATM adaptation layer (AAL), the ATM layer, and the ATM physical layer:

ATM adaptation layer (AAL)
ATM layer
ATM physical layer

FIGURE 1.29 The three ATM layers

| Application layer (HTTP, FTP, and so on) |
| Transport layer (TCP or UDP) |
| Network layer (IP) |
| AAL5 |
| ATM layer |
| ATM physical layer |

FIGURE 1.30   Internet-over-ATM protocol stack

The **ATM physical layer** deals with voltages, bit timings, and framing on the physical medium. The **ATM layer** is the core of the ATM standard. It defines the structure of the ATM cell. The **ATM adaptation layer** is roughly analogous to the transport layer in the Internet protocol stack. ATM includes many different types of AALs to support many different types of services.

Currently, ATM is often used as a link-layer technology within localized regions of the Internet. A special AAL type, AAL5, has been developed to allow TCP/IP to interface with ATM. At the IP-to-ATM interface, AAL5 prepares IP datagrams for ATM transport; at the ATM-to-IP interface, AAL5 reassembles ATM cells into IP datagrams. Figure 1.30 shows the protocol stack for the regions of the Internet that use ATM.

Note that in this configuration, the three ATM layers have been squeezed into the lower two layers of the Internet protocol stack. In particular, the Internet's network layer "sees" ATM as a link-layer protocol.

This concludes our brief introduction to ATM. We will return to ATM from time to time throughout this book.

SUMMARY

In this chapter we've covered a tremendous amount of material! We've looked at the various pieces of hardware and software that make up the Internet in particular, and computer networks in general. We started at the "edge" of the network, looking at end systems and applications, and at the transport service provided to the applications running on the end systems. Using network-based distributed applications as examples, we introduced the notion of a protocol—a key concept in networking. We then dove deeper inside the network, into the network core, identifying packet switching and circuit switching as the two basic approaches for transporting data through a telecommunication network, and examining the strengths and weaknesses of each approach. We then looked at the lowest (from an architectural standpoint) parts of the network—the link layer technologies and physical media typically found in the access network.

In the second part of this introductory chapter, we took the broader view on networking. From a performance standpoint, we identified the causes of packet delay and packet loss in the Internet. We identified key architectural principles (layering, service models) in networking. We then examined the structure of today's Internet.

We finished our introduction to networking with a brief history of computer networking. The first chapter in itself constitutes a mini-course in computer networking.

So, we have indeed covered a tremendous amount of ground in this first chapter! If you're a bit overwhelmed, don't worry. In the following chapters we will revisit all of these ideas, covering them in much more detail (that's a promise, not a threat!). At this point, we hope you leave this chapter with a still-developing intuition for the pieces that make up a network, a still-developing command for the vocabulary of networking (don't be shy to refer back to this chapter), and an ever-growing desire to learn more about networking. That's the task ahead of us for the rest of this book.

Roadmapping This Book

Before starting any trip, we should always glance at a roadmap in order to become familiar with the major roads and junctures that lie between us and our ultimate destination. For the trip we are about to embark on, the ultimate destination is a deep understanding of the how, what, and why of computer networks. Our roadmap is the sequence of chapters of this book:

1. Computer Networks and the Internet
2. Application Layer
3. Transport Layer
4. Network Layer and Routing
5. Link Layer and Local Area Networks
6. Multimedia Networking
7. Security in Computer Networks
8. Network Management

Taking a look at this roadmap, we identify Chapters 2 through 5 as the four core chapters of this book. You should notice that there is one chapter for each of the top four layers of the Internet protocol stack. Further note that our journey will begin at the top of the Internet protocol stack, namely, the application layer, and will work its way downward. The rationale behind this top-down journey is that once we understand the applications, we can then understand the network services needed to support these applications. We can then, in turn, examine the various ways in which such services might be implemented by a network architecture. Covering applications early thus provides motivation for the remainder of the text.

The second half of the book—Chapters 6 through 8—zoom in on three enormously important (and somewhat independent) topics in modern computer networking. In Chapter 6 (Multimedia Networking), we examine audio and video applications such as Internet phone, video conferencing, and streaming of stored media. We also look at how a packet-switched network can be designed to provide consistent quality of service to audio and video applications. In Chapter 7 (Security in Computer Networks), we first look at the underpinnings of encryption and network security, and then examine how the basic theory is being applied in a broad range of Internet contexts, including electronic mail and Internet commerce. The last chapter (Network Management) examines the key issues in network management as well as the Internet protocols that address these issues.

HOMEWORK PROBLEMS AND QUESTIONS

Chapter 1

Review Questions

Sections 1.1–1.4

1. What are the two types of services that the Internet provides to its applications? What are some of characteristics of each of these services?

2. It has been said that flow control and congestion control are equivalent. Is this true for the Internet's connection-oriented service? Are the objectives of flow control and congestion control the same?

3. Briefly describe how the Internet's connection-oriented service provides reliable transport.

4. What advantage does a circuit-switched network have over a packet-switched network? What advantages does TDM have over FDM in a circuit-switched network?

5. Suppose that between a sending host and a receiving host there is exactly one packet switch. The transmission rates between the sending host and the switch and between the switch and the receiving host are R_1 and R_2, respectively. Assuming that the router uses store-and-forward packet switching, what is the total end-to-end delay to send a packet of length L? (Ignore queuing and propagation delay.)

6. What are some of the networking technologies that use virtual circuits? (Find good URLs that discuss and explain these technologies.)

7. What is meant by connection state information in a virtual circuit network?

8. Suppose you are developing a standard for a new type of network. You need to decide whether your network will use VCs or datagram routing. What are the pros and cons for using VCs?

Sections 1.5–1.7

9. Is HFC bandwidth dedicated or shared among users? Are collisions possible in a downstream HFC channel? Why or why not?

10. What is the transmission rate of Ethernet LANs? For a given transmission rate, can each user on the LAN continuously transmit at that rate?

11. What are some of the physical media that Ethernet can run over?

12. Dial-up modems, ISDN, HFC, and ADSL are all used for residential access. For each of these access technologies, provide a range of transmission rates and comment on whether the bandwidth is shared or dedicated.

13. Consider sending a series of packets from a sending host to a receiving host over a fixed route. List the delay components in the end-to-end delay for a single packet. Which of these delays are constant and which are fixed?

14. Review the car-caravan analogy in Section 1.6. Again assume a propagation speed of 100 km/hour.

    a. Suppose the caravan travels 200 km, beginning in front of one toll booth, passing through a second toll booth, and finishing just before a third toll booth. What is the end-to-end delay?

b. Repeat (a), now assuming that there are seven cars in the caravan instead of 10.

15. List five tasks that a layer can perform. It is possible that one (or more) of these tasks could be performed by two (or more) layers?

16. What are the five layers in the Internet protocol stack? What are the principle responsibilities for each of these layers?

17. Which layers in the Internet protocol stack does a router process?

PROBLEMS

1. Design and describe an application-level protocol to be used between an automatic teller machine and a bank's centralized computer. Your protocol should allow a user's card and password to be verified, the account balance (which is maintained at the centralized computer) to be queried, and an account withdrawal (that is, when money is given to the user) to be made. Your protocol entities should be able to handle the all-too-common case in which there is not enough money in the account to cover the withdrawal. Specify your protocol by listing the messages exchanged, and the action taken by the automatic teller machine or the bank's centralized computer on transmission and receipt of messages. Sketch the operation of your protocol for the case of a simple withdrawal with no errors, using a diagram similar to that in Figure 1.2. Explicitly state the assumptions made by your protocol about the underlying end-to-end transport service.

2. Consider an application that transmits data at a steady rate (for example, the sender generates a N-bit unit of data every k time units, where k is small and fixed). Also, when such an application starts, it will stay on for a relatively long period of time. Answer the following questions, briefly justifying your answer:

   a. Would a packet-switched network or a circuit-switched network be more appropriate for this application? Why?

   b. Suppose that a packet-switching network is used and the only traffic in this network comes from such applications as described above. Furthermore, assume that the sum of the application data rates is less that the capacities of each and every link. Is some form of congestion control needed? Why?

3. Consider sending a file of $F = M \cdot L$ bits over a path of Q links. Each link transmits at R bps. The network is lightly loaded so that there are no queuing delays. When a form of packet switching is used, the $M \cdot L$ bits are broken up into M packets, each packet with L bits. Propagation delay is negligible.

   a. Suppose the network is a packet-switched virtual circuit network. Denote the VC set-up time by t_s seconds. Suppose the sending layers add a total of h bits of header to each packet. How long does it take to send the file from source to destination?

   b. Suppose the network is a packet-switched datagram network and a connectionless service is used. Now suppose each packet has $2h$ bits of header. How long does it take to send the file?

   c. Repeat (b), but assume message switching is used (that is, $2h$ bits are added to the message, and the message is not segmented).

d. Finally, suppose that the network is a circuit-switched network. Further suppose that the transmission rate of the circuit between source and destination is R bps. Assuming t_s set-up time and h bits of header appended to the entire file, how long does it take to send the file?

4. Experiment with the message-switching Java applet in this chapter. Do the delays in the applet correspond to the delays in the previous question? How do link propagation delays affect the overall end-to-end delay for packet switching and for message switching?

5. Consider sending a large file of F bits from Host A to Host B. There are two links (and one switch) between A and B, and the links are uncongested (that is, no queuing delays). Host A segments the file into segments of S bits each and adds 40 bits of header to each segment, forming packets of $L = 40 + S$ bits. Each link has a transmission rate of R bps. Find the value of S that minimizes the delay of moving the packet from Host A to Host B. Neglect propagation delay.

6. This elementary problem begins to explore propagation delay and transmission delay, two central concepts in data networking. Consider two hosts, Hosts A and B, connected by a single link of rate R bps. Suppose that the two hosts are separated by m meters, and suppose the propagation speed along the link is s meters/sec. Host A is to send a packet of size L bits to Host B.

   a. Express the propagation delay, d_{prop} in terms of m and s.

   b. Determine the transmission time of the packet, d_{trans} in terms of L and R.

   c. Ignoring processing and queuing delays, obtain an expression for the end-to-end delay.

   d. Suppose Host A begins to transmit the packet at time $t = 0$. At time $t = d_{trans}$, where is the last bit of the packet?

   e. Suppose d_{prop} is greater than d_{trans}. At time $t = d_{trans}$, where is the first bit of the packet?

   f. Suppose d_{prop} is less than d_{trans}. At time $t = d_{trans}$, where is the first bit of the packet?

   g. Suppose $s = 2.5 \cdot 10^8$, $L = 100$ bits and $R = 28$ kbps. Find the distance m so that d_{prop} equals d_{trans}.

7. In this problem we consider sending voice from Host A to Host B over a packet-switched network (for example, Internet phone). Host A converts on-the-fly analog voice to a digital 64 Kbps bit stream. Host A then groups the bits into 48-byte packets. There is one link between host A and B; its transmission rate is 1 Mbps and its propagation delay is 2 msec. As soon as Host A gathers a packet, it sends it to Host B. As soon as Host B receives an entire packet, it coverts the packet's bits to an analog signal. How much time elapses from when a bit is created (from the original analog signal at A) until a bit is decoded (as part of the analog signal at B)?

8. Suppose users share a 1-Mbps link. Also suppose each user requires 100 Kbps when transmitting, but each user only transmits 10% of the time. (See the discussion on "Packet Switching versus Circuit Switching.")

   a. When circuit-switching is used, how many users can be supported?

   b. For the remainder of this problem, suppose packet-switching is used. Find the probability that a given user is transmitting.

    c. Suppose there are 40 users. Find the probability that at any given time, n users are transmitting simultaneously.

    d. Find the probability that there are 10 or more users transmitting simultaneously.

9. Consider the queuing delay in a router buffer (preceding an outbound link). Suppose all packets are L bits, the transmission rate is R bps, and that N packets arrive to the buffer every L/RN seconds. Find the average queuing delay of a packet.

10. Consider the queuing delay in a router buffer. Let I denote traffic intensity, that is, $I = La/R$. Suppose that the queuing delay takes the form $LR/(1 - I)$ for $I < 1$.

    a. Provide a formula for the "total delay," that is, the queuing delay plus the transmission delay.

    b. Plot the transmission delay as a function of L/R.

11. a. Generalize the end-to-end delay formula in Section 1.6 for heterogeneous processing rates, transmission rates, and propagation delays.

    b. Repeat (a), but now also suppose that there is an average queuing delay of d_{queue} at each node.

12. Perform a `traceroute` between source and destination on the same continent at three different hours of the day. Find the average and standard deviation of the delays. Do the same for a source and destination on different continents.

13. Recall that ATM uses 53 byte packets consisting of 5 header bytes and 48 payload bytes. Fifty-three bytes is unusually small for fixed-length packets; most networking protocols (IP, Ethernet, frame relay, and so forth) use packets that are, on average, significantly larger. One of the drawbacks of a small packet size is that a large fraction of link bandwidth is consumed by overhead bytes; in the case of ATM, almost 10% of the bandwidth is "wasted" by the ATM header. In this problem we investigate why such a small packet size was chosen. To this end, suppose that the ATM cell consists of P bytes (possibly different from 48) and 5 bytes of header.

    a. Consider sending a digitally encoded voice source directly over ATM. Suppose the source is encoded at a constant rate of 64 kbps. Assume each cell is entirely filled before the source sends the cell into the network. The time required to fill a cell is the **packetization delay.** In terms of L, determine the packetization delay in milliseconds.

    b. Packetization delays greater than 20 msecs can cause noticeable and unpleasant echo. Determine the packetization delay for $L = 1,500$ bytes (roughly corresponding to a maximum-size Ethernet packet) and for $L = 48$ (corresponding to an ATM cell).

    c. Calculate the store-and-forward delay at a single ATM switch for a link rate of $R = 155$ Mbps (a popular link speed for ATM) for $L = 1,500$ bytes and $L = 48$ bytes.

    d. Comment on the advantages of using a small cell size.

DISCUSSION QUESTIONS

1. Write a one-paragraph description for each of three major projects currently under way at the World Wide Web Consortium (W3C).

2. What is Internet phone? Describe some of the existing products for Internet phone. Find some of the Web sites of companies that are in the Internet phone business.

3. What is Internet audio-on-demand? Describe some of the existing products for Internet audio-on-demand. Find some of the Web sites of companies that are in the Internet audio-on-demand business. Find some Web sites that provide audio-on-demand content.

4. What is Internet video conferencing? Describe some of the existing products for Internet video conferencing. Find some of the Web sites of companies that are in the Internet video-conferencing business.

5. Surf the Web to find a company that is offering HFC Internet access. What is the transmission rate of the cable modem? Is this rate always guaranteed for each user on the network?

6. Suppose you are developing an application for the Internet. Would you have your application run over TCP or UDP? Elaborate. (We will explore this question in some detail in subsequent chapters. For now appeal to your intuition to answer the question.)

7. What are some of the current activities of the The World Wide Web Consortium (W3C)? What are some of the current activities of the National Laboratory for Applied Network Research or NLANR?

8. What does the current topological structure of the Internet (that is, backbone ISPs, regional ISPs, and local ISPs) have in common with the topological structure of the telephone networks in the United States? How is pricing in the Internet the same as or different from pricing in the phone system?

Chapter 2 | Application Layer

2.1 PRINCIPLES OF APPLICATION LAYER PROTOCOLS

Network applications are the *raisons d'etre* of a computer network. If we couldn't conceive of any useful applications, there wouldn't be any need to design networking protocols to support them. But over the past thirty years, many people have devised numerous ingenious and wonderful networking applications. These applications include the classic text-based applications that became popular in the 1980s, including remote access to computers, electronic mail, file transfers, newsgroups, and chat. But they also include more recently conceived multimedia applications, such as the World Wide Web, Internet telephony, video conferencing, and audio and video on demand.

Although network applications are diverse and have many interacting components, software is almost always at their core. Recall from Section 1.2 that a network application's software is distributed among two or more end systems (that is, host computers). For example, with the Web there are two pieces of software that communicate with each other: the browser software in the user's host (PC, Mac, or workstation), and the Web server software in the Web server. With Telnet, there are again two pieces of software in two hosts: software in the local host and software in the remote host. With multiparty video conferencing, there is a software piece in each host that participates in the conference.

In the jargon of operating systems, it is not actually software pieces (that is, programs) that are communicating but in truth **processes** that are communicating. A process can be thought of as a program that is *running* within an end system. When communicating processes are running on the same end system, they communicate with each other using interprocess communication. The rules for interprocess communication are governed by the end system's operating system. But in this book we are not interested in how processes on the same host communicate, but instead in how processes running on *different* end systems (with potentially different operating systems) communicate. Processes on two different end systems communicate with each other by exchanging **messages** across the computer network. A sending process creates and sends messages into the network; a receiving process receives these messages and possibly responds by sending messages back. Networking applications have **application-layer protocols** that define the format and order of the messages exchanged between processes, as well as define the actions taken on the transmission or receipt of a message.

The application layer is a particularly good place to start our study of protocols. It's familiar ground. We're acquainted with many of the applications that rely on the protocols we will study. It will give us a good feel for what protocols are all about and will introduce us to many of the same issues that we'll see again when we study transport, network, and data-link layer protocols.

2.1.1 Application-Layer Protocols

It is important to distinguish between **network applications** and **application-layer protocols.** An application-layer protocol is only one piece (albeit, a big piece) of a network application. Let's look at a couple of examples. The Web is a network application that allows users to obtain "documents" from Web servers on demand. The Web application consists of many components, including a standard for document formats (that is, HTML), Web browsers (for example, Netscape Navigator and Internet Explorer), Web servers (for example, Apache, Microsoft, and Netscape servers), and an application-layer protocol. The Web's application-layer protocol, HTTP (the HyperText Transfer Protocol [RFC 2068]), defines how messages are passed between browser and Web server. Thus, HTTP is only one piece (a big piece) of the Web application. As another example, consider the Internet electronic mail application. Internet electronic mail also has many components, including mail servers that house user mailboxes, mail readers that allow users to read and create messages, a standard for defining the structure of an e-mail message (that is, MIME) and application-layer protocols that define how messages are passed between servers, how messages are passed between servers and mail readers, and how the contents of certain parts of the mail message (for example, a mail message header) are to be interpreted. The principal application-layer protocol for electronic mail is SMTP (Simple Mail Transfer Protocol [RFC 821]). Thus, SMTP is only one piece (albeit, a big piece) of the e-mail application.

As noted above, an application-layer protocol defines how an application's processes, running on different end systems, pass messages to each other. In particular, an application layer protocol defines:

- the types of messages exchanged, for example, request messages and response messages
- the syntax of the various message types, such as, the fields in the message and how the fields are delineated
- the semantics of the fields, that is, the meaning of the information in the fields
- rules for determining when and how a process sends messages and responds to messages

Some application-layer protocols are specified in RFCs and are therefore in the public domain. For example, HTTP is available as an RFC. If a browser developer follows the rules of the HTTP RFC, the browser will be able to retrieve Web pages from any Web server (more precisely, any Web server that has also followed the rules of the HTTP RFC). Many other application-layer protocols are proprietary and intentionally not available in the public domain. For example, many of the existing Internet phone products use proprietary application-layer protocols.

Clients and servers.   A network application protocol typically has two parts or "sides," a **client side** and a **server side.** The client side in one end system communicates with the server side in another end system. For example, a Web browser implements the client side of HTTP, and a Web server implements the server side of HTTP. In another example, in e-mail, the sending mail server implements the client side of SMTP, and the receiving mail server implements the server side of SMTP.

For many applications, a host will implement both the client and server sides of an application. For example, consider a Telnet session between Hosts A and B. (Recall that Telnet is a popular remote login application.) If Host A initiates the Telnet session (so that a user at Host A is logging onto Host B), then Host A runs the client side of the application and Host B runs the server side. On the other hand, if Host B initiates the Telnet session, then Host B runs the client side of the application. FTP, used for transferring files between two hosts, provides another example. When an FTP session exists between two hosts, then either host can transfer a file to the other host during the session. However, as is the case for almost all network applications, *the host that initiates the session is labeled the client.* Furthermore, a host can actually act as both a client and a server at the same time for a given application. For example, a mail server host runs the client side of SMTP (for sending mail) as well as the server side of SMTP (for receiving mail).

Processes communicating across a network.   As noted above, an application involves two processes in two different hosts communicating with each other over a network. (Actually, a multicast application can involve communication among more than two hosts. We shall address this issue in Chapter 4.) The two processes communicate with each other by sending and receiving messages through their *sockets.* A process's socket can be thought of as the process's door: A process sends messages into, and receives message from, the network through its socket. When a process wants to send a message to another process on another host, it shoves the message out its door. The process assumes that there is a transportation infrastructure on the other side of the door that will transport the message to the door of the destination process.

Figure 2.1 illustrates socket communication between two processes that communicate over the Internet. (The figure assumes that the underlying transport protocol is TCP, although the UDP protocol could be used as well in the Internet.) As shown in this figure, a **socket** is the interface between the application layer and the transport layer within a host. It is also referred to as the **API (application programmers' interface)** between the application and the network, since the socket is the programming interface with which networked applications are built in the Internet. The application developer has control of everything on the application-layer side of the socket but has little control of the transport-layer side of the socket. The only control that the application developer has on the transport-layer

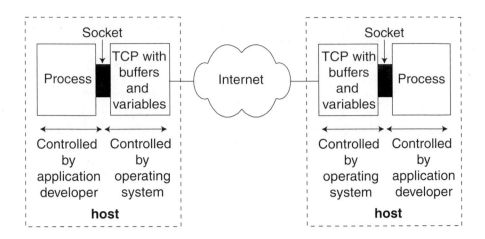

FIGURE 2.1 Application processes, sockets, and the underlying transport protocol

side is (1) the choice of transport protocol and (2) perhaps the ability to fix a few transport-layer parameters such as maximum buffer and maximum segment sizes. Once the application developer chooses a transport protocol (if a choice is available), the application is built using the transport layer of the services offered by that protocol. We will explore sockets in some detail in Sections 2.6 and 2.7.

Addressing processes.   In order for a process on one host to send a message to a process on another host, the sending process must identify the receiving process. To identify the receiving process, one must typically specify two pieces of information: (1) the name or address of the host machine, and (2) an identifier that specifies the identity of the receiving process on the destination host.

Let us first consider host addresses. In Internet applications, the destination host is specified by its **IP address.** We will discuss IP addresses in great detail in Chapter 4. For now, it suffices to know that the IP address is a 32-bit quantity that *uniquely* identifies the end system (more precisely, it uniquely identifies the interface that connects that host to the Internet). Since the IP address of any end system connected to the public Internet must be *globally* unique, the assignment of IP addresses must be carefully managed, as discussed in Section 4.4. ATM networks have a different addressing standard. The ITU-T has specified telephone number-like addresses, called E.164 addresses [ITU 1997], for use in public ATM networks. E.164 addresses consist of between 7 and 15 digits, with each digit encoded as a byte (yielding an address of between 56 and 120 bits in length). The assignment of these addresses is carefully managed by country- or region-specific standards bodies; in the United States, the American National Standards Institute (ANSI) provides this address registration service. We will not cover ATM end-system addressing in depth in this book; see [Fritz 1997, Cisco Addressing 1999] for more details.

In addition to knowing the address of the end system to which a message is destined, a sending application must also specify information that will allow the receiving end system to direct the message to the appropriate process on that system. A receive-side **port number** serves this purpose in the Internet. Popular application-layer protocols have been assigned specific port numbers. For example, a Web server process (that uses the HTTP protocol) is identified by port number 80. A mail server (using the SMTP) protocol is identified by port number 25.

A list of well-known port numbers for all Internet standard protocols can be found in [RFC 1700]. When a developer creates a new network application, the application must be assigned a new port number.

User agents.   Before we begin a more detailed study of application-layer protocols, it is useful to discuss the notion of a **user agent.** The user agent is an interface between the user and the network application. For example, consider the Web. For this application, the user agent is a browser such as Netscape Navigator or Microsoft Explorer. The browser allows a user to view Web pages, to navigate in the Web, to provide input to forms, to interact with Java applets, and so on. The browser also implements the client side of the HTTP protocol. Thus, when activated, the browser is a process that, along with providing an interface to the user, sends messages into a socket. As another example, consider the electronic mail application. In this case, the user agent is a "mail reader" that allows a user to compose and read messages. Many companies market mail readers (for example, Eudora, Netscape Messenger) with a graphical user interface that can run on PCs, Macs, and workstations. Mail readers running on PCs also implement the client side of application-layer protocols; typically they implement the client side of SMTP for sending mail and the client side of a mail retrieval protocol, such as POP3 or IMAP (see Section 2.4), for receiving mail.

2.1.2   What Services Does an Application Need?

Recall that a socket is the interface between the application process and the transport protocol. The application at the sending side sends messages through the door. At the other side of the door, the transport protocol has the responsibility of moving the messages across the network to the door at the receiving process. Many networks, including the Internet, provide more than one transport protocol. When you develop an application, you must choose one of the available transport protocols. How do you make this choice? Most likely, you will study the services that are provided by the available transport protocols, and you will pick the protocol with the services that best match the needs of your application. The situation is similar to choosing either train or airplane transport for travel between two cities (say, New York and Boston). You have to choose one or the other, and each transport mode offers different services. (For example, the train offers downtown pick up and drop off, whereas the plane offers shorter transport time.)

What services might a network application need from a transport protocol? We can broadly classify an application's service requirements along three dimensions: data loss, bandwidth, and timing.

Data loss.   Some applications, such as electronic mail, file transfer, remote host access, Web document transfers, and financial applications require fully reliable data transfer, that is, no data loss. In particular, a loss of file data, or data in a financial transaction, can have devastating consequences (in the latter case, for either the bank or the customer!). Other **loss tolerant applications,** most notably multimedia applications such as real-time audio/video or stored audio/video, can tolerate some amount of data loss. In these latter applications, lost data might result in a small glitch in the played-out audio/video—not a crucial impairment. The effects of such loss on application quality, and actual amount of tolerable packet loss, will depend strongly on the coding scheme used.

Bandwidth. Some applications must be able to transmit data at a certain rate in order to be effective. For example, if an Internet telephony application encodes voice at 32 Kbps, then it must be able to send data into the network and have data delivered to the receiving application at this rate. If this amount of bandwidth is not available, the application needs to encode at a different rate (and receive enough bandwidth to sustain this different coding rate) or it should give up because receiving half of the needed bandwidth is of no use to such a **bandwidth-sensitive application.** Many current multimedia applications are bandwidth sensitive, but future multimedia applications may use adaptive coding techniques to encode at a rate that matches the currently available bandwidth. While bandwidth-sensitive applications require a given amount of bandwidth, **elastic applications** can make use of as much or as little bandwidth as happens to be available. Electronic mail, file transfer, remote access, and Web transfers are all elastic applications. Of course, the more bandwidth, the better. There's an adage that says that one cannot be too rich, too thin, or have too much bandwidth.

Timing. The final service requirement is that of timing. Interactive real-time applications, such as Internet telephony, virtual environments, teleconferencing, and multiplayer games require tight timing constraints on data delivery in order to be effective. For example, many of these applications require that end-to-end delays be on the order of a few hundred milliseconds or less. (See Chapter 6 and [Gauthier 1999, Ramjee 1994].) Long delays in Internet telephony, for example, tend to result in unnatural pauses in the conversation; in a multiplayer game or virtual interactive environment, a long delay between taking an action and seeing the response from the environment (for example, from another player on the end of an end-to-end connection) makes the application feel less realistic. For non-real-time applications, lower delay is always preferable to higher delay, but no tight constraint is placed on the end-to-end delays.

Figure 2.2 summarizes the reliability, bandwidth, and timing requirements of some popular and emerging Internet applications.

Figure 2.2 outlines only a few of the key requirements of a few of the more popular Internet applications. Our goal here is not to provide a complete classification, but simply to identify a few of the most important axes along which network application requirements can be classified.

2.1.3 Services Provided by the Internet Transport Protocols

The Internet (and, more generally, TCP/IP networks) makes available two transport protocols to applications, namely, **UDP** (User Datagram Protocol) and **TCP** (Transmission Control Protocol). When a developer creates a new application for the Internet, one of the first decisions that the developer must make is whether to use UDP or TCP. Each of these protocols offers a different service model to the invoking applications.

TCP services. The TCP service model includes a connection-oriented service and a reliable data transfer service. When an application invokes TCP for its transport protocol, the application receives both of these services from TCP.

Connection-oriented service: TCP has the client and server exchange transport-layer control information with each other *before* the application-level

Application	Data loss	Bandwidth	Time sensitive?
file transfer	no loss	elastic	no
electronic mail	no loss	elastic	no
Web documents	no loss	elastic	no
real-time audio/video	loss-tolerant	**audio:** few Kbps to 1Mbps	yes: 100s of msec
		video: 10s of Kbps to 5 Mbps	
Stored audio/video	loss-tolerant	same as interactive audio/video	yes: few seconds
Interactive games	loss-tolerant	few Kbps to 10s Kbps	yes: 100s msecs
Financial applications	required	elastic	yes and no

FIGURE 2.2   Requirements of selected network applications

messages begin to flow. This so-called handshaking procedure (that is part of the TCP protocol) alerts the client and server, allowing them to prepare for an onslaught of packets. After the handshaking phase, a **TCP connection** is said to exist between the sockets of the two processes. The connection is a full-duplex connection in that the two processes can send messages to each other over the connection at the same time. When the application is finished sending messages, it must tear down the connection. The service is referred to as a "connection-oriented" service rather than a "connection" service (or a "virtual circuit" service), because the two processes are connected in a very loose manner. In Chapter 3 we will discuss connection-oriented service in detail and examine how it is implemented.

Reliable transport service: The communicating processes can rely on TCP to deliver all messages sent without error and in the proper order. When one side of the application passes a stream of bytes into a socket, it can count on TCP to deliver the same stream of data to the receiving socket, with no missing or duplicate bytes.

TCP also includes a congestion-control mechanism, a service for the general welfare of the Internet rather than for the direct benefit of the communicating processes. The TCP congestion-control mechanism throttles a process (client or server) when the network is congested. In particular, as we shall see in Chapter 3, TCP congestion control attempts to limit each TCP connection to its fair share of network bandwidth.

The throttling of the transmission rate can have a very harmful effect on real-time audio and video applications that have minimum bandwidth requirements.

Moreover, real-time applications are loss-tolerant and do not need a fully reliable transport service. In fact, the TCP acknowledgments and retransmissions that provide the reliable transport service (discussed in Chapter 3) can further slow down the transmission rate of useful real-time data. For these reasons, developers of real-time applications usually run their applications over UDP rather than TCP.

Having outlined the services provided by TCP, let us say a few words about the services that TCP does *not* provide. First, TCP does not guarantee a minimum transmission rate. In particular, a sending process is not permitted to transmit at any rate it pleases; instead the sending rate is regulated by TCP congestion control, which may force the sender to send at a low average rate. Second, TCP does not provide any delay guarantees. In particular, when a sending process passes a message into a TCP socket, the message will eventually arrive at the receiving socket, but TCP guarantees absolutely no limit on how long the data may take to get there. As many of us have experienced with the world wide wait, one can sometimes wait tens of seconds or even minutes for TCP to deliver a message (containing, for example, an HTML file) from Web server to Web client. In summary, TCP guarantees delivery of all data, but provides no guarantees on the rate of delivery or on the delays experienced by individual messages.

UDP services.   UDP is a no-frills, lightweight transport protocol with a minimalist service model. UDP is connectionless, so there is no handshaking before the two processes start to communicate. UDP provides an unreliable data transfer service; that is, when a process sends a message into a UDP socket, UDP provides *no* guarantee that the message will ever reach the receiving socket. Furthermore, messages that do arrive to the receiving socket may arrive out of order. Returning to our houses/doors analogy for processes/sockets, UDP is like having a long line of taxis waiting for passengers on the other side of the sender's door. When a passenger (analogous to an application message) exits the house, it hops in one of the taxis. Some of the taxis may break down, so they don't ever deliver the passenger to the receiving door; taxis may also take different routes, so that passengers arrive at the receiving door out of order.

On the other hand, UDP does not include a congestion-control mechanism, so a sending process can pump data into a UDP socket at any rate it pleases. Although all the data may not make it to the receiving socket, a large fraction of the data may arrive. Also, because UDP does not use acknowledgments or retransmissions that can slow down the delivery of useful real-time data, developers of real-time applications often choose to run their applications over UDP. Similar to TCP, UDP provides no guarantee on delay. As many of us know, a taxi can be stuck in a traffic jam for a very long time (while the meter continues to run!).

Figure 2.3 indicates the transport protocols used by some popular Internet applications. We see that e-mail, remote terminal access, the Web, and file transfer all use TCP. These applications have chosen TCP primarily because TCP provides the reliable data transfer service, guaranteeing that all data will eventually get to its destination. We also see that Internet telephony typically runs over UDP. Each side of an Internet phone application needs to send data across the network at some minimum rate (see Figure 2.2); this is more likely to be possible with UDP than with TCP. Also, Internet phone applications are loss-tolerant, so they do not need the reliable data transfer service (and the acknowledgments and retransmissions that implement the service) provided by TCP.

Application	Application-layer protocol	Underlying transport protocol
Electronic mail	SMTP [RFC 821]	TCP
Remote terminal access	Telnet [RFC 854]	TCP
Web	HTTP [RFC 2068]	TCP
File transfer	FTP [RFC 959]	TCP
Remote file server	NFS [McKusik 1996]	UDP or TCP
Streaming multimedia	proprietary (for example, Real Networks)	UDP or TCP
Internet telephony	proprietary (for example, Vocaltec)	typically UDP

FIGURE 2.3   Popular Internet applications, their application-layer protocols, and their underlying transport protocols

As noted earlier, neither TCP nor UDP offer timing guarantees. Does this mean that time-sensitive applications cannot run in today's Internet? The answer is clearly no—the Internet has been hosting time-sensitive applications for many years. These applications often work pretty well because they have been designed to cope, to the greatest extent possible, with this lack of guarantee. We shall investigate several of these design tricks in Chapter 6. Nevertheless, clever design has its limitations when delay is excessive, as is often the case in the public Internet. In summary, today's Internet can often provide satisfactory service to time-sensitive applications, but it cannot provide any timing or bandwidth guarantees. In Chapter 6, we shall also discuss emerging Internet service models that provide new services, including guaranteed delay service for time-sensitive applications.

2.1.4   Network Applications Covered in this Book

New public domain and proprietary Internet applications are being developed everyday. Rather than treating a large number of Internet applications in an encyclopedic manner, we have chosen to focus on a small number of important and popular applications. In this chapter we discuss in some detail four popular applications: the Web, file transfer, electronic mail, and directory service. We first discuss the Web, not only because the Web is an enormously popular application, but also because its application-layer protocol, HTTP, is relatively simple and illustrates many key principles of network protocols. We then discuss file transfer, as it provides a nice contrast to HTTP and enables us to highlight some additional principles. We discuss electronic mail, the Internet's first highly popular application. We shall see that modern electronic mail makes use of not one, but of several, application-layer protocols. The Web, file transfer, and electronic mail have common service requirements: They all require a reliable transfer service, none of them have special timing requirements, and they all welcome an elastic bandwidth offering. The services provided by TCP are largely sufficient for these three applications. The fourth application, Domain Name System (DNS), provides a directory service for the Internet. Most users do not interact with DNS directly; instead, users invoke DNS indirectly through other applications (including the Web, file transfer, and electronic mail). DNS illustrates nicely how a distributed database can be implemented in the Internet. None of the four applications discussed in this chapter are particularly time sensitive; we will defer our discussion of such time-sensitive applications until Chapter 6.

2.2　THE WORLD WIDE WEB: HTTP

In the 1980s the Internet was used by researchers, academics, and university students to login to remote hosts, to transfer files from local hosts to remote hosts and vice versa, to receive and send news, and to receive and send electronic mail. Although these applications were (and continue to be) extremely useful, the Internet was essentially unknown outside the academic and research communities. Then, in the early 1990s, the Internet's killer application arrived on the scene—the World Wide Web. The Web is the Internet application that caught the general public's eye. It is dramatically changing how people interact inside and outside their work environments. It has spawned thousands of start up companies. It has elevated the Internet from just one of many data networks (including online networks such as Prodigy, America OnLine, and Compuserve, national data networks such as Minitel/Transpac in France, private X.25, and frame relay networks) to essentially the one and only data network.

History is sprinkled with the arrival of electronic communication technologies that have had major societal impacts. The first such technology was the telephone, invented in the 1870s. The telephone allowed two persons to orally communicate in real-time without being in the same physical location. It had a major impact on society—both good and bad. The next electronic communication technology was broadcast radio/television, which arrived in the 1920s and 1930s. Broadcast radio/ television allowed people to receive vast quantities of audio and video information. It also had a major impact on society—both good and bad. The third major communication technology that has changed the way people live and work is the Web. Perhaps what appeals the most to users about the Web is that it operates *on demand*. Users receive what they want, when they want it. This is unlike broadcast radio and television, which force users to "tune in" when the content provider makes the content available. In addition to being on demand, the Web has many other wonderful features that people love and cherish. It is enormously easy for any individual to make any information available over the Web; everyone can become a publisher at extremely low cost. Hyperlinks and search engines help us navigate through an ocean of Web sites. Graphics and animated graphics stimulate our senses. Forms, Java applets, Active X components, as well as many other devices enable us to interact with pages and sites. And more and more, the Web provides a menu interface to vast quantities of audio and video material stored in the Internet, audio and video that can be accessed on demand.

2.2.1 Overview of HTTP

The Hypertext Transfer Protocol (HTTP), the Web's application-layer protocol, is at the heart of the Web. HTTP is implemented in two programs: a client program and a server program. The client program and server programs, executing on different end systems, talk to each other by exchanging HTTP messages. HTTP defines the structure of these messages and how the client and server exchange the messages. Before explaining HTTP in detail, it is useful to review some Web terminology.

A **Web page** (also called a document) consists of objects. An **object** is simply a file—such as an HTML file, a JPEG image, a GIF image, a Java applet, an audio clip, and so on—that is addressable by a single URL. Most Web pages consist of a **base HTML file** and several referenced objects. For example, if a Web page contains HTML text and five JPEG images, then the Web page has six objects: the base HTML file plus the five images. The base HTML file references the other objects in the page with the objects' URLs. Each URL has two components: the host name of the server that houses the object and the object's path name. For example, the URL

```
www.someSchool.edu/someDepartment/picture.gif
```

has `www.someSchool.edu` for a host name and `/someDepartment/picture.gif` for a path name. A **browser** is a user agent for the Web; it displays to the user the requested Web page and provides numerous navigational and configuration features. Web browsers also implement the client side of HTTP. Thus, in the context of the Web, we will interchangeably use the words "browser" and "client." Popular Web browsers include Netscape Communicator and Microsoft Explorer. A **Web server** houses Web objects, each addressable by a URL. Web servers also implement the server side of HTTP. Popular Web servers include Apache, Microsoft Internet Information Server, and the Netscape Enterprise Server. (Netcraft provides a nice survey of Web server penetration [Netcraft].)

HTTP defines how Web clients (that is, browsers) request Web pages from servers (that is, Web servers) and how servers transfer Web pages to clients. We discuss the interaction between client and server in detail below, but the general idea is illustrated in Figure 2.4. When a user requests a Web page (for example, clicks on a hyperlink), the browser sends HTTP request messages for the objects in the page to the server. The server receives the requests and responds with HTTP response messages that contain the objects. Through 1997 essentially all browsers and Web servers implemented version HTTP/1.0, which is defined in [RFC 1945]. Beginning in 1998, Web servers and browsers began to implement version HTTP/1.1, which is defined in [RFC 2068]. HTTP/1.1 is backward compatible with HTTP/1.0; a Web server running 1.1 can "talk" with a browser running 1.0, and a browser running 1.1 can "talk" with a server running 1.0.

Both HTTP/1.0 and HTTP/1.1 use TCP as their underlying transport protocol (rather than running on top of UDP). The HTTP client first initiates a TCP connection with the server. Once the connection is established, the browser and the server processes access TCP through their socket interfaces. As described in Section 2.1, on the client side the socket interface is the "door" between the client process and the TCP connection; on the server side it is the "door" between the

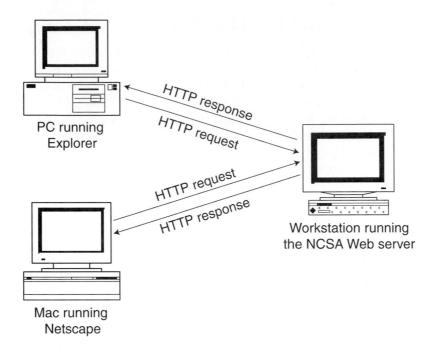

FIGURE 2.4   HTTP request-response behavior

server process and the TCP connection. The client sends HTTP request messages into its socket interface and receives HTTP response messages from its socket interface. Similarly, the HTTP server receives request messages from its socket interface and sends response messages into the socket interface. Once the client sends a message into its socket interface, the message is "out of the client's hands" and is "in the hands of TCP." Recall from Section 2.1 that TCP provides a reliable data transfer service to HTTP. This implies that each HTTP request message emitted by a client process eventually arrives intact at the server; similarly, each HTTP response message emitted by the server process eventually arrives intact at the client. Here we see one of the great advantages of a layered architecture—HTTP need not worry about lost data, or the details of how TCP recovers from loss or reordering of data within the network. That is the job of TCP and the protocols in the lower layers of the protocol stack.

TCP also employs a congestion control mechanism that we shall discuss in detail in Chapter 3. We mention here only that this mechanism forces each new TCP connection to initially transmit data at a relatively slow rate, but then allows each connection to ramp up to a relatively high rate when the network is uncongested. The initial slow-transmission phase is referred to as **slow start.**

It is important to note that the server sends requested files to clients without storing any state information about the client. If a particular client asks for the same object twice in a period of a few seconds, the server does not respond by saying that it just served the object to the client; instead, the server resends the object, as it has completely forgotten what it did earlier. Because an HTTP server maintains no information about the clients, HTTP is said to be a **stateless protocol.**

2.2.2   Nonpersistent and Persistent Connections

HTTP can use both nonpersistent connections and persistent connections. Non-persistent connections is the default mode for HTTP/1.0. Conversely, persistent connections is the default mode for HTTP/1.1.

Nonpersistent connections.   Let us walk through the steps of transferring a Web page from server to client for the case of nonpersistent connections. Suppose the page consists of a base HTML file and 10 JPEG images, and that all 11 of these objects reside on the same server. Suppose the URL for the base HTML file is

`www.someSchool.edu/someDepartment/home.index`.

Here is what happens:

1. The HTTP client initiates a TCP connection to the server `www.some-School.edu`. Port number 80 is used as the default port number at which the HTTP server will be listening for HTTP clients that want to retrieve documents using HTTP.
2. The HTTP client sends a HTTP request message into the socket associated with the TCP connection that was established in Step 1. The request message either includes the entire URL or simply the path name `/someDepartment/home.index`. (We will discuss the HTTP messages in some detail below.)
3. The HTTP server receives the request message via the socket associated with the connection that was established in Step 1, retrieves the object `/someDepartment/home.index` from its storage (RAM or disk), encapsulates the object in an HTTP response message, and sends the response message into the TCP connection.
4. The HTTP server tells TCP to close the TCP connection. (But TCP doesn't actually terminate the connection until the client has received the response message intact.)
5. The HTTP client receives the response message. The TCP connection terminates. The message indicates that the encapsulated object is an HTML file. The client extracts the file from the response message, parses the HTML file, and finds references to the 10 JPEG objects.
6. The first four steps are then repeated for each of the referenced JPEG objects.

As the browser receives the Web page, it displays the page to the user. Two different browsers may interpret (that is, display to the user) a Web page in somewhat different ways. HTTP has nothing to do with how a Web page is interpreted by a client. The HTTP specifications ([RFC 1945] and [RFC 2068]) only define the communication protocol between the client HTTP program and the server HTTP program.

The steps above use nonpersistent connections because each TCP connection is closed after the server sends the object—the connection does not persist for other objects. Note that each TCP connection transports exactly one request message and one response message. Thus, in this example, when a user requests the Web page, 11 TCP connections are generated.

In the steps described above, we were intentionally vague about whether the client obtains the 10 JPEGs over 10 serial TCP connections, or whether some of the JPEGs are obtained over parallel TCP connections. Indeed, users can configure modern browsers to control the degree of parallelism. In their default modes, most browsers open 5 to 10 parallel TCP connections, and each of these connections handles one request-response transaction. If the user prefers, the maximum number of parallel connections can be set to 1, in which case the 10 connections are established serially. As we shall see in the next chapter, the use of parallel connections shortens the response time since it cuts out some of the RTT and slow-start delays. Parallel TCP connections can also allow the requesting browser to steal a larger share of its fair share of the end-to-end transmission bandwidth.

Before continuing, let's do a back-of-the-envelope calculation to estimate the amount of time from when a client requests the base HTML file until the file is received by the client. To this end we define the **round-trip time (RTT),** which is the time it takes for a small packet to travel from client to server and then back to the client. The RTT includes packet-propagation delays, packet-queuing delays in intermediate routers and switches, and packet-processing delays. (These delays were discussed in Section 1.6.) Now consider what happens when a user clicks on a hyperlink. This causes the browser to initiate a TCP connection between the browser and the Web server; this involves a "three-way handshake"—the client sends a small TCP message to the server, the server acknowledges and responds with a small message, and, finally, the client acknowledges back to the server. One RTT elapses after the first two parts of the three-way handshake. After completing the first two parts of the handshake, the client sends the HTTP request message into the TCP connection, and TCP "piggybacks" the last acknowledgment (the third part of the three-way handshake) onto the request message. Once the request message arrives at the server, the server sends the HTML file into the TCP connection. This HTTP request/response eats up another RTT. Thus, roughly, the total response time is two RTTs plus the transmission time at the server of the HTML file.

Persistent connections. Nonpersistent connections have some shortcomings. First, a brand new connection must be established and maintained for *each requested object*. For each of these connections, TCP buffers must be allocated and TCP variables must be kept in both the client and server. This can place a serious burden on the Web server, which may be serving requests from hundreds of different clients simultaneously. Second, as we just described, each object suffers two RTTs—one RTT to establish the TCP connection and one RTT to request and receive an object. Finally, each object suffers from TCP slow start because every TCP connection begins with a TCP slow-start phase. However, the accumulation of RTT and slow-start delays is partially alleviated by the use of parallel TCP connections.

With persistent connections, the server leaves the TCP connection open after sending responses. Subsequent requests and responses between the same client and server can be sent over the same connection. In particular, an entire Web page (in the example above, the base HTML file and the 10 images) can be sent over a single persistent TCP connection; moreover, multiple Web pages residing on the same server can be sent over one persistent TCP connection. Typically, the HTTP server closes the connection when it isn't used for a certain time (the timeout interval), which is often configurable. There are two versions of persistent connections: **without pipelining** and **with pipelining.** For the version without pipelining, the client issues a new request only when the previous response has been received. In this case, each of the referenced objects (the 10 images in the example above) experiences one RTT in order to request and receive the object. Although this is an improvement over nonpersistent's two RTTs, the RTT delay can be further reduced with pipelining. Another disadvantage of no pipelining is that after the server sends an object over the persistent TCP connection, the connection hangs—does nothing—while it waits for another request to arrive. This hanging wastes server resources.

The default mode of HTTP/1.1 uses persistent connections with pipelining. In this case, the HTTP client issues a request as soon as it encounters a reference. Thus the HTTP client can make back-to-back requests for the referenced objects. When the server receives the requests, it can send the objects back to back. If all the requests are sent back-to-back and all the responses are sent back-to-back, then only one RTT is expended for all the referenced objects (rather than one RTT per referenced object when pipelining isn't used). Furthermore, the pipelined TCP connection hangs for a smaller fraction of time. In addition to reducing RTT delays, persistent connections (with or without pipelining) have a smaller slow-start delay than nonpersistent connections. The reason is that after sending the first object, the persistent server does not have to send the next object at the initial slow rate since it continues to use the same TCP connection. Instead, the server can pick up at the rate where the first object left off. We shall quantitatively compare the performance of nonpersistent and persistent connections in the homework problems of Chapter 3. The interested reader is also encouraged to see [Heidemann 1997] and [Nielsen 1997].

2.2.3   HTTP Message Format

The HTTP specifications 1.0 ([RFC 1945] and 1.1 [RFC 2068]) define the HTTP message formats. There are two types of HTTP messages, request messages and response messages, both of which are discussed below.

HTTP request message.   Below we provide a typical HTTP request message:

```
GET /somedir/page.html HTTP/1.1
Connection: close
User-agent: Mozilla/4.0
Accept: text/html, image/gif, image/jpeg
Accept-language:fr
(extra carriage return, line feed)
```

We can learn a lot by taking a good look at this simple request message. First of all, we see that the message is written in ordinary ASCII text, so that your ordinary computer-literate human being can read it. Second, we see that the message consists of five lines, each followed by a carriage return and a line feed. The last line is followed by an additional carriage return and line feed. Although this particular request message has five lines, a request message can have many more lines or as little as one line. The first line of an HTTP request message is called the

request line; the subsequent lines are called the **header lines.** The request line has three fields: the method field, the URL field, and the HTTP version field. The method field can take on several different values, including GET, POST, and HEAD. The great majority of HTTP request messages use the GET method. The GET method is used when the browser requests an object, with the requested object identified in the URL field. In this example, the browser is requesting the object /somedir/page.html. (The browser doesn't have to specify the host name in the URL field since the TCP connection is already connected to the host (server) that serves the requested file.) The version is self-explanatory; in this example, the browser implements version HTTP/1.1.

Now let's look at the header lines in the example. By including the Connection:close header line, the browser is telling the server that it doesn't want to use persistent connections; it wants the server to close the connection after sending the requested object. Thus the browser that generated this request message implements HTTP/1.1 but it doesn't want to bother with persistent connections. The User-agent: header line specifies the user agent, that is, the browser type that is making the request to the server. Here the user agent is Mozilla/4.0, a Netscape browser. This header line is useful because the server can actually send different versions of the same object to different types of user agents. (Each of the versions is addressed by the same URL.) The Accept: header line tells the server the type of objects the browser is prepared to accept. In this case, the client is prepared to accept HTML text, a GIF image or a JPEG image. If the file /somedir/page.html contains a Java applet (and who says it can't!), then the server shouldn't send the file, since the browser cannot handle that object type. Finally, the Accept-language: header indicates that the user prefers to receive a French version of the object, if such an object exists on the server; otherwise, the server should send its default version.

Having looked at an example, let us now look at the general format for a request message, as shown in Figure 2.5.

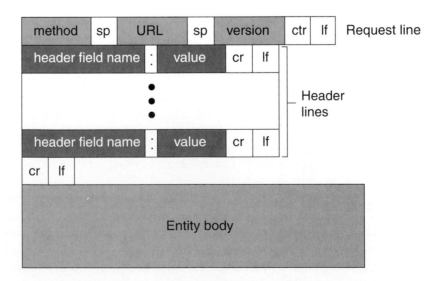

FIGURE 2.5 General format of a request message

We see that the general format follows closely the example request message seen earlier. You may have noticed, however, that after the header lines (and the additional carriage return and line feed) there is an "entity body." The entity body is not used with the GET method, but is used with the POST method. The HTTP client uses the POST method when the user fills out a form—for example, when a user gives search words to a search engine such as Yahoo. With a POST message, the user is still requesting a Web page from the server, but the specific contents of the Web page depend on what the user wrote in the form fields. If the value of the method field is POST, then the entity body contains what the user typed into the form fields. The HEAD method is similar to the POST method. When a server receives a request with the HEAD method, it responds with an HTTP message but it leaves out the requested object. The HEAD method is often used by HTTP server developers for debugging.

HTTP response message.   Below we provide a typical HTTP response message. This response message could be the response to the example request message just discussed.

```
HTTP/1.1 200 OK
Connection: close
Date: Thu, 06 Aug 1998 12:00:15 GMT
Server: Apache/1.3.0 (Unix)
Last-Modified: Mon, 22 Jun 1998 09:23:24 GMT
Content-Length: 6821
Content-Type: text/html
data data data data data ...
```

Let's take a careful look at this response message. It has three sections: an initial **status line,** six **header lines,** and then the **entity body.** The entity body is the meat of the message—it contains the requested object itself (represented by data data data data data ...). The status line has three fields: the protocol version field, a status code, and a corresponding status message. In this example, the status line indicates that the server is using HTTP/1.1 and that everything is OK (that is, the server has found, and is sending, the requested object).

Now let's look at the header lines. The server uses the Connection: close header line to tell the client that it is going to close the TCP connection after sending the message. The Date: header line indicates the time and date when the HTTP response was created and sent by the server. Note that this is not the time when the object was created or last modified; it is the time when the server retrieves the object from its file system, inserts the object into the response message, and sends the response message. The Server: header line indicates that the message was generated by an Apache Web server; it is analogous to the User-agent: header line in the HTTP request message. The Last-Modified: header line indicates the time and date when the object was created or last modified. The Last-Modified: header, which we will cover in more detail, is critical for object caching, both in the local client and in network cache servers (also known as proxy servers). The Content-Length: header line indicates the number of bytes in the object being sent. The Content-Type: header line indicates that the object in the entity body is HTML text. (The object type is officially indicated by the `Content-Type:` header and not by the file extension.)

Note that if the server receives an HTTP/1.0 request, it will not use persistent connections, even if it is an HTTP/1.1 server. Instead, the HTTP/1.1 server will close the TCP connection after sending the object. This is necessary because an HTTP/1.0 client expects the server to close the connection.

Having looked at an example, let us now examine the general format of a response message, which is shown in Figure 2.6. This general format of the response message matches the previous example of a response message. Let's say a few additional words about status codes and their phrases. The status code and associated phrase indicate the result of the request. Some common status codes and associated phrases include:

- `200 OK`: Request succeeded and the information is returned in the response.
- `301 Moved Permanently`: Requested object has been permanently moved; new URL is specified in `Location:` header of the response message. The client software will automatically retrieve the new URL.
- `400 Bad Request`: A generic error code indicating that the request could not be understood by the server.
- `404 Not Found`: The requested document does not exist on this server.
- `505 HTTP Version Not Supported`: The requested HTTP protocol version is not supported by the server.

How would you like to see a real HTTP response message? This is very easy to do! First Telnet into your favorite Web server. Then type in a one-line request message for some object that is housed on the server. For example, if you can logon to a Unix machine, type:

```
telnet www.eurecom.fr 80
GET /~ross/index.html HTTP/1.0
```

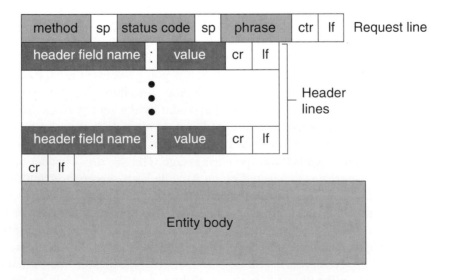

FIGURE 2.6   General format of a response message

(Hit the carriage return twice after typing the second line.) This opens a TCP connection to port 80 of the host `www.eurecom.fr` and then sends the HTTP `GET` command. You should see a response message that includes the base HTML file of Professor Ross's homepage. If you'd rather just see the HTTP message lines and not receive the object itself, replace `GET` with `HEAD`. Finally, replace `/~ross/index.html` with `/~ross/banana.html` and see what kind of response message you get.

In this section we discussed a number of header lines that can be used within HTTP request and response messages. The HTTP specification (especially HTTP/1.1) defines many, many more header lines that can be inserted by browsers, Web servers, and network cache servers. We have only covered a small number of the totality of header lines. We will cover a few more below and another small number when we discuss network Web caching at the end of this chapter. A readable and comprehensive discussion of HTTP headers and status codes is given in [Luotonen 1998]. An excellent introduction to the technical issues surrounding the Web is [Yeager 1996].

How does a browser decide which header lines to include in a request message? How does a Web server decide which header lines to include in a response message? A browser will generate header lines as a function of the browser type and version (for example, an HTTP/1.0 browser will not generate any 1.1 header lines), the user configuration of the browser (for example, preferred language), and whether the browser currently has a cached, but possibly out-of-date, version of the object. Web servers behave similarly: There are different products, versions, and configurations, all of which influence which header lines are included in response messages.

2.2.4 User-Server Interaction: Authentication and Cookies

We mentioned above that an HTTP server is stateless. This simplifies server design, and has permitted engineers to develop very high-performing Web servers. However, it is often desirable for a Web site to identify users, either because the server wishes to restrict user access or because it wants to serve content as a function of the user identity. HTTP provides two mechanisms to help a server identify a user: authentication and cookies.

Authentication. Many sites require users to provide a username and a password in order to access the documents housed on the server. This requirement is referred to as **authentication.** HTTP provides special status codes and headers to help sites perform authentication. Let us walk through an example to get a feel for how these special status codes and headers work. Suppose a client requests an object from a server, and the server requires user authorization.

The client first sends an ordinary request message with no special header lines. The server then responds with empty entity body and with a `401 Authorization Required` status code. In this response message the server includes the `WWW-Authenticate:` header, which specifies the details about how to perform authentication. (Typically, it indicates that the user needs to provide a username and a password.)

The client receives the response message and prompts the user for a username and password. The client resends the request message, but this time includes an `Authorization:` header line, which includes the username and password.

After obtaining the first object, the client continues to send the username and password in subsequent requests for objects on the server. (This typically continues until the client closes his browser. However, while the browser remains open, the username and password are cached, so the user is not prompted for a username and password for each object it requests!) In this manner, the site can identify the user for every request.

We will see in Chapter 7 that HTTP performs a rather weak form of authentication, one that would not be difficult to break. We will study more secure and robust authentication schemes later in Chapter 7.

Cookies.   Cookies are an alternative mechanism for sites to keep track of users. They are defined in [RFC 2109]. Some Web sites use cookies and others don't. Let's walk through an example. Suppose a client contacts a Web site for the first time, and this site uses cookies. The server's response will include a `Set-cookie:` header. Often this header line contains an identification number generated by the Web server. For example, the header line might be:

```
Set-cookie: 1678453
```

When the HTTP client receives the response message, it sees the `Set-cookie:` header and identification number. It then appends a line to a special cookie file that is stored in the client machine. This line typically includes the host name of the server and user's associated identification number. In subsequent requests to the same server, say one week later, the client includes a `Cookie:` request header, and this header line specifies the identification number for that server. In the current example, the request message includes the header line:

```
Cookie: 1678453
```

In this manner, the server does not know the username of the user, but the server does know that this user is the same user that made a specific request one week ago. Web servers use cookies for many different purposes:

- If a server requires authentication but doesn't want to hassle a user with a username and password prompt every time the user visits the site, it can set a cookie.
- If a server wants to remember a user's preferences so that it can provide targeted advertising during subsequent visits, it can set a cookie.
- If a user is shopping at a site (for example, buying several CDs), the server can use cookies to keep track of the items that the user is purchasing, that is, to create a virtual shopping cart.

We mention, however, that cookies pose problems for mobile users who access the same site from different machines. The site will treat the same user as a different user for each different machine used. We conclude by pointing the reader to the page Persistent Client State HTTP Cookies, which provides an in-depth but readable introduction to cookies. We also recommend Cookies Central, which includes extensive information on the cookie controversy.

2.2.5   The Conditional GET

By storing previously retrieved objects, Web caching can reduce object-retrieval delays and diminish the amount of Web traffic sent over the Internet. Web caches can reside in a client or in an intermediate network cache server. We will discuss network caching at the end of this chapter. In this subsection, we restrict our attention to client caching.

Although Web caching can reduce user-perceived response times, it introduces a new problem—a copy of an object residing in the cache may be *stale*. In other words, the object housed in the Web server may have been modified since the copy was cached at the client. Fortunately, HTTP has a mechanism that allows the client to employ caching while still ensuring that all objects passed to the browser are up to date. This mechanism is called the **conditional GET.** An HTTP request message is a so-called conditional GET message if (1) the request message uses the GET method and (2) the request message includes an If-Modified-Since: header line.

To illustrate how the conditional GET operates, let's walk through an example. First, a browser requests an uncached object from some Web server:

```
GET /fruit/kiwi.gif HTTP/1.0
User-agent: Mozilla/4.0
Accept: text/html, image/gif, image/jpeg
```

Second, the Web server sends a response message with the object to the client:

```
HTTP/1.0 200 OK
Date: Wed, 12 Aug 1998 15:39:29
Server: Apache/1.3.0 (Unix)
Last-Modified: Mon, 22 Jun 1998 09:23:24
Content-Type: image/gif
data data data data data ...
```

The client displays the object to the user but also saves the object in its local cache. Importantly, the client also caches the last-modified date along with the object. Third, one week later, the user requests the same object and the object is still in the cache. Since this object may have been modified at the Web server in the past week, the browser performs an up-to-date check by issuing a conditional GET. Specifically, the browser sends

```
GET /fruit/kiwi.gif HTTP/1.0
User-agent: Mozilla/4.0
Accept: text/html, image/gif, image/jpeg
If-modified-since: Mon, 22 Jun 1998 09:23:24
```

Note that the value of the If-modified-since: header line is exactly equal to the value of the Last-Modified: header line that was sent by the server one week ago. This conditional GET is telling the server to send the object only if the object has been modified since the specified date. Suppose the object has not been modified since 22 Jun 1998 09:23:24. Then, fourth, the Web server sends a response message to the client:

```
HTTP/1.0 304 Not Modified
Date: Wed, 19 Aug 1998 15:39:29
Server: Apache/1.3.0 (Unix)
```
(*empty entity body*)

We see that in response to the conditional GET, the Web server still sends a response message, but it doesn't bother to include the requested object in the response message. Including the requested object would only waste bandwidth and increase user perceived response time, particularly if the object is large (such as a high resolution image). Note that this last response message has in the status line 304 Not Modified, which tells the client that it can go ahead and use its cached copy of the object.

2.2.6   Web Caches

A **Web cache**—also called a **proxy server**—is a network entity that satisfies HTTP requests on the behalf of a client. The Web cache has its own disk storage and keeps in this storage copies of recently requested objects. As shown in Figure 2.7, users configure their browsers so that all of their HTTP requests are first directed to the Web cache. (This is a straightforward procedure with Microsoft and Netscape browsers.) Once a browser is configured, each browser request for an object is first directed to the Web cache. As an example, suppose a browser is requesting the object http://www.someschool.edu/campus.gif.

- The browser establishes a TCP connection to the proxy server and sends an HTTP request for the object to the Web cache.
- The Web cache checks to see if it has a copy of the object stored locally. If it does, the Web cache forwards the object within an HTTP response message to the client browser.
- If the Web cache does not have the object, the Web cache opens a TCP connection to the origin server, that is, to www.someschool.edu. The Web cache then sends an HTTP request for the object into the TCP connection. After receiving this request, the origin server sends the object within an HTTP response to the Web cache.
- When the Web cache receives the object, it stores a copy in its local storage and forwards a copy, within an HTTP response message, to the client browser (over the existing TCP connection between the client browser and the Web cache).

Note that a cache is both a server and a client at the same time. When it receives requests from and sends responses to a browser, it is a server. When it sends requests to and receives responses from an origin server it is a client.

So why bother with a Web cache? What advantages does it have? Web caches are enjoying wide-scale deployment in the Internet for at least three reasons. First, a Web cache can substantially reduce the response time for a client request, particularly if the bottleneck bandwidth between the client and the origin server is much

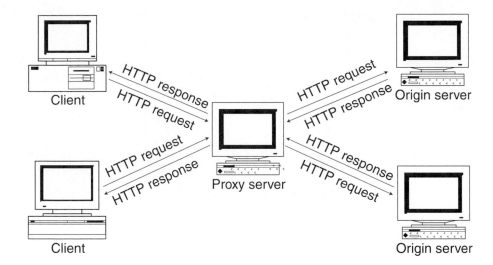

FIGURE 2.7   Clients requesting objects through a Web cache

less than the bottleneck bandwidth between the client and the cache. If there is a high-speed connection between the client and the cache, as there often is, and if the cache has the requested object, then the cache will be able to rapidly deliver the object to the client. Second, as we will soon illustrate with an example, Web caches can substantially reduce traffic on an institution's access link to the Internet. By reducing traffic, the institution (for example, a company or a university) does not have to upgrade bandwidth as quickly, thereby reducing costs. Furthermore, Web caches can substantially reduce Web traffic in the Internet as a whole, thereby improving performance for all applications. In 1998, over 75% of Internet traffic was Web traffic, so a significant reduction in Web traffic can translate into a significant improvement in Internet performance [Claffy 1998]. Third, an Internet dense with Web caches—such as, at institutional, regional, and national levels— provides an infrastructure for rapid distribution of content, even for content providers who run their sites on low-speed servers behind low-speed access links. If such a "resource-poor" content provider suddenly has popular content to distribute, this popular content will quickly be copied into the Internet caches, and high user demand will be satisfied.

To gain a deeper understanding of the benefits of caches, let us consider an example in the context of Figure 2.8. In this figure, there are two networks—the institutional network and the Internet. The institutional network is a high-speed LAN. A router in the institutional network and a router in the Internet are connected by a 1.5 Mbps link. The institutional network consists of a high-speed LAN that is connected to the Internet through a 1.5 Mbps access link. The origin servers are attached to the Internet, but located all over the globe. Suppose that the average object size is 100 Kbits and that the average request rate from the institution's browsers to the origin servers is 15 requests per second. Also suppose that the amount of time it takes from when the router on the Internet side of the access link in Figure 2.8 forwards an HTTP request (within an IP datagram) until it receives the IP datagram (typically, many IP datagrams) containing the corresponding

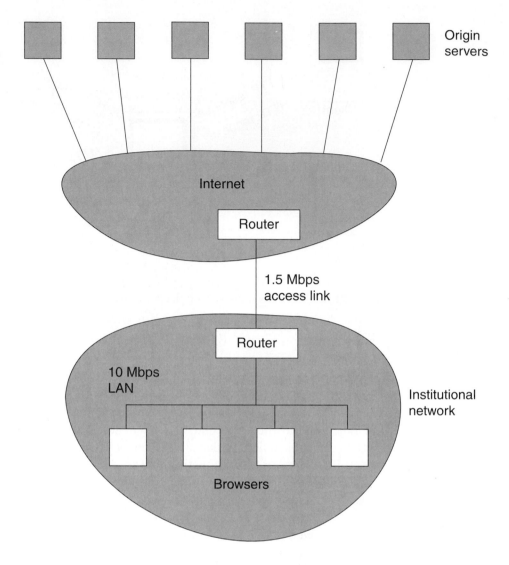

FIGURE 2.8 Bottleneck between an institutional network and the Internet

response is two seconds on average. Informally, we refer to this last delay as the "Internet delay."

The total response time—that is, the time from the browser's request of an object until its receipt of the object—is the sum of the LAN delay, the access delay (that is, the delay between the two routers), and the Internet delay. Let us now do a very crude calculation to estimate this delay. The traffic intensity on the LAN (see Section 1.6) is

$$(15 \text{ requests/sec}) * (100 \text{ Kbits/request})/(10\text{Mbps}) = 0.15$$

whereas the traffic intensity on access link (from Internet router to institution router) is

$$(15 \text{ requests/sec}) * (100 \text{ Kbits/request})/(1.5 \text{ Mbps}) = 1$$

A traffic intensity of 0.15 on a LAN typically results in, at most, tens of milliseconds of delay; hence, we can neglect the LAN delay. However, as discussed in Section 1.6, as the traffic intensity approaches 1 (as is the case of the access link in Figure 2.8), the delay on a link becomes very large and grows without bound. Thus, the average response time to satisfy requests is going to be on the order of minutes, if not more, which is unacceptable for the institution's users. Clearly something must be done.

One possible solution is to increase the access rate from 1.5 Mbps to, say, 10 Mbps. This will lower the traffic intensity on the access link to 0.15, which translates to negligible delays between the two routers. In this case, the total response time will roughly be 2 seconds, that is, the Internet delay. But this solution also means that the institution must upgrade its access link from 1.5 Mbps to 10 Mbps, which can be very costly.

Now consider the alternative solution of not upgrading the access link but instead installing a Web cache in the institutional network. This solution is illustrated in Figure 2.9. Hit rates—the fraction of requests that are satisfied by a cache—typically range from 0.2 to 0.7 in practice. For illustrative purposes, let us suppose that the cache provides a hit rate of 0.4 for this institution. Because the clients and the cache are connected to the same high-speed LAN, 40% of the requests will be satisfied almost immediately, say within 10 milliseconds, by the cache. Nevertheless, the remaining 60% of the requests still need to be satisfied by the origin servers. But with only 60% of the requested objects passing through the access link, the traffic intensity on the access link is reduced from 1.0 to 0.6. Typically a traffic intensity less than 0.8 corresponds to a small delay, say tens of milliseconds, on a 1.5 Mbps link, which is negligible compared with the 2-second Internet delay. Given these considerations, average delay therefore is

$$0.4 * (0.010 \text{ seconds}) + 0.6 * (2.01 \text{ seconds})$$

which is just slightly greater than 1.2 seconds. Thus, this second solution provides an even lower response time then the first solution, and it doesn't require the institution to upgrade its access rate. The institution does, of course, have to purchase and install a Web cache. But this cost is low—many caches use public-domain software that run on inexpensive servers and PCs.

Cooperative caching.   Multiple Web caches, located at different places in the Internet, can cooperate and improve overall performance. For example, an institutional cache can be configured to send its HTTP requests to a cache in a backbone ISP at the national level. In this case, when the institutional cache does not have the requested object in its storage, it forwards the HTTP request to the national cache. The national cache then retrieves the object from its own storage or, if the object is not in storage, from the origin server. The national cache then sends the object (within an HTTP response message) to the institutional cache, which in turn forwards the object to the requesting browser. Whenever an object passes through a cache (institutional or national), the cache leaves a copy in its local storage. The advantage of passing through a higher-level cache, such as a national cache, is that it has a larger user population and therefore higher hit rates.

An example of a cooperative caching system is the NLANR caching system, which consists of a number of backbone caches in the United States providing

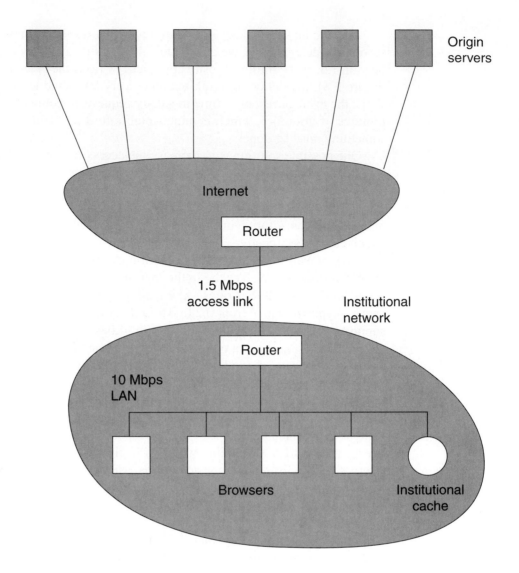

FIGURE 2.9   Adding a cache to the institutional network

service to institutional and regional caches from all over the globe [NLANR]. The NLANR caching hierarchy is shown in Figure 2.10 [Huffaker 1998]. The caches obtain objects from each other using a combination of HTTP and ICP (Internet Caching Protocol). ICP is an application-layer protocol that allows one cache to quickly ask another cache if it has a given document [RFC 2186]; a cache can then use HTTP to retrieve the object from the other cache. ICP is used extensively in many cooperative caching systems and is fully supported by Squid, a popular public-domain software for Web caching [Squid]. If you are interested in learning more about ICP, you are encouraged to see [Luotonen 1998], [Ross 1998], and the ICP RFC [RFC 2186].

An alternative form of cooperative caching involves clusters of caches, often co-located on the same LAN. A single cache is often replaced with a cluster of

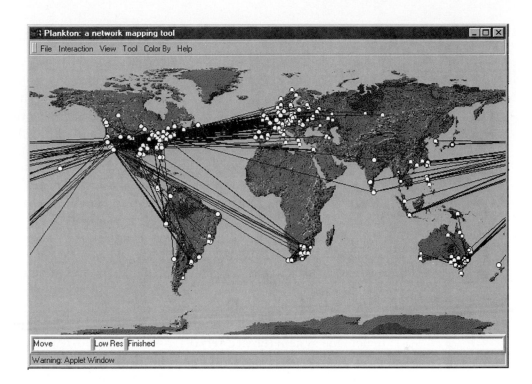

FIGURE 2.10 The NLANR caching hierarchy (Courtesy of [Huffaker 1998])

caches when the single cache is not sufficient to handle the traffic or provide sufficient storage capacity. Although cache clustering is a natural way to scale as traffic increases, their use introduces a new problem: When a browser wants to request a particular object, to which cache in the cache cluster should it send the request? This problem can be elegantly solved using hash routing. (If you are not familiar with hash functions, you can read about them in Chapter 7.) In the simplest form of hash routing, the browser hashes the URL, and depending on the result of the hash, the browser directs its request message to one of the caches in the cluster. By having all the browsers use the same hash function, an object will never be present in more than one cache in the cluster, and if the object is indeed in the cache cluster, the browser will always direct its request to the correct cache. Hash routing is the essence of the Cache Array Routing Protocol (CARP). If you are interested in learning more about hash routing or CARP, see [Valloppillil 1997], [Luotonen 1998], [Ross 1997] and [Ross 1998].

Web caching is a rich and complex subject; over two thirds (40 pages) of the HTTP/1.1 RFC is devoted to Web caching [RFC 2068]! Web caching has also enjoyed extensive research and product development in recent years. Furthermore, caches are now being built to handle streaming audio and video. Caches will likely play an important role as the Internet begins to provide an infrastructure for the large-scale, on-demand distribution of music, television shows, and movies in the Internet.

FILE TRANSFER: FTP

FTP (File Transfer Protocol) is a protocol for transferring a file from one host to another host. The protocol dates back to 1971 (when the Internet was still an experiment), but remains enormously popular. FTP is described in [RFC 959]. Figure 2.11 provides an overview of the services provided by FTP.

In a typical FTP session, the user is sitting in front of one host (the local host) and wants to transfer files to or from a remote host. In order for the user to access the remote account, the user must provide a user identification and a password. After providing this authorization information, the user can transfer files from the local file system to the remote file system and vice versa. As shown in Figure 2.11, the user interacts with FTP through an FTP user agent. The user first provides the hostname of the remote host, causing the FTP client process in the local host to establish a TCP connection with the FTP server process in the remote host. The user then provides the user identification and password, which get sent over the TCP connection as part of FTP commands. Once the server has authorized the user, the user copies one or more files stored in the local file system into the remote file system (or vice versa).

HTTP and FTP are both file transfer protocols and have many common characteristics; for example, they both run on top of TCP, the Internet's connection-oriented, transport-layer, reliable data transfer protocol. However, the two application-layer protocols have some important differences. The most striking difference is that FTP uses two parallel TCP connections to transfer a file, a **control connection** and a **data connection.** The control connection is used for sending control information between the two hosts—information such as user identification, password, commands to change remote directory, and commands to "put" and "get" files. The data connection is used to actually send a file. Because FTP uses a separate control connection, FTP is said to send its control information **out-of-band.** In Chapter 6 we shall see that the RTSP protocol, which is used for controlling the transfer of continuous media such as audio and video, also sends its control information out-of-band. HTTP, as you recall, sends request and

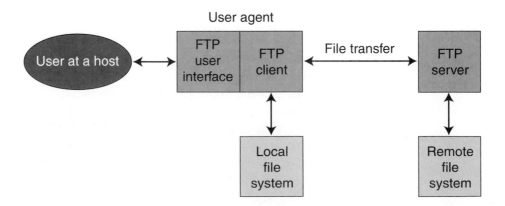

FIGURE 2.11   FTP moves files between local and remote file systems

response header lines into the same TCP connection that carries the transferred file itself. For this reason, HTTP is said to send its control information **in-band.** In the next section we shall see that SMTP, the main protocol for electronic mail, also sends control information in-band. The FTP control and data connections are illustrated in Figure 2.12.

When a user starts an FTP session with a remote host, FTP first sets up a control TCP connection on server port number 21. The client side of FTP sends the user identification and password over this control connection. The client side of FTP also sends, over the control connection, commands to change the remote directory. When the user requests a file transfer (either to, or from, the remote host), FTP opens a TCP data connection on server port number 20. FTP sends exactly one file over the data connection and then closes the data connection. If, during the same session, the user wants to transfer another file, FTP opens another data TCP connection. Thus, with FTP, the control connection remains open throughout the duration of the user session, but a new data connection is created for each file transferred within a session (that is, the data connections are nonpersistent).

Throughout a session, the FTP server must maintain **state** about the user. In particular, the server must associate the control connection with a specific user account, and the server must keep track of the user's current directory as the user wanders about the remote directory tree. Keeping track of this state information for each ongoing user session significantly impedes the total number of sessions that FTP can maintain simultaneously. HTTP, on the other hand, is **stateless**—it does not have to keep track of any user state.

2.3.1   FTP Commands and Replies

We end this section with a brief discussion of some of the more common FTP commands. The commands, from client to server, and replies, from server to client, are sent across the control TCP connection in seven-bit ASCII format. Thus, like HTTP commands, FTP commands are readable by people. In order to delineate successive commands, a carriage return and line feed end each command (and reply). Each command consists of four uppercase ASCII characters, some with optional arguments. Some of the more common commands are given below (with options in italics):

- USER *username:* Used to send the user identification to server.
- PASS *password:* Used to send the user password to the server.

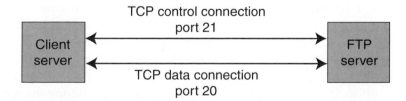

FIGURE 2.12   Control and data connections

- LIST: Used to ask the server to send back a list of all the files in the current remote directory. The list of files is sent over a (new and nonpersistent) data TCP connection and not over the control TCP connection.
- RETR *filename*: Used to retrieve (that is, get) a file from the current directory of the remote host.
- STOR *filename*: Used to store (that is, put) a file into the current directory of the remote host.

There is typically a one-to-one correspondence between the command that the user issues and the FTP command sent across the control connection. Each command is followed by a reply, sent from server to client. The replies are three-digit numbers, with an optional message following the number. This is similar in structure to the status code and phrase in the status line of the HTTP response message; the inventors of HTTP intentionally included this similarity in the HTTP response messages. Some typical replies, along with their possible messages, are as follows:

- 331 Username OK, password required
- 125 Data connection already open; transfer starting
- 425 Can't open data connection
- 452 Error writing file

Readers who are interested in learning about the other FTP commands and replies are encouraged to read [RFC 959].

2.4 ELECTRONIC MAIL IN THE INTERNET

Along with the Web, electronic mail is one of the most popular Internet applications. Just like ordinary "snail mail," e-mail is asynchronous—people send and read messages when it is convenient for them, without having to coordinate with other peoples' schedules. In contrast with snail mail, electronic mail is fast, easy to distribute, and inexpensive. Moreover, modern electronic mail messages can include hyperlinks, HTML formatted text, images, sound, and even video. In this section we will examine the application-layer protocols that are at the heart of Internet electronic mail. But before we jump into an in-depth discussion of these protocols, let's take a bird's eye view of the Internet mail system and its key components.

Figure 2.13 presents a high-level view of the Internet mail system. We see from this diagram that it has three major components: **user agents, mail servers,** and the **Simple Mail Transfer Protocol (SMTP).** We now describe each of these components in the context of a sender, Alice, sending an e-mail message to a recipient, Bob. User agents allow users to read, reply to, forward, save, and compose messages. (User agents for electronic mail are sometimes called *mail readers,* although we will generally avoid this term in this book.) When Alice is finished composing her message, her user agent sends the message to her mail server, where the message is placed in the mail server's outgoing message queue. When Bob wants to read a message, his user agent obtains the message from his

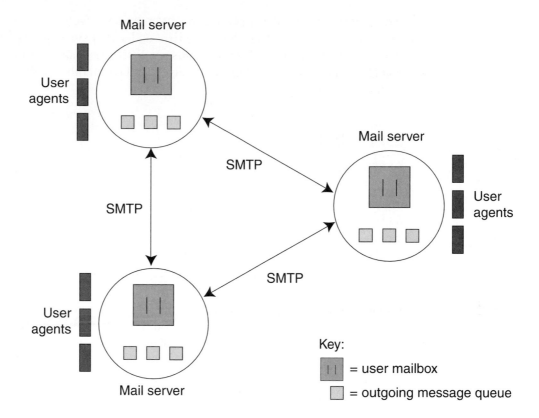

FIGURE 2.13   A bird's eye view of the Internet e-mail system

mailbox in his mail server. In the late 1990s, GUI (graphical user interface) user agents became popular, allowing users to view and compose multimedia messages. Currently, Eudora, Microsoft's Outlook Express, and Netscape's Messenger are among the popular GUI user agents for e-mail. There are also many text-based e-mail user interfaces in the public domain, including mail, pine, and elm.

Mail servers form the core of the e-mail infrastructure. Each recipient, such as Bob, has a **mailbox** located in one of the mail servers. Bob's mailbox manages and maintains the messages that have been sent to him. A typical message starts its journey in the sender's user agent, travels to the sender's mail server, and then travels to the recipient's mail server, where it is deposited in the recipient's mailbox. When Bob wants to access the messages in his mailbox, the mail server containing the mailbox authenticates Bob (with user names and passwords). Alice's mail server must also deal with failures in Bob's mail server. If Alice's server cannot deliver mail to Bob's server, Alice's server holds the message in a *message queue* and attempts to transfer the message later. Reattempts are often done every 30 minutes or so; if there is no success after several days, the server removes the message and notifies the sender (Alice) with an e-mail message.

The Simple Mail Transfer Protocol (SMTP) is the principal application-layer protocol for Internet electronic mail. It uses the reliable data transfer service of TCP to transfer mail from the sender's mail server to the recipient's mail server. As with most application-layer protocols, SMTP has two sides: a client side, which executes on the sender's mail server, and a server side, which executes on the recipient's mail server. Both the client and server sides of SMTP run on every mail server. When a mail server sends mail (to other mail servers), it acts as an SMTP client. When a mail server receives mail (from other mail servers) it acts as an SMTP server.

2.4.1   SMTP

SMTP, defined in [RFC 821], is at the heart of Internet electronic mail. As mentioned above, SMTP transfers messages from senders' mail servers to the recipients' mail servers. SMTP is much older than HTTP. (The SMTP RFC dates back to 1982, and SMTP was around long before that.) Although SMTP has numerous wonderful qualities, as evidenced by its ubiquity in the Internet, it is nevertheless a legacy technology that possesses certain "archaic" characteristics. For example, it restricts the body (not just the headers) of all mail messages to be in simple seven-bit ASCII. This restriction was not bothersome in the early 1980s when transmission capacity was scarce and no one was e-mailing large attachments or large image, audio, or video files. But today, in the multimedia era, the seven-bit ASCII restriction is a bit of a pain—it requires binary multimedia data to be encoded to ASCII before being sent over SMTP; and it requires the corresponding ASCII message to be decoded back to binary after SMTP transport. Recall from Section 2.3 that HTTP does not require multimedia data to be ASCII encoded before transfer.

To illustrate the basic operation of SMTP, let's walk through a common scenario. Suppose Alice wants to send Bob a simple ASCII message:

- Alice invokes her user agent for e-mail, provides Bob's e-mail address (for example, `bob@someschool.edu`), composes a message, and instructs the user agent to send the message.
- Alice's user agent sends the message to her mail server, where it is placed in a message queue.
- The client side of SMTP, running on Alice's mail server, sees the message in the message queue. It opens a TCP connection to an SMTP server, running on Bob's mail server.
- After some initial SMTP handshaking, the SMTP client sends Alice's message into the TCP connection.
- At Bob's mail server host, the server side of SMTP receives the message. Bob's mail server then places the message in Bob's mailbox.
- Bob invokes his user agent to read the message at his convenience.

The scenario is summarized in Figure 2.14.

It is important to observe that SMTP does not use intermediate mail servers for sending mail, even when the two mail servers are located at opposite ends of the world. If Alice's server is in Hong Kong and Bob's server is in Mobile, Alabama, the TCP "connection" is a direct connection between the Hong Kong and

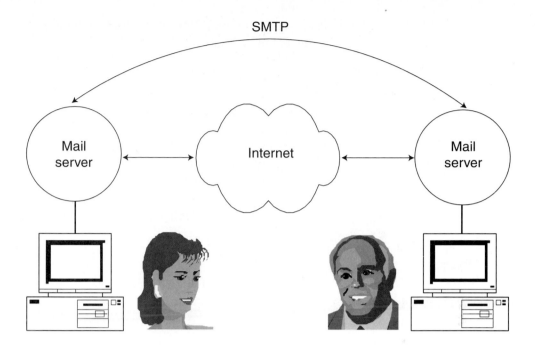

FIGURE 2.14   Alice's mail server transfers Alice's message to Bob's mail server

Mobile servers. In particular, if Bob's mail server is down, the message remains in Alice's mail server and waits for a new attempt—the message does not get placed in some intermediate mail server.

Let's now take a closer look at how SMTP transfers a message from a sending mail server to a receiving mail server. We will see that the SMTP protocol has many similarities with protocols that are used for face-to-face human interaction. First, the client SMTP (running on the sending mail server host) has TCP establish a connection on port 25 to the server SMTP (running on the receiving mail server host). If the server is down, the client tries again later. Once this connection is established, the server and client perform some application-layer handshaking. Just as humans often introduce themselves before transferring information from one to another, SMTP clients and servers introduce themselves before transferring information. During this SMTP handshaking phase, the SMTP client indicates the e-mail address of the sender (the person who generated the message) and the e-mail address of the recipient. Once the SMTP client and server have introduced themselves to each other, the client sends the message. SMTP can count on the reliable data transfer service of TCP to get the message to the server without errors. The client then repeats this process over the same TCP connection if it has other messages to send to the server; otherwise, it instructs TCP to close the connection.

Let us take a look at an example transcript between client (C) and server (S). The host name of the client is `crepes.fr` and the host name of the server is `hamburger.edu`. The ASCII text prefaced with `C:` are exactly the lines the client sends into its TCP socket; and the ASCII text prefaced with `S:` are exactly the lines the server sends into its TCP socket. The following transcript begins as soon as the TCP connection is established:

```
S: 220 hamburger.edu
C: HELO crepes.fr
S: 250 Hello crepes.fr, pleased to meet you
C: MAIL FROM: <alice@crepes.fr>
S: 250 alice@crepes.fr... Sender ok
C: RCPT TO: <bob@hamburger.edu>
S: 250 bob@hamburger.edu ... Recipient ok
C: DATA
S: 354 Enter mail, end with "." on a line by itself
C: Do you like ketchup?
C: How about pickles?
C: .
S: 250 Message accepted for delivery
C: QUIT
S: 221 hamburger.edu closing connection
```

In the above example, the client sends a message ("Do you like ketchup? How about pickles?") from mail server crepes.fr to mail server hamburger.edu. The client issued five commands: HELO (an abbreviation for HELLO), MAIL FROM, RCPT TO, DATA, and QUIT. These commands are self explanatory. The server issues replies to each command, with each reply having a reply code and some (optional) English-language explanation. We mention here that SMTP uses persistent connections: If the sending mail server has several messages to send to the same receiving mail server, it can send all of the messages over the same TCP connection. For each message, the client begins the process with a new HELO crepes.fr and only issues QUIT after all messages have been sent.

It is highly recommended that you use Telnet to carry out a direct dialogue with an SMTP server. To do this, issue telnet serverName 25 where serverName is the name of the remote mail server. When you do this, you are simply establishing a TCP connection between your local host and the mail server. After typing this line, you should immediately receive the 220 reply from the server. Then issue the SMTP commands HELO, MAIL FROM, RCPT TO, DATA, and QUIT at the appropriate times. If you Telnet into your friend's SMTP server, you should be able to send mail to your friend in this manner (that is, without using your mail user agent).

2.4.2 Comparison with HTTP

Let us now briefly compare SMTP to HTTP. Both protocols are used to transfer files from one host to another; HTTP transfers files (or objects) from Web server to Web user agent (that is, the browser); SMTP transfers files (that is, e-mail messages) from one mail server to another mail server. When transferring the files, both persistent HTTP and SMTP use persistent connections; that is, they can send multiple files over the same TCP connection. Thus the two protocols have common characteristics. However, there are important differences. First, HTTP is principally a **pull protocol**—someone loads information on a Web server and users use HTTP to pull the information off the server at their convenience. In particular, the TCP connection is initiated by the machine that wants to receive the file. On the other hand, SMTP is primarily a **push protocol**—the sending mail server pushes the file to the receiving mail server. In particular, the TCP connection is initiated by the machine that wants to send the file.

A second important difference, which we alluded to earlier, is that SMTP requires each message, including the body of each message, to be in seven-bit ASCII format. Furthermore, the SMTP RFC requires the body of every message to end with a line consisting of only a period—that is, in ASCII jargon, the body of each message ends with "CRLF.CRLF," where CR and LF stand for carriage return and line feed, respectively. In this manner, while the SMTP server is receiving a series of messages from an SMTP client over a persistent TCP connection, the server can delineate the messages by searching for "CRLF.CRLF" in the byte stream. (This operation of searching through a character stream is referred to as "parsing.") Now suppose that the body of one of the messages is not ASCII text but instead binary data (for example, a JPEG image). It is possible that this binary data might accidentally have the bit pattern associated with ASCII representation of "CRLF.CRLF" in the middle of the bit stream. This would cause the SMTP server to incorrectly conclude that the message has terminated. To get around this and related problems, binary data is first encoded to ASCII in such a way that certain ASCII characters (including ".") are not used. Returning to our comparison with HTTP, we note that neither nonpersistent nor persistent HTTP has to bother with the ASCII conversion. For nonpersistent HTTP, each TCP connection transfers exactly one object; when the server closes the connection, the client knows it has received one entire response message. For persistent HTTP, each response message includes a Content-length: header line, enabling the client to delineate the end of each message.

A third important difference concerns how a document consisting of text and images (along with possibly other media types) is handled. As we learned in Section 2.3, HTTP encapsulates each object in its own HTTP response message. Internet mail, as we shall discuss in greater detail below, places all of the message's objects into one message.

2.4.3 Mail Message Formats and MIME

When Alice sends an ordinary snail-mail letter to Bob, she puts the letter into an envelope, on which there is all kinds of peripheral information such as Bob's address, Alice's return address, and the date (supplied by the postal service). Similarly, when an e-mail message is sent from one person to another, a header containing peripheral information precedes the body of the message itself. This peripheral information is contained in a series of header lines, which are defined in [RFC 822]. The header lines and the body of the message are separated by a blank line (that is, by CRLF). RFC 822 specifies the exact format for mail header lines as well as their semantic interpretations. As with HTTP, each header line contains readable text, consisting of a keyword followed by a colon followed by a value. Some of the keywords are required and others are optional. Every header must have a From: header line and a To: header line; a header may include a Subject: header line as well as other optional header lines. It is important to note that these header lines are *different* from the SMTP commands we studied in the section in this chapter on SMTP (even though they contain some common words such as "from" and "to"). The commands in that section were part of the SMTP handshaking protocol; the header lines examined in this section are part of the mail message itself.

A typical message header looks like this:

```
From: alice@crepes.fr
To: bob@hamburger.edu
Subject: Searching for the meaning of life.
```

After the message header, a blank line follows, then the message body (in ASCII) follows. The message terminates with a line containing only a period, as discussed above. It is highly recommended that you use Telnet to send to a mail server a message that contains some header lines, including the `Subject:` header line. To do this, issue `telnet serverName 25`. The actual message is sent into the TCP connection right after the `SMTP DATA` command. The message consists of the message headers, the blank line, and the message body. The final line with a single period indicates the end of the message.

The MIME extension for non-ASCII data.   While the message headers described in RFC 822 are satisfactory for sending ordinary ASCII text, they are not sufficiently rich enough for multimedia messages (for example, messages with images, audio, and video) or for carrying non-ASCII text formats (for example, characters used by languages other than English). To send content different from ASCII text, the sending user agent must include additional headers in the message. These extra headers are defined in [RFC 2045] and [RFC 2046], the MIME extension to [RFC 822]. Two key MIME headers for supporting multimedia are the `Content-Type:` header and the `Content-Transfer-Encoding:` header. The `Content-Type:` header allows the receiving user agent to take an appropriate action on the message. For example, by indicating that the message body contains a JPEG image, the receiving user agent can direct the message body to a JPEG decompression routine. To understand the need of the `Content-Transfer-Encoding:` header, recall that non-ASCII text messages must be encoded to an ASCII format that isn't going to confuse SMTP. The `Content-Transfer-Encoding:` header alerts the receiving user agent that the message body has been ASCII-encoded and the type of encoding used. Thus, when a user agent receives a message with these two headers, it first uses the value of the `Content-Transfer-Encoding:` header to convert the message body to its original non-ASCII form, and then uses the `Content-Type:` header to determine what actions it should take on the message body.

Let's take a look at a concrete example. Suppose Alice wants to send Bob a JPEG image. To do this, Alice invokes her user agent for e-mail, specifies Bob's e-mail address, specifies the subject of the message, and inserts the JPEG image into the message body of the message. (Depending on the user agent Alice uses, she might insert the image into the message as an "attachment.") When Alice finishes composing her message, she clicks on "Send." Alice's user agent then generates a MIME message, which might look something like this:

```
From: alice@crepes.fr
To: bob@hamburger.edu
Subject: Picture of yummy crepe.
```

```
MIME-Version: 1.0
Content-Transfer-Encoding: base64
Content-Type: image/jpeg
base64 encoded data .....
........................
......base64 encoded data
```

We observe from the above MIME message that Alice's user agent encoded the JPEG image using base64 encoding. This is one of several encoding techniques standardized in the MIME [RFC 2045] for conversion to an acceptable seven-bit ASCII format. Another popular encoding technique is quoted-printable content-transfer-encoding, which is typically used to convert an ordinary ASCII message to ASCII text void of undesirable character strings (for example, a line with a single period.)

When Bob reads his mail with his user agent, his user agent operates on this same MIME message. When Bob's user agent observes the `Content-Transfer-Encoding: base64` header line, it proceeds to decode the base64-encoded message body. The message also includes a `Content-Type: image/jpeg` header line; this indicates to Bob's user agent that the message body (after base64 decoding) should be JPEG decompressed. Finally, the message includes the `MIME-Version:` header, which, of course, indicates the MIME version that is being used. Note that the message otherwise follows the standard RFC 822/SMTP format. In particular, after the message header there is a blank line and then the message body; and after the message body, there is a line with a single period.

Let's now take a closer look at the `Content-Type:` header. According to the MIME specification, [RFC 2046], this header has the following format:

```
Content-Type: type/subtype; parameters
```

where the "parameters" (along with the semi-colon) is optional. Paraphrasing [RFC 2046], the `Content-Type` field is used to specify the nature of the data in the body of a MIME entity, by giving media type and subtype names. After the type and subtype names, the remainder of the header field consists of a set of parameters. In general, the top-level type is used to declare the general type of data, whereas the subtype specifies a specific format for that type of data. The parameters are modifiers of the subtype, and as such do not fundamentally affect the nature of the content. The set of meaningful parameters depends on the type and subtype. Most parameters are associated with a single specific subtype. MIME has been carefully designed to be extensible, and it is expected that the set of media type/subtype pairs and their associated parameters will grow significantly over time. In order to ensure that the set of such types/subtypes is developed in an orderly, well-specified, and public manner, MIME sets up a registration process that uses the Internet Assigned Numbers Authority (IANA) as a central registry for MIME's various areas of extensibility. The registration process for these areas is described in [RFC 2048].

Currently there are seven top-level types defined. For each type, there is a list of associated subtypes, and the lists of subtypes are growing every year. We describe five of these types below:

- **text:** The text type is used to indicate to the receiving user agent that the message body contains textual information. One extremely common type/subtype pair is `text/plain`. The subtype `plain` indicates plain text containing no formatting commands or directives. Plain text is to be displayed as is; no special software is required to get the full meaning of the text, aside from support for the indicated character set. If you take a glance at the MIME headers in some of the messages in your mailbox, you will almost certainly see content type header lines with `text/plain; charset=us-ascii` or `text/plain; charset="ISO-8859-1"`. The parameters indicate the character set used to generate the message. Another type/subtype pair that is gaining popularity is `text/html`. The `html` subtype indicates to the mail reader that it should interpret the embedded HTML tags that are included in the message. This allows the receiving user agent to display the message as a Web page, which might include a variety of fonts, hyperlinks, applets, and so on.

- **image:** The image type is used to indicate to the receiving user agent that the message body is an image. Two popular type/subtype pairs are `image/gif` and `image/jpeg`. When the receiving user agent encounters `image/gif`, it knows that it should decode the GIF image and then display it.

- **audio:** The audio type requires an audio output device (such as a speaker or a telephone) to render the contents. Some of the standardized subtypes include `basic` (basic eight-bit mu-law encoded) and `32kadpcm` (a 32 Kbps format defined in [RFC 1911]).

- **video:** The video type includes `mpeg`, and `quicktime` for subtypes.

- **application:** The application type is for data that does not fit in any of the other categories. It is often used for data that must be processed by an application before it is viewable or usable by a user. For example, when a user attaches a Microsoft Word document to an e-mail message, the sending user agent typically uses `application/msword` for the type/subtype pair. When the receiving user agent observes the content type `application/msword`, it launches the Microsoft Word application and passes the body of the MIME message to the application. A particularly important subtype for the application type is `octet-stream`, which is used to indicate that the body contains arbitrary binary data. Upon receiving this type, a mail reader will prompt the user, providing the option to save the message to disk for later processing.

There is one MIME type that is particularly important and requires special discussion, namely, the **multipart** type. Just as a Web page can contain many objects (such as text, images, applets), so can an e-mail message. Recall that the Web sends each of the objects within independent HTTP response messages. Internet e-mail, on the other hand, places all the objects (or "parts") in the same message. In particular, when a multimedia message contains more than one object (such as multiple images or some ASCII text and some images) the message typically has `Content-type: multipart/mixed`. This content type header line indicates to the receiving user agent that the message contains multiple objects. With all the objects in the same message, the receiving user agent needs a means to determine (1) where each object begins and ends, (2) how each non-ASCII object was transfer-encoded, and (3) the content type of each message. This is done by placing *boundary characters* between each object and preceding each object in the message with `Content-type:` and `Content-Transfer-Encoding:` header lines.

To obtain a better understanding of `multipart/mixed`, let's look at an example. Suppose that Alice wants to send a message to Bob consisting of some ASCII text, followed by a JPEG image, followed by more ASCII text. Using her user agent, Alice types some text, attaches a JPEG image, and then types some more text. Her user agent then generates a message something like this:

```
From: alice@crepes.fr
To: bob@hamburger.edu
Subject: Picture of yummy crepe with commentary
MIME-Version: 1.0
Content-Type: multipart/mixed; Boundary=StartOfNextPart
—StartOfNextPart
Dear Bob,
Please find a picture of an absolutely scrumptious crepe.
—StartOfNextPart
Content-Transfer-Encoding: base64
Content-Type: image/jpeg
base64 encoded data .....
.........................
......base64 encoded data
—StartOfNextPart
Let me know if you would like the recipe.
```

Examining the above message, we note that the `Content-Type:` line in the header indicates how the various parts in the message are separated. The separation always begins with two dashes and ends with `CRLF`.

As mentioned earlier, the list of registered MIME types grows every year. The RFC [2048] describes the registration procedures that use the Internet Assigned Numbers Authority (IANA) as a central registry for such values. A list of the current MIME subtypes is maintained at numerous sites. The reader is also encouraged to glance at Yahoo's MIME Category Page [Yahoo-MIME 99].

The received message. As we have discussed, an e-mail message consists of many components. The core of the message is the message body, which is the actual data being sent from sender to receiver. For a multipart message, the message body itself consists of many parts, with each part preceded by one or more lines of peripheral information. Preceding the message body is a blank line and then a number of header lines. These header lines include RFC 822 header lines such as `From:`, `To:`, and `Subject:` header lines. The header lines also include MIME header lines such as `Content-type:` and `Content-transfer-encoding:` header lines. But we would be remiss if we didn't mention another class of header lines that are inserted by the SMTP *receiving* server. Indeed, the receiving server, upon receiving a message with RFC 822 and MIME header lines, appends a `Received:` header line to the top of the message; this header line specifies the name of the SMTP server that sent the message ("from"), the name of the SMTP server that received the message ("by") and the time at which the receiving server received the message. Thus, the message seen by the destination user takes the following form:

```
Received: from crepes.fr by hamburger.edu; 12 Oct 98
15:27:39 GMT
From: alice@crepes.fr
To: bob@hamburger.edu
Subject: Picture of yummy crepe.
MIME-Version: 1.0
Content-Transfer-Encoding: base64
Content-Type: image/jpeg
base64 encoded data .......
.........................................
.......base64 encoded data
```

Almost everyone who has used electronic mail has seen the `Received:` header line (along with the other header lines) preceding e-mail messages. (This line is often directly seen on the screen or when the message is sent to a printer.) You may have noticed that a single message sometimes has multiple `Received:` header lines and a more complex `Return-Path:` header line. This is because a message may be received by more than one SMTP server in the path between sender and recipient. For example, if Bob has instructed his e-mail server `hamburger.edu` to forward all his messages to `sushi.jp`, then the message read by Bob's user agent would begin with something like:

```
Received: from hamburger.edu by sushi.jp; 12 Oct 98 15:30:01 GMT
Received: from crepes.fr by hamburger.edu; 12 Oct 98 15:27:39 GMT
```

These header lines provide the receiving user agent a trace of the SMTP servers visited as well as timestamps of when the visits occurred. You can learn more about the syntax of these header lines in the SMTP RFC, which is one of the more readable of the many RFCs.

2.4.4 Mail Access Protocols

Once SMTP delivers the message from Alice's mail server to Bob's mail server, the message is placed in Bob's mailbox. Throughout this discussion we have tacitly assumed that Bob reads his mail by logging onto the server host (most likely through Telnet) and then executes a mail reader (such as, mail or elm) on that host. Up until the early 1990s this was the standard way of doing things. But today a typical user reads mail with a user agent that executes on his or her local PC (or Mac), whether that PC be an office PC, a home PC, or a portable PC. By executing the user agent on a local PC, users enjoy a rich set of features, including the ability to view multimedia messages and attachments. Popular mail user agents that run on local PCs include Eudora, Microsoft's Outlook Express, and Netscape's Messenger.

Given that Bob (the recipient) executes his user agent on his local PC, it is natural to consider placing a mail server on his local PC as well. There is a problem with this approach, however. Recall that a mail server manages mailboxes and runs the client and server sides of SMTP. If Bob's mail server were to reside on his local PC, then Bob's PC would have to remain constantly on, and connected to the Internet, in order to receive new mail, which can arrive at any time. This is impractical for the great majority of Internet users. Instead, a typical user runs a user agent on the local PC but accesses a mailbox from a shared mail server—a mail server that is always running, that is always connected to the Internet, and that is shared with other users. The mail server is typically maintained by the user's ISP, which could be a residential or an institutional (university or company) ISP.

With user agents running on users' local PCs and mail servers hosted by ISPs, a protocol is needed to allow the user agent and the mail server to communicate. Let us first consider how a message that originates at Alice's local PC makes its way to Bob's SMTP mail server. This task could simply be done by having Alice's user agent communicate directly with Bob's mail server in the language of SMTP. Alice's user agent would initiate a TCP connection to Bob's mail server, issue the SMTP handshaking commands, upload the message with the DATA command, and then close the connection. This approach, although perfectly feasible, is not commonly employed, primarily because it doesn't offer Alice's user agent any recourse to a crashed destination mail server. Instead, Alice's user agent initiates a SMTP dialogue with her own mail server (rather than with the recipient's mail server) and uploads the message. Alice's mail server then establishes a new SMTP session with Bob's mail server and *relays* the message to Bob's mail server. If Bob's mail server is down, then Alice's mail server holds the message and tries again later. The SMTP RFC defines how the SMTP commands can be used to relay a message across multiple SMTP servers.

But there is still one missing piece to the puzzle! How does a recipient like Bob, running a user agent on his local PC, obtain his messages, which are sitting on a mail server within Bob's ISP? The puzzle is completed by introducing a special access protocol that transfers the messages from Bob's mail server to the local PC. There are currently two popular mail access protocols: **POP3** (Post Office Protocol—Version 3) and **IMAP** (Internet Mail Access Protocol). We shall discuss both of these protocols below. Note that Bob's user agent can't use SMTP to obtain the messages because obtaining the messages is a pull operation whereas SMTP is a push protocol. Figure 2.15 provides a summary of the protocols that are used for Internet mail: SMTP is used to transfer mail from the sender's mail server to the recipient's mail server; SMTP is also used to transfer mail from the sender's user agent to the sender's mail server. POP3 or IMAP are used to transfer mail from the recipient's mail server to the recipient's user agent.

POP3. POP3, defined in [RFC 1939], is an extremely simple mail access protocol. Because the protocol is so simple, its functionality is rather limited. POP3 begins when the user agent (the client) opens a TCP connection to the mail server (the server) on port 110. With the TCP connection established, POP3 progresses through three phases: authorization, transaction, and update. During the first phase, authorization, the user agent sends a user name and a password to authenticate the user downloading the mail. During the second phase, transaction, the user agent retrieves messages. During the transaction phase, the user agent can also mark messages for deletion, remove deletion marks, and obtain mail statistics. The third phase, update, occurs after the client has issued the

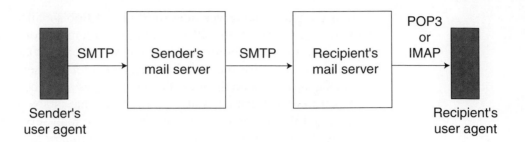

FIGURE 2.15 E-mail protocols and their communicating entities

`quit` command ending the POP3 session; at this time, the mail server deletes the messages that were marked for deletion.

In a POP3 transaction, the user agent issues commands, and the server responds to each command with a reply. There are two possible responses: `+OK` (sometimes followed by server-to-client data), whereby the server is saying that the previous command was fine; and `-ERR`, whereby the server is saying that something was wrong with the previous command.

The authorization phase has two principle commands: `user<user name>` and `pass<password>`. To illustrate these two commands, we suggest that you Telnet directly into a POP3 server, using port 110, and issue these commands. Suppose that `mailServer` is the name of your mail server. You will see something like:

```
telnet mailServer 110
+OK POP3 server ready
user alice
+OK
pass hungry
+OK user successfully logged on
```

If you misspell a command, the POP3 server will reply with an `-ERR` message.

Now let's take a look at the transaction phase. A user agent using POP3 can often be configured (by the user) to "*download and delete*" or to "*download and keep*." The sequence of commands issued by a POP3 user agent depend on which of these two modes the user agent is operating in. In the download-and-delete mode, the user agent will issue the `list`, `retr`, and `dele` commands. As an example, suppose the user has two messages in his or her mailbox. In the dialogue below, `C:` (standing for client), is the user agent and `S:` (standing for server) is the mail server. The transaction will look something like:

```
C: list
S: 1 498
S: 2 912
S: .
C: retr 1
S: blah blah ...
```

```
S:  . . . . . . . . . . . . . . . .
S:  . . . . . . . . . .blah
S:  .
C:  dele 1
C:  retr 2
S:  blah blah ...
S:  . . . . . . . . . . . . . . . .
S:  . . . . . . . . . .blah
S:  .
C:  dele 2
C:  quit
S:  +OK POP3 server signing off
```

The user agent first asks the mail server to list the size of each of the stored messages. The user agent then retrieves and deletes each message from the server. Note that after the authorization phase, the user agent employed only four commands: `list`, `retr`, `dele`, and `quit`. The syntax for these commands is defined in [RFC 1939]. After processing the quit command, the POP3 server enters the update phase and removes messages 1 and 2 from the mailbox.

A problem with this download-and-delete mode is that the recipient, Bob, may be nomadic and want to access his mail from multiple machines, including the office PC, the home PC, and a portable computer. The download-and-delete mode scatters Bob's mail over all the local machines; in particular, if Bob first reads a message on a home PC, he will not be able to reread the message on his portable later in the evening. In the download-and-keep mode, the user agent leaves the messages on the mail server after downloading them. In this case, Bob can reread messages from different machines; he can access a message from work, and then access it again later in the week from home.

During a POP3 session between a user agent and the mail server, the POP3 server maintains some state information; in particular, it keeps track of which messages have been marked deleted. However, the POP3 server is not required to carry state information across POP3 sessions. For example, no message is marked for deletion at the beginning of each session. This lack of state information across sessions greatly simplifies the implementation of a POP3 server.

IMAP.   Once Bob has downloaded his messages to the local machine using POP3, he can create mail folders and move the downloaded messages into the folders. Bob can then delete messages, move messages across folders, and search for messages (by sender name or subject). But this paradigm—folders and messages in the local machine—poses a problem for the nomadic user, who would prefer to maintain a folder hierarchy on a remote server that can be accessed from any computer. This is not possible with POP3.

To solve this and other problems, the Internet Mail Access Protocol (IMAP), defined in [RFC 1730], was invented. Like POP3, IMAP is a mail access protocol. It has many more features than POP3, but it is also significantly more complex. (And thus the client and server side implementations are significantly more complex.) IMAP is designed to allow users to manipulate remote mailboxes as if they were local. In particular, IMAP enables Bob to create and maintain multiple message folders at the mail server. Bob can put messages in folders and move messages from one folder to another. IMAP also provides commands that allow Bob to search remote folders for messages matching specific criteria. One reason why an IMAP implementation is much more complicated than a POP3 implementation is that the IMAP server must maintain a folder hierarchy for each of its users. This state information persists across a particular user's successive accesses to the IMAP server. Recall that a POP3 server, by contrast, does not maintain anything about a particular user once the user quits the POP3 session.

Another important feature of IMAP is that it has commands that permit a user agent to obtain components of messages. For example, a user agent can obtain just the message header of a message or just one part of a multipart MIME message. This feature is useful when there is a low-bandwidth connection between the user agent and its mail server, for example, a wireless or slow-speed modem connection. With a low-bandwidth connection, the user may not want to download all the messages in its mailbox, particularly avoiding long messages that might contain, for example, an audio or video clip.

An IMAP session consists of the establishment of a connection between the client (that is, the user agent) and the IMAP server, an initial greeting from the server, and client-server interactions. The client/server interactions are similar to, but richer than, those of POP3. They consist of a client command, server data, and a server completion result response. The IMAP server is always in one of four states. In the *nonauthenticated state,* which starts when the connection starts, the user must supply a user name and password before most commands will be permitted. In the *authenticated state,* the user must select a folder before sending commands that affect messages. In the *selected state,* the user can issue commands that affect messages (retrieve, move, delete, retrieve a part in a multipart message, etc.). Finally, the *logout state* is when the session is being terminated. The IMAP commands are organized by the state in which the command is permitted. You can read all about IMAP at the official IMAP site [IMAP 1999].

HTTP.   More and more users today are using browser-based e-mail services such as Hotmail or Yahoo! Mail. With these servers, the user agent is an ordinary Web browser and the user communicates with its mailbox on its mailserver via HTTP. When a recipient, such as Bob, wants to access the messages in his mailbox, the messages are sent from Bob's mail server to Bob's browser using the HTTP protocol rather than the POP3 or IMAP protocol. When a sender with an account on an HTTP-based e-mail server, such as Alice, wants to send a message, the message is sent from her browser to her mail server over HTTP rather than over SMTP. The mail server, however, still sends messages to, and receives messages from, other mail servers using SMTP. This solution to mail access is enormously convenient for the user on the go. The user need only to be able to access a browser in order to send and receive messages. The browser can be in an Internet cafe, in a friend's house, in a hotel room with a Web TV, and so on. As with IMAP, users can organize their messages in a hierarchy of folders on the remote server. In fact, Web-based e-mail is so convenient that it may replace POP3 and IMAP access in the upcoming years. Its principle disadvantage is that it can be slow, as the server is typically far from the client and interaction with the server is done through CGI scripts.

2.4.5   Continuous Media E-mail

Continuous-media (CM) e-mail is e-mail that includes audio or video. CM e-mail is appealing for asynchronous communication among friends and family. For example, a young child who cannot type would prefer sending an audio message to his or her grandparents. Furthermore, CM e-mail can be desirable in many corporate contexts, as an office worker may be able to record a CM message more quickly than typing a text message. (English can be spoken at a rate of 180 words per minute, whereas the average office worker types words at a much slower rate.) Continuous-media e-mail resembles in some respects ordinary voice-mail messaging in the telephone system. However, continuous-media e-mail is much more powerful. Not only does it provide the user with a graphical interface to the user's mailbox, but it also allows the user to annotate and reply to CM messages and to forward CM messages to a large number of recipients.

CM e-mail differs from traditional text mail in many ways. CM e-mail can have much larger messages, more stringent end-to-end delay requirements, and greater sensitivity to recipients with highly heterogeneous Internet access rates and local storage capabilities. Unfortunately, the current e-mail infrastructure has several inadequacies that obstruct the widespread adoption of CM e-mail [Turner 1999]. First, many existing mail servers do not have the capacity to store large CM objects; recipient mail servers typically reject such messages, which makes sending CM messages to such recipients impossible. Second, the existing mail paradigm of transporting *entire* messages to the recipient's mail server before recipient rendering can lead to excessive waste of bandwidth and storage. Indeed, stored CM is often not rendered in its entirety [Padhye 1999], so that bandwidth and recipient storage is wasted by receiving data that is never rendered. (For example, one can imagine listening to the first fifteen seconds of a long audio e-mail from a rather long-winded colleague, and then deciding to delete the remaining 20 minutes of the message without listening to it.) Third, current mail access protocols (POP3, IMAP, and HTTP) are inappropriate for streaming CM to recipients. (Streaming CM is discussed in detail in Chapter 6.) In particular, the current mail access protocols do not provide functionality that allows a user to pause/resume a message or to reposition within a message; furthermore, streaming over TCP often leads to poor reception (see Chapter 6). These inadequacies will hopefully be addressed in the upcoming years. Possible solutions are discussed in [Gay 1997], [Hess 1998], [Schurmann 1996], and [Turner 1999].

2.5   DNS—THE INTERNET'S DIRECTORY SERVICE

We human beings can be identified in many ways. For example, we can be identified by the names that appear on our birth certificates. We can be identified by our social security numbers. We can be identified by our driver's license numbers. Although each of these identifiers can be used to identify people, within a given context, one identifier may be more appropriate than another. For example, the computers at the IRS (the infamous tax collecting agency in the United States) prefers to use fixed-length social security numbers rather than birth-certificate names. On the other hand, ordinary people prefer the more mnemonic birth-certificate names rather than social security numbers. (Indeed, can you imagine saying, "Hi. My name is 132-67-9875. Please meet my husband, 178-87-1146.")

Just as humans can be identified in many ways, so too can Internet hosts. One identifier for a host is its **hostname.** Hostnames—such as `cnn.com`, `www.yahoo.com`, `gaia.cs.umass.edu`, and `surf.eurecom.fr`—are mnemonic and are therefore appreciated by humans. However, hostnames provide little, if any, information about the location within the Internet of the host. (A hostname such as `surf.eurecom.fr`, which ends with the country code `.fr`, tells us that the host is probably in France, but doesn't say much more.) Furthermore, because hostnames can consist of variable-length alphanumeric characters, they would be difficult to process by routers. For these reasons, hosts are also identified by so-called **IP addresses.** We will discuss IP addresses in some detail in Chapter 4, but it is useful to say a few brief words about them now. An IP address consists of four bytes and has a rigid hierarchical structure. An IP address looks like `121.7.106.83`, where each period separates one of the bytes expressed in decimal notation from 0 to 127. An IP address is hierarchical because as we scan the address from left to right, we obtain more and more specific information about where (that is, within which network, in the network of networks) the host is located in the Internet. (Just as when we scan a postal address from bottom to top we obtain more and more specific information about where the residence is located.) An IP address is included in the header of each IP datagram, and Internet routers use this IP address to route a datagram toward its destination.

2.5.1 Services Provided by DNS

We have just seen that there are two ways to identify a host—by a hostname and by an IP address. People prefer the more mnemonic hostname identifier, while routers prefer fixed-length, hierarchically structured IP addresses. In order to reconcile these different preferences, we need a directory service that translates hostnames to IP addresses. This is the main task of the Internet's **Domain Name System (DNS).** The DNS is (1) a distributed database implemented in a hierarchy of **name servers** and (2) an application-layer protocol that allows hosts and name servers to communicate in order to provide the translation service. Name servers are usually Unix machines running the Berkeley Internet Name Domain (BIND) software. The DNS protocol runs over UDP and uses port 53. On the Web site for this book, at http://www.seas.upenn.edu/~ross/book/apps/nslookup.htm we provide interactive links to DNS programs that allow you to translate arbitrary hostnames, among other things.

DNS is commonly employed by other application-layer protocols—including HTTP, SMTP, and FTP—to translate user-supplied host names to IP addresses. As an example, consider what happens when a browser (that is, an HTTP client), running on some user's machine, requests the URL `www.someschool.edu/index.html`. In order for the user's machine to be able to send an HTTP request message to the Web server `www.someschool.edu`, the user's machine must obtain the IP address of `www.someschool.edu`. This is done as follows. The same user machine runs the client-side of the DNS application. The browser extracts the hostname, `www.someschool.edu`, from the URL and passes the hostname to the client-side of the DNS application. As part of a DNS query message, the DNS client sends a query containing the hostname to a DNS server. The DNS client eventually receives a reply, which includes the IP address for the hostname. The browser then opens a TCP connection to the HTTP server process located at that IP address. All IP datagrams sent from the client to the server as part of this connection will include this IP address in the destination address field of the datagrams. In particular, the IP datagram(s) that encapsulate the HTTP request message use this IP address. We see from this example that DNS adds an additional delay—sometimes substantial—to the Internet applications that use DNS. Fortunately, as we shall discuss below, the desired IP address is often cached in a "nearby" DNS name server, which helps to reduce the DNS network traffic as well as the average DNS delay.

Like HTTP, FTP, and SMTP, the DNS protocol is an application-layer protocol since (1) it runs between communicating end systems (again using the client-server paradigm), and (2) it relies on an underlying end-to-end transport protocol (that is, UDP) to transfer DNS messages between communicating end systems. In another sense, however, the role of the DNS is quite different from Web, file transfer, and e-mail applications. Unlike these applications, the DNS is not an application with which a user directly interacts. Instead, the DNS provides a core Internet function—namely, translating hostnames to their underlying IP addresses, for user applications and other software in the Internet. We noted earlier in Section 1.2 that much of the "complexity" in the Internet architecture is located at the "edges" of the network. The DNS, which implements the critical name-to-address translation process using clients and servers located at the edge of the network, is yet another example of that design philosophy.

DNS provides a few other important services in addition to translating hostnames to IP addresses:

Host aliasing.   A host with a complicated hostname can have one or more alias names. For example, a hostname such as `relay1.west-coast.enterprise.com` could have, say, two aliases such as `enterprise.com` and `www.enterprise.com`. In this case, the hostname `relay1.west-coast.enterprise.com` is said to be a **canonical hostname.** Alias hostnames, when present, are typically more mnemonic than a canonical hostname. DNS can be invoked by an application to obtain the canonical hostname for a supplied alias hostname as well as the IP address of the host.

Mail server aliasing.   For obvious reasons, it is highly desirable that e-mail addresses be mnemonic. For example, if Bob has an account with Hotmail, Bob's e-mail address might be as simple as `bob@hotmail.com`. However, the hostname of the Hotmail mail server is more complicated and much less mnemonic than simply `hotmail.com` (for example, the canonical hostname might be something like `relay1.west-coast.hotmail.com`). DNS can be invoked by a mail application to obtain the canonical hostname for a supplied alias hostname as well as the IP address of the host. In fact, DNS permits a company's mail server and Web server to have identical (aliased) hostnames; for example, a company's Web server and mail server can both be called `enterprise.com`.

Load distribution.   Increasingly, DNS is also being used to perform load distribution among replicated servers, such as replicated Web servers. Busy sites, such as `cnn.com`, are replicated over multiple servers, with each server running on a different end system, and having a different IP address. For replicated Web servers, a set of IP addresses is thus associated with one canonical hostname. The DNS database contains this set of IP addresses. When clients make a DNS query for a name mapped to a set of addresses, the server responds with the entire set of IP addresses, but rotates the ordering of the addresses within each reply. Because a client typically sends its HTTP request message to the IP address that is listed first in the set, DNS rotation distributes the traffic among all the replicated servers. DNS rotation is also used for e-mail so that multiple mail servers can have the same alias name.

The DNS is specified in [RFC 1034] and [RFC 1035], and updated in several additional RFCs. It is a complex system, and we only touch upon key aspects of its operation here. The interested reader is referred to these RFCs and the book [Abitz 1993].

2.5.2 Overview of How DNS Works

We now present a high-level overview of how DNS works. Our discussion will focus on the hostname-to-IP-address translation service. From the client's perspective, the DNS is a black box. The client sends a DNS query message into the black box, specifying the hostname that needs to be translated to an IP address. On many Unix-based machines, `gethostbyname()` is the library routine that an application calls in order to issue the query message. In Section 2.7, we shall present a Java program that begins by issuing a DNS query. After a delay, ranging from milliseconds to tens of seconds, the client receives a DNS reply message that provides the desired mapping. Thus, from the client's perspective, DNS is a simple, straightforward translation service. But in fact, the black box that implements the service is complex, consisting of a large number of name servers distributed around the globe, as well as an application-layer protocol that specifies how the name servers and querying hosts communicate.

A simple design for DNS would have one Internet name server that contains all the mappings. In this centralized design, clients simply direct all queries to the single name server, and the name server responds directly to the querying clients. Although the simplicity of this design is attractive, it is completely inappropriate for today's Internet, with its vast (and growing) number of hosts. The problems with a centralized design include:

- **A single point of failure.** If the name server crashes, so too does the entire Internet!
- **Traffic volumes.** A single name server would have to handle all DNS queries (for all the HTTP requests and e-mail messages generated from millions of hosts).
- **Distant centralized database.** A single name server cannot be "close to" all the querying clients. If we put the single name server in New York City, then all queries from Australia must travel to the other side of the globe, perhaps over slow and congested links. This can lead to significant delays (thereby increasing the "world wide wait" for the Web and other applications).
- **Maintenance.** The single name server would have to keep records for all Internet hosts. Not only would this centralized database be huge, but it would have to be updated frequently to account for every new host. There are also authentication and authorization problems associated with allowing any user to register a host with the centralized database.

In summary, a centralized database in a single name server simply *doesn't scale*. Consequently, the DNS is distributed by design. In fact, the DNS is a wonderful example of how a distributed database can be implemented in the Internet.

In order to deal with the issue of scale, the DNS uses a large number of name servers, organized in a hierarchical fashion and distributed around the world. No one name server has all of the mappings for all of the hosts in the Internet. Instead, the mappings are distributed across the name servers. To a first approximation, there are three types of name servers: local name servers, root name servers, and authoritative name servers. These name servers, again to a first approximation, interact with each other and with the querying host as follows:

- **Local name servers.** Each ISP—such as a university, an academic department, an employee's company, or a residential ISP—has a local name server (also called a default name server). When a host issues a DNS query message, the message is first sent to the host's local name server. The IP address of the local name server is typically configured by hand in a host. (On a Windows 95/98 machine, you can find the IP address of the local name server used by your PC by opening the Control Panel, and then selecting "Network," then selecting an installed TCP/IP component, and then selecting the DNS configuration folder tab.) The local name server is typically "close to" the client; in the case of an institutional ISP, it may be on the same LAN as the client host; for a regional ISP, the name server is typically separated from the client host by no more than a few routers. If a host requests a translation for another host that is part of the same local ISP, then the local name server will be able to immediately provide the requested IP address. For example, when the host `surf.eurecom.fr` requests the IP address for `baie.eurecom.fr`, the local name server at Eurecom will be able to provide the requested IP address without contacting any other name servers.

- **Root name servers.** In the Internet there are a dozen or so root name servers, most of which are currently located in North America. A February 1998 map of the root servers is shown in Figure 2.16. When a local name server cannot immediately satisfy a query from a host (because it does not have a record for the hostname being requested), the local name server behaves as a DNS client and queries one of the root name servers. If the root name server has a record for the hostname, it sends a DNS reply message to the local name server, and the local name server then sends a DNS reply to the querying host. But the root name server may not have a record for the hostname. Instead, the root-name server knows the IP address of an "authoritative name server" that has the mapping for that particular hostname.

- **Authoritative name servers.** Every host is registered with an authoritative name server. Typically, the authoritative name server for a host is a name server in the host's local ISP. (Actually, each host is required to have at least two authoritative name servers, in case of failures.) By definition, a name server is authoritative for a host if it always has a DNS record that translates the host's hostname to that host's IP address. When an authoritative name server is queried by a root server, the authoritative name server responds with a DNS reply that contains the requested mapping. The root server then forwards the mapping to the local name server, which in turn forwards the

DNS Root Servers
Designation, Responsibility, and Locations

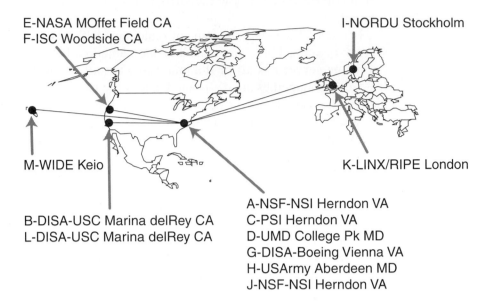

E-NASA MOffet Field CA
F-ISC Woodside CA

I-NORDU Stockholm

M-WIDE Keio

K-LINX/RIPE London

B-DISA-USC Marina delRey CA
L-DISA-USC Marina delRey CA

A-NSF-NSI Herndon VA
C-PSI Herndon VA
D-UMD College Pk MD
G-DISA-Boeing Vienna VA
H-USArmy Aberdeen MD
J-NSF-NSI Herndon VA

FIGURE 2.16   A February 1998 map of the DNS root servers. Obtained from the WIA alliance Web site (`http://www.wia.org/`)

mapping to the requesting host. Many name servers act as both local and authoritative name servers.

Let's take a look at a simple example. Suppose the host `surf.eurecom.fr` desires the IP address of `gaia.cs.umass.edu`. Also suppose that Eurecom's local name server is called `dns.eurecom.fr` and that an authoritative name server for `gaia.cs.umass.edu` is called `dns.umass.edu`. As shown in Figure 2.17, the host `surf.eurecom.fr` first sends a DNS query message to its local name server, `dns.eurecom.fr`. The query message contains the hostname to be translated, namely, `gaia.cs.umass.edu`. The local name server forwards the query message to a root name server. The root name server forwards the query message to the name server that is authoritative for all the hosts in the domain `umass.edu`, namely, to `dns.umass.edu`. The authoritative name server then sends the desired mapping to the querying host, via the root name server and the local name server. Note that in this example, in order to obtain the mapping for one hostname, six DNS messages were sent: three query messages and three reply messages.

Our discussion up to this point has assumed that the root name server knows the IP address of an authoritative name server for *every* hostname. This assumption may be incorrect. For a given hostname, the root name server may only know the IP address of an intermediate name server that in turn knows the IP address of an authoritative name server for the hostname. To illustrate this, consider once again the above example with the host `surf.eurecom.fr` querying for the IP address of `gaia.cs.umass.edu`. Suppose now that the University of Massachusetts has a name server for the university, called `dns.umass.edu`. Also suppose

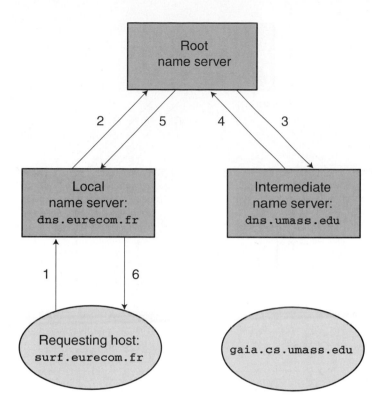

FIGURE 2.17   Recursive queries to obtain the mapping for gaia.cs.umass.edu

that each of the departments at the University of Massachusetts has its own name server, and that each departmental name server is authoritative for all the hosts in the department. As shown in Figure 2.18, when the root name server receives a query for a host with hostname ending with umass.edu it forwards the query to the name server dns.umass.edu. This name server forwards all queries with hostnames ending with .cs.umass.edu to the name server dns.cs.umass.edu, which is authoritative for all hostnames ending with .cs.umass.edu. The authoritative name server sends the desired mapping to the intermediate name server, dns.umass.edu, which forwards the mapping to the root name server, which forwards the mapping to the local name server, dns.eurecom.fr, which forwards the mapping to the requesting host! In this example, eight DNS messages are sent. Actually, even more DNS messages can be sent in order to translate a single hostname—there can be two or more intermediate name servers in the chain between the root name server and the authoritative name server!

The examples up to this point assumed that all queries are **recursive queries.** When a host or name server A makes a recursive query to a name server B, then name server B obtains the requested mapping *on behalf* of A and then forwards the mapping to A. The DNS protocol also allows for **iterative queries** at any step in the chain between requesting host and authoritative name server. When a name server A makes an iterative query to name server B, if name server B does not

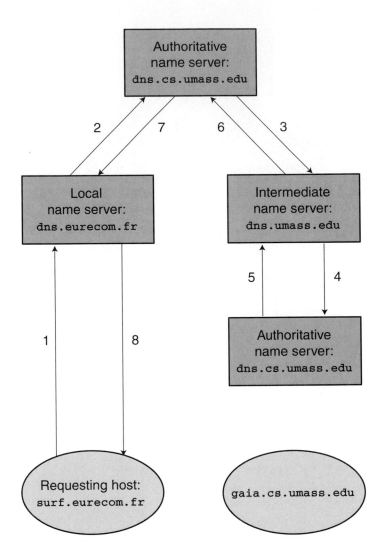

FIGURE 2.18 Recursive queries with an intermediate name server between the root and authoritative name servers

have the requested mapping, it immediately sends a DNS reply to A that contains the IP address of the next name server in the chain, say, name server C. Name server A then sends a query directly to name server C.

In the sequence of queries that are required to translate a hostname, some of the queries can be iterative and others recursive. Such a combination of recursive and iterative queries is illustrated in Figure 2.19. Typically, all queries in the query chain are recursive except for the query from the local name server to the root name server, which is iterative. (Because root servers handle huge volumes of queries, it is preferable to use the less burdensome iterative queries for root servers.)

Our discussion this far has not touched on one important feature of the DNS: **DNS caching.** In reality, DNS extensively exploits caching in order to improve the delay performance and to reduce the number of DNS messages in the network. The idea is very simple. When a name server receives a DNS mapping for some hostname, it caches the mapping in local memory (disk or RAM) while passing the message along the name server chain. Given a cached hostname/IPaddress

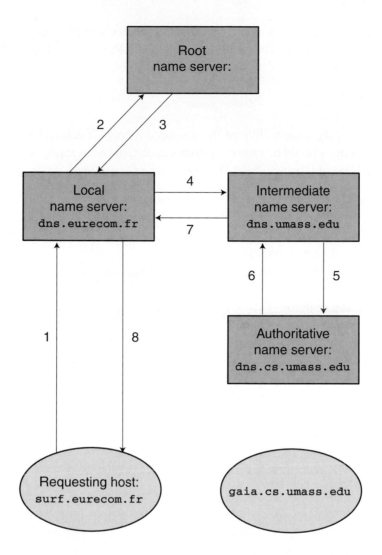

FIGURE 2.19 A query chain with recursive and iterative queries

translation pair, if another query arrives to the name server for the same hostname, the name server can provide the desired IP address, even if it is not authoritative for the hostname. In order to deal with the ephemeral hosts, a cached record is discarded after a period of time (often set to two days). As an example, suppose that `surf.eurecom.fr` queries the DNS for the IP address for the hostname `cnn.com`. Furthermore suppose that a few hours later, another Eurecom host, say, `baie.eurecom.fr`, also queries DNS with the same hostname. Because of caching, the local name server at Eurecom will be able to immediately return the IP address to the requesting host without having to query name servers on another continent. Any name server may cache DNS mappings.

2.5.3 DNS Records

The name servers that together implement the DNS distributed database, store **resource records (RR)** for the hostname to IP address mappings. Each DNS reply message carries one or more resource records. In this and the following subsection, we provide a brief overview of DNS resource records and messages; more details can be found in [Abitz 1993] or in the DNS RFCs [RFC 1034], [RFC 1035].

A resource record is a four-tuple that contains the following fields:

```
(Name, Value, Type, TTL)
```

TTL is the time to live of the resource record; it determines the time at which a resource should be removed from a cache. In the example records given below, we will ignore the TTL field. The meaning of Name and Value depend on Type:

- If Type=A, then Name is a hostname and Value is the IP address for the hostname. Thus, a Type A record provides the standard hostname to IP address mapping. As an example, (relay1.bar.foo.com, 145.37.93.126, A) is a Type A record.
- If Type=NS, then Name is a domain (such as foo.com) and Value is the hostname of a server that knows how to obtain the IP addresses for hosts in the domain. This record is used to route DNS queries further along in the query chain. As an example, (foo.com, dns.foo.com, NS) is a Type NS record.
- If Type=CNAME, then Value is a canonical hostname for the alias hostname Name. This record can provide querying hosts the canonical name for a hostname. As an example, (foo.com, relay1.bar.foo.com, CNAME) is a CNAME record.
- If Type=MX, then Value is a hostname of a mail server that has an alias hostname Name. As an example, (foo.com. mail.bar.foo.com, MX) is an MX record. MX records allow the hostnames of mail servers to have simple aliases.

If a name server is authoritative for a particular hostname, then the name server will contain a Type A record for the hostname. (Even if the name server is not authoritative, it may contain a Type A record in its cache.) If a server is not authoritative for a hostname, then the server will contain a Type NS record for the domain that includes the hostname; it will also contain a Type A record that provides the IP address of the name server in the Value field of the NS record. As an example, suppose a root server is not authoritative for the host gaia.cs.umass.edu. Then the root server will contain a record for a domain that includes the host cs.umass.edu, for example, (umass.edu, dns.umass.edu, NS).

The root server would also contain a Type A record, which maps the name server dns.umass.edu to an IP address, for example, (dns.umass.edu, 128.119.40.111, A).

2.5.4 DNS Messages

Earlier in this section we alluded to DNS query and reply messages. These are the only two kinds of DNS messages. Furthermore, both request and reply messages have the same format, as shown in Figure 2.20.

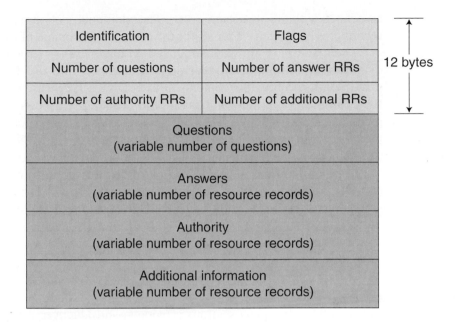

Identification	Flags
Number of questions	Number of answer RRs
Number of authority RRs	Number of additional RRs
Questions (variable number of questions)	
Answers (variable number of resource records)	
Authority (variable number of resource records)	
Additional information (variable number of resource records)	

12 bytes

FIGURE 2.20   DNS message format

The semantics of the various fields in a DNS message are as follows:

The first 12 bytes is the *header section,* which has a number of fields. The first field is a 16-bit number that identifies the query. This identifier is copied into the reply message to a query, allowing the client to match received replies with sent queries. There are a number of flags in the flag field. A one-bit query/reply flag indicates whether the message is a query (0) or a reply (1). A one-bit authoritative flag is set in a reply message when a name server is an authoritative server for a queried name. A one-bit recursion-desired flag is set when a client (host or name server) desires that the name server perform recursion when it doesn't have the record. A one-bit recursion available field is set in a reply if the name server supports recursion. In the header, there are also four "number of" fields. These fields indicate the number of occurrences of the four types of "data" sections that follow the header.

The *question section* contains information about the query that is being made. This section includes (1) a name field that contains the name that is being queried, and (2) a type field that indicates the type of question being asked about the name (for example, a host address associated with a name—type A, or the mail server for a name—type MX).

In a reply from a name server, the *answer section* contains the resource records for the name that was originally queried. Recall that in each resource record there is the `Type` (for example, A, NS, CSNAME, and MX), the `Value` and the `TTL`. A reply can return multiple RRs in the answer, since a hostname can have multiple IP addresses (for example, for replicated Web servers, as discussed earlier in this section).

The *authority section* contains records of other authoritative servers.

The *additional section* contains other "helpful" records. For example, the answer field in a reply to an MX query will contain the hostname of a mail server associated with the alias name `Name`. The additional section will contain a Type A record providing the IP address for the canonical hostname of the mail server.

The discussion above has focused on how data is retrieved from the DNS database. You might be wondering how data gets into the database in the first place? Until recently, the contents of each DNS server was configured statically, for example, from a configuration file created by a system manager. More recently, an `UPDATE` option has been added to the DNS protocol to allow data to be dynamically added or deleted from the database via DNS messages. [RFC 2136] specifies DNS dynamic updates.

DNSNet provides a nice collection of documents pertaining to DNS [DNS-Net]. The Internet Software Consortium provides many resources for **BIND,** a popular public-domain name server for Unix machines [BIND].

2.6 SOCKET PROGRAMMING WITH TCP

This and the subsequent sections provide an introduction to network application development. Recall from Section 2.1 that the core of a network application consists of a pair of programs—a client program and a server program. When these two programs are executed, a client and server process are created, and these two processes communicate with each other by reading from and writing to sockets. When creating a networking application, the developer's main task is to write the code for both the client and server programs.

There are two sorts of client-server applications. One sort is a client-server application that is an *implementation* of a protocol standard defined in an RFC. For such an implementation, the client and server programs must conform to the rules dictated by the RFC. For example, the client program could be an implementation of the FTP client, defined in [RFC 959], and the server program could be an implementation of the FTP server, also defined in [RFC 959]. If one developer writes code for the client program and an independent developer writes code for the server program, and both developers carefully follow the rules of the RFC, then the two programs will be able to interoperate. Indeed, most of today's network applications involve communication between client and server programs that have been created by independent developers. (For example, a Netscape browser communicating with an Apache Web server, or an FTP client on a PC uploading a file to a Unix FTP server.) When a client or server program implements a protocol defined in an RFC, it should use the port number associated with the protocol. (Port numbers were briefly discussed in Section 2.1. They will be covered in more detail in the next chapter.)

The other sort of client-server application is a *proprietary* client-server application. In this case the client and server programs do not necessarily conform to any existing RFC. A single developer (or development team) creates both the client and server programs, and the developer has complete control over what goes in the code. But because the code does not implement a public-domain protocol, other independent developers will not be able to develop code that interoperates with the application. When developing a proprietary application, the developer must be careful not to use one of the well-known port numbers defined in the RFCs.

In this and the next section, we will examine the key issues for the development of a proprietary client-server application. During the development phase, one of the first decisions the developer must make is whether the application is to run over TCP or over UDP. TCP is connection-oriented and provides a *reliable byte stream channel* through which data flows between two end systems. UDP is connectionless and sends *independent packets* of data from one end system to the other, without any guarantees about delivery.

In this section we develop a simple-client application that runs over TCP; in the subsequent section, we develop a simple-client application that runs over UDP.

We present these simple TCP and UDP applications in Java. We could have written the code in C or C++, but we opted for Java for several reasons. First, the applications are more neatly and cleanly written in Java; with Java there are fewer lines of code, and each line can be explained to the novice programmer without much difficulty. Second, client-server programming in Java is becoming increasingly popular, and may even become the norm in upcoming years. Java is platform independent, it has exception mechanisms for robust handling of common problems that occur during I/O and networking operations, and its threading facilities provide a way to easily implement powerful servers. But there is no need to be frightened if you are not familiar with Java. You should be able to follow the code if you have experience programming in another language.

For readers who are interested in client-server programming in C, there are several good references available, including [Stevens 1990], [Frost 1994], and [Kurose 1996].

2.6.1   Socket Programming with TCP

Recall from Section 2.1 that processes running on different machines communicate with each other by sending messages into sockets. We said that each process was analogous to a house and the process's socket is analogous to a door. As shown in Figure 2.21, the socket is the door between the application process and TCP. The application developer has control of everything on the application-layer side of the socket; however, it has little control of the transport-layer side. (At the

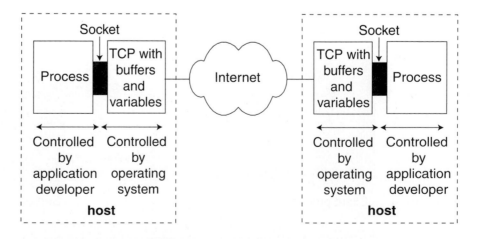

FIGURE 2.21   Processes communicating through TCP sockets

very most, the application developer has the ability to fix a few TCP parameters, such as maximum buffer size and maximum segment sizes.)

Now let's take a little closer look at the interaction of the client and server programs. The client has the job of initiating contact with the server. In order for the server to be able to react to the client's initial contact, the server has to be ready. This implies two things. First, the server program cannot be dormant; it must be running as a process before the client attempts to initiate contact. Second, the server program must have some sort of door (that is, socket) that welcomes some initial contact from a client (running on an arbitrary machine). Using our house/door analogy for a process/socket, we will sometimes refer to the client's initial contact as "knocking on the door."

With the server process running, the client process can initiate a TCP connection to the server. This is done in the client program by creating a socket object. When the client creates its socket object, it specifies the address of the server process, namely, the IP address of the server and the port number of the process. Upon creation of the socket object, TCP in the client initiates a three-way handshake and establishes a TCP connection with the server. The three-way handshake is completely transparent to the client and server programs.

During the three-way handshake, the client process knocks on the welcoming door of the server process. When the server "hears" the knocking, it creates a new door (that is, a new socket) that is dedicated to that particular client. In our example below, the welcoming door is a `ServerSocket` object that we call the `welcomeSocket`. When a client knocks on this door, the program invokes `welcomeSocket`'s `accept()` method, which creates a new door for the client. At the end of the handshaking phase, a TCP connection exists between the client's socket and the server's new socket. Henceforth, we refer to the new socket as the server's *connection socket*.

From the application's perspective, the TCP connection is a direct virtual pipe between the client's socket and the server's connection socket. The client process can send arbitrary bytes into its socket; TCP guarantees that the server process will receive (through the connection socket) each byte in the order sent. Furthermore, just as people can go in and out the same door, the client process can also receive bytes from its socket and the server process can also send bytes into its connection socket. This is illustrated in Figure 2.22.

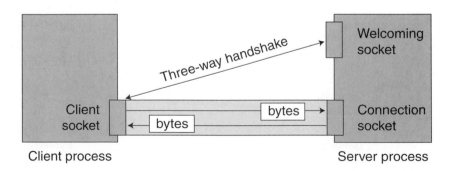

FIGURE 2.22 Client socket, welcoming socket, and connection socket

Because sockets play a central role in client-server applications, client-server application development is also referred to as **socket programming.** Before providing our example client-server application, it is useful to discuss the notion of a stream. A **stream** is a flowing sequence of characters that flow into or out of a process. Each stream is either an **input stream** for the process or an **output stream** for the process. If the stream is an input stream, then it is attached to some input source for the process, such as standard input (the keyboard) or a socket into which characters flow from the Internet. If the stream is an output stream, then it is attached to some output source for the process, such as standard output (the monitor) or a socket out of which characters flow into the Internet.

2.6.2   An Example Client-Server Application in Java

We shall use the following simple client-server application to demonstrate socket programming for both TCP and UDP:

A client reads a line from its **standard input** (keyboard) and sends the line out its socket to the server.

The server reads a line from its connection socket.

The server converts the line to uppercase.

The server sends the modified line out its connection socket to the client.

The client reads the modified line from its socket and prints the line on its **standard output** (monitor).

Below we provide the client-server program pair for a TCP implementation of the application. We provide a detailed, line-by-line analysis after each program. The client program is called `TCPClient.java`, and the server program is called `TCPServer.java`. In order to emphasize the key issues, we intentionally provide code that is to the point but not bullet proof. "Good code" would certainly have a few more auxiliary lines.

Once the two programs are compiled on their respective hosts, the server program is first executed at the server, which creates a process at the server. As discussed above, the server process waits to be contacted by a client process. When the client program is executed, a process is created at the client, and this process contacts the server and establishes a TCP connection with it. The user at the client may then "use" the application to send a line and then receive a capitalized version of the line.

TCPClient.java.   Here is the code for the client side of the application:

```
import java.io.*;
import java.net.*;
class TCPClient {

    public static void main(String argv[]) throws Exception
    {
        String sentence;
        String modifiedSentence;
```

```
        BufferedReader inFromUser =
          new BufferedReader(
                          new InputStreamReader(System.in));
        Socket clientSocket = new Socket("hostname", 6789);
        DataOutputStream outToServer =
          new DataOutputStream(
                          clientSocket.getOutputStream());
        BufferedReader inFromServer =
          new BufferedReader(new InputStreamReader(
                          clientSocket.getInputStream()));
        sentence = inFromUser.readLine();
        outToServer.writeBytes(sentence + '\n');
        modifiedSentence = inFromServer.readLine();
        System.out.println("FROM SERVER: " +
                                        modifiedSentence);
        clientSocket.close();
    }
}
```

The program `TCPClient` creates three streams and one socket, as shown in Figure 2.23.

The socket is called `clientSocket`. The stream `inFromUser` is an input stream to the program; it is attached to the standard input (that is, the keyboard). When the user types characters on the keyboard, the characters flow into the stream `inFromUser`. The stream `inFromServer` is another input stream to the program; it is attached to the socket. Characters that arrive from the network flow into the stream `inFromServer`. Finally, the stream `outToServer` is an output

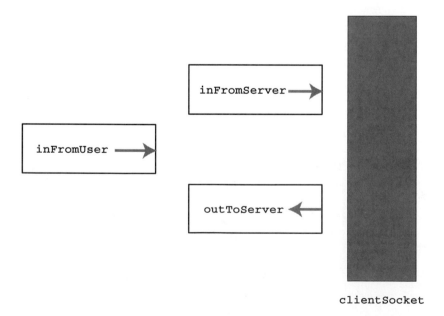

FIGURE 2.23 `TCPClient` has three streams and one socket

stream from the program; it is also attached to the socket. Characters that the client sends to the network flow into the stream outToServer.

Let's now take a look at the various lines in the code.

```
import java.io.*;
import java.net.*;
```

java.io and java.net are java packages. The java.io package contains classes for input and output streams. In particular, the java.io package contains the BufferedReader and DataOutputStream classes, classes that the program uses to create the three streams previously illustrated. The java.net package provides classes for network support. In particular, it contains the Socket and Server-Socket classes. The clientSocket object of this program is derived from the Socket class.

```
class TCPClient {
    public static void main(String argv[]) throws Exception
        {......}
              }
```

The above is standard stuff that you see at the beginning of most java code. The first line is the beginning of a class definition block. The keyword class begins the class definition for the class named TCPClient. A class contains variables and methods. The variables and methods of the class are embraced by the curly brackets that begin and end the class definition block. The class TCPClient has no class variables and exactly one method, the main() method. Methods are similar to the functions or procedures in languages such as C; the main method in the Java language is similar to the main function in C and C++. When the Java interpreter executes an application (by being invoked upon the application's controlling class), it starts by calling the class's main method. The main method then calls all the other methods required to run the application. For this introduction into socket programming in Java, you may ignore the keywords public, static, void, main, and throws Exceptions (although you must include them in the code).

```
String sentence;
String modifiedSentence;
```

These above two lines declare objects of type String. The object sentence is the string typed by the user and sent to the server. The object modifiedSentence is the string obtained from the server and sent to the user's standard output.

```
BufferedReader inFromUser =
        new BufferedReader(
                    new InputStreamReader(System.in));
```

The above line creates the stream object inFromUser of type BufferedReader. The input stream is initialized with System.in, which attaches the stream to the standard input. The command allows the client to read text from its keyboard.

```
Socket clientSocket = new Socket("hostname", 6789);
```

The above line creates the object `clientSocket` of type `Socket`. It also initiates the TCP connection between client and server. The variable "host name" must be replaced with the host name of the server (for example, "`fling.seas.upenn.edu`"). Before the TCP connection is actually initiated, the client performs a DNS look-up on the hostname to obtain the host's IP address. The number 6789 is the port number. You can use a different port number; but you must make sure that you use the same port number at the server side of the application. As discussed earlier, the host's IP address along with the applications port number identifies the server process.

```
DataOutputStream outToServer =
    new DataOutputStream(clientSocket.getOutputStream());
BufferedReader inFromServer =
    new BufferedReader(new inputStreamReader(
                             clientSocket.getInputStream()));
```

The above two lines create stream objects that are attached to the socket. The `outToServer` stream provides the process output to the socket. The `inFromServer` stream provides the process input from the socket (see Figure 2.23).

```
sentence = inFromUser.readLine();
```

The above line places a line typed by the user into the string `sentence`. The string sentence continues to gather characters until the user ends the line by typing a carriage return. The line passes from standard input through the stream `inFromUser` into the string `sentence`.

```
outToServer.writeBytes(sentence + '\n');
```

The above line sends the string `sentence` augmented with a carriage return into the `outToServer` stream. The augmented sentence flows through the client's socket and into the TCP pipe. The client then waits to receive characters from the server.

```
modifiedSentence = inFromServer.readLine();
```

When characters arrive from the server, they flow through the stream `inFromServer` and get placed into the string `modifiedSentence`. Characters continue to accumulate in `modifiedSentence` until the line ends with a carriage return character.

```
System.out.println("FROM SERVER " + modifiedSentence);
```

The above line prints to the monitor the string `modifiedSentence` returned by the server.

```
clientSocket.close();
```

This last line closes the socket and, hence, closes the TCP connection between the client and the server. It causes TCP in the client to send a TCP message to TCP in the server (see Section 3.5).

TCPServer.java.   Now let's take a look at the server program.

```java
import java.io.*;
import java.net.*;
class TCPServer {
  public static void main(String argv[]) throws Exception
    {
      String clientSentence;
      String capitalizedSentence;
      ServerSocket welcomeSocket = new ServerSocket(6789);

      while(true) {
          Socket connectionSocket = welcomeSocket.accept();
          BufferedReader inFromClient =
            new BufferedReader(new InputStreamReader(
                    connectionSocket.getInputStream()));
          DataOutputStream outToClient =
            new DataOutputStream(
                    connectionSocket.getOutputStream());
          clientSentence = inFromClient.readLine();
          capitalizedSentence =
                    clientSentence.toUpperCase() + '\n';
          outToClient.writeBytes(capitalizedSentence);
      }
    }
}
```

`TCPServer` has many similarities with `TCPClient`. Let us now take a look at the lines in `TCPServer.java`. We will not comment on the lines which are identical or similar to commands in `TCPClient.java`.

The first line in `TCPServer` that is substantially different from what we saw in `TCPClient` is:

```java
ServerSocket welcomeSocket = new ServerSocket(6789);
```

That line creates the object `welcomeSocket`, which is of type `ServerSocket`. The `WelcomeSocket`, as discussed above, is a sort of door that waits for a knock from some client. The port number 6789 identifies the process at the server. The next line is:

```java
Socket connectionSocket = welcomeSocket.accept();
```

This line creates a new socket, called `connectionSocket`, when some client knocks on `welcomeSocket`. TCP then establishes a direct virtual pipe between `clientSocket` at the client and `connectionSocket` at the server. The client and server can then send bytes to each other over the pipe, and all bytes sent arrive at the other side in order. With `connectionSocket` established, the server can continue to listen for other requests from other clients for the application using `welcomeSocket`. (This version of the program doesn't actually listen for more connection requests, but it can be modified with threads to do so.) The program then creates several stream objects, analogous to the stream objects created in `clientSocket`. Now consider:

```
capitalizedSentence = clientSentence.toUpperCase() + '\n';
```

This command is the heart of the application. It takes the line sent by the client, capitalizes it and adds a carriage return. It uses the method `toUpperCase()`. All the other commands in the program are peripheral; they are used for communication with the client.

That completes our analysis of the TCP program pair. Recall that TCP provides a reliable data transfer service. This implies, in particular, that if one of the user's characters gets corrupted in the network, then the client host will retransmit the character, thereby providing correct delivery of the data. These retransmissions are completely transparent to the application programs. The DNS lookup is also transparent to the application programs.

To test the program pair, you install and compile `TCPClient.java` in one host and `TCPServer.java` in another host. Be sure to include the proper host name of the server in `TCPClient.java`. You then execute `TCPServer.class`, the compiled server program, in the server. This creates a process in the server that idles until it is contacted by some client. Then you execute `TCPClient.class`, the compiled client program, in the client. This creates a process in the client and establishes a TCP connection between the client and server processes. Finally, to use the application, you type a sentence followed by a carriage return.

To develop your own client-server application, you can begin by slightly modifying the programs. For example, instead of converting all the letters to uppercase, the server can count the number of times the letter "s" appears and return this number.

2.7   SOCKET PROGRAMMING WITH UDP

We learned in the previous section that when two processes communicate over TCP, from the perspective of the processes it is as if there is a pipe between the two processes. This pipe remains in place until one of the two processes closes it. When one of the processes wants to send some bytes to the other process, it simply inserts the bytes into the pipe. The sending process does not have to attach a destination address to the bytes because the pipe is logically connected to the destination. Furthermore, the pipe provides a reliable byte stream channel—the sequence of bytes received by the receiving process is exactly the sequence of bytes that the sender inserted into the pipe.

UDP also allows two (or more) processes running on different hosts to communicate. However, UDP differs from TCP in many fundamental ways. First, UDP is a connectionless service—there isn't an initial handshaking phase during which a pipe is established between the two processes. Because UDP doesn't have a pipe, when a process wants to send a batch of bytes to another process, the sending process must attach the destination process's address to the batch of bytes. And this must be done for each batch of bytes the sending process sends. Thus,

UDP is similar to a taxi service—each time a group of people get in a taxi, the group has to inform the driver of the destination address. As with TCP, the destination address is a tuple consisting of the IP address of the destination host and the port number of the destination process. We shall refer to the batch of information bytes along with the IP destination address and port number as the "packet."

After having created a packet, the sending process pushes the packet into the network through a socket. Continuing with our taxi analogy, at the other side of the socket, there is a taxi waiting for the packet. The taxi then drives the packet in the direction of the packet's destination address. However, the taxi does not guarantee that it will eventually get the datagram to its ultimate destination; the taxi could break down. In other terms, *UDP provides an unreliable transport service to its communication processes*—it makes no guarantees that a datagram will reach its ultimate destination.

In this section we will illustrate UDP client-server programming by redeveloping the same application of the previous section, but this time over UDP. We shall also see that the Java code for UDP is different from the TCP code in many important ways. In particular, we shall see that there is (1) no initial handshaking between the two processes, and therefore no need for a welcoming socket, (2) no streams are attached to the sockets, (3) the sending hosts create packets by attaching the IP destination address and port number to each batch of bytes it sends, and (4) the receiving process must unravel each received packet to obtain the packet's information bytes. Recall once again our simple application:

A client reads a line from its standard input (keyboard) and sends the line out its socket to the server.

The server reads a line from its socket.

The server converts the line to uppercase.

The server sends the modified line out its socket to the client.

The client reads the modified line through its socket and prints the line on its standard output (monitor).

UDPClient.java. Here is the code for the client side of the application:

```
import java.io.*;
import java.net.*;
class UDPClient {
    public static void main(String args[]) throws Exception
    {
        BufferedReader inFromUser =
          new BufferedReader(new InputStreamReader(System.in));
        DatagramSocket clientSocket = new DatagramSocket();
        InetAddress IPAddress =
                        InetAddress.getByName("hostname");
        byte[] sendData = new byte[1024];
        byte[] receiveData = new byte[1024];
        String sentence = inFromUser.readLine();
        sendData = sentence.getBytes();
```

```
            DatagramPacket sendPacket =
               new DatagramPacket(sendData, sendData.length,
                               IPAddress, 9876);
            clientSocket.send(sendPacket);
            DatagramPacket receivePacket =
              new DatagramPacket(receiveData, receiveData.length);
            clientSocket.receive(receivePacket);
            String modifiedSentence =
                new String(receivePacket.getData());
            System.out.println("FROM SERVER:" + modifiedSentence);
            clientSocket.close();
        }
}
```

The program `UDPClient.java` constructs one stream and one socket, as shown
in Figure 2.24. The socket is called `clientSocket`, and it is of type `Datagram-`
`Socket`. Note that UDP uses a different kind of socket than TCP at the client. In
particular, with UDP our client uses a `DatagramSocket` whereas with TCP our
client used a `Socket`. The stream `inFromUser` is an input stream to the program;
it is attached to the standard input, that is, to the keyboard. We had an equivalent
stream in our TCP version of the program. When the user types characters on the
keyboard, the characters flow into the stream `inFromUser`. But in contrast with
TCP, there are no streams (input or output) attached to the socket. Instead of feed-
ing bytes to the stream attached to a `Socket` object, UDP will push individual
packets through the `DatagramSocket` object.

Let's now take a look at the lines in the code that differ significantly from
`TCPClient.java`.

```
DatagramSocket clientSocket = new DatagramSocket();
```

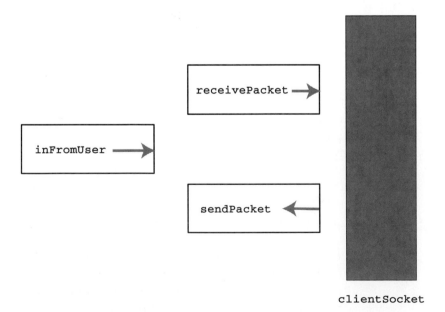

FIGURE 2.24   `UDPClient.java` has one stream and one socket

The previous line creates the object `clientSocket` of type `DatagramSocket`. In contrast with `TCPClient.java`, this line does not initiate a TCP connection. In particular, the client host does not contact the server host upon execution of this line. For this reason, the constructor `DatagramSocket()` does not take the server hostname or port number as arguments. Using our door/pipe analogy, the execution of the above line creates a door for the client process but does not create a pipe between the two processes.

```
InetAddress IPAddress = InetAddress.getByName("hostname");
```

In order to send bytes to a destination process, we shall need to obtain the address of the process. Part of this address is the IP address of the destination host. The above line invokes a DNS look up that translates the hostname (in this example, supplied in the code by the developer) to an IP address. DNS was also invoked by the TCP version of the client, although it was done there implicitly rather than explicitly. The method `getByName()` takes as an argument the hostname of the server and returns the IP address of this same server. It places this address in the object `IPAddress` of type `InetAddress`.

```
byte[] sendData = new byte[1024];
byte[] receiveData = new byte[1024];
```

The byte arrays `sendData` and `receiveData` will hold the data the client sends and receives, respectively.

```
sendData = sentence.getBytes();
```

The above line essentially performs a type conversion. It takes the string `sentence` and renames it as `sendData`, which is an array of bytes.

```
DatagramPacket sendPacket =
    new DatagramPacket(sendData, sendData.length, IPAddress,
                       9876);
```

The above line constructs the packet, `sendPacket`, that the client will pop into the network through its socket. This packet includes that data that is contained in the packet, `sendData`, the length of this data, the IP address of the server, and the port number of the application (which we have set to 9876). Note that `sendPacket` is of type `DatagramPacket`.

```
clientSocket.send(sendPacket);
```

In the above line, the method `send()` of the object `clientSocket` takes the packet just constructed and pops it into the network through `clientSocket`. Once again, note that UDP sends the line of characters in a manner very different from TCP. TCP simply inserted the line into a stream, which had a logical direct connection to the server; UDP creates a packet that includes the address of the server. After sending the packet, the client then waits to receive a packet from the server.

```
DatagramPacket receivePacket =
   new DatagramPacket(receiveData, receiveData.length);
```

In the above line, while waiting for the packet from the server, the client creates a place holder for the packet, `receivePacket`, an object of type DatagramPacket.

```
clientSocket.receive(receivePacket);
```

The client idles until it receives a packet; when it does receive a packet, it puts the packet in `receivePacket`.

```
String modifiedSentence =
   new String(receivePacket.getData());
```

The above line extracts the data from `receivePacket` and performs a type conversion, converting an array of bytes into the string `modifiedSentence`.

```
System.out.println("FROM SERVER:" + modifiedSentence);
```

This line, which is also present in `TCPClient`, prints out the string `modifiedSentence` at the client's monitor.

```
clientSocket.close();
```

This last line closes the socket. Because UDP is connectionless, this line does not cause the client to send a transport-layer message to the server (in contrast with `TCPClient`).

UDPServer.java.   Let's now take a look at the server side of the application:

```
import java.io.*;
import java.net.*;
class UDPServer {
  public static void main(String args[]) throws Exception
    {
      DatagramSocket serverSocket = new DatagramSocket(9876);
      byte[] receiveData = new byte[1024];
      byte[] sendData = new byte[1024];
      while(true)
        {
          DatagramPacket receivePacket =
             new DatagramPacket(receiveData,
                                   receiveData.length);
          serverSocket.receive(receivePacket);
          String sentence = new String(
                                    receivePacket.getData());
          InetAddress IPAddress = receivePacket.getAddress();
          int port = receivePacket.getPort();
          String capitalizedSentence =
                                    sentence.toUpperCase();
```

```
        sendData = capitalizedSentence.getBytes();
        DatagramPacket sendPacket =
            new DatagramPacket(sendData, sendData.length,
                                IPAddress, port);
        serverSocket.send(sendPacket);
      }
   }
}
```

The program UDPServer.java constructs one socket, as shown in Figure 2.25. The socket is called serverSocket. It is an object of type DatagramSocket, as was the socket in the client side of the application. Once again, no streams are attached to the socket.

Let's now take a look at the lines in the code that differ from TCP-Server.java.

```
DatagramSocket serverSocket = new DatagramSocket(9876);
```

The above line constructs the DatagramSocket serverSocket at port 9876. All data sent and received will pass through this socket. Because UDP is connectionless, we do not have to spawn a new socket and continue to listen for new connection requests, as done in TCPServer.java. If multiple clients access this application, they will all send their packets into this single door, server-Socket.

```
String sentence = new String(receivePacket.getData());
InetAddress IPAddress = receivePacket.getAddress();
int port = receivePacket.getPort();
```

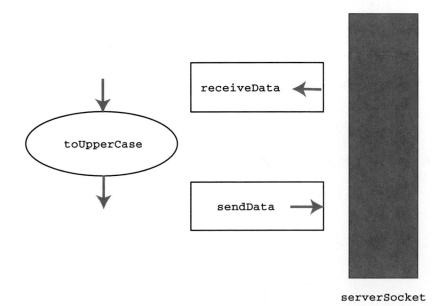

FIGURE 2.25 UDPServer.java has one socket

The above three lines unravel the packet that arrives from the client. The first of the three lines extracts the data from the packet and places the data in the `String sentence`; it has an analogous line in `UDPClient`. The second line extracts the IP address; the third line extracts the *client port number,* which is chosen by the client and is different from the server port number 9876. (We will discuss client port numbers in some detail in the next chapter.) It is necessary for the server to obtain the address (IP address and port number) of the client, so that it can send the capitalized sentence back to the client.

That completes our analysis of the UDP program pair. To test the application, you install and compile `UDPClient.java` in one host and `UDPServer.java` in another host. (Be sure to include the proper hostname of the server in `UDPClient.java`.) Then execute the two programs on their respective hosts. Unlike with TCP, you can first execute the client side and then the server side. This is because, when you execute the client side, the client process does not attempt to initiate a connection with the server. Once you have executed the client and server programs, you may use the application by typing a line at the client.

2.8   BUILDING A SIMPLE WEB SERVER

Now that we have studied HTTP in some detail and have learned how to write client-server applications in Java, let us combine this new-found knowledge and build a simple Web server in Java. We will see that the task is remarkably easy.

2.8.1   Web Server Functions

Our goal is to build a server that does the following:

- Handles only one HTTP request
- Accepts and parses the HTTP request
- Gets the requested file from the server's file system
- Creates an HTTP response message consisting of the requested file preceded by header lines
- Sends the response directly to the client

Let's try to make the code as simple as possible in order to shed insight on the networking concerns. The code that we present will be far from bullet proof! For example, let's not worry about handling exceptions. And let's assume that the client requests an object that is in server's file system.

WebServer.java.   Here is the code for a simple Web server:

```
import java.io.*;
import java.net.*;
import java.util.*;
class WebServer {
    public static void main(String argv[]) throws Exception {
        String requestMessageLine;
```

```java
      String fileName;
      ServerSocket listenSocket = new ServerSocket(6789);
      Socket connectionSocket = listenSocket.accept();
      BufferedReader inFromClient =
        new BufferedReader(new InputStreamReader(
                  connectionSocket.getInputStream()));
      DataOutputStream outToClient =
        new DataOutputStream(
                  connectionSocket.getOutputStream());
      requestMessageLine = inFromClient.readLine();
      StringTokenizer tokenizedLine =
        new StringTokenizer(requestMessageLine);
      if (tokenizedLine.nextToken().equals("GET")){
        fileName = tokenizedLine.nextToken();
        if (fileName.startsWith("/") == true )
                    fileName = fileName.substring(1);
        File file = new File(fileName);
        int numOfBytes = (int) file.length();
        FileInputStream inFile = new FileInputStream (
                                        fileName);
        byte[] fileInBytes = new byte[numOfBytes];
        inFile.read(fileInBytes);
        outToClient.writeBytes(
                "HTTP/1.0 200 Document Follows\r\n");
        if (fileName.endsWith(".jpg"))
              outToClient.writeBytes("Content-Type:
                                    image/jpeg\r\n");
        if (fileName.endsWith(".gif"))
              outToClient.writeBytes("Content-Type:
                                    image/gif\r\n");
        outToClient.writeBytes("Content-Length: " +
                          numOfBytes + "\r\n");
        outToClient.writeBytes("\r\n");
        outToClient.write(fileInBytes, 0, numOfBytes);
        connectionSocket.close();
        }
    else System.out.println("Bad Request Message");
    }
}
```

Let us now take a look at the code. The first half the program is almost identical to `TCPServer.java`. As with `TCPServer.java`, we import the `java.io` and `java.net` packages. In addition to these two packages we also import the `java.util` package, which contains the `StringTokenizer` class, which is used for parsing HTTP request messages. Looking now at the lines within the class `WebServer`, we define two string objects:

```java
String requestMessageLine;
String fileName;
```

The object `requestMessageLine` is a string that will contain the first line in the HTTP request message. The object `fileName` is a string that will contain the file name of the requested file. The next set of commands is identical to the corresponding set of commands in `TCPServer.java`.

```
ServerSocket listenSocket = new ServerSocket(6789);
Socket connectionSocket = listenSocket.accept();
BufferedReader inFromClient =
  new BufferedReader(new InputStreamReader
                     (connectionSocket.getInputStream()));
  DataOutputStream outToClient =
    new DataOutputStream(connectionSocket.getOutputStream());
```

Two socket-like objects are created. The first of these objects is `listenSocket`, which is of type `ServerSocket`. The object `listenSocket` is created by the server program before receiving a request for a TCP connection from a client. It listens at port 6789 and waits for a request from some client to establish a TCP connection. When a request for a connection arrives, the `accept()` method of `listenSocket` creates a new object, `connectionSocket`, of type `Socket`. Next two streams are created: the `BufferedReader inFromClient` and the `DataOutputStream outToClient`. The HTTP request message comes from the network, through `connectionSocket` and into `inFromClient`; the HTTP response message goes into `outToClient`, through `connectionSocket` and into the network. The remaining portion of the code differs significantly from `TCPServer.java`.

```
requestMessageLine = inFromClient.readLine();
```

The above command reads the first line of the HTTP request message. This line is supposed to be of the form:

```
GET file_name HTTP/1.0
```

Our server must now parse the line to extract the filename.

```
StringTokenizer tokenizedLine =
                    new StringTokenizer(requestMessageLine);
if (tokenizedLine.nextToken().equals("GET")){
  fileName = tokenizedLine.nextToken();
  if (fileName.startsWith("/") == true )
    fileName = fileName.substring(1);
```

The above commands parse the first line of the request message to obtain the requested filename. The object `tokenizedLine` can be thought of as the original request line with each of the "words" `GET`, `file_name`, and `HTTP/1.0` placed in a separate placeholder called a token. The server knows from the HTTP RFC that the file name for the requested file is contained in the token that follows the token containing "`GET`." This file name is put in a string called `fileName`. The purpose of the last `if` statement in the above code is to remove the backslash that may precede the filename.

```
FileInputStream inFile = new FileInputStream (fileName);
```

The above command attaches a stream, `inFile`, to the file `fileName`.

```
byte[] fileInBytes = new byte[numOfBytes];
inFile.read(fileInBytes);
```

These commands determine the size of the file and construct an array of bytes of that size. The name of the array is `fileInBytes`. The last command reads from the stream `inFile` to the byte array `fileInBytes`. The program must convert to bytes because the output stream `outToClient` may only be fed with bytes.

Now we are ready to construct the HTTP response message. To this end we must first send the HTTP response header lines into the `DataOutputStream` `outToClient`:

```
outToClient.writeBytes("HTTP/1.0 200 Document Follows\r\n");
if (fileName.endsWith(".jpg"))
    outToClient.writeBytes("Content-Type: image/jpeg\r\n");
if (fileName.endsWith(".gif"))
    outToClient.writeBytes("Content-Type: image/gif\r\n");
outToClient.writeBytes("Content-Length: " + numOfBytes +
                       "\r\n");
outToClient.writeBytes("\r\n");
```

The above set of commands are particularly interesting. These commands prepare the header lines for HTTP response message and send the header lines to the TCP send buffer. The first command sends the mandatory status line: `HTTP/1.0 200 Document Follows`, followed by a carriage return and a line feed. The next two command lines prepare a single content-type header line. If the server is to transfer a GIF image, then the server prepares the header line `Content-Type: image/gif`. If, on the other hand, the server is to transfer a JPEG image, then the server prepares the header line `Content-Type: image/jpeg`. (In this simple Web server, no content line is sent if the object is neither a GIF nor a JPEG image.) The server then prepares and sends a content-length header line and a mandatory blank line to precede the object itself that is to be sent. We now must send the file `FileName` into the `DataOutputStream` `outToClient`.

We can now send the requested file:

```
outToClient.write(fileInBytes, 0, numOfBytes);
```

The above command sends the requested file, `fileInBytes`, to the TCP send buffer. TCP will concatenate the file, `fileInBytes`, to the header lines just created, segment the concatenation if necessary, and send the TCP segments to the client.

```
connectionSocket.close();
```

After serving one request for one file, the server performs some housekeeping by closing the socket `connectionSocket`.

To test this Web server, install it on a host. Also put some files in the host. Then use a browser running on any machine to request a file from the server. When you request a file, you will need to use the port number that you include in the server code (for example, 6789). So if your server is located at `some-host.somewhere.edu`, the file is `somefile.html`, and the port number is 6789, then the browser should request the following:

```
http://somehost.somewhere.edu:6789/somefile.html
```

SUMMARY

In this chapter we've studied both the conceptual and the implementation aspects of network applications. We've learned about the ubiquitous client-server paradigm adopted by Internet applications and seen its use in the HTTP, FTP, SMTP, POP3, and DNS protocols. We've studied these important application-level protocols, and their associated applications (the Web, file transfer, e-mail, and the Domain Name System) in some detail. We've examined how the socket API can be used to build network applications and we've walked through not only the use of sockets over connection-oriented (TCP) and connectionless (UDP) end-to-end transport services, but also built a simple Web server using this API. The first step in our top-down journey "down" the layered network architecture is complete.

At the very beginning of this book, in Section 1.2, we gave a rather vague, bare bones definition of a protocol as defining "the format and the order of messages exchanged between two communicating entities, as well as the actions taken on the transmission and/or receipt of a message or other event." The material in this chapter, and in particular the detailed study of the HTTP, FTP, SMTP, POP3, and DNS protocols, has now added considerable substance to this definition. Protocols are a key concept in networking; our study of applications protocols has now given us the opportunity to develop a more intuitive feels for what protocols are all about.

In Section 2.1 we described the service models that TCP and UDP offer to applications that invoke them. We took an even closer look at these service models when we developed simple applications that run over TCP and UDP in Sections 2.6–2.7. However, we have said little about *how* TCP and UDP provide these service models. For example, we have said very little about how TCP provides a reliable data transfer service to its applications. In the next chapter we shall take a careful look at not only the *what*, but also the *how* and *why*, of transport protocols.

Armed with a knowledge about Internet application structure and application-level protocols, we're now ready to head further down the protocol stack and examine the transport layer in Chapter 3.

HOMEWORK PROBLEMS AND QUESTIONS

Chapter 2

Review Questions

Section 2.1

1. List five nonproprietary Internet applications and the application-layer protocols that they use.

2. For a communication session between two hosts, which host is the client and which is the server?

3. What information is used by a process running on one host to identify a process running on another host?

4. List the various network-application user agents that you use on a daily basis.

5. Referring to Figure 2.2, we see that none of the applications listed in the figure require both "no data loss" and "timing." Can you conceive of an application that requires no data loss and that is also highly time sensitive?

Sections 2.2–2.5

6. What is meant by a handshaking protocol?

7. Why do HTTP, FTP, SMTP, POP3, and IMAP run on top of TCP rather than UDP?

8. Consider an e-commerce site that wants to keep a purchase record for each of its customers. Describe how this can be done with HTTP authentication. Describe how this can be done with cookies.

9. What is the difference between persistent HTTP with pipelining and persistent HTTP without pipelining? Which of the two is used by HTTP/1.1?

10. Telnet into a Web server and send a multiline request message. Include in the request message the `If-modified-since:` header line to force a response message with the `304 Not Modified` status code.

11. Why is it said that FTP sends control information "out of band"?

12. Suppose Alice with a Web-based e-mail account (such as Yahoo! mail or Hotmail) sends a message to Bob, who accesses his mail from his mail server using POP3. Discuss how the message gets from Alice's host to Bob's host. Be sure to list the series of application-layer protocols that are used to move the message between the two hosts.

13. Suppose that you send an e-mail message whose only data is a Microsoft Excel attachment. What might the header lines (including MIME lines) look like?

14. Print out the header of a message that you have recently received. How many `Received:` header lines are there? Analyze each of the header lines in the message.

15. From a user's perspective, what is the difference between the download-and-delete mode and the download-and-keep mode in POP3?

16. Redraw Figure 2.19 for the case in which all queries from the local name server are iterative.

17. Each Internet host will have at least one local name server and one authoritative name server. What role does each of these servers have in DNS?

18. Is it possible that an organization's Web server and mail server have exactly the same alias for a hostname (for example, `foo.com`)? What would be the type for the RR that contains the hostname of the mail server?

19. Use `nslookup` to find a Web server that has multiple IP addresses. Does the Web server of your institution (school or company) have multiple IP addresses?

Sections 2.6–2.9

20. The UDP server described in Section 2.7 needed only one socket, whereas the TCP server described in Section 2.6 needed two sockets. Why? If the TCP server were to support *n* simultaneous connections, each from a different client host, how many sockets would the TCP server need?

21. For the client-server application over TCP described in Section 2.6, why must the server program be executed before the client program? For the client-server application over UDP described in Section 2.7, why may the client program be executed before the server program?

PROBLEMS

1. True or false?
   a. Suppose a user requests a Web page that consists of some text and two images. For this page the client will send one request message and receive three response messages.
   b. Two distinct Web pages (for example, `www.mit.edu/research.html` and `www.mit.edu/students.html`) can be sent over the same persistent connection.
   c. With nonpersistent connections between browser and origin server, it is possible for a single TCP segment to carry two distinct HTTP request messages.
   d. The `Date:` header in the HTTP response message indicates when the object in the response was last modified.

2. Read RFC 959 for FTP. List all of the client commands that are supported by the RFC.

3. Read RFC 1700. What are the well-known port numbers for the simple file transfer protocol (sftp)? For the network news transfer protocol (nntp)?

4. Suppose within your Web browser you click on a link to obtain a Web page. Suppose that the IP address for the associated URL is not cached in your local host, so that a DNS look-up is necessary to obtain the IP address. Suppose that *n* DNS servers are visited before your host receives the IP address from DNS; the successive visits incur a RTT of $RTT_1, \ldots, RTT_n$. Further suppose that the Web page associated with the link contains exactly one object, a small amount of HTML text. Let RTT_0 denote the RTT between the local host and the server containing the object. Assuming zero transmission time of the object, how much time elapses from when the client clicks on the link until the client receives the object?

5. Referring to problem 4, suppose the page contains three very small objects. Neglecting transmission times, how much time elapses with (a) nonpersistent HTTP with no parallel TCP connections, (b) nonpersistent HTTP with parallel connections, (c) persistent HTTP with pipelining?

6. Two HTTP request methods are `GET` and `POST`. Are there any other methods in HTTP/1.0? If so, what are they used for? How about HTTP/1.1?

7. Write a simple TCP program for a server that accepts lines of input from a client and prints the lines onto the server's standard output. (You can do this by

modifying the `TCPServer.java program` in the text.) Compile and execute your program. On any other machine that contains a Web browser, set the proxy server in the browser to the machine in which your server program is running; also configure the port number appropriately. Your browser should now send its `GET` request messages to your server, and your server should display the messages on its standard output. Use this platform to determine whether your browser generates conditional `GET` messages for objects that are locally cached.

8. Read the POP3 RFC, RFC 1939. What is the purpose of the UIDL POP3 command?

9. Install and compile the Java programs `TCPClient` and `UDPClient` on one host and `TCPServer` and `UDPServer` on another host.

   a. Suppose you run `TCPClient` before you run `TCPServer`. What happens? Why?

   b. Suppose you run `UDPClient` before you run `UDPServer`. What happens? Why?

   c. What happens if you use different port numbers for the client and server sides?

10. Rewrite `TCPServer.java` so that it can accept multiple connections. (*Hint:* You will need to use threads.)

DISCUSSION QUESTIONS

1. What is a CGI script? Give examples of two popular Web sites that use CGI scripts. Explain how these sites use CGI. Which languages are CGI scripts typically written in?

2. How can you configure your browser for local caching? What kinds of options do you have?

3. Can you configure your browser to open multiple simultaneous connections to a Web site? What are the advantages and disadvantages of having a large number of simultaneous TCP connections?

4. Consider SMTP, POP3, and IMAP. Are these stateless protocols? Why or why not?

5. We have seen that Internet TCP sockets treat the data being sent as a byte stream but UDP sockets recognize message boundaries. What is one advantage and one disadvantage of byte-oriented API versus having the API explicitly recognize and preserve application-defined message boundaries?

6. Would it be possible to implement a connection-oriented service (for example, SMTP or HTTP) on top of a connectionless service? What would be some of the difficulties involved in doing so, and how could these be overcome?

Chapter 3 | Transport Layer

TRANSPORT-LAYER SERVICES AND PRINCIPLES

Residing between the application and network layers, the transport layer is in the core of the layered network architecture. It has the critical role of providing communication services directly to the application processes running on different hosts. In this chapter we'll examine the possible services provided by a transport-layer protocol and the principles underlying various approaches towards providing these services. We'll also look at how these services are implemented and instantiated in existing protocols; as usual, particular emphasis will be given to the Internet protocols, namely, the TCP and UDP transport-layer protocols.

In the previous two chapters we touched on the role of the transport layer and the services that it provides. Let's quickly review what we have already learned about the transport layer:

A transport layer protocol provides for **logical communication** between application processes running on different hosts. By logical communication, we mean that although the communicating application processes are not *physically* connected to each other (indeed, they may be on different sides of the planet, connected via numerous routers and a wide range of link types), from the applications' viewpoint, it is as if they were physically connected. Application processes use the logical communication provided by the transport layer to send messages to each other, free from the worry of the details of the physical infrastructure used to carry these messages. Figure 3.1 illustrates the notion of logical communication.

As shown in Figure 3.1, transport-layer protocols are implemented in the end systems but not in network routers. Network routers only act on the network-layer fields of the layer-3 PDUs; they do not act on the transport-layer fields.

On the sending side, the transport layer converts the messages it receives from a sending application process into 4-PDUs (that is, transport-layer protocol data units). This is done by (possibly) breaking the application messages into smaller

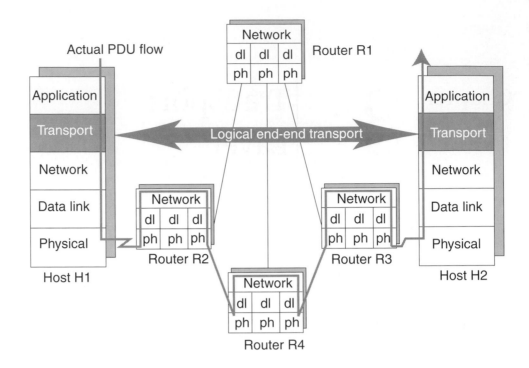

FIGURE 3.1 The transport layer provides logical rather than physical communication between applications.

chunks and adding a transport-layer header to each chunk to create 4-PDUs. The transport layer then passes the 4-PDUs to the network layer, where each 4-PDU is encapsulated into a 3-PDU. On the receiving side, the transport layer receives the 4-PDUs from the network layer, removes the transport header from the 4-PDUs, reassembles the messages, and passes them to a receiving application process.

A computer network can make more than one transport-layer protocol available to network applications. For example, the Internet has two protocols—TCP and UDP. Each of these protocols provides a different set of transport-layer services to the invoking application.

All transport-layer protocols provide an application multiplexing/demultiplexing service. This service will be described in detail in the next section. As discussed in Section 2.1, in addition to a multiplexing/demultiplexing service, a transport protocol can possibly provide other services to invoking applications, including reliable data transfer, bandwidth guarantees, and delay guarantees.

3.1.1 Relationship between Transport and Network Layers

From the perspective of network applications, the transport layer *is* the underlying communication infrastructure. Of course, there is more to the communication infrastructure than just the transport layer. For example, the network layer lies just below the transport layer in the protocol stack. Whereas a transport-layer protocol provides *logical communication between processes* running on different hosts, a network-layer protocol provides *logical communication between hosts*. This distinction is subtle but important. Let's examine this distinction with the aid of a household analogy.

Consider two houses, one on the East Coast and the other on the West Coast, with each house being home to a dozen kids. The kids in the East Coast household are cousins of the kids in the West Coast household. The kids in the two households love to write to each other—each kid writes each cousin every week, with each letter delivered by the traditional postal service in a separate envelope. Thus, each household sends 144 letters to the other household every week. (These kids would save a lot of money if they had e-mail!) In each of the households there is one kid—Ann in the West Coast house and Bill in the East Coast house—responsible for mail collection and mail distribution. Each week Ann visits all her brothers and sisters, collects the mail, and gives the mail to a postal-service mail person who makes daily visits to the house. When letters arrive at the West Coast house, Ann also has the job of distributing the mail to her brothers and sisters. Bill has a similar job on the East Coast.

In this example, the postal service provides logical communication between the two houses—the postal service moves mail from house to house, not from person to person. On the other hand, Ann and Bill provide logical communication between the cousins—Ann and Bill pick up mail from and deliver mail to their brothers and sisters. Note that, from the cousins' perspective, Ann and Bill *are* the mail service, even though Ann and Bill are only a part (the end system part) of the end-to-end delivery process. This household example serves as a nice analogy for explaining how the transport layer relates to the network layer:

hosts (also called end systems) = houses

processes = cousins

application messages = letters in envelopes

network layer protocol = postal service (including mail persons)

transport-layer protocol = Ann and Bill

Continuing with this analogy, observe that Ann and Bill do all their work within their respective homes; they are not involved, for example, in sorting mail in any intermediate mail center or in moving mail from one mail center to another. Similarly, transport-layer protocols live in the end systems. Within an end system, a transport protocol moves messages from application processes to the network edge (that is, the network layer) and vice versa; but it doesn't have any say about how the messages are moved within the network core. In fact, as illustrated in Figure 3.1, intermediate routers neither act on, nor recognize, any information that the transport layer may have appended to the application messages.

Continuing with our family saga, suppose now that when Ann and Bill go on vacation, another cousin pair—say, Susan and Harvey—substitute for them and provide the household-internal collection and delivery of mail. Unfortunately for the two families, Susan and Harvey do not do the collection and delivery in exactly the same way as Ann and Bill. Being younger kids, Susan and Harvey pick up and drop off the mail less frequently and occasionally lose letters (which are sometimes chewed up by the family dog). Thus, the cousin-pair Susan and Harvey do not provide the same set of services (that is, the same service model) as Ann and Bill. In an analogous manner, a computer network may make available multiple transport protocols, with each protocol offering a different service model to applications.

The possible services that Ann and Bill can provide are clearly constrained by the possible services that the postal service provides. For example, if the postal service doesn't provide a maximum bound on how long it can take to deliver mail between the two houses (for example, three days), then there is no way that Ann and Bill can guarantee a maximum delay for mail delivery between any of the cousin pairs. In a similar manner, the services that a transport protocol can provide are often constrained by the service model of the underlying network-layer protocol. If the network-layer protocol cannot provide delay or bandwidth guarantees for 4-PDUs sent between hosts, then the transport-layer protocol cannot provide delay or bandwidth guarantees for the messages sent between processes.

Nevertheless, certain services *can* be offered by a transport protocol even when the underlying network protocol doesn't offer the corresponding service at the network layer. For example, as we'll see in this chapter, a transport protocol can offer reliable data transfer service to an application even when the underlying network protocol is unreliable, that is, even when the network protocol loses, garbles, and duplicates packets. As another example (which we'll explore in Chapter 7 when we discuss network security), a transport protocol can use encryption to guarantee that application messages are not read by intruders, even when the network layer cannot guarantee the secrecy of 4-PDUs.

3.1.2 Overview of the Transport Layer in the Internet

Recall that the Internet, and more generally a TCP/IP network, makes available two distinct transport-layer protocols to the application layer. One of these protocols is **UDP** (User Datagram Protocol), which provides an unreliable, connectionless service to the invoking application. The second of these protocols is **TCP** (Transmission Control Protocol), which provides a reliable, connection-oriented service to the invoking application. When designing a network application, the application developer must specify one of these two transport protocols. As we saw in Sections 2.6 and 2.7, the application developer selects between UDP and TCP when creating sockets.

To simplify terminology, when in an Internet context, we refer to the 4-PDU as a **segment.** We mention, however, that the Internet literature (for example, the RFCs) also refers to the PDU for TCP as a segment but often refers to the PDU for UDP as a **datagram.** But this same Internet literature also uses the terminology datagram for the network-layer PDU! For an introductory book on computer networking such as this, we believe that it is less confusing to refer to both TCP and UDP PDUs as segments, and reserve the terminology datagram for the network-layer PDU.

Before preceding with our brief introduction of UDP and TCP, it is useful to say a few words about the Internet's network layer. (The network layer is examined in detail in Chapter 4.) The Internet's network-layer protocol has a name—IP, for Internet Protocol. The IP provides logical communication between hosts. The IP service model is a *best-effort delivery service.* This means that IP makes its "best effort" to deliver segments between communicating hosts, *but it makes no guarantees.* In particular, it does not guarantee segment delivery, it does not guarantee orderly delivery of segments, and it does not guarantee the integrity of the data in the segments. For these reasons, IP is said to be an **unreliable service.** We

also mention here that every host has an IP address. We will examine IP addressing in detail in Chapter 4; for this chapter we need only keep in mind that each
host has a *unique* IP address.

Having taken a glimpse at the IP service model, let's now summarize the service model of UDP and TCP. The most fundamental responsibility of UDP and
TCP is to extend IP's delivery service between two end systems to a delivery service between two processes running on the end systems. Extending host-to-host
delivery to process-to-process delivery is called **application multiplexing** and
demultiplexing. We'll discuss application multiplexing and demultiplexing in the
next section. UDP and TCP also provide integrity checking by including error-
detection fields in their headers. These two minimal transport-layer services—
host-to-host data delivery and error checking—are the only two services that UDP
provides! In particular, like IP, UDP is an unreliable service—it does not guarantee that data sent by one process will arrive intact to the destination process. UDP
is discussed in detail in Section 3.3.

TCP, on the other hand, offers several additional services to applications. First
and foremost, it provides **reliable data transfer.** Using flow control, sequence
numbers, acknowledgments, and timers (techniques we'll explore in detail in this
chapter), TCPs guarantee of reliable data transfer ensures that data is delivered
from sending process to receiving process, correctly and in order. TCP thus converts IP's unreliable service between end systems into a reliable data transport service between processes. TCP also uses **congestion control.** Congestion control is
not so much a service provided to the invoking application as it is a service for the
Internet as a whole, a service for the general good. In loose terms, TCP congestion
control prevents any one TCP connection from swamping the links and switches
between communicating hosts with an excessive amount of traffic. In principle,
TCP permits TCP connections traversing a congested network link to equally
share that link's bandwidth. This is done by regulating the rate at which the sending-
side TCPs can send traffic into the network. UDP traffic, on the other hand, is
unregulated. An application using UDP transport can send traffic at any rate it
pleases, for as long as it pleases.

A protocol that provides reliable data transfer and congestion control is necessarily complex. We will need several sections to cover the principles of reliable
data transfer and congestion control, and additional sections to cover the TCP protocol itself. These topics are investigated in Sections 3.4 through 3.8. The
approach taken in this chapter is an alternative between basic principles and the
TCP protocol. For example, we first discuss reliable data transfer in a general setting and then discuss how TCP specifically provides reliable data transfer. Similarly, we first discuss congestion control in a general setting and then discuss how
TCP uses congestion control. But before getting into all this good stuff, let's first
look at application multiplexing and demultiplexing in the next section.

3.2   MULTIPLEXING AND DEMULTIPLEXING APPLICATIONS

In this section we discuss multiplexing and demultiplexing network applications.
In order to keep the discussion concrete, we shall discuss this basic transport-layer
service in the context of the Internet. We emphasize, however, that a multiplexing/
demultiplexing service is needed for all computer networks.

Although the multiplexing/demultiplexing service is not among the most exciting services that can be provided by a transport-layer protocol, it is absolutely critical. To understand why it is so critical, consider the fact that IP delivers data between two end systems, with each end system identified with a unique IP address. IP does *not* deliver data between the application processes that run on these end systems. Extending host-to-host delivery to a process-to-process delivery is the job of application multiplexing and demultiplexing.

At the destination host, the transport layer receives segments (that is, transport-layer PDUs) from the network layer just below. The transport layer has the responsibility of delivering the data in these segments to the appropriate application process running in the host. Let's take a look at an example. Suppose you are sitting in front of your computer, and you are downloading Web pages while running one FTP session and two Telnet sessions. You therefore have four network application processes running—two Telnet processes, one FTP process, and one HTTP process. When the transport-layer in your computer receives data from the network layer below, it needs to direct the received data to one of these four processes. Let's now examine how this is done.

Each transport-layer segment has a field that specifies the process to which the segment's data is to be delivered. At the receiving end, the transport layer can then examine this field to determine the receiving process, and then direct the segment to that process. This job of delivering the data in a transport-layer segment to the correct application process is called **demultiplexing.** The job of gathering data at the source host from different application processes, enveloping the data with header information (which will later be used in demultiplexing) to create segments, and passing the segments to the network layer is called **multiplexing.**

To illustrate the demultiplexing job, let us return to the household saga in the previous section. Each of the kids is distinguished by his or her name. When Bill receives a batch of mail from the mail person, he performs a demultiplexing operation by observing to whom the letters are addressed and then hand delivers the mail to his brothers and sisters. Ann performs a multiplexing operation when she collects letters from her brothers and sisters and gives the collected mail to the mail person.

UDP and TCP perform the demultiplexing and multiplexing jobs by including two special fields in the segment headers: the **source port-number field** and the **destination port-number field.** These two fields are illustrated in Figure 3.2. When taken together, the fields uniquely identify an application process running

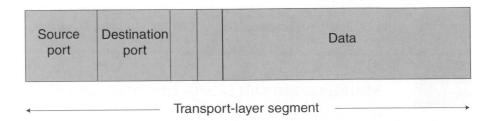

FIGURE 3.2   Source and destination port-number fields in a transport layer segment

on the destination host. (The UDP and TCP segments have other fields as well, and they will be addressed in the subsequent sections of this chapter.)

The notion of port numbers was briefly introduced in Sections 2.6–2.7, in which we studied application development and socket programming. The port number is a 16-bit number, ranging from 0 to 65535. The port numbers ranging from 0 to 1023 are called **well-known port numbers** and are restricted, which means that they are reserved for use by well-known application protocols such as HTTP and FTP. HTTP uses port number 80; FTP uses port number 21. The list of well-known port numbers is given in [RFC 1700]. When we develop a new application (such as one of the applications developed in Sections 2.6–2.8), we must assign the application a port number.

Given that each *type* of application running on an end system has a unique port number, then why is it that the transport-layer segment has fields for two port numbers, a source port number and a destination port number? The answer is simple: An end system may be running two processes of the same type at the same time, and thus the port number of an application may not suffice to identify a specific process. For example, a Web server may spawn a new HTTP process for every request it processes; whenever such a Web server is servicing more than one request (which is by no means uncommon), the server is running more than one process with port number 80. Therefore, in order to uniquely identify processes, a second port number is needed.

How is this second port number created? Which port number goes in the source port-number field of a segment? Which goes in the destination port-number field of a segment? To answer these questions, recall from Section 2.1 that networking applications are organized around the client-server model. Typically, the host that initiates the application is the client and the other host is the server. Now let us look at a specific example. Suppose the application has port number 23 (the port number for Telnet). Consider a transport-layer segment leaving the client (that is, the host that initiated the Telnet session) and destined for the server. What are the destination and source port numbers for this segment? For the destination port number, this segment has the port number of the application, namely, 23. For the source port number, the client uses a number that is not being used by any of its other ongoing Telnet client processes. (This is done automatically by the transport-layer software running on the client and is transparent to the application developer.) Let's say the client chooses port number x. Then each segment that this process sends will have its source port number set to x and destination port number set to 23. When the segment arrives at the server, the source and destination port numbers in the segment enable the server host to pass the data of the segment to the correct application process. The destination port number 23 identifies a Telnet process and the source port number x identifies the specific Telnet process.

The situation is reversed for the segments flowing from the server to the client. The source port number is now the application port number, 23. The destination port number is now x (the *same* x used for the source port number for the segments sent from client to server). When a segment arrives at the client, the source and destination port numbers in the segment will enable the client host to pass the data of the segment to the correct application process, which is identified by the port number pair. Figure 3.3 summarizes the discussion.

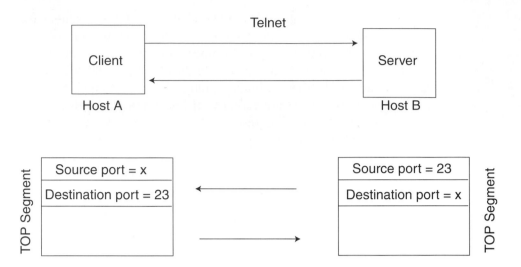

FIGURE 3.3   Use of source and destination port numbers in a client-server application

Now you may be wondering, what happens if two different clients establish a Telnet session to a server and each of these clients choose the same source port number x? How will the server be able to demultiplex the segments when the two sessions have exactly the same port-number pair? The answer to this question is that the server also uses the IP addresses in the IP datagrams carrying these segments. (We will discuss IP datagrams and addressing in detail in Chapter 4.) The situation is illustrated in Figure 3.4, in which host A initiates two Telnet sessions to host C, and host A initiates one Telnet session to host C. Hosts A, B, and C each have their own unique IP address; host A has IP address A, host B has IP address B, and host C has IP address C. Host A assigns two different source port (SP) numbers (x and y) to the two Telnet connections emanating from host A. But because host B is choosing source port numbers independently from A, it can also assign SP = x to its Telnet connection. Nevertheless, host C is still able to demultiplex the two connections since the two connections have different source IP addresses. In summary, we see that when a destination host receives data from the network layer, the triplet (source IP address, source port number, destination port number) is used to forward the data to the appropriate process.

Now that we've shown how the transport layer can multiplex and demultiplex network applications, let's move on and discuss one of the Internet's transport protocols, UDP. In the next section we shall see that UDP adds little more to the network layer protocol than multiplexing/demultiplexing service.

3.3   CONNECTIONLESS TRANSPORT: UDP

Recall that the Internet makes two transport protocols available to its applications, UDP and TCP. In this section, we take a close look at UDP, how UDP works, and what it does. The reader is encouraged to refer back to material in Section 2.1,

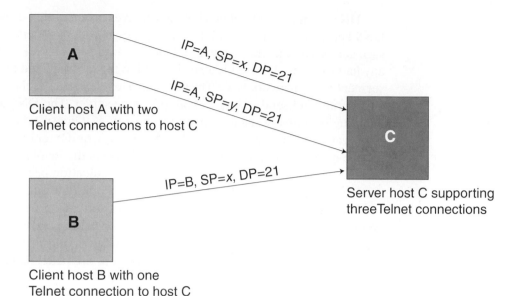

FIGURE 3.4 Two clients, using the same port numbers to communicate with the same server application

which includes an overview of the UDP service model, and to the material in Section 2.7, which discusses socket programming over UDP.

To motivate our discussion about UDP, suppose you were interested in designing a no-frills, bare-bones transport protocol. How might you go about doing this? You might first consider using a vacuous transport protocol. In particular, on the sending side, you might consider taking the messages from the application process and passing them directly to the network layer; and on the receiving side, you might consider taking the messages arriving from the network layer and passing them directly to the application process. But as we learned in the previous section, we have to do a little more than nothing. At the very least, the transport layer has to provide the multiplexing/demultiplexing service in order to pass data between the network layer and the correct application.

UDP, defined in [RFC 768], does just about as little as a transport protocol can. Aside from the multiplexing/demultiplexing function and some light error checking, it adds nothing to IP. In fact, if the application developer chooses UDP instead of TCP, then the application is almost directly talking with IP. UDP takes messages from the application process, attaches source and destination port number fields for the multiplexing/demultiplexing service, adds two other fields of minor importance, and passes the resulting segment to the network layer. The network layer encapsulates the segment into an IP datagram and then makes a best-effort attempt to deliver the segment to the receiving host. If the segment arrives at the receiving host, UDP uses the port numbers and the IP destination address to deliver the data in the segment to the correct application process. Note that with UDP there is no handshaking between sending and receiving transport-layer entities before sending a segment. For this reason, UDP is said to be *connectionless*.

DNS is an example of an application-layer protocol that uses UDP. When the DNS application in a host wants to make a query, it constructs a DNS query message and passes the message to a UDP socket (see Section 2.7). Without performing any handshaking, UDP adds a header field to the message and passes the resulting segment to the network layer. The network layer encapsulates the UDP segment into a datagram and sends the datagram to a name server. The DNS application at the querying host then waits for a reply to its query. If it doesn't receive a reply (possibly because the underlying network lost the query or the reply), it either tries sending the query to another nameserver, or it informs the invoking application that it can't get a reply. We mention that the DNS specification permits DNS to run over TCP instead of UDP; in practice, however, DNS almost always runs over UDP.

Now you might be wondering why an application developer would ever choose to build an application over UDP rather than over TCP. Isn't TCP always preferable to UDP since TCP provides a reliable data transfer service and UDP does not? The answer is no, as many applications are better suited for UDP for the following reasons:

- *No connection establishment.* As we shall discuss later, TCP uses a three-way handshake before it starts to transfer data. UDP just blasts away without any formal preliminaries. Thus UDP does not introduce any delay to establish a connection. This is probably the principal reason why DNS runs over UDP rather than TCP—DNS would be much slower if it ran over TCP. HTTP uses TCP rather than UDP, since reliability is critical for Web pages with text. But, as we briefly discussed in Section 2.2, the TCP connection-establishment delay in HTTP is an important contributor to the "world wide wait."

- *No connection state.* TCP maintains connection state in the end systems. This connection state includes receive and send buffers, congestion control parameters, and sequence and acknowledgment number parameters. We will see in Section 3.5 that this state information is needed to implement the reliable data transfer service and to provide congestion control. UDP, on the other hand, does not maintain a connection state and does not track any of these parameters. For this reason, a server devoted to a particular application can typically support many more active clients when the application runs over UDP rather than TCP.

- *Small packet header overhead.* The TCP segment has 20 bytes of header overhead in every segment, whereas UDP only has 8 bytes of overhead.

- *Unregulated send rate.* TCP has a congestion control mechanism that throttles the sender when one or more links between sender and receiver become excessively congested. This throttling can have a severe impact on real-time applications, which can tolerate some packet loss but require a minimum send rate. On the other hand, the speed at which UDP sends data is only constrained by the rate at which the application generates data, the capabilities of the source (CPU, clock rate, and so on) and the access bandwidth to the Internet. We should keep in mind, however, that the receiving host does not necessarily receive all the data. When the network is congested, a fraction of the data could be lost due to router buffer overflow. Thus, the receive rate is limited by network congestion even if the sending rate is not constrained.

Figure 3.5 lists popular Internet applications and the transport protocols that they use. As we expect, e-mail, remote terminal access, the Web, and file transfer

Application	Application-layer protocol	Underlying transport protocol
Electronic mail	SMTP	TCP
Remote terminal access	Telnet	TCP
Web	HTTP	TCP
File transfer	FTP	TCP
Remote file server	NFS	typically UDP
Streaming multimedia	proprietary	typically UDP
Internet telephony	proprietary	typically UDP
Network management	SNMP	typically UDP
Routing protocol	RIP	typically UDP
Name translation	DNS	typically UDP

FIGURE 3.5   Popular Internet applications and their underlying transport protocols

run over TCP—all these applications need the reliable data transfer service of TCP. Nevertheless, many important applications run over UDP rather than TCP. UDP is used for RIP routing table updates (see Chapter 4 on the network layer), because the updates are sent periodically (typically every five minutes), so that lost updates are replaced by more recent updates. UDP is used to carry network management (SNMP; see Chapter 8) data. UDP is preferred to TCP in this case, since network management must often run when the network is in a stressed state—precisely when reliable, congestion-controlled data transfer is difficult to achieve. Also, as we mentioned earlier, DNS runs over UDP, thereby avoiding TCP's connection-establishment delays.

As shown in Figure 3.5, UDP is also commonly used today with multimedia applications, such as Internet phone, real-time video conferencing, and streaming of stored audio and video. We shall take a close look at these applications in Chapter 6. We just mention now that all of these applications can tolerate a small fraction of packet loss, so that reliable data transfer is not absolutely critical for the success of the application. Furthermore, real-time applications, like Internet phone and video conferencing, react very poorly to TCP's congestion control. For these reasons, developers of multimedia applications often choose to run the applications over UDP instead of TCP. Finally, because TCP cannot be employed with multicast, multicast applications run over UDP.

Although commonly done today, running multimedia applications over UDP is controversial to say the least. As we mentioned above, UDP has no congestion control. But congestion control is needed to prevent the network from entering a state in which very little useful work is done. If everyone were to start streaming high-bit-rate video without using any congestion control, there would be so much packet overflow at routers that no one would see anything. Thus, the lack of congestion control in UDP is a potentially serious problem. Many researchers have proposed new mechanisms to force all sources, including UDP sources, to perform adaptive congestion control [Mahdavi].

Before discussing the UDP segment structure, we mention that it is possible for an application to have reliable data transfer when using UDP. This can be done if reliability is built into the application itself (for example, by adding acknowledgment and retransmission mechanisms, such as those we shall study in the next section). But this is a nontrivial task that would keep an application developer busy debugging for a long time. Nevertheless, building reliability directly into the application allows the application to "have its cake and eat it too." That is, application processes can communicate reliably without having to succumb to the transmission rate constraints imposed by TCP's congestion-control mechanism. Many of today's proprietary streaming applications do just this—they run over UDP, but they have built acknowledgments and retransmissions into the application in order to reduce packet loss.

3.3.1 UDP Segment Structure

The UDP segment structure, shown in Figure 3.6, is defined in [RFC 768]. The application data occupies the data field of the UDP datagram. For example, for DNS, the data field contains either a query message or a response message. For a streaming audio application, audio samples fill the data field. The UDP header has only four fields, each consisting of four bytes. As discussed in the previous section, the port numbers allow the destination host to pass the application data to the correct process running on the destination (that is, the demultiplexing function). The checksum is used by the receiving host to check if errors have been intro-

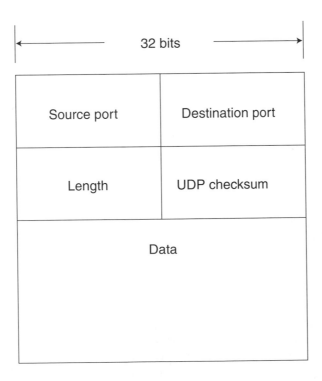

FIGURE 3.6 UDP segment structure

duced into the segment. (Basic principles of error detection are described in Section 5.1.) The UDP checksum is the one's complement of the sum of all the 16-bit words in the segment. (In truth, the checksum is also calculated over a few of the fields in the IP header in addition to the UDP segment. But we ignore this detail in order to see the forest through the trees.) We shall discuss the checksum calculation below.

3.3.2   UDP Checksum

The UDP checksum provides for error detection. UDP at the sender side performs the one's complement of the sum of all the 16-bit words in the segment. This result is put in the checksum field of the UDP segment. Here we give a simple example of the checksum calculation. You can find details about efficient implementation of the calculation in the [RFC 1071]. As an example, suppose that we have the following three 16-bit words:

> 0110011001100110
> 0101010101010101
> 0000111100001111

The sum of first of these 16-bit words is

> 0110011001100110
> 0101010101010101
> ―――――――――――――――――
> 1011101110111011

Adding the third word to the above sum gives

> 1011101110111011
> 0000111100001111
> ―――――――――――――――――
> 1100101011001010

The 1's complement is obtained by converting all the 0s to 1s and converting all the 1s to 0s. Thus the 1's complement of the sum `1100101011001010` is `0011010100110101`, which becomes the checksum. At the receiver, all four 16-bit words are added, including the checksum. If no errors are introduced into the packet, then clearly the sum at the receiver will be 1111111111111111. If one of the bits is a zero, then we know that errors have been introduced into the packet.

You may wonder why UDP provides a checksum in the first place, as many link-layer protocols (including the popular Ethernet protocol) also provide error checking. The reason is that there is no guarantee that all the links between source and destination provide error checking—one of the links may use a protocol that does not provide error checking. Because IP is supposed to run over just about any layer-2 protocol, it is useful for the transport layer to provide error checking as a safety measure. Although UDP provides error checking, it does not do anything to recover from an error. Some implementations of UDP simply discard the damaged segment; others pass the damaged segment to the application with a warning.

That wraps up our discussion of UDP. We will soon see that TCP offers reliable data transfer to its applications as well as other services that UDP doesn't offer. Naturally, TCP is also more complex than UDP. Before discussing TCP, however, it will be useful to step back and first discuss the underlying principles of reliable data transfer, which we do in the subsequent section. We will then explore TCP in Section 3.5, where we will see that TCP has it foundations in these underlying principles.

3.4   PRINCIPLES OF RELIABLE DATA TRANSFER

In this section, we consider the problem of reliable data transfer in a general context. This is appropriate since the problem of implementing reliable data transfer occurs not only at the transport layer, but also at the link layer and the application layer as well. The general problem is thus of central importance to networking. Indeed, if one had to identify a "top-10" list of fundamentally important problems in all of networking, this would be a top candidate to lead that list. In the next section we will examine TCP and show, in particular, that TCP exploits many of the principles that we are about to describe.

Figure 3.7 illustrates the framework for our study of reliable data transfer. The service abstraction provided to the upper layer entities is that of a reliable channel through which data can be transferred. With a reliable channel, no transferred data bits are corrupted (flipped from 0 to 1, or vice versa) or lost, and all are delivered in the order in which they were sent. This is precisely the service model offered by TCP to the Internet applications that invoke it.

It is the responsibility of a **reliable data transfer protocol** to implement this service abstraction. This task is made difficult by the fact that the layer *below* the reliable data transfer protocol may be unreliable. For example, TCP is a reliable data transfer protocol that is implemented on top of an unreliable (IP) end-end network layer. More generally, the layer beneath the two reliably communicating endpoints might consist of a single physical link (for example, as in the case of a

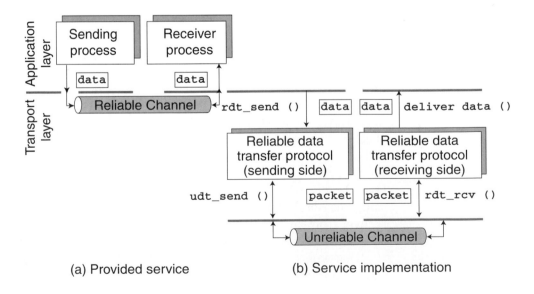

(a) Provided service   (b) Service implementation

FIGURE 3.7   Reliable data transfer: Service model and service implementation

link-level data transfer protocol) or a global internetwork (for example, as in the case of a transport-level protocol). For our purposes, however, we can view this lower layer simply as an unreliable point-to-point channel.

In this section, we will incrementally develop the sender and receiver sides of a reliable data transfer protocol, considering increasingly complex models of the underlying channel. Figure 3.7(b) illustrates the interfaces for our data transfer protocol. The sending side of the data transfer protocol will be invoked from above by a call to `rdt_send()`. It will be passed the data to be delivered to the upper layer at the receiving side. (Here `rdt` stands for "reliable data transfer" protocol and `_send` indicates that the sending side of `rdt` is being called. The first step in developing any protocol is to choose a good name!) On the receiving side, `rdt_rcv()` will be called when a packet arrives from the receiving side of the channel. When the `rdt` protocol wants to deliver data to the upper layer, it will do so by calling `deliver_data()`. In the following we use the terminology "packet" rather than "segment" for the protocol data unit. Because the theory developed in this section applies to computer networks in general and not just to the Internet transport layer, the generic term "packet" is perhaps more appropriate here.

In this section we consider only the case of **unidirectional** data transfer, that is, data transfer from the sending to receiving side. The case of reliable **bidirectional** (that is, full duplex) data transfer is conceptually no more difficult but considerably more tedious to explain. Although we consider only unidirectional data transfer, it is important to note that the sending and receiving sides of our protocol will nonetheless need to transmit packets in *both* directions, as indicated in Figure 3.7. We will see shortly that, in addition to exchanging packets containing the data to be transferred, the sending and receiving sides of `rdt` will also need to exchange control packets back and forth. Both the send and receive sides of `rdt` send packets to the other side by a call to `udt_send()` (where `udt` stands for unreliable data transfer).

3.4.1   Building a Reliable Data Transfer Protocol

We now step through a series of protocols, each one becoming more complex, arriving at a flawless reliable data transfer protocol.

Reliable data transfer over a perfectly reliable channel: `rdt1.0`.   We first consider the simplest case in which the underlying channel is completely reliable. The protocol itself, which we will call `rdt1.0`, is trivial. The **finite state machine (FSM)** definitions for the `rdt1.0` sender and receiver are shown in Figure 3.8. The sender and receiver FSMs in Figure 3.8 each have just one state. The arrows

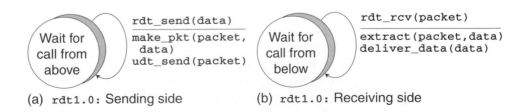

FIGURE 3.8   `rdt1.0`—A protocol for a completely reliable channel

in the FSM description indicate the transition of the protocol from one state to another. (Since each FSM in Figure 3.8 has just one state, a transition is necessarily from the one state back to itself; we'll see more complicated state diagrams shortly.) The event causing the transition is shown above the horizontal line labeling the transition, and the action(s) taken when the event occurs are shown below the horizontal line.

The sending side of `rdt` simply accepts data from the upper layer via the `rdt_send(data)` event, puts the data into a packet (via the action `make_pkt(packet,data)`) and sends the packet into the channel. In practice, the `rdt_send(data)` event would result from a procedure call (for example, to `rdt_send()`) by the upper-layer application.

On the receiving side, `rdt` receives a packet from the underlying channel via the `rdt_rcv(packet)` event, removes the data from the packet (via the action `extract(packet,data)`) and passes the data up to the upper layer. In practice, the `rdt_rcv(packet)` event would result from a procedure call (for example, to `rdt_rcv()`) from the lower-layer protocol.

In this simple protocol, there is no difference between a unit of data and a packet. Also, all packet flow is from the sender to receiver; with a perfectly reliable channel there is no need for the receiver side to provide any feedback to the sender since nothing can go wrong!

Reliable data transfer over a channel with bit errors: `rdt2.0`.   A more realistic model of the underlying channel is one in which bits in a packet may be corrupted. Such bit errors typically occur in the physical components of a network as a packet is transmitted, propagates, or is buffered. We'll continue to assume for the moment that all transmitted packets are received (although their bits may be corrupted) in the order in which they were sent.

Before developing a protocol for reliably communicating over such a channel, first consider how people might deal with such a situation. Consider how you yourself might dictate a long message over the phone. In a typical scenario, the message taker might say "OK" after each sentence has been heard, understood, and recorded. If the message taker hears a garbled sentence, you're asked to repeat the garbled sentence. This message dictation protocol uses both **positive acknowledgments** ("OK") and **negative acknowledgments** ("Please repeat that."). These control messages allow the receiver to let the sender know what has been received correctly, and what has been received in error and thus requires repeating. In a computer network setting, reliable data transfer protocols based on such retransmission are known ARQ (Automatic Repeat reQuest) protocols.

Fundamentally, two additional protocol capabilities are required in ARQ protocols to handle the presence of bit errors:

■ *Error detection.* First, a mechanism is needed to allow the receiver to detect when bit errors have occurred. Recall from the previous section of this chapter that the UDP transport protocol uses the Internet checksum field for exactly this purpose. In Chapter 5 we'll examine error detection and correction techniques in greater detail; these techniques allow the receiver to detect and possibly correct packet bit errors. For now, we need only know that these techniques require that extra bits (beyond the bits of original data to be transferred) be sent from the sender to receiver; these bits will be gathered into the packet checksum field of the `rdt2.0` data packet.

- *Receiver feedback.* Since the sender and receiver are typically executing on different end systems, possibly separated by thousands of miles, the only way for the sender to learn of the receiver's view of the world (in this case, whether or not a packet was received correctly) is for the receiver to provide explicit feedback to the sender. The positive (ACK) and negative (NAK) acknowledgment replies in the message dictation scenario are examples of such feedback. Our `rdt2.0` protocol will similarly send ACK and NAK packets back from the receiver to the sender. In principle, these packets need only be one bit long; for example, a 0 value could indicate a NAK and a value of 1 could indicate an ACK.

Figure 3.9 shows the FSM representation of `rdt2.0`, a data transfer protocol employing error detection, positive acknowledgments, and negative acknowledgments.

The send side of `rdt2.0` has two states. In one state, the send-side protocol is waiting for data to be passed down from the upper layer. In the other state, the sender protocol is waiting for an ACK or a NAK packet from the receiver. If an

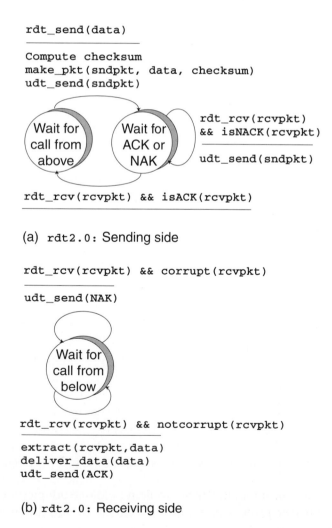

(a) `rdt2.0`: Sending side

(b) `rdt2.0`: Receiving side

FIGURE 3.9 `rdt2.0`—A protocol for a channel with bit errors

ACK packet is received (the notation `rdt_rcv(rcvpkt) && isACK(rcvpkt)` in Figure 3.9 corresponds to this event), the sender knows the most recently transmitted packet has been received correctly and thus the protocol returns to the state of waiting for data from the upper layer. If a NAK is received, the protocol retransmits the last packet and waits for an ACK or NAK to be returned by the receiver in response to the retransmitted data packet. It is important to note that when the receiver is in the wait-for-ACK-or-NAK state, it *cannot* get more data from the upper layer; that will only happen after the sender receives an ACK and leaves this state. Thus, the sender will not send a new piece of data until it is sure that the receiver has correctly received the current packet. Because of this behavior, protocols such as `rdt2.0` are known as **stop-and-wait** protocols.

The receiver-side FSM for `rdt2.0` still has a single state. On packet arrival, the receiver replies with either an ACK or a NAK, depending on whether or not the received packet is corrupted. In Figure 3.9, the notation `rdt_rcv(rcvpkt) && corrupt(rcvpkt)` corresponds to the event where a packet is received and is found to be in error.

Protocol `rdt2.0` may look as if it works but, unfortunately, it has a fatal flaw. In particular, we haven't accounted for the possibility that the ACK or NAK packet could be corrupted! (Before proceeding on, you should think about how this problem may be fixed.) Unfortunately, our slight oversight is not as innocuous as it may seem. Minimally, we will need to add checksum bits to ACK/NAK packets in order to detect such errors. The more difficult question is how the protocol should recover from errors in ACK or NAK packets. The difficulty here is that if an ACK or NAK is corrupted, the sender has no way of knowing whether or not the receiver has correctly received the last piece of transmitted data.

Consider three possibilities for handling corrupted ACKs or NAKs:

- For the first possibility, consider what a human might do in the message dictation scenario. If the speaker didn't understand the "OK" or "Please repeat that" reply from the receiver, the speaker would probably ask "What did you say?" (thus introducing a new type of sender-to-receiver packet to our protocol). The speaker would then repeat the reply. But what if the speaker's "What did you say" is corrupted? The receiver, having no idea whether the garbled sentence was part of the dictation or a request to repeat the last reply, would probably then respond with "What did *you* say?" And then, of course, that response might be garbled. Clearly, we're heading down a difficult path.

- A second alternative is to add enough checksum bits to allow the sender to not only detect, but to recover from, bit errors. This solves the immediate problem for a channel that can corrupt packets but not lose them.

- A third approach is for the sender to simply resend the current data packet when it receives a garbled ACK or NAK packet. This method, however, introduces **duplicate packets** into the sender-to-receiver channel. The fundamental difficulty with duplicate packets is that the receiver doesn't know whether the ACK or NAK it last sent was received correctly at the sender. Thus, it cannot know a priori whether an arriving packet contains new data or is a retransmission!

A simple solution to this new problem (and one adopted in almost all existing data transfer protocols including TCP) is to add a new field to the data packet and have the sender number its data packets by putting a **sequence number** into this field. The receiver then need only check this sequence number to determine whether or not the received packet is a retransmission. For this simple case of a stop-and-wait protocol, a 1-bit sequence number will suffice, since it will allow the receiver to know whether the sender is resending the previously transmitted packet (the sequence number of the received packet has the same sequence number as the most recently received packet) or a new packet (the sequence number changes, moving "forward" in modulo-2 arithmetic). Since we are currently assuming a channel that does not lose packets, ACK and NAK packets do not themselves need to indicate the sequence number of the packet they are acknowledging. The sender knows that a received ACK or NAK packet (whether garbled or not) was generated in response to its most recently transmitted data packet.

Figures 3.10 and 3.11 show the FSM description for `rdt2.1`, our fixed version of `rdt2.0`. The `rdt2.1` sender and receiver FSM's each now have twice as many states as before. This is because the protocol state must now reflect whether the packet currently being sent (by the sender) or expected (at the receiver) should have a sequence number of 0 or 1. Note that the actions in those states where a 0-numbered packet is being sent or expected are mirror images of those where

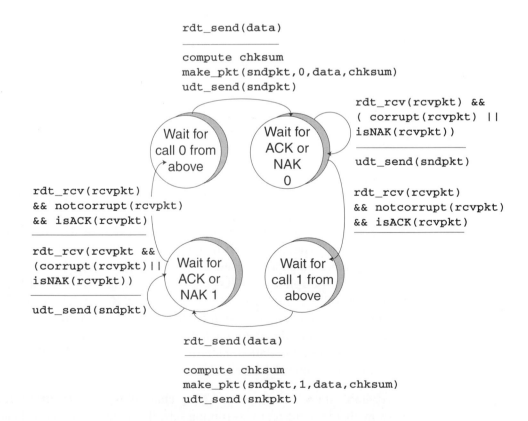

FIGURE 3.10 `rdt2.1` sender

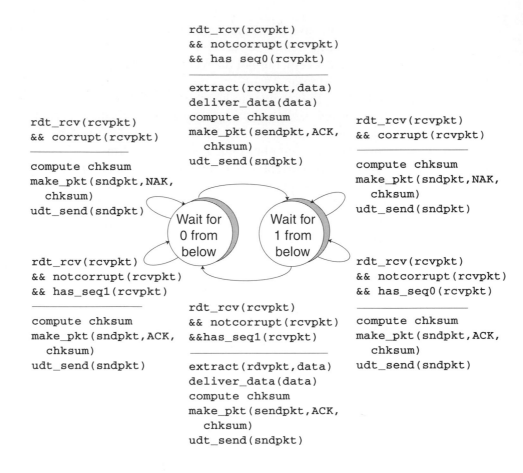

FIGURE 3.11 `rdt2.1` receiver

a 1-numbered packet is being sent or expected; the only differences have to do with the handling of the sequence number.

Protocol `rdt2.1` uses both positive and negative acknowledgments from the receiver to the sender. A negative acknowledgment is sent whenever a corrupted packet or an out-of-order packet is received. We can accomplish the same effect as a NAK if, instead of sending a NAK, we instead send an ACK for the last correctly received packet. A sender that receives two ACKs for the same packet (that is, receives **duplicate ACKs**) knows that the receiver did not correctly receive the packet following the packet that is being ACKed twice. Many TCP implementations use the receipt of so-called "triple duplicate ACKs" (three ACK packets all acknowledging the same packet) to trigger a retransmission at the sender. Our NAK-free reliable data transfer protocol for a channel with bit errors is `rdt2.2`, shown in Figures 3.12 and 3.13.

Reliable data transfer over a lossy channel with bit errors: `rdt3.0`. Suppose now that in addition to corrupting bits, the underlying channel can *lose* packets as well, a not-uncommon event in today's computer networks (including the Internet).

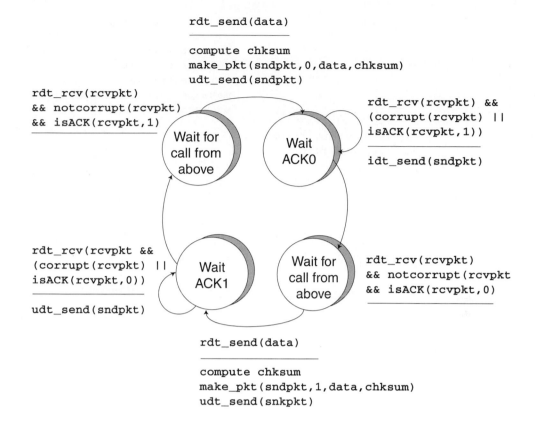

FIGURE 3.12   `rdt2.2` sender

Two additional concerns must now be addressed by the protocol: how to detect packet loss and what to do when packet loss occurs. The use of checksumming, sequence numbers, ACK packets, and retransmissions—the techniques already developed in `rdt2.2`—will allow us to answer the latter concern. Handling the first concern will require adding a new protocol mechanism.

There are many possible approaches towards dealing with packet loss (several more of which are explored in the exercises at the end of the chapter). Here, we'll put the burden of detecting and recovering from lost packets on the sender. Suppose that the sender transmits a data packet and either that packet, or the receiver's ACK of that packet, gets lost. In either case, no reply is forthcoming at the sender from the receiver. If the sender is willing to wait long enough so that it is *certain* that a packet has been lost, it can simply retransmit the data packet. You should convince yourself that this protocol does indeed work.

But how long must the sender wait to be certain that something has been lost? The sender must clearly wait at least as long as a round-trip delay between the sender and receiver (which may include buffering at intermediate routers or gateways) plus whatever amount of time is needed to process a packet at the receiver. In many networks, this worst-case maximum delay is very difficult to even estimate, much less know with certainty. Moreover, the protocol should ideally

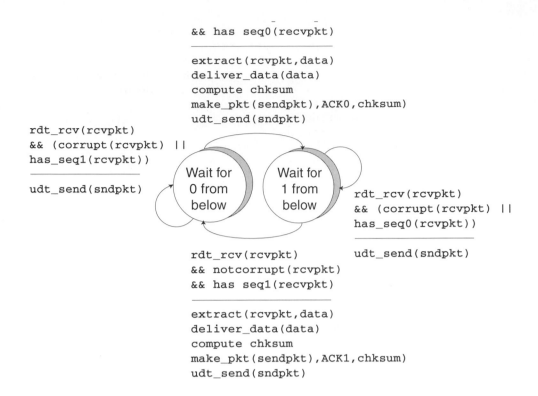

```
                                    && has seq0(recvpkt)
                                    ─────────────────────────
                                    extract(rcvpkt,data)
                                    deliver_data(data)
                                    compute chksum
                                    make_pkt(sendpkt),ACK0,chksum)
                                    udt_send(sndpkt)
rdt_rcv(rcvpkt)
&& (corrupt(rcvpkt) ||
has_seq1(rcvpkt))
─────────────────────
udt_send(sndpkt)        Wait for      Wait for
                        0 from        1 from       rdt_rcv(rcvpkt)
                        below         below        && (corrupt(rcvpkt) ||
                                                   has_seq0(rcvpkt))
                                                   ─────────────────────
                    rdt_rcv(rcvpkt)                udt_send(sndpkt)
                    && notcorrupt(rcvpkt)
                    && has seq1(recvpkt)
                    ─────────────────────
                    extract(rcvpkt,data)
                    deliver_data(data)
                    compute chksum
                    make_pkt(sendpkt),ACK1,chksum)
                    udt_send(sndpkt)
```

FIGURE 3.13 `rdt2.2` receiver

recover from packet loss as soon as possible; waiting for a worst-case delay could mean a long wait until error recovery is initiated. The approach thus adopted in practice is for the sender to "judiciously" choose a time value such that packet loss is likely, although not guaranteed, to have happened. If an ACK is not received within this time, the packet is retransmitted. Note that if a packet experiences a particularly large delay, the sender may retransmit the packet even though neither the data packet nor its ACK have been lost. This introduces the possibility of **duplicate data packets** in the sender-to-receiver channel. Happily, protocol `rdt2.2` already has enough functionality (that is, sequence numbers) to handle the case of duplicate packets.

From the sender's viewpoint, retransmission is a panacea. The sender does not know whether a data packet was lost, an ACK was lost, or if the packet or ACK was simply overly delayed. In all cases, the action is the same: retransmit. In order to implement a time-based retransmission mechanism, a **countdown timer** will be needed that can interrupt the sender after a given amount of timer has expired. The sender will thus need to be able to (1) start the timer each time a packet (either a first-time packet, or a retransmission) is sent, (2) respond to a timer interrupt (taking appropriate actions), and (3) stop the timer.

The existence of sender-generated duplicate packets and packet (data, ACK) loss also complicates the sender's processing of any ACK packet it receives. If an

ACK is received, how is the sender to know if it was sent by the receiver in response to its (sender's) own most recently transmitted packet, or is a delayed ACK sent in response to an earlier transmission of a different data packet? The solution to this dilemma is to augment the ACK packet with an **acknowledgment field.** When the receiver generates an ACK, it will copy the sequence number of the data packet being acknowledged into this acknowledgment field. By examining the contents of the acknowledgment field, the sender can determine the sequence number of the packet being positively acknowledged.

Figure 3.14 shows the sender FSM for rdt3.0, a protocol that reliably transfers data over a channel that can corrupt or lose packets. Figure 3.15 shows how the protocol operates with no lost or delayed packets, and how it handles lost data packets. In Figure 3.15, time moves forward from the top of the diagram towards the bottom of the diagram; note that a receive time for a packet is necessarily later than the send time for a packet as a result of transmission and propagation delays. In Figures 3.15b–d, the send-side brackets indicate the times at which a timer is

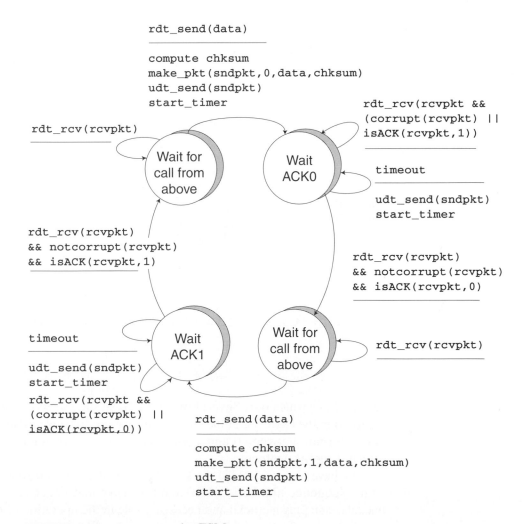

FIGURE 3.14 rdt3.0 sender FSM

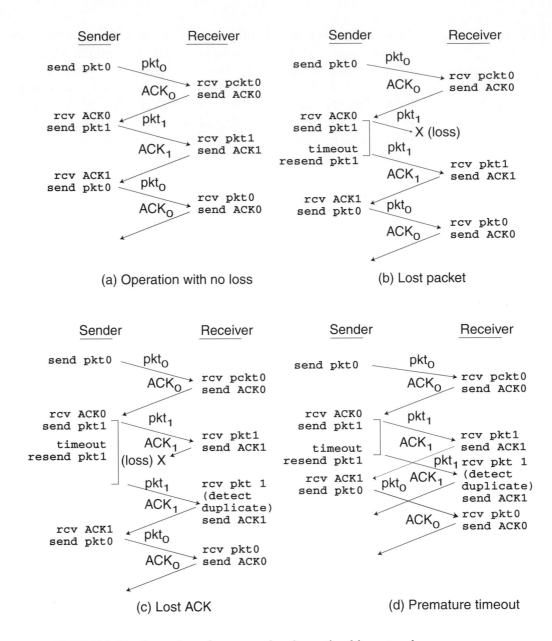

FIGURE 3.15 Operation of `rdt3.0`, the alternating bit protocol

set and later times out. Several of the more subtle aspects of this protocol are explored in the exercises at the end of this chapter. Because packet sequence numbers alternate between 0 and 1, protocol `rdt3.0` is sometimes known as the **alternating bit protocol.**

We have now assembled the key elements of a data transfer protocol. Checksums, sequence numbers, timers, and positive and negative acknowledgment packets each play a crucial and necessary role in the operation of the protocol. We now have a working reliable data transfer protocol!

3.4.2 Pipelined Reliable Data Transfer Protocols

Protocol `rdt3.0` is a functionally correct protocol, but it is unlikely that anyone would be happy with its performance, particularly in today's high-speed networks. At the heart of `rdt3.0`'s performance problem is the fact that it is a stop-and-wait protocol.

To appreciate the performance impact of this stop-and-wait behavior, consider an idealized case of two end hosts, one located on the West Coast of the United States and the other located on the East Coast. The speed-of-light propagation delay, T_{prop}, between these two end systems is approximately 15 milliseconds. Suppose that they are connected by a channel with a capacity, C, of 1 Gigabit ($10**9$ bits) per second. With a packet size, SP, of 1K bytes per packet including both header fields and data, the time needed to actually transmit the packet into the 1Gbps link is

$$T_{trans} = SP/C = (8 \text{ Kbits/packet})/(10^9 \text{ bits/sec}) = 8 \text{ microseconds}$$

With our stop-and-wait protocol, if the sender begins sending the packet at $t = 0$, then at $t = 8$ microseconds, the last bit enters the channel at the sender side. The packet then makes its 15-msec cross-country journey, as depicted in Figure 3.16a, with the last bit of the packet emerging at the receiver at $t = 15.008$ msec. Assuming for simplicity that ACK packets are the same size as data packets and that the receiver can begin sending an ACK packet as soon as the last bit of a data packet is received, the last bit of the ACK packet emerges back at the receiver at $t = 30.016$ msec. Thus, in 30.016 msec, the sender was only busy (sending or receiving) for 0.016 msec. If we define the **utilization** of the sender (or the channel) as the fraction of time the sender is actually busy sending bits into the channel, we have a rather dismal sender utilization, U_{sender}, of

$$U_{sender} = (.008/30.016) = 0.00015$$

That is, the sender was busy only 1.5 hundredths of one percent of the time. Viewed another way, the sender was only able to send 1 kilobytes in 30.016 milliseconds, an effective throughput of only 33 kilobytes per second—even though a 1 gigabit per second link was available! Imagine the unhappy network manager

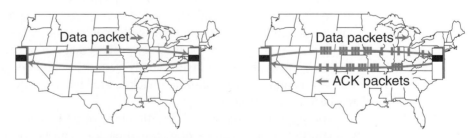

(a) A stop-and-wait protocol in operation   (b) A pipelined protocol in operation

FIGURE 3.16 Stop-and-wait versus pipelined protocol

who just paid a fortune for a gigabit capacity link but manages to get a throughput of only 33 kilobytes! This is a graphic example of how network protocols can limit the capabilities provided by the underlying network hardware. Also, we have neglected lower-layer protocol-processing times at the sender and receiver, as well as the processing and queuing delays that would occur at any intermediate routers between the sender and receiver. Including these effects would only serve to further increase the delay and further accentuate the poor performance.

The solution to this particular performance problem is a simple one: rather than operate in a stop-and-wait manner, the sender is allowed to send multiple packets without waiting for acknowledgments, as shown in Figure 3.16(b). Since the many in-transit sender-to-receiver packets can be visualized as filling a pipeline, this technique is known as **pipelining.** Pipelining has several consequences for reliable data transfer protocols:

- The range of sequence numbers must be increased, since each in-transit packet (not counting retransmissions) must have a unique sequence number and there may be multiple, in-transit, unacknowledged packets.
- The sender and receiver sides of the protocols may have to buffer more than one packet. Minimally, the sender will have to buffer packets that have been transmitted, but not yet acknowledged. Buffering of correctly received packets may also be needed at the receiver, as discussed below.

The range of sequence numbers needed and the buffering requirements will depend on the manner in which a data transfer protocol responds to lost, corrupted, and overly delayed packets. Two basic approaches towards pipelined error recovery can be identified: **Go-Back-N** and **selective repeat.**

3.4.3 Go-Back-N (GBN)

In a Go-Back-N (GBN) protocol, the sender is allowed to transmit multiple packets (when available) without waiting for an acknowledgment, but is constrained to have no more than some maximum allowable number, N, of unacknowledged packets in the pipeline. Figure 3.17 shows the sender's view of the range of sequence numbers in a GBN protocol. If we define base to be the sequence number of the oldest unacknowledged packet and nextseqnum to be the smallest unused sequence number (that is, the sequence number of the next packet to be sent), then four intervals in the range of sequence numbers can be identified. Sequence numbers in the interval [0,base−1] correspond to packets that have already been transmitted and acknowledged. The interval [base,nextseqnum−1] corresponds to packets that have been sent but not yet acknowledged. Sequence numbers in the interval [nextseqnum,base+N−1] can be used for packets that can be sent immediately, should data arrive from the upper layer. Finally, sequence numbers greater than or equal to base+N cannot be used until an unacknowledged packet currently in the pipeline has been acknowledged.

As suggested by Figure 3.17, the range of permissible sequence numbers for transmitted but not-yet-acknowledged packets can be viewed as a "window" of size N over the range of sequence numbers. As the protocol operates, this window slides forward over the sequence number space. For this reason, N is often referred to as the **window size** and the GBN protocol itself as a **sliding window protocol.** You might be wondering why even limit the number of outstanding,

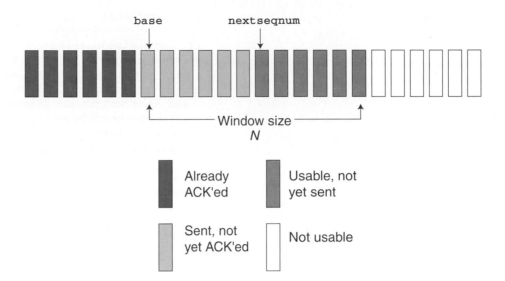

FIGURE 3.17   Sender's view of sequence numbers in Go-Back-N

unacknowledged packets to a value of N in the first place. Why not allow an unlimited number of such packets? We will see in Section 3.5 that flow control is one reason to impose a limit on the sender. We'll examine another reason to do so in Section 3.7, when we study TCP congestion control.

In practice, a packet's sequence number is carried in a fixed-length field in the packet header. If k is the number of bits in the packet sequence number field, the range of sequence numbers is thus $[0,2^k - 1]$. With a finite range of sequence numbers, all arithmetic involving sequence numbers must then be done using modulo 2^k arithmetic. (That is, the sequence number space can be thought of as a ring of size 2^k, where sequence number $2^k - 1$ is immediately followed by sequence number 0.) Recall that `rtd3.0` had a 1-bit sequence number and a range of sequence numbers of [0,1]. Several of the problems at the end of this chapter explore consequences of a finite range of sequence numbers. We will see in Section 3.5 that TCP has a 32-bit sequence-number field, where TCP sequence numbers count bytes in the byte stream rather than packets.

Figures 3.18 and 3.19 give an extended-FSM description of the sender and receiver sides of an ACK-based, NAK-free, GBN protocol. We refer to this FSM description as an **extended FSM** since we have added variables (similar to programming language variables) for `base` and `nextseqnum`, and also added operations on these variables and conditional actions involving these variables. Note that the extended FSM specification is now beginning to look somewhat like a programming language specification. [Bochman 84] provides an excellent survey of additional extensions to FSM techniques as well as other programming language-based techniques for specifying protocols.

The GBN sender must respond to three types of events:

- *Invocation from above.* When `rdt_send()` is called from above, the sender first checks to see if the window is full, that is, whether there are N outstanding, unacknowledged packets. If the window is not full, a packet is created

```
rdt_send(data)
_____

if(nextseqnum<base+N){
compute chksum
  make_pkt(sndpk(nextseqnum)),
    nextseqnum,data,chksum)
  udt_send(sndpkt(nexseqnum))
  if(base==nextseqnum)
    start_timer
  nextseqnum=nextseqnum+1
  }
else
  refuse_data(data)
```

```
rdt_rcv(rcv_pkt)
&& notcorrupt(rcvpkt)
_____

base=getacknum(rcvpkt)+1
if(base==nextseqnum)
  stop_timer
else
  start_timer
```

```
timeout
_____

start_timer
udt_send(sndpkt(base))
udt_send(sndpkt(base+1)
..
udt_send(sndpkt
  (nextseqnum-1))
```

WAIT

FIGURE 3.18   Extended FSM description of GBN sender

and sent, and variables are appropriately updated. If the window is full, the sender simply returns the data back to the upper layer, an implicit indication that the window is full. The upper layer would presumably then have to try again later. In a real implementation, the sender would more likely have either buffered (but not immediately sent) this data, or would have a synchronization mechanism (for example, a semaphore or a flag) that would allow the upper layer to call `rdt_send()` only when the window is not full.

■ *Receipt of an ACK.* In our GBN protocol, an acknowledgment for packet with sequence number *n* will be taken to be a **cumulative acknowledgment,** indicating that all packets with a sequence number up to and including *n* have

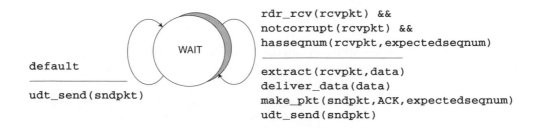

```
default
_____

udt_send(sndpkt)
```

WAIT

```
rdr_rcv(rcvpkt) &&
notcorrupt(rcvpkt) &&
hasseqnum(rcvpkt,expectedseqnum)
_____

extract(rcvpkt,data)
deliver_data(data)
make_pkt(sndpkt,ACK,expectedseqnum)
udt_send(sndpkt)
```

FIGURE 3.19   Extended FSM description of GBN receiver

been correctly received at the receiver. We'll come back to this issue shortly when we examine the receiver side of GBN.

▪ *A timeout event.* The protocol's name, "Go-Back-N," is derived from the sender's behavior in the presence of lost or overly delayed packets. As in the stop-and-wait protocol, a timer will again be used to recover from lost data or acknowledgment packets. If a timeout occurs, the sender resends *all* packets that have been previously sent but that have not yet been acknowledged. Our sender in Figure 3.18 uses only a single timer, which can be thought of as a timer for the oldest transmitted-but-not-yet-acknowledged packet. If an ACK is received but there are still additional transmitted-but-yet-to-be-acknowledged packets, the timer is restarted. If there are no outstanding unacknowledged packets, the timer is stopped.

The receiver's actions in GBN are also simple. If a packet with sequence number n is received correctly and is in-order (that is, the data last delivered to the upper layer came from a packet with sequence number $n - 1$), the receiver sends an ACK for packet n and delivers the data portion of the packet to the upper layer. In all other cases, the receiver discards the packet and resends an ACK for the most recently received in-order packet. Note that since packets are delivered one-at-a-time to the upper layer, if packet k has been received and delivered, then all packets with a sequence number lower than k have also been delivered. Thus, the use of cumulative acknowledgments is a natural choice for GBN.

In our GBN protocol, the receiver discards out-of-order packets. While it may seem silly and wasteful to discard a correctly received (but out-of-order) packet, there is some justification for doing so. Recall that the receiver must deliver data, in-order, to the upper layer. Suppose now that packet n is expected, but packet $n + 1$ arrives. Since data must be delivered in order, the receiver *could* buffer (save) packet $n + 1$ and then deliver this packet to the upper layer after it had later received and delivered packet n. However, if packet n is lost, both it and packet $n + 1$ will eventually be retransmitted as a result of the GBN retransmission rule at the sender. Thus, the receiver can simply discard packet $n + 1$. The advantage of this approach is the simplicity of receiver buffering—the receiver need not buffer *any* out-of-order packets. Thus, while the sender must maintain the upper and lower bounds of its window and the position of `nextseqnum` within this window, the only piece of information the receiver need maintain is the sequence number of the next in-order packet. This value is held in the variable `expectedseqnum`, shown in the receiver FSM in Figure 3.20. Of course, the disadvantage of throwing away a correctly received packet is that the subsequent retransmission of that packet might be lost or garbled and thus even more retransmissions would be required.

Figure 3.20 shows the operation of the GBN protocol for the case of a window size of four packets. Because of this window size limitation, the sender sends packets 0 through 3 but then must wait for one or more of these packets to be acknowledged before proceeding. As each successive ACK (for example, ACK0 and ACK1) is received, the window slides forwards and the sender can transmit one new packet (pkt4 and pkt5, respectively). On the receiver side, packet 2 is lost and thus packets 3, 4, and 5 are found to be out-of-order and are discarded.

Before closing our discussion of GBN, it is worth noting that an implementation of this protocol in a protocol stack would likely be structured similar to that

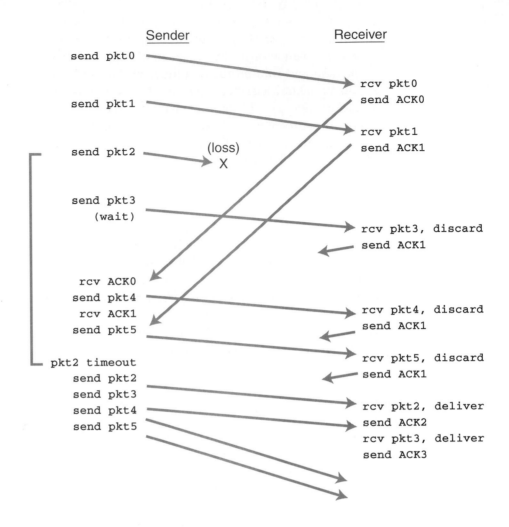

FIGURE 3.20 Go-Back-N in operation

of the extended FSM in Figure 3.18. The implementation would also likely be in the form of various procedures that implement the actions to be taken in response to the various events that can occur. In such **event-based programming,** the various procedures are called (invoked) either by other procedures in the protocol stack, or as the result of an interrupt. In the sender, these events would be (1) a call from the upper-layer entity to invoke `rdt_send()`, (2) a timer interrupt, and (3) a call from the lower layer to invoke `rdt_rcv()` when a packet arrives. The programming exercises at the end of this chapter will give you a chance to actually implement these routines in a simulated, but realistic, network setting.

We note here that the GBN protocol incorporates almost all of the techniques that we will encounter when we study the reliable data transfer components of TCP in Section 3.5. These techniques include the use of sequence numbers, cumulative acknowledgments, checksums, and a time-out/retransmit operation. Indeed, TCP is often referred to as a GBN-style of protocol. There are, however, some differences. Many TCP implementations will buffer correctly received but out-of-order segments [Stevens 1994]. A proposed modification to TCP, the so-called selective acknowledgment [RFC 2581], will also allow a TCP receiver to selectively acknowledge a single out-of-order packet rather than cumulatively acknowledge the last correctly received packet. The notion of a selective acknowledgment is at the heart of the second broad class of pipelined protocols: the so-called selective repeat protocols.

3.4.4   Selective Repeat (SR)

The GBN protocol allows the sender to potentially "fill the pipeline" in Figure 3.16 with packets, thus avoiding the channel utilization problems we noted with stop-and-wait protocols. There are, however, scenarios in which GBN itself will suffer from performance problems. In particular, when the window size and bandwidth-delay product are both large, many packets can be in the pipeline. A single packet error can thus cause GBN to retransmit a large number of packets, many of which may be unnecessary. As the probability of channel errors increases, the pipeline can become filled with these unnecessary retransmissions. Imagine in our message dictation scenario, if every time a word was garbled, the surrounding 1,000 words (for example, a window size of 1,000 words) had to be repeated. The dictation would be slowed by all of the reiterated words.

As the name suggests, Selective Repeat (SR) protocols avoid unnecessary retransmissions by having the sender retransmit only those packets that it suspects were received in error (that is, were lost or corrupted) at the receiver. This individual, as-needed, retransmission will require that the receiver *individually* acknowledge correctly received packets. A window size of *N* will again be used to limit the number of outstanding, unacknowledged packets in the pipeline. However, unlike GBN, the sender will have already received ACKs for some of the packets in the window. Figure 3.21 shows the SR sender's view of the sequence number space. Figure 3.22 details the various actions taken by the SR sender.

The SR receiver will acknowledge a correctly received packet whether or not it is in-order. Out-of-order packets are buffered until any missing packets (that is, packets with lower sequence numbers) are received, at which point a batch of packets can be delivered in-order to the upper layer. Figure 3.23 itemizes the various actions taken by the SR receiver. Figure 3.24 shows an example of SR operation in the presence of lost packets. Note that in Figure 3.24, the receiver initially buffers packets 3 and 4, and delivers them together with packet 2 to the upper layer when packet 2 is finally received.

It is important to note that in step 2 in Figure 3.23, the receiver re-acknowledges (rather than ignores) already received packets with certain sequence numbers *below* the current window base. You should convince yourself that this re-acknowledgment is indeed needed. Given the sender and receiver sequence-number spaces in Figure 3.21 for example, if there is no ACK for packet `sendbase` propagating from the receiver to the sender, the sender will eventually retransmit packet `sendbase`, even though it is clear (to us, not the sender!) that the receiver has already received that packet. If the receiver were not to acknowledge this packet, the sender's window would never move forward! This example illustrates an important aspect of SR protocols (and many other protocols as well). The sender and receiver will not always have an identical view of what has been

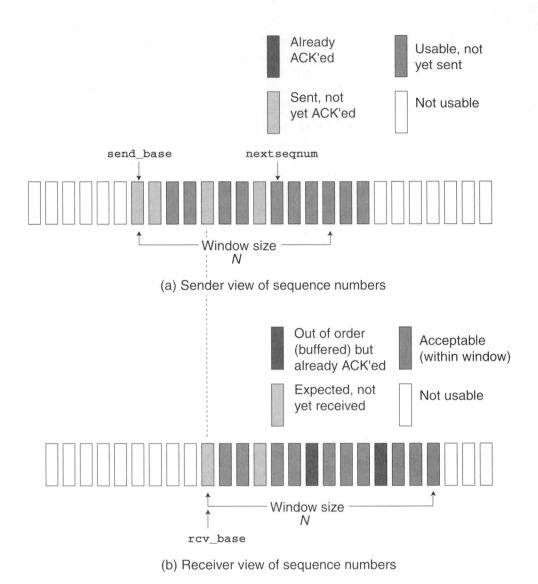

FIGURE 3.21   Selective Repeat (SR) sender and receiver views of sequence-number space

received correctly and what has not. For SR protocols, this means that the sender and receiver windows will not always coincide.

The lack of synchronization between sender and receiver windows has important consequences when we are faced with the reality of a finite range of sequence numbers. Consider what could happen, for example, with a finite range of four packet sequence numbers, 0, 1, 2, 3 and a window size of three. Suppose packets 0 through 2 are transmitted and correctly received and acknowledged at the receiver. At this point, the receiver's window is over the fourth, fifth, and sixth packets, which have sequence numbers 3, 0, and 1, respectively. Now consider two scenarios. In the first scenario, shown in Figure 3.25a, the ACKs for the first three packets are lost and the sender retransmits these packets. The receiver thus next receives a packet with sequence number 0—a copy of the first packet sent.

1. *Data received from above.* When data is received from above, the SR sender checks the next available sequence number for the packet. If the sequence number is within the sender's window, the data is packetized and sent; otherwise it is either buffered or returned to the upper layer for later transmission, as in GBN.

2. *Timeout.* Timers are again used to protect against lost packets. However, each packet must now have its own logical timer, since only a single packet will be transmitted on timeout. A single hardware timer can be used to mimic the operation of multiple logical timers.

3. *ACK received.* If an ACK is received, the SR sender marks that packet as having been received, provided it is in the window. If the packet's sequence number is equal to `sendbase`, the window base is moved forward to the unacknowledged packet with the smallest sequence number. If the window moves and there are untransmitted packets with sequence numbers that now fall within the window, these packets are transmitted.

FIGURE 3.22 Selective Repeat (SR) sender events and actions

In the second scenario, shown in Figure 3.25b, the ACKs for the first three packets are all delivered correctly. The sender thus moves its window forward and sends the fourth, fifth, and sixth packets, with sequence numbers 3, 0, 1, respectively. The packet with sequence number 3 is lost, but the packet with sequence number 0 arrives—a packet containing *new* data.

Now consider the receiver's viewpoint in Figure 3.25, which has a figurative curtain between the sender and the receiver, since the receiver cannot "see" the actions taken by the sender. All the receiver observes is the sequence of messages

1. *Packet with sequence number in* [`rcvbase`, `rcvbase+N`−1] *is correctly received.* In this case, the received packet falls within the receiver's window and a selective ACK packet is returned to the sender. If the packet was not previously received, it is buffered. If this packet has a sequence number equal to the base of the receive window (`rcvbase` in Figure 3.21), then this packet, and any previously buffered and consecutively numbered (beginning with `rcvbase`) packets are delivered to the upper layer. The receive window is then moved forward by the number of packets delivered to the upper layer. As an example, consider Figure 3.24. When a packet with a sequence number of `rcvbase=2` is received, it and packets `rcvbase+1` and `rcvbase+2` can be delivered to the upper layer.

2. *Packet with sequence number in* [`rcvbase-N`, `rcvbase`−1] *is received.* In this case, an ACK must be generated, even though this is a packet that the receiver has previously acknowledged.

3. *Otherwise.* Ignore the packet.

FIGURE 3.23 Selective Repeat (SR) receiver events and actions

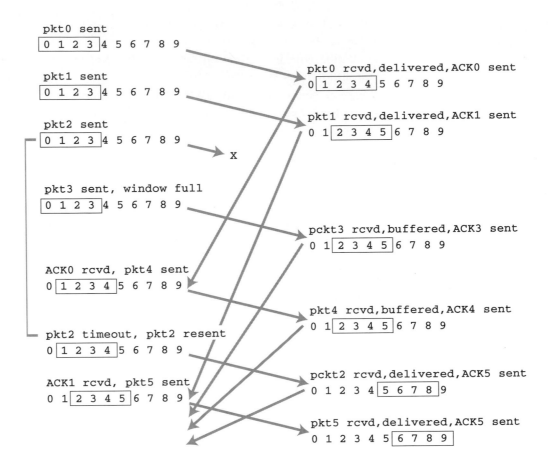

FIGURE 3.24 SR operation

it receives from the channel and sends into the channel. As far as it is concerned, the two scenarios in Figure 3.25 are *identical*. There is no way of distinguishing the retransmission of the first packet from an original transmission of the fifth packet. Clearly, a window size that is 1 less than the size of the sequence number space won't work. But how small must the window size be? A problem at the end of the chapter asks you to show that the window size must be less than or equal to half the size of the sequence-number space.

Let us conclude our discussion of reliable data transfer protocols by considering one remaining assumption in our underlying channel model. Recall that we have assumed that packets cannot be reordered within the channel between the sender and receiver. This is generally a reasonable assumption when the sender and receiver are connected by a single physical wire. However, when the "channel" connecting the two is a network, packet reordering can occur. One manifestation of packet ordering is that old copies of a packet with a sequence or acknowledgment number of x can appear, even though neither the sender's nor the receiver's window contains x. With packet reordering, the channel can be thought of as essentially buffering packets and spontaneously emitting these packets at

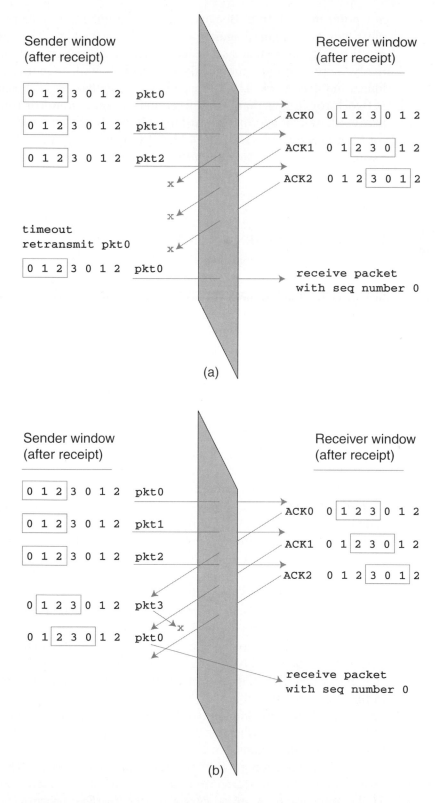

FIGURE 3.25   SR receiver dilemma with too-large windows: A new packet or a retransmission?

any point in the future. Because sequence numbers may be reused, some care must be taken to guard against such duplicate packets. The approach taken in practice is to ensure that a sequence number is not reused until the sender is relatively "sure" than any previously sent packets with sequence number x are no longer in the network. This is done by assuming that a packet cannot "live" in the network for longer than some fixed maximum amount of time. A maximum packet lifetime of approximately three minutes is assumed in the TCP extensions for high-speed networks [RFC 1323]. [Sunshine 1978] describes a method for using sequence numbers such that reordering problems can be completely avoided.

3.5 CONNECTION-ORIENTED TRANSPORT: TCP

Now that we have covered the underlying principles of reliable data transfer, let's turn to TCP—the Internet's transport-layer, connection-oriented, reliable transport protocol. In this section, we'll see that in order to provide reliable data transfer, TCP relies on many of the underlying principles discussed in the previous section, including error detection, retransmissions, cumulative acknowledgments, timers, and header fields for sequence and acknowledgment numbers. TCP is defined in [RFC 793], [RFC 1122], [RFC 1323], [RFC 2018] and [RFC 2581].

3.5.1 The TCP Connection

TCP provides multiplexing, demultiplexing, and error detection (but not recovery) in exactly the same manner as UDP. Nevertheless, TCP and UDP differ in many ways. The most fundamental difference is that UDP is **connectionless,** while TCP is **connection-oriented.** UDP is connectionless because it sends data without ever establishing a connection. TCP is connection-oriented because before one application process can begin to send data to another, the two processes must first "handshake" with each other—that is, they must send some preliminary segments to each other to establish the parameters of the ensuing data transfer. As part of the TCP connection establishment, both sides of the connection will initialize many TCP "state variables" (many of which will be discussed in this section and in Section 3.7) associated with the TCP connection.

The TCP "connection" is not an end-to-end TDM or FDM circuit as in a circuit-switched network. Nor is it a virtual circuit (see Chapter 1), as the connection state resides entirely in the two end systems. Because the TCP protocol runs only in the end systems and not in the intermediate network elements (routers and bridges), the intermediate network elements do not maintain TCP connection state. In fact, the intermediate routers are completely oblivious to TCP connections; they see datagrams, not connections.

A TCP connection provides for **full duplex** data transfer. That is, application-level data can be transferred in both directions between two hosts. If there is a TCP connection between process A on one host and process B on another host, then application-level data can flow from A to B at the same time as application-level data flows from B to A. TCP connection is also always **point-to-point,** that is, between a single sender and a single receiver. So called "multicasting" (see

Section 4.8)—the transfer of data from one sender to many receivers in a single send operation—is not possible with TCP. With TCP, two hosts are company and three are a crowd!

Let us now take a look at how a TCP connection is established. Suppose a process running in one host wants to initiate a connection with another process in another host. Recall that the host that is initiating the connection is called the **client host,** while the other host is called the **server host.** The client application process first informs the client TCP that it wants to establish a connection to a process in the server. Recall from Section 2.6, a Java client program does this by issuing the command:

```
Socket clientSocket = new Socket("hostname", "port number");
```

The TCP in the client then proceeds to establish a TCP connection with the TCP in the server. We will discuss in some detail the connection establishment procedure at the end of this section. For now it suffices to know that the client first sends a special TCP segment; the server responds with a second special TCP segment; and finally the client responds again with a third special segment. The first two segments contain no "payload," that is, no application-layer data; the third of these segments may carry a payload. Because three segments are sent between the two hosts, this connection establishment procedure is often referred to as a **three-way handshake.**

Once a TCP connection is established, the two application processes can send data to each other; because TCP is full-duplex they can send data at the same time. Let us consider the sending of data from the client process to the server process. The client process passes a stream of data through the socket (the door of the process), as described in Section 2.6. Once the data passes through the door, the data is now in the hands of TCP running in the client. As shown in Figure 3.26, TCP directs this data to the connection's **send buffer,** which is one of the buffers that is set aside during the initial three-way handshake. From time to time, TCP will "grab" chunks of data from the send buffer. The maximum amount of data that can be grabbed and placed in a segment is limited by the **Maximum Segment Size (MSS).** The MSS depends on the TCP implementation (determined by the operating system) and can often be configured; common values are 1,500 bytes, 536 bytes, and 512 bytes. (These segment sizes are often chosen in order to avoid

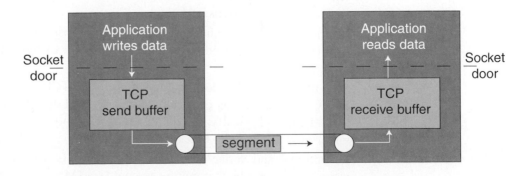

FIGURE 3.26 TCP send and receive buffers

IP fragmentation, which will be discussed in the next chapter.) Note that the MSS is the maximum amount of application-level data in the segment, not the maximum size of the TCP segment including headers. (This terminology is confusing, but we have to live with it, as it is well entrenched.)

TCP encapsulates each chunk of client data with a TCP header, thereby forming **TCP segments.** The segments are passed down to the network layer, where they are separately encapsulated within network-layer IP datagrams. The IP datagrams are then sent into the network. When TCP receives a segment at the other end, the segment's data is placed in the TCP connection's **receive buffer.** The application reads the stream of data from this buffer. Each side of the connection has its own send buffer and its own receive buffer. The send and receive buffers for data flowing in one direction are shown in Figure 3.26.

We see from this discussion that a TCP connection consists of buffers, variables, and a socket connection to a process in one host, and another set of buffers, variables, and a socket connection to a process in another host. As mentioned earlier, no buffers or variables are allocated to the connection in the network elements (routers, bridges, and repeaters) between the hosts.

3.5.2 TCP Segment Structure

Having taken a brief look at the TCP connection, let's examine the TCP segment structure. The TCP segment consists of header fields and a data field. The data field contains a chunk of application data. As mentioned above, the MSS limits the maximum size of a segment's data field. When TCP sends a large file, such as an encoded image as part of a Web page, it typically breaks the file into chunks of size MSS (except for the last chunk, which will often be less than the MSS). Interactive applications, however, often transmit data chunks that are smaller than the MSS; for example, with remote login applications like Telnet, the data field in the TCP segment is often only one byte. Because the TCP header is typically 20 bytes (12 bytes more than the UDP header), segments sent by Telnet may only be 21 bytes in length.

Figure 3.27 shows the structure of the TCP segment. As with UDP, the header includes **source and destination port numbers,** that are used for multiplexing/demultiplexing data from/to upper layer applications. Also, as with UDP, the header includes a **checksum field.** A TCP segment header also contains the following fields:

- The 32-bit **sequence number field,** and the 32-bit **acknowledgment number field** are used by the TCP sender and receiver in implementing a reliable data transfer service, as discussed below.
- The 16-bit **window size** field is used for the purposes of flow control. We will see shortly that it is used to indicate the number of bytes that a receiver is willing to accept.
- The 4-bit **length field** specifies the length of the TCP header in 32-bit words. The TCP header can be of variable length due to the TCP options field, discussed below. (Typically, the options field is empty, so that the length of the typical TCP header is 20 bytes.)
- The optional and variable length **options field** is used when a sender and receiver negotiate the maximum segment size (MSS) or as a window scaling factor for use in high-speed networks. A timestamping option is also defined. See [RFC 854], [RFC1323] for additional details.

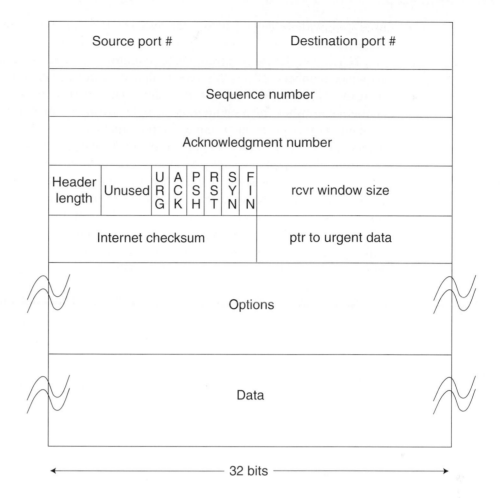

Source port #							Destination port #
Sequence number							
Acknowledgment number							
Header length	Unused	URG	ACK	PSH	RST	SYN	FIN	rcvr window size
Internet checksum							ptr to urgent data
Options							
Data							

◄——————— 32 bits ———————►

FIGURE 3.27   TCP segment structure

- The **flag field** contains 6 bits. The **ACK bit** is used to indicate that the value carried in the acknowledgment field is valid. The **RST, SYN,** and **FIN** bits are used for connection setup and teardown, as we will discuss at the end of this section. When the **PSH** bit is set, this is an indication that the receiver should pass the data to the upper layer immediately. Finally, the **URG** bit is used to indicate that there is data in this segment that the sending-side upper layer entity has marked as "urgent." The location of the last byte of this urgent data is indicated by the 16-bit urgent data pointer. TCP must inform the receiving-side upper layer entity when urgent data exists and pass it a pointer to the end of the urgent data. (In practice, the PSH, URG, and pointer to urgent data are not used. However, we mention these fields for completeness.)

3.5.3   Sequence Numbers and Acknowledgment Numbers

Two of the most important fields in the TCP segment header are the sequence number field and the acknowledgment number field. These fields are a critical part of TCP's reliable data transfer service. But before discussing how these fields are used to provide reliable data transfer, let us first explain what exactly TCP puts in these fields.

TCP views data as an unstructured, but ordered, stream of bytes. TCP's use of sequence numbers reflects this view in that sequence numbers are over the stream of transmitted bytes and *not* over the series of transmitted segments. The **sequence number for a segment** is the byte-stream number of the first byte in the segment. Let's look at an example. Suppose that a process in host A wants to send a stream of data to a process in host B over a TCP connection. The TCP in host A will implicitly number each byte in the data stream. Suppose that the data stream consists of a file consisting of 500,000 bytes, that the MSS is 1,000 bytes, and that the first byte of the data stream is numbered zero. As shown in Figure 3.28, TCP constructs 500 segments out of the data stream. The first segment gets assigned sequence number 0, the second segment gets assigned sequence number 1000, the third segment gets assigned sequence number 2000, and so on. Each sequence number is inserted in the sequence number field in the header of the appropriate TCP segment.

Now let us consider acknowledgment numbers. These are a little trickier than sequence numbers. Recall that TCP is full duplex, so that host A may be receiving data from host B while it sends data to host B (as part of the same TCP connection). Each of the segments that arrive from host B have a sequence number for the data flowing from B to A. *The acknowledgment number that host A puts in its segment is the sequence number of the next byte host A is expecting from host B.* It is good to look at a few examples to understand what is going on here. Suppose that host A has received all bytes numbered 0 through 535 from B and suppose that it is about to send a segment to host B. In other words, host A is waiting for byte 536 and all the subsequent bytes in host B's data stream. So host A puts 536 in the acknowledgment number field of the segment it sends to B.

As another example, suppose that host A has received one segment from host B containing bytes 0 through 535 and another segment containing bytes 900 through 1,000. For some reason host A has not yet received bytes 536 through 899. In this example, host A is still waiting for byte 536 (and beyond) in order to recreate B's data stream. Thus, A's next segment to B will contain 536 in the acknowledgment number field. Because TCP only acknowledges bytes up to the first missing byte in the stream, TCP is said to provide **cumulative acknowledgments.**

This last example also brings up an important but subtle issue. Host A received the third segment (bytes 900 through 1,000) before receiving the second segment (bytes 536 through 899). Thus, the third segment arrived out of order.

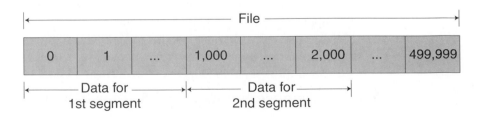

FIGURE 3.28 Dividing file data into TCP segments

The subtle issue is: What does a host do when it receives out of order segments in a TCP connection? Interestingly, the TCP RFCs do not impose any rules here, and leave the decision up to the people programming a TCP implementation. There are basically two choices: either (1) the receiver immediately discards out-of-order bytes; or (2) the receiver keeps the out-of-order bytes and waits for the missing bytes to fill in the gaps. Clearly, the latter choice is more efficient in terms of network bandwidth, whereas the former choice significantly simplifies the TCP code. Throughout the remainder of this introductory discussion of TCP, we focus on the former implementation, that is, we assume that the TCP receiver discards out-of-order segments.

In Figure 3.28 we assumed that the initial sequence number was zero. In truth, both sides of a TCP connection randomly choose an initial sequence number. This is done to minimize the possibility that a segment that is still present in the network from an earlier, already-terminated connection between two hosts is mistaken for a valid segment in a later connection between these same two hosts (who also happen to be using the same port numbers as the old connection) [Sunshine 1978].

3.5.4 Telnet: A Case Study for Sequence and Acknowledgment Numbers

Telnet, defined in [RFC 854], is a popular application-layer protocol used for remote login. It runs over TCP and is designed to work between any pair of hosts. Unlike the bulk-data transfer applications discussed in Chapter 2, Telnet is an interactive application. We discuss a Telnet example here, as it nicely illustrates TCP sequence and acknowledgment numbers.

Suppose one host, 88.88.88.88, initiates a Telnet session with host 99.99.99.99. (Anticipating our discussion on IP addressing in the next chapter, we take the liberty to use IP addresses to identify the hosts.) Because host 88.88.88.88 initiates the session, it is labeled the client, and host 99.99.99.99 is labeled the server. Each character typed by the user (at the client) will be sent to the remote host; the remote host will send back a copy of each character, which will be displayed on the Telnet user's screen. This "echo back" is used to ensure that characters seen by the Telnet user have already been received and processed at the remote site. Each character thus traverses the network twice between when the user hits the key and when the character is displayed on the user's monitor.

Now suppose the user types a single letter, 'C', and then grabs a coffee. Let's examine the TCP segments that are sent between the client and server. As shown in Figure 3.29, we suppose the starting sequence numbers are 42 and 79 for the client and server, respectively. Recall that the sequence number of a segment is the sequence number of the first byte in the data field. Thus, the first segment sent from the client will have sequence number 42; the first segment sent from the server will have sequence number 79. Recall that the acknowledgment number is the sequence number of the next byte of data that the host is waiting for. After the TCP connection is established but before any data is sent, the client is waiting for byte 79 and the server is waiting for byte 42.

As shown in Figure 3.29, three segments are sent. The first segment is sent from the client to the server, containing the one-byte ASCII representation of the letter 'C' in its data field. This first segment also has 42 in its sequence number

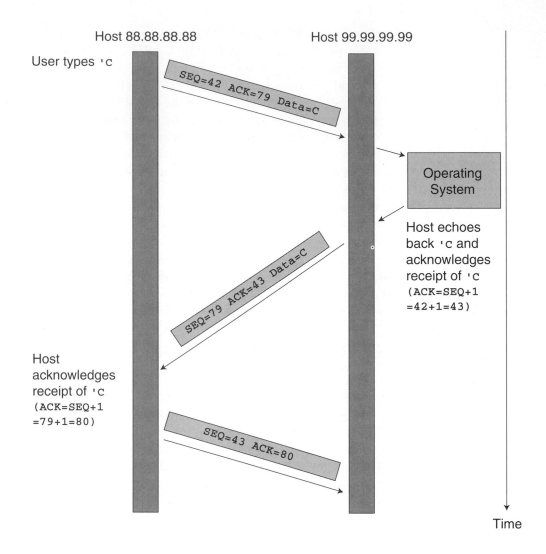

Host 88.88.88.88   Host 99.99.99.99

User types 'c

SEQ=42 ACK=79 Data=C

Operating System

Host echoes
back 'c and
acknowledges
receipt of 'c
(ACK=SEQ+1
=42+1=43)

SEQ=79 ACK=43 Data=C

Host
acknowledges
receipt of 'c
(ACK=SEQ+1
=79+1=80)

SEQ=43 ACK=80

Time

FIGURE 3.29   Sequence and acknowledgment numbers for a simple Telnet application over TCP

field, as we just described. Also, because the client has not yet received any data from the server, this first segment will have 79 in its acknowledgment number field.

The second segment is sent from the server to the client. It serves a dual purpose. First it provides an acknowledgment for the data the client has received. By putting 43 in the acknowledgment field, the server is telling the client that it has successfully received everything up through byte 42 and is now waiting for bytes 43 onward. The second purpose of this segment is to echo back the letter 'C'. Thus, the second segment has the ASCII representation of 'C' in its data field. This second segment has the sequence number 79, the initial sequence number of the server-to-client data flow of this TCP connection, as this is the very first byte of data that the server is sending. Note that the acknowledgment for client-to-server data is carried in a segment carrying server-to-client data; this acknowledgment is said to be **piggybacked** on the server-to-client data segment.

The third segment is sent from the client to the server. Its sole purpose is to acknowledge the data it has received from the server. (Recall that the second segment contained data—the letter 'C'—from the server to the client.) This segment has an empty data field (that is, the acknowledgment is not being piggybacked with any client-to-server data). The segment has 80 in the acknowledgment number field because the client has received the stream of bytes up through byte sequence number 79 and it is now waiting for bytes 80 onward. You might think it odd that this segment also has a sequence number since the segment contains no data. But because TCP has a sequence number field, the segment needs to have some sequence number.

3.5.5   Reliable Data Transfer

Recall that the Internet's network layer service (IP service) is unreliable. IP does not guarantee datagram delivery, does not guarantee in-order delivery of datagrams, and does not guarantee the integrity of the data in the datagrams. With IP service, datagrams can overflow router buffers and never reach their destination, datagrams can arrive out of order, and bits in the datagram can get corrupted (flipped from 0 to 1 and vice versa). Because transport-layer segments are carried across the network by IP datagrams, transport-layer segments can also suffer from these problems as well.

TCP creates a **reliable data transfer** service on top of IP's unreliable best-effort service. Many popular application protocols—including FTP, SMTP, NNTP, HTTP, and Telnet—use TCP rather than UDP primarily because TCP provides reliable data transfer service. TCP's reliable data transfer service ensures that the data stream that a process reads out of its TCP receive buffer is uncorrupted, without gaps, without duplication, and in sequence, that is, the byte stream is exactly the same byte stream that was sent by the end system on the other side of the connection. In this subsection, we provide an overview of how TCP provides reliable data transfer. We shall see that the reliable data transfer service of TCP uses many of the principles that we studied in Section 3.4.

Retransmissions.   Retransmission of lost and corrupted data is crucial for providing reliable data transfer. TCP provides reliable data transfer by using positive acknowledgments and timers in much the same way as we studied in Section 3.4. TCP acknowledges data that has been received correctly, and retransmits segments when segments or their corresponding acknowledgments are thought to be lost or corrupted. Just as in the case of our reliable data transfer protocol, rdt3.0, TCP cannot itself tell for certain if a segment, or its ACK, is lost, corrupted, or overly delayed. In all cases, TCP's response will be the same: retransmit the segment in question.

TCP also uses **pipelining,** allowing the sender to have multiple transmitted but yet-to-be-acknowledged segments outstanding at any given time. We saw in the previous section that pipelining can greatly improve the throughput of a TCP connection when the ratio of the segment size to round trip delay is small. The specific number of outstanding unacknowledged segments that a sender can have is determined by TCP's flow control and congestion control mechanisms. TCP flow control is discussed at the end of this section; TCP congestion control is discussed in Section 3.7. For the time being, we must simply be aware that the sender can have multiple transmitted, but unacknowledged, segments at any given time.

Figure 3.30 shows the three major events related to data transmission/retransmission at a simplified TCP sender. Let us consider a TCP connection between host A and B and focus on the data stream being sent from host A to host B. At the sending host (A), TCP is passed application-layer data, which it frames into segments and then passes on to IP. The passing of data from the application to TCP and the subsequent framing and transmission of a segment is the first important event that the TCP sender must handle. Each time TCP releases a segment to IP, it starts a timer for that segment. If this timer expires, an interrupt event is generated at host A. TCP responds to the timeout event, the second major type of event that the TCP sender must handle, by retransmitting the segment that caused the timeout.

The third major event that must be handled by the TCP sender is the arrival of an acknowledgment segment (ACK) from the receiver (more specifically, a segment containing a valid ACK field value). Here, the sender's TCP must determine

```
/* assume sender is not constrained by TCP flow or congestion control,
that data from above is less than MSS in size, and that data transfer is
in one direction only */
sendbase = initial_sequence number /* see Figure 3.17 */
nextseqnum = initial_sequence number
loop (forever) {
    switch(event)
          event: data received from application above
                create TCP segment with sequence number nextseqnum
                start timer for segment nextseqnum
                pass segment to IP
                nextseqnum = nextseqnum + length(data)
          event: timer timeout for segment with sequence number y
                retransmit segment with sequence number y
                compute new timeout interval for segment y
                restart timer for sequence number y
          event: ACK received, with ACK field value of y
                if (y > sendbase) { /* cumulative ACK of all data up to y */
                    cancel all timers for segments with sequence numbers < y
                    sendbase = y
                    }
                else { /* a duplicate ACK for already ACKed segment */
                    increment number of duplicate ACKs received for y
                    if (number of duplicate ACKS received for y == 3) {
                        /* TCP fast retransmit */
                        resend segment with sequence number y
                        restart timer for segment y
          }
} /* end of loop forever */
```

FIGURE 3.30   Simplified TCP sender

Table 3.1 TCP ACK generation recommendations [RFC 1122, RFC 2581]

Event	TCP receiver action
Arrival of in-order segment with expected sequence number. All data up to expected sequence number already acknowledged. No gaps in the received data.	Delayed ACK. Wait up to 500 ms for arrival of another in-order segment. If next in-order segment does not arrive in this interval, send an ACK.
Arrival of in-order segment with expected sequence number. One other in-order segment waiting for ACK transmission. No gaps in the received data.	Immediately send single cumulative ACK, ACKing both in-order segments.
Arrival of out-of-order segment with higher-than-expected sequence number. Gap detected.	Immediately send duplicate ACK, indicating sequence number of next expected byte.
Arrival of segment that partially or completely fills in gap in received data.	Immediately send ACK, provided that segment starts at the lower end of gap.

whether the ACK is a **first-time ACK** for a segment that the sender has yet to receive an acknowledgment for, or a so-called **duplicate ACK** that re-acknowledges a segment for which the sender has already received an earlier acknowledgment. In the case of the arrival of a first-time ACK, the sender now knows that *all* data up to the byte being acknowledged has been received correctly at the receiver. The sender can thus update its TCP state variable that tracks the sequence number of the last byte that is known to have been received correctly and in-order at the receiver.

To understand the sender's response to a duplicate ACK, we must look at why the receiver sends a duplicate ACK in the first place. Table 3.1 summarizes the TCP receiver's ACK generation policy. When a TCP receiver receives a segment with a sequence number that is larger than the next, expected, in-order sequence number, it detects a gap in the data stream—that is, a missing segment. Since TCP does not use negative acknowledgments, the receiver cannot send an explicit negative acknowledgment back to the sender. Instead, it simply re-acknowledges (that is, generates a duplicate ACK for) the last in-order byte of data it has received. If the TCP sender receives three duplicate ACKs for the same data, it takes this as an indication that the segment following the segment that has been ACKed three times has been lost. In this case, TCP performs a **fast retransmit** [RFC 2581], retransmitting the missing segment *before* that segment's timer expires.

A few interesting scenarios. We end this discussion by looking at a few simple scenarios. Figure 3.31 depicts the scenario where host A sends one segment to host B. Suppose that this segment has sequence number 92 and contains 8 bytes of data. After sending this segment, host A waits for a segment from B with acknowledgment number 100. Although the segment from A is received at B, the acknowledgment from B to A gets lost. In this case, the timer expires, and host A retransmits the same segment. Of course, when host B receives the retransmission, it will observe that the bytes in the segment duplicate bytes it has already

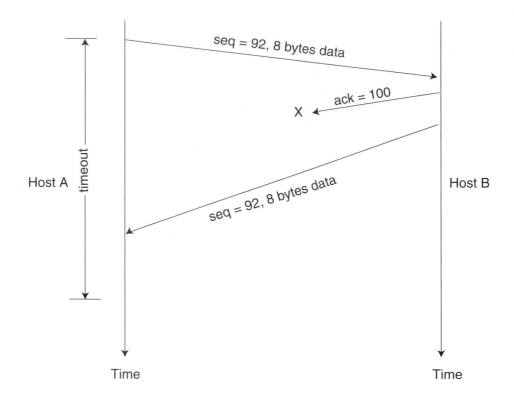

Host A

timeout

seq = 92, 8 bytes data

X ← ack = 100

seq = 92, 8 bytes data

Host B

Time   Time

FIGURE 3.31   Retransmission due to a lost acknowledgment

deposited in its receive buffer. Thus, TCP in host B will discard the bytes in the retransmitted segment.

In a second scenario, host A sends two segments back to back. The first segment has sequence number 92 and 8 bytes of data, and the second segment has sequence number 100 and 20 bytes of data. Suppose that both segments arrive intact at B, and B sends two separate acknowledgments for each of these segments. The first of these acknowledgments has acknowledgment number 100; the second has acknowledgment number 120. Suppose now that neither of the acknowledgments arrive at host A before the timeout of the first segment. When the timer expires, host A resends the first segment with sequence number 92. Now, you may ask, does A also resend the second segment? According to the rules described above, host A resends the segment only if the timer expires before the arrival of an acknowledgment with an acknowledgment number of 120 or greater. Thus, as shown in Figure 3.32, if the second acknowledgment does not get lost and arrives before the timeout of the second segment, A does not resend the second segment.

In a third and final scenario, suppose host A sends the two segments, exactly as in the second example. The acknowledgment of the first segment is lost in the network, but just before the timeout of the first segment, host A receives an acknowledgment with acknowledgment number 120. Host A therefore knows that host B has received *everything* up through byte 119; so host A does not resend either of the two segments. This scenario is illustrated in the Figure 3.33.

Recall that in the previous section we said that TCP is a Go-Back-N style protocol. This is because acknowledgments are cumulative and correctly-received but

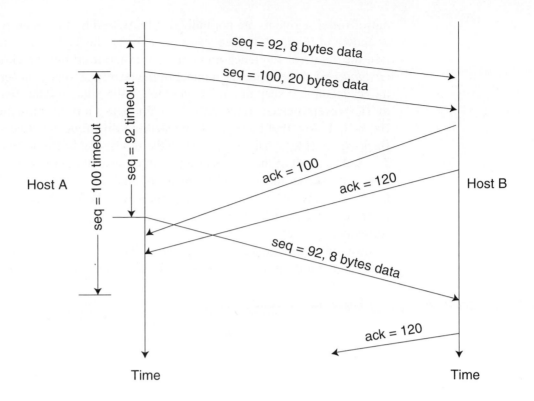

FIGURE 3.32   Segment is not retransmitted because its acknowledgment arrives before the timeout

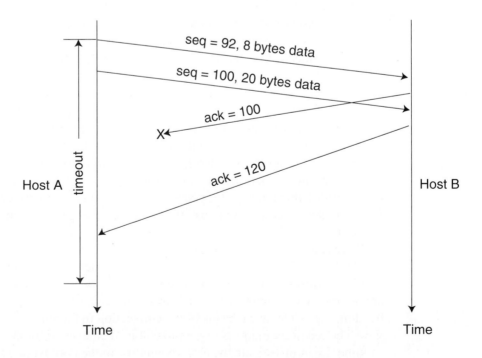

FIGURE 3.33   A cumulative acknowledgment avoids retransmission of first segment

out-of-order segments are not individually ACKed by the receiver. Consequently, as shown in Figure 3.30 (see also Figure 3.17), the TCP sender need only maintain the smallest sequence number of a transmitted but unacknowledged byte (*sendbase*) and the sequence number of the next byte to be sent (*nextseqnum*). But the reader should keep in mind that although the reliable-data-transfer component of TCP resembles Go-Back-N, it is by no means a pure implementation of Go-Back-N. To see that there are some striking differences between TCP and Go-Back-N, consider what happens when the sender sends a sequence of segments *1, 2, . . ., N,* and all of the segments arrive in order without error at the receiver. Further suppose that the acknowledgment for packet $n < N$ gets lost, but the remaining $N - 1$ acknowledgments arrive at the sender before their respective timeouts. In this example, Go-Back-N would retransmit not only packet *n*, but also all of the subsequent packets $n + 1, n + 2, . . ., N$. TCP, on the other hand, would retransmit at most, one segment, namely, segment *n*. Moreover, TCP would not even retransmit segment *n* if the acknowledgment for segment $n + 1$ arrives before the timeout for segment *n*.

There have recently been several proposals [RFC 2581, Fall 1996, Mathis 1996] to extend the TCP ACKing scheme to be more similar to a selective repeat protocol. The key idea in these proposals is to provide the sender with explicit information about which segments have been received correctly, and which are still missing at the receiver.

3.5.6   Flow Control

Recall that the hosts on each side of a TCP connection each set aside a receive buffer for the connection. When the TCP connection receives bytes that are correct and in sequence, it places the data in the receive buffer. The associated application process will read data from this buffer, but not necessarily at the instant the data arrives. Indeed, the receiving application may be busy with some other task and may not even attempt to read the data until long after it has arrived. If the application is relatively slow at reading the data, the sender can very easily overflow the connection's receive buffer by sending too much data too quickly. TCP thus provides a **flow control service** to its applications by eliminating the possibility of the sender overflowing the receiver's buffer. Flow control is thus a speed matching service—matching the rate at which the sender is sending to the rate at which the receiving application is reading. As noted earlier, a TCP sender can also be throttled due to congestion within the IP network; this form of sender control is referred to as **congestion control,** a topic we will explore in detail in Sections 3.6 and 3.7. While the actions taken by flow and congestion control are similar (the throttling of the sender), they are obviously taken for very different reasons. Unfortunately, many authors use the term interchangeably, and the savvy reader would be careful to distinguish between the two cases. Let's now discuss how TCP provides its flow control service.

TCP provides flow control by having the sender maintain a variable called the **receive window.** Informally, the receive window is used to give the sender an idea about how much free buffer space is available at the receiver. In a full-duplex connection, the sender at each side of the connection maintains a distinct receive window. The receive window is dynamic, that is, it changes throughout a connection's lifetime. Let's investigate the receive window in the context of a file transfer. Suppose that host A is sending a large file to host B over a TCP connection. Host B allocates a receive buffer to this connection; denote its size by `RcvBuffer`. From time to time, the application process in host B reads from the buffer. Define the following variables:

`LastByteRead` = the number of the last byte in the data stream read from the buffer by the application process in B.

`LastByteRcvd` = the number of the last byte in the data stream that has arrived from the network and has been placed in the receive buffer at B.

Because TCP is not permitted to overflow the allocated buffer, we must have:

`LastByteRcvd - LastByteRead <= RcvBuffer`

The receive window, denoted `RcvWindow`, is set to the amount of spare room in the buffer:

`RcvWindow = RcvBuffer - [LastByteRcvd - LastByteRead]`

Because the spare room changes with time, `RcvWindow` is dynamic. The variable `RcvWindow` is illustrated in Figure 3.34.

How does the connection use the variable `RcvWindow` to provide the flow control service? Host B informs host A of how much spare room it has in the connection buffer by placing its current value of `RcvWindow` in the window field of every segment it sends to A. Initially, host B sets `RcvWindow` = `RcvBuffer`. Note that to pull this off, host B must keep track of several connection-specific variables.

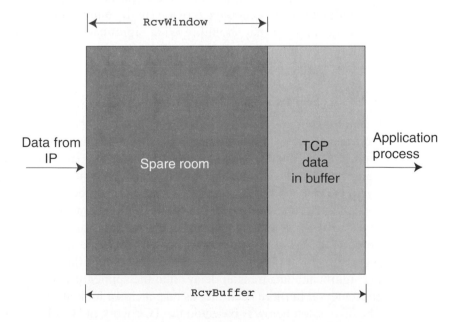

FIGURE 3.34   The receive window (`RcvWindow`) and the receive buffer (`RcvBuffer`)

Host A in turn keeps track of two variables, `LastByteSent` and `LastByteAcked`, which have obvious meanings. Note that the difference between these two variables, `LastByteSent` − `LastByteAcked`, is the amount of unacknowledged data that A has sent into the connection. By keeping the amount of unacknowledged data less than the value of `RcvWindow`, host A is assured that it is not overflowing the receive buffer at host B. Thus, host A makes sure throughout the connection's life that

$$\texttt{LastByteSent} - \texttt{LastByteAcked} <= \texttt{RcvWindow}$$

There is one minor technical problem with this scheme. To see this, suppose host B's receive buffer becomes full so that `RcvWindow` = 0. After advertising `RcvWindow` = 0 to host A, also suppose that B has *nothing* to send to A. As the application process at B empties the buffer, TCP does not send new segments with new `RcvWindows` to host A—TCP will only send a segment to host A if it has data to send or if it has an acknowledgment to send. Therefore, host A is never informed that some space has opened up in host B's receive buffer: host A is blocked and can transmit no more data! To solve this problem, the TCP specification requires host A to continue to send segments with one data byte when B's receive window is zero. These segments will be acknowledged by the receiver. Eventually the buffer will begin to empty and the acknowledgments will contain a non-zero `RcvWindow` value.

Having described TCP's flow control service, we briefly mention here that UDP does not provide flow control. To understand the issue here, consider sending a series of UDP segments from a process on host A to a process on host B. For a typical UDP implementation, UDP will append the segments (more precisely, the data in the segments) in a finite-size queue that "precedes" the corresponding socket (that is, the door to the process). The process reads one entire segment at a time from the queue. If the process does not read the segments fast enough from the queue, the queue will overflow and segments will get lost.

Following this section we provide (in the online version of this text) an interactive Java applet that should provide significant insight into the TCP receive window.

3.5.7 Round Trip Time and Timeout

Recall that when a host sends a segment into a TCP connection, it starts a timer. If the timer expires before the host receives an acknowledgment for the data in the segment, the host retransmits the segment. The time from when the timer is started until when it expires is called the **timeout** of the timer. A natural question is, how large should timeout be? Clearly, the timeout should be larger than the connection's round-trip time, that is, the time from when a segment is sent until it is acknowledged. Otherwise, unnecessary retransmissions would be sent. But the timeout should not be much larger than the round-trip time; otherwise, when a segment is lost, TCP would not quickly retransmit the segment, thereby introducing significant data transfer delays into the application. Before discussing the timeout interval in more detail, let us take a closer look at the round-trip time (RTT). The discussion below is based on the TCP work in [Jacobson 1988].

Estimating the average round-trip time.   The sample RTT, denoted `SampleRTT`, for a segment is the time from when the segment is sent (that is, passed to IP) until an acknowledgment for the segment is received. Each segment sent will have its own associated `SampleRTT`. Obviously, the `SampleRTT` values will fluctuate from segment to segment due to congestion in the routers and to the varying load on the end systems. Because of this fluctuation, any given `SampleRTT` value may be atypical. In order to estimate a typical RTT, it is therefore natural to take some sort of average of the `SampleRTT` values. TCP maintains an average, called `EstimatedRTT`, of the `SampleRTT` values. Upon receiving an acknowledgment and obtaining a new `SampleRTT`, TCP updates `EstimatedRTT` according to the following formula:

```
EstimatedRTT = (1 - x) EstimatedRTT + x SampleRTT.
```

The above formula is written in the form of a programming language statement—the new value of `EstimatedRTT` is a weighted combination of the previous value of `Estimated RTT` and the new value for `SampleRTT`. A typical value of x is x = 0.1, in which case the above formula becomes:

```
EstimatedRTT = 0.9 EstimatedRTT + 0.1 SampleRTT.
```

Note that `EstimatedRTT` is a weighted average of the `SampleRTT` values. As we will see in the homework, this weighted average puts more weight on recent samples than on old samples, This is natural, as the more recent samples better reflect the current congestion in the network. In statistics, such an average is called an **exponential weighted moving average** (EWMA). The word "exponential" appears in EWMA because the weight of a given `SampleRTT` decays exponentially fast as the updates proceed. In the homework problems you will be asked to derive the exponential term in `EstimatedRTT`.

Setting the timeout.   The timeout should be set so that a timer expires early (that is, before the delayed arrival of a segment's ACK) only on rare occasions. It is therefore natural to set the timeout equal to the `EstimatedRTT` plus some margin. The margin should be large when there is a lot of fluctuation in the `SampleRTT` values; it should be small when there is little fluctuation. TCP uses the following formula:

```
Timeout = EstimatedRTT + 4*Deviation,
```

where `Deviation` is an estimate of how much `SampleRTT` typically deviates from `EstimatedRTT`:

```
Deviation = (1 - x) Deviation + x | SampleRTT - EstimatedRTT |
```

Note that `Deviation` is an EWMA of how much `SampleRTT` deviates from `EstimatedRTT`. If the `SampleRTT` values have little fluctuation, then `Deviation` is small and `Timeout` is hardly more than `EstimatedRTT`; on the other hand, if there is a lot of fluctuation, `Deviation` will be large and `Timeout` will be much larger than `EstimatedRTT`.

3.5.8 TCP Connection Management

In this subsection, we take a closer look at how a TCP connection is established and torn down. Although this particular topic may not seem particularly exciting, it is important because TCP connection establishment can significantly add to perceived delays (for example, when surfing the Web). Let's now take a look at how a TCP connection is established. Suppose a process running in one host wants to initiate a connection with another process in another host. The host that is initiating the connection is called the **client host** whereas the other host is called the **server host.** The client application process first informs the client TCP that it wants to establish a connection to a process in the server. Recall from Section 2.6, that a Java client program does this by issuing the command:

```
Socket clientSocket = new Socket("hostname", "port number");
```

The TCP in the client then proceeds to establish a TCP connection with the TCP in the server in the following manner:

- **Step 1.** The client-side TCP first sends a special TCP segment to the server-side TCP. This special segment contains no application-layer data. It does, however, have one of the flag bits in the segment's header (see Figure 3.27), the so-called SYN bit, set to 1. For this reason, this special segment is referred to as a **SYN segment.** In addition, the client chooses an initial sequence number (`client_isn`) and puts this number in the sequence number field of the initial TCP SYN segment. This segment is encapsulated within an IP datagram and sent into the Internet.

- **Step 2.** Once the IP datagram containing the TCP SYN segment arrives at the server host (assuming it does arrive!), the server extracts the TCP SYN segment from the datagram, allocates the TCP buffers and variables to the connection, and sends a connection-granted segment to client TCP. This connection-granted segment also contains no application-layer data. However, it does contain three important pieces of information in the segment header. First, the SYN bit is set to 1. Second, the acknowledgment field of the TCP segment header is set to `client_isn+1`. Finally, the server chooses its own initial sequence number (`server_isn`) and puts this value in the sequence number field of the TCP segment header. This connection granted segment is saying, in effect, "I received your SYN packet to start a connection with your initial sequence number, `client_isn`. I agree to establish this connection. My own initial sequence number is `server_isn`." The connection-granted segment is sometimes referred to as a **SYNACK** segment.

- **Step 3.** Upon receiving the connection-granted segment, the client also allocates buffers and variables to the connection. The client host then sends the server yet another segment; this last segment acknowledges the server's connection-granted segment (the client does so by putting the value `server_isn+1` in the acknowledgment field of the TCP segment header). The SYN bit is set to 0, since the connection is established.

Once the previous three steps have been completed, the client and server hosts can send segments containing data to each other. In each of these future segments, the SYN bit will be set to zero. Note, that in order to establish the connection, three packets are sent between the two hosts, as illustrated in Figure 3.35. For this reason, this connection establishment procedure is often referred to as a **three-way handshake.** Several aspects of the TCP three-way handshake (Why are initial sequence numbers needed? Why is a three-way handshake, as opposed to a two-way handshake, needed?) are explored in the homework problems.

All good things must come to an end, and the same is true with a TCP connection. Either of the two processes participating in a TCP connection can end the connection. When a connection ends, the "resources" (that is, the buffers and variables) in the hosts are de-allocated. As an example, suppose the client decides to close the connection. The client application process issues a close command. This causes the client TCP to send a special TCP segment to the server process. This special segment has a flag bit in the segment's header, the so-called FIN bit (see Figure 3.27), set to 1. When the server receives this segment, it sends the client an acknowledgment segment in return. The server then sends its own shut-down segment, which has the FIN bit set to 1. Finally, the client acknowledges the server's shut-down segment. At this point, all the resources in the two hosts are now de-allocated.

During the life of a TCP connection, the TCP protocol running in each host makes transitions through various **TCP states.** Figure 3.36 illustrates a typical sequence of TCP states that are visited by the *client* TCP. The client TCP begins in the closed state. The application on the client side initiates a new TCP connection (by creating a Socket object in our Java examples). This causes TCP in the client to send a SYN segment to TCP in the server. After having sent the SYN segment, the client TCP enters the SYN_SENT sent. While in the SYN_STATE, the client TCP waits for a segment from the server TCP that includes an acknowledgment for the

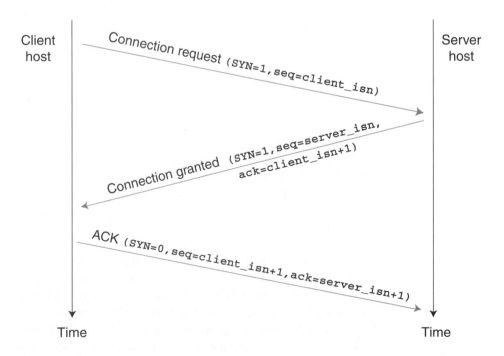

FIGURE 3.35 TCP three-way handshake: segment exchange

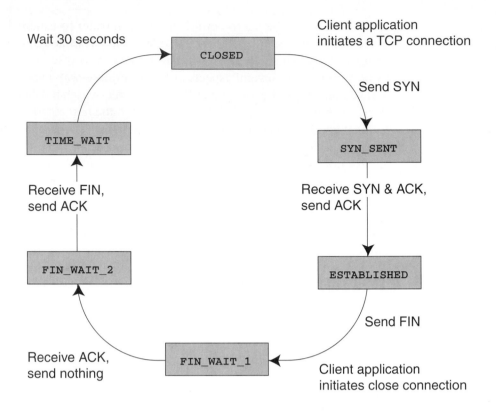

FIGURE 3.36 A typical sequence of TCP states visited by a client TCP

client's previous segment as well as the SYN bit set to 1. Once having received such a segment, the client TCP enters the ESTABLISHED state. While in the ESTAB-LISHED state, the TCP client can send and receive TCP segments containing pay-load (that is, application-generated) data.

Suppose that the client application decides it wants to close the connection. This causes the client TCP to send a TCP segment with the FIN bit set to 1 and to enter the FIN_WAIT_1 state. While in the FIN_WAIT state, the client TCP waits for a TCP segment from the server with an acknowledgment. When it receives this segment, the client TCP enters the FIN_WAIT_2 state. While in the FIN_WAIT_2 state, the client waits for another segment from the server with the FIN bit set to 1; after receiving this segment, the client TCP acknowledges the server's segment and enters the TIME_WAIT state. The TIME_WAIT state lets the TCP client resend the final acknowledgment in case the ACK is lost. The time spent in the TIME-WAIT state is implementation dependent, but typical values are 30 sec-onds, 1 minute, and 2 minutes. After the wait, the connection formally closes and all resources on the client side (including port numbers) are released.

Figure 3.37 illustrates the series of states typically visited by the server-side TCP; the transitions are self-explanatory. In these two state transition diagrams, we have only shown how a TCP connection is normally established and shut down. We are not going to describe what happens in certain pathological scenarios, for exam-ple, when both sides of a connection want to shut down at the same time. If you are interested in learning about this and other advanced issues concerning TCP, you are encouraged to see Steven's comprehensive book [Stevens 1994].

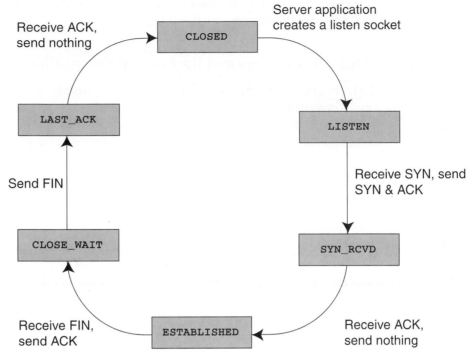

FIGURE 3.37 A typical sequence of TCP states visited by a server-side TCP

This completes our introduction to TCP. In Section 3.7 we will return to TCP and look at TCP congestion control in some depth. Before doing so, in the next section we step back and examine congestion control issues in a broader context.

3.6 PRINCIPLES OF CONGESTION CONTROL

In the previous sections, we've examined both the general principles and specific TCP mechanisms used to provide for a reliable data transfer service in the face of packet loss. We mentioned earlier that, in practice, such loss typically results from the overflowing of router buffers as the network becomes congested. Packet retransmission thus treats a symptom of network congestion (the loss of a specific transport-layer packet) but does not treat the cause of network congestion—too many sources attempting to send data at too high a rate. To treat the *cause* of network congestion, mechanisms are needed to throttle the sender in the face of network congestion.

In this section, we consider the problem of congestion control in a general context, seeking to understand *why* congestion is a "bad thing," *how* network congestion is manifested in the performance received by upper-layer applications, and various approaches that can be taken to avoid, or react to, network congestion. This more general study of congestion control is appropriate since, as with reliable data transfer, it is high on the "top-10" list of fundamentally important problems in networking. We conclude this section with a discussion of congestion control in the ATM ABR protocol. The following section contains a detailed study of TCP's congestion-control algorithm.

3.6.1 The Causes and the Costs of Congestion

Let's begin our general study of congestion control by examining three increasingly complex scenarios in which congestion occurs. In each case, we'll look at why congestion occurs in the first place and at the cost of congestion (in terms of resources not fully utilized and poor performance received by the end systems).

Scenario 1: Two senders, a router with infinite buffers.   We begin by considering perhaps the simplest congestion scenario possible: two hosts (A and B) each have a connection that shares a single hop between source and destination, as shown in Figure 3.38.

Let's assume that the application in Host A is sending data into the connection (for example, passing data to the transport-level protocol via a socket) at an average rate of λ_{in} bytes/sec. These data are "original" in the sense that each unit of data is sent into the socket only once. The underlying transport-level protocol is a simple one. Data is encapsulated and sent; no error recovery (for example, retransmission), flow control, or congestion control is performed. Host B operates in a similar manner, and we assume for simplicity that it too is sending at a rate of λ_{in} bytes/sec. Packets from hosts A and B pass through a router and over a shared outgoing link of capacity C. The router has buffers that allow it to store incoming packets when the packet-arrival rate exceeds the outgoing link's capacity. In this first scenario, we'll assume that the router has an infinite amount of buffer space.

Figure 3.39 plots the performance of Host A's connection under this first scenario. The left graph plots the **per-connection throughput** (number of bytes per second at the receiver) as a function of the connection sending rate. For a sending rate between 0 and $C/2$, the throughput at the receiver equals the sender's sending rate—everything sent by the sender is received at the receiver with a finite delay. When the sending rate is above $C/2$, however, the throughput is only $C/2$. This upper limit on throughput is a consequence of the sharing of link capacity

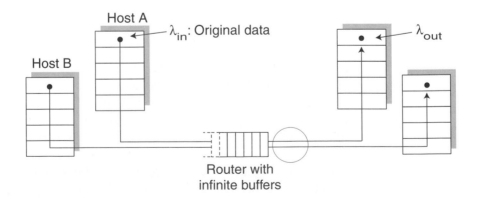

FIGURE 3.38   Congestion scenario 1: Two connections sharing a single hop with infinite buffers

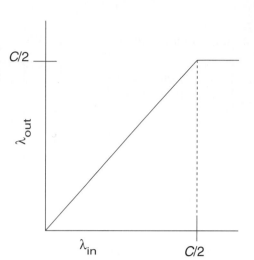
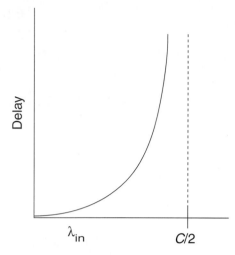

FIGURE 3.39   Congestion scenario 1: Throughput and delay as a function of host sending rate

between two connections. The link simply cannot deliver packets to a receiver at a steady-state rate that exceeds $C/2$. No matter how high Hosts A and B set their sending rates, they will each never see a throughput higher than $C/2$.

Achieving a per-connection throughput of $C/2$ might actually appear to be a "good thing," as the link is fully utilized in delivering packets to their destinations. The right-hand graph in Figure 3.39, however, shows the consequences of operating near link capacity. As the sending rate approaches $C/2$ (from the left), the average delay becomes larger and larger. When the sending rate exceeds $C/2$, the average number of queued packets in the router is unbounded, and the average delay between source and destination becomes infinite (assuming that the connections operate at these sending rates for an infinite period of time). Thus, while operating at an aggregate throughput of near C may be ideal from a throughput standpoint, it is far from ideal from a delay standpoint. *Even in this (extremely) idealized scenario, we've already found one cost of a congested network—large queuing delays are experienced as the packet-arrival rate nears the link capacity.*

Scenario 2: Two senders, a router with finite buffers.   Let us now slightly modify scenario 1 in the following two ways (see Figure 3.40). First, the amount of router buffering is assumed to be finite. Second, we assume that each connection is reliable. If a packet containing a transport-level segment is dropped at the router, it will eventually be retransmitted by the sender. Because packets can be retransmitted, we must now be more careful with our use of the term "sending rate." Specifically, let us again denote the rate at which the application sends original data into the socket by λ_{in} bytes/sec. The rate at which the transport layer sends segments (containing original data *or* retransmitted data) into the network will be denoted λ_{in}' bytes/sec. λ_{in}' is sometimes referred to as the **offered load** to the network.

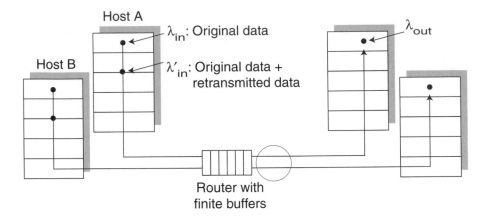

FIGURE 3.40 Scenario 2: Two hosts (with retransmissions) and a router with finite buffers

The performance realized under scenario 2 will now depend strongly on how retransmission is performed. First, consider the unrealistic case that Host A is able to somehow (magically!) determine whether or not a buffer is free in the router and thus sends a packet only when a buffer is free. In this case, no loss would occur, λ_{in} would be equal to λ_{in}', and the throughput of the connection would be equal to λ_{in}. This case is shown in Figure 3.41(a). From a throughput standpoint, performance is ideal—everything that is sent is received. Note that the average host sending rate cannot exceed $C/2$ under this scenario, since packet loss is assumed never to occur.

Consider next the slightly more realistic case that the sender retransmits only when a packet is known for certain to be lost. (Again, this assumption is a bit of a stretch. However, it possible that the sending host might set its timeout large enough to be virtually assured that a packet that has not been acknowledged has been lost.) In this case, the performance might look something like that shown in Figure 3.41(b). To appreciate what is happening here, consider the case that the offered load, λ_{in}' (the rate of original data transmission plus retransmissions), equals $0.6C$. According to Figure 3.41(b), at this value of the offered load, the rate at which data are delivered to the receiver application is $C/3$. Thus, out of the $0.6C$ units of data transmitted, 0.3333 bytes/sec (on average) are original data and 0.26666 bytes per second (on average) are retransmitted data. *We see here another cost of a congested network—the sender must perform retransmissions in order to compensate for dropped (lost) packets due to buffer overflow.*

Finally, let us consider the more realistic case that the sender may timeout prematurely and retransmit a packet that has been delayed in the queue, but not yet lost. In this case, both the original data packet and the retransmission may both reach the receiver. Of course, the receiver needs but one copy of this packet and will discard the retransmission. In this case, the "work" done by the router in forwarding the retransmitted copy of the original packet was "wasted," as the receiver will have already received the original copy of this packet. The router would have better used the link transmission capacity transmitting a different

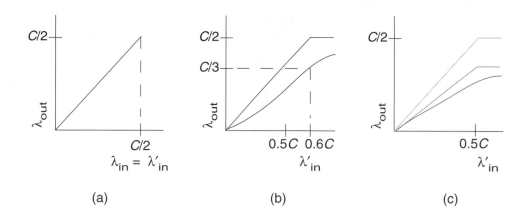

FIGURE 3.41 Scenario 2 performance: (a) No retransmissions, (b) only needed retransmissions, (c) extraneous, unneeded retransmissions

packet instead. *Here then is yet another cost of a congested network—unneeded retransmissions by the sender in the face of large delays may cause a router to use its link bandwidth to forward unneeded copies of a packet.* Figure 3.41(c) shows the throughput versus offered load when each packet is assumed to be forwarded (on average) at least twice by the router. Since each packet is forwarded twice, the throughput achieved will be bounded above by the two-segment curve with the asymptotic value of $C/4$.

Scenario 3: Four senders, routers with finite buffers, and multihop paths. In our final congestion scenario, four hosts transmit packets, each over overlapping two-hop paths, as shown in Figure 3.42. We again assume that each host uses a timeout/retransmission mechanism to implement a reliable data transfer service, that all hosts have the same value of λ_{in}, and that all router links have capacity C bytes/sec.

Let us consider the connection from Host A to Host C, passing through Routers R1 and R2. The A–C connection shares router R1 with the D–B connection and shares router R2 with the B–D connection. For extremely small values of λ_{in}, buffer overflows are rare (as in congestion scenarios 1 and 2), and the throughput approximately equals the offered load. For slightly larger values of λ_{in}, the corresponding throughput is also larger, as more original data is being transmitted into the network and delivered to the destination, and overflows are still rare. Thus, for small values of λ_{in}, an increase in λ_{in} results in an increase in λ_{out}.

Having considered the case of extremely low traffic, let us next examine the case that λ_{in} (and hence λ_{in}') is extremely large. Consider router R2. The A–C traffic arriving to router R2 (which arrives at R2 after being forwarded from R1) can have an arrival rate at R2 that is at most C, the capacity of the link from R1 to R2, regardless of the value of λ_{in}. If λ_{in}' is extremely large for all connections (including the B–D connection), then the arrival rate of B–D traffic at R2 can be much larger than that of the A–C traffic. Because the A–C and B–D traffic must compete at router R2 for the limited amount of buffer space, the amount of A–C traffic that successfully gets through R2 (that is, is not lost due to buffer overflow)

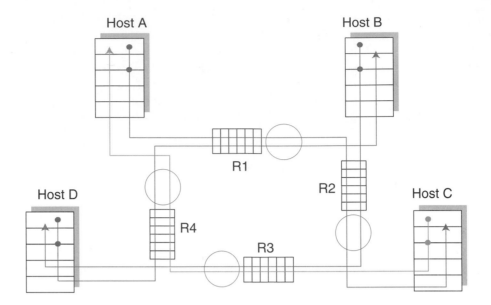

FIGURE 3.42   Four senders, routers with finite buffers, and multihop paths

becomes smaller and smaller as the offered load from B–D gets larger and larger. In the limit, as the offered load approaches infinity, an empty buffer at R2 is immediately filled by a B–D packet and the throughput of the A–C connection at R2 goes to zero. This, in turn, *implies that the A–C end-end throughput goes to zero* in the limit of heavy traffic. These considerations give rise to the offered load versus throughput tradeoff shown in Figure 3.43.

The reason for the eventual decrease in throughput with increasing offered load is evident when one considers the amount of wasted "work" done by the network. In the high-traffic scenario outlined above, whenever a packet is dropped at a second-hop router, the "work" done by the first-hop router in forwarding a packet to the second-hop router ends up being "wasted." The network would have been equally well off (more accurately, equally bad off) if the first router had simply discarded that packet and remained idle. More to the point, the transmission capacity used at the first router to forward the packet to the second router could have been much more profitably used to transmit a different packet. (For example, when selecting a packet for transmission, it might be better for a router to give priority to packets that have already traversed some number of upstream routers.) *So here we see yet another cost of dropping a packet due to congestion—when a packet is dropped along a path, the transmission capacity that was used at each of the upstream routers to forward that packet to the point at which it is dropped ends up having been wasted.*

3.6.2   Approaches toward Congestion Control

In Section 3.7, we will examine TCP's specific approach towards congestion control in great detail. Here, we identify the two broad approaches that are taken in

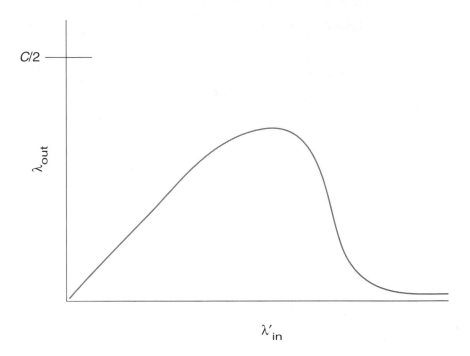

FIGURE 3.43   Scenario 2 performance with finite buffers and multihop paths

practice towards congestion control, and discuss specific network architectures and congestion-control protocols embodying these approaches.

At the broadest level, we can distinguish among congestion control approaches based on whether or not the network layer provides any explicit assistance to the transport layer for congestion-control purposes:

- *End-end congestion control.* In an end-end approach towards congestion control, the network layer provides *no explicit support* to the transport layer for congestion-control purposes. Even the presence of congestion in the network must be inferred by the end systems based only on observed network behavior (for example, packet loss and delay). We will see in Section 3.7 that TCP must necessarily take this end-end approach towards congestion control, since the IP layer provides no feedback to the end systems regarding network congestion. TCP segment loss (as indicated by a timeout or a triple duplicate acknowledgment) is taken as an indication of network congestion and TCP decreases its window size accordingly. We will also see that new proposals for TCP use increasing round-trip delay values as indicators of increased network congestion.

- *Network-assisted congestion control.* With network-assisted congestion control, network-layer components (that is, routers) provide explicit feedback to the sender regarding the congestion state in the network. This feedback may be as simple as a single bit indicating congestion at a link. This approach was taken in the early IBM SNA [Schwartz 1982] and DEC DECnet [Jain 1989] [Ramakrishnan 1990] architectures, was recently proposed for TCP/IP

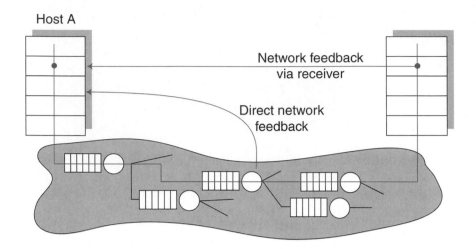

FIGURE 3.44 Two feedback pathways for network-indicated congestion information

networks [Floyd TCP 1994] [RFC 2481], and is used in ATM available bit-rate (ABR) congestion control as well, as discussed below. More sophisticated network-feedback is also possible. For example, one form of ATM ABR congestion control that we will study shortly allows a router to explicitly inform the sender of the transmission rate it (the router) can support on an outgoing link.

For network-assisted congestion control, congestion information is typically fed back from the network to the sender in one of two ways, as shown in Figure 3.44. Direct feedback may be sent from a network router to the sender. This form of notification typically takes the form of a **choke packet** (essentially saying, "I'm congested!"). The second form of notification occurs when a router marks/updates a field in a packet flowing from sender to receiver to indicate congestion. Upon receipt of a marked packet, the receiver then notifies the sender of the congestion indication. Note that this latter form of notification takes at least a full round-trip time.

3.6.3 ATM ABR Congestion Control

Our detailed study of TCP congestion control in Section 3.7 will provide an in-depth case study of an end-end approach towards congestion control. We conclude this section with a brief case study of the network-assisted congestion-control mechanisms used in ATM ABR service. ABR has been designed as an elastic data transfer service in a manner reminiscent of TCP. When the network is under-loaded, ABR service should be able to take advantage of the spare available bandwidth; when the network is congested, ABR service should throttle its transmission rate to some predetermined minimum transmission rate. A detailed tutorial on ATM ABR congestion control and traffic management is provided in [Jain 1996].

Figure 3.45 shows the framework for ATM ABR congestion control. In our discussion below we adopt ATM terminology (for example, using the term "switch" rather than "router," and the term "cell" rather than "packet"). With ATM ABR service, data cells are transmitted from a source to a destination through a series of intermediate switches. Interspersed with the data cells are so-called resource-management cells, **RM cells;** we will see shortly that these RM cells can be used to convey congestion-related information among the hosts and switches. When an RM cell is at a destination, it will be "turned around" and sent back to the sender (possibly after the destination has modified the contents of the RM cell). It is also possible for a switch to generate an RM cell itself and send this RM cell directly to a source. RM cells can thus be used to provide both direct network feedback and network-feedback-via-the-receiver, as shown in Figure 3.45.

ATM ABR congestion control is a rate-based approach. That is, the sender explicitly computes a maximum rate at which it can send and regulates itself accordingly. ABR provides three mechanisms for signaling congestion-related information from the switches to the receiver:

- *EFCI bit.* Each *data cell* contains an **EFCI (explicit forward congestion indication) bit.** A congested network switch can set the EFCI bit in a data cell to 1 to signal congestion to the destination host. The destination must check the EFCI bit in all received data cells. When an RM cell arrives at the destination, if the most recently received data cell had the EFCI bit set to 1, then the destination sets the congestion indication bit (the CI bit) of the RM cell to 1 and sends the RM cell back to the sender. Using the EFCI in data cells and the CI bit in RM cells, a sender can thus be notified about congestion at a network switch.

- *CI and NI bits.* As noted above, sender-to-receiver RM cells are interspersed with data cells. The rate of RM cell interspersion is a tunable parameter, with one RM cell every 32 data cells being the default value. These RM cells have a CI (congestion indication) bit and an NI (no increase) bit that can be set by a congested network switch. Specifically, a switch can set the NI bit in a passing RM cell to 1 under mild congestion and can set the CI bit to 1 under severe congestion conditions. When a destination host receives an RM cell, it will send the RM cell back to the sender with its CI and NI bits intact (except that CI may be set to 1 by the destination as a result of the EFCI mechanism described above).

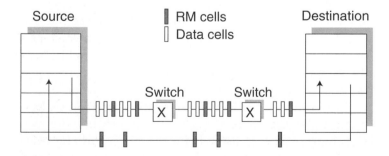

FIGURE 3.45 Congestion control framework for ATM ABR service

- *ER setting.* Each RM cell also contains a two-byte **ER (explicit rate) field.** A congested switch may lower the value contained in the ER field in a passing RM cell. In this manner, the ER field will be set to the minimum supportable rate of all switches on the source-to-destination path.

An ATM ABR source adjusts the rate at which it can send cells as a function of the CI, NI, and ER values in a returned RM cell. The rules for making this rate adjustment are rather complicated and tedious. The interested reader is referred to [Jain 1996] for details.

3.7   TCP CONGESTION CONTROL

In this section we return to our study of TCP. As we learned in Section 3.5, TCP provides a reliable transport service between two processes running on different hosts. Another extremely important component of TCP is its congestion-control mechanism. As we indicated in the previous section, TCP must use end-to-end congestion control rather than network-assisted congestion control, since the IP layer provides no feedback to the end systems regarding network congestion. Before diving into the details of TCP congestion control, let's first get a high-level view of TCP's congestion-control mechanism, as well as the overall goal that TCP strives for when multiple TCP connections must share the bandwidth of a congested link.

A TCP connection controls its transmission rate by limiting its number of transmitted-but-yet-to-be-acknowledged segments. Let us denote this number of permissible unacknowledged segments as w, often referred to as the TCP **window size.** Ideally, TCP connections should be allowed to transmit as fast as possible (that is, to have as large a number of outstanding unacknowledged packets as possible) as long as segments are not lost (dropped at routers) due to congestion. In very broad terms, a TCP connection starts with a small value of w and then "probes" for the existence of additional unused link bandwidth at the links on its end-to-end path by increasing w. A TCP connection continues to increase w until a segment loss occurs (as detected by a timeout or duplicate acknowledgments). When such a loss occurs, the TCP connection reduces w to a "safe level" and then begins probing again for unused bandwidth by slowly increasing w.

An important measure of the performance of a TCP connection is its throughput—the rate at which it transmits data from the sender to the receiver. Clearly, throughput will depend on the value of w. If a TCP sender transmits all w segments back-to-back, it must then wait for one round trip time (RTT) until it receives acknowledgments for these segments, at which point it can send w additional segments. If a connection transmits w segments of size *MSS* bytes every *RTT* seconds, then the connection's throughput, or transmission rate, is $(w * MSS)/RTT$ bytes per second.

Suppose now that K TCP connections are traversing a link of capacity R. Suppose also that there are no UDP packets flowing over this link, that each TCP connection is transferring a very large amount of data, and that none of these TCP connections traverse any other congested link. Ideally, the window sizes in the TCP connections traversing this link should be such that each connection achieves a throughput of R/K. More generally, if a connection passes through N links, with link n having transmission rate R_n and supporting a total of K_n TCP connections, then ideally this connection should achieve a rate of R_n/K_n on the nth link. However, this connection's end-to-end average rate cannot exceed the minimum rate achieved at all of the links along the end-to-end path. That is, the end-to-end transmission rate for this connection is $r = \min\{R_1/K_1, \ldots, R_N/K_N\}$. The goal of TCP is to provide this connection with this end-to-end rate, r. (In actuality, the formula for r is more complicated, as we should take into account the fact that one or more of the intervening connections may be bottlenecked at some other link that is not on this end-to-end path and hence cannot use their bandwidth share, R_n/K_n. In this case, the value of r would be higher than $\min\{R_1/K_1, \ldots, R_N/K_N\}$.)

3.7.1 Overview of TCP Congestion Control

In Section 3.5 we saw that each side of a TCP connection consists of a receive buffer, a send buffer, and several variables (LastByteRead, RcvWin, and so on.) The TCP congestion-control mechanism has each side of the connection keep track of two additional variables: the **congestion window** and the **threshold.** The congestion window, denoted CongWin, imposes an additional constraint on how much traffic a host can send into a connection. Specifically, the amount of unacknowledged data that a host can have within a TCP connection may not exceed the minimum of CongWin and RcvWin, that is:

    LastByteSent - LastByteAcked <= min{CongWin, RcvWin}

The threshold, which we discuss in detail below, is a variable that effects how CongWin grows.

Let us now look at how the congestion window evolves throughout the lifetime of a TCP connection. In order to focus on congestion control (as opposed to flow control), let us assume that the TCP receive buffer is so large that the receive window constraint can be ignored. In this case, the amount of unacknowledged data that a host can have within a TCP connection is solely limited by CongWin. Further let's assume that a sender has a very large amount of data to send to a receiver.

Once a TCP connection is established between the two end systems, the application process at the sender writes bytes to the sender's TCP send buffer. TCP grabs chunks of size MSS, encapsulates each chunk within a TCP segment, and passes the segments to the network layer for transmission across the network. The TCP congestion window regulates the times at which the segments are sent into the network (that is, passed to the network layer). Initially, the congestion window is equal to one MSS. TCP sends the first segment into the network and waits for an acknowledgment. If this segment is acknowledged before its timer times out, the sender increases the congestion window by one MSS and sends out two maximum-size segments. If these segments are acknowledged before their timeouts, the sender increases the congestion window by one MSS for each of the acknowledged segments, giving a congestion window of four MSS, and sends out four maximum-sized segments. This procedure continues as long as (1) the congestion window is below the threshold and (2) the acknowledgments arrive before their corresponding timeouts.

During this phase of the congestion-control procedure, the congestion window increases exponentially fast. The congestion window is initialized to one MSS; after one RTT, the window is increased to two segments; after two round-trip times, the window is increased to four segments; after three round-trip times, the window is increased to eight segments, and so forth. This phase of the algorithm is called **slow start** because it begins with a small congestion window equal to one MSS. (The transmission rate of the connection starts slowly but accelerates rapidly.)

The slow-start phase ends when the window size exceed the value of `threshold`. Once the congestion window is larger than the current value of `threshold`, the congestion window grows linearly rather than exponentially. Specifically, if w is the current value of the congestion window, and w is larger than `threshold`, then after w acknowledgments have arrived, TCP replaces w with $w + 1$. This has the effect of increasing the congestion window by 1 in each RTT for which an entire window's worth of acknowledgments arrives. This phase of the algorithm is called **congestion avoidance.**

The congestion-avoidance phase continues as long as the acknowledgments arrive before their corresponding timeouts. But the window size, and hence the rate at which the TCP sender can send, cannot increase forever. Eventually, the TCP rate will be such that one of the links along the path becomes saturated, at which point loss (and a resulting timeout at the sender) will occur. When a time-out occurs, the value of `threshold` is set to half the value of the current congestion window, and the congestion window is reset to one MSS. The sender then again grows the congestion window exponentially fast using the slow-start procedure until the congestion window hits the threshold.

In summary:

- When the congestion window is below the threshold, the congestion window grows exponentially.
- When the congestion window is above the threshold, the congestion window grows linearly.
- Whenever there is a timeout, the threshold is set to one-half of the current congestion window and the congestion window is then set to 1.

If we ignore the slow-start phase, we see that TCP essentially increases its window size by 1 each RTT (and thus increases its transmission rate by an additive factor) when its network path is not congested, and decreases its window size by a factor of 2 each RTT when the path is congested. For this reason, TCP is often referred to as an **additive-increase, multiplicative-decrease (AIMD)** algorithm.

The evolution of TCP's congestion window is illustrated in Figure 3.46. In this figure, the threshold is initially equal to 8 ∗ *MSS*. The congestion window climbs exponentially fast during slow start and hits the threshold at the third transmission. The congestion window then climbs linearly until loss occurs, just after transmission 7. Note that the congestion window is 12 ∗ *MSS* when loss occurs. The threshold is then set to 0.5 ∗ `CongWin` = 6 ∗ *MSS* and the congestion window is set 1. And the process continues. This congestion-control algo-

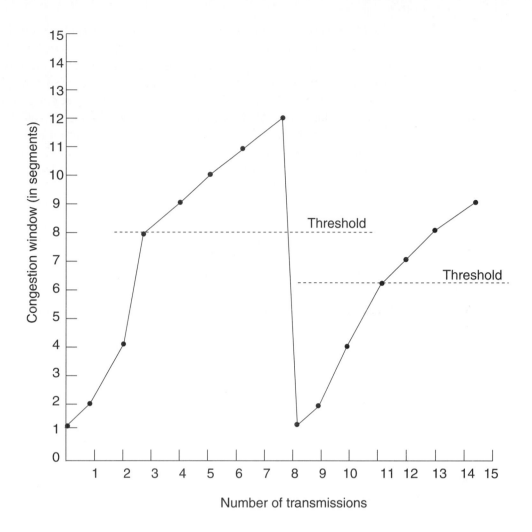

FIGURE 3.46 Evolution of TCP's congestion window

rithm is due to V. Jacobson [Jacobson 1988]; a number of modifications to Jacobson's initial algorithm are described in [Stevens 1994] and [RFC 2581].

A trip to Nevada: Tahoe, Reno, and Vegas.   The TCP congestion-control algorithm just described is often referred to as **Tahoe.** One problem with the Tahoe algorithm is that, when a segment is lost, the sender side of the application may have to wait a long period of time for the timeout. For this reason, a variant of Tahoe, called **Reno,** is implemented by most operating systems. Like Tahoe, Reno sets its congestion window to one segment upon the expiration of a timer. However, Reno also includes the fast retransmit mechanism that we examined in Section 3.5. Recall that fast retransmission triggers the transmission of a dropped segment if three duplicate ACKs for a segment are received before the occurrence of the segment's timeout. Reno also employs a **fast-recovery** mechanism, which essentially cancels the slow-start phase after a fast retransmission. The interested reader is encouraged to see [Stevens 1994] and [RFC 2581] for details.

Most TCP implementations currently use the Reno algorithm. There is, how-ever, another algorithm in the literature, the Vegas algorithm, that can improve Reno's performance. Whereas Tahoe and Reno react to congestion (that is, to overflowing router buffers), Vegas attempts to avoid congestion while maintaining good throughput. The basic idea of Vegas is to (1) detect congestion in the routers between source and destination *before* packet loss occurs, and (2) lower the rate linearly when this imminent packet loss is detected. Imminent packet loss is pre-dicted by observing the round-trip times. The longer the round-trip times of the packets, the greater the congestion in the routers. The Vegas algorithm is dis-cussed in detail in [Brakmo 1995]; a study of its performance is given in [Ahn 1995]. As of 1999, Vegas is not a part of the most popular TCP implementations.

We emphasize that TCP congestion control has evolved over the years, and is still evolving. What was good for the Internet when the bulk of the TCP connec-tions carried SMTP, FTP, and Telnet traffic is not necessarily good for today's Web-dominated Internet or for the Internet of the future, which will support who-knows-what kinds of services.

Does TCP ensure fairness? In the above discussion, we noted that the goal of TCP's congestion-control mechanism is to share a bottleneck link's bandwidth evenly among the TCP connections traversing that link. But why should TCP's additive-increase, multiplicative-decrease algorithm achieve that goal, particularly given that different TCP connections may start at different times and thus may have different window sizes at a given point in time? [Chiu 1989] provides an ele-gant and intuitive explanation of why TCP congestion control converges to pro-vide an equal share of a bottleneck link's bandwidth among competing TCP connections.

Let's consider the simple case of two TCP connections sharing a single link with transmission rate R, as shown in Figure 3.47. We'll assume that the two con-nections have the same MSS and RTT (so that if they have the same congestion window size, then they have the same throughput), that they have a large amount of data to send, and that no other TCP connections or UDP datagrams traverse this

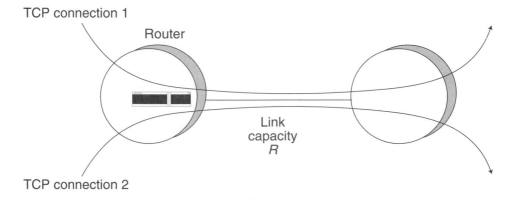

FIGURE 3.47 Two TCP connections sharing a single bottleneck link

shared link. Also, we'll ignore the slow-start phase of TCP and assume the TCP connections are operating in congestion-avoidance mode (additive-increase, multiplicative-decrease) at all times.

Figure 3.48 plots the throughput realized by the two TCP connections. If TCP is to equally share the link bandwidth between the two connections, then the realized throughput should fall along the 45-degree arrow ("equal bandwidth share") emanating from the origin. Ideally, the sum of the two throughputs should equal R. (Certainly, each connection receiving an equal, but zero, share of the link capacity is not a desirable situation!) So the goal should be to have the achieved throughputs fall somewhere near the intersection of the "equal bandwidth share" line and the "full bandwidth utilization" line in Figure 3.48.

Suppose that the TCP window sizes are such that at a given point in time, connections 1 and 2 realize throughputs indicated by point A in Figure 3.48. Because the amount of link bandwidth jointly consumed by the two connections is less than R, no loss will occur, and both connections will increase their window by 1 per RTT as a result of TCP's congestion-avoidance algorithm. Thus, the joint throughput of the two connections proceeds along a 45-degree line (equal increase for both connections) starting from point A. Eventually, the link bandwidth jointly

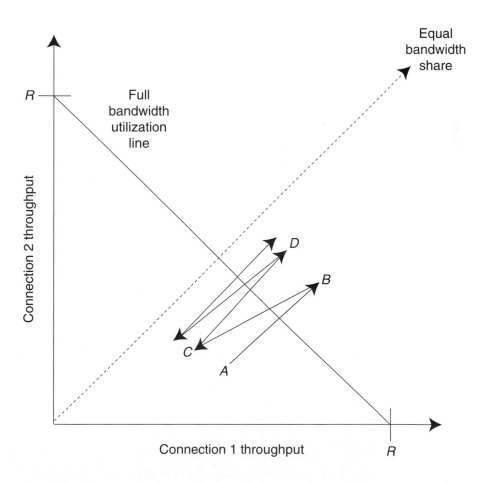

FIGURE 3.48   Throughput realized by TCP connections 1 and 2

consumed by the two connections will be greater than R and eventually packet loss will occur. Suppose that connections 1 and 2 experience packet loss when they realize throughputs indicated by point B. Connections 1 and 2 then decrease their windows by a factor of two. The resulting throughputs realized are thus at point C, halfway along a vector starting at B and ending at the origin. Because the joint bandwidth use is less than R at point C, the two connections again increase their throughputs along a 45-degree line starting from C. Eventually, loss will again occur, for example, at point D, and the two connections again decrease their window sizes by a factor of two, and so on. You should convince yourself that the bandwidth realized by the two connections eventually fluctuates along the equal bandwidth share line. You should also convince yourself that the two connections will converge to this behavior regardless of where they are in the two-dimensional space! Although a number of idealized assumptions lay behind this scenario, it still provides an intuitive feel for why TCP results in an equal sharing of bandwidth among connections.

In our idealized scenario, we assumed that only TCP connections traverse the bottleneck link, and that only a single TCP connection is associated with a host-destination pair. In practice, these two conditions are typically not met, and client-server applications can thus obtain very unequal portions of link bandwidth.

Many network applications run over TCP rather than UDP because they want to make use of TCP's reliable transport service. But an application developer choosing TCP gets not only reliable data transfer but also TCP congestion control. We have just seen how TCP congestion control regulates an application's transmission rate via the congestion-window mechanism. Many multimedia applications do not run over TCP for this very reason—they do not want their transmission rate throttled, even if the network is very congested. In particular, many Internet telephone and Internet video conferencing applications typically run over UDP. These applications prefer to pump their audio and video into the network at a constant rate and occasionally lose packets, rather than reduce their rates to "fair" levels at times of congestion and not lose any packets. From the perspective of TCP, the multimedia applications running over UDP are not being fair—they do not cooperate with the other connections nor adjust their transmission rates appropriately. A major challenge in the upcoming years will be to develop congestion-control mechanisms for the Internet that prevent UDP traffic from bringing the Internet's throughput to a grinding halt.

But even if we could force UDP traffic to behave fairly, the fairness problem would still not be completely solved. This is because there is nothing to stop an application running over TCP from using multiple parallel connections. For example, Web browsers often use multiple parallel TCP connections to transfer a Web page. (The exact number of multiple connections is configurable in most browsers.) When an application uses multiple parallel connections, it gets a larger fraction of the bandwidth in a congested link. As an example, consider a link of rate R supporting nine on-going client-server applications, with each of the applications using one TCP connection. If a new application comes along and also uses one TCP connection, then each application gets approximately the same transmission rate of $R/10$. But if this new application instead uses 11 parallel TCP connections, then the new application gets an unfair allocation of $R/2$. Because Web traffic is so pervasive in the Internet, multiple parallel connections are not uncommon.

Macroscopic description of TCP dynamics. Consider sending a very large file over a TCP connection. If we take a macroscopic view of the traffic sent by the source, we can ignore the slow-start phase. Indeed, the connection is in the slow-start phase for a relatively short period of time because the connection grows out of the phase exponentially fast. When we ignore the slow-start phase, the congestion window grows linearly, gets chopped in half when loss occurs, grows linearly, gets chopped in half when loss occurs, and so on. This gives rise to the saw-tooth behavior of TCP [Stevens 1994] shown in Figure 3.46.

Given this saw-tooth behavior, what is the average throughput of a TCP connection? During a particular round-trip interval, the rate at which TCP sends data is a function of the congestion window and the current RTT. When the window size is $w * MSS$ and the current round-trip time is *RTT,* then TCP's transmission rate is $(w * MSS)/RTT$. During the congestion-avoidance phase, TCP probes for additional bandwidth by increasing w by one each RTT until loss occurs. (Denote by W the value of w at which loss occurs.) Assuming that *RTT* and W are approximately constant over the duration of the connection, the TCP transmission rate ranges from

$$(W * MSS)/(2\ RTT) \text{ to } (W * MSS)/RTT$$

These assumptions lead to a highly simplified macroscopic model for the steady-state behavior of TCP. The network drops a packet from the connection when the connection's window size increases to $W * MSS$; the congestion window is then cut in half and then increases by one MSS per round-trip time until it again reaches W. This process repeats itself over and over again. Because the TCP throughput increases linearly between the two extreme values, we have:

$$\text{Average throughput of a connection} = (0.75 * W * MSS)/RTT$$

Using this highly idealized model for the steady-state dynamics of TCP, we can also derive an interesting expression that relates a connection's loss rate to its available bandwidth [Mahdavi 1997]. This derivation is outlined in the homework problems.

3.7.2 Modeling Latency: Static Congestion Window

Many TCP connections transport relatively small files from one host to another. For example, with HTTP/1.0, each object in a Web page is transported over a separate TCP connection, and many of these objects are small text files or tiny icons. When transporting a small file, TCP connection establishment and slow start may have a significant impact on the latency. In this section we present an analytical model that quantifies the impact of connection establishment and slow start on latency. For a given object, we define the **latency** as the time from when the client initiates a TCP connection until the time at which the client receives the requested object in its entirety.

The analysis presented here assumes that the network is uncongested, that is, that the TCP connection transporting the object does not have to share link bandwidth with other TCP or UDP traffic. (We comment on this assumption below.) Also, in order to not to obscure the central issues, we carry out the analysis in the

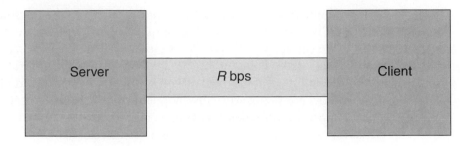

FIGURE 3.49   A simple one-link network connecting a client and a server

context of the simple one-link network as shown in Figure 3.49. (This link might model a single bottleneck on an end-to-end path. See also the homework problems for an explicit extension to the case of multiple links.)

We also make the following simplifying assumptions:

- The amount of data that the sender can transmit is solely limited by the sender's congestion window. (Thus, the TCP receive buffers are large.)
- Packets are neither lost nor corrupted, so that there are no retransmissions.
- All protocol header overheads—including TCP, IP, and link-layer headers— are negligible and ignored.
- The object (that is, file) to be transferred consists of an integer number of segments of size MSS (maximum segment size).
- The only packets that have non-negligible transmission times are packets that carry maximum-size TCP segments. Request packets, acknowledgments and TCP connection establishment packets are small and have negligible transmission times.
- The initial threshold in the TCP congestion control mechanism is a large value that is never attained by the congestion window.

We also introduce the following notation:

- The size of the object to be transferred is O bits.
- The MSS (maximum size segment) is S bits (for example, 536 bytes).
- The transmission rate of the link from the server to the client is R bps.
- The round-trip time is denoted by *RTT*.

In this section we define the *RTT* to be the time elapsed for a small packet to travel from client to server and then back to the client, *excluding the transmission time of the packet.* It includes the two end-to-end propagation delays between the two end systems and the processing times at the two end systems. We shall assume that the RTT is also equal to the roundtrip time of a packet beginning at the server.

Although the analysis presented in this section assumes an uncongested network with a single TCP connection, it nevertheless sheds insight on the more realistic case of multilink congested network. For a congested network, R roughly represents the amount of bandwidth received in steady state in the end-to-end network connection, and RTT represents a round-trip delay that includes queuing delays at the routers preceding the congested links. In the congested network case, we model each TCP connection as a constant-bit-rate connection of rate R bps preceded by a single slow-start phase. (This is roughly how TCP Tahoe behaves when losses are detected with triple duplicate acknowledgments.) In our numerical examples, we use values of R and RTT that reflect typical values for a congested network.

Before beginning the formal analysis, let us try to gain some intuition. Let us consider what would be the latency if there were no congestion-window constraint; that is, if the server were permitted to send segments back-to-back until the entire object is sent. To answer this question, first note that one RTT is required to initiate the TCP connection. After one RTT, the client sends a request for the object (which is piggybacked onto the third segment in the three-way TCP handshake). After a total of two RTTs, the client begins to receive data from the server. The client receives data from the server for a period of time O/R, the time for the server to transmit the entire object. Thus, in the case of no congestion-window constraint, the total latency is $2\ RTT + O/R$. This represents a lower bound; the slow-start procedure, with its dynamic congestion window, will of course elongate this latency.

Static congestion window. Although TCP uses a dynamic congestion window, it is instructive to first analyze the case of a static congestion window. Let W, a positive integer, denote a **fixed-size static congestion window.** For the static congestion window, the server is not permitted to have more than W unacknowledged outstanding segments. When the server receives the request from the client, the server immediately sends W segments back-to-back to the client. The server then sends one segment into the network for each acknowledgment it receives from the client. The server continues to send one segment for each acknowledgment until all of the segments of the object have been sent. There are two cases to consider:

1. $WS/R > RTT + S/R$. In this case, the server receives an acknowledgment for the first segment in the first window before the server completes the transmission of the first window.

2. $WS/R < RTT + S/R$. In this case, the server transmits the first window's worth of segments before the server receives an acknowledgment for the first segment in the window.

Let us first consider case 1, which is illustrated in Figure 3.50. In this figure the window size is $W = 4$ segments.

One RTT is required to initiate the TCP connection. After one RTT, the client sends a request for the object (which is piggybacked onto the third segment in the three-way TCP handshake). After a total of two RTTs, the client begins to receive data from the server. Segments arrive periodically from the server every S/R seconds, and the client acknowledges every segment it receives from the server. Because the server receives the first acknowledgment before it completes sending a window's worth of segments, the server continues to transmit segments after having transmitted the first window's worth of segments. And because the acknowledgments arrive periodically at the server every S/R seconds from the time when the first acknowledgment arrives, the server transmits segments continuously until it has transmitted the entire object. Thus, once the server starts

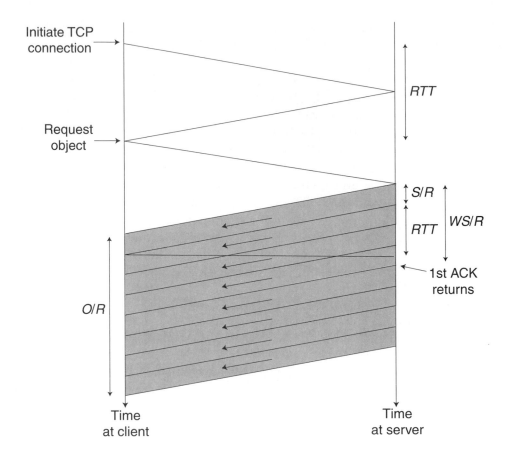

FIGURE 3.50   The case that $WS/R > RTT + S/R$

to transmit the object at rate R, it continues to transmit the object at rate R until the entire object is transmitted. The latency therefore is $2\,RTT + O/R$.

Now let us consider case 2, which is illustrated in Figure 3.51. In this figure, the window size is $W = 2$ segments.

Once again, after a total of two RTTs, the client begins to receive segments from the server. These segments arrive periodically every S/R seconds, and the client acknowledges every segment it receives from the server. But now the server completes the transmission of the first window before the first acknowledgment arrives from the client. Therefore, after sending a window, the server must stall and wait for an acknowledgment before resuming transmission. When an acknowledgment finally arrives, the server sends a new segment to the client. Once the first acknowledgment arrives, a window's worth of acknowledgments arrive, with each successive acknowledgment spaced by S/R seconds. For each of these acknowledgments, the server sends exactly one segment. Thus, the server alternates between two states: a transmitting state, during which it transmits W segments, and a stalled state, during which it transmits nothing and waits for an acknowledgment. The latency is equal to $2\,RTT$ plus the time required for the

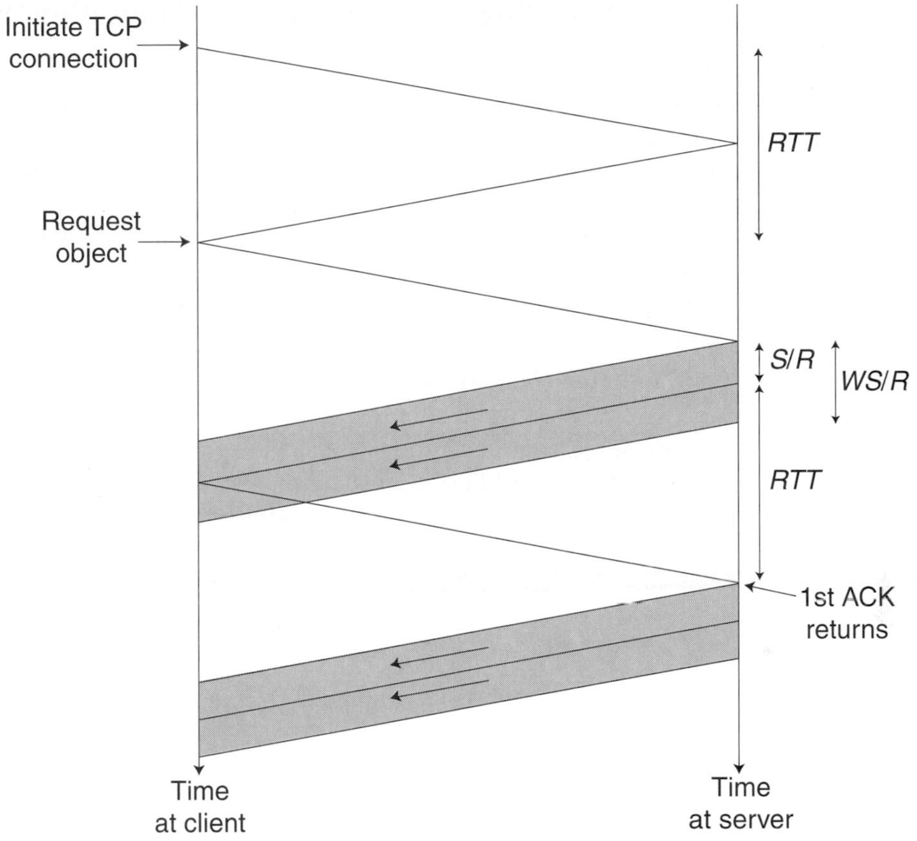

FIGURE 3.51 The case that $WS/R < RTT + S/R$

server to transmit the object, O/R, plus the amount of time that the server is in the stalled state. To determine the amount of time the server is in the stalled state, let $K = O/WS$; if O/WS is not an integer, then round K up to the nearest integer. Note that K is the number of windows of data there are in the object of size O. The server is in the stalled state between the transmission of each of the windows, that is, for $K - 1$ periods of time, with each period lasting $RTT - (W - 1)S/R$ (see Figure 3.51). Thus, for case 2,

$$\text{Latency} = 2\,RTT + O/R + (K - 1)\,[S/R + RTT - WS/R]$$

Combining the two cases, we obtain

$$\text{Latency} = 2\,RTT + O/R + (K - 1)\,[S/R + RTT - WS/R]^+$$

where $[x]^+ = \max(x,0)$.

This completes our analysis of static windows. The following analysis for dynamic windows is more complicated, but parallels that for static windows.

3.7.3 Modeling Latency: Dynamic Congestion Window

We now investigate the latency for a file transfer when TCP's dynamic congestion window is in force. Recall that the server first starts with a congestion window of one segment and sends one segment to the client. When it receives an acknowledgment for the segment, it increases its congestion window to two segments and sends two segments to the client (spaced apart by S/R seconds). As it receives the acknowledgments for the two segments, it increases the congestion window to four segments and sends four segments to the client (again spaced apart by S/R seconds). The process continues, with the congestion window doubling every RTT. A timing diagram for TCP is illustrated in Figure 3.52.

Note that O/S is the number of segments in the object; in the above diagram, $O/S = 15$. Consider the number of segments that are in each of the windows. The first window contains one segment, the second window contains two segments, and the third window contains four segments. More generally, the kth window contains 2^{k-1} segments. Let K be the number of windows that cover the object; in the preceding diagram, $K = 4$. In general, we can express K in terms of O/S as follows:

$$
\begin{aligned}
K &= \min\left\{k : 2^0 + 2^1 + \cdots + 2^{k-1} \geq \frac{O}{S}\right\} \\[2mm]
&= \min\left\{k : 2^k - 1 \geq \frac{O}{S}\right\} \\[2mm]
&= \min\left\{k : k \geq \log_2\left(\frac{O}{S} + 1\right)\right\} \\[2mm]
&= \left\lceil \log_2\left(\frac{O}{S} + 1\right) \right\rceil
\end{aligned}
$$

After transmitting a window's worth of data, the server may stall (that is, stop transmitting) while it waits for an acknowledgment. In Figure 3.52, the server stalls after transmitting the first and second windows, but not after transmitting the third. Let us now calculate the amount of stall time after transmitting the kth window. The time the server begins to transmit the kth window until the time when the server receives an acknowledgment for the first segment in the window is $S/R + RTT$. The transmission time of the kth window is $(S/R) \, 2^{k-1}$. The stall time is the difference of these two quantities, that is,

$$
[S/R + RTT - 2^{k-1}(S/R)]^+.
$$

The server can potentially stall after the transmission of each of the first $k - 1$ windows. (The server is done after the transmission of the kth window.) We can now calculate the latency for transferring the file. The latency has three components: $2\,RTT$ for setting up the TCP connection and requesting the file, O/R, the

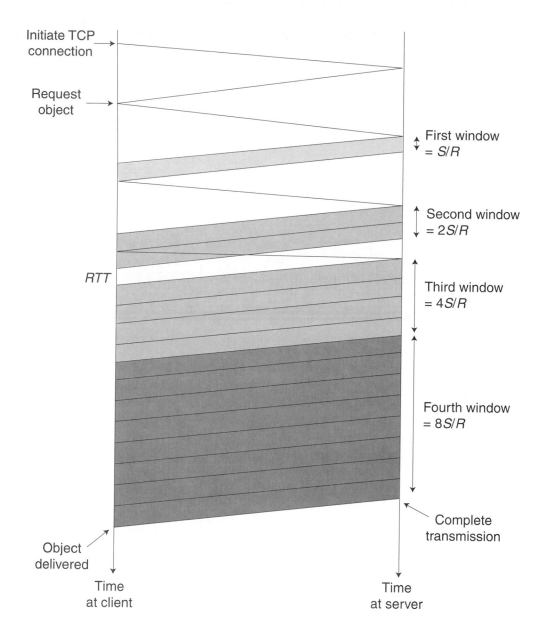

FIGURE 3.52 TCP timing during slow start

transmission time of the object, and the sum of all the stalled times. Thus,

$$Latency = 2RTT + \frac{O}{R} + \sum_{k=1}^{K-1} \left[\frac{S}{R} + RTT - 2^{k-1}\frac{S}{R} \right]^{+}$$

The reader should compare the above equation for the latency equation for static congestion windows; all the terms are exactly the same except the term WS/R for static windows has been replaced by $2^{k-1}(S/R)$ for dynamic windows. To obtain a more compact expression for the latency, let Q be the number of times the server would stall if the object contained an infinite number of segments:

$$Q = \max\left\{k : RTT + \frac{S}{R} - \frac{S}{R}2^{k-1} \geq 0\right\}$$

$$= \max\left\{k : 2^{k-1} \leq 1 + \frac{RTT}{S/R}\right\}$$

$$= \max\left\{k : k \leq \log_2\left(1 + \frac{RTT}{S/R}\right) + 1\right\}$$

$$= \left\lfloor \log_2\left(1 + \frac{RTT}{S/R}\right)\right\rfloor + 1.$$

The actual number of times the server stalls is $P = \min\{Q, K-1\}$. In Figure 3.52, $P = Q = 2$. Combining the above two equations gives

$$Latency = \frac{O}{R} + 2RTT + \sum_{k=1}^{P}\left(RTT + \frac{S}{R} - \frac{S}{R}2^{k-1}\right)$$

We can further simplify the above formula for latency by noting

$$\sum_{k=1}^{P} 2^{k-1} = 2^P - 1$$

Combining the above two equations gives the following closed-form expression for the latency:

$$Latency = 2RTT + \frac{O}{R} + P\left[RTT + \frac{S}{R}\right] - (2^P - 1)\frac{S}{R}$$

Thus to calculate the latency, we simple must calculate K and Q, set $P = \min\{Q, K-1\}$, and plug P into the above formula.

It is interesting to compare the TCP latency to the latency that would occur if there were no congestion control (that is, no congestion window constraint). Without congestion control, the latency is $2\,RTT + O/R$, which we define to be the *minimum latency*. It is a simple exercise to show that

$$\frac{Latency}{MinimumLatency} \leq 1 + \frac{P}{[(O/R)/RTT] + 2}$$

We see from the above formula that TCP slow start will not significantly increase latency if $RTT \ll O/R$, that is, if the round-trip time is much less than the transmission time of the object. Thus, if we are sending a relatively large object over an uncongested high-speed link, then slow start has an insignificant affect on latency. However, with the Web, we are often transmitting many small objects over congested links, in which case slow start can significantly increase latency (as we shall see in the following subsection).

Let us now take a look at some example scenarios. In all the scenarios we set $S = 536$ bytes, a common default value for TCP. We shall use an *RTT* of 100 msec, which is not an atypical value for a continental or intercontinental delay over moderately congested links. First consider sending a rather large object of size $O = 100$ Kbytes. The number of windows that cover this object is $K = 8$. For a number of transmission rates, the following chart examines the effect of the slow-start mechanism on the latency.

R	*O/R*	P	Minimum Latency: *O/R + 2 RTT*	Latency with slow start
28 Kbps	28.6 sec	1	28.8 sec	28.9 sec
100 Kbps	8 sec	2	8.2 sec	8.4 sec
1 Mbps	800 msec	5	1 sec	1.5 sec
10 Mbps	80 msec	7	0.28 sec	0.98 sec

We see from the above chart that for a large object, slow-start adds appreciable delay only when the transmission rate is high. If the transmission rate is low, then acknowledgments come back relatively quickly, and TCP quickly ramps up to its maximum rate. For example, when $R = 100$ Kbps, the number of stall periods is $P = 2$ whereas the number of windows to transmit is $K = 8$; thus the server stalls only after the first two of eight windows. On other hand, when $R = 10$ Mbps, the server stalls between each window, which causes a significant increase in the delay.

Now consider sending a small object of size $O = 5$ Kbytes. The number of windows that cover this object is $K = 4$. For a number of transmission rates, the following chart examines the effect of the slow-start mechanism.

R	*O/R*	P	Minimum latency: *O/R + 2 RTT*	Latency with slow start
28 Kbps	1.43 sec	1	1.63 sec	1.73 sec
100 Kbps	0.4 sec	2	0.6 sec	0.757 sec
1 Mbps	40 msec	3	0.24 sec	0.52 sec
10 Mbps	4 msec	3	0.20 sec	0.50 sec

Once again, slow start adds an appreciable delay when the transmission rate is high. For example, when $R = 1$ Mbps, the server stalls between each window, which causes the latency to be more than twice that of the minimum latency.

For a larger *RTT,* the effect of slow start becomes significant for small objects for smaller transmission rates. The following chart examines the effect of slow start for RTT = 1 second and O = 5 Kbytes (K = 4).

R	*O/R*	P	Minimum latency: *O/R + 2 RTT*	Latency with slow start
28 Kbps	1.43 sec	3	3.4 sec	5.8 sec
100 Kbps	0.4 sec	3	2.4 sec	5.2 sec
1 Mbps	40 msec	3	2.0 sec	5.0 sec
10 Mbps	4 msec	3	2.0 sec	5.0 sec

In summary, slow start can significantly increase latency when the object size is relatively small and the RTT is relatively large. Unfortunately, this is often the scenario when sending objects over the World Wide Web.

An example: HTTP. As an application of the latency analysis, let's now calculate the response time for a Web page sent over nonpersistent HTTP. Suppose that the page consists of one base HTML page and M referenced images. To keep things simple, let us assume that each of the $M + 1$ objects contains exactly O bits.

With nonpersistent HTTP, each object is transferred independently, one after the other. The response time of the Web page is therefore the sum of the latencies for the individual objects. Thus

$$response\ time\ =\ (M + 1)\left\{ 2RTT + \frac{O}{R} + P\left[RTT + \frac{S}{R}\right] - (2^P - 1)\frac{S}{R} \right\}$$

Note that the response time for nonpersistent HTTP takes the form:

Response time = $(M + 1)O/R$ + $2(M + 1)$RTT + latency due to TCP slow-start for each of the $M + 1$ objects.

Clearly, if there are many objects in the Web page and if *RTT* is large, then non-persistent HTTP will have poor response-time performance. In the homework problems, we will investigate the response time for other HTTP transport schemes, including persistent connections and nonpersistent connections with parallel connections. The reader is also encouraged to see [Heidemann 1997] for a related analysis.

SUMMARY

We began this chapter by studying the services that a transport layer protocol can provide to network applications. At one extreme, the transport layer protocol can be very simple and offer a no-frills service to applications, providing only the multiplexing/demultiplexing function for communicating processes. The Internet's UDP protocol is an example of such a no-frills (and no-thrills, from the perspective of someone interested in networking) transport-layer protocol. At the other extreme, a transport layer protocol can provide a variety of guarantees to applications, such as reliable delivery of data, delay guarantees, and bandwidth guarantees. Nevertheless, the services that a transport protocol can provide are often constrained by the service model of the underlying network-layer protocol. If the network layer protocol cannot provide delay or bandwidth guarantees to transport-layer segments, then the transport-layer protocol cannot provide delay or bandwidth guarantees for the messages sent between processes.

We learned in Section 3.4 that a transport-layer protocol can provide reliable data transfer even if the underlying network layer is unreliable. We saw that providing reliable data transfer has many subtle points, but that the task can be accomplished by carefully combining acknowledgments, timers, retransmissions, and sequence numbers.

Although we covered reliable data transfer in this chapter, we should keep in mind that reliable data transfer can be provided by link, network, transport, or application-layer protocols. Any of the upper four layers of the protocol stack can implement acknowledgments, timers, retransmissions, and sequence numbers and provide reliable data transfer to the layer above. In fact, over the years, engineers and computer scientists have independently designed and implemented link, network, transport, and application-layer protocols that provide reliable data transfer (although many of these protocols have quietly disappeared).

In Section 3.5 we took a close look at TCP, the Internet's connection-oriented and reliable transport-layer protocol. We learned that TCP is complex, involving connection management, flow control, round-trip time estimation, as well as reliable data transfer. In fact, TCP is actually more complex than our description—we intentionally did not discuss a variety of TCP patches, fixes, and improvements that are widely implemented in various versions of TCP. All of this complexity, however, is hidden from the network application. If a client on one host wants to reliably send data to a server on another host, it simply opens a TCP socket to the server and then pumps data into that socket. The client-server application is oblivious to all of TCP's complexity.

In Section 3.6 we examined congestion control from a broad perspective, and in Section 3.7 we showed how TCP implements congestion control. We learned that congestion control is imperative for the well-being of the network. Without congestion control, a network can easily become gridlocked, with little or no data being transported end-to-end. In Section 3.7 we learned that TCP implements an end-to-end congestion-control mechanism that additively increases its transmission rate when the TCP connection's path is judged to be congestion-free, and multiplicatively decreases its transmission rate when loss occurs. This mechanism also strives to give each TCP connection passing through a congested link an equal share of the link bandwidth. We also examined in some depth the impact of TCP connection establishment and slow start on latency. We observed that in many important scenarios, connection establishment and slow start significantly contribute to end-to-end delay. We emphasize once more that while TCP congestion control has evolved over the years, it remains an area of intensive research, and will likely continue to evolve in the upcoming years.

In Chapter 1 we said that a computer network can be partitioned into the "network edge" and the "network core." The network edge covers everything that happens in the end systems. Having now covered the application layer and the transport layer, our discussion of the network edge is now complete. It is time to explore the network core! This journey begins in the next chapter, where we'll study the network layer, and continues into Chapter 5, where we'll study the link layer.

HOMEWORK PROBLEMS AND QUESTIONS

Chapter 3

Review Questions

Sections 3.1–3.3

1. Consider a TCP connection between host A and host B. Suppose that the TCP segments traveling from host A to host B have source port number x and destination port number y. What are the source and destination port numbers for the segments traveling from host B to host A?

2. Describe why an application developer may choose to run its application over UDP rather than TCP.

3. Is it possible for an application to enjoy reliable data transfer even when the application runs over UDP? If so, how?

Section 3.5

4. True or False:
   a. Host A is sending host B a large file over a TCP connection. Assume host B has no data to send A. Host B will not send acknowledgments to host A because host B cannot piggyback the acknowledgments on data.
   b. The size of the TCP `RcvWindow` never changes throughout the duration of the connection.
   c. Suppose host A is sending host B a large file over a TCP connection. The number of unacknowledged bytes that A sends cannot exceed the size of the receive buffer.
   d. Suppose host A is sending a large file to host B over a TCP connection. If the sequence number for a segment of this connection is m, then the sequence number for the subsequent segment will necessarily be m + 1.
   e. The TCP segment has a field in its header for `RcvWindow`.
   f. Suppose that the last `SampleRTT` in a TCP connection is equal to 1 sec. Then `Timeout` for the connection will necessarily be set to a value >= 1 sec.
   g. Suppose host A sends host B one segment with sequence number 38 and 4 bytes of data. Then in this same segment the acknowledgment number is necessarily 42.

5. Suppose A sends two TCP segments back-to-back to B. The first segment has sequence number 90; the second has sequence number 110. (a) How much data is the first segment? (b) Suppose that the first segment is lost, but the second segment arrives at B. In the acknowledgment that B sends to A, what will be the acknowledgment number?

6. Consider the Telent example discussed in Section 3.5. A few seconds after the user types the letter 'C' the user types the letter 'R'. After typing the letter 'R' how many segments are sent and what is put in the sequence number and acknowledgment fields of the segments?

Section 3.7

7. Suppose two TCP connections are present over some bottleneck link of rate R bps. Both connections have a huge file to send (in the same direction over the bottleneck link). The transmissions of the files start at the same time. What is the transmission rate that TCP would like to give to each of the connections?

8. True or False: Consider congestion control in TCP. When a timer expires at the sender, the threshold is set to one half of its previous value.

PROBLEMS

1. Suppose client A initiates an FTP session with server S. At about the same time, client B also initiates an FTP session with server S. Provide possible source and destination port numbers for:
   a. the segments sent from A to S.
   b. the segments sent from B to S.
   c. the segments sent from S to A.
   d. the segments sent from S to B.
   e. If A and B are different hosts, is it possible that the source port numbers in the segments from A to S are the same as those from B to S?
   f. How about if they are the same host?

2. UDP and TCP use 1's complement for their checksums. Suppose you have the following three 8-bit words: 01010101, 01110000, 11001100. What is the 1's complement of the sum of these words? Show all work. Why is it that UDP takes the 1's complement of the sum, that is, why not just use the sum? With the 1's complement scheme, how does the receiver detect errors? Is it possible that a 1-bit error will go undetected? How about a 2-bit error?

3. Protocol rdt2.1 uses both ACKs and NAKs. Redesign the protocol, adding whatever additional protocol mechanisms are needed, for the case that only ACK messages are used. Assume that packets can be corrupted, but not lost. Give the sender and receiver FSMs, and a trace of your protocol in operation (using traces as in Figure 3.15). Show also how the protocol works in the case of no errors, and show how your protocol recovers from channel bit errors.

4. Consider our motivation for correcting protocol rtd2.1.

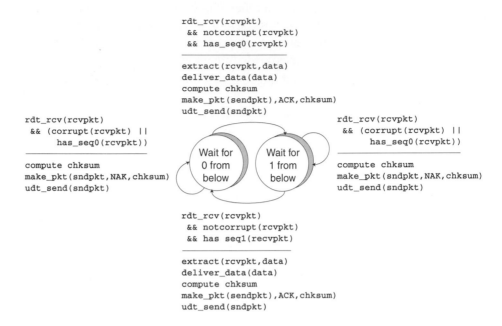

Show that this receiver, when operating with the sender shown in Figure 3.11, can lead the sender and receiver to enter into a deadlock state, where each is waiting for an event that will never occur.

5. In protocol rdt3.0, the ACK packets flowing from the receiver to the sender do not have sequence numbers (although they do have an ACK field that contains the sequence number of the packet they are acknowledging). Why is it that our ACK packets do not require sequence numbers?

6. Draw the FSM for the receiver side of protocol rdt 3.0.

7. Give a trace of the operation of protocol rdt3.0 when data packets and acknowledgments packets are garbled. Your trace should be similar to that used in Figure 3.15.

8. Consider a channel that can lose packets but has a maximum delay that is known. Modify protocol rdt2.1 to include sender timeout and retransmit. Informally argue why your protocol can communicate correctly over this channel.

9. The sender side of rdt3.0 simply ignores (that is, takes no action on) all received packets that are either in error, or have the wrong value in the acknum field of an acknowledgment packet. Suppose that in such circumstances, rdt3.0 were to simply retransmit the current data packet. Would the protocol still work? (Hint: Consider what would happen in the case that there are only bit errors; no packet losses and no premature timeouts occur. Consider how many times the nth packet is sent, in the limit as n approaches infinity.)

10. Consider the cross-country example shown in Figure 3.16. How big would the window size have to be for the channel utilization to be greater than 90%?

11. Design a reliable, pipelined, data transfer protocol that uses only negative acknowledgments. How quickly will your protocol respond to lost packets when the arrival rate of data to the sender is low? Is high?

12. Consider transferring an enormous file of L bytes from host A to host B. Assume an MSS of 1460 bytes.

    a. What is the maximum value of L such that TCP sequence numbers are not exhausted? Recall that the TCP number field has four bytes.

    b. For the L you obtain in (a), find how long it takes to transmit the file. Assume that a total of 66 bytes of transport, network, and data-link header are added to each segment before the resulting packet is sent out over a 10 Mbps link. Ignore flow control and congestion control, so A can pump out the segments back-to-back and continuously.

13. In Figure 3.30, we see that TCP waits until it has received three duplicate ACK before performing a fast retransmit. Why do you think the TCP designers chose not to perform a fast retransmit after the first duplicate ACK for a segment is received?

14. Consider the TCP procedure for estimating RTT. Suppose that $x = .1$. Let `SampleRTT`$_1$ be the most recent sample RTT, let `SampleRTT`$_2$ be the next most recent sample RTT, etc. (a) For a given TCP connection, suppose 4 acknowledgments have been returned with corresponding sample RTTs `SampleRTT`$_4$, `SampleRTT`$_3$, `SampleRTT`$_2$, and `SampleRTT`$_1$. Express `Esti-matedRTT` in terms of the four sample RTTs. (b) Generalize your formula for n sample round-trip times. (c) For the formula in part (b) let n approach infinity. Comment on why this averaging procedure is called an exponential moving average.

15. Refer to Figure 3.48 that illustrates the convergence of TCP's additive increase, multiplicative decrease algorithm. Suppose that instead of a multiplicative decrease, TCP decreased the window size by a constant amount. Would the resulting additive increase additive decrease converge to an equal share algorithm? Justify your answer using a diagram similar to Figure 3.48.

16. Recall the idealized model for the steady-state dynamics of TCP. In the period of time from when the connection's window size varies from (W*MSS)/2 to W*MSS, only one packet is lost (at the very end of the period).

    a. Show that the loss rate is equal to

    $$L = \text{loss rate} = 1/[(3/8) * W^2 - W/4]$$

    b. Use the above result to show that if a connection has loss rate L, then its average bandwidth is approximately given by:

    $$\text{Average bandwidth of connection} \sim 1.22 * MSS/[RTT * \text{sqrt}(L)]$$

17. Consider sending an object of size O = 100 Kbytes from server to client. Let S = 536 bytes and RTT = 100 msec. Suppose the transport protocol uses static windows with window size W.

    a. For a transmission rate of 28 Kbps, determine the minimum possible latency. Determine the minimum window size that achieves this latency.

    b. Repeat (a) for 100 Kbps.

    c. Repeat (a) for 1 Mbps.

    d. Repeat (a) for 10 Mbps.

18. Suppose TCP increased its congestion window by two rather than by one for each received acknowledgment during slow start. Thus, the first window consists of one segment, the second of three segments, the third of nine segments, etc. For this slow-start procedure:

    a. Express K in terms of O and S.

    b. Express Q in terms of RTT, S, and R.

    c. Express latency in terms of $P = \min(K - 1, Q)$, O, R, and *RTT*.

19. Consider the case RTT = 1 second and O = 100 Kbytes. Prepare a chart (similar to the charts in Section 3.5.2) that compares the minimum latency ($O/R + 2$ *RTT*) with the latency with slow start for R = 28 Kbps, 100 Kbps, 1 Mbps, and 10 Mbps.

20. True or False?

    a. If a Web page consists of exactly one object, then non-persistent and persistent connections have exactly the same response time performance.

    b. Consider sending one object of size O from server to browser over TCP. If O > S, where S is the maximum segment size, then the server will stall at least once.

    c. Suppose a Web page consists of 10 objects, each of size O bits. For persistent HTTP, the RTT portion of the response time is 20 RTT.

    d. Suppose a Web page consists of 10 objects, each of size O bits. For non-persistent HTTP with 5 parallel connections, the RTT portion of the response time is 12 RTT.

21. The analysis for dynamic windows in the text assumes that there is one link between server and client. Redo the analysis for *T* links between server and client. Assume the network has no congestion, so the packets experience no queuing delays. The packets do experience a store-and-forward delay, however. The definition of RTT is the same as that given in the section on TCP congestion control. (Hint: The time for the server to send out the first segment until it receives the acknowledgment is *TS/R + RTT*.)

22. Recall the discussion at the end of Section 3.7.3 on the response time for a Web page. For the case of non-persistent connections, determine a general expression for the *fraction* of the response time that is due to TCP slow start.

23. With persistent HTTP, all objects are sent over the same TCP connection. As we discussed in Chapter 2, one of the motivations behind persistent HTTP (with pipelining) is to diminish the effects of TCP connection establishment and slow start on the response time for a Web page. In this problem we investigate the response time for persistent HTTP. Assume that the client requests all the images at once, but only when it has received the *entire* HTML base page. Let $M + 1$ denote the number of objects and let O denote the size of each object.

    a. Argue that the response time takes the form $(M + 1)O/R + 3RTT +$ latency due to slow-start. Compare the contribution of the RTTs in this expression with that in non-persistent HTTP.

    b. Assume that $K = \log_2 (O/R + 1)$ is an integer; thus, the last window of the base HTML file transmits an entire window's worth of segments, that is, window K transmits 2^{K-1} segments. Let $P' = \min\{Q, K' - 1\}$ and

$$K' = \left\lceil \log_2\left((M + 1)\frac{O}{S}\right) + 1 \right\rceil$$

Note that K' is the number of windows that cover an object of size $(M + 1)O$ and P' is the number of stall periods when sending the large object over a single TCP connection. Suppose (incorrectly) the server can send the images without waiting for the formal request for the images from the client. Show that the response time is that of sending one large object of size $(M + 1)O$:

$$approx\ response\ time\ =\ 2RTT + \frac{(M+1)O}{R} + P'\left[RTT + \frac{S}{R}\right] - (2^{P'} - 1)\frac{S}{R}$$

c. The actual response time for persistent HTTP is somewhat larger than the approximation. This is because the server must wait for a request for the images before sending the images. In particular, the stall time between the Kth and $(K + 1)$st window is not $[S/R + RTT - 2^{K-}(S/R)]^+$ but is instead RTT. Show that

$$response\ time\ =\ 3RTT + \frac{(M+1)O}{R} + P'\left[RTT + \frac{S}{R}\right] -$$

$$(2^{P'} - 1)\frac{S}{R} - \left[\frac{S}{R} + RTT - \frac{S}{R}2^{K-1}\right]^+$$

24. Consider the scenario of $RTT = 100$ msec, $O = 5$ Kbytes, and $M = 10$. Construct a chart that compares the response times for non-persistent and persistent connections for 28 kbps, 100 kbps, 1 Mbps, and 10 Mbps. Note that persistent HTTP has substantially lower response time than non-persistent HTTP for all the transmission rates except 28 Kbps.

25. Repeat the above question for the case of $RTT = 1$ sec, $O = 5$ Kbytes, $M = 10$. Note that for these parameters, persistent HTTP gives a significantly lower response time than non-persistent HTTP for all the transmission rates.

26. Consider now non-persistent HTTP with parallel TCP connections. Recall that browsers typically operate in this mode when using HTTP/1.0. Let X denote the maximum number of parallel connections that the client (browser) is permitted to open. In this mode, the client first uses one TCP connection to obtain the base HTML file. Upon receiving the base HTML file, the client establishes M/X sets of TCP connections, with each set having X parallel connections. Argue that the total response time takes the form:

Response time = $(M + 1)O/R + 2(M/X + 1)\ RTT$ + latency due to slow-start stalling

Compare the contribution of the term involving RTT to that of persistent connections and non-persistent (non-parallel) connections.

DISCUSSION QUESTION

1. Consider streaming stored audio. Does it make sense to run the application over UDP or TCP? Which one does RealNetworks use? Why? Are there any other streaming stored audio products? Which transport protocol do they use and why?

PROGRAMMING ASSIGNMENT

In this programming assignment, you will be writing the sending and receiving transport-level code for implementing a simple reliable data transfer protocol—for either the alternating bit protocol or a Go-Back-N protocol. This should be fun since your implementation will differ very little from what would be required in a real-world situation.

Since you presumably do not have standalone machines (with an OS that you can modify), your code will have to execute in a simulated hardware/software environment. However, the programming interface provided to your routines (that is, the code that would call your entities from above (from layer 5) and from below (from layer 3)) is very close to what is done in an actual UNIX environment. (Indeed, the software interfaces described in this programming assignment are much more realistic than the infinite loop senders and receivers that many textbooks describe.) Stopping/starting of timers are also simulated, and timer interrupts will cause your timer handling routine to be activated.

You can find full details of the programming assignment, as well as C code that you will need to create the simulated hardware/software environment at `http://gaia.cs.umass.edu/kurose/transport/programming_assignment.htm`.

Chapter 4

Network Layer and Routing

INTRODUCTION AND NETWORK SERVICE MODELS

We saw in the previous chapter that the transport layer provides communication service between two processes running on two different hosts. In order to provide this service, the transport layer relies on the services of the network layer, which provides a communication service between hosts. In particular, the network layer moves transport-layer segments from one host to another. At the sending host, the transport-layer segment is passed to the network layer. The network layer then "somehow" gets the segment to the destination host and passes the segment up the protocol stack to the transport layer. Exactly how the network layer moves a segment from the transport layer of an origin host to the transport layer of the destination host is the subject of this chapter. We will see that unlike the transport layers, the network layer *requires the coordination of each and every host and router in the network.* Because of this, network-layer protocols are among the most challenging (and therefore interesting!) in the protocol stack.

Figure 4.1 shows a simple network with two hosts (H1 and H2) and four routers (R1, R2, R3, and R4). The role of the network layer in a sending host is to begin the packet on its journey to the receiving host. For example, if H1 is sending to H2, the network layer in host H1 transfers these packets to its nearby router R2. At the receiving host (for example, H2), the network layer receives the packet from its nearby router (in this case, R3) and delivers the packet up to the transport layer at H2. The primary role of the routers is to "switch" packets from input links to output links. Note that the routers in Figure 4.1 are shown with a truncated protocol stack, that is, with no upper layers above the network layer, because (except for control purposes) routers do not run transport- and application-layer protocols such as those we examined in Chapters 2 and 3.

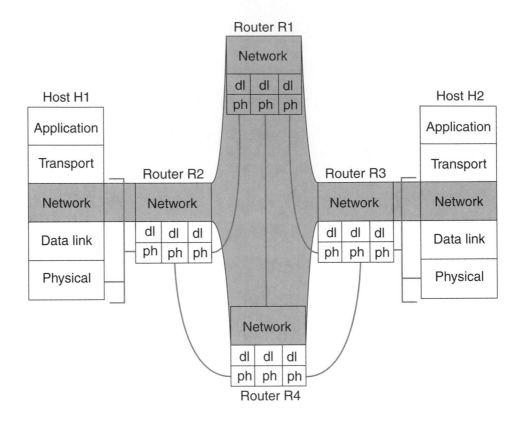

FIGURE 4.1 The network layer

The role of the network layer is thus deceptively simple—to transport packets from a sending host to a receiving host. To do so, three important network-layer functions can be identified:

- *Path Determination.* The network layer must determine the route or path taken by packets as they flow from a sender to a receiver. The algorithms that calculate these paths are referred to as *routing algorithms*. A routing algorithm would determine, for example, whether packets from H1 to H2 flow along the path R2-R1-R3 or path R2-R4-R3 (or any other path between H1 and H2). Much of this chapter will focus on routing algorithms. In Section 4.2 we will study the theory of routing algorithms, concentrating on the two most prevalent classes of routing algorithms: link state routing and distance vector routing. We will see that the complexity of routing algorithms grows considerably as the number of routers in the network increases. This motivates the use of hierarchical routing, a topic we cover in Section 4.3. In Section 4.8 we cover multicast routing—the routing algorithms, switching functions, and call setup mechanisms that allow a packet that is sent just once by a sender to be delivered to multiple destinations.

- *Switching.* When a packet arrives at the input to a router, the router must move it to the appropriate output link. For example, a packet arriving from host H1 to router R2 must either be forwarded towards H2 either along the link from

R2 to R1 or along the link from R2 to R4. In Section 4.6, we look inside a router and examine how a packet is actually switched (moved) from an input link to an output link.

- *Call Setup.* Recall that in our study of TCP, a three-way handshake was required before data actually flowed from sender to receiver. This allowed the sender and receiver to setup the needed state information (for example, sequence number and initial flow control window size). In an analogous manner, some network layer architectures (for example, ATM) require that the routers along the chosen path from source to destination handshake with each other in order to setup state before data actually begins to flow. In the network layer, this process is referred to as **call setup.** The network layer of the Internet architecture does not perform any such call setup.

Before delving into the details of the theory and implementation of the network layer, however, let us first take the broader view and consider what different types of *service* might be offered by the network layer.

4.1.1   Network Service Model

When the transport layer at a sending host transmits a packet into the network (that is, passes it down to the network layer at the sending host), can the transport layer count on the network layer to deliver the packet to the destination? When multiple packets are sent, will they be delivered to the transport layer in the receiving host in the order in which they were sent? Will the amount of time between the sending of two sequential packet transmissions be the same as the amount of time between their reception? Will the network provide any feedback about congestion in the network? What is the abstract view (properties) of the channel connecting the transport layer in the two hosts? The answers to these questions and others are determined by the *service model* provided by the network layer. The network service model defines the characteristics of end-to-end transport of data between one "edge" of the network and the other, that is, between sending and receiving end systems.

Datagram or virtual circuit?   Perhaps the most important abstraction provided by the network layer to the upper layers is whether or not the network layer uses **virtual circuits (VCs).** You may recall from Chapter 1 that a virtual-circuit packet network behaves much like a telephone network, which uses "real circuits" as opposed to "virtual circuits." There are three identifiable phases in a virtual circuit:

- *VC setup.* During the setup phase, the sender contacts the network layer, specifies the receiver address, and waits for the network to setup the VC. The network layer determines the path between sender and receiver, that is, the series of links and switches through which all packets of the VC will travel. As discussed in Chapter 1, this typically involves updating tables in each of the packet switches in the path. During VC setup, the network layer may also reserve resources (for example, bandwidth) along the path of the VC.
- *Data transfer.* Once the VC has been established, data can begin to flow along the VC.

- *Virtual circuit teardown.* This is initiated when the sender (or receiver) informs the network layer of its desire to terminate the VC. The network layer will then typically inform the end system on the other side of the network of the call termination and update the tables in each of the packet switches on the path to indicate that the VC no longer exists.

There is a subtle but important distinction between VC setup at the network layer and connection setup at the transport layer (for example, the TCP 3-way handshake we studied in Chapter 3). Connection setup at the transport layer only involves the two end systems. The two end systems agree to communicate and together determine the parameters (for example, initial sequence number, flow control window size) of their transport layer connection before data actually begins to flow on the transport-level connection. Although the two end systems are aware of the transport-layer connection, the switches within the network are completely oblivious to it. On the other hand, with a virtual-circuit network layer, *packet switches are involved in virtual-circuit setup, and each packet switch is fully aware of all the VCs passing through it.*

The messages that the end systems send to the network to indicate the initiation or termination of a VC, and the messages passed between the switches to set up the VC (that is, to modify switch tables) are known as **signaling messages** and the protocols used to exchange these messages are often referred to as **signaling protocols.** VC setup is shown pictorially in Figure 4.2.

We mentioned in Chapter 1 that ATM uses virtual circuits, although virtual circuits in ATM jargon are called virtual channels. Thus ATM packet switches receive and process VC setup and tear down messages, and they also maintain VC state tables. Frame relay and X.25, which will be covered in Chapter 5, are two other networking technologies that use virtual circuits.

With a **datagram network layer,** each time an end system wants to send a packet, it stamps the packet with the address of the destination end system, and

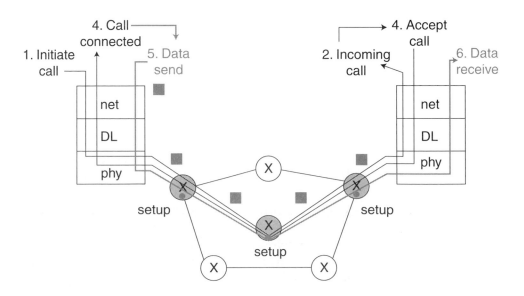

FIGURE 4.2 Virtual circuit service model

then pops the packet into the network. As shown in Figure 4.3, this is done without any VC setup. Packet switches (called "routers" in the Internet) do not maintain any state information about VCs because there are no VCs! Instead, packet switches route a packet towards its destination by examining the packet's destination address, indexing a routing table with the destination address, and forwarding the packet in the direction of the destination. (As discussed in Chapter 1, datagram routing is similar to routing ordinary postal mail.) Because routing tables can be modified at any time, a series of packets sent from one end system to another may follow different paths through the network and may arrive out of order. The Internet uses a datagram network layer.

You may recall from Chapter 1 that a packet-switched network typically offers either a VC service or a datagram service to the transport layer, but not both services. For example, an ATM network offers only a VC service to the ATM transport layer (more precisely, to the ATM adaptation layer), and the Internet offers only a datagram service to the transport layer. The transport layer in turn offers services to communicating processes at the application layer. For example, TCP/IP networks (such as the Internet) offer a connection-oriented service (using TCP) and connectionless service (UDP) to their communicating processes.

An alternative terminology for VC service and datagram service is **network-layer connection-oriented service** and **network-layer connectionless service,** respectively. Indeed, the VC service is a sort of connection-oriented service, as it involves setting up and tearing down a connection-like entity, and maintaining connection state information in the packet switches. The datagram service is a sort of connectionless service in that it does not employ connection-like entities. Both sets of terminology have advantages and disadvantages, and both sets are commonly used in the networking literature. In this book we decided to use the "VC service" and "datagram service" terminology for the network layer, and reserve the "connection-oriented service" and "connectionless service" terminology for the transport layer. We believe this decision will be useful in helping the reader delineate the services offered by the two layers.

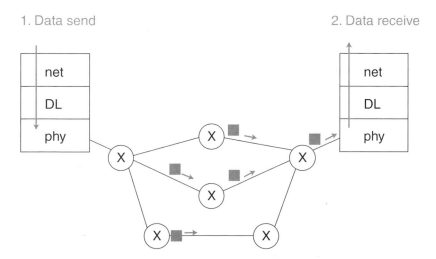

FIGURE 4.3   Datagram service model

The key aspects of the service model of the Internet and ATM network architectures are summarized in Table 4.1. We do not want to delve deeply into the details of the service models here (it can be quite "dry" and detailed discussions can be found in the standards themselves [ATM Forum 1997]). A comparison between the Internet and ATM service models is, however, quite instructive.

The current Internet architecture provides only one service model, the datagram service, which is also known as "**best effort service.**" From Table 4.1, it might appear that best effort service is a euphemism for "no service at all." With best effort service, timing between packets is not guaranteed to be preserved, packets are not guaranteed to be received in the order in which they were sent, nor is the eventual delivery of transmitted packets guaranteed. Given this definition, a network which delivered *no* packets to the destination would satisfy the definition of best effort delivery service. (Indeed, today's congested public Internet might sometimes appear to be an example of a network that does so!) As we will discuss shortly, however, there are sound reasons for such a minimalist network service model. The Internet's best-effort only service model is currently being extended to include so-called "integrated services" and "differentiated service." We will cover these still-evolving service models later in Chapter 6.

Let us next turn to the ATM service models. As noted in our overview of ATM in Chapter 1, there are two ATM standards bodies (the ITU and The ATM Forum). Their network service model definitions contain only minor differences and we adopt here the terminology used in the ATM Forum standards. The ATM architecture provides for multiple service models (that is, each of the two ATM standards each has multiple service models). This means that within the same network, different connections can be provided with different classes of service.

Constant Bit Rate (CBR) network service was the first ATM service model to be standardized, probably reflecting the fact that telephone companies were the early prime movers behind ATM, and CBR network service is ideally suited for

Table 4.1 Internet and ATM Network Service Models

Network Architecture	Service Model	Bandwidth Guarantee	No Loss Guarantee	Ordering	Timing	Congestion Indication
Internet	Best Effort	None	None	Any order possible	Not maintained	None
ATM	CBR	Guaranteed constant rate	Yes	In order	Maintained	Congestion will not occur
ATM	VBR	Guaranteed rate	Yes	In order	Maintained	Congestion will not occur
ATM	ABR	Guaranteed minimum	None	In order	Not maintained	Congestion indication provided
ATM	UBR	None	None	In order	Not maintained	None

carrying real-time, constant-bit-rate audio (for example, a digitized telephone call) and video traffic. The goal of CBR service is conceptually simple—to make the network connection look like a dedicated copper or fiber connection between the sender and receiver. With CBR service, ATM cells are carried across the network in such a way that the end-to-end delay experienced by a cell (the so-called Cell Transfer Delay, CDT), the variability in the end-end delay (often referred to as "jitter" or Cell Delay Variation, CDV), and the fraction of cells that are lost or delivered late (the so-called Cell Loss Rate, CLR) are guaranteed to be less than some specified values. Also, an allocated transmission rate (the Peak Cell Rate, PCR) is defined for the connection and the sender is expected to offer data to the network at this rate. The values for the PCR, CDT, CDV, and CLR are agreed upon by the sending host and the ATM network when the CBR connection is first established.

A second conceptually simple ATM service class is **Unspecified Bit Rate (UBR) network service.** Unlike CBR service, which guarantees rate, delay, delay jitter, and loss, UBR makes no guarantees at all other than in-order delivery of cells (that is, cells that are fortunate enough to make it to the receiver). With the exception of in-order delivery, UBR service is thus equivalent to the Internet best effort service model. As with the Internet best effort service model, UBR also provides no feedback to the sender about whether or not a cell is dropped within the network. For reliable transmission of data over a UBR network, higher layer protocols (such as those we studied in the previous chapter) are needed. UBR service might be well suited for non-interactive data transfer applications such as email and newsgroups.

If UBR can be thought of as a "best effort" service, then **Available Bit Rate (ABR) network service** might best be characterized as a "better" best effort service model. The two most important additional features of ABR service over UBR service are:

▪ A minimum cell transmission rate (MCR) is guaranteed to a connection using ABR service. If, however, the network has enough free resources at a given time, a sender may actually be able to successfully send traffic at a *higher* rate than the MCR.

▪ Congestion feedback from the network. An ATM network provides feedback to the sender (in terms of a congestion notification bit, or a lower rate at which to send) that controls how the sender should adjust its rate between the MCR and some peak cell rate (PCR). ABR senders must decrease their transmission rates in accordance with such feedback.

ABR provides a minimum bandwidth guarantee, but on the other hand will attempt to transfer data as fast as possible (up to the limit imposed by the PCR). As such, ABR is well suited for data transfer where it is desirable to keep the transfer delays low (for example, Web browsing).

The final ATM service model is **Variable Bit Rate (VBR) network service.** VBR service comes in two flavors (and, in the ITU specification of VBR-like service, comes in *four* flavors—perhaps indicating a service class with an identity crisis!). In real-time VBR service, the acceptable cell loss rate, delay, and delay jitter are specified as in CBR service. However, the actual source rate is allowed to vary according to parameters specified by the user to the network. The declared variability in rate may be used by the network (internally) to more efficiently allocate resources to its connections, but in terms of the loss, delay, and jitter seen by the sender, the service is essentially the same as CBR service. While early efforts in defining a VBR service model were clearly targeted towards real-time services (for example, as evidenced by the PCR, CDT, CDV, and CLR parameters), a second flavor of VBR service is now targeted towards non real-time services and provides a cell loss rate guarantee. An obvious question with VBR is what advantages it offers over CBR (for real-time applications) and over UBR and ABR for non real-time applications. Currently, there is not enough (any?) experience with VBR service to answer these questions.

An excellent discussion of the rationale behind various aspects of the ATM Forum's Traffic Management Specification 4.0 [ATM Forum 1996] for CBR, VBR, ABR, and UBR service is [Garrett 1996].

4.1.2 Origins of Datagram and Virtual Circuit Service

The evolution of the Internet and ATM network service models reflects their origins. With the notion of a virtual circuit as a central organizing principle, and an early focus on CBR services, ATM reflects its roots in the telephony world (which uses "real circuits"). The subsequent definition of UBR and ABR service classes acknowledges the importance of the types of data applications developed in the data networking community. Given the VC architecture and a focus on supporting real-time traffic with *guarantees* about the level of received performance (even with data-oriented services such as ABR), the network layer is *significantly more complex* than the best effort Internet. This too is in keeping with the ATM's telephony heritage. Telephone networks, by necessity, had their "complexity" within the network, since they were connecting "dumb" end-system devices such as a rotary telephone. (For those too young to know, a rotary phone is a non-digital telephone with no buttons—only a dial.)

The Internet, on the other hand, grew out of the need to connect computers (that is, more sophisticated end devices) together. With sophisticated end-systems devices, the Internet architects chose to make the network service model (best effort) as simple as possible and to implement any additional functionality (for example, reliable data transfer), as well as any new application level network services at a higher layer, at the end systems. This inverts the model of the telephone network, with some interesting consequences:

- The resulting network service model which made minimal (no!) service guarantees (and hence posed minimal requirements on the network layer) also made it easier to *interconnect* networks that used very different link layer technologies (for example, satellite, Ethernet, fiber, or radio) which had very different characteristics (transmission rates, loss characteristics). We will address the interconnection of IP networks in detail Section 4.4.
- As we saw in Chapter 2, applications such as email, the Web, and even a network-layer-centric service such as the DNS are implemented in hosts (servers) at the edge of the network. The ability to add a new service simply by attaching a host to the network and defining a new higher layer protocol (such as HTTP) has allowed new services such as the WWW to be adopted in a breathtakingly short period of time.

As we will see in Chapter 6, however, there is considerable debate in the Internet community about how the network layer architecture must evolve in order to support the real-time services such as multimedia. An interesting comparison of the ATM and the proposed next generation Internet architecture is given in [Crowcroft 95].

4.2 ROUTING PRINCIPLES

In order to transfer packets from a sending host to the destination host, the network layer must determine the *path* or *route* that the packets are to follow. Whether the network layer provides a datagram service (in which case different packets between a given host-destination pair may take different routes) or a virtual circuit service (in which case all packets between a given source and destination will take the same path), the network layer must nonetheless determine the path for a packet. This is the job of the network layer **routing protocol.**

At the heart of any routing protocol is the algorithm (the "routing algorithm") that determines the path for a packet. The purpose of a routing algorithm is simple: given a set of routers, with links connecting the routers, a routing algorithm finds a "good" path from source to destination. Typically, a "good" path is one which has "least cost." But we will see that in practice, "real-world" concerns such as policy issues (for example, a rule such as "router X, belonging to organization Y should not forward any packets originating from the network owned by organization Z") also come into play to complicate the conceptually simple and elegant algorithms whose theory underlies the practice of routing in today's networks.

The graph abstraction used to formulate routing algorithms is shown in Figure 4.4. (To view some graphs representing real network maps, see [Dodge 1999]; for a discussion of how well different graph-based models model the Internet, see [Zegura 1997]). Here, nodes in the graph represent routers—the points at which

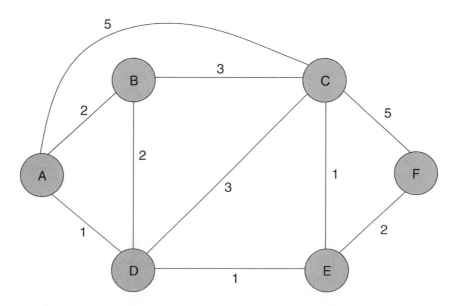

FIGURE 4.4　Abstract model of a network

packet routing decisions are made—and the lines ("edges" in graph theory termi-nology) connecting these nodes represent the physical links between these rout-ers. A link also has a value representing the "cost" of sending a packet across the link. The cost may reflect the level of congestion on that link (for example, the current average delay for a packet across that link) or the physical distance tra-versed by that link (for example, a transoceanic link might have a higher cost than a short-haul terrestrial link). For our current purposes, we will simply take the link costs as a given and won't worry about how they are determined.

Given the graph abstraction, the problem of finding the least cost path from a source to a destination requires identifying a series of links such that:

- the first link in the path is connected to the source
- the last link in the path is connected to the destination
- for all *i*, the *i* and *i-1*st link in the path are connected to the same node
- for the **least cost path,** the sum of the cost of the links on the path is the min-imum over all possible paths between the source and destination. Note that if all link costs are the same, the least cost path is also the **shortest path** (that is, the path crossing the smallest number of links between the source and the des-tination).

In Figure 4.4, for example, the least cost path between nodes A (source) and C (destination) is along the path ADEC. (We will find it notationally easier to refer to the path in terms of the nodes on the path, rather than the links on the path.)

As a simple exercise, try finding the least cost path from nodes A to F, and reflect for a moment on how you calculated that path. If you are like most people, you found the path from A to F by examining Figure 4.4, tracing a few routes from A to F, and somehow convincing yourself that the path you had chosen was the least cost among all possible paths. (Did you check all of the 12 possible paths between A and F? Probably not!) Such a calculation is an example of a centralized routing algorithm. Broadly, one way in which we can classify routing algorithms is according to whether they are *centralized* or *decentralized:*

- A **global routing algorithm** computes the least cost path between a source and destination using complete, global knowledge about the network. That is, the algorithm takes the connectivity between all nodes and all link costs as inputs. This then requires that the algorithm somehow obtain this infor-mation before actually performing the calculation. The calculation itself can be run at one site (a centralized global routing algorithm) or replicated at multiple sites. The key distinguishing feature here, however, is that a global algorithm has *complete* information about connectivity and link costs. In practice, algorithms with global state information are often referred to as **link state algorithms,** since the algorithm must be aware of the state (cost) of each link in the network. We will study a global link state algorithm in Section 4.2.1.
- In a **decentralized routing algorithm,** the calculation of the least cost path is carried out in an iterative, distributed manner. No node has complete informa-tion about the costs of all network links. Instead, each node begins with only the knowledge of the costs of its own directly attached links and then, through an iterative process of calculation and exchange of information with its neigh-boring nodes (that is, nodes which are at the "other end" of links to which it

itself is attached), gradually calculates the least cost path to a destination or set of destinations. We will study a decentralized routing algorithm known as a **distance vector algorithm** in Section 4.2.2. It is called a distance vector algorithm because a node never actually knows a complete path from source to destination. Instead, it only knows the direction (which neighbor) to which it should forward a packet in order to reach a given destination along the least cost path, and the cost of that path from itself to the destination.

A second broad way to classify routing algorithms is according to whether they are **static** or **dynamic.** In static routing algorithms, routes change very slowly over time, often as a result of human intervention (for example, a human manually editing a router's forwarding table). Dynamic routing algorithms change the routing paths as the network traffic loads (and the resulting delays experienced by traffic) or topology change. A dynamic algorithm can be run either periodically or in direct response to topology or link cost changes. While dynamic algorithms are more responsive to network changes, they are also more susceptible to problems such as routing loops and oscillation in routes, issues we will consider in Section 4.2.2.

Only two types of routing algorithms are typically used in the Internet: a dynamic global link state algorithm, and a dynamic decentralized distance vector algorithm. We cover these algorithms in Section 4.2.1 and 4.2.2 respectively. Other routing algorithms are surveyed briefly in Section 4.2.3.

4.2.1   A Link State Routing Algorithm

Recall that in a link state algorithm, the network topology and all link costs are known; that is, available as input to the link state algorithm. In practice this is accomplished by having each node **broadcast** the identities and costs of its attached links to *all* other routers in the network. This **link state broadcast,** [Perlman 1999], can be accomplished without the nodes having to initially know the identities of all other nodes in the network. A node need only know the identities and costs to its directly-attached neighbors; it will then learn about the topology of the rest of the network by receiving link state broadcasts from other nodes. (In Chapter 5, we will learn how a router learns the identities of its directly-attached neighbors). The result of the nodes' link state broadcast is that all nodes have an identical and complete view of the network. Each node can then run the link state algorithm and compute the same set of least cost paths as every other node.

The link state algorithm we present below is known as Dijkstra's algorithm, named after its inventor (a closely related algorithm is Prim's algorithm; see [Corman 1990] for a general discussion of graph algorithms). It computes the least cost path from one node (the source, which we will refer to as A) to all other nodes in the network. Dijkstra's algorithm is iterative and has the property that after the kth iteration of the algorithm, the least cost paths are known to k destination nodes, and among the least cost paths to all destination nodes, these k paths will have the k smallest costs. Let us define the following notation:

- $c(i,j)$: link cost from node i to node j. If nodes i and j are not directly connected, then $c(i,j) = \infty$. We will assume for simplicity that $c(i,j)$ equals $c(j,i)$.

- $D(v)$: the cost of the path from the source node to destination v that has currently (as of this iteration of the algorithm) the least cost
- $p(v)$: previous node (neighbor of v) along the current least cost path from the source to v
- N: set of nodes whose shortest path from the source is definitively known

The link state algorithm consists of an initialization step followed by a loop. The number of times the loop is executed is equal to the number of nodes in the network. Upon termination, the algorithm will have calculated the shortest paths from the source node to every other node in the network.

Link State (LS) Algorithm:

```
1   Initialization:
2     N = {A}
3     for all nodes v
4       if v adjacent to A
5         then D(v) = c(A,v)
6         else D(v) = ∞
7
8   Loop
9     find w not in N such that D(w) is a minimum
10    add w to N
11    update D(v) for all v adjacent to w and not in N:
12        D(v) = min( D(v), D(w) + c(w,v) )
13    /* new cost to v is either old cost to v or known
14      shortest path cost to w plus cost from w to v */
15  until all nodes in N
```

As an example, let us consider the network in Figure 4.4 and compute the shortest path from A to all possible destinations. A tabular summary of the algorithm's computation is shown in Table 4.2, where each line in the table gives the

Table 4.2   Running the link state algorithm on the network in Figure 4.4

step	N	D(B),p(B)	D(C),P(C)	D(D),P(D)	D(E),P(E)	D(F),p(F)
0	A	2,A	5,A	1,A	∞	∞
1	AD	2,A	4,D		2,D	∞
2	ADE	2,A	3,E			4,E
3	ADEB		3,E			4,E
4	ADEBC					4,E
5	ADEBCF					

values of the algorithm's variables at the end of the iteration. Let us consider the few first steps in detail:

- **In the initialization step,** the currently known least path costs from A to its directly attached neighbors, B, C, and D are initialized to 2, 5, and 1 respectively. Note in particular that the cost to C is set to 5 (even though we will soon see that a lesser cost path does indeed exist) since this is the cost of the direct (one hop) link from A to C. The costs to E and F are set to infinity because they are not directly connected to A.

- **In the first iteration,** we look among those nodes not yet added to the set N and find that node with the least cost as of the end of the previous iteration. That node is D, with a cost of 1, and thus D is added to the set N. Line 12 of the LS algorithm is then performed to update $D(v)$ for all nodes v, yielding the results shown in the second line (step 1) in Table 4.2. The cost of the path to B is unchanged. The cost of the path to C (which was 5 at the end of the initialization) through node D is found to have a cost of 4. Hence this lower cost path is selected and C's predecessor along the shortest path from A is set to D. Similarly, the cost to E (through D) is computed to be 2, and the table is updated accordingly.

- **In the second iteration,** nodes B and E are found to have the shortest path costs (2), and we break the tie arbitrarily and add E to the set N so that N now contains A, D, and E. The cost to the remaining nodes not yet in N, that is, nodes B, C, and F, are updated via line 12 of the LS algorithm, yielding the results shown in the third row in the Table 4.2.

- and so on . . .

When the LS algorithm terminates, we have, for each node, its predecessor along the least cost path from the source node. For each predecessor, we also have *its* predecessor and so in this manner we can construct the entire path from the source to all destinations.

What is the computational complexity of this algorithm? That is, given n nodes (not counting the source), how much computation must be done in the worst case to find the least cost paths from the source to all destinations? In the first iteration, we need to search through all n nodes to determine the node, w, not in N that has the minimum cost. In the second iteration, we need to check $n - 1$ nodes to determine the minimum cost; in the third iteration $n - 2$ nodes, and so on. Overall, the total number of nodes we need to search through over all the iterations is $n * (n + 1)/2$, and thus we say that the above implementation of the link state algorithm has worst case complexity of order n squared: $O(n^2)$. (A more sophisticated implementation of this algorithm, using a data structure known as a heap, can find the minimum in line 9 in logarithmic rather than linear time, thus reducing the complexity.)

Before completing our discussion of the LS algorithm, let us consider a pathology that can arise with the use of link state routing. Figure 4.5 shows a simple network topology where link costs are equal to the load carried on the link, for example, reflecting the delay that would be experienced. In this example, link costs are not symmetric, that is, $c(A,B)$ equals $c(B,A)$ only if the load carried on both directions on the AB link is the same. In this example, node D originates a

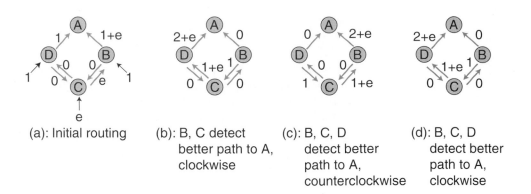

FIGURE 4.5   Oscillations with Link State routing

unit of traffic destined for A, node B also originates a unit of traffic destined for A, and node C injects an amount of traffic equal to e, also destined for A. The initial routing is shown in Figure 4.5(a) with the link costs corresponding to the amount of traffic carried.

When the LS algorithm is next run, node C determines (based on the link costs shown in Figure 4.5a) that the clockwise path to A has a cost of 1, while the counterclockwise path to A (which it had been using) has a cost of $1 + e$. Hence C's least cost path to A is now clockwise. Similarly, B determines that its new least cost path to A is also clockwise, resulting in costs shown in Figure 4.5b. When the LS algorithm is run next, nodes B, C, and D all detect a zero cost path to A in the counterclockwise direction and all route their traffic to the counterclockwise routes. The next time the LS algorithm is run, B, C, and D all then route their traffic to the clockwise routes.

What can be done to prevent such oscillations in the LS algorithm? One solution would be to mandate that link costs not depend on the amount of traffic carried—an unacceptable solution since one goal of routing is to avoid highly congested (for example, high delay) links. Another solution is to insure that all routers do not run the LS algorithm at the same time. This seems a more reasonable solution, since we would hope that even if routers run the LS algorithm with the same periodicity, the execution instance of the algorithm would not be the same at each node. Interestingly, researchers have recently noted that routers in the Internet can self-synchronize among themselves [Floyd Synchronization 1994]. That is, even though they initially execute the algorithm with the same period but at different instants of time, the algorithm execution instance can eventually become, and remain, synchronized at the routers. One way to avoid such self-synchronization is to purposefully introduce randomization into the period between execution instants of the algorithm at each node.

Having now studied the link state algorithm, let's next consider the other major routing algorithm that is used in practice today—the distance vector routing algorithm.

4.2.2   A Distance Vector Routing Algorithm

While the LS algorithm is an algorithm using global information, the **distance vector (DV)** algorithm is iterative, *asynchronous, and distributed.* It is distributed in that each node receives some information from one or more of its *directly-attached* neighbors, performs a calculation, and may then distribute the results of its calculation back to its neighbors. It is iterative in that this process continues on until no more information is exchanged between neighbors. (Interestingly, we will see that the algorithm is self terminating—there is no "signal" that the computation should stop; it just stops.) The algorithm is asynchronous in that it does not require all of the nodes to operate in lock step with each other. We'll see that an asynchronous, iterative, self terminating, distributed algorithm is much more "interesting" and "fun" than a centralized algorithm.

The principal data structure in the DV algorithm is the **distance table** maintained at each node. Each node's distance table has a row for each destination in the network and a column for each of its directly attached neighbors. Consider a node X that is interested in routing to destination Y via its directly attached neighbor Z. Node X's **distance table entry**, $D^X(Y,Z)$ is the sum of the cost of the direct one hop link between X and Z, $c(X,Z)$, plus neighbor Z's currently known minimum cost path from itself (Z) to Y. That is:

$$D^x(Y,Z) = c(X,Z) + \min_w\{D^z(Y,w)\}$$

The $\min_w$ term in the equation is taken over all of Z's directly attached neighbors (including X, as we shall soon see).

The equation suggests the form of the neighbor-to-neighbor communication that will take place in the DV algorithm—each node must know the cost of each of its neighbors' minimum cost path to each destination. Thus, whenever a node computes a new minimum cost to some destination, it must inform its neighbors of this new minimum cost.

Before presenting the DV algorithm, let's consider an example that will help clarify the meaning of entries in the distance table. Consider the network topology and the distance table shown for node E in Figure 4.6. This is the distance table in node E once the DV algorithm has converged. Let's first look at the row for destination A.

- Clearly the cost to get to A from E via the direct connection to A has a cost of 1. Hence $D^E(A,A) = 1$.
- Let's now consider the value of $D^E(A,D)$—the cost to get from E to A, given that the first step along the path is D. In this case, the distance table entry is the cost to get from E to D (a cost of 2) plus whatever the minimum cost it is to get from D to A. Note that the minimum cost from D to A is 3—a path that passes right back through E! Nonetheless, we record the fact that the minimum cost from E to A given that the first step is via D has a cost of 5. We're left, though, with an uneasy feeling that the fact that the path from E via D loops back through E may be the source of problems down the road (it will!).
- Similarly, we find that the distance table entry via neighbor B is $D^E(A,B) = 14$. Note that the cost is *not* 15. (Why?)

A circled entry in the distance table gives the cost of the least cost path to the corresponding destination (row). The column with the circled entry identifies the next node along the least cost path to the destination. Thus, a node's **routing table** (which indicates which outgoing link should be used to forward packets to a given destination) is easily constructed from the node's distance table.

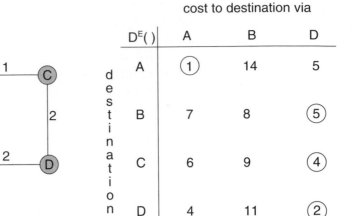

FIGURE 4.6 A distance table example

In discussing the distance table entries for node *E* above, we informally took a global view, knowing the costs of all links in the network. The distance vector algorithm we will now present is *decentralized* and does not use such global information. Indeed, the only information a node will have are the costs of the links to its directly attached neighbors, and information it receives from these directly attached neighbors. The distance vector algorithm we will study is also known as the Bellman-Ford algorithm, after its inventors. It is used in many routing algorithms in practice, including: Internet BGP, ISO IDRP, Novell IPX, and the original ARPAnet.

Distance Vector (DV) algorithm. At each node, *X*:

```
1   Initialization:
2     for all adjacent nodes v:
3       DˣX(*,v) = ∞          /* the * operator means "for all rows" */
4       DˣX(v,v) = c(X,v)
5     for all destinations, y
6       send min_wD(y,w) to each neighbor   /* w over all X's neighbors */
7
8   loop
9     wait (until I see a link cost change to neighbor V
10          or until I receive an update from neighbor V)
11
12    if (c(X,V) changes by d)
13      /* change cost to all dest's via neighbor v by d */
14      /* note: d could be positive or negative */
15      for all destinations y: Dˣ(y,V) = Dˣ(y,V) + d
16
17    else if (update received from V wrt destination Y)
```

```
18          /* shortest path from V to some Y has changed */
19          /* V has sent a new value for its min_w D^V(Y,w) */
20          /* call this received new value "newval" */
21          for the single destination y: D^X(Y,V) = c(X,V) + newval
22
23   if we have a new min_w D^X(Y,w) for any destination Y
24       send new value of min_w D^X(Y,w) to all neighbors
25
26   forever
```

The key steps are lines 15 and 21, where a node updates its distance table entries in response to either a change of cost of an attached link or the receipt of an update message from a neighbor. The other key step is line 24, where a node sends an update to its neighbors if its minimum cost path to a destination has changed.

Figure 4.7 illustrates the operation of the DV algorithm for the simple three node network shown at the top of the figure. The operation of the algorithm is illustrated in a synchronous manner, where all nodes simultaneously receive messages from their neighbors, compute new distance table entries, and inform their neighbors of any changes in their new least path costs. After studying this example, you should convince yourself that the algorithm operates correctly in an asynchronous manner as well, with node computations and update generation/reception occurring at any times.

The circled distance table entries in Figure 4.7 show the current least path cost to a destination. A double-circled entry indicates that a new minimum cost has been computed (in either line 4 of the DV algorithm (initialization) or line 21). In such cases an update message will be sent (line 24 of the DV algorithm) to the node's neighbors as represented by the arrows between columns in Figure 4.7.

The leftmost column in Figure 4.7 shows the distance table entries for nodes X, Y, and Z after the initialization step.

Let us now consider how node X computes the distance table shown in the middle column of Figure 4.7 after receiving updates from nodes Y and Z. As a result of receiving the updates from Y and Z, X computes in line 21 of the DV algorithm:

$$\begin{aligned}
D^X(Y,Z) &= c(X,Z) + \min_w D^Z(Y,w) \\
&= 7 + 1 \\
&= 8 \\
D^X(Z,Y) &= c(X,Y) + \min_w D^Y(Z,w) \\
&= 2 + 1 \\
&= 3
\end{aligned}$$

It is important to note that the only reason that X knows about the terms $\min_w D^Z(Y,w)$ and $\min_w D^Y(Z,w)$ is because nodes Z and Y have sent those values to X (and are received by X in line 10 of the DV algorithm). As an exercise, verify the distance tables computed by Y and Z in the middle column of Figure 4.7.

The value $D^X(Z,Y) = 3$ means that X's minimum cost to Z has changed from 7 to 3. Hence, X sends updates to Y and Z informing them of this new least cost to Z. Note that X need not update Y and Z about its cost to Y since this has not changed.

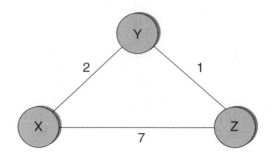

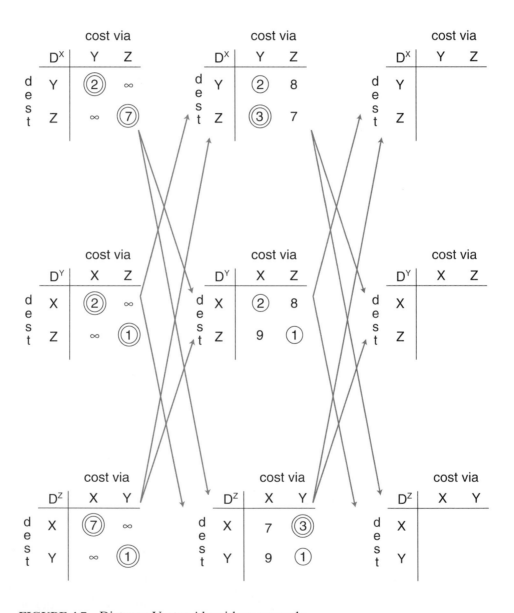

FIGURE 4.7 Distance Vector Algorithm: example

Note also that Y's recomputation of its distance table in the middle column of Figure 4.7 *does* result in new distance entries, but *does not* result in a change of Y's least cost path to nodes X and Z. Hence Y does *not* send updates to X and Z.

The process of receiving updated costs from neighbors, recomputation of distance table entries, and updating neighbors of changed costs of the least cost path to a destination continues until no update messages are sent. At this point, since no update messages are sent, no further distance table calculations will occur and the algorithm enters a quiescent state; that is, all nodes are performing the wait in line 9 of the DV algorithm. The algorithm would remain in the quiescent state until a link cost changes, as discussed below.

The Distance Vector Algorithm: Link Cost Changes and Link Failure. When a node running the DV algorithm detects a change in the link cost from itself to a neighbor (line 12), it updates its distance table (line 15) and, if there is a change in the cost of the least cost path, updates its neighbors (lines 23 and 24). Figure 4.8 illustrates this behavior for a scenario where the link cost from Y to X changes from 4 to 1. We focus here only on Y and Z's distance table entries to destination (row) X.

- At time t_0, Y detects the link cost change (the cost has changed from 4 to 1) and informs its neighbors of this change since the cost of a minimum cost path has changed.

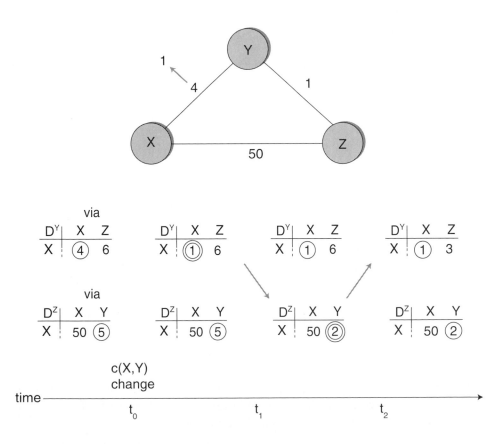

FIGURE 4.8   Link cost change: good news travels fast

- At time t_1, Z receives the update from Y and then updates its table. Since it computes a new least cost to X (it has decreased from a cost of 5 to a cost of 2), it informs its neighbors.
- At time t_2, Y receives Z's update and updates its distance table. Y's least costs have not changed (although its cost to X via Z has changed) and hence Y does *not* send any message to Z. The algorithm comes to a quiescent state.

In Figure 4.8, only two iterations are required for the DV algorithm to reach a quiescent state. The "good news" about the decreased cost between X and Y has propagated fast through the network.

Let's now consider what can happen when a link cost *increases*. Suppose that the link cost between X and Y increases from 4 to 60.

- At time t_0, Y detects the link cost change (the cost has changed from 4 to 60). Y computes its new minimum cost path to X to have a cost of 6 via node Z. Of course, with our global view of the network, we can see that this new cost via Z is *wrong*. But the only information node Y has is that its direct cost to X is 60 and that Z has last told Y that Z could get to X with a cost of 5. So in order to get to X, Y would now route through Z, fully expecting that Z will be able to get to X with a cost of 5. As of t_1 we have a **routing loop**—in order to get to X, Y routes through Z, and Z routes through Y. A routing loop is like a black hole—a packet arriving at Y or Z as of t_1 will bounce back and forth between these two nodes forever (or until the routing tables are changed).
- Since node Y has computed a new minimum cost to X, it informs Z of this new cost at time t_1.
- Sometime after t_1, Z receives the new least cost to X via Y (Y has told Z that Y's new minimum cost is 6). Z knows it can get to Y with a cost of 1 and hence computes a new least cost to X (still via Y) of 7. Since Y's least cost to X has increased, it then informs Y of its new cost at t_2.
- In a similar manner, Y then updates its table and informs Z of a new cost of 9. Z then updates its table and informs Y of a new cost of 10, etc.

How long will the process continue? You should convince yourself that the loop will persist for 44 iterations (message exchanges between Y and Z)—until Z eventually computes its path via Y to be larger than 50. At this point, Z will (finally!) determine that its least cost path to X is via its direct connection to X. Y will then route to X via Z. The result of the "bad news" about the increase in link cost has indeed traveled slowly! What would have happened if the link cost change of $c(Y,X)$ had been from 4 to 10,000 and the cost $c(Z,X)$ had been 9,999? Because of such scenarios, the problem we have seen is sometimes referred to as the "count-to-infinity" problem.

Distance Vector Algorithm: Adding Poisoned Reverse. The specific looping scenario illustrated in Figure 4.9 can be avoided using a technique known as poisoned reverse. The idea is simple—if Z routes through Y to get to destination X, then Z will advertise to Y that its (Z's) distance to X is infinity. Z will continue telling this little "white lie" to Y as long as it routes to X via Y. Since Y believes that Z has no path to X, Y will never attempt to route to X via Z, as long as Z continues to route to X via Y (and lie about doing so).

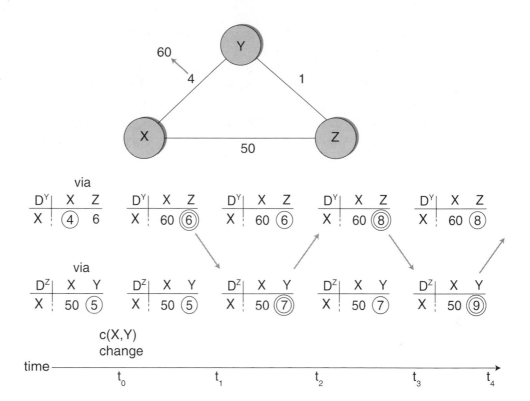

FIGURE 4.9 Link cost changes: bad news travels slowly and causes loops.

Figure 4.10 illustrates how poisoned reverse solves the particular looping problem we encountered before in Figure 4.9. As a result of the poisoned reverse, *Y*'s distance table indicates an infinite cost when routing to *X* via *Z* (the result of *Z* having informed *Y* that *Z*'s cost to *X* was infinity). When the cost of the *XY* link changes from 4 to 60 at time t_0, *Y* updates its table and continues to route directly to *X*, albeit at a higher cost of 60, and informs *Z* of this change in cost. After receiving the update at t_1, *Z* immediately shifts its route to *X* to be via the direct *ZX* link at a cost of 50. Since this is a new least cost to *X*, and since the path no longer passes through *Y*, *Z* informs *Y* of this new least cost path to *X* at t_2. After receiving the update from *Z*, *Y* updates its distance table to route to *X* via *Z* at a least cost of 51. Also, since *Z* is now on *Y*'s least path to *X*, *Y* poisons the reverse path from *Z* to *X* by informing *Z* at time t_3 that it (*Y*) has an infinite cost to get to *X*. The algorithm becomes quiescent after t_4, with distance table entries for destination *X* shown in the rightmost column in Figure 4.10.

Does poison reverse solve the general count-to-infinity problem? It does not. You should convince yourself that loops involving *three* or more nodes (rather than simply two immediately neighboring nodes, as we saw in Figure 4.10) will not be detected by the poison reverse technique.

A Comparison of Link State and Distance Vector Routing Algorithms. Let us conclude our study of link state and distance vector algorithms with a quick comparison of some of their attributes.

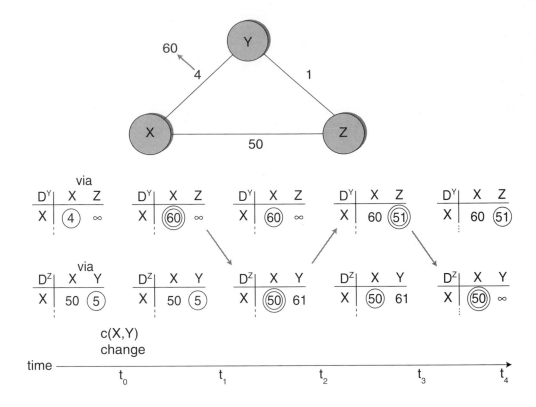

FIGURE 4.10 Poisoned reverse

- *Message Complexity.* We have seen that LS requires each node to know the cost of each link in the network. This requires $O(nE)$ messages to be sent, where n is the number of nodes in the network and E is the number of links. Also, whenever a link cost changes, the new link cost must be sent to *all* nodes. The DV algorithm requires message exchanges between directly connected neighbors at each iteration. We have seen that the time needed for the algorithm to converge can depend on many factors. When link costs change, the DV algorithm will propagate the results of the changed link cost *only* if the new link cost results in a changed least cost path for one of the nodes attached to that link.

- *Speed of Convergence.* We have seen that our implementation of the LS is an $O(n^2)$ algorithm requiring $O(nE)$ messages, and that potentially suffers from oscillations. The DV algorithm can converge slowly (depending on the relative path costs, as we saw in Figure 4.10) and can have routing loops while the algorithm is converging. DV also suffers from the count-to-infinity problem.

- *Robustness.* What can happen if a router fails, misbehaves, or is sabotaged? Under LS, a router could broadcast an incorrect cost for one of its attached links (but no others). A node could also corrupt or drop any LS broadcast packets it receives as part of a link state broadcast. But an LS node is only computing its own routing tables; other nodes are performing the similar calculations for themselves. This means route calculations are somewhat separated under LS, providing a degree of robustness. Under DV, a node can advertise incorrect least path costs to any/all destinations. (Indeed, in 1997, a malfunctioning router in a small ISP provided national backbone routers with erroneous routing tables. This caused other routers to flood the malfunctioning router with traffic, and caused large portions of the Internet to become disconnected for up to several hours [Neumann 1997].) More generally, we note that at each iteration, a node's calculation in DV is passed on to its neighbor and then indirectly to its neighbor's neighbor on the next iteration. In this sense, an incorrect node calculation can be diffused through the entire network under DV.

In the end, neither algorithm is a "winner" over the other; as we will see in Section 4.4, both algorithms are used in the Internet.

4.2.3   Other Routing Algorithms

The LS and DV algorithms we have studied are not only widely used in practice, they are essentially the only routing algorithms used in practice today.

Nonetheless, many routing algorithms have been proposed by researchers over the past 30 years, ranging from the extremely simple to the very sophisticated and complex. One of the simplest routing algorithms proposed is **hot potato routing.** The algorithm derives its name from its behavior—a router tries to get rid of (forward) an outgoing packet as soon as it can. It does so by forwarding it on *any* outgoing link that is not congested, regardless of destination. Although initially proposed quite some time ago, interest in hot-potato-like routing has recently been revived for routing in highly structured networks, such as the so-called Manhattan street network [Brassil 1994].

Another broad class of routing algorithms are based on viewing packet traffic as flows between sources and destinations in a network. In this approach, the routing problem can be formulated mathematically as a constrained optimization problem known as a network flow problem [Bertsekas 1991]. Let us define λ_{ij} as the amount of traffic (for example, in packets/sec) entering the network for the first time at node i and destined for node j. The set of flows, $\{\lambda_{ij}\}$ for all i,j, is sometimes referred to as the network **traffic matrix.** In a network flow problem, traffic flows must be assigned to a set of network links subject to constraints such as:

- The sum of the flows between all source destination pairs passing though link m must be less than the capacity of link m.
- The amount of λ_{ij} traffic entering any router r (either from other routers, or directly entering that router from an attached host) must equal the amount of λ_{ij} traffic leaving the router either via one of r's outgoing links or to an attached host at that router. This is a **flow conservation** constraint.

Let us define $\lambda_{ij}{}^{m}$ as the amount of source i, destination j traffic passing through link m. The optimization problem then is to find the set of link flows, $\{\lambda_{ij}{}^{m}\}$ for all links m and all sources, i, and destinations, j, that satisfies the constraints above and optimizes a performance measure that is a function of $\{\lambda_{ij}{}^{m}\}$. The solution to this optimization problem then defines the routing used in the network. For example, if the solution to the optimization problem is such that $\lambda_{ij}{}^{m} = \lambda_{ij}$ for some link m, then all i-to-j traffic will be routed over link m. In particular, if link m is attached to node i, then m is the first hop on the optimal path from source i to destination j.

But what performance function should be optimized? There are many possible choices. If we make certain assumptions about the size of packets and the manner in which packets arrive at the various routers, we can use the so-called M/M/1 queuing theory formula [Kleinrock 1975] to express the average delay at link as:

$$D_m = 1/(R_m - \Sigma_i \Sigma_j \lambda_{ij}^m),$$

where R_m is link m's capacity (measured in terms of the average number of packets/sec it can transmit) and $\Sigma_i \Sigma_j \lambda_{ij}^m$ is the total arrival rate of packets (in packets/sec) that arrive to link m. The overall network-wide performance measure to be optimized might then be the sum of all link delays in the network, or some other suitable performance metric. A number of elegant distributed algorithms exist for computing the optimum link flows (and hence routing determines the routing paths, as discussed above). The reader is referred to [Bertsekas 1991] for a detailed study of these algorithms.

The final set of routing algorithms we mention here are those derived from the telephony world. These *circuit-switched* routing algorithms are of interest to packet-switched data networking in cases where per-link resources (for example, buffers, or a fraction of the link bandwidth) are to be reserved (that is, set aside) for each connection that is routed over the link. While the formulation of the routing problem might appear quite different from the least cost routing formulation we have seen in this chapter, we will see that there are a number of similarities, at least as far as the path finding algorithm (routing algorithm) is concerned. Our goal here is to provide a brief introduction for this class of routing algorithms. The reader is referred to [Ash 1998], [Ross 1995], and [Girard 1990] for a detailed discussion of this active research area.

The circuit-switched routing problem formulation is illustrated in Figure 4.11. Each link has a certain amount of resources (for example, bandwidth). The easiest (and a quite accurate) way to visualize this is to consider the link to be a bundle of

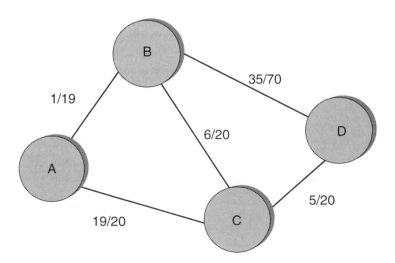

FIGURE 4.11 Circuit-switched routing

circuits, with each call that is routed over the link requiring the dedicated use of one of the link's circuits. A link is thus characterized both by its total number of circuits, as well as the number of these circuits currently in use. In Figure 4.11, all links except *AB* and *BD* have 20 circuits; the number to the left of the number of circuits indicates the number of circuits currently in use.

Suppose now that a call arrives at node *A*, destined to node *D*. What path should be taken? In **shortest path first (SPF)** routing, the shortest path (least number of links traversed) is taken. We have already seen how the Dijkstra LS algorithm can be used to find shortest path routes. In Figure 4.11, either that ABD or ACD path would thus be taken. In **least loaded path** (LLP) routing, the *load* at a link is defined as the ratio of the number of used circuits at the link and the total number of circuits at that link. The path load is the maximum of the loads of all links in the path. In LLP routing, the path taken is that with the smallest path load. In Figure 4.11, the LLP path is ABCD. In **maximum free circuit** (MFC) routing, the number of free circuits associated with a path is the minimum of the number of free circuits at each of the links on a path. In MFC routing, the path with the maximum number of free circuits is taken. In Figure 4.11, the path ABD would be taken with MFC routing.

Given these examples from the circuit switching world, we see that the path selection algorithms have much the same flavor as LS routing. All nodes have complete information about the network's link states. Note however, that the potential consequences of old or inaccurate state information are more severe with circuit-oriented routing—a call may be routed along a path only to find that the circuits it had been expecting to be allocated are no longer available. In such a case, the call setup is blocked and another path must be attempted. Nonetheless, the main differences between connection-oriented, circuit-switched routing and connectionless packet-switched routing come not in the path selection mechanism, but rather in the actions that must be taken when a connection is set up, or torn down, from source to destination.

4.3   HIERARCHICAL ROUTING

In the previous section, we viewed "the network" simply as a collection of interconnected routers. One router was indistinguishable from another in the sense that all routers executed the same routing algorithm to compute routing paths through the entire network. In practice, this model and its view of a homogenous set of routers all executing the same routing algorithm is a bit simplistic for at least two important reasons:

- *Scale.* As the number of routers becomes large, the overhead involved in computing, storing, and communicating the routing table information (for example, link-state updates or least-cost path changes) becomes prohibitive. Today's public Internet consists of millions of interconnected routers and more than 50 million hosts. Storing routing table entries to each of these hosts and routers would clearly require enormous amounts of memory. The overhead required to broadcast link state updates among millions of routers would leave no bandwidth left for sending the data packets! A distance vector algorithm that iterated among millions of routers would surely never converge!

Clearly, something must be done to reduce the complexity of route computation in networks as large as the public Internet.

- *Administrative autonomy.* Although engineers tend to ignore issues such as a company's desire to run its routers as it pleases (for example, to run whatever routing algorithm it chooses), or to "hide" aspects of the networks' internal organization from the outside, these are important considerations. Ideally, an organization should be able to run and administer its network as it wishes, while still being able to connect its network to other "outside" networks.

Both of these problems can be solved by aggregating routers into "regions" or "autonomous systems" (ASs). Routers within the same AS all run the same routing algorithm (for example, an LS or DV algorithm) and have full information about each other—exactly as was the case in our idealized model in the previous section. The routing algorithm running within an autonomous system is called an **intra-autonomous system routing protocol.** It will be necessary, of course, to connect ASs to each other, and thus one or more of the routers in an AS will have the added task of being responsible for routing packets to destinations outside the AS. Routers in an AS that have the responsibility of routing packets to destinations outside the AS are called **gateway routers.** In order for gateway routers to route packets from one AS to another (possibly passing through multiple other ASs before reaching the destination AS), the gateways must know how to route (that is, determine routing paths) among themselves. The routing algorithm that gateways use to route among the various ASs is known as an **inter-autonomous system routing protocol.**

In summary, the problems of scale and administrative authority are solved by defining autonomous systems. Within an AS, all routers run the same intra-autonomous system routing protocol. Special gateway routers in the various ASs run an inter-autonomous system routing protocol that determines routing paths among the ASs. The problem of scale is solved since an intra-AS router need only know about routers within its AS and the gateway router(s) in its AS. The problem of administrative authority is solved since an organization can run whatever intra-AS routing protocol it chooses, as long as the AS's gateway(s) is able to run an inter-AS routing protocol that can connect the As to other ASs.

Figure 4.12 illustrates this scenario. Here, there are three routing ASs, A, B, and C. Autonomous system A has four routers, A.a, A.b, A.c, and A.d, which run the intra-AS routing protocol used within autonomous system A. These four routers have complete information about routing paths within autonomous system A. Similarly, autonomous systems B and C have three and two routers, respectively. Note that the intra-AS routing protocols running in A, B, and C need not be the same. The gateway routers are A.a, A.c, B.a, and C.b. In addition to running the intra-AS routing protocol in conjunction with other routers in their ASs, these four routers run an inter-AS routing protocol among themselves. The topological view they use for their inter-AS routing protocol is shown at the higher level, with "links" shown in light gray. Note that a "link" at the higher layer may be an actual physical link, for example, the link connection A.c and B.a, or a logical link, such as the link connecting A.c and A.a. Figure 4.13 illustrates that the gateway router A.c must run an intra-AS routing protocol with its neighbors A.b and A.d, as well as an inter-AS protocol with gateway router B.a.

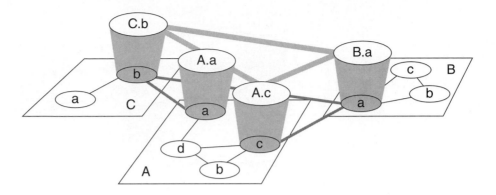

FIGURE 4.12   Intra-AS and Inter-AS routing

Suppose now that a host h1 attached to router A.d needs to route a packet to destination h2 in autonomous system B, as shown in Figure 4.14. Assuming that A.d's routing table indicates that router A.c is responsible for routing its (A.d's) packets outside the AS, the packet is first routed from A.d to A.c using A's intra-AS routing protocol. It is important to note that router A.d does not know about the internal structure of autonomous systems B and C and indeed need not even know about the topology connecting autonomous systems A, B, and C. Router A.c will receive the packet and see that it is destined to an autonomous system outside of A. A.c's routing table for the inter-AS protocol would indicate that a packet destined to autonomous system B should be routed along the A.c to B.a link. When the packet arrives at B.a, B.a's *inter-AS* routing sees that the packet is destined for autonomous system B. The packet is then "handed over" to the

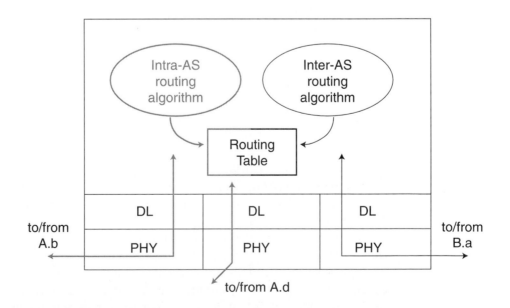

FIGURE 4.13   Internal architecture of gateway router A.c

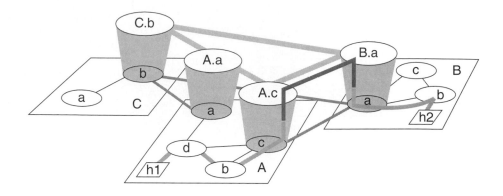

FIGURE 4.14 The route from A.d to B.b: intra-AS and inter-AS path segments

intra-AS routing protocol within B, which routes the packet to its final destination, h2. In Figure 4.14, the portion of the path routed using A's intra-AS protocol is shown on the lower plane in light shading, the portion using the inter-AS routing protocol is shown in the upper plane in dark shading, and the portion of the path routed using B's intra-AS protocol is shown on the lower plane in light shading. We will examine specific inter-AS and intra-AS routing protocols used in the Internet in Section 4.5.

4.4 INTERNET PROTOCOL

So far in this chapter we have examined the underlying principles of the network layer. We have discussed the network layer service models, including virtual circuit service and datagram service, the routing algorithms commonly used to determine paths between origin and destination hosts, and how problems of scale are addressed with hierarchical routing. We are now going to turn our attention to the Internet's network layer.

As we mentioned in Section 4.1, the Internet's network layer does not provide a virtual-circuit service, but instead a connectionless datagram service. When the network layer at the sending host receives a segment from the transport layer, it encapsulates the segment within an IP datagram, writes the destination address of the host (as well as other fields) on the datagram, and drops the datagram into the network. As we mentioned in Chapter 1, this process is similar to a person writing a letter, inserting the letter in an envelope, writing the destination address on the envelope, and dropping the envelope into a mailbox. Neither the Internet's network layer nor the postal service make any kind of preliminary contact with the destination before moving its "parcel" to the destination. Furthermore, as discussed in Section 4.1, the network layer service is a best effort service. It does not guarantee that the datagram will arrive within a certain time, it does not guarantee that a series of datagrams will arrive in the same order sent; in fact, it does not even guarantee that the datagram will ever arrive at its destination.

As we discussed in Section 4.1, the network layer for a datagram network, such as the Internet, has two major components. First, it has a network protocol component, which defines network-layer addressing, the fields in the datagram (that is, the network layer PDU), and how the end systems and routers act on these fields. The network protocol in the Internet is called the Internet Protocol, or more commonly, the **IP Protocol.** There are currently two versions of the IP protocol in use today. In this section, we examine the more widespread version, namely, Internet Protocol version 4, which is specified in [RFC 791] and which is more commonly known as IPv4. In Section 4.7 we shall examine IPv6, which is expected to slowly replace IPv4 in the upcoming years. The second major component of the network layer is the path determination component, which determines the route a datagram follows from origin to destination. We study the path determination component in the next section.

4.4.1   IP Addressing

Before discussing IP addressing, we need to say a few words about hosts and routers. A host (also called an end system) typically has one link into the network. When IP in the host wants to send a datagram, it passes the datagram to its link. The boundary between the host and the link is called the **interface.** A router is fundamentally different from a host in that it has two or more links that connect to it. When a router forwards a datagram, it forwards the datagram over one of its links. The boundary between the router and any one of its links is also called an **interface.** Thus, a router has multiple interfaces, one for each of its links. Because every interface (for a host or router) is capable of sending and receiving IP datagrams, IP requires each interface to have an IP address.

Each IP address is 32 bits long (equivalently, four bytes). IP addresses are typically written in so-called "dot-decimal notation," whereby each byte of the address is written in its decimal form and is separated by a period. For example, a typical IP address would be 193.32.216.9. The 193 is the decimal equivalent for the first 8 bits of the address; the 32 is the decimal equivalent for the second 8 bits of the address, etc. Thus, the address 193.32.216.9 in binary notation is:

```
11000001 00100000 11011000 00001001
```

(A space has been added between the bytes for visual purposes.) Because each IP address is 32 bits long, there are 2^{32} possible IP addresses.

Figure 4.15 provides an example of IP addressing and interfaces. In this figure there is one router that interconnects three LANs. (LANs, also known as local area networks, were briefly discussed in Chapter 1 and will be studied in detail in the next chapter.) In the jargon of IP, each of these LANs is called an **IP network** or more simply a "**network.**" There are several things to observe from this diagram. First, the router has three interfaces, labeled 1, 2, and 3. Each of the router interfaces has its own IP address, which are provided in Figure 4.16; each host also has its own interface and IP address. Second, all of the interfaces attached to LAN 1, including a router interface, have an IP address of the form 223.1.1.xxx. Similarly, all the interfaces attached to LAN 2 and LAN 3 have IP addresses of the form 223.1.2.xxx and 233.1.3.xxx, respectively. In other words, each address has two parts: the first part (the first three bytes in this example) that specifies the network, and the second part (the last byte in this example) that addresses a specific host on the network.

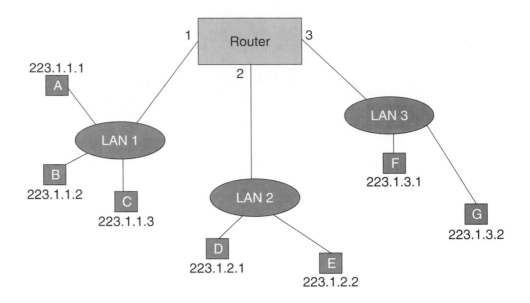

FIGURE 4.15 LANs are networks in IP jargon

The IP definition of a "network" is not restricted to a LAN. To get some insight here, let us now take a look at another example. Figure 4.17 shows several LANs interconnected with three routers. All of the interfaces attached to LAN 1, including the router R1 interface that is attached to LAN 1, have an IP address of the form 223.1.1.xxx. Similarly, all the interfaces attached to LAN 2 and to LAN 3 have the form 223.1.2.xxx and 223.1.3.xxx, respectively. Each of the three LANs again constitute their own network (that is, IP network). But note that there are three additional "networks" in this example: one network for the interfaces that connect Router 1 to Router 2; another network for the interfaces that connect Router 2 to Router 3; and a third network for the interfaces that connect Router 3 to Router 1.

For a general interconnected system of routers and hosts (such as the Internet), we use the following recipe to define the "networks" in the system. We first detach each router interface from its router and each host interface from its host. This creates "islands" of isolated networks, with "interfaces" terminating all the

Router Interface	IP Address
1	223.1.1.4
2	223.1.2.9
3	223.1.3.27

FIGURE 4.16 IP addresses for router interfaces

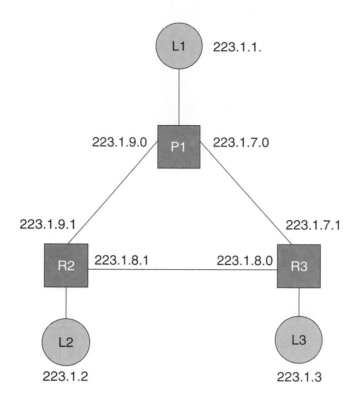

FIGURE 4.17   An interconnected system consisting of six networks

leaves of the isolated networks. We then call each of these isolated networks a **network.** Indeed, if we apply this procedure to the interconnected system in Figure 4.17, we get six islands or "networks." The current Internet consists of millions of networks. (In the next chapter we will consider bridges. We mention here that when applying this recipe, we do not detach interfaces from bridges. Thus, each bridge lies within the interior of some network.)

Now that we have defined a network, we are ready to discuss IP addressing in more detail. IP addresses are globally unique, that is, no two interfaces in the world have the same IP address. Figure 4.18 shows the four possible formats of an IP address. (A fifth address, beginning with 11110, is reserved for future use.) In general, each interface (for a host or router) belongs to a network; the network part of the address identifies the network to which the interface belongs. The host part identifies the specific interface within the network. (We would prefer to use the terminology "interface part of the address" rather than "host part of the address" because an IP address is really for an interface and not for a host; but the terminology "host part" is commonly used in practice.) For a class A address, the first 8 bits identify the network, and the last 24 bits identify the interface within that network. Thus, with a class A we can have up to 2^7 networks (the first of the eight bits is fixed as 0) and 2^{24} interfaces. Note that the interfaces in Figures 4.15 and 4.17 use class A addresses. The class B address space allows for 2^{14} networks, with up to 2^{16} interfaces within each network. A class C address uses 21 bits to identify the network and leaves only 8 bits for the interface identifier. Class D addresses are reserved for so-called multicast

class

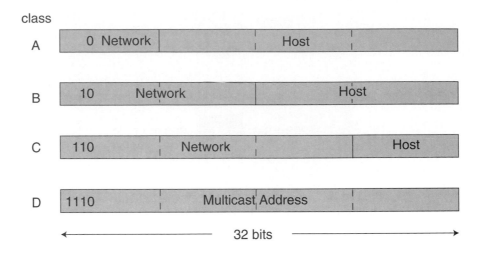

FIGURE 4.18 IPv4 address formats

addresses. As we will see in Section 4.7, these addresses do not identify a specific interface but rather provide a mechanism through which multiple hosts can receive a copy of each single packet sent by a sender.

Assigning addresses. Having introduced IP addressing, one question that immediately comes to mind is how does a host get its own IP address? We have just learned that an IP address has two parts, a network part and a host part. The host part of the address can be assigned in several different ways, including:

- *Manual configuration.* The IP address is configured into the host (typically in a file) by the system administrator.
- *Dynamic Host Configuration Protocol (DHCP)* [RFC 2131]. DHCP is an extension of the BOOTP [RFC 1542] protocol, and is sometimes referred to as Plug and Play. With DHCP, a DHCP server in a network (for example, in a LAN) receives DHCP requests from a client and in the case of dynamic address allocation, allocates an IP address back to the requesting client. DHCP is used extensively in LANs and in residential Internet access.

The network part of the address is the same for all the hosts in the network. To obtain the network part of the address for a network, the network administrator might first contact the network's ISP, which would provide addresses from a larger block of addressees that have already been allocated to the ISP. But how does an ISP get a block of addresses? IP addresses are managed under the authority of the Internet Assigned Numbers Authority (IANA), under the guidelines set forth in [RFC 2050]. The actual assignment of addresses is now managed by regional Internet registries. As of mid-1998, there are three such regional registries: the American Registry for Internet Number (ARIN, which handles registrations for North and South America, as well as parts of Africa. ARIN has recently taken over a number of the functions previously provided by Network Solutions), the Reseaux IP Europeans (RIPE, which covers Europe and nearby countries), and the Asia Pacific Network Information Center (APNIC).

Before leaving our discussion of addressing, we want to mention that mobile hosts may change the network to which they are attached, either dynamically while in motion or on a longer time scale. Because routing is to a network first, and then to a host within the network, this means that the mobile host's IP address must change when the host changes networks. Techniques for handling such issues are now under development within the IETF and the research community [RFC2002] [RFC2131].

4.4.2 The Big Picture: Transporting a Datagram from Source to Destination

Now that we have defined interfaces and networks, and have a basic understanding of IP addressing, we take a step back and discuss how IP transports a datagram from source to destination. To this end, a high level view of an IP datagram is shown in Figure 4.19. Note that every IP datagram has a destination address field and a source address field. The source host fills the source address field with its own 32-bit IP address and fills the destination address field with the 32-bit IP address of the host to which it wants to send the datagram. Note that these actions are analogous to what you do when you send a letter: on the envelope of the letter, you provide a destination address and a return (source) address. The data field of the datagram is typically filled with a TCP or UDP segment. We will discuss the remaining IP datagram fields a little later in this section.

Once the source host creates the IP datagram, how does the network layer transport the datagram from the source host to the destination host? Let us answer this question in the context of network Figure 4.15. First suppose host A wants to send an IP datagram to host B. The datagram is transported from host A to host B as follows. IP in host A first extracts the network portion of the address, 223.1.1., and scans its *routing table,* which is shown in Figure 4.20. In this table, the "number of hops to destination" is defined to be the number of networks that need to be traversed, including the destination network. Scanning the table, host A finds a match in the first row, and observes that the number of hops to the destination is 1. This indicates to host A that the destination host is on the same network. Host A then passes the IP datagram to the link layer protocol and indicates to the link layer protocol that the destination is on the same LAN. The link layer protocol then has the responsibility of transporting the datagram to host B. (We will study how the link layer transports a datagram between two interfaces on the same network in Chapter 5.)

Now consider the more interesting case of host A sending an IP datagram to host E, which has IP address 223.1.2.2 and is on a different LAN. Host A again scans its routing table, but now finds a match in the second row. Because the number of hops to the destination is 2, host A knows that the destination is on another

Other Header Fields	Source Address	Destination Address	Data

FIGURE 4.19 The key fields in an IP datagram

Destination Network	Next Router	Number of Hops to Destination
223.1.1.	—	1
223.1.2.	223.1.1.4	2
223.1.3.	223.1.1.4	2

FIGURE 4.20 Routing table in host A

network. The routing table also tells host A that in order to get the datagram to host E, host A should first send the datagram to router address 223.1.1.4. IP in host A then passes the datagram down to the link layer, and indicates to the link layer that it should first send the datagram to IP address 223.1.1.4. The link layer then transports the datagram to the router interface 1. The datagram is now in the router, and it is the job of the router to move the datagram toward the datagram's ultimate destination. The router extracts the network portion of the destination address of the IP datagram, namely 223.1.2., and scans its routing table, which is shown in Figure 4.21. The router finds a match in the second row of the table. The table tells the router that the datagram should be forwarded on router interface 2; also the number of hops to the destination is 1, which indicates to the router that the destination host is on the LAN directly attached to interface 2. The router moves the datagram to interface 2. (The moving of a datagram from an input interface to an output interface within a router will be covered in Section 4.6.) Once the datagram is at interface 2, the router passes the datagram to link layer protocol and indicates to the link layer protocol that the destination host is on the same LAN. The link layer protocol has the job of transporting the datagram from the router interface 2 to host E, both of which are attached to the same LAN.

In Figure 4.21, note that the entries in the "next router" column are all empty. This is because all of the networks (223.1.1., 223.1.2., and 223.1.3.) are each

Destination Network	Next Router	Number of Hops to Destination	Interface
223.1.1.	—	1	1
223.1.2.	—	1	2
223.1.3.	—	1	3

FIGURE 4.21 Routing table in router

directly attached to the router, that is, there is no need to go through an intermediate router to get to the destination host. However, if host A and host E were separated by two routers, then within the routing table of the first router along the path from A to B, the appropriate row would indicate 2 hops to the destination and would specify the IP address of the second router along the path. The first router would then forward the datagram to the second router, using the link layer protocol that connects the two routers. The second router then forwards the datagram to the destination host, using the link layer protocol that connects the second router to the destination host.

You may recall from Chapter 1 that we said that routing a datagram in the Internet is similar to a person driving a car and asking gas station attendants at each intersection along the way how to get to the ultimate destination. It should now be clear why this an appropriate analogy for routing in the Internet. As a datagram travels from source to destination, it visits a series of routers. At each router in the series, it stops and asks the router how to get to its ultimate destination. Unless the router is on the same LAN as the ultimate destination, the routing table essentially says to the datagram: "I don't know exactly how to get to the ultimate destination, put I do know that the ultimate destination is in the direction of the link (analogous to a road) connected to interface 3." The datagram then sets out on the link connected to interface 3, arrives at a new router, and again asks for new directions.

From this discussion we see that the routing tables in the routers play a central role in routing datagrams through the Internet. But how are these routing tables configured and maintained for large networks with multiple paths between sources and destinations (such as in the Internet)? Clearly, these routing tables should be configured so that the datagrams follow good (if not optimal) routes from source to destination. As you probably guessed, routing algorithms—like those studied in Section 4.2—have the job of configuring and maintaining the routing tables. Furthermore, as discussed in Section 4.3, the Internet is partitioned into autonomous systems (ASs): intra-AS routing algorithms independently configure the routing tables within the autonomous systems; inter-AS routing algorithms have the job of configuring routing tables so that datagrams can pass through multiple autonomous systems. We will discuss the Internet's intra-AS and inter-AS routing algorithms in Section 4.5. But before moving on to routing algorithms, we cover three more important topics for the IP protocol, namely, the datagram format, datagram fragmentation, and the Internet Control Message Protocol (ICMP).

4.4.3 Datagram Format

The IPv4 datagram format is shown in Figure 4.22.

The key fields in the IPv4 datagram are the following:

- *Version Number.* These 4 bits specify the IP protocol version of the datagram. By looking at the version number, the router can then determine how to interpret the remainder of the IP datagram. Different versions of IP use different datagram formats. The datagram format for the "current" version of IP, IPv4, is shown in Figure 4.22. The datagram format for the "new" version of IP (IPv6) is discussed in Section 4.7.

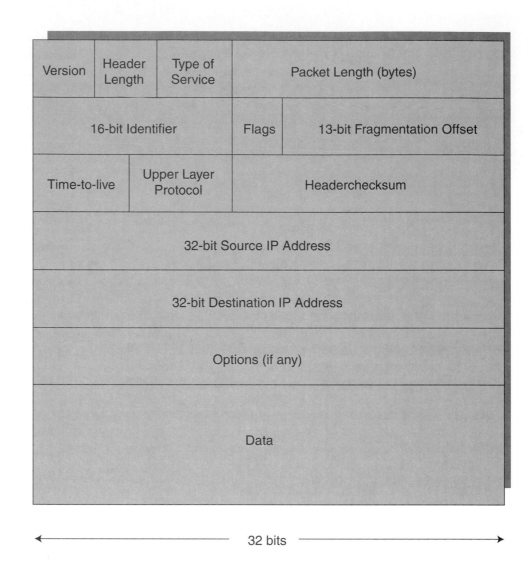

Version	Header Length	Type of Service	Packet Length (bytes)	
16-bit Identifier			Flags	13-bit Fragmentation Offset
Time-to-live	Upper Layer Protocol		Headerchecksum	
32-bit Source IP Address				
32-bit Destination IP Address				
Options (if any)				
Data				

◄─────────────── 32 bits ───────────────►

FIGURE 4.22 IPv4 datagram format

- *Header Length.* Because an IPv4 datagram can contain a variable number of options (which are included in the IPv4 datagram header) these 4 bits are needed to determine where in the IP datagram the data actually begins. Most IP datagrams do not contain options so the typical IP datagram has a 20 byte header.

- *TOS.* The type of service (TOS) bits were included in the IPv4 header to allow different "types" of IP datagrams to be distinguished from each other, presumably so that they could be handled differently in times of overload. When the network is overloaded, for example, it would be useful to be able to distinguish network control datagrams (for example, see the ICMP discussion in Section 4.4.5) from datagrams carrying data (for example, HTTP messages). It would also be useful to distinguish real-time datagrams (for example, used by an IP telephony application) from non-real-time traffic (for example, FTP). More recently, one major routing vendor (Cisco) interprets the first three TOS bits as defining differential levels of service that can be provided by the router. The specific level of service to be provided is a policy issue determined by the router's administrator. We shall explore the topic of differentiated service in detail in Chapter 6.

- *Datagram Length.* This is the total length of the IP datagram (header plus data) measured in bytes. Since this field is 16 bits long, the theoretical maximum size of the IP datagram is 65,535 bytes. However, datagrams are rarely greater than 1500 bytes, and are often limited in size to 576 bytes.

- *Identifier, Flags, Fragmentation Offset.* These three fields have to do with so-called IP fragmentation, a topic we will consider in depth shortly. Interestingly, the new version of IP, IPv6, simply does not allow for fragmentation.

- *Time-to-live.* The time-to-live (TTL) field is included to ensure that datagrams do not circulate forever (due to, for example, a long lived router loop) in the network. This field is decremented by one each time the datagram is processed by a router. If the TTL field reaches 0, the datagram must be dropped.

- *Protocol.* This field is only used when an IP datagram reaches its final destination. The value of this field indicates the transport-layer protocol at the destination to which the data portion of this IP datagram will be passed. For example, a value of 6 indicates that the data portion is passed to TCP, while a value of 17 indicates that the data is passed to UDP. For a listing of all possible numbers, see [RFC 1700]. Note that the protocol number in the IP datagram has a role that is fully analogous to the role of the port number field in the transport-layer segment. The protocol number is the "glue" that holds the network and transport layers together, whereas the port number is the "glue" that holds the transport and application layers together. We will see in Chapter 5 that the link layer frame also has a special field which glues the link layer to the network layer.

- *Header Checksum.* The header checksum aids a router in detecting bit errors in a received IP datagram. The header checksum is computed by treating each 2 bytes in the header as a number and summing these numbers using 1's complement arithmetic. As discussed in Section 3.3, the 1's complement of this sum, known as the Internet checksum, is stored in the checksum field. A router computes the Internet checksum for each received IP datagram and detects an error condition if the checksum carried in the datagram does not equal the computed checksum. Routers typically discard datagrams for which an error has been detected. Note that the checksum must be recomputed and restored at each router, as the TTL field, and possibly options fields as well, may change. An interesting discussion of fast algorithms for computing the Internet checksum is [RFC 1071]. A question often asked at this point is, why does TCP/IP perform error checking at both the transport and network layers? There are many reasons for this. First, routers are not required to perform error checking, so the transport layer cannot count on the network layer to do the job. Second, TCP/UDP and IP do not necessarily have to both belong to the same protocol stack. TCP can, in principle, run over a different protocol (for example, ATM) and IP can carry data without passing through TCP/UDP (for example, RIP data).

- *Source and Destination IP Address.* These fields carry the 32 bit IP address of the source and final destination for this IP datagram. The use and importance of the destination address is clear. The source IP address (along with the source and destination port numbers) is used at the destination host to direct the application data to the proper socket.

- *Options.* The optional options fields allows an IP header to be extended. Header options were meant to be used rarely—hence the decision to save overhead by not including the information in options fields in every datagram header. However, the mere existence of options does complicate matters— since datagram headers can be of variable length, one cannot determine *a priori* where the data field will start. Also, since some datagrams may require options processing and others may not, the amount of time needed to process an IP datagram can vary greatly. These considerations become particularly important for IP processing in high performance routers and hosts. For these reasons and others, IP options were dropped in the IPv6 header.

- *Data (payload).* Finally, we come to the last, and most important field—the *raison d'être* for the datagram in the first place! In most circumstances, the data field of the IP datagram contains the transport-layer segment (TCP or UDP) to be delivered to the destination. However, the data field can carry other types of data, such ICMP messages (discussed in Section 4.4.5).

Note that IP datagram has a total of 20 bytes of header (assuming it has no options). If the IP datagram carries a TCP segment, then each (non-fragmented) datagram carries a total of 40 bytes of header (20 IP bytes and 20 TCP bytes) along with the application-layer data.

4.4.4   IP Fragmentation and Reassembly

We will see in Chapter 5 that not all link layer protocols can carry packets of the same size. Some protocols can carry "big" packets whereas other protocols can only carry "little" packets. For example, Ethernet packets can carry no more than 1500 bytes of data, whereas packets for many wide-area links can carry no more than 576 bytes. The maximum amount of data that a link-layer packet can carry is called the **MTU (maximum transfer unit).** Because each IP datagram is encapsulated within the link-layer packet for transport from one router to the next router, the MTU of the link-layer protocol places a hard limit on the length of an IP datagram. Having a hard limit on the size of an IP datagram is not much of a problem. What is a problem is that each of the links along the route between sender and destination can use different link-layer protocols, and each of these protocols can have different MTUs.

To understand the problem better, imagine that *you* are a router that interconnects several links, each running different link-layer protocols with different MTUs. Suppose you receive an IP datagram from one link, you check your routing table to determine the outgoing link, and this outgoing link has an MTU that is smaller than the length of the IP datagram. Time to panic—how are you going to squeeze this oversized IP packet into the payload field of the link-layer packet? The solution to this problem is to "fragment" the data in the IP datagram among two or more smaller IP datagrams, and then send these smaller datagrams over the outgoing link. Each of these smaller datagrams is referred to as a **fragment.**

Fragments need to be reassembled before they reach the transport layer at the destination. Indeed, both TCP and UDP are expecting to receive from the network layer complete, un-fragmented segments. The designers of IPv4 felt that reassembling (and possibly re-fragmenting) datagrams in the routers would introduce significant complication into the protocol and put a damper on router performance. (If you were a router, would you want to be reassembling fragments on top of everything else you have to do?) Sticking to end-to-end principle for the Internet, the designers of IPv4 decided to put the job of datagram reassembly in the end systems rather than in the network interior.

When a destination host receives a series of datagrams from the same source, it needs to determine if any of these datagrams are fragments of some "original" bigger datagram. If it does determine that some datagrams are fragments, it must further determine when it has received the last fragment and how the fragments it has received should be pieced back together to form the original datagram. To allow the destination host to perform these reassembly tasks, the designers of IP (version 4) put *identification, flag,* and *fragmentation* fields in the IP datagram. When a datagram is created, the sending host stamps the datagram with an identification number as well as a source and destination address. The sending host increments the identification number for each datagram it sends. When a router needs to fragment a datagram, each resulting datagram (that is, "fragment") is stamped with the source address, destination address, and identification number of the original datagram. When the destination receives a series of datagrams from the same sending host, it can examine the identification numbers of the datagrams to determine which of the datagrams are actually fragments of the same bigger datagram. Because IP is an unreliable service, one or more of the fragments may never arrive at the destination. For this reason, in order for the destination host to be absolutely sure it has received the last fragment of the original datagram, the last fragment has a flag bit set to 0 whereas all the other fragments have this flag bit set to 1. Also, in order for the destination host to determine if a fragment is missing (and also to be able to reassemble the fragments in the proper order), the offset field is used to specify where the fragment fits within the original IP datagram. This bit is set to 1 in all except the last fragment.

Figure 4.23 illustrates an example. A datagram of 3,980 bytes arrives at a router, and this datagram must be forwarded to a link with an MTU of 1500 bytes. This implies that the 3,980 data bytes in the original datagram must be allocated to three separate fragments (each of which are also IP datagrams). Suppose that the original datagram is stamped with an identification number of 777. The characteristics of the three fragments are shown in Table 4.3.

FIGURE 4.23 IP Fragmentation

Table 4.3   IP Fragments

Fragment	Bytes	ID	Offset	Flag
1st fragment	1480 bytes in the data field of the IP datagram	identification = 777	offset = 0 (meaning the data should be inserted beginning at byte 0)	flag = 1 (meaning there is more)
2nd fragment	1480 byte information field	identification = 777	offset = 1,480 (meaning the data should be inserted beginning at byte 1,480	flag = 1 (meaning there is more)
3rd fragment	1020 byte (=3980-1480-1480) information field	identification = 777	offset = 2,960 (meaning the data should be inserted beginning at byte 2,960)	flag = 0 (meaning this is the last fragment)

The payload of the datagram is only passed to the transport layer once the IP layer has fully reconstructed the original IP datagram. If one or more of the fragments does not arrive to the destination, the datagram is "lost" and not passed to the transport layer. But, as we learned in the previous chapter, if TCP is being used at the transport layer, then TCP will recover from this loss by having the source retransmit the data in the original datagram.

Fragmentation and reassembly puts an additional burden on Internet routers (the additional effort to create fragments out of a datagram) and on the destination hosts (the additional effort to reassemble fragments). For this reason it is desirable to keep fragmentation to a minimum. This is often done by limiting the TCP and UDP segments to a relatively small size, so that the fragmentation of the corresponding datagrams is unlikely. Because all data link protocols supported by IP are supposed to have MTUs of at least 576 bytes, fragmentation can be entirely eliminated by using an MSS of 536 bytes, 20 bytes of TCP segment header and 20 bytes of IP datagram header. This is why most TCP segments for bulk data transfer (such as with HTTP) are 512-536 bytes long. (You may have noticed while surfing the Web that 500 or so bytes of data often arrive at a time.)

Following this section in the online version of this text, we provide a Java applet that generates fragments. You provide the incoming datagram size, the MTU and the incoming datagram identification. It automatically generates the fragments for you. See http://www.seas.upenn.edu/~ross/book/net_layer.

4.4.5   ICMP: Internet Control Message Protocol

We conclude this section with a discussion of the Internet Control Message Protocol, ICMP, which is used by hosts, routers, and gateways to communicate network layer information to each other. ICMP is specified in [RFC 792]. The most typical use of ICMP is for error reporting. For example, when running a Telnet, FTP, or HTTP session, you may have encountered an error message such as "Destination network unreachable." This message had its origins in ICMP. At some point, an IP router was unable to find a path to the host specified in your Telnet, FTP, or HTTP application. That router created and sent a type-3 ICMP message to your host indicating the error. Your host received the ICMP message and returned the error code to the TCP code that was attempting to connect to the remote host. TCP, in turn, returned the error code to your application.

ICMP is often considered part of IP, but architecturally lies just above IP, as ICMP messages are carried inside IP packets. That is, ICMP messages are carried as IP payload, just as TCP or UDP packets are carried as IP payload. Similarly, when a host receives an IP packet with ICMP specified as the upper layer protocol, it demultiplexes the packet to ICMP, just as it would demultiplex a packet to TCP or UDP.

ICMP messages have a type and a code field, and also contain the first 8 bytes of the IP datagram that caused the ICMP message to be generated in the first place (so that the sender can determine which packet sent caused the error). Selected ICMP messages are shown below in Figure 4.24. Note that ICMP messages are

Table 4.4   Selected ICMP messages

ICMP Type	Code	Description
0	0	echo reply (to ping)
3	0	destination network unreachable
3	1	destination host unreachable
3	2	destination protocol unreachable
3	3	destination port unreachable
3	6	destination network unknown
3	7	destination host unknown
4	0	source quench (congestion control)
8	0	echo request
9	0	router advertisement
10	0	router discovery
11	0	TTL expired
12	0	IP header bad

FIGURE 4.24   IP Fragmentation

used not only for signaling error conditions. The well-known `ping` program ICMP. `ping` sends an ICMP type 8 code 0 message to the specified host. The destination host, seeing the echo request, sends back a type 0 code 0 ICMP echo reply. Another interesting ICMP message is the source quench message. This message is seldom used in practice. Its original purpose was to perform congestion control—to allow a congested router to send an ICMP source quench message to a host to force that host to reduce its transmission rate. We have seen in Chapter 3 that TCP has its own congestion control mechanism that operates at the transport layer, without the use of network layer support such as the ICMP source quench message.

In Chapter 1 we introduced the `Traceroute` program, which enabled you to trace the route from a few given hosts to any host in the world. Interesting enough, `Traceroute` also uses ICMP messages. To determine the names and addresses of the routers between source and destination, `Traceroute` in the source sends a series of ordinary IP datagrams to the destination. The first of these datagrams has a TTL of 1, the second of 2, the third of 3, etc. The source also starts timers for each of the datagrams. When the nth datagram arrives at the nth router, the nth router observes that the TTL of the datagram has just expired. According to the rules of the IP protocol, the router discards the datagram (because there may be a routing loop) and sends an ICMP warning message to the source (type 11 code 0). This warning message includes the name of the router and its IP address. When the ICMP message corresponding to the nth datagram arrives at the source, the source obtains the round-trip time from the timer and the name and IP address from the ICMP message. Now that you understand how `Traceroute` works, you may want to go back and play with it some more.

4.5 ROUTING IN THE INTERNET

The Internet consists of interconnected autonomous systems (ASs). An AS typically consists of many networks, where a network (also called an IP network) was defined in the previous section. Recall from Section 4.3 that each autonomous system is administered independently. The administrator of an autonomous system chooses the intra-AS routing algorithm for that AS, and is responsible for administering that AS and no others. Datagrams must also be routed among the ASs, and this is the job of inter-AS routing protocols. As discussed in Section 4.3, this hierarchical organization of the Internet has permitted the Internet to scale. In this section, we examine the intra-AS and inter-AS routing protocols that are commonly used in the Internet.

4.5.1 Intra-Autonomous System Routing in the Internet

An intra-AS routing protocol is used to configure and maintain the routing tables within an autonomous system (AS). Once the routing tables are configured, datagrams are routed within the AS as described in the previous section. Intra-AS routing protocols are also known as **interior gateway protocols.** Historically, three routing protocols have been used extensively for routing within an autonomous system in the Internet: **RIP** (the Routing Information Protocol), **OSPF** (Open Shortest Path First), and **IGRP** (Cisco's propriety Interior Gateway Routing Protocol).

RIP: Routing Information Protocol.   The Routing Information Protocol (RIP) was one of the earliest intra-AS Internet routing protocols and is still in widespread use today. It traces its origins and its name to the Xerox Network Systems (XNS) architecture. The widespread deployment of RIP was due in great part to its inclusion in 1982 of the Berkeley Software Distribution (BSD) version of UNIX supporting TCP/IP. RIP version 1 is defined in [RFC 1058], with a backwards compatible version 2 defined in [RFC 1723].

RIP is a distance vector protocol that operates in a manner very close to the idealized protocol we examined in Section 4.2.3. The version of RIP specified in RFC 1058 uses hop count as a cost metric; that is, each link has a cost of 1, and limits the maximum cost of a path to 15. This limits the use of RIP to autonomous systems that are less than 15 hops in diameter. Recall that in distance vector protocols, neighboring routers exchange routing information with each other. In RIP, the routing tables are exchanged between neighbors every 30 seconds using a so-called **response message,** with each *response* message containing that host's routing table entries for up to 25 destination networks. These response messages containing routing tables are also called **advertisements.**

Let us take a look at a simple example of how RIP advertisements work. Consider the portion of an AS shown in Figure 4.25. In this figure, the rectangles denote routers and the lines connecting the rectangles denote networks. Note that the routers are labeled A, B, C, etc. and the networks are labeled 1, 10, 20, 30, etc. For visual convenience, some of the routers and networks are not labeled. Dotted lines in the figure indicate that the autonomous system continues on and perhaps loops back. Thus this autonomous system has many more routers and links than are shown in the figure.

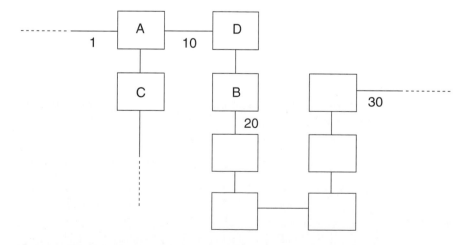

FIGURE 4.25   A portion of an autonomous system

Destination Network	Next Router	Number of Hops to Destination
1	A	2
20	B	2
30	B	7
10	—	1
....	....	....

FIGURE 4.26   Routing table in router D before receiving advertisement from router A

Now suppose that the routing table for router D is as shown in Figure 4.26. Note that the routing table has three columns. The first column is for the destination network, the second column indicates the next router along the shortest path to the destination network, and the third column indicates the number of hops (that is, the number of networks that have to be traversed, including the destination network, to get to the destination network along the shortest path). For this example, the table indicates that to send a datagram from router D to destination network 1, the datagram should be first sent to neighboring router A; moreover, the table indicates that destination network 1 is two hops away along the shortest path. Also note that the table indicates that network 30 is seven hops away via router B. In principle, the routing table should have one row for each network in the AS, although aggregation, a topic beyond the scope of this book, can be used to aggregate entries. It should also have at least one row for networks that are outside of the AS. The table in Figure 4.26, and the subsequent tables to come, are only partially complete.

Now suppose that 30 seconds later, router D receives from router A the advertisement shown in Figure 4.27. Note that this advertisement is nothing other but

Destination Network	Next Router	Number of Hops to Destination
30	C	4
1	—	1
10	—	1
....	....	....

FIGURE 4.27   Advertisement from router A

the routing table in router A! This routing table says, in particular, that network 30 is only 4 hops away from router A.

Router D, upon receiving this advertisement, merges the advertisement (Figure 4.27) with the "old" routing table (Figure 4.26). In particular, router D learns that there is now a path through router A to network 30 that is shorter than the path through router B. Thus, router D updates its routing table to account for the "shorter" shortest path, as shown in Figure 4.28. How is it, you might ask, that the shortest path to network 30 became shorter. This is because either this decentralized distance vector algorithm was still in the process of converging (see Section 4.2), or new links and/or routers were added to the AS, which changed the actual shortest paths in the network.

Returning now to the general properties of RIP, if a router does not hear from its neighbor at least once every 180 seconds, that neighbor is considered to be no longer reachable; that is, either the neighbor has died or the connecting link has gone down. When this happens, RIP modifies its local routing table and then propagates this information by sending advertisements to its neighboring routers (the ones that are still reachable). A router can also request information about its neighbor's cost to a given destination using RIP's *request* message. Routers send RIP request and response messages to each other over UDP using port number 520. The UDP packet is carried between routers in a standard IP packet. The fact that RIP uses a transport layer protocol (UDP) on top of a network layer protocol (IP) to implement network layer functionality (a routing algorithm) may seem rather convoluted (it is!). Looking a little deeper at how RIP is implemented will clear this up.

Figure 4.29 sketches how RIP is typically implemented in a UNIX system, for example, for example, a UNIX workstation serving as a router. A process called *routed* (pronounced "route dee") executes the RIP protocol, that is, maintains the routing table and exchanges messages with *routed* processes running in neighboring routers. Because RIP is implemented as an application-layer process (albeit a very special one that is able to manipulate the routing tables within the UNIX kernel), it can send and receive messages over a standard socket and use a standard transport protocol. Thus, RIP is an application-layer protocol (see Chapter 2) running over UDP.

Destination Network	Next Router	Number of Hops to Destination
1	A	2
20	B	2
30	A	5
....	....	....

FIGURE 4.28 Routing table in router D after receiving advertisement from router A

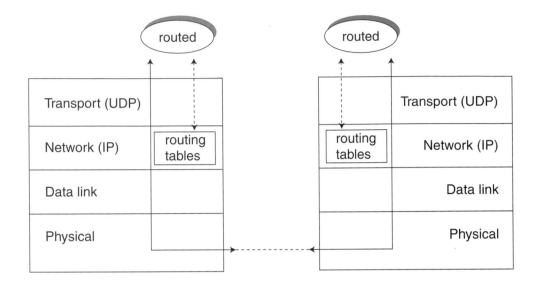

FIGURE 4.29 Implementation of RIP as the *routed* daemon

Finally, let us take a quick look at an RIP routing table. The RIP routing table in Figure 4.30 is taken from a UNIX router `giroflee.eurecom.fr`. If you give a `netstat -rn` command on a UNIX system, you can view the routing table for that host or router. Performing a `netstat` command on `giroflee.eure-com.fr` yields the routing table in Figure 4.30.

The router `giroflee` is connected to three networks. The second, third, and fourth rows in the table tell us that these three networks are attached to `giroflee` via `giroflee`'s network interfaces `fa0`, `le0` and `qaa0`. These giroflee interfaces have IP addresses 192.168.2.5, 193.55.114.6, and 192.168.3.5, respectively. To transmit a packet to any host belonging to one of these three networks, `giroflee` will simply send the outgoing IP datagram over the appropriate interface. Of particular interest to us is the **default route.** Any IP datagram that is not destined for one of the networks explicitly listed in the routing table will be forwarded to the router with IP address 193.55.114.129; this router is reached by sending the datagram over the default network interface. The first entry in the routing table is the so-called loopback interface. When IP sends a datagram to the loopback interface,

```
Destination     Gateway          Flags    Ref     Use      Interface
-----------     -------------    -----    ----    ------    --------
127.0.0.1       127.0.0.1        UH       0       26492     lo0
192.168.2.      192.168.2.5      U        2       13        fa0
193.55.114.     193.55.114.6     U        3       58503     le0
192.168.3.      192.168.3.5      U        2       25        qaa0
224.0.0.0       193.55.114.6     U        3       0         le0
default         193.55.114.129   UG       0       143454
```

FIGURE 4.30 RIP routing table from `giroflee.eurecom.fr`

the packet is simply returned back to IP; this is useful for debugging purposes. The address 224.0.0.0 is a special multicast (Class D) IP address. We will examine IP multicast in Section 4.8.

OSPF: Open Shortest Path First.   Like RIP, Open Shortest Path First (OSPF) routing is used for intra-AS routing. The "Open" in OSPF indicates that the routing protocol specification is publicly available (for example, as opposed to Cisco's IGRP protocol). The most recent version of OSPF, version 2, is defined in RFC 2178—a public document.

OSPF was conceived as the successor to RIP and as such has a number of advanced features. At its heart, however, OSPF is a link-state protocol that uses flooding of link state information and a Dijkstra least-cost-path algorithm. With OSPF, a router constructs a complete topological map (that is, a directed graph) of the entire autonomous system. The router then locally runs Dijkstra's shortest path algorithm to determine a shortest path tree to all networks with itself as the root node. The router's routing table is then obtained from this shortest path tree. Individual link costs are configured by the network administrator.

Let us now contrast and compare the advertisements sent by RIP and OSPF. With OSPF, a router periodically sends routing information to *all* other routers in the autonomous system, not just to its neighboring routers. This routing information sent by a router has one entry for each of the router's neighbors; the entry gives the distance (that is, link state) from the router to the neighbor. On the other hand, a RIP advertisement sent by a router contains information about all the networks in the autonomous system, although this information is only sent to its neighboring routers. In a sense, the advertising techniques of RIP and OSPF are duals of each other.

Some of the advances embodied in OSPF include the following:

- *Security.* All exchanges between OSPF routers (for example, link state updates) are authenticated. This means that only trusted routers can participate in the OSPF protocol within a domain, thus preventing malicious intruders (or networking students taking their newfound knowledge out for a joyride) from injecting incorrect information into router tables.

- *Multiple same-cost paths.* When multiple paths to a destination have the same cost, OSPF allows multiple paths to be used (that is, a single path need not be chosen for carrying all traffic when multiple equal cost paths exist).

- *Different cost metrics for different TOS traffic.* OSPF allows each link to have different costs for different TOS (type of service) IP packets. For example, a high bandwidth satellite link might be configured to have a low cost (and hence be attractive) for non-time critical traffic, but a very high cost metric for delay-sensitive traffic. In essence, OSPF sees different network topologies for different classes of traffic, and hence can compute different routes for each type of traffic.

- *Integrated support for unicast and multicast routing.* Multicast OSPF [RFC 1584] provides simple extensions to OSPF to provide for multicast routing (a topic we cover in more depth in Section 4.8). MOSPF uses the existing OSPF link database and adds a new type of link state advertisement to the existing OSPF link state broadcast mechanism.

■ *Support for hierarchy within a single routing domain.* Perhaps the most significant advance in OSPF is the ability to hierarchically structure an autonomous system. Section 4.3 has already looked at the many advantages of hierarchical routing structures. We cover the implementation of OSPF hierarchical routing in the remainder of this section.

As OSPF autonomous system can be configured into "areas." Each area runs its own OSPF link state routing algorithm, with each router in an area broadcasting its link state to all other routers in that area. The internal details of an area thus remain invisible to all routers outside the area. Intra-area routing involves only those routers within the same area.

Within each area, one of more **area border routers** are responsible for routing packets outside the area. Exactly one OSPF area in the AS is configured to be the **backbone** area. The primary role of the backbone area is to route traffic between the other areas in the AS. The backbone always contains all area border routers in the AS and may contain non-border routers as well. Inter-area routing within the AS requires that the packet be first routed to an area border router (intra AS routing), then routed though the backbone to the area border router that is in the destination area, and then routed to the final destination.

A diagram of a hierarchically structured OSPF network is shown in Figure 4.19. We can identify four types of OSPF routers in Figure 4.31:

■ *Internal routers.* These routers, shaded in black, are in non-backbone areas and only perform intra-AS routing.

■ *Area border routers.* These routers, shaded in gray, belong to both an area and the backbone.

■ *Backbone routers (non-border routers).* These routers, shaded very lightly, perform routing within the backbone but themselves are not area border routers. Within a non-backbone area, internal routers learn of the existence of routes to other areas from information (essentially a link state advertisement, but advertising the cost of a route to another area, rather than a link cost) broadcast within the area by its backbone routers.

■ *Boundary routers.* A boundary router, shown with a black ring and white center, exchanges routing information with routers belonging to other autonomous systems. This router might, for example, use BGP to perform inter-AS routing. It is through such a boundary router that other routers learn about paths to external networks.

IGRP: Internal Gateway Routing Protocol. The Interior Gateway Routing Protocol (IGRP) [Cisco IGRP 1997] is a proprietary routing algorithm developed by Cisco Systems, Inc. in the mid-1980's as a successor for RIP. IGRP is a distance vector protocol. Several cost metrics (including delay, bandwidth, reliability, and load) can be used in making routing decisions, with the weight given to each of the metrics being determined by the network administrator. This ability to use administrator-defined costs in making route selections is an important difference from RIP; we will see shortly that so-called policy-based inter-AS Internet routing protocols such as BGP also allow administratively defined routing decisions to be made. Other important differences from RIP include the use of a reliable transport protocol to communicate routing information, the use of update messages that are sent only when routing table costs change (rather than periodi-

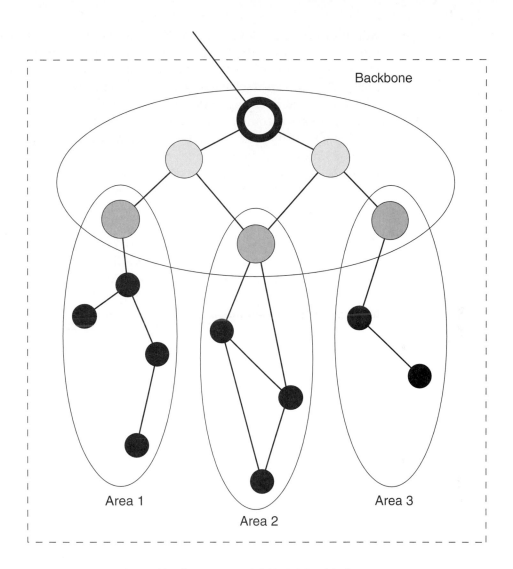

FIGURE 4.31   Hierarchically structured OSPF AS with four areas

cally), and the use of a distributed diffusing update routing algorithm [Garcia-Luna-Aceves 1991] to quickly compute loop free routing paths.

4.5.2   Inter-Autonomous System Routing

The Border Gateway Protocol version 4, specified in [RFC 1771] (see also [RFC 1772, RFC 1773]), is the *de facto* standard interdomain routing protocol in today's Internet. It is commonly referred to as BGP4 or simply as BGP. As an inter-autonomous system routing protocol, it provides for routing between autonomous systems (that is, administrative domains).

   While BGP has the same general flavor as the distance vector protocol that we studied in Section 4.2, it is more appropriately characterized as a **path vector protocol.** This is because BGP in a router does not propagate cost information (for example, number of hops to a destination), but instead propagates path information, such as the sequence of ASs on a route to a destination AS. We will examine the path information in detail shortly. We note though that while this information includes the names of the ASs on a route to the destination, they do *not* contain cost information. Nor does BGP specify how a specific route to a particular destination should be chosen among the routes that have been advertised. That decision is a *policy* decision that is left up to the domain's administrator. Each domain can thus choose its routes according to whatever criteria it chooses (and need not even inform its neighbors of its policy!)—allowing a significant degree of autonomy in route selection. In essence, BGP provides the *mechanisms* to distribute path information among the interconnected autonomous systems, but leaves the policy for making the actual route selections up to the network administrator.

Let's begin with a grossly simplified description of how BGP works. This will help us see the forest through the trees. As discussed in Section 4.3, as far as BGP is concerned, the whole Internet is a graph of ASs, and each AS is identified by an AS number. At any instant of time, a given AS X may, or may not, know of a path of ASs that lead to a given destination AS Z. As an example, suppose X has listed in its BGP table such a path $XY_1Y_2Y_3Z$ from itself to Z. This means that X knows that it can send datagrams to Z through the ASs X, Y_1, Y_2 and Y_3, Z. When X sends updates to its BGP neighbors (that is, the neighbors in the graph), X actually sends the entire path information, $XY_1Y_2Y_3Z$, to its neighbors (as well as other paths to other ASs). If, for example, W is a neighbor of X, and W receives an advertisement that includes the path $XY_1Y_2Y_3Z$, then W can list a new entry $WXY_1Y_2Y_3Z$ in its BGP table. However, we should keep in mind that W may decide to *not* create this new entry for one of several reasons. For example, W would not create this entry if W is equal to (say) Y_2, thereby creating an undesirable loop in the routing; or if W already has a path to Z in its tables, and this existing path is preferable (with respect to the metric used by BGP at W) to $WXY_1Y_2Y_3Z$; or, finally, if W has a policy decision to not forward datagrams through (say) Y_2.

In BGP jargon, the immediate neighbors in the graph of ASs are called **peers.** BGP information is propagated through the network by exchanges of BGP messages between peers. The BGP protocol defines the four types of messages: `OPEN`, `UPDATE`, `NOTIFICATION`, and `KEEPALIVE`.

- *OPEN.* BGP peers communicate using the TCP protocol and port number 179. TCP thus provides for reliable and congestion controlled message exchange between peers. In contrast, recall that we earlier saw that two RIP peers, for example, the *routed's* in Figure 4.29 communicate via unreliable UDP. When a BGP gateway wants to first establish contact with a BGP peer (for example, after the gateway itself or a connecting link has just been booted), an `OPEN` message is sent to the peer. The `OPEN` message allows a BGP gateway to identify and authenticate itself, and provide timer information. If the `OPEN` is acceptable to the peer, it will send back a `KEEPALIVE` message.

- *UPDATE.* A BGP gateway uses the `UPDATE` message to advertise a path to a given destination (for example, $XY_1Y_2Y_3Z$) to the BGP peer. The `UPDATE` message can also be used to *withdraw* routes that had previously been advertised (that is, to tell a peer that a route that it had previously advertised is no longer a valid route).

- *KEEPALIVE.* This BGP message is used to let a peer know that the sender is alive but that the sender doesn't have other information to send. It also serves as an acknowledgment to a received `OPEN` message.

▪ *NOTIFICATION.* This BGP message is used to inform a peer that an error has been detected (for example, in a previously transmitted BGP message) or that the sender is about to close the BGP session.

Recall from our discussion above that BGP provides mechanisms for distributing path information but does not mandate policies for selecting a route from those available. Within this framework, it is thus possible for an AS such as Hatfield.net to implement a policy such as "traffic from my AS should not cross the AS McCoy.net," since it knows the identities of all AS's on the path. (The Hatfields and the McCoys are two famous feuding families in the US.) But what about a policy that would prevent the McCoys from sending traffic through the Hatfield's network? The only means for an AS to control the traffic it passes though its AS (known as "transit" traffic—traffic that neither originates in, nor is destined for, the network, but instead is "just passing through") is by controlling the paths that it advertises. For example, if the McCoys are immediate neighbors of the Hatfields, the Hatfields could simply not advertise any routes to the McCoys that contain the Hatfield network. But restricting transit traffic by controlling an AS's route advertisement can only be partially effective. For example, if the Jones' are between the Hatfields and the McCoys, and the Hatfields advertise routes to the Jones' that pass through the Hatfields, then the Hatfields cannot prevent (using BGP mechanisms) the Jones' from advertising these routes to the McCoys.

Very often an AS will have multiple gateway routers that provide connections to other ASs. Even though BGP is an inter-AS protocol, it can still be used inside an AS as a pipe to exchange BGP updates among gateway routers belonging to the same AS. BGP connections inside an AS are called Internal **BGP (IBGP),** whereas BGP connections between ASs are called External **BGP (EBGP).**

As noted above, BGP, which is the successor to EGP, is becoming the *de facto* standard for inter-AS routing for the public Internet. BGP is used, for example, at the major network access points (NAP's) where major Internet carriers connect to each other and exchange traffic. To see the contents of today's (less than four hours out of date) BGP routing table (large!) at one of the major NAP's in the US (which include Chicago and San Francisco), see http://www.merit.edu/ipma/routing_table/.

This completes our brief introduction of BGP. Although BGP is complex, it plays a central role in the Internet. We encourage readers to see the references [Halabi 1997] and [Huitema 1995] to learn more about BGP.

4.5.3 Why are there Different Inter-AS and Intra-AS Routing Protocols?

Having now studied the details of specific inter-AS and intra-AS routing protocols deployed in today's Internet, let us conclude by considering perhaps the most fundamental question we could ask about these protocols in the first place (hopefully, you have been wondering this all along, and have not lost the forest for the trees!):

Why are different inter-AS and intra-AS routing protocols used?

The answer to this question gets at the heart of the differences between the goals of routing within an AS and among ASs:

▪ *Policy.* Among ASs, policy issues dominate. It may well be important that traffic originating in a given AS specifically not be able to pass through another specific AS. Similarly, a given AS may well want to control what transit traffic it carries between other ASs. We have seen that BGP specifically carries path attributes and provides for controlled distribution of routing information so that such policy-based routing decisions can be made. Within an AS, everything is nominally under the same administrative control, and thus policy issues play a much less important role in choosing routes within the AS.

- *Scale.* The ability of a routing algorithm and its data structures to scale to handle routing to/among large numbers of networks is a critical issue in inter-AS routing. Within an AS, scalability is less of a concern. For one thing, if a single administrative domain become too large, it is always possible to divide it into two ASs and perform inter-AS routing between the two new ASs. (Recall that OSPF allows such a hierarchy to be built by splitting an AS into "areas".)

- *Performance.* Because inter-AS routing is so policy-oriented, the quality (for example, performance) of the routes used is often of secondary concern (that is, a longer or more costly route that satisfies a certain policy criteria may well be taken over a route that is shorter but does not meet that criteria). Indeed, we saw that among ASs, there is not even the notion of preference or costs associated with routes. Within a single AS, however, such policy concerns can be ignored, allowing routing to focus more on the level of performance realized on a route.

4.6 WHAT'S INSIDE A ROUTER?

Our study of the network layer so far has focused on network layer service models, the routing algorithms that control the routes taken by packets through the network, and the protocols that embody these routing algorithms. These topics, however, are only part (albeit *important* ones) of what goes on in the network layer. We have yet to consider the **switching function** of a router—the actual transfer of datagrams from a router's incoming links to the appropriate outgoing links. Studying just the control and service aspects of the network layer is like studying a company and considering only its management (which controls the company but typically performs very little of the actual "grunt" work that makes a company run!) and its public relations ("Our product will provide this wonderful service to you!"). To fully appreciate what really goes on within a company, one needs to consider the workers. In the network layer, the real work (that is, the reason the network layer exists in the first place) is the forwarding of datagrams. A key component in this forwarding process is the transfer of a datagram from a router's incoming link to an outgoing link. In this section, we study how this is accomplished. Our coverage here is necessarily brief, as an entire course would be needed to cover router design in depth. Consequently, we'll make a special effort in this section to provide pointers to material that covers this topic in more depth.

A high level view of a generic router architecture is shown in Figure 4.32. Four components of a router can be identified:

- *Input ports.* The input port performs several functions. It performs the physical layer functionality (the leftmost box of the input port and the rightmost box of the output port in Figure 4.32) of terminating an incoming physical link to a router. It performs the data link layer functionality (shown in the middle boxes in the input and output ports) needed to interoperate with the data link layer functionality (see Chapter 5) on the other side of the incoming

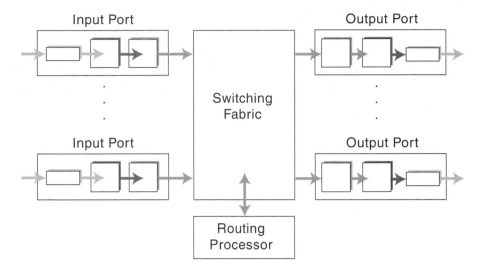

FIGURE 4.32 Router architecture

link. It also performs a lookup and forwarding function (the rightmost box of the input port and the leftmost box of the output port) so that a datagram forwarded into the switching fabric of the router emerges at the appropriate output port. Control packets (for example, packets carrying routing protocol information such as RIP, OSPF or IGMP) are forwarded from the input port to the routing processor. In practice, multiple ports are often gathered together on a single *line card* within a router.

■ *Switching fabric.* The switching fabric connects the router's input ports to its output ports. This switching fabric is completely contained with the router—a network inside of a network router!

■ *Output ports.* An output port stores the datagrams that have been forwarded to it through the switching fabric, and then transmits the datagrams on the outgoing link. The output port thus performs the reverse data link and physical layer functionality as the input port.

■ *Routing processor.* The routing processor executes the routing protocols (for example, the protocols we studied in Section 4.5), maintains the routing tables, and performs network management functions (see Chapter 8), within the router. Since we cover these topics elsewhere in this book, we defer discussion of these topics to elsewhere.

In the following, we'll take a look at input ports, the switching fabric, and output ports in more detail. [Turner 1988, Giacopelli 1990, McKeown 1997a, Partridge 1998] provide a discussion of some specific router architectures. [McKeown 1997b] provides a particularly readable overview of modern router architectures, using the Cisco 12000 router as an example.

4.6.1 Input ports

A more detailed view of input port functionality is given in Figure 4.33. As discussed above, the input port's line termination function and data link processing implement the physical and data link layers associated with an individual input

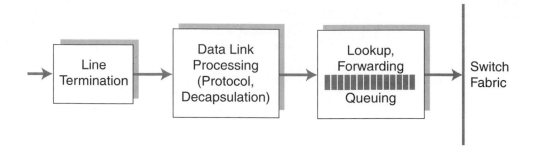

FIGURE 4.33 Input port processing

link to the router. The lookup/forwarding function of the input port is central to the switching function of the router. In many routers, it is here that the router determines the output port to which an arriving datagram will be forwarded via the switching fabric. The choice of the output port is made using the information contained in the routing table. Although the routing table is computed by the routing processor, a "shadow copy" of the routing table is typically stored at each input port and updated, as needed, by the routing processor. With local copies of the routing table, the switching decision can be made locally, at each input port, without invoking the centralized routing processor. Such *decentralized* switching avoids creating a forwarding bottleneck at a single point within the router.

In routers with limited processing capabilities at the input port, the input port may simply forward the packet to the centralized routing processor, which will then perform the routing table lookup and forward the packet to the appropriate output port. This is the approach taken when a workstation or server serves as a router (for example, [Microsoft Routing 1998]); here, the "routing processor" is really just the workstation's CPU and the "input port" is really just a network interface card (for example, an Ethernet card).

Given the existence of a routing table, the routing table lookup is conceptually simple—we just search through the routing table, looking for a destination entry that matches the destination address of the datagram, or a default route if the destination entry is missing. In practice, however, life is not so simple. Perhaps the most important complicating factor is that backbone routers must operate at high speeds, being capable of performing millions of lookups per second. Indeed, it is desirable for the input port processing to be able to proceed at **line speed,** that is, that a lookup can be done in less than the amount of time needed to receive a packet at the input port. In this case, input processing of a received packet can be completed before the next receive operation is complete. To get an idea of the performance requirements for a lookup, consider that a so-called OC48 link runs at 2.5 Gbps. With 256 byte-long packets, this implies a lookup speed of approximately a million lookups per second.

Given the need to operate at today's high link speeds, a linear search through a large routing table is impossible. A more reasonable technique is to store the routing table entries in a tree data structure. Each level in the tree can be thought of as corresponding to a bit in the destination address. To lookup an address, one simply starts at the root node of the tree. If the first address bit is a zero, then the left subtree will contain the routing table entry for a destination address; otherwise it will be in the right subtree. The appropriate subtree is then traversed using the remaining address bits—if the next address bit is a zero, the left subtree of the initial subtree is chosen; otherwise, the right subtree of the initial subtree is chosen. In this manner, one can lookup the routing table entry in N steps, where N is the number of bits in the address. (The reader will note that this is essentially a binary search through an address space of size 2^N.) Refinements of this approach are discussed in [Doeringer 1996].

But even with $N = 32$ (for example, a 32-bit IP address) steps, the lookup speed is not fast enough for today's backbone routing requirements. For example, assuming a memory access at each step, less than a million address lookups/sec could be performed with 40 ns memory access times. Several techniques have thus been explored to increase lookup speeds. Content addressable memories (CAMs) allow a 32-bit IP address to be presented to the CAM, which then returns the content of the routing table entry for that address in essentially constant time. The Cisco 8500 series router [Cisco 8500 1999] has a 64K CAM for each input port. Another technique for speeding lookup is to keep recently accessed routing table entries in a cache [Feldmeier 1998]. Here, the potential concern is the size of the cache. Measurements in [Thompson 1997] suggest that even for an OC-3 speed link, approximately 256,000 source-destination pairs might be seen in one minute in a backbone router. Most recently, even faster data structures, which allow routing table entries to be located in $\log(N)$ steps [Waldvogel 1997], or which compress routing tables in novel ways [Brodnik 1997], have been proposed. A hardware-based approach to lookup that is optimized for the common case that the address being looked up has 24 or fewer significant bits is discussed in [Gupta 1998].

Once the output port for a packet has been determined via the lookup, the packet can be forwarded into the switching fabric. However, as we'll see below, a packet may be temporarily **blocked** from entering the switching fabric (due to the fact that packets from other input ports are currently using the fabric). A blocked packet must thus be queued at the input port and then scheduled to cross the switching fabric at a later point in time. We'll take a closer look at the blocking, queuing, and scheduling of packets (at both input ports and output ports) within a router in Section 4.6.4.

4.6.2 Switching Fabrics

The switching fabric is at the very heart of a router. It is through this switching fabric that the datagrams are actually moved from an input port to an output port. Switching can be accomplished in a number of ways, as indicated in Figure 4.34:

- *Switching via memory.* The simplest, earliest routers were often traditional computers, with switching between input and output port, being done under direct control of the CPU (routing processor). Input and output ports functioned as traditional I/O devices in a traditional operating system. An input port with an arriving datagram first signaled the routing processor via an interrupt. The packet was then copied from the input port into processor memory. The routing processor then extracted the destination address from the

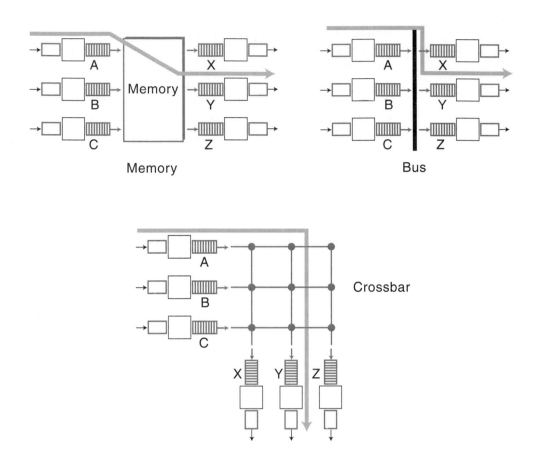

FIGURE 4.34   Three switching techniques

header, looked up the appropriate output port in the routing table, and copied the packet to the output port's buffers. Note that if the memory bandwidth is such that B packets/sec can be written into, or read from, memory, then the overall switch throughput (the total rate at which packets are transferred from input ports to output ports) must be less than B/2.

Many modern routers also switch via memory. A major difference from early routers, however, is that the lookup of the destination address and the storing (switching) of the packet into the appropriate memory location is performed by processors on the input line cards. In some ways, routers that switch via memory look very much like shared memory multiprocessors, with the processors on a line card storing datagrams into the memory of the appropriate output port. Cisco's Catalyst 8500 series switches [Cisco 8500 1999] and Bay Networks Accelar 1200 Series routers switch packets via a shared memory.

- *Switching via a bus.* In this approach, the input ports transfer a datagram directly to the output port over a shared bus, without intervention by the routing processor (Note that when switching via memory, the datagram must also cross the system bus going to/from memory). Although the routing processor is not involved in the bus transfer, since the bus is shared, only one packet at a time can be transferred over the bus. A datagram arriving at an input port and finding the bus busy with the transfer of another datagram is blocked from passing through the switching fabric and queued at the input port. Because every packet must cross the single bus, the switching bandwidth of the router is limited to the bus speed.

Given that bus bandwidths of over a gigabit per second are possible in today's technology, switching via a bus is often sufficient for routers that operate in access and enterprise networks (for example, local area and corporate networks). Bus-based switching has been adopted in a number of current router products, including the Cisco 1900 [Cisco Switches 1999], which switches packets over a 1Gbps Packet Exchange Bus. 3Com's CoreBuilder 5000 systems [Kapoor 1997] interconnects ports that reside on different switch modules over its PacketChannel data bus, with a bandwidth of 2 Gbps.

- *Switching via an interconnection network.* One way to overcome the bandwidth limitation of a single, shared bus is to use a more sophisticated interconnection network, such as those that have been used in the past to interconnect processors in a multiprocessor computer architecture. A crossbar switch is an interconnection network consisting of $2N$ busses that connect N input ports to N output ports, as shown in Figure 4.34. A packet arriving at an input port travels along the horizontal bus attached to the input port until it intersects with the vertical bus leading to the desired output port. If the vertical bus leading to the output port is free, the packet is transferred to the output port. If the vertical bus is being used to transfer a packet from another input port to this same output port, the arriving packet is blocked and must be queued at the input port.

  Delta and Omega switching fabrics have also been proposed as an interconnection network between input and output ports. See [Tobagi 1990] for a survey of switch architectures. Cisco 12000 Family switches [Cisco 12000 1998] use an interconnection network, providing up to 60 Gbps through the switching fabric. One current trend in interconnection network design [Keshav 1998] is to fragment a variable length IP datagram into fixed length cells, and then tag and switch the fixed length cells through the interconnection network. The cells are then reassembled into the original datagram at the output port. The fixed length cell and internal tag can considerably simplify and speed up the switching of the packet through the interconnection network.

4.6.3   Output Ports

Output port processing, shown in Figure 4.35, takes the datagrams that have been stored in the output port's memory and transmits them over the outgoing link. The data link protocol processing and line termination are the send-side link- and physical-layer functionality that interact with the input port on the other end of the outgoing link, as discussed above in Section 4.6.2. The queuing and buffer management functionality are needed when the switch fabric delivers packets to the output port at a rate that exceeds the output link rate; we'll cover output port queuing below.

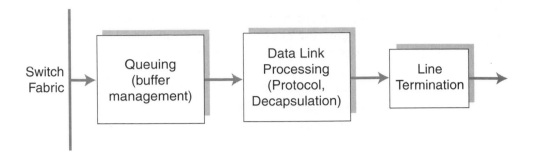

FIGURE 4.35 Output port processing

4.6.4 Where Does Queuing Occur?

Looking at the input and output port functionality and the configurations shown in Figure 4.34, it is evident that packet queues can form at both the input ports *and* the output ports. It is important to consider these queues in a bit more detail, since as these queues grow large, the router's buffer space will eventually be exhausted and **packet loss** will occur. Recall that in our earlier discussions, we said rather vaguely that packets were lost "within the network" or "dropped at a router." It is here, at these queues within a router, where such packets are dropped and lost. The actual location of packet loss (either at the input port queues or the output port queues) will depend on the traffic load, the relative speed of the switching fabric and the line speed, as discussed below.

Suppose that the input line speeds and output line speeds are all identical, and that there are n input ports and n output ports. If the switching fabric speed is at least n times as fast as the input line speed, then no queuing can occur at the input ports. This is because even in the worst case that all n input lines are receiving packets, the switch will be able to transfer n packets from input port to output port in the time it takes each of the n input ports to (simultaneously) receive a *single* packet. But what can happen at the output ports? Let us suppose still that the switching fabric is at least n times as fast as the line speeds. In the worst case, the packets arriving at each of the n input ports will be destined to the *same* output port. In this case, in the time it takes to receive (or send) a single packet, n packets will arrive at this output port. Since the output port can only transmit a single packet in a unit of time (the packet transmission time), the n arriving packets will have to queue (wait) for transmission over the outgoing link. n more packets can then possibly arrive in the time it takes to transmit just one of the n packets that had previously been queued. And so on. Eventually, buffers can grow large enough to exhaust the memory space at the output port, in which case packets are dropped.

Output port queuing is illustrated in Figure 4.36. At time t, a packet has arrived at each of the incoming input ports, each destined for the uppermost outgoing port. Assuming identical line speeds and a switch operating at three times the line speed, one time unit later (that is, in the time needed to receive or send a packet), all three original packets have been transferred to the outgoing port and

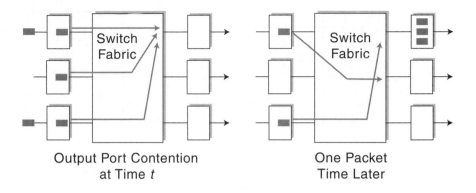

Output Port Contention
at Time *t*

One Packet
Time Later

FIGURE 4.36 Output port queuing

are queued awaiting transmission. In the next time unit, one of these three packets will have been transmitted over the outgoing link. In our example, two *new* packets have arrived at the incoming side of the switch; one of these packets is destined for this uppermost output port.

A consequence of output port queuing is that a **packet scheduler** at the output port must choose one packet among those queued for transmission. This selection might be done on a simple basis such as first-come-first-served (FCFS) scheduling, or a more sophisticated scheduling discipline such as weighted fair queuing (WFQ), which shares the outgoing link "fairly" among the different end-to-end connections that have packets queued for transmission. Packet scheduling plays a crucial role in providing **quality of service guarantees.** We will cover this topic extensively in Section 6.6. A discussion of output port packet scheduling disciplines used in today's routers is [Cisco Queue 1995].

If the switch fabric is not fast enough (relative to the input line speeds) to transfer *all* arriving packets through the fabric without delay, then packet queuing will also occur at the input ports, as packets must join input port queues to wait their turn to be transferred through the switching fabric to the output port. To illustrate an important consequence of this queuing, consider a crossbar switching fabric and suppose that (1) all link speeds are identical, (2) that one packet can be transferred from any one input port to a given output port in the same amount of time it takes for a packet to be received on an input link, and (3) packets are moved from a given input queue to their desired output queue in a FCFS manner. Multiple packets can be transferred in parallel, as long as their output ports are different. However, if two packets at the front of two input queues are destined to the same output queue, then one of the packets will be blocked and must wait at the input queue—the switching fabric can only transfer one packet to a given output port at a time.

Figure 4.37 shows an example where two packets (shaded black) at the front of their input queues are destined for the same upper right output port. Suppose that the switch fabric chooses to transfer the packet from the front of the upper left queue. In this case, the black packet in the lower left queue must wait. But not only must this black packet wait, but so too must the white packet that is queued behind that packet in the lower left queue, even though there is *no* contention for

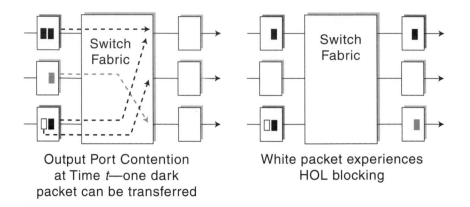

Output Port Contention
at Time *t*—one dark
packet can be transferred

White packet experiences
HOL blocking

FIGURE 4.37 HOL blocking at an input queued switch

the middle right output port (the destination for the white packet). This phenomenon is known as **head-of-the-line (HOL) blocking** in an input-queued switch—a queued packet in an input queue must wait for transfer through the fabric (even though its output port is free) due to the blocking of another packet at the head-of-the-line. [Karol 1987] shows that due to HOL blocking, the input queue will grow to unbounded length (informally, this is equivalent to saying that significant packet loss will occur) as soon as the packet arrival rate on the input links reaches only 58% of their capacity. A number of solutions to HOL blocking are discussed in [McKeown 1997b].

4.7 IPv6

In the early 1990's, the Internet Engineering Task Force began an effort to develop a successor to the IPv4 protocol. A prime motivation for this effort was the realization that the 32-bit IP address space was beginning to be used up, with new networks and IP nodes being attached to the Internet (and being allocated unique IP addresses) at a breathtaking rate. To respond to this need of a large IP address space, a new IP protocol, IPv6, was developed. The designers of IPv6 also took this opportunity to tweak and augment other aspects of IPv4, based on the accumulated operational experience with IPv4.

The point in time when IPv4 addresses would have been completely allocated (and hence no new networks could have attached to the Internet) was the subject of considerable debate. Based on current trends in address allocation, the estimates of the two leaders of the IETF's Address Lifetime Expectations working group were that addresses would become exhausted in 2008 and 2018 respectively [Solensky 1996]. In 1996, the American Registry for Internet Numbers (ARIN) reported that all of the IPv4 class A addresses had been assigned, 62% of the class B addresses had been assigned, and 37% of the class C addresses had been assigned [ARIN 1996]. While these estimates and numbers suggested that a considerable amount of time might be left until the IPv4 address space became exhausted, it was realized that considerable time would be needed to deploy a new technology on such an extensive scale, and so the "Next Generation IP" (IPng) effort [Bradner 1996], [RFC1752] was begun. An excellent on-line source of information about IPv6 is The IP Next Generation Homepage. An excellent book is also available on the subject [Huitema 1997].

4.7.1 IPv6 Packet Format

The format of the IPv6 packet is shown in Figure 4.38. The most important changes introduced in IPv6 are evident in the packet format:

- *Expanded addressing capabilities.* IPv6 increases the size of the IP address from 32 to 128 bits. This ensures that the world won't run out of IP addresses. Now, every grain of sand on the planet can be IP-addressable. In addition, the address space contains new hierarchical structure, allocating portions of the enlarged address space to geographical regions [RFC 1884]. In addition to unicast and multicast addresses, a new type of address, called an **anycast address,** has also been introduced, which allows a packet addressed to an anycase address to be delivered to any one of a group of hosts. (This feature could be used, for example, to send an HTTP GET to the nearest of a number of mirror sites that contain a given document.)
- *A streamlined 40 byte header.* As discussed below, a number of IPv4 fields have been dropped or made optional. The resulting 40-byte fixed-length header allows for faster processing of the IP packet. A new encoding of options allows for more flexible options processing.
- *Flow labeling and priority.* IPv6 has an elusive definition of a "**flow.**" [RFC 1752] and [RFC 2460] state that this allows "labeling of packets belonging to particular flows for which the sender requests special handling, such as a non-default quality of service or real-time service." For example, audio and video transmission might likely be treated as a flow. On the other hand, the

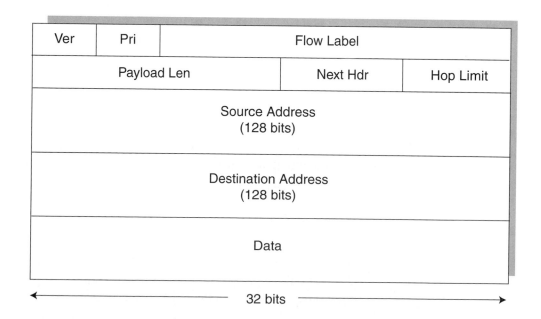

FIGURE 4.38 IPv6 packet format

more traditional applications, such as file transfer and email might not be treated as flows. It is possible that the traffic carried by a high-priority user (for example, someone paying for better service for their traffic) might also be treated as a flow. What is clear, however, is that the designers of IPv6 foresee the eventual need to be able to differentiate among the "flows," even if the exact meaning of a flow has not yet been determined. The IPv6 header also has a 4-bit **priority** field. This field, as the TOS field in IPv4, can be used to give priority to certain packets within a flow, or it can be used to give priority to datagrams from certain applications (for example, ICMP packets) over packets from other applications (for example, network news).

The IPv6 datagram format is shown in Figure 4.38. As noted above, a comparison of Figure 4.38 with Figure 4.22 reveals the simpler, more streamlined structure of the IPv6 datagram. The following fields are defined in IPv6:

- *Version.* This four-bit field identifies the IP version number. Not surprisingly, IPv6 carries a value of "6" in this field. Note that putting a "4" in this field does not create a valid IPv4 packet (if it did, life would be a lot simpler—see the discussion below regarding the transition from IPv4 to IPv6.

- *Priority.* This four bit field is similar in spirit to the ToS field we saw in IP version 4. [RFC 2460] states that values 0 through 7 are to be used for priority among traffic that is congestion-controlled (that is, for which the source will back off on detection of congestion), while values 8 through 15 are used for non-congestion controlled traffic, such as constant bit rate real-time traffic.

- *Flow label.* As discussed above, this field is used to identify a "flow" of packets.

- *Payload length.* This 16-bit value is treated as an unsigned integer giving the number of bytes in the IPv6 packet following the fixed length, 40 byte packet header.

- *Next header.* This field identifies the protocol to which the contents (data field) of this packet will be delivered (for example, to TCP or UDP). The field uses the same values as the Protocol field in the IPv4 header.

- *Hop limit.* The contents of this field are decremented by one by each router that forwards the packet. If the hop limit count reaches zero, the packet is discarded.

- *Source and destination address.* An IPv6 address has the following structure:

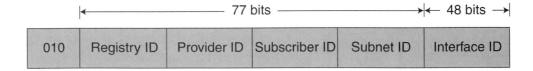

FIGURE 4.39   IPv6 address structure

- *Data.* This is the payload portion of the IPv6 packet. When the packet reaches its destination, the payload will be removed from the IP packet and passed on to the protocol specified in the next header field.

The discussion above identified the purpose of the fields that *are* included in the IPv6 packet. Comparing the IPv6 packet format in Figure 4.38 with the IPv4 packet format that we saw earlier in Figure 4.22, we notice that several fields appearing in the IPv4 packet are no longer present in the IPv6 packet:

- *Fragmentation/Reassembly.* IPv6 does not provide for fragmentation and reassembly. If an IPv6 datagram received by a router is too large to be forwarded over the outgoing link, the router simply drops the datagram and sends a "Packet Too Big" ICMP error message (see below) back to the sender. The sender can then resend the data, using a smaller IP datagram size. Fragmentation and reassembly is a time-consuming operation; removing this functionality from the routers and placing it squarely in the end systems considerably speeds up IP forwarding within the network.

- *Checksum.* Because the transport layer (for example, TCP and UDP) and data link (for example, Ethernet) protocols in the Internet layers perform checksumming, the designers of IP probably felt that this functionality was sufficiently redundant in the network layer that it could be removed. Once again, fast processing of IP packets was a central concern. Recall from our discussion of IPv4 in Section 4.4.1, that since the IPv4 header contains a TTL field (similar to the hop limit field in IPv6), the IPv4 header checksum needed to be recomputed at every router. As with fragmentation and reassembly, this too was a costly operation in IPv4.

- *Options.* An options field is no longer a part of the standard IP header. However, it has not gone away. Instead, the options field is one of the possible "next headers" pointed to from within the IPv6 header. That is, just as TCP or UDP protocol headers can be the next header within an IP packet, so too can an options field. The removal of the options field results in a fixed length, 40 byte IP header.

A new ICMP for IPv6. Recall from our discussion in Section 4.4, that the ICMP protocol is used by IP nodes to report error conditions and provide limited information (for example, the echo reply to a ping message) to an end system. A new version of ICMP has been defined for IPv6 in [RFC 2463]. In addition to reorganizing the existing ICMP type and code definitions, ICMPv6 also added new types and codes required by the new IPv6 functionality. These include the "Packet Too Big" type, and an "unrecognized IPv6 options" error code. In addition, ICMPv6 subsumes the functionality of the Internet Group Management Protocol (IGMP) that we will study in Section 4.8. IGMP, which is used to manage a host's joining and leaving of so-called multicast groups, was previously a separate protocol from ICMP in IPv4.

4.7.2 Transitioning from IPv4 to IPv6

Now that we have seen the technical details of IPv6, let us consider a very practical matter: how will the public Internet, which is based on IPv4, be transitioned to IPv6? The problem is that while new IPv6-capable systems can be made "backwards compatible," that is, can send, route, and receive IPv4 datagrams, already deployed IPv4-capable systems are not capable of handling IPv6 datagrams. Several options are possible.

One option would be to declare a "flag day"—a given time and date when all Internet machines would be turned off, be upgraded from IPv4 to IPv6. The last major technology transition (from using NCP to using TCP for reliable transport service) occurred almost 20 years ago. Even back then [RFC 801], when the Internet was tiny and still being administered by a small number of "wizards," it was realized the such a flag day was not possible. A flag day involving hundreds of millions of machines and millions of network administrators and users is even more unthinkable today. [RFC 1993] describes two approaches (which can be used either alone or together) for gradually integrating IPv6 hosts and routers into an IPv4 world (with the long term goal, of course, of having all IPv4 nodes eventually transition to IPv6).

Probably the most straightforward way to introduce IPv6-capable nodes is a **dual stack** approach, where IPv6 nodes also have a complete IPv4 implementation as well. Such a node, referred to as an IPv6/IPv4 node in [RFC 1993], has the ability to send and receive both IPv4 and IPv6 datagrams. When interoperating with an IPv4 node, an IPv6/IPv4 node can use IPv4 datagrams; when interoperating with an IPv6 node, it can speak IPv6. IPv6/IPv4 nodes must have both IPv6 and IPv4 addresses. They must furthermore be able to determine whether another node is IPv6-capable or IPv4-only. This problem can be solved using the DNS (see Chapter 2), which can return an IPv6 address if the node name being resolved is IPv6 capable, or otherwise return an IPv4 address. Of course, if the node issuing the DNS request in only IPv4 capable, the DNS returns only an IPv4 address.

In the dual stack approach, if either the sender or the receiver is only IPv4-capable, an IPv4 datagram must be used. As a result, it is possible that two IPv6-capable nodes can end up, in essence, sending IPv4 datagrams to each other. This is illustrated in Figure 4.40. Suppose node A is IPv6 capable and wants to send an IP datagram to node F, which is also IPv6-capable. Nodes A and B can exchange an IPv6 packet. However, node B must create an IPv4 datagram to send to C. Certainly, the data field of the IPv6 packet can be copied into the data field of the IPv4 datagram and appropriate address mapping can be done. However, in performing the conversion from IPv6 to IPv4, there will be IPv6-specific fields in the IPv6

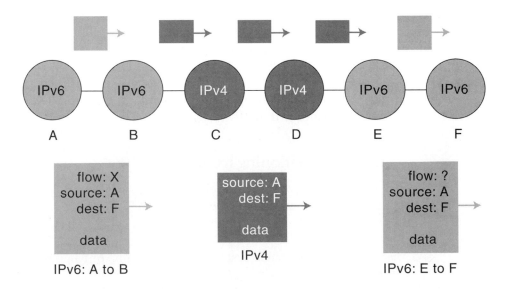

FIGURE 4.40 A dual stack approach

datagram (for example, the flow identifier field) that have no counterpart in IPv4. The information in these fields will be lost. Thus, even though E and F can exchange IPv6 datagrams, the arriving IPv4 datagrams at E from D do not contain all of the fields that were in the original IPv6 datagram sent from A.

An alternative to the dual stack approach, also discussed in [RFC 1993], is known as **tunneling.** Tunneling can solve the problem noted above, allowing, for example, E to receive the IPv6 datagram originated by A. The basic idea behind tunneling is the following. Suppose two IPv6 nodes (for example, B and E in Figure 4.40) want to interoperate using IPv6 datagrams, but are connected to each other by intervening IPv4 routers. We refer to the intervening set of IPv4 routers between two IPv6 routers as a **tunnel,** as illustrated in Figure 4.41. With tunneling, the IPv6 node on the sending side of the tunnel (for example, B) takes the *entire* IPv6 datagram, and puts it in the data (payload) field of an IPv4 datagram. This IPv4 datagram is then addressed to the IPv6 node on the receiving side of the tunnel (for example, E) and sent to the first node in the tunnel (for example, C). The intervening IPv4 routers in the tunnel route this IPv4 datagram amongst themselves, just as they would any other datagram, blissfully unaware that the IPv4 datagram itself contains a complete IPv6 datagram. The IPv6 node on the receiving side of the tunnel eventually receives the IPv4 datagram (it is the destination of the IPv4 datagram!), determines that the IPv4 datagram contains an IPv6 datagram, extracts the IPv6 datagram, and then routes the IPv6 datagram exactly as it would if it had received the IPv6 datagram from a directly-connected IPv6 neighbor.

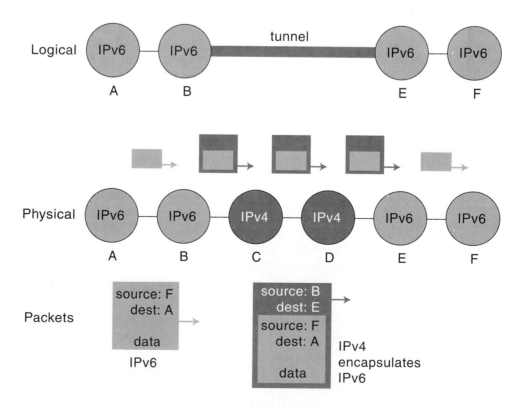

FIGURE 4.41   Tunneling

We end this section by mentioning that there is currently some doubt about whether IPv6 will make significant inroads into the Internet in the near future (2000–2002) or even ever at all [Garber 1999]. Indeed, at the time of this writing, a number of North American ISPs have said they don't plan to buy IPv6-enabled networking equipment. These ISPs say that there is little customer demand for IPv6's capabilities when IPv4, with some patches (such as network address translator boxes), is working well enough. On the other hand, there appears to be more interest in IPv6 in Europe and Asia. Thus the fate of IPv6 remains an open question.

One important lesson that we can learn from the IPv6 experience is that it is enormously difficult to change network-layer protocols. Since the early 1990s, numerous new network-layer protocols have been trumpeted as the next major revolution for the Internet, but most of these protocols have had limited penetration to date. These protocols include IPv6, multicast protocols (Section 4.8), and resource reservation protocols (Section 6.9). Indeed, introducing new protocols into the network layer is like replacing the foundation of a house—it is difficult to do without tearing the whole house down or at least temporarily relocated the house's residents. On the other hand, the Internet has witnessed rapid deployment of new protocols at the application layer. The classic example, of course, is HTTP and the Web; other examples include audio and video streaming and chat. Introducing new application layer protocols is like adding a new layer of paint to a house—it is relatively easy to do, and if you choose an attractive color, others in the neighborhood will copy you. In summary, in the future we can expect to see changes in the Internet's network layer, but these changes will likely occur on a time scale that is much slower than the changes that will occur at the application layer.

4.8   MULTICAST ROUTING

The transport and network layer protocols we have studied so far provide for the delivery of packets from a single source to a single destination. Protocols involving just one sender and one receiver are often referred to as **unicast protocols.**

A number of emerging network applications require the delivery of packets from one or more senders to a *group of receivers.* These applications include bulk data transfer (for example, the transfer of a software upgrade from the software developer to users needing the upgrade), streaming continuous media (for example, the transfer of the audio, video, and text of a live lecture to a set of distributed lecture participants), shared data applications (for example, a whiteboard or teleconferencing application that is shared among many distributed participants), data feeds (for example, stock quotes), and interactive gaming (for example, distributed interactive virtual environments or multiplayer games such as Quake). For each of these applications, an extremely useful abstraction is the notion of a **multicast:** the sending of a packet from one sender to multiple receivers with a single "transmit" operation.

In this section we consider the network layer aspects of multicast. We continue our primary focus on the Internet here, as multicast is much more mature (although it is still undergoing significant development and evolution) in the Internet than in ATM networks. We will see that as in the unicast case, routing algorithms again play a central role in the network layer. We will also see, however, that unlike the unicast case, Internet multicast is *not* a connectionless service—state information for a multicast connection must be established and maintained in routers that handle multicast packets sent among hosts in a so-called multicast group. This, in turn, will require a combination of signaling and routing protocols in order to set up, maintain, and tear down connection state in the routers.

4.8.1   Introduction: The Internet Multicast Abstraction and Multicast Groups

From a networking standpoint, the multicast *abstraction*—a single send operation that results in copies of the sent data being delivered to many receivers—can be *implemented* in many ways. One possibility is for the sender to use a separate unicast transport connection to each of the receivers. An application-level data unit that is passed to the transport layer is then duplicated at the sender and transmitted over each of the individual connections. This approach implements a one-sender-to-many-receivers multicast abstraction using an underlying unicast network layer [Talpade 1997]. It requires no explicit multicast support from the network layer to implement the multicast abstraction; multicast is emulated using multiple point-to-point unicast connections. This is shown in the left of Figure 4.42, with network routers shaded in white to indicate that they are not actively involved in supporting the multicast. Here, the multicast sender uses three *separate* unicast connections to reach the three receivers.

A second alternative is to provide explicit multicast support at the network layer. In this latter approach, a *single* datagram is transmitted from the sending host. This datagram (or a copy of this datagram) is then replicated at a network router whenever it must be forwarded on multiple outgoing links in order to reach the receivers. The right side of Figure 4.42 illustrates this second approach, with certain routers shaded gray to indicate that they are actively involved in supporting the multicast. Here, a single datagram is transmitted by the sender. That datagram is then duplicated by the router within the network; one copy is forwarded to the uppermost receiver and another copy is forwarded towards the rightmost receivers. At the rightmost router, the multicast datagram is broadcast over the Ethernet that connects the two receivers to the rightmost router. Clearly, this second approach towards multicast makes more efficient use of network bandwidth in that only a *single* copy of a datagram will ever traverse a link. On the other

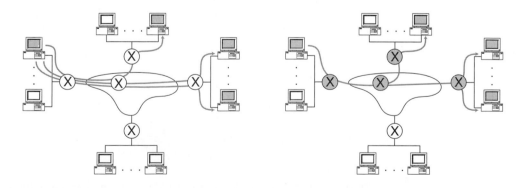

FIGURE 4.42   Two approaches toward implementing the multicast abstraction

hand, considerable network layer support is needed to implement a multicast-aware network layer. For the remainder of this section we will focus on a multicast-aware network layer, as this approach is implemented in the Internet and poses a number of interesting challenges.

With multicast communication, we are immediately faced with two problems that are much more complicated than in the case of unicast—how to identify the receivers of a multicast datagram and how to address a datagram sent to these receivers.

In the case of unicast communication, the IP address of the receiver (destination) is carried in each IP unicast datagram and identifies the single recipient. But in the case of multicast, we now have multiple receivers. Does it make sense for each multicast datagram to carry the IP addresses of all of the multiple recipients? While this approach might be workable with a small number of recipients, it would not scale well to the case of hundreds or thousands of receivers; the amount of addressing information in the datagram would swamp the amount of data actually carried in the datagram's payload field. Explicit identification of the receivers by the sender also requires that the sender know the identities and addresses of all of the receivers. We will see shortly that there are cases where this requirement might be undesirable.

For these reasons, in the Internet architecture (and the ATM architecture as well), a multicast datagram is addressed using **address indirection.** That is, a single "identifier" is used for the group of receivers, and *a copy of the datagram that is addressed to the group using this single "identifier" is delivered to all of the multicast receivers associated with that group.* In the Internet, the single "identifier" that represents a group of receivers is a Class D multicast address, as we saw earlier in Section 4.4. The group of receivers associated with a class D address is referred to as a **multicast group.** The multicast group abstraction is illustrated in Figure 4.43. Here, four hosts (shown with shaded gray screens) are associated

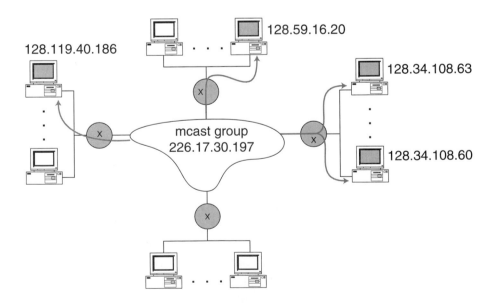

FIGURE 4.43 The multicast group: a datagram addressed to the group is delivered to all members of the multicast group

with the multicast group address of 226.17.30.197 and will receive all datagrams addressed to that multicast address. The difficulty that we must still address is the fact that each host has a unique IP unicast address that is completely independent of the address of the multicast group in which it is participating.

While the multicast group abstraction is simple, it raises a host (pun intended) of questions. How does a group get started and how does it terminate? How is the group address chosen? How are new hosts added to the group (either as senders or receivers)? Can anyone join a group (and send to, or receive from, that group) or is group membership restricted and if so, by whom? Do group members know the identities of the other group members as part of the network layer protocol? How do the network routers interoperate with each other to deliver a multicast datagram to all group members? For the Internet, the answers to all of these questions involve the Internet Group Management Protocol [RFC 2236]. So, let us next consider the IGMP protocol and then return to these broader questions.

4.8.2 The IGMP Protocol

The **Internet Group Management Protocol, IGMP** version 2 [RFC 2236], operates between a host and its directly attached router (informally, think of the directly-attached router as the "first-hop" router that a host would see on a path to any other host outside its own local network, or the "last-hop" router on any path to that host), as shown in Figure 4.44. Figure 4.44 shows three first-hop multicast routers, each connected to its attached hosts via one outgoing local interface. This local interface is attached to a LAN in this example, and while each LAN has multiple attached hosts, at most a few of these hosts will typically belong to a given multicast group at any given time.

IGMP provides the means for a host to inform its attached router that an application running on the host wants to join a specific multicast group. Given that the scope of IGMP interaction is limited to a host and its attached router, another protocol is clearly required to coordinate the multicast routers (including the

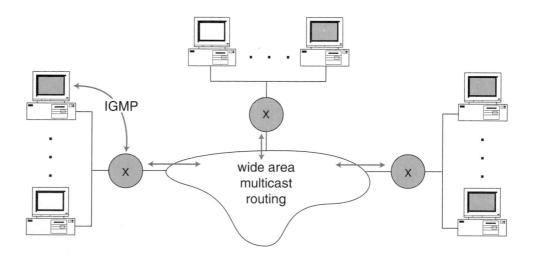

FIGURE 4.44 The two components of network layer multicast: IGMP and multicast routing protocols

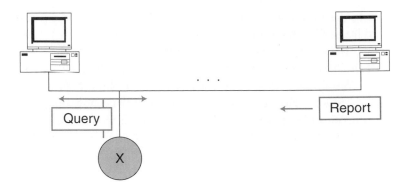

FIGURE 4.45 IGMP member query and membership report

attached routers) throughout the Internet, so that multicast datagrams are routed to their final destinations. This latter functionality is accomplished by the **network layer multicast routing algorithms** such as PIM, DVMRP, MOSFP and BGP. We will study multicast routing algorithms in Sections 4.8.3 and 4.8.4. Network-layer multicast in the Internet thus consists of two complementary components: IGMP and multicast routing protocols.

Although IGMP is referred to as a "group membership protocol," the term is a bit misleading since IGMP operates *locally,* between a host and an attached router. Despite its name, IGMP is *not* a protocol that operates among all the hosts that have joined a multicast group, hosts that may be spread around the world. Indeed, there is *no* network-layer multicast group membership protocol that operates among all the Internet hosts in a group. There is no protocol, for example, that allows a host to determine the identities of all of the other hosts, network-wide, that have joined the multicast group. (See the homework problems for a further exploration of the consequences of this design choice.)

IGMP version 2 [RFC 2236] has only three message types, as shown in Table 4.4. A general `membership_query` message is sent by a router to all hosts on an attached interface (for example, to all hosts on a local area network) to determine the set of all multicast groups that have been joined by the hosts on that interface. A router can also determine if a specific multicast group has been joined by hosts on an attached interface using a specific `membership_query`. The specific query includes the multicast address of the group being queried in the multicast group

Table 4.4   IGMP v2 Message types

IGMP Message Types	Sent by	Purpose
Membership query: general	router	query multicast groups joined by attached hosts
Membership query: specific	router	query if specific multicast group joined by attached hosts
Membership report	host	report host wants to join or is joined to given multicast group
Leave group	host	report leaving given multicast group

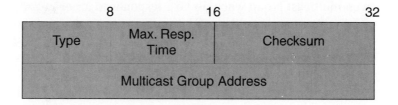

FIGURE 4.46 IGMP message format

address field of the IGMP `membership_query` message, as shown in Figure 4.46.

Hosts respond to a `membership_query` message with an IGMP `membership_report` message, as illustrated in Figure 4.45. `Membership_report` messages can also be generated by a host when an application first joins a multicast group without waiting for a `membership_query` message from the router. `Membership_report` messages are received by the router, as well as all hosts on the attached interface (for example, in the case of a LAN). Each `membership_report` contains the multicast address of a single group that the responding host has joined. Note that an attached router doesn't really care *which* hosts have joined a given multicast group or even *how many* hosts on the same LAN have joined the same group. (In either case, the router's work is the same—it must run a multicast routing protocol together with other routers to ensure that it receives the multicast datagrams for the appropriate multicast groups.) Since a router really only cares about whether one or more of its attached hosts belong to a given multicast group, it would ideally like to hear from only one of the attached hosts that belongs to each group (why waste the effort to receive identical responses from multiple hosts?). IGMP thus provides an explicit mechanism aimed at decreasing the number of `membership_report` messages generated when multiple attached hosts belong to the same multicast group.

Specifically, each `membership_query` message sent by a router also includes a "maximum response time" value field, as shown in Figure 4.46. After receiving a `membership_query` message and before sending a `membership_report` message for a given multicast group, a host waits a random amount of time between zero and the maximum response time value. If the host observes a `membership_report` message from some *other* attached host for that given multicast group, it *suppresses* (discards) its own pending `membership_report` message, since the host now knows that the attached router already knows that one or more hosts are joined to that multicast group. This form of **feedback suppression** is thus a performance optimization—it avoids the transmission of unnecessary `membership_report` messages. Similar feedback suppression mechanisms have been used in a number of Internet protocols, including reliable multicast transport protocols [Floyd 1997].

The final type of IGMP message is the `leave_group` message. Interestingly, this message is optional! But if it is optional, how does a router detect that there are no longer any hosts on an attached interface that are joined to a given multicast group? The answer to this question lies in the use of the IGMP `membership_query` message. The router infers that no hosts are joined to a given multicast group when no host responds to a `membership_query` message with the given group address. This is an example of what is sometimes called **soft state** in an Internet protocol. In a soft state protocol, the state (in this case of IGMP, the fact that there are hosts joined to a given multicast group) is removed via a timeout event (in this case, via a periodic `membership_query` message from the router) if it is not explicitly refreshed (in this case, by a `membership_report` message from an attached host). It has been argued that soft-state protocols result in simpler control than hard-state protocols, which not only require state to be explicitly added and removed, but also require mechanisms to recover from the situation where the entity responsible for removing state has terminated prematurely or failed [Sharma 1997]. An excellent discussion of soft state can be found in [Raman 1999].

The IGMP message format is summarized in Figure 4.46. Like ICMP, IGMP messages are carried (encapsulated) within an IP datagram, with an IP protocol number of 2.

Having examined the protocol for joining and leaving multicast groups we are now in a better position to reflect on the current Internet multicast service model, which is based on the work of Steve Deering [RFC 1112, Deering 1991]. In this multicast service model, any host can "join" a multicast group at the network layer. A host simply issues a `membership_report` IGMP message to its attached router. That router, working in concert with other Internet routers, will soon begin delivering multicast datagrams to the host. Joining a multicast group is thus receiver-driven. A sender need not be concerned with explicitly adding receivers to the multicast group (as is the case with multicast in ATM) but neither can it control who joins the group and therefore receives datagrams sent to that group. Indeed, recall that it is not possible at the network layer to even know which hosts, network-wide, have joined a multicast group. Similarly, there is no control over who sends to the multicast group. Datagrams sent by different hosts can be arbitrarily interleaved at the various receivers (with different interleavings possible at different receivers). A malicious sender can inject datagrams into the multicast group datagram flow. Even with benign senders, since there is no network layer coordination of the use of multicast addresses, it is possible that two different multicast groups will choose to use the same multicast address. From a multicast application viewpoint, this will result in interleaved extraneous multicast traffic.

These problems may seem to be insurmountable drawbacks for developing multicast applications. All is not lost, however. Although the network layer does *not* provide for filtering, ordering, or privacy of multicast datagrams, these mechanisms *can* all be implemented at the application layer. There is also on-going work aimed at adding some of this functionality into the network layer [Cain 1999]. In many ways, the current Internet multicast service model reflects the same philosophy as the Internet unicast service model—an extremely simple network layer with additional functionality being provided in the upper layer protocols in the hosts of the "edges" of the network. This philosophy has been unquestionably successful for the unicast case; whether the minimalist network layer philosophy will be equally successful for the multicast service model still remains an open question. An interesting discussion of an alternate multicast service model is [Holbrook 1999].

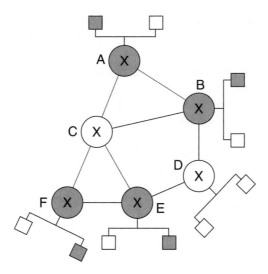

FIGURE 4.47   Multicast hosts, their attached routers, and other routers

4.8.3   Multicast Routing: The General Case

In the previous section we have seen how the IGMP protocol operates at the "edge" of the network between a router and its attached hosts, allowing a router to determine what multicast group traffic it needs to receive for forwarding to its attached hosts. We can now focus our attention on just the multicast routers: how should they route packets amongst themselves in order to insure that each router receives the multicast group traffic that it needs?

Figure 4.47 illustrates the setting for the **multicast routing problem.** Let us consider a single multicast group and assume that any router that has an attached host that has joined this group may either send or receive traffic addressed to this group.[1] In Figure 4.47, hosts joined to the multicast group are represented by shaded gray squares; their immediately attached router is also shaded in gray. As shown in Figure 4.47, among the population of multicast routers, only a *subset* of these routers (those with attached hosts that are joined to the multicast group) actually *need* to receive the multicast traffic. In Figure 4.47, only routers A, B, E and F need to receive the multicast traffic. Since none of the attached hosts to router D are joined to the multicast group and since router C has no attached hosts, neither C nor D *need* to receive the multicast group traffic.

The goal of multicast routing then is to find a tree of links that connects all of the routers that have attached hosts belonging to the multicast group. Multicast packets will then be routed along this tree from the sender to all of the hosts belonging to the multicast tree. Of course, the tree may contain routers that do not

---

1. For simplicity, we will assume throughout this section that the hosts sending to the multicast group are all members of the group (for example, have used IGMP to join the multicast group). We have seen in Section 4.6.1, however, that in the Internet multicast model, any host can send to a multicast group (that is, a host need not have explicitly joined the group in order to send to the group).

have attached hosts belonging to the multicast group (for example, in Figure 4.47, it is impossible to connect routers A, B, E, and F in a tree without involving either routers C and/or D).

In practice, two approaches have been adopted for determining the multicast routing tree. The two approaches differ according to whether a single tree is used to distribute the traffic for *all* senders in the group, or whether a source-specific routing tree is constructed for each individual sender:

- *Group-shared tree.* In the group-shared tree approach, only a *single* routing tree is constructed for the entire multicast group. For example, the single multicast tree shown with thick shaded lines in the left of Figure 4.48, connects routers A, B, C, E, and F. (Following our conventions from Figure 4.47, router C is not shaded in gray. Although it participates in the multicast tree, it has no attached hosts that are members of the multicast group). Multicast packets will flow only over those links shaded in gray. Note that the links are bi-directional, since packets can flow in either direction on a link.

- *Source-based trees.* In a source-based approach, an individual routing tree is constructed for *each* sender in the multicast group. In a multicast group with *N* hosts, *N* different routing trees will be constructed for that *single* multicast group. Packets will be routed to multicast group members in a source-specific manner. In the right of Figure 4.48, two source-specific multicast trees are shown, one rooted at A and another rooted at B. Note that not only are there different links than in the group-shared tree case, (for example, the link from BC is used in the source-specific tree routed at B, but not in the group-shared tree in the left of Figure 4.48), but that some links may also be used only in a single direction.

Multicast routing using a group-shared tree. Let us first consider the case where all packets sent to a multicast group are to be routed along the same single multicast tree, regardless of the sender. In this case, the multicast routing problem appears quite simple: find a tree within the network that connects all routers having an attached host belonging to that multicast group. In Figure 4.48 (left), the tree composed of thick gray links is one such tree. Note that the tree contains routers that have attached hosts belonging to the multicast group (that is, routers A, B,

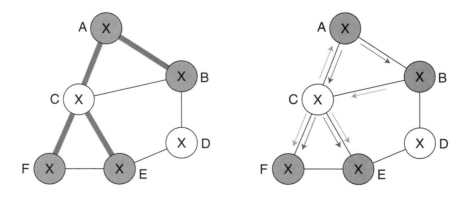

FIGURE 4.48 A single, shared tree (left), and two source-based trees (right)

E and F) as well as routers that have no attached hosts belonging to the multicast group. Ideally, one might also want the tree to have minimal "cost." If we assign a "cost" to each link (as we did for unicast routing in Section 4.2.2) then an optimal multicast routing tree is one having the smallest sum of the tree link costs. For the link costs given in Figure 4.49, the optimum multicast tree (with a cost of 7) is shown with thick gray lines.

The problem of finding a minimum cost tree is known as the **Steiner Tree problem** [Hakimi 1971]. Solving this problem has been shown to be NP-complete [Garey 1978], but the approximation algorithm in [Kou 1981] has been proven to be within a constant of the optimal solution. Other studies have shown that, in general, approximation algorithms for the Steiner tree problem do quite well in practice [Wall 1980, Waxman 1988, Wei 1993].

Even though good heuristics exist for the Steiner tree problem, it is interesting to note that none of the existing Internet multicast routing algorithms have been based on this approach. Why? One reason is that information is needed about all links in the network. Another reason is that in order for a minimum cost tree to be maintained, the algorithm needs to be re-run whenever link costs change. Finally, we will see that other considerations, such as the ability to leverage the routing tables that have already been computed for unicast routing, play an important role in judging the suitability of a multicast routing algorithm. In the end, performance (and optimality) is but one of many concerns.

An alternate approach towards determining the group-shared multicast tree, one that is used in practice by several Internet multicast routing algorithms, is based on the notion of defining a *center* node (also known as a *rendezvous point* or a *core*) in the single shared multicast routing tree. In the **center-based approach,** a center node is first identified for the multicast group. Routers with attached hosts belonging to the multicast group then unicast so-called "join" messages addressed to the center node. A join message is forwarded using unicast routing towards the center until it either arrives at a router that already belongs to the multicast tree or arrives at the center. In either case, the path that the join message has followed defines the branch of the routing tree between the edge router that initiated the join message and the center. One can think of this new path as being "grafted" onto the existing multicast tree for the group.

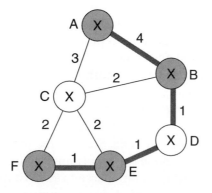

FIGURE 4.49   A minimum cost multicast tree

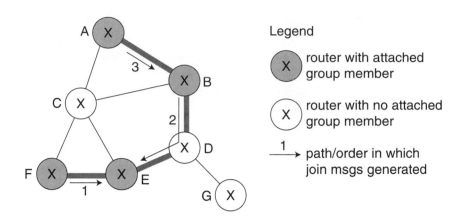

FIGURE 4.50 Constructing a center-based tree

Figure 4.50 illustrates the construction of a center-based multicast routing tree. Suppose that router E is selected as the center of the tree. Node F first joins the multicast group and forwards a join message to E. The single link EF becomes the initial multicast tree. Node B then joins the multicast tree by sending its join message to E. Suppose that the unicast path route to E from B is via D. In this case, the join message results in the path BDE being grafted onto the multicast tree. Finally, node A joins the multicast group by forwarding its join message towards E. Let us assume that A's unicast path to E is through B. Since B has already joined the multicast tree, the arrival of A's join message at B will result in the AB link being immediately grafted on to the multicast tree.

A critical question for center-based tree multicast routing is the process used to select the center. Center selection algorithms are discussed in [Wall 1980, Thaler 1997, Estrin 1997]. [Wall 1980] shows that centers can be chosen so that the resulting tree is within a constant factor of optimum (the solution to the Steiner tree problem).

Multicast routing using a source-based tree.   While the multicast routing algorithms we have studied above construct a single, shared routing tree that is used to route packets from *all* senders, the second broad class of multicast routing algorithms construct a multicast routing tree for *each* source in the multicast group.

We have already studied an algorithm (Dijkstra's link-state routing algorithm, in Section 4.2.1) that computes the unicast paths that are individually the least cost paths from the source to all destinations. The union of these paths might be thought of as forming a **least unicast-cost path tree** (or a **shortest unicast path tree,** if all link costs are identical). Figure 4.51 shows the construction of the least cost path tree rooted at A. By comparing the tree in Figure 4.51 with that of Figure 4.49, it is evident that the least cost path tree is *not* the same as the minimum over-all cost tree computed as the solution to the Steiner tree problem. The reason for this difference is that the goals of these two algorithms are different: least unicast-cost path tree minimizes the cost from the source to each of the destinations (that is, there is no other tree that has a shorter distance path from the source to any of the destinations), while the Steiner tree minimizes the sum of the link costs in the tree. You might also want to convince yourself that the least unicast-cost path tree

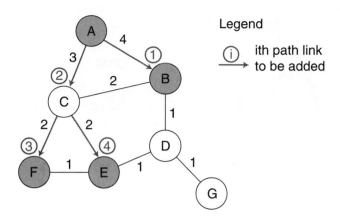

Legend

(i)   ith path link
─→   to be added

FIGURE 4.51   Construction of a least-cost path routing tree

often differs from one source to another (for example, the source tree rooted at A is different from the source tree rooted at E in Figure 4.51).

The least cost path multicast routing algorithm is a link-state algorithm. It requires that each router know the state of each link in the network in order to be able to compute the least cost path tree from the source to all destinations. A simpler multicast routing algorithm, one which requires much less link state information than the least cost path routing algorithm, is the **reverse path forwarding (RPF)** algorithm.

The idea behind reverse path forwarding is simple, yet elegant. When a router receives a multicast packet with a given source address, it transmits the packet on *all* of its outgoing links (except the one on which it was received) *only* if the packet arrived on the link that is on *its own* shortest path back *to* the sender. Otherwise the router simply discards the incoming packet without forwarding it on any of its outgoing links. Such a packet can be dropped because the router knows it either will receive, or has already received, a copy of this packet on the link that is on its own shortest path back to the sender. (You might want to convince yourself that this will, in fact, happen.) Note that reverse path forwarding does *not* require that a router know the complete shortest path from itself to the source; it need only know the next hop on its unicast shortest path to the sender.

Figure 4.52 illustrates RPF. Suppose that the links with shaded thicker gray lines represent the least cost paths *from* the receivers *to* the source (A). Router A initially multicasts a source-S packet to routers C and B. Router B will forward the source-S packet it has received from A (since A is on its least cost path to A) to both C and D. B will *ignore* (drop, without forwarding) any source-S packets it receives from any other routers (for example, from routers C or D).

Let us now consider router C, which will receive a source-S packet directly from A as well as from B. Since B is not on C's own shortest path back to A, C will ignore (drop) any source-S packets it receives from B. On the other hand, when C receives an source-S packet directly from A, it will forward the packet to routers B, E, and F.

RPF is a nifty idea. But consider what happens at router D in Figure 4.52. It will forward packets to router G, even though router G has no attached hosts that are joined to the multicast group. While this is not so bad for this case where D

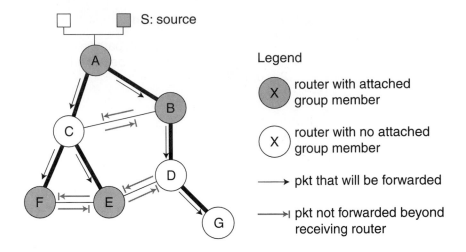

FIGURE 4.52 Reverse path forwarding

has only a single downstream receiver, G, imagine what would happen if there were thousands of routers downstream from D! Each of these thousands of routers would receive unwanted multicast packets. (This scenario is not as far-fetched as it might seem. The initial MBone [Casner 1992, Macedonia 1994], the first global multicast network suffered from *precisely* this problem at first!)

The solution to the problem of receiving unwanted multicast packets under RPF is known as **pruning.** A multicast router that receives multicast packets and has no attached hosts joined to that group will send a prune message to its upstream router. If a router receives prune messages from each of its downstream routers, then it can forward a prune message upstream. Pruning is illustrated in Figure 4.53.

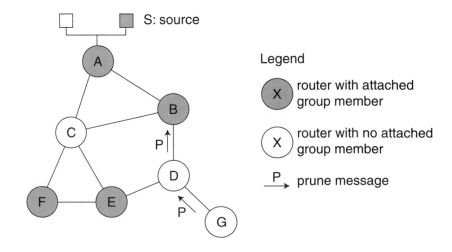

FIGURE 4.53 Pruning an RPF tree.

While pruning is conceptually straightforward, two subtle issues arise. First, pruning requires that a router know which routers downstream are dependent on it for receiving their multicast packets. This requires additional information beyond that required for RPF alone. A second complication is more fundamental: if a router sends a prune message upstream, then what should happen if a router later needs to join that multicast group? Recall that under RPF, multicast packets are "pushed" down the RPF tree to all routers. If a prune message removes a branch from that tree, then some mechanism is needed to restore that branch. One possibility is to add a graft message that allows a router to "unprune" a branch. Another option is to allow pruned branches to time-out and be added again to the multicast RPF tree; a router can then re-prune the added branch if the multicast traffic is still not wanted.

4.8.4   Multicast Routing in the Internet

Having now studied multicast routing algorithms in the abstract, let's now consider how these algorithms are put into practice in today's Internet by examining the three currently-standardized Internet multicast routing protocols: DVMRP, MOSPF, and PIM.

DVMRP: Distance Vector Multicast Routing Protocol.   The first multicast routing protocol used in the Internet and the most widely supported multicast routing algorithm [IP Multicast Initiative 1998] is the Distance Vector Multicast Routing Protocol (DVMRP) [RFC 1075]. DVMRP implements source-based trees with reverse path forwarding, pruning, and grafting. DVMRP uses a distance vector algorithm (see Section 4.2) that allows each router to compute the outgoing link (next hop) that is on its shortest path back to each possible source. This information is then used in the RPF algorithm, as discussed above. A public copy of DVMRP software is available at [mrouted 1996].

In addition to computing next hop information, DVMRP also computes a list of dependent downstream routers for pruning purposes. When a router has received a prune message from all of its dependent downstream routers for a given group, it will propagate a prune message upstream to the router from which it receives its multicast traffic for that group. A DVMRP prune message contains a prune lifetime (with a default value of two hours) that indicates how long a pruned branch will remain pruned before being automatically restored. DVMRP graft messages are sent by a router to its upstream neighbor to force a previously-pruned branch to be added back on to the multicast tree.

Before examining other multicast routing algorithms, let us consider how multicast routing can be deployed in the Internet. The crux of the problem is that only a small fraction of the Internet routers are multicast capable. If one router is multicast capable but all of its immediate neighbors are not, is this lone island of multicast routing lost in a sea of unicast routers? Most decidedly not! Tunneling, a technique we examined earlier in the context of IP version 6 (Section 4.7), can be used to create a virtual network of multicast capable routers on top of a physical network that contains a mix of unicast and multicast routers. This is the approach taken in the Internet MBone.

Multicast tunnels are illustrated in Figure 4.54. Suppose that multicast router A wants to forward a multicast datagram to multicast router B. Suppose that A

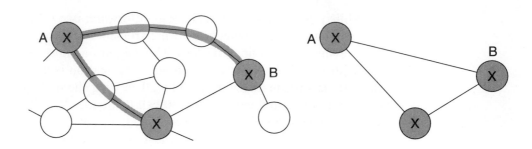

FIGURE 4.54 Multicast tunnels

and B are not physical connected to each other and that the intervening routers between A and B are not multicast capable. To implement tunneling, router A takes the multicast datagram and "encapsulates" it [RFC 2003] inside a standard unicast datagram. That is, the entire multicast datagram (including source and multicast address fields) is carried as the payload of an IP unicast datagram—a complete multicast IP datagram inside of a unicast IP datagram! The unicast datagram is then addressed to the unicast address of router B and forwarded towards B by router A. The unicast routers between A and B dutifully forward the unicast packet to B, blissfully unaware that the unicast datagram itself contains a multicast datagram. When the unicast datagram arrives at B, B then extracts the multicast datagram. B may then forward the multicast datagram on to one of its attached hosts, forward the packet to a directly attached neighboring router that is multicast capable, or forward the multicast datagram to another logical multicast neighbor via another tunnel.

MOSPF: Multicast Open Shortest Path First.   The Multicast Open Shortest Path First protocol (MOSPF) [RFC 1584] operates in an autonomous system (AS) that uses the OSPF protocol (see Section 4.5) for unicast routing. MOSPF extends OSPF by having routers add their multicast group membership to the link state advertisements that are broadcast by routers as part of the OSPF protocol. With this extension, all routers have not only complete topology information, but also know which edge routers have attached hosts belonging to various multicast groups. With this information, the routers within the AS can build source-specific, pre-pruned, shortest path trees for each multicast group.

CBT: Core-Based Trees.   The core-based tree (CBT) multicast routing protocol [RFC 2201, RFC 2189] builds a bi-directional, group-shared tree with a single "core" (center). A CBT edge router unicasts a JOIN_REQUEST message towards the tree core. The core, or the first router that receives this JOIN_REQUEST and itself has already successfully joined the tree, will respond with a JOIN_ACK message to the edge router. Once a multicast routing tree has been built, it is maintained by having a downstream router send keepalive messages (ECHO_REQUEST) to its immediate upstream router. The immediate upstream router responds with an ECHO_REPLY message. These messages are exchanged at a time granularity of minutes. If a downstream router receives no reply to its ECHO_REQUEST, it will retry sending the ECHO_REQUEST for a small number of times. If no ECHO_REPLY is received, the router will dissolve the downstream tree by sending a FLUSH_TREE message downstream.

PIM: Protocol Independent Multicast. The Protocol Independent Multicast (PIM) routing protocol [Deering 1996, RFC 2362, Estrin 1998b] explicitly envisions two different multicast distribution scenarios. In so-called **dense mode,** multicast group members are densely located, that is, many or most of the routers in the area need to be involved in routing multicast datagrams. In **sparse mode,** the number of routers with attached group members is small with respect to the total number of routers; group members are widely dispersed.

The PIM designers noted several consequences of the sparse-dense dichotomy. In dense mode, since most routers will be involved in multicast (for example, have attached group members), it is reasonable to assume that each and every router should be involved in multicast. Thus, an approach like RPF that floods datagrams to every multicast router (unless a router explicitly prunes itself), is well-suited to this scenario. On the other hand, in sparse mode, the routers that need to be involved in multicast forwarding are few and far between. In this case, a data-driven multicast technique like RPF, which *forces* a router to constantly do work (prune) simply to avoid receiving multicast traffic is much less satisfactory. In sparse mode, the default assumption should be that a router is not involved in a multicast distribution; the router should *not* have to do any work unless it wants to join a multicast group. This argues for a center-based approach, where routers send explicit join messages, but are otherwise uninvolved in multicast forwarding. One can think of the sparse mode approach as being receiver-driven (that is, nothing happens until a receiver explicitly joins a group) versus the dense mode approach as being data-driven (that is, that datagrams are multicast everywhere, unless explicitly pruned).

PIM accommodates this dense versus sparse dichotomy by offering two explicit modes of operation: dense mode and sparse mode. PIM Dense Mode is a flood-and-prune reverse path forwarding technique similar in spirit to DVMRP. Recall that PIM is "protocol independent," that is, independent of the underlying unicast routing protocol. A better description might be that it can interoperate with any underlying unicast routing protocol. Because PIM makes no assumptions about the underlying routing protocol, its reverse path forwarding algorithm is slightly simpler, although slightly less efficient than DVMRP.

PIM Sparse Mode is a center-based approach. PIM routers send JOIN messages towards a rendezvous point (center) to join the tree. As with CBT, intermediate routers set up multicast state and forward the JOIN message towards the rendezvous point. Unlike CBT, there is no acknowledgment generated in response to a JOIN message. JOIN message are periodically sent upstream to refresh/maintain the PIM routing tree. One novel feature of PIM is the ability to switch from a group-shared tree to a source-specific tree after joining the rendezvous point. A source-specific tree may be preferred due to the decreased traffic concentration that occurs when multiple source-specific trees are used (see homework problems).

In PIM Sparse Mode, the router that receives a datagram to send from one of its attached hosts will unicast the datagram to the rendezvous point. The rendezvous point then multicasts the datagram via the group-shared tree. A sender is notified by the RP that it must stop sending to the RP whenever there are no routers joined to the tree (that is, no one is listening!).

PIM is implemented in numerous router platforms [IP Multicast Initiative 1998] and has been deployed in UUnet as part of their streaming multimedia delivery effort [LaPolla 1997].

Inter-Autonomous System Multicast Routing.   In our discussion above, we have implicitly assumed that all routers are running the same multicast routing protocol. As we saw with unicasting, this will typically be the case within a single autonomous system (AS). However, different AS's may choose to run different multicast routing protocols. One AS might choose to run PIM within its autonomous system, while another may choose to run MOSPF. Interoperability rules have been defined for all of the major Internet multicast routing protocols. (This is a particularly messy issue due to the very different approaches taken to multicast routing by sparse and dense mode protocols.) What is still missing, however, is an *inter-AS* multicast routing protocol to route multicast datagrams among different AS's.

Today, DVMRP is the *defacto* inter-AS multicast routing protocol. However, as a dense mode protocol, it is not particularly well-suited to the rather sparse set of routers participating in today's Internet MBone. The development of an inter-AS multicast protocol is an active area of research and development being carried out by the *idmr* working group of the IETF [IDRM 1998]. BGMP, the Border Gateway Multicast Protocol, is an interdomain multicast protocol being developed in *idmr*. It takes a group-shared tree approach towards routing. An interesting problem that arises in the interdomain case is the location of the tree's center. In the intra-AS case, all routers are within the same AS. In the inter-AS case, however, a center could conceivably be chosen in an autonomous system that does not even contain any hosts in the multicast group; such *third party dependency* would not only "unfairly" burden the autonomous system (which, after all, has no interest in the multicast group), but also may unnecessarily subject the multicast group to performance dependencies on ASs outside of those participating in the group. BGMP is described in [Kumar 1998].

Having now considered the multicast routing problem and a number of multicast protocols embodying the group-shared tree and source-based tree approaches, let us conclude by enumerating some of the factors involved in evaluating a multicast protocol:

- *Scalability.* What is the amount of state required in the routers by a multicast routing protocol? How does the amount of state change as the number of groups, or number of senders in a group, change?
- *Reliance on underlying unicast routing.* To what extent does a multicast protocol rely on information maintained by an underlying unicast routing protocol? We have seen solutions that range from reliance on one specific underlying unicast routing protocol (MOSPF), to a solution that is completely independent of the underlying unicast routing (PIM) to a solution that implements much of the same distance vector functionality that we saw earlier for the unicast case (DVMRP).
- *Excess (un-needed) traffic received.* We have seen solutions where a router receives data only if it has an attached host in the multicast group (MOSPF, PIM-Sparse Mode) to solutions where the default is for a router to receive all traffic for all multicast groups (DVMRP, PIM Dense Mode).

- *Traffic concentration.* The group-shared tree approach tends to concentrate traffic on a smaller number of links (those in the single tree), whereas source-specific trees tend to distribute multicast traffic more evenly.
- *Optimality of forwarding paths.* We have seen that determining the minimum cost multicast tree (that is, solving the Steiner problem) is difficult and that this approach has not been adopted in practice. Instead, heuristic approaches, based on either using the tree of shortest paths, or selecting a center router from which to "grow" the routing multicast tree, have been adopted in practice.

SUMMARY

In this chapter, we began our journey into the network core. We learned that the network layer requires the coordination of each and every host and router in the network. Because of this, network layer protocols are among the most challenging in the protocol stack.

We learned that one of the biggest challenges in the network layer is routing datagrams through a network of millions of hosts and routers. We saw that this scaling problem is solved by partitioning large networks into independent administrative domains, which are called autonomous systems (ASs) in the jargon of computer networking. Each AS independently routes its datagrams through the AS, just as each country independently routes its postal mail through the country. In the Internet, the two most popular protocols for intra-AS routing are currently RIP and OSPF. To route packets among ASs, an inter-AS routing protocol is needed. The dominant inter-AS protocol today is BGP4.

Performing routing on two levels—one level for within each of the ASs and another level for among the ASs—is referred to as hierarchical routing. We saw that the scaling problem of routing packets through millions of hosts and routers is largely solved by a hierarchical organization of the network. This is a general principle we should keep in mind when designing protocols, particularly for network-layer protocols: scaling problems can often be solved by hierarchical organization. It is interesting to note that this principle has been applied throughout the ages to many other disciplines besides computer networking, including corporate, government, religious, and military organizations.

In this chapter, we also learned about a second scaling issue: For large computer networks, a router may need to process millions of flows of packets between different source-destination pairs at the same time. To permit a router to process such a large number of flows, network designers have learned over the years that the router's tasks should be as simple as possible. Many measures can be taken to make the router's job easier, including using a datagram network layer rather than a virtual-circuit network layer, using a streamlined and fixed-sized header (as in IPv6), eliminating fragmentation (also done in IPv6) and providing the one and only best-effort service. Perhaps the most important trick here is to *not* keep track of individual flows, but instead base routing decisions solely on hierarchical-structured destination addresses in the packets. It is interesting to note that the postal service has been using this same trick for many years.

In this chapter, we also looked at the underlying principles of routing algorithms. We learned that designers of routing algorithms abstract the computer network to a graph with nodes and links. With this abstraction, we can exploit the rich theory of shortest-path routing in graphs, which has been developed over the past 40 years in the operations research and algorithms communities. We saw that there are two broad approaches, a centralized approach in which each node obtains a complete map of the network and applies independently a shortest-path routing algorithm; and a decentralized approach, in which individual nodes only have a partial picture of the entire network, yet the nodes work together to deliver packets along the shortest routes. Routing algorithms in computer networks had been an active research area for many years, and will undoubtedly remain so.

At the end of this chapter, we examined two advanced subjects, reflecting current trends in computer networking and the Internet. The first subject is IPv6, which provides a streamlined network layer and resolves the IPv4 address space problem. The second subject is multicast routing, which can potentially save tremendous amounts of bandwidth, router, and server resources in a computer network. It will be interesting to see how the deployment of IPv6 and multicast routing protocols play out over the next decade of computer networking.

Having completed our study of the network layer, our journey now takes us one further step down the protocol stack, namely, to the link layer. Like the network layer, the link layer is also part of the network core. But we will see in the next chapter that the link layer has the much more localized task of moving packets between nodes on the same link or LAN. Although this task may appear on the surface trivial compared to that of the network layer's tasks, we will see that the link layer involves a number of important and fascinating issues that can keep us busy for a long time.

HOMEWORK PROBLEMS AND QUESTIONS

Chapter 4

Review Questions

Sections 4.1-4.4

1. What are the two main functions of a datagram-based network layer? What additional functions does a VC-based network layer have?
2. List and describe the ATM network service models.
3. Compare and contrast link-state and distance-vector routing algorithms.
4. Discuss how a hierarchical organization of the Internet has helped to scale to millions of users.
5. Is it necessary that every autonomous system use the same intra-autonomous system routing algorithm? Why or why not?

Section 4.5

6. What is the 32-bit binary equivalent of the IP address 223.1.3.27 ?
7. Consider a LAN to which ten host interfaces and three router interfaces are attached. Suppose all three LANs use class C addresses. The IP addresses for the 13 devices will be identical in which of the first 32 bits?

8. Consider a router with three interfaces. Suppose all three interfaces use class C addresses. Will the IP addresses of the three interfacess necessarily have the same first 8 bits?

9. Suppose there are three routers between source and destination hosts. Ignoring fragmentation, an IP segment sent from source host to destination host will travel over how many interfaces? How many routing tables will be indexed to move the datagram from source to destination?

10. Suppose an application generates chunks of 40 bytes of data every 20 msec, and each chunk gets encapsulated in a TCP segment and then an IP datagram. What percentage of each datagram will be overhead and what percentage will be application data?

11. Consider sending a 3000 byte datagram into a link that has an MTU of 500 bytes. Suppose the original datagram is stamped with the identification number 422. How many fragments are generated? What are their characteristics?

12. Consider Figure 4.25. Starting with the original table in D, suppose that D receives from A the following advertisement:

Destination network	Next router	Number of hops to destination
30	C	10
1	--	1
10	--	1
....	....	....

Will the table in A change? If so how?

13. Contrast and compare the advertisements used by RIP and OSPF.

14. RIP advertisements typically announce the number of hops to various destinations. BGP updates, on the otherhand, announce the _____ (fill in the blank) to the various destinations.

15. Why are different inter-AS and intra-AS protocols used in the Internet?

Section 4.6

16. Describe three different types of switching fabrics commonly used in packet switches.

17. Why are buffers needed at the output ports of switches? Why are buffers needed at the input port of switches?

Section 4.7

18. Compare and contrast the IPv4 and the IPv6 header fields. Do they have any fields in common?

19. It has been said that IPv6 tunnels through IPv4 routers, IPV6 treats the IPv4 tunnels as link layer protocols. Do you agree with this statement? Why or why not?

Section 4.8

20. What is an important difference between implementing the multicast abstract via multiple unicasts, and a single network (router) supported multicast group?

21. True or False: when a host joins a multicst group, it must change its IP address to be that of the multicast group it is joining.

22. What are the roles played by the IGMP protocol and a wide-area multicast routing protocol?

23. What is the difference between a group-shared tree and a source-based tree in the context of multicast routing?

24. True or False: In reverse path forwarding, a node will receive multiple copies of the same packet. True or False: In reverse path forwarding, a node may forward multiple copies of a packet over the same outgoing link.

25. Classify each of the following multicast routing algorithms as either a source-based tree approach or a group-shared tree approach: DVMRP, MOSPF, CBT, PIM Sparse Mode, PIM Dense Mode.

PROBLEMS

1. Let us consider some of the pros and cons of a connection-oriented versus connectionless architecture.

   a. Suppose that in the network layer, routers were subjected to "stressful" conditions that might cause them to fail fairly often. At a high level, what actions would need to be taken on such router failure. Does this argue for a connection-oriented or a connectionless environment?

   b. Suppose that in order to provide a *guarantee* regarding the level of performance (e.g., delay) that would be seen along a source-to-destination path, the network requires a sender to declare its peak traffic rate. If the declared peak traffic rate and the existing declared traffic rates that have been declared are such that there is no way to get traffic from the source to the destination that meets the required delay requirements, the source is not allowed access to the network. Would such an approach be more easily accomplished within a connection-oriented or connectionless paradigm?

2. In Figure 4.4, enumerate the paths from A to F that do not contain any loops.

3. Consider the network shown on the following page. With the indicated link costs, use Dijkstra's shortest path algorithm to compute the shortest past from F to all network nodes. Show how the algorithm works by computing a table similar to Table 4.2.

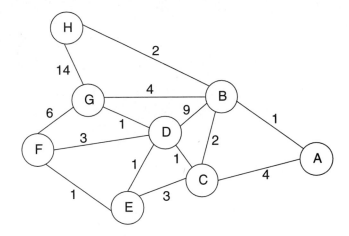

4. Consider the network shown below and assume that each node initially knows the costs to each of its neighbors. Consider the distance vector algorithm and show the distance table entries at node E.

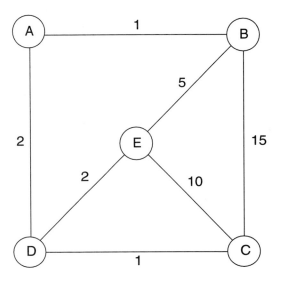

5. Consider a general topology (i.e., not the specific network shown above) and a synchronous version of the distance vector algorithm. Suppose that at each iteration, a node exchanges its minimum costs with its neighbors and receives their minimum costs. Assuming that the algorithm begins with each node knowing only the costs to its immediate neighbors, what is the maximum number of iterations required until the distributed algorithm converges? Justify your answer.

6. Consider the network fragment shown on the next page. X has only two attached neighbors, W and Y. W has a minimum cost path to destination A of 5 and Y has a minimum cost path to A of 6. The complete paths from W and Y to A (and between W and Y) are not shown. All link costs in the network have strictly positive integer values.

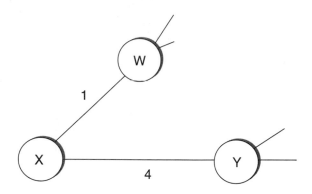

   a. Give X's distance table (row) entries for destinations X, Y, and A.

   b. Give a link cost change for either c(X,W) or c(X,Y) such that X will inform its neighbors of a new minimum cost path to A as a result of executing lines 15 and 24 of the distance vector algorithm.

   c. Give a link cost change for either c(X,W) or c(X,Y) such that X will *not* inform its neighbors of a new minimum cost path to A as a result of executing lines 15 and 24 of the distance vector algorithm.

7. Compute the distance tables for X, Y, and Z shown in the rightmost column of Figure 4.7. After the computation of the new distance tables, which nodes will send which updated values to which neighbors?

8. Consider the three node topology shown in Figure 4.7. Rather than having the link costs shown in Figure 4.7, the link costs are c(X,Y)=5, c(Y,Z)=6, c(Z,X)=2. Compute the distance tables after the initialization step and after each iteration of a synchronous version of the distance vector algorithm (as we did in our earlier discussion of Figure 4.7.)

9. Consider the 8-node network (with nodes labeled A-H) above. Show the minimal cost spanning tree rooted at A that includes (as end hosts) nodes C, D, E, and G. Informally argue why your spanning tree is a minimal cost spanning tree.

10. We saw in Section 4.8 that there is no network layer protocol that can be used to identify the hosts participating in a multicast group. Given this, how can multicast applications learn the identities of the hosts that are participating in a multicast group?

11. Consider the two basic approaches identified toward achieving multicast: unicast emulation and network-layer-multicast. Consider a single sender and 32 receivers. Suppose the sender is connected to the receiver through a binary tree of routers. What is the cost of sending a multicast packet, in the case of unicast emulation and network-layer multicast, for this topology? Here, each time a packet (or copy of a packet) is sent over a single link, it incurs a unit of "cost". What topology for interconnecting the sender, receivers, and routers will bring the cost of unicast emulation and true network-layer-multicast as far apart as possible.? You can choose as many routers as you'd like.

12. Design (give a pseudocode description of) an application-level protocol that maintains the host addresses of all hosts participating in a multicast group. Specifically identify the network service (unicast or multicast) that is used by

your protocol, and indicate whether your protocol is sending messages in-band or out-of-band (with respect to the application-data flow among the multicast group participants), and why.

13. Consider the topology from Figure 4.49. Suppose the link cost from B to D changes from 1 to 10. Find the Steiner tree that connects all of the shaded routers. (Note: you are not being asked here to program a solution to the Steiner tree problem. Instead, you should be able to construct the minimum cost tree by inspection and informally convince yourself that it is the minimum cost tree). If you were asked (you are *not* being asked to actually do so!), how would you prove that your tree is indeed a minimum cost tree?

14. Center-based routing. Consider the topology shown in Figure 4.49. Suppose node C is chosen as the center in a center-based multicast routing algorithm. Assuming that each attached router in the multicast group uses its least cost path to node C to send join messages to C, draw the resulting center-based multicast routing tree. Is the resulting tree a minimum cost Steiner tree? Justify your answer.

15. Least unicast-cost path routing. Consider Figure 4.49. Suppose that node E is chosen as the source. Compute the least unicast-cost path multicast routing tree from E to multicast routers A, B, and F.

16. Reverse path forwarding. Consider the topology and link costs shown in Figure 4.49 and suppose that node E is the multicast source. Using arrows like those shown in Figure 4.52, indicate links over which packets will be forwarded using RPF, and links over which packets will not be forwarded, given that node E is the source.

17. Suppose that the cost of transmitting a multicast packet on a link is completely independent of the cost of transmitting a unicast packet on a link. Will reverse path forwarding still work in this case? Justify your answer.

18. Traffic concentration in center-based trees. Consider the simple topology shown in Figure 4.49. Suppose that each of the multicast routers receive one unit of traffic per unit of time from an attached host. This traffic must be forwarded to the other three multicast routers. Suppose that node C is chosen as the center node in a center-based, multicast routing protocol (see homework problem above). Given the resulting routing tree, compute the rate of traffic on each link in the topology. (Compute the total amount of traffic on each link, regardless of the direction of the traffic flow). Suppose next that RPF is used to build four source-specific routing trees rooted at each of the routers A, B, E, F. Recompute the rate of traffic on each of the links in this second scenario. In this example, does a center-based tree or source-specific trees tend to concentrate traffic?

19. Suppose that a network has G multicast groups, each with S group members (hosts), each of which can be a sender. Under DVMRP, each router must thus maintain up to S pieces of routing information (the outgoing link on the shortest reverse path to the sender, for each of the S senders) for each group. Thus, in the worst case, each router must maintain S*G pieces of routing information, when taking all groups into account. What is the worst case amount of routing information needed by MOSPF, PIM Sparse Mode, and PIM Dense Mode? Justify your answers.

20. Birthday problem. What is the size of the multicast address space? Suppose now that two different multicast groups randomly choose a multicast address. What is the probability that they choose the same address? Suppose now that 1000 multicast groups are ongoing at the same time and chose their multicast group addresses at random. What is the probability that they interfere with each other?

21. Recall that in our discussion of multicast tunneling, we said that an IP multicast datagram is carried inside of an IP unicast datagram. How does the IP router at the end of the multicast tunnel know that the unicast datagram contains an IP multicast datagram (as opposed to simply being an IP unicast datagram that should be forwarded along)?

DISCUSSION QUESTIONS

1. Suppose AS X and Z are not directly connected but instead connected by AS Y. Further suppose that X has a peering agreement with Y, and that Y has a peering agreement with Z. Finally, suppose that Z wants to transit all of Y's traffic but does not want to transit X's traffic. Does BGP allow Z to implement this policy?

2. In Section 4.7, we indicated that deployment of IPv6 has been slow to date. Why has it been slow? What is needed to accelerate its deployment? (See article by L. Garber.)

3. In Section 4.8.1 we saw that the multicast abstraction can be implemented by having a sender open an individual connection to each of the receivers. What are the drawbacks of this approach compared to the approach that provides native multicast support at the network layer? What are the advantages of this approach?

4. In Section 4.8 we identified a number of multicast applications. Which of these applications are well-suited for the minimalist Internet multicast service model? Why? Which applications are not particularly well-suited for this service model?

5. Given the CBT soft state mechanism for maintaining a tree, why do you think there is a separate FLUSH_TREE message? What would happen if the FLUSH_TREE message were lost?

PROGRAMMING ASSIGNMENT

In this third programming assignment, you will be writing a "distributed" set of procedures that implement a distributed asynchronous distance vector routing for the network shown on the next page:

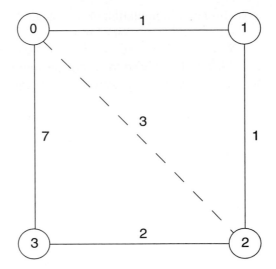

You are to write the following routines that will "execute" asynchronously within the emulated environment provided for this assignment. For node 0, you will write the routines:

- *rtinit0()* This routine will be called once at the beginning of the emulation. *rtinit0()* has no arguments. It should initialize your distance table in node 0 to reflect the direct costs of 1, 3, and 7 to nodes 1, 2, and 3, respectively. In the figure above, all links are bi-directional and the costs in both directions are identical. After initializing the distance table, and any other data structures needed by your node 0 routines, it should then send its directly-connected neighbors (in this case, 1, 2, and 3) the cost of its minimum cost paths to all other network nodes. This minimum cost information is sent to neighboring nodes in a routing update packet by calling the routine *tolayer2()*, as described in the full assignment. The format of the routing update packet is also described in the full assignment

- *rtupdate0(struct rtpkt *rcvdpkt)*. This routine will be called when node 0 receives a routing packet that was sent to it by one if its directly connected neighbors. The parameter *rcvdpkt* is a pointer to the packet that was received. *rtupdate0()* is the "heart" of the distance vector algorithm. The values it receives in a routing update packet from some other node *i* contain *i*'s current shortest path costs to all other network nodes. *rtupdate0()* uses these received values to update its own distance table (as specified by the distance vector algorithm). If its own minimum cost to another node changes as a result of the update, node 0 informs its directly connected neighbors of this change in minimum cost by sending them a routing packet. Recall that in the distance vector algorithm, only directly connected nodes will exchange routing packets. Thus, nodes 1 and 2 will communicate with each other, but nodes 1 and 3 will not communicate with each other.

Similar routines are defined for nodes 1, 2, and 3. Thus, you will write 8 procedures in all: *rtinit0(), rtinit1(), rtinit2(), rtinit3(), rtupdate0(), rtupdate1(), rtupdate2(), rtupdate3().*These routines will together implement a distributed, asynchronous computation of the distance tables for the topology and costs shown in the figure on the previous page.

You can find the full details of the programming assignment, as well as C code that you will need to create the simulated hardware/software environment at http://gaia.cs.umass.edu/kurose/network/programming_assignment.htm.

Chapter 5 | Link Layer and Local Area Networks

THE DATA LINK LAYER: INTRODUCTION, SERVICES

In the previous chapter we learned that the network layer provides a communication service between two hosts. As shown in Figure 5.1, this communication path starts at the source host, passes through a series of routers, and ends at the destination host. We'll find it convenient here to refer to the hosts and the routers simply

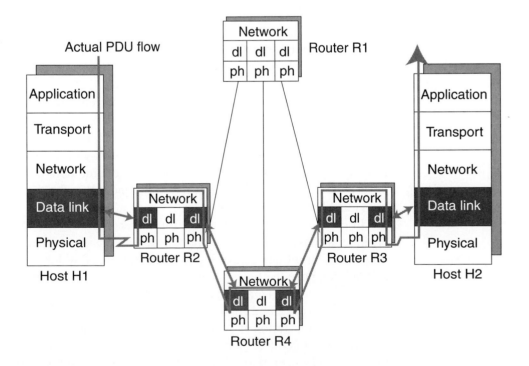

FIGURE 5.1   The data link layer

as **nodes** (since, as we'll see shortly, we will not be particularly concerned whether a node is a router or a host), and to the communication channels that connect adjacent nodes along the communication path as **links.** In order to move a datagram from source host to destination host, the datagram must be moved over each of the *individual links* in the path. In this chapter, we focus on the **data link layer,** which is responsible for transferring a datagram across an individual link. We'll first identify and study the services provided by the link layer. In Sections 5.2 through 5.4, we'll then examine important principles behind the protocols that provide these services (including the topics of error detection and correction, so-called multiple access protocols that are used share a single physical link among multiple nodes, and link-level addressing). We'll see that many different types of link-level technology can be used to connect two nodes. In Sections 5.5 through 5.10, we'll examine specific link-level architectures and protocols in more detail.

5.1.1   The Services Provided by the Link Layer

A link-layer protocol is used to move a datagram over an individual link. The **link-layer protocol** defines the format of the packets exchanged between the nodes at the ends of the link, as well as the actions taken by these nodes when sending and receiving packets. Recall from Chapter 1 that the packets exchanged by a link-layer protocol are called **frames,** and that each link-layer frame typically encapsulates one network-layer datagram. As we shall see shortly, the actions taken by a link-layer protocol when sending and receiving frames include error detection, retransmission, flow control, and random access. Examples of link-layer protocols include Ethernet, token ring, FDDI, and PPP; in some contexts, ATM and frame relay can be considered link-layer protocols as well. We will cover these protocols in detail in the latter half of this chapter.

Whereas the network layer has the end-to-end job of moving transport-layer segments from the source host to the destination host, a link-layer protocol has the node-to-node job of moving a network-layer datagram over a *single link* in the path. An important characteristic of the link layer is that a datagram may be handled by different link-layer protocols on the different links in the path. For example, a datagram may be handled by Ethernet on the first link, PPP on the last link, and frame relay on all intermediate links. It is important to note that the services provided by the different link-layer protocols may be different. For example, a link-layer protocol may or may not provide reliable delivery. Thus, the network layer must be able to accomplish its end-to-end job in the face of a varying set of individual link-layer services.

In order to gain insight to the link layer and how it relates to the network layer, let's consider a transportation analogy. Consider a travel agent who is planning a trip for a tourist traveling from Princeton, New Jersey to Lausanne, Switzerland. Suppose the travel agent decides that it is most convenient for the tourist to take a limousine from Princeton to JFK airport, then a plane from JFK airport to Geneva airport, and finally a train from Geneva to Lausanne's train station. (There is a train station at Geneva's airport.) Once the travel agent makes the three reservations, it is the responsibility of the Princeton limousine company to get the tourist from Princeton to JFK; it is the responsibility of the airline company to get the tourist from JFK to Geneva; and it is responsibility of the Swiss train service to get the tourist from Geneva to Lausanne. Each of the three segments of the trip is "direct" between two "adjacent" locations. Note that the three transportation segments are managed by different companies and use entirely different transportation modes (limousine, plane, and train). Although the transportation modes are different, they each provide the basic service of moving passengers from one location to an adjacent location. This *service* is used by the travel agent to plan the tourist's trip. In this transportation analogy, the tourist is analogous to a datagram, each transportation segment is analogous to a communication link, the transportation mode is analogous to the link-layer protocol, and the travel agent who plans the trip is analogous to a routing protocol.

The basic service of the link layer is to "move" a datagram from one node to an adjacent node over a single communication link. But the details of the link-layer service depend on the specific link-layer protocol that is employed over the link. Possible services that can be offered by a link-layer protocol include:

- *Framing and link access.* Almost all link-layer protocols encapsulate each network-layer datagram within a link-layer frame before transmission onto the link. A frame consists of a data field, in which the network-layer datagram is inserted, and a number of header fields. (A frame may also include trailer fields; however, we will refer to both header and trailer fields as header fields.) A data link protocol specifies the structure of the frame, as well as a channel access protocol that specifies the rules by which a frame is transmitted onto the link. For point-to-point links that have a single sender on one end of the link and a single receiver at the other end of the link, the link access protocol is simple (or non-existent)—the sender can send a frame whenever the link is idle. The more interesting case is when multiple nodes share a single broadcast link—the so-called multiple access problem. Here, the channel access protocol serves to coordinate the frame transmissions of the many nodes; we cover multiple access protocols in detail in Section 5.3. We'll see several different frame formats when we examine specific link-layer protocols in the second half of this chapter. In Section 5.3, we'll see that frame headers also often include fields for a node's so-called **physical address,** which is completely *distinct* from the node's network layer (for example, IP) address.

- *Reliable delivery.* If a link-layer protocol provides the reliable-delivery service, then it guarantees to move each network-layer datagram across the link without error. Recall that transport-layer protocols (such as TCP) may also provide a reliable-delivery service. Similar to a transport-layer reliable-delivery service, a link-layer reliable-delivery service is achieved with acknowledgments and retransmissions (see Section 3.4). A link-layer reliable-delivery service is often used for links that are prone to high error rates, such as a wireless link, with the goal of correcting an error locally, on the link at which the error occurs, rather than forcing an end-to-end retransmission of the data by transport- or application-layer protocol. However, link-layer reliable delivery is often considered to be unnecessary overhead for low bit-error links, including fiber, coax, and many twisted-pair copper links. For this reason, many of the most popular link-layer protocols do not provide a reliable-delivery service.

- *Flow control.* The nodes on each side of a link have a limited amount of packet buffering capacity. This is a potential problem, as a receiving node may receive frames at a rate faster than it can process the frames (over some time interval). Without flow control, the receiver's buffer can overflow and frames can get lost. Similar to the transport layer, a link-layer protocol can provide flow control in order to prevent the sending node on one side of a link from overwhelming the receiving node on the other side of the link.

■ *Error detection.* A node's receiver can incorrectly decide that a bit in a frame is zero when it was transmitted as a one (and *vice versa*). These errors are introduced by signal attenuation and electromagnetic noise. Because there is no need to forward a datagram that has an error, many link-layer protocols provide a mechanism for a node to detect the presence of one or more errors. This is done by having the transmitting node set error detection bits in the frame, and having the receiving node perform an error check. Error detection is a very common service among link-layer protocols. Recall from Chapters 3 and 4 that the transport layer and network layers in the Internet also provide a limited form of error detection. Error detection in the link layer is usually more sophisticated and implemented in hardware.

■ *Error correction.* Error correction is similar to error detection, except that a receiver can not only detect whether errors have been introduced in the frame but can also determine exactly where in the frame the errors have occurred (and hence correct these errors). Some protocols (such as ATM) provide link-layer error correction for the packet header rather than for the entire packet. We cover error detection and correction in Section 5.2.

■ *Half-Duplex and Full-Duplex.* With full-duplex transmission, both nodes at the ends of a link may transmit packets at the same time. With half-duplex transmission, a node cannot both transmit and receive at the same time.

As noted above, many of the services provided by the link layer have strong parallels with services provided at the transport layer. For example, both the link layer and the transport layer can provide reliable delivery. Although the mechanisms used to provide reliable delivery in the two layers are similar (see Section 3.4), the two reliable delivery services are not the same. A transport protocol provides reliable delivery between two processes on an end-to-end basis; a reliable link-layer protocol provides the reliable-delivery service between two nodes connected by a single link. Similarly, both link-layer and transport-layer protocols can provide flow control and error detection; again, flow control in a transport-layer protocol is provided on an end-to-end basis, whereas it is provided in a link-layer protocol on a node-to-adjacent-node basis.

5.1.2 Adapters Communicating

For a given communication link, the link-layer protocol is, for the most part, implemented in **adapters.** An adapter is a board (or a PCMCIA card) that typically contains RAM, DSP chips, a host bus interface, and a link interface. Adapters are also commonly known as *network interface cards* or *NICs*. As shown in Figure 5.2, the network layer in the transmitting node (that is, a host or router) passes a network-layer datagram to the adapter that handles the sending side of the communication link. The adapter encapsulates the datagram in a frame and then transmits the frame into the communication link. At the other side, the receiving adapter receives the entire frame, extracts the network-layer datagram,

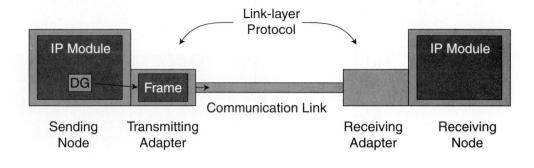

Legend:
DG = datagram

FIGURE 5.2   The link-layer protocol for a communication link is implemented in the adapters at the two ends of the link

and passes it to the network layer. If the link-layer protocol provides error detection, then it is the sending adapter that sets the error detection bits and it is the receiving adapter that performs the error checking. If the link-layer protocol provides reliable delivery, then the mechanisms for reliable delivery (for example, sequence numbers, timers, and acknowledgments) are entirely implemented in the adapters. If the link-layer protocol provides random access (see Section 5.3), then the random access protocol is entirely implemented in the adapters.

A computer in itself, an adapter is a semi-autonomous unit. For example, an adapter can receive a frame, determine if a frame is in error and discard the frame without notifying its "parent" node. An adapter that receives a frame only interrupts its parent node when it wants to pass a network-layer datagram up the protocol stack. Similarly, when a node passes a datagram down the protocol stack to an adapter, the node fully delegates to the adapter the task of transmitting the datagram across that link. On the other hand, an adapter is not an completely autonomous unit. Although we have shown the adapter as a separate "box" in Figure 5.3, the adapter is typically housed in the same physical box as the rest of the node, shares power and busses with the rest of the node, and is ultimately under the control of the node.

As shown in Figure 5.3, the main components of an adapter are the bus interface and the link interface. The bus interface is responsible for communicating with the adapter's parent node. It sends to and receives from the parent node network-layer datagrams and control information. The link interface is responsible for implementing the link-layer protocol. In addition to framing and de-framing datagrams, it may provide error detection, random access, and other link-layer functions. It also includes the transmit and receive circuitry. For popular link-layer technologies, such as Ethernet, the link interface is implemented by chip set that can be bought on the commodity market. For this reason, Ethernet adapters are incredibly cheap—often less than $30 for 10 Mbps and 100 Mbps transmission rates.

Adapter design has become very sophisticated over the years. One of the critical issues in adapter performance has always been whether the adapter can move

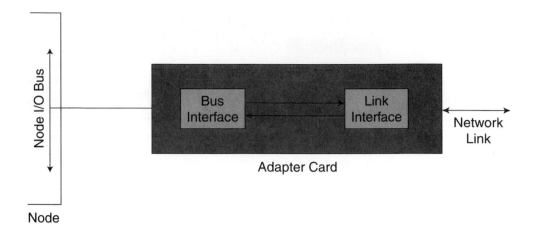

FIGURE 5.3 The adapter is a semi-autonomous unit

data in and out of a node at the full line speed, that is, at the transmission rate of the link. You can learn more about adapter architecture for 10Mbps Ethernet, 100 Mbps Ethernet, and 155 Mbps ATM by visiting the 3Com adapter page [3Com 1999]. *Data Communications* magazine provides a nice introduction to Gbps Ethernet adapters [GigaAdapter].

5.2 ERROR DETECTION AND CORRECTION TECHNIQUES

In the previous section, we noted that bit-level error detection and correction—detecting and correcting the corruption of bits in a data-link-layer frame sent from one node to another physically-connected neighboring node—are two services often provided by the data link layer. We saw in Chapter 3 that error detection and correction services are also often offered at the transport layer as well. In this section, we'll examine a few of the simplest techniques that can be used to detect and, in some cases, correct such bit errors. A full treatment of the theory and implementation of this topic is itself the topic of many textbooks (for example, [Schwartz 1980]), and our treatment here is necessarily brief. Our goal here is to develop an intuitive feel for the capabilities that error detection and correction techniques provide, and to see how a few simple techniques work and are used in practice in the data link layer.

Figure 5.4 illustrates the setting for our study. At the sending node, data, D, to be "protected" against bit errors is augmented with error detection and correction bits, EDC. Typically, the data to be protected includes not only the datagram passed down from the network layer for transmission across the link, but also link-level addressing information, sequence numbers, and other fields in the data link frame header. Both D and EDC are sent to the receiving node in a link-level frame. At the receiving node, a sequence of bits, D' and EDC' are received. Note that D' and EDC' may differ from the original D and EDC as a result of in-transit bit flips.

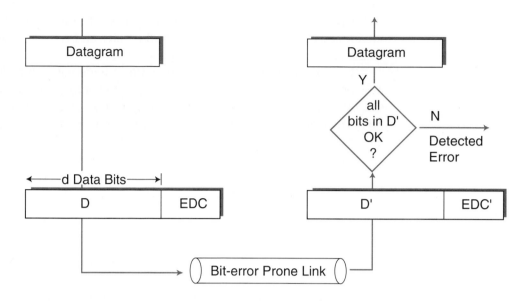

FIGURE 5.4   Error detection and correction scenario

The receiver's challenge is to determine whether or not D' is the same as the original D, given that it has only received D' and EDC'. The exact wording of the receiver's decision in Figure 5.4 (we ask whether an error is detected, not whether an error has occurred!) is important. Error detection and correction techniques allow the receiver to sometimes, *but not always,* detect that bit errors have occurred. That is, even with the use of error detection bits there will still be a possibility that **undetected bit errors** will occur, that is, that the receiver will be unaware that the received information contains bit errors. As a consequence, the receiver might deliver a corrupted datagram to the network layer, or be unaware that the contents of some other field in the frame's header have been corrupted. We thus want to choose an error detection scheme so that the probability of such occurrences is small. Generally, more sophisticated error detection and correction techniques (that is, those that have a smaller probability of allowing undetected bit errors) incur a larger overhead—more computation is need to compute and transmit a larger number of error detection and correction bits.

Let's now examine three techniques for detecting errors in the transmitted data—parity checks (to illustrate the basic ideas behind error detection and correction), checksumming methods (which are more typically employed in the transport layer) and cyclic redundancy checks (which are typically employed in the data link layer).

5.2.1   Parity Checks

Perhaps the simplest form of error detection is the use of a single **parity bit.** Suppose that the information to be sent, D in Figure 5.4, has d bits. In an even parity scheme, the sender simply includes one additional bit and chooses its value such that the total number of 1's in the $d + 1$ bits (the original information plus a parity bit) is even. For odd parity schemes, the parity bit value is chosen such that there are an odd number of 1's. Figure 5.5 illustrates an even parity scheme, with the single parity bit being stored in a separate field.

Receiver operation is also simple with a single parity bit. The receiver need only count the number of 1's in the received $d + 1$ bits. If an odd number of 1-valued bits are found with an even parity scheme, the receiver knows that at least one bit error has occurred. More precisely, it knows that some *odd* number of bit errors have occurred.

But what happens if an even number of bit errors occur? You should convince yourself that this would result in an undetected error. If the probability of bit errors is small and errors can be assumed to occur independently from one bit to the next, the probability of multiple bit errors in a packet would be extremely small. In this case, a single parity bit might suffice. However, measurements have shown that rather than occurring independently, errors are often clustered together in "bursts." Under burst error conditions, the probability of undetected errors in a frame protected by single-bit-parity can approach 50 percent [Spragins 1991]. Clearly, a more robust error detection scheme is needed (and, fortunately, is used in practice!). But before examining error detection schemes that are used in practice, let's consider a simple generalization of one-bit parity that will provide us with insight into error correction techniques.

Figure 5.6 shows a two-dimensional generalization of the single-bit parity scheme. Here, the d bits in D are divided into i rows and j columns. A parity value is computed for each row and for each column. The resulting $i + j + 1$ parity bits are the data link frame's error detection bits.

Suppose now that a single bit error occurs in the original d bits of information. With this **two-dimensional parity** scheme, the parity of both the column and the row containing the flipped bit will be in error. The receiver can thus not only *detect* the fact that a single bit error has occurred, but can use the column and row indices of the column and row with parity errors to actually identify the bit that was corrupted and *correct* that error! Figure 5.6 shows an example in which the 0-valued bit in position (1,1) is corrupted and switched to a 1—an error that is both detectable and correctable at the receiver. Although our discussion has focused on the original d bits of information, a single error in the parity bits themselves is also detectable and correctable. Two dimensional parity can also detect (but not correct!) any combination of two errors in a packet. Other properties of the two-dimensional parity scheme are explored in the problems at the end of the chapter.

The ability of the receiver to both detect and correct errors is known as **forward error correction (FEC)**. These techniques are commonly used in audio storage and playback devices such as audio CD's. In a network setting, FEC tech-

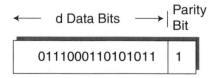

FIGURE 5.5   One-bit even parity

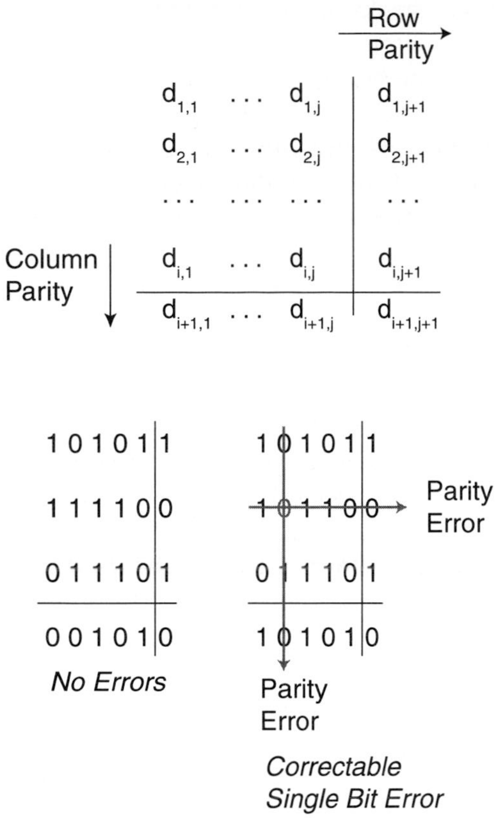

FIGURE 5.6 Two-dimensional even parity

niques can be used by themselves, or in conjunction with the ARQ techniques we examined in Chapter 3. FEC techniques are valuable because they can decrease the number of sender retransmissions required. Perhaps more importantly, they allow for immediate correction of errors at the receiver. This avoids having to wait for the round-trip propagation delay needed for the sender to receive a NAK packet and for the retransmitted packet to propagate back to the receiver—a potentially important advantage for real-time network applications [Rubenstein 1998]. Recent work examining the use of FEC in error control protocols include [Biersack 1992, Nonnenmacher 1998, Byers 1998, Shacham 1990].

5.2.2 Checksumming Methods

In checksumming techniques, the d bits of data in Figure 5.4 are treated as a sequence of k-bit integers. One simple checksumming method is to simply sum these k-bit integers and use the resulting sum as the error detection bits. The so-called **Internet checksum** is based on this approach—bytes of data are treated as 16-bit integers and their ones-complement sum forms the Internet checksum. A receiver calculates the checksum over the received data and checks whether it matches the checksum carried in the received packet. RFC 1071 discusses the Internet checksum algorithm and its implementation in detail. In the TCP/IP protocols, the Internet checksum is computed over all fields (header and data fields included). In other protocols, for example, XTP [Strayer 1992], one checksum is computed over the header, with another checksum computed over the entire packet.

McAuley [McAuley 1994] describes improved weighted checksum codes that are suitable for high-speed software implementation and Feldmeier [Feldmeier 1995] presents fast software implementation techniques for not only weighted checksum codes, but CRC (see below) and other codes as well.

5.2.3 Cyclic Redundancy Check (CRC)

An error detection technique used widely in today's computer networks is based on **cyclic redundancy check (CRC) codes.** CRC codes are also known as **polynomial codes,** since it is possible to view the bit string to be sent as a polynomial whose coefficients are the 0 and 1 values in the bit string, with operations on the bit string interpreted as polynomial arithmetic.

CRC codes operate as follows. Consider the *d-bit* piece of data, D, that the sending node wants to send to the receiving node. The sender and receiver must first agree on an $r + 1$ bit pattern, known as a **generator,** which we will denote as G. We will require that the most significant (leftmost) bit of G be a 1. The key idea behind CRC codes is shown in Figure 5.7. For a given piece of data, D, the sender will choose r additional bits, R, and append them to D such that the resulting $d + r$ bit pattern (interpreted as a binary number) is exactly divisible by G using modulo 2 arithmetic. The process of error checking with CRC's is thus simple: the receiver divides the $d + r$ received bits by G. If the remainder is non-zero, the receiver knows that an error has occurred; otherwise the data is accepted as being correct.

All CRC calculations are done in modulo 2 arithmetic without carries in addition or borrows in subtraction. This means that addition and subtraction are identical, and both are equivalent to the bitwise exclusive-or (XOR) of the operands. Thus, for example,

```
1011 XOR 0101 = 1110
1001 XOR 1101 = 0100
```

Also, we similarly have

```
1011 - 0101 = 1110
1001 - 1101 = 0100
```

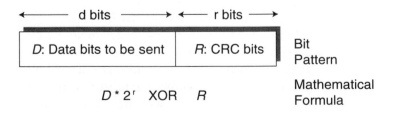

FIGURE 5.7   CRC codes

Multiplication and division arc the same as in base 2 arithmetic, except that any required addition or subtraction is done without carries or borrows. As in regular binary arithmetic, multiplication by 2^k left shifts a bit pattern by k places. Thus, given D and R, the quantity $D * 2^r$ XOR R yields the $d + r$ bit pattern shown in Figure 5.7. We'll use this algebraic characterization of the $d + r$ bit pattern from Figure 5.7 in our discussion below.

Let us now turn to the crucial question of how the sender computes R. Recall that we want to find R such that there is an n such that

$$D * 2^r \text{ XOR } R = nG$$

That is, we want to choose R such that G divides into $D * 2^r$ XOR R without remainder. If we exclusive-or (that is, add modulo 2, without carry) R to both sides of the above equation, we get

$$D * 2^r = nG \text{ XOR } R$$

This equation tells us that if we divide $D * 2^r$ by G, the value of the remainder is precisely R. In other words, we can calculate R as

$$R = \text{remainder} (D * 2^r/G)$$

Figure 5.8 illustrates this calculation for the case of $D = 101110$, $d = 6$ and $G = 1001$, $r = 3$. The nine bits transmitted in this case are `101110 011`. You should check these calculations for yourself and also check that indeed $D2^r = 101011 *$ G XOR R.

International standards have been defined for 8-, 12-, 16- and 32-bit generators, G. An 8-bit CRC is used to protect the 5-byte header in ATM cells. The CRC-

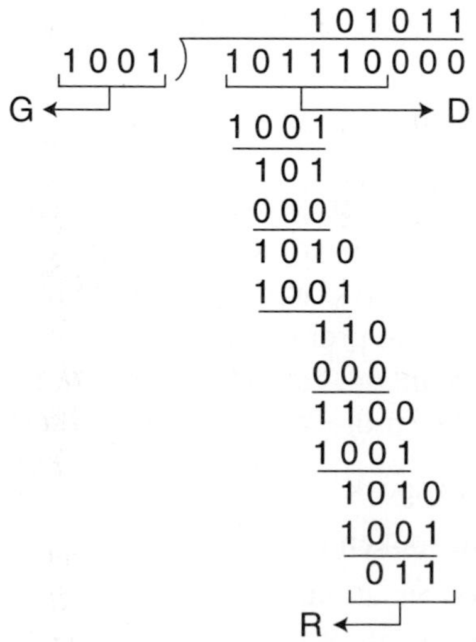

FIGURE 5.8 An example CRC calculation

32 32-bit standard, which has been adopted in a number of link-level IEEE protocols, uses a generator of

$$G_{CRC-32} = 100000100110000010001110110110111$$

Each of the CRC standards can detect burst errors of less than $r + 1$ bits and any odd number of bit errors. Furthermore, under appropriate assumptions, a burst of length greater than $r + 1$ bits is detected with probability $1 - 0.5^r$. The theory behind CRC codes and even more powerful codes is beyond the scope of this text. The text [Schwartz 1980] provides an excellent introduction to this topic.

5.3   MULTIPLE ACCESS PROTOCOLS AND LANs

In the introduction to this chapter, we noted that there are two types of network links: point-to-point links, and broadcast links. A **point-to-point link** consists of a single sender on one end of the link, and a single receiver at the other end of the link. Many link-layer protocols have been designed for point-to-point links; PPP (the point-to-point protocol) and HDLC are two such protocols that we'll cover later in this chapter. The second type of link, a **broadcast link,** can have multiple sending and receiving nodes all connected to the same, single, shared broadcast channel. The term "broadcast" is used here because when any one node transmits a frame, the channel broadcasts the frame and each of the other nodes receives a copy. Ethernet is probably the most widely deployed broadcast link technology; we'll cover Ethernet in detail in Section 5.5. In this section we'll take step back from specific link layer protocols and first examine a problem of central importance to the data link layer: how to coordinate the access of multiple sending and receiving nodes to a shared broadcast channel—the so-called **multiple access problem.** Broadcast channels are often used in **local area networks (LANs),** networks that are geographically concentrated in a single building (or on a corporate or university campus). Thus, we'll also look at how multiple access channels are used in LANs at the end of this section.

We are all familiar with the notion of broadcasting, as television has been using it since its invention. But traditional television is a one-way broadcast (that is, one fixed node transmitting to many receiving nodes), while nodes on a computer network broadcast channel can both send and receive. Perhaps a more apt human analogy for a broadcast channel is a cocktail party, where many people gather together in a large room (the air providing the broadcast medium) to talk and listen. A second good analogy is something many readers will be familiar with—a classroom—where teacher(s) and student(s) similarly share the same, single, broadcast medium. A central problem in both scenarios is that of determining who gets to talk (that is, transmit into the channel), and when. As humans, we've evolved an elaborate set of protocols for sharing the broadcast channel

"Give everyone a chance to speak."

"Don't speak until you are spoken to."

"Don't monopolize the conversation."

"Raise your hand if you have question."

"Don't interrupt when someone is speaking."

"Don't fall asleep when someone else is talking."

Computer networks similarly have protocols—so-called multiple access protocols—by which nodes regulate their transmission onto the shared broadcast channel. As shown in Figure 5.9, multiple access protocols are needed in a wide variety of network settings, including both wired and wireless local area networks, and satellite networks. Figure 5.10 takes a more abstract view of the broadcast channel and of the nodes sharing that channel. Although technically each node accesses the broadcast channel through its adapter, in this section we will refer to the *node* as the sending and receiving device. In practice, hundreds or even thousands of nodes can directly communicate over a broadcast channel.

Because all nodes are capable of transmitting frames, more than two nodes can transmit frames at the same time. When this happens, all of the nodes receive multiple frames at the same time, that is, the transmitted frames **collide** at all of the receivers. Typically, when there is a collision, none of the receiving nodes can make any sense of any of the frames that were transmitted; in a sense, the signals of the colliding frame become inextricably tangled together. Thus, all the frames

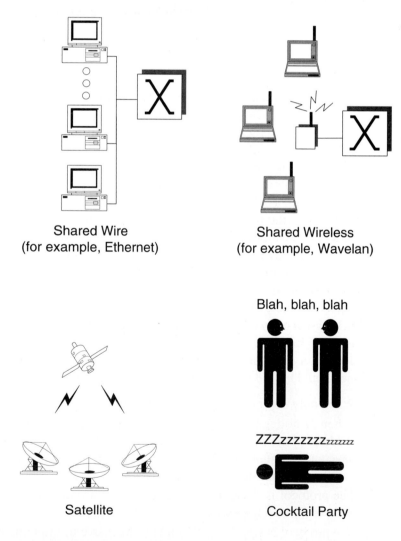

Shared Wire
(for example, Ethernet)

Shared Wireless
(for example, Wavelan)

Satellite

Cocktail Party

FIGURE 5.9   Various multiple access channels

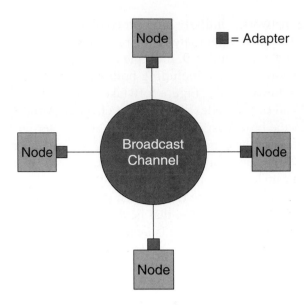

FIGURE 5.10 A broadcast channel interconnecting four nodes

involved in the collision are lost, and the broadcast channel is wasted during the collision interval. Clearly, if many nodes want to frequently transmit frames, many transmissions will result in collisions, and much of the bandwidth of the broadcast channel will be wasted.

In order to ensure that the broadcast channel performs useful work when multiple nodes are active, it is necessary to somehow coordinate the transmissions of the active nodes. This coordination job is the responsibility of the **multiple access protocol.** Over the past thirty years, thousands of papers and hundreds of Ph.D. dissertations have been written on multiple access protocols; a comprehensive survey of this body of work is [Rom 1990]. Furthermore, dozens of different protocols have been implemented in a variety of link-layer technologies. Nevertheless, we can classify just about any multiple access protocol as belonging to one of three categories: **channel partitioning protocols, random access protocols,** and **taking-turns protocols.** We'll cover these categories of multiple access protocols in the following three subsections. Let us conclude this overview by noting that ideally, a multiple access protocol for a broadcast channel of rate R bits per second should have the following desirable characteristics:

1. When only one node has data to send, that node has a throughput of R bps.
2. When M nodes have data to send, each of these nodes has a throughput of R/M bps. This need not necessarily imply that each of the M nodes always have an instantaneous rate of R/M, but rather that each node should have an average transmission rate of R/M over some suitably-defined interval of time.
3. The protocol is decentralized, that is, there are no master nodes that can fail and bring down the entire system.
4. The protocol is simple, so that it is inexpensive to implement.

5.3.1   Channel Partitioning Protocols

Recall from our early discussion back in Section 1.4 that Time Division Multiplexing (TDM) and Frequency Division Multiplexing (FDM) are two techniques that can be used to partition a broadcast channel's bandwidth among all nodes sharing that channel. As an example, suppose the channel supports N nodes and that the transmission rate of the channel is R bps. TDM divides time into **time frames** (not to be confused with the unit of data, the frame, at the data link layer) and further divides each time frame into N **time slots.** Each slot time is then assigned to one of the N nodes. Whenever a node has a frame to send, it transmits the frame's bits during its assigned time slot in the revolving TDM frame. Typically, frame sizes are chosen so that a single frame can be transmitting during a slot time. Figure 5.11 shows a simple four-node TDM example. Returning to our cocktail party analogy, a TDM-regulated cocktail party would allow one partygoer to speak for a fixed period of time, and then allow another partygoer to speak for the same amount of time, and so on. Once everyone has had their chance to talk, the pattern repeats.

TDM is appealing as it eliminates collisions and is perfectly fair: each node gets a dedicated transmission rate of R/N bps during each slot time. However, it has two major drawbacks. First, a node is limited to an average rate of R/N bps even when it is the only node with frames to send. A second drawback is that a node must always wait for its turn in the transmission sequence—again, even when it is the only node with a frame to send. Imagine the partygoer who is the only one with anything to say (and imagine that this is the even rarer circumstance where everyone at the party wants to hear what that one person has to say).

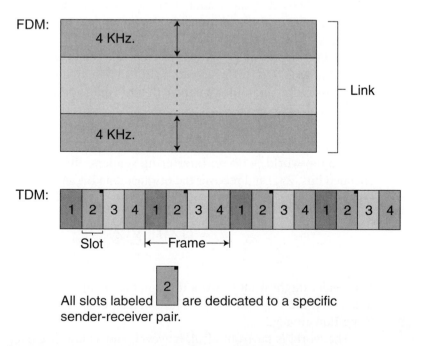

FIGURE 5.11   A four-node TDM and FDM example

Clearly, TDM would be a poor choice for a multiple access protocol for this particular party.

While TDM shares the broadcast channel in time, FDM divides the R bps channel into different frequencies (each with a bandwidth of R/N) and assigns each frequency to one of the N nodes. FDM thus creates N "smaller" channels of R/N bps out of the single, "larger" R bps channel. FDM shares both the advantages and drawbacks of TDM. It avoids collisions and divides the bandwidth fairly among the N nodes. However, FDM also shares a principal disadvantage with TDM—a node is limited to a bandwidth of R/N, even when it is the only node with frames to send.

A third channel partitioning protocol is **Code Division Multiple Access (CDMA).** While TDM and FDM assign time slots and frequencies, respectively, to the nodes, CDMA assigns a different *code* to each node. Each node then uses its unique code to encode the data bits it sends, as discussed below. We'll see that CDMA allows different nodes to transmit *simultaneously* and yet have their respective receivers correctly receive a sender's encoded data bits (assuming the receiver knows the sender's code) in spite of "interfering" transmissions by other nodes. CDMA has been used in military systems for some time (due to its anti-jamming properties) and is now beginning to find widespread civilian use, particularly for use in wireless multiple access channels.

In a CDMA protocol, each bit being sent by the sender is encoded by multiplying the bit by a signal (the code) that changes at a much faster rate (known as the **chipping rate**) than the original sequence of data bits. Figure 5.12 shows a simple, idealized CDMA encoding/decoding scenario. Suppose that the rate at which original data bits reach the CDMA encoder defines the unit of time; that is, each original data bit to be transmitted requires one bit-slot time. Let d_i be the value of the data bit for the ith bit slot. Each bit slot is further subdivided into M mini-slots; in Figure 5.12, $M = 8$, although in practice M is much larger. The CDMA code used by the sender consists of a sequence of M values, c_m, $m = 1, \ldots, M$, each taking a $+1$ or -1 value. In the example in Figure 5.12, the M-bit CDMA code being used by the sender is $(1, 1, 1, -1, 1, -1, -1, -1)$.

To illustrate how CDMA works, let us focus on the ith data bit, d_i. For the mth mini-slot of the bit-transmission time of d_i, the output of the CDMA encoder, $Z_{i,m}$, is the value of d_i multiplied by the mth bit in the assigned CDMA code, c_m:

$$Z_{i,m} = d_i \cdot c_m \tag{5.1}$$

In a simple world, with no interfering senders, the receiver would receive the encoded bits, $Z_{i,m}$, and recover the original data bit, d_i, by computing:

$$d_i = (1/M) \sum_{m=1}^{m} Z_{i,m} \cdot c_m \tag{5.2}$$

The reader might want to work through the details of the example in Figure 5.12 to see that the original data bits are indeed correctly recovered at the receiver using Equation 5.2.

The world is far from ideal, however, and as noted above, CDMA must work in the presence of interfering senders that are encoding and transmitting their data using a different assigned code. But how can a CDMA receiver recover a sender's original data bits when those data bits are being tangled with bits being transmit-

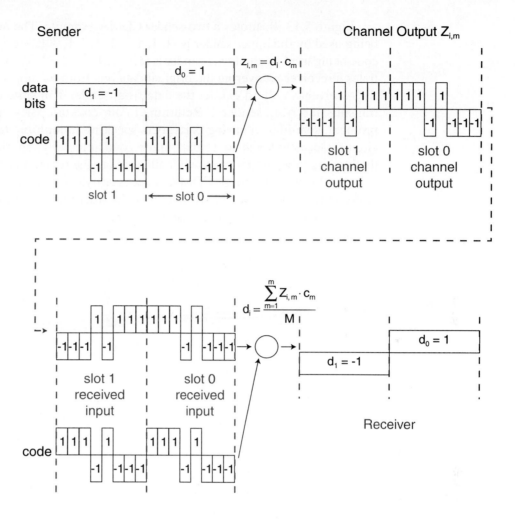

FIGURE 5.12 A simple CDMA example: sender encoding, receiver decoding

ted by other senders? CDMA works under the assumption that the interfering transmitted bit signals are additive, for example, that if three senders send a 1 value, and a fourth sender sends a -1 value during the same minislot, then the received signal at all receivers during that minislot is a 2 (since $1 + 1 + 1 - 1 = 2$). In the presence of multiple senders, sender s computes its encoded transmissions, $Z_{i,m}{}^s$, in exactly the same manner as in Equation 5.1. The value received at a receiver during the mth minislot of the ith bit slot, however, is now the *sum* of the transmitted bits from all N senders during that minislot:

$$Z_{i,m}^* = \sum_{s=1}^{n} Z_{i,m}^s$$

Amazingly, if the senders' codes are chosen carefully, each receiver can recover the data sent by a given sender out of the aggregate signal simply by using the sender's code in exactly the same manner as in Equation 5.2:

$$d_i = (1/M) \sum_{m=1}^{m} Z_{im}^* \cdot c_m \tag{5.3}$$

Figure 5.13 illustrates a two-sender CDMA example. The *M*-bit CDMA code being used by the upper sender is $(1, 1, 1, -1, 1, -1, -1, -1)$, while the CDMA code being used by the lower sender is $(1, -1, 1, 1, 1, -1, 1, 1)$. Figure 5.13 illustrates a receiver recovering the original data bits from the upper sender. Note that the receiver is able to extract the data from sender 1 in spite of the interfering transmission from sender 2. Returning to our cocktail party analogy, a CDMA protocol is similar to having partygoers speaking in multiple languages; in such circumstances humans are actually quite good at locking into the conversation in the language they understand, while filtering out the remaining conversations.

Our discussion here of CDMA is necessarily brief and a number of difficult issues must be addressed in practice. First, in order for the CDMA receivers to be able to extract out a particular sender's signal, the CDMA codes must be carefully

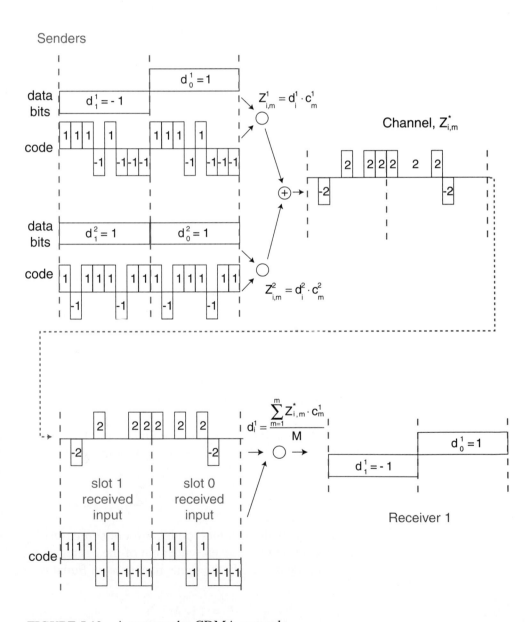

FIGURE 5.13 A two-sender CDMA example

chosen. Secondly, our discussion has assumed that the received signal strengths from various senders at a receiver are the same; this can be difficult to achieve in practice. There is a considerable body of literature addressing these and other issues related to CDMA; see [Pickholtz 1982, Viterbi 1995] for details.

5.3.2 Random Access Protocols

The second broad class of multiple access protocols are so-called random access protocols. In a random access protocol, a transmitting node always transmits at the full rate of the channel, namely, R bps. When there is a collision, each node involved in the collision repeatedly retransmits its frame until the frame gets through without a collision. But when a node experiences a collision, it doesn't necessarily retransmit the frame right away. *Instead it waits a random delay before retransmitting the frame.* Each node involved in a collision chooses independent random delays. Because after a collision the random delays are independently chosen, it is possible that one of the nodes will pick a delay that is sufficiently less than the delays of the other colliding nodes, and will therefore be able to "sneak" its frame into the channel without a collision.

There are dozens if not hundreds of random access protocols described in the literature [Rom 1990, Bertsekas 1991]. In this section we'll describe a few of the most commonly used random access protocols—the ALOHA protocols [Abramson 1970, Abramson 1985] and the Carrier Sense Multiple Access (CSMA) protocols [Kleinrock 1975a]. Later, in Section 5.5, we'll cover the details of Ethernet [Metcalfe 1976], a popular and widely deployed CSMA protocol.

Slotted ALOHA. Let's begin our study of random access protocols with one of the most simple random access protocols, the so-called slotted ALOHA protocol. In our description of slotted ALOHA, we assume the following:

- All frames consist of exactly L bits.
- Time is divided into slots of size L/R seconds (that is, a slot equals the time to transmit one frame).
- Nodes start to transmit frames only at the beginnings of slots.
- The nodes are synchronized so that each node knows when the slots begin.
- If two or more frames collide in a slot, then all the nodes detect the collision event before the slot ends.

Let p be a probability, that is, a number between 0 and 1. The operation of slotted ALOHA in each node is simple:

- When the node has a fresh frame to send, it waits until the beginning of the next slot and transmits the entire frame in the slot.
- If there isn't a collision, the node won't consider retransmitting the frame. (The node can prepare a new frame for transmission, if it has one.)
- If there is a collision, the node detects the collision before the end of the slot. The node retransmits its frame in each subsequent slot with probability p until the frame is transmitted without a collision.

By retransmitting with probability p, we mean that the node effectively tosses a biased coin; the event heads corresponds to retransmit, which occurs with probability p. The event tails corresponds to "skip the slot and toss the coin again in the next slot"; this occurs with probability $(1 - p)$. Each of the nodes involved in the collision toss their coins independently.

Slotted ALOHA would appear to have many advantages. Unlike channel partitioning, slotted ALOHA allows a single active node (that is, a node with a frame to send) to continuously transmit frames at the full rate of the channel. Slotted ALOHA is also highly decentralized, because each node detects collisions and independently decides when to retransmit. (Slotted ALOHA does, however, require the slots to be synchronized in the nodes; we'll shortly discuss an unslotted version of the ALOHA protocol, as well as CSMA protocols, none of which require such synchronization and are therefore fully decentralized.) Slotted ALOHA is also an extremely simple protocol.

Slotted ALOHA works well when there is only one active node, but how efficient is it when there are multiple active nodes? There are two possible efficiency concerns here. First, as shown in Figure 5.14, when there are multiple active nodes, a certain fraction of the slots will have *collisions* and will therefore be "wasted." The second concern is that another fraction of the slots will be *empty* because all active nodes refrain from transmitting as a result of the probabilistic transmission policy. The only "unwasted" slots will be those in which exactly one node transmits. A slot in which exactly one node transmits is said to be a **successful slot.** The **efficiency** of a slotted multiple access protocol is defined to be the long-run fraction of successful slots when there are a large number of active nodes, with each node having a large number of frames to send. Note that if no form of access control were used, and each node were to immediately retransmit after each collision, the efficiency would be zero. Slotted ALOHA clearly increases the efficiency beyond zero, but by how much?

We now proceed to outline the derivation of the maximum efficiency of slotted ALOHA. To keep this derivation simple, let's modify the protocol a little and assume that each node attempts to transmit a frame in each slot with probability p. (That is, we assume that each node always has a frame to send and that the node transmits with probability p for a fresh frame as well as for a frame that has

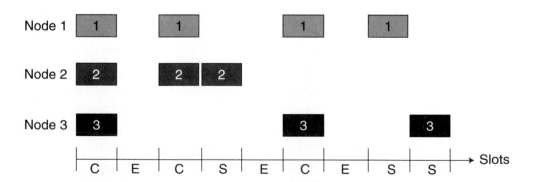

FIGURE 5.14 Nodes 1, 2, and 3 collide in the first slot. Node 2 finally succeeds in the fourth slot, node 1 in the eighth slot, and node 3 in the ninth slot. The notation C, E, and S represent "collision slot," "empty slot," and "successful slot," respectively.

already suffered a collision.) Suppose first there are N nodes. Then the probability that a given slot is a successful slot is the probability that one of the nodes transmits and that the remaining N-1 nodes do not transmit. The probability that a given node transmits is p; the probability that the remaining nodes do not transmit is $(1 - p)^{N-1}$. Therefore the probability a given node has a success is $p(1 - p)^{N-1}$. Because there are N nodes, the probability that an arbitrary node has a success is $Np(1 - p)^{N-1}$.

Thus, when there are N active nodes, the efficiency of slotted ALOHA is $Np(1 - p)^{N-1}$. To obtain the *maximum* efficiency for N active nodes, we have to find the p^* that maximizes this expression. (See the homework problems for a general outline of this derivation.) And to obtain the maximum efficiency for a large number of active nodes, we take the limit of $Np^*(1 - p^*)^{N-1}$ as N approaches infinity. (Again, see the homework problems.) After performing these calculations, we'll find that the maximum efficiency of the protocol is given by $1/e = 0.37$. That is, when a large number of nodes have many frames to transmit, then (at best) only 37% of the slots do useful work. Thus the effective transmission rate of the channel is not R bps but only $0.37 R$ bps! A similar analysis also shows that 37% of the slots go empty and 26% of slots have collisions. Imagine the poor network administrator who has purchased a 100 Mbps slotted ALOHA system, expecting to be able to use the network to transmit data among a large number of users at an aggregate rate of, say, 80 Mbps! Although the channel is capable of transmitting a given frame at the full channel rate of 100Mbps, in the long term, the successful throughput of this channel will be less that 37 Mbps.

ALOHA. The slotted ALOHA protocol required that all nodes synchronize their transmissions to start at the beginning of a slot. The first ALOHA protocol [Abramson 1970] was actually an unslotted, fully decentralized protocol. In so-called pure ALOHA, when a frame first arrives (that is, a network layer datagram is passed down from the network layer at the sending node), the node immediately transmits the frame in its entirety into the broadcast channel. If a transmitted frame experiences a collision with one or more other transmissions, the node will then immediately (after completely transmitting its collided frame) retransmit the frame with probability p. Otherwise, the node waits for a frame transmission time. After this wait, it then transmits the frame with probability p, or waits (remaining idle) for another frame time with probability $1 - p$.

To determine the maximum efficiency of pure ALOHA, we focus on an individual node. We'll make the same assumptions as in our slotted ALOHA analysis and take the frame transmission time to be the unit of time. At any given time, the probability that a node is transmitting a frame is p. Suppose this frame begins transmission at time t_0. As shown in Figure 5.15, in order for this frame to be successfully transmitted, no other nodes can begin their transmission in the interval of time $[t_0 - 1, t_0]$. Such a transmission would overlap with the beginning of the transmission of node i's frame. The probability that all other nodes do not begin a transmission in this interval is $(1 - p)^{N-1}$. Similarly, no other node can begin a transmission while node i is transmitting, as such a transmission would overlap with the latter part of node i's transmission. The probability that all other nodes do not begin a transmission in this interval is also $(1 - p)^{N-1}$. Thus, the probability that a given node has a successful transmission is $p(1 - p)^{2(N-1)}$. By taking limits

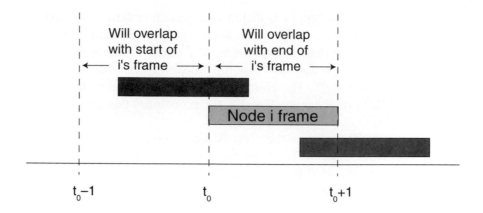

FIGURE 5.15 Interfering transmissions in pure ALOHA

as in the slotted ALOHA case, we find that the maximum efficiency of the pure ALOHA protocol is only $1/(2e)$—exactly half that of slotted ALOHA. This then is the price to be paid for a fully decentralized ALOHA protocol.

CSMA—Carrier Sense Multiple Access. In both slotted and pure ALOHA, a node's decision to transmit is made independently of the activity of the other nodes attached to the broadcast channel. In particular, a node neither pays attention to whether another node happens to be transmitting when it begins to transmit, nor stops transmitting if another node begins to interfere with its transmission. In our cocktail party analogy, ALOHA protocols are quite like a boorish partygoer who continues to chatter away regardless of whether other people are talking. As humans, we have human protocols that allow us to not only behave with more civility, but also to decrease the amount of time spent "colliding" with each other in conversation and consequently increasing the amount of data we exchange in our conversations. Specifically, there are two important rules for polite human conversation:

- *Listen before speaking.* If someone else is speaking, wait until they are done. In the networking world, this is termed **carrier sensing**—a node listens to the channel before transmitting. If a frame from another node is currently being transmitted into the channel, a node then waits ("backs off") a random amount of time and then again senses the channel. If the channel is sensed to be idle, the node then begins frame transmission. Otherwise, the node waits another random amount of time and repeats this process.

- *If someone else begins talking at the same time, stop talking.* In the networking world, this is termed **collision detection**—a transmitting node listens to the channel while it is transmitting. If it detects that another node is transmitting an interfering frame, it stops transmitting and uses some protocol to determine when it should next attempt to transmit.

These two rules are embodied in the family of **CSMA** (Carrier Sense Multiple Access) and **CSMA/CD** (CSMA with Collision Detection) protocols [Kleinrock 1975a, Metcalfe 1976, Lam 1980, Rom 1990]. Many variations on CSMA and

CSMA/CD have been proposed, with the differences being primarily in the manner in which nodes perform backoff. The reader can consult these references for the details of these protocols. We'll study the CSMA/CD scheme used in Ethernet in detail in Section 5.5. Here, we'll consider a few of the most important, and fundamental, characteristics of CSMA and CSMA/CD.

The first question that one might ask about CSMA is that if all nodes perform carrier sensing, why do collisions occur in the first place? After all, a node will refrain from transmitting whenever it senses that another node is transmitting. The answer to the question can best be illustrated using space-time diagrams [Molle 1987]. Figure 5.16 shows a space-time diagram of four nodes (A, B, C, D)

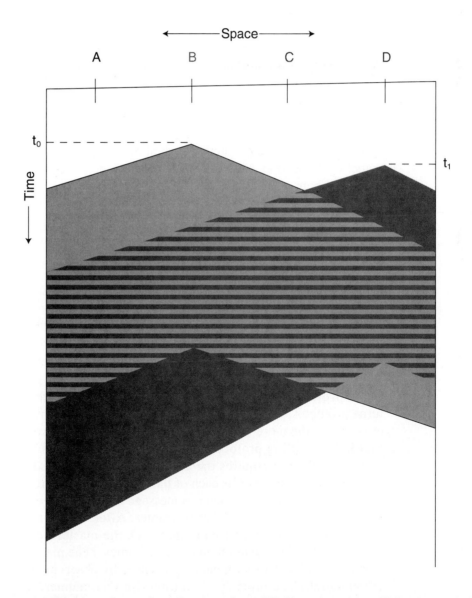

FIGURE 5.16   Space-time diagram of two CSMA nodes with colliding transmissions

attached to a linear broadcast bus. The horizontal axis shows the position of each node in space; the vertical axis represents time.

At time t_0, node B senses the channel is idle, as no other nodes are currently transmitting. Node B thus begins transmitting, with its bits propagating in both directions along the broadcast medium. The downward propagation of B's bits in Figure 5.16 with increasing time indicates that a non-zero amount of time is needed for B's bits to actually propagate (albeit at near the speed-of-light) along the broadcast medium. At time t_1 ($t_1 > t_0$), node D has a frame to send. Although node B is currently transmitting at time t_1, the bits being transmitted by B have yet to reach D, and thus D senses the channel idle at t_1. In accordance with the CSMA protocol, D thus begins transmitting its frame. A short time later, B's transmission begins to interfere with D's transmission at D. From Figure 5.16, it is evident that the end-to-end **channel propagation delay** of a broadcast channel—the time it takes for a signal to propagate from one of the channel to another—will play a crucial role in determining its performance. The longer this propagation delay, the larger the chance that a carrier-sensing node is not yet able to sense a transmission that has already begun at another node in the network.

In Figure 5.16, nodes do not perform collision detection; both B and D continue to transmit their frames in their entirety even though a collision has occurred. When a node performs collision detection, it will cease transmission as soon as it detects a collision. Figure 5.17 shows the same scenario as in Figure 5.16, except that the two nodes each abort their transmission a short time after detecting a collision. Clearly, adding collision detection to a multiple access protocol will help protocol performance by not transmitting a useless, damaged (by interference with a frame from another node) frame in its entirety. The Ethernet protocol we will study in Section 5.5 is a CSMA protocol that uses collision detection.

5.3.3   Taking-Turns Protocols

Recall that two desirable properties of a multiple access protocol are (1) when only one node is active, the active node has a throughput of R bps, and (2) when M nodes are active, then each active node has a throughput of nearly R/M bps. The ALOHA and CSMA protocols have this first property but not the second. This has motivated researchers to create another class of protocols—the **taking-turns protocols.** As with random-access protocols, there are dozens of taking-turns protocols, and each one of these protocols has many variations. We'll discuss two of the more important protocols here. The first one is the **polling protocol.** The polling protocol requires one of the nodes to be designated as a "master node" (or requires the introduction of a new node serving as the master). The master node **polls** each of the nodes in a round-robin fashion. In particular, the master node first sends a message to node 1, saying that it can transmit up to some maximum number of frames. After node 1 transmits some frames (from zero up to the maximum number), the master node tells node 2 it can transmit up to the maximum number of frames. (The master node can determine when a node has finished sending its frames by observing the lack of a signal on the channel.) The procedure continues in this manner, with the master node polling each of the nodes in a cyclic manner.

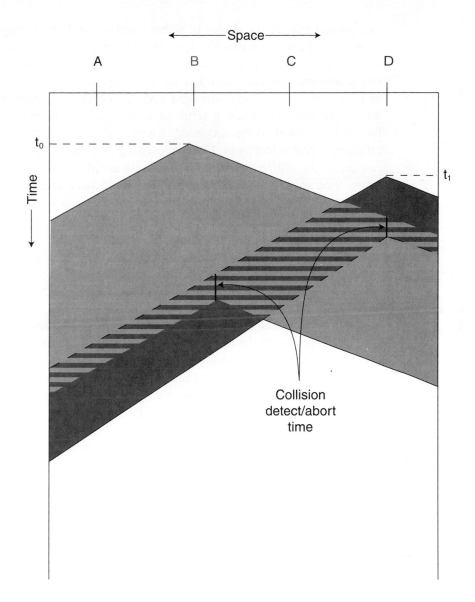

FIGURE 5.17 CSMA with collision detection

The polling protocol eliminates the collisions and the empty slots that plague the random access protocols. This allows it to have a much higher efficiency. But it also has a few drawbacks. The first drawback is that the protocol introduces a polling delay, the amount of time required to notify a node that it can transmit. If, for example, only one node is active, then the node will transmit at a rate less than R bps, as the master node must poll each of the inactive nodes in turn, each time the active node sends its maximum number of frames. The second drawback, which is potentially more serious, is that if the master node fails, the entire channel becomes inoperative.

The second taking-turn protocol is the **token-passing protocol.** In this protocol there is no master node. A small, special-purpose frame known as a **token** is exchanged among the nodes in some fixed order. For example, node 1 might always send the token to node 2, node 2 might always send the token to node 3, node N might always send the token to node 1. When a node receives a token, it holds onto the token only if it has some frames to transmit; otherwise, it immediately forwards the token to the next node. If a node does have frames to transmit when it receives the token, it sends up to a maximum number of frames and then forwards the token to the next node. Token passing is decentralized and has a high efficiency. But it has its problems as well. For example, the failure of one node can crash the entire channel. Or if a node accidentally neglects to release the token, then some recovery procedure must be invoked to get the token back in circulation. Over the years many token-passing products have been developed, and each one had to address these as well as other sticky issues.

5.3.4   Local Area Networks (LANs)

Multiple access protocols are used in conjunction with many different types of broadcast channels. They have been used for satellite and wireless channels, whose nodes transmit over a common frequency spectrum. They are currently used in the upstream channel for cable access to the Internet (see Section 1.5), and they are extensively used in local area networks (LANs).

Recall that a **LAN** is a computer network that is concentrated in a geographical area, such as in a building or on a university campus. When a user accesses the Internet from a university or corporate campus, the access is almost always by way of a LAN. For this type of Internet access, the user's host is a node on the LAN, and the LAN provides access to the Internet through a router, as shown in Figure 5.18. The LAN is a single "link" between each user host and the router; it therefore uses a link-layer protocol, which incorporates a multiple access protocol. The transmission rate, R, of most LANs is very high. Even in the early 1980s,

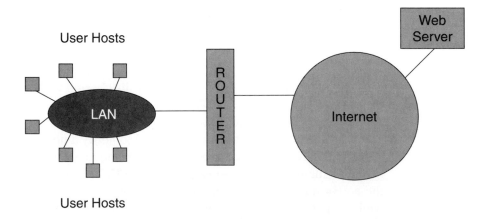

FIGURE 5.18   User hosts access an Internet Web server through a LAN. The broadcast channel between a user host and the router consists of "one" link.

10 Mbps LANs were common; today, 100 Mbps LANs are common, and 1 Gbps LANs are available.

In the 1980s and the early 1990s, two classes of LAN technologies were popular in the workplace. The first class consists of the Ethernet LANs (also known as 802.3 LANs [IEEE 802.3 1998, Spurgeon 1999]), which are random-access based. The second class of LAN technologies are token-passing technologies, including *token ring* (also known as IEEE 802.5 [IEEE 802.5 1998]) and *FDDI* (also known as Fiber Distributed Data Interface [Jain 1994]). Because we shall explore the Ethernet technologies in some detail in Section 5.4, we focus our discussion here on the token-passing LANs. Our discussion on token-passing technologies is intentionally brief, since these technologies have become relatively minor players in the face of relentless Ethernet competition. Nevertheless, in order to provide examples about token-passing technology and to give a little historical perspective, it is useful to say a few words about token rings.

In a token ring LAN, the *N* nodes of the LAN (hosts and routers) are connected in a ring by direct links. The topology of the token ring defines the token-passing order. When a node obtains the token and sends a frame, the frame propagates around the entire ring, thereby creating a virtual broadcast channel. The node that sends the frame has the responsibility of removing the frame from the ring. FDDI was designed for geographically larger LANs (so called MANs, that is, metropolitan area networks). For geographically large LANs (spread out over several kilometers) it is inefficient to let a frame propagate back to the sending node once the frame has passed the destination node. FDDI has the destination node remove the frame from the ring. (Strictly speaking, FDDI is not a pure broadcast channel, as every node does not receive every transmitted frame.) You can learn more about token ring and FDDI by visiting the 3Com adapter page [3Com 1999].

5.4   LAN ADDRESSES AND ARP

As we learned in the previous section, nodes in LANs send frames to each other over a broadcast channel. This means that when a node in a LAN transmits a frame, every other node connected to the LAN receives the frame. But usually, a node in the LAN doesn't want to send a frame to *all* of the other LAN nodes but instead wants to send to some *particular* LAN node. To provide this functionality, the nodes on the LAN need to be able to address each other when sending frames, that is, the nodes need LAN addresses and the frame needs a field for a destination LAN address. In this manner, when a node receives a frame, it can determine whether the frame was intended for it or for some other node in the LAN:

- If the destination address of the frame matches a receiving node's LAN address, then the node extracts the network-layer datagram from the data link layer frame and passes the datagram up the protocol stack.
- If the destination address does not match the address of the receiving node, the node simply discards the frame.

5.4.1 LAN Addresses

In truth, it is not a node that has a LAN address but instead a node's adapter that has a LAN address. This is illustrated in Figure 5.19. A **LAN address** is also variously called a **physical address,** an **Ethernet address,** or a **MAC** (media access control) **address.** For most LANs (including Ethernet and token-passing LANs), the LAN address is six-bytes long, giving 2^{48} possible LAN addresses. These six-byte addresses are typically expressed in hexadecimal notation, with each byte of the address expressed by a pair of hexadecimal numbers. An adapter's LAN address is permanent—when an adapter is manufactured, a LAN address is burned into the adapter's ROM.

One interesting property of LAN addresses is that no two adapters have the same address. This might seem surprising given that adapters are manufactured in many different countries by many different companies. How does a company manufacturing adapters in Taiwan make sure that it is using different addresses from a company manufacturing adapters in Belgium? The answer is that IEEE manages the physical address space. In particular, when a company wants to manufacture adapters, it purchases a chunk of the address space consisting of 2^{24} addresses for a nominal fee. IEEE allocates the chunk of 2^{24} addresses by fixing the first 24 bits of a physical address and letting the company create unique combinations of the last 24 bits for each adapter.

An adapter's LAN address has a flat structure (as opposed to a hierarchical structure), and doesn't change no matter where the adapter goes. A portable computer with an Ethernet card always has the same LAN address, no matter where the portable goes. Recall that, in contrast, an IP address has a hierarchical structure (that is, a network part and a host part), and a node's IP address needs to be changed when the host moves. An adapter's LAN address is analogous to a person's social security number, which also has a flat addressing structure and which

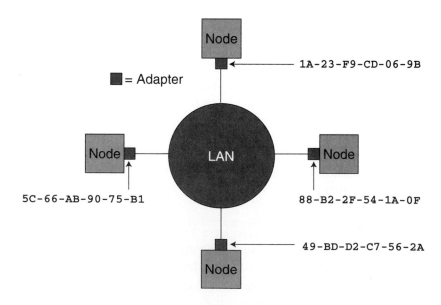

FIGURE 5.19 Each adapter connected to a LAN has a unique LAN address

also doesn't change no matter where the person goes. An IP address is analogous to a person's postal address, which is hierarchical and which needs to be changed whenever a person moves.

One natural question at this juncture is, because all nodes also have IP addresses, why do they have to have LAN addresses as well? There are several good answers to this question. First, LANs are designed for "arbitrary" network-layer protocols, not just for IP. If adapters were to get assigned IP addresses rather than "neutral" LAN addresses, then the adapters would not be able to easily support other network-layer protocols (for example, IPX or DECNet). Second, if adapters were to use IP addresses instead of LAN addresses, the IP address would have to be stored in adapter RAM and configured every time the adapter were moved (or powered up). Another option is to not use any addresses in the adapters, and have each adapter pass the data (that is, the IP datagram) of each frame it receives to its parent node. The parent node could then check for a matching IP address. One problem with this option is that the parent node will be interrupted by every frame sent on the LAN, including by the frames that are destined for other nodes on the LAN.

As we described at the beginning of this section, when an adapter wants to send a frame to some destination adapter on the same LAN, the sending adapter inserts the destination LAN address into the frame. When the destination adapter receives the frame, it extracts the enclosed datagram and passes the datagram up the protocol stack. All the other adapters on the LAN also receive the frame; but these other adapters discard the frame without passing the network-layer datagram up the protocol stack. Thus, these other adapters do not have to interrupt their hosts when they receive datagrams destined to other hosts. Having said this, sometimes a sending adapter *does* want all the other adapters on the LAN to receive and *process* the frame it is about to send. In this case, the sending adapter inserts a special **LAN broadcast address** into the destination address field of the frame. For LANs that use the six-byte addresses (such as Ethernet and token-passing LANs), the broadcast address is a string of 48 consecutive 1s (that is, `FF-FF-FF-FF-FF-FF` in hexadecimal notation).

5.4.2   Address Resolution Protocol

Because there are both network-layer addresses (for example, Internet IP addresses) and link-layer addresses (that is, LAN addresses), there is a need to translate between them. For the Internet, this is the job of the Address Resolution Protocol (ARP) [RFC 826]. Every Internet host and router on a LAN has an **ARP module.** To motivate ARP, consider the network shown in Figure 5.20. In this figure, each node has an IP address and each node's adapter has a LAN address. As usual, IP addresses are shown in dotted-decimal notation and LAN addresses are shown in hexadecimal notation. Now suppose that the node with IP address `222.222.222.220` wants to send an IP datagram to node `222.222.222.222`. To accomplish this task, the sending node must give its adapter not only the IP datagram but also the LAN address for node `222.222.222.222`. When passed the IP datagram and the LAN address, the sending node's adapter can construct a data link layer frame and send the frame into the LAN. But how does the sending node determine the LAN address for

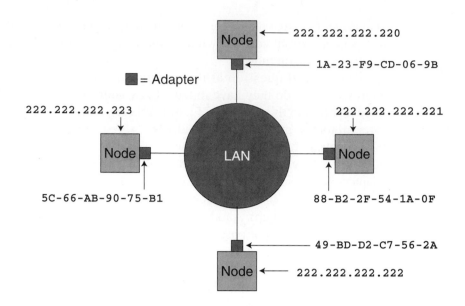

FIGURE 5.20   Each node on a LAN has an IP address, and each node's adapter has a LAN address

the node with IP address `222.222.222.222`? It does this by providing its ARP module with the IP address `222.222.222.222`. ARP then responds with the corresponding LAN address, namely, `49-BD-D2-C7-56-2A`.

So we see that ARP resolves an IP address to a LAN address. In many ways it is analogous to DNS (studied in Section 2.5), which resolves hostnames to IP addresses. However, one important difference between the two resolvers is that DNS resolves hostnames for hosts anywhere in the Internet, whereas ARP only resolves IP addresses for nodes on the same LAN. If a node in California were to try to use ARP to resolve the IP address for a node in Mississippi, ARP would return with an error.

Now that we have explained what ARP does, let's look at how it works. The ARP module in each node has a table in its RAM called an ARP table. This table contains the mappings of IP addresses to LAN addresses. Figure 5.21 shows what an ARP table in node `222.222.222.220` might look like. For each address mapping the table also contains a time-to-live (TTL) entry, which indicates when the entry will be deleted. Note that the table does not necessarily contain an entry for

IP address	LAN address	TTL
222.222.222.221	88-B2-2F-54-1A-0F	13:45:00
222.222.222.223	5C-66-AB-90-75-B1	13:52:00

FIGURE 5.21   A possible ARP table in node `222.222.222.220`

every node on the LAN; some nodes may have had entries that expired over time, whereas other nodes may have never been entered into the table. We note that a typical expiration time for an entry is 20 minutes from when an entry is placed in an ARP table.

Now suppose that node `222.222.222.220` wants to send a datagram that is IP-addressed to another node on that LAN. As we indicated above, the sending node needs to obtain the LAN address of the destination node, given the IP address of that node. This task is easy if the sending node's ARP table has an entry for the destination node. But what if the ARP table doesn't currently have an entry for the destination node? In particular, suppose node `222.222.222.220` wants to send a datagram to node `222.222.222.222`. In this case, the sending node uses the ARP protocol to resolve the address. First, the sending node constructs a special packet called an **ARP packet.** An ARP packet has several fields, including the sending and receiving IP and LAN addresses. Both ARP query and response packets have the same format. The purpose of the ARP query packet is to query all the other nodes on the LAN to determine the LAN address corresponding to the IP address that is being resolved.

Returning to the example, node `222.222.222.220` passes an ARP query packet to the adapter along with an indication that the adapter should send the packet to the LAN broadcast address, namely, `FF-FF-FF-FF-FF-FF`. The adapter encapsulates the ARP packet in a data link frame, uses the broadcast address for the frame's destination address, and transmits the frame into the LAN. Recalling our social security number/postal address analogy, note that an ARP query is equivalent to a person shouting out in a crowded room of cubicles in some company (say, AnyCorp): "What is the social security number of the person whose postal address is Cubicle 13, Room 112, AnyCorp, Palo Alto, CA?" The frame containing the ARP query is received by all the other adapters on the LAN, and (because of the broadcast address) each adapter passes the ARP packet within the frame up to its parent node. Each node that receives the ARP packet checks to see if its IP address matches the destination IP address in the ARP packet. The one node with a match sends back to the querying node a response ARP packet with the desired mapping. The querying node (`222.222.222.220`) can then update its ARP table and send its IP datagram.

There are a couple of interesting things to note about the ARP protocol. First, the query ARP message is sent within a broadcast frame whereas the response ARP message is sent within a standard frame. Before reading on you should think about why this is so. Second, ARP is plug-and-play, that is, a node's ARP table gets built automatically—it doesn't have to be configured by a systems administrator. And if a node is disconnected from the LAN, its entry is eventually deleted from the table.

Sending a datagram to a node off the LAN.   It should now be clear how ARP operates when a node wants to send a datagram to another node *on the same LAN*. But now let's look at the more complicated situation when a node on a LAN wants to send a network-layer datagram to a node *off the LAN*. Let us discuss this issue in the context of Figure 5.22, which shows a simple network consisting of two LANs interconnected by a router.

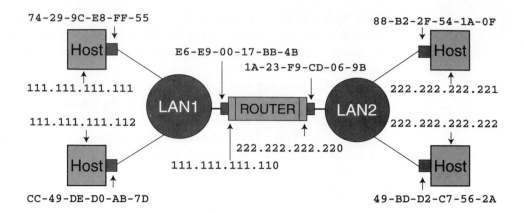

FIGURE 5.22   Two LANs interconnected by a router

There are several interesting things to note about Figure 5.22. First, there are two types of nodes: hosts and routers. Each host has exactly one IP address and one adapter. But, as discussed in Section 4.4, a router has an IP address for *each* of its interfaces. Each router interface also has its own ARP module (in the router) and its own adapter. Because the router in Figure 5.22 has two interfaces, it has two IP addresses, two ARP modules, and two adapters. Of course, each adapter in the network has its own LAN address.

Also note that all of the interfaces connected to LAN 1 have addresses of the form `111.111.111.xxx` and all of the interfaces connected to LAN 2 have the form `222.222.222.xxx`. Thus, in this example, the first three bytes of the IP address specifies the "network" whereas the last byte specifies the specific interface on a network.

Now suppose that host `111.111.111.111` wants to send an IP datagram to host `222.222.222.222`. The sending host passes the datagram to its adapter, as usual. But the sending host must also indicate to its adapter an appropriate destination LAN address. What LAN address should the adapter use? One might venture to guess that the appropriate LAN address is the address of the adapter for host `222.222.222.222`, namely, `49-BD-D2-C7-58-2A`. This guess is, however, wrong. If the sending adapter were to use that LAN address, then none of the adapters on LAN 1 would bother to pass the IP datagram up to its network layer; the datagram would just die and go to datagram heaven.

If we look carefully at Figure 5.22, we see that in order for a datagram to go from `111.111.111.111` to a node on LAN 2, the datagram must first be sent to the router interface `111.111.111.110`. Thus, the appropriate LAN address for the frame is the address of the adapter for router interface `111.111.111.110`, namely, `E6-E9-00-17-BB-4B`. How does the sending host acquire the LAN address of `111.111.111.110`? By using ARP, of course! Once the sending adapter has this LAN address, it creates a frame and sends the frame into LAN 1. The router adapter on LAN 1 sees that the data link frame is addressed to it, and therefore passes the frame to the network layer of the router. Hooray, the IP datagram has successfully been moved from source host to the router! But we are not done. We still have to move the datagram from the router to the destination! The router now has to determine the correct interface on which the datagram is to be forwarded. As discussed in Section 4.4, this is done by consulting a routing table in the router. The routing table tells the router that the datagram is to be forwarded router interface 222.222.222.220. This interface then passes the datagram to its adapter, which encapsulates the datagram in a new frame and sends the frame into LAN 2. This time, the destination LAN address of the frame is indeed the LAN address of the ultimate destination. And how does the router obtain this destination LAN address? From ARP, of course!

ARP for Ethernet is defined in [RFC 826]. A nice introduction to ARP is given in the TCP/IP tutorial, [RFC 1180]. We shall explore ARP in more detail in the homework problems.

5.5 ETHERNET

Ethernet has pretty much taken over the LAN market. As recently as the 1980s and the early 1990s, Ethernet faced many challenges from other LAN technologies, including token ring, FDDI, and ATM. Some of these other technologies succeeded at capturing a part of the market share for a few years. But since its invention in the mid-1970, Ethernet has continued to evolve and grow, and has held on to its dominant market share. Today, Ethernet is by far the most prevalent LAN technology, and is likely to remain so for the foreseeable future. One might say that Ethernet has been to local area networking what the Internet has been to global networking.

There are many reasons for Ethernet's success. First, Ethernet was the first widely-deployed high-speed LAN. Because it was deployed early, network administrators became intimately familiar with Ethernet—its wonders and its quirks—and were reluctant to switch over to other LAN technologies when they came on the scene. Second, token ring, FDDI, and ATM are more complex and expensive than Ethernet, which further discouraged network administrators from switching over. Third, the most compelling reason to switch to another LAN technology (such as FDDI or ATM) was usually the higher data rate of the new technology; however, Ethernet always fought back, producing versions that operated at equal data rates or higher. Switched Ethernet was also introduced in the early 1990s, which further increased its effective data rates. Finally, because Ethernet has been so popular, Ethernet hardware (in particular, network interface cards) has become a commodity and is remarkably cheap. This low cost is also due to the fact that Ethernet's multiple access protocol, CSMA/CD, is totally decentralized, which has also contributed to a simple design.

The original Ethernet LAN, as shown in Figure 5.23, was invented in the mid 1970s by Bob Metcalfe. An excellent source of online information about Ethernet is Spurgeon's Ethernet Web Site [Spurgeon 1999].

5.5.1 Ethernet Basics

Today Ethernet comes in many shapes and forms. An Ethernet LAN can have a "bus topology" or a "star topology." An Ethernet LAN can run over coaxial cable,

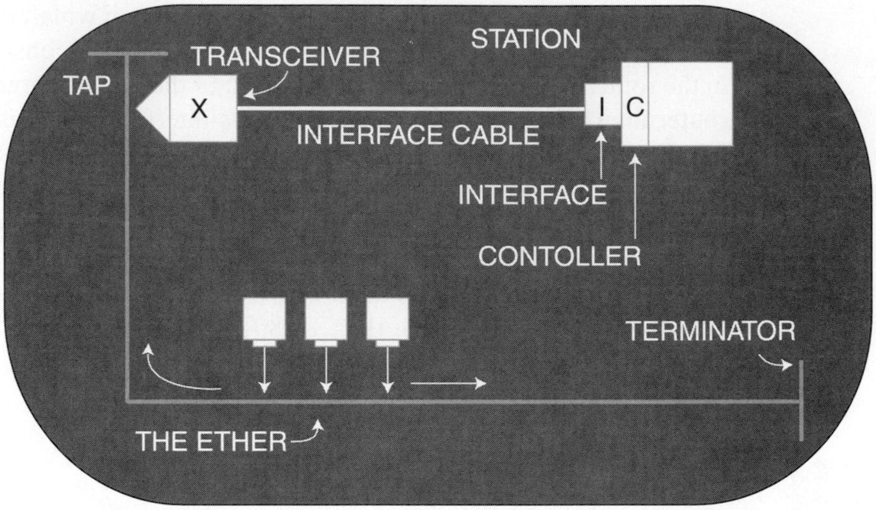

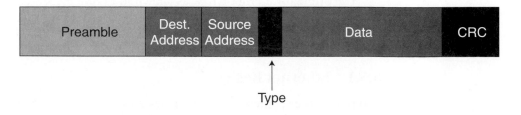

FIGURE 5.23   The original Metcalfe design led to the 10Base5 Ethernet standard, which included an interface cable that connected the Ethernet adapter (that is, interface) to an external transceiver.

twisted-pair copper wire, or fiber optics. Furthermore, Ethernet can transmit data at different rates, specifically, at 10 Mbps, 100 Mbps, and 1 Gbps. But even though Ethernet comes in many flavors, all of the Ethernet technologies share a few important characteristics. Before examining the different technologies, let's first take a look at the common characteristics.

Ethernet frame structure.   Given that there are many different Ethernet technologies on the market today, what do they have in common, what binds them together with a common name? First and foremost is the Ethernet frame structure. All of the Ethernet technologies—whether they use coaxial cable or copper wire, whether they run at 10 Mbps, 100 Mbps or 1 Gbps—use the same frame structure.

The Ethernet frame is shown in Figure 5.24. Once we understand the Ethernet frame, we will already know a lot about Ethernet. To put our discussion of the Ethernet frame in a tangible context, let us consider sending an IP datagram from one host to another host, with both hosts on the same Ethernet LAN. Let the sending

FIGURE 5.24   Ethernet frame structure

adapter, adapter A, have the physical address `AA-AA-AA-AA-AA-AA` and the receiving adapter, adapter B, have the physical address `BB-BB-BB-BB-BB-BB`. The sending adapter encapsulates the IP datagram within an Ethernet frame and passes the frame to the physical layer. The receiving adapter receives the frame from the physical layer, extracts the IP datagram, and passes the IP datagram to the network layer. In this context, let us now examine the six fields of the Ethernet frame:

- *Data Field (46 to 1500 bytes).* This field carries the IP datagram. The Maximum Transfer Unit (MTU) of Ethernet is 1500 bytes. This means that if the IP datagram exceeds 1500 bytes, then the host has to fragment the datagram, as discussed in Section 4.4. The minimum size of the data field is 46 bytes. This means that if the IP datagram is less than 46 bytes, the data field has to be "stuffed" to fill it out to 46 bytes. When stuffing is used, the data passed to the network layer contains the stuffing as well as an IP datagram. The network layer uses the length field in the IP datagram header to remove the stuffing.

- *Destination Address (6 bytes).* This field contains the LAN address of the destination adapter, namely, `BB-BB-BB-BB-BB-BB`. When adapter B receives an Ethernet frame with destination address *other* than its own physical address, `BB-BB-BB-BB-BB-BB`, or the LAN broadcast address, it discards the frame. Otherwise, it passes the contents of the data field to the network layer.

- *Source Address (6 bytes).* This field contains the LAN address of the adapter that transmits the frame onto the LAN, namely, `AA-AA-AA-AA-AA-AA`.

- *Type Field (two bytes).* The type field permits Ethernet to "multiplex" network-layer protocols. To understand this idea, we need to keep in mind that hosts can use other network-layer protocols besides IP. In fact, a given host may support multiple network layer protocols, and use different protocols for different applications. For this reason, when the Ethernet frame arrives at adapter B, adapter B needs to know to which network-layer protocol it should pass the contents of the data field. IP and other data-link layer protocols (for example, Novell IPX or AppleTalk) each have there own, standardized type number. Furthermore, the ARP protocol (discussed in the previous section) has its own type number. Note that the type field is analogous to the protocol field in the network-layer datagram and the port number fields in the transport-layer segment; all of these fields serve to glue a protocol at one layer to a protocol at the layer above.

- *Cyclic Redundancy Check (CRC) (4 bytes).* As discussed in Section 5.2, the purpose of the CRC field is to allow the receiving adapter, adapter B, to detect whether any errors have been introduced into the frame, that is, if bits in the frame have been toggled. Causes of bit errors include attenuation in signal strength and ambient electromagnetic energy that leaks into the Ethernet cables and interface cards. Error detection is performed as follows. When host A constructs the Ethernet frame, it calculates a CRC field, which is obtained from a mapping of the other bits in frame (except for the preamble bits). When host B receives the frame, it applies the same mapping to the frame and checks to see if the result of the mapping is equal to what is in the CRC field. This operation at the receiving host is called the **CRC check.** If the CRC check fails (that is, if the result of the mapping does not equal the contents of the CRC field), then host B knows that there is an error in the frame.

- *Preamble (8 bytes).* The Ethernet frame begins with an eight-byte preamble field. Each of the first seven bytes of the preamble is `10101010`; the last byte is `10101011`. The first seven bytes of the preamble serve to "wake up" the receiving adapters and to synchronize their clocks to that of the sender's clock. Why should the clocks be out of synchronization? Keep in mind that adapter A aims to transmit the frame at 10 Mbps, 100 Mbps, or 1 Gbps, depending on the type of Ethernet LAN. However, because nothing is absolutely perfect, adapter A will not transmit the frame at exactly the target rate; there will always be some *drift* from the target rate, a drift which is not known *a priori* by the other adapters on the LAN. A receiving adapter can lock onto adapter A's clock by simply locking onto the bits in the first seven bytes of the preamble. The last two bits of the eighth byte of the preamble (the first two consecutive 1s) alert adapter B that the "important stuff" is about to come. When host B sees the two consecutive 1s, it knows that the next six bytes are the destination address. An adapter can tell when a frame ends by simply detecting absence of current.

An unreliable connectionless service. All of the Ethernet technologies provide **connectionless service** to the network layer. That is to say, when adapter A wants to send a datagram to adapter B, adapter A encapsulates the datagram in an Ethernet frame and sends the frame into the LAN, without first "handshaking" with adapter B. This layer-2 connectionless service is analogous to IP's layer-3 datagram service and UDP's layer-4 connectionless service.

All the Ethernet technologies provide an **unreliable service** to the network layer. In particular when adapter B receives a frame from A, adapter B does not send an acknowledgment when a frame passes the CRC check (nor does it send a negative acknowledgment when a frame fails the CRC check). Adapter A hasn't the slightest idea whether a frame arrived correctly or incorrectly. When a frame fails the CRC check, adapter B simply discards the frame. This lack of reliable transport (at the link layer) helps to make Ethernet simple and cheap. But it also means that the stream of datagrams passed to the network layer can have gaps.

If there are gaps due to discarded Ethernet frames, does the application-layer protocol at host B see gaps as well? As we learned in Chapter 3, this solely depends on whether the application is using UDP or TCP. If the application is using UDP, then the application-layer protocol in host B will indeed suffer from gaps in the data. On the other hand, if the application is using TCP, then TCP in host B will not acknowledge the discarded data, causing TCP in host A to retransmit. Note that when TCP retransmits data, Ethernet retransmits the data as well. But we should keep in mind that Ethernet doesn't know that it is retransmitting. Ethernet thinks it is receiving a brand new datagram with brand new data, even though this datagram contains data that has already been transmitted at least once.

Baseband transmission and manchester encoding. Ethernet uses baseband transmission, that is, the adapter sends a digital signal directly into the broadcast channel. The interface card does not shift the signal into another frequency band, as do ADSL and cable modem systems. Ethernet also uses Manchester encoding, as shown in Figure 5.25. With Manchester encoding, each bit contains a transition; a 1 has a transition from up to down, whereas a zero has a transition from

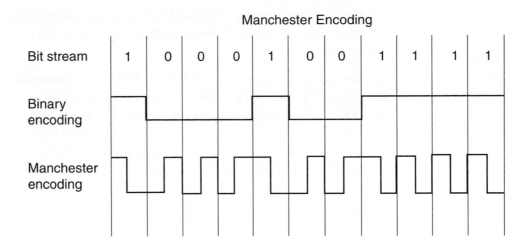

FIGURE 5.25   Manchester encoding

down to up. The reason for Manchester encoding is that the clocks in the sending and receiving adapters are not perfectly synchronized. By including a transition in the middle of each bit, the receiving host can synchronize its clock to that of the sending host. Once the receiving adapter's clock is synchronized, the receiver can delineate each bit and determine whether it is a one or zero. Manchester encoding is a physical layer operation rather than a link-layer operation; however, we have briefly described it here as it is used extensively in Ethernet.

5.5.2   CSMA/CD: Ethernet's Multiple Access Protocol

Nodes in an Ethernet LAN are interconnected by a broadcast channel, so that when an adapter transmits a frame, all the adapters on the LAN receive the frame. As we mentioned in Section 5.3, Ethernet uses a CSMA/CD multiple access algorithm. Summarizing our discussion from Section 5.3, recall that CSMA/CD employs the following mechanisms:

1. An adapter may begin to transmit at any time, that is, no slots are used.
2. An adapter never transmits a frame when it senses that some other adapter is transmitting, that is, it uses carrier-sensing.
3. A transmitting adapter aborts its transmission as soon as it detects that another adapter is also transmitting, that is, it uses collision detection.
4. Before attempting a retransmission, an adapter waits a random time that is typically small compared to a frame time.

These mechanisms give CSMA/CD much better performance than slotted ALOHA in a LAN environment. In fact, if the maximum propagation delay between stations is very small, the efficiency of CSMA/CD can approach 100%. But note that the second and third mechanisms listed above require each Ethernet adapter to be able to (1) sense when some other adapter is transmitting, and (2) detect a collision while it is transmitting. Ethernet adapters perform these two tasks by measuring voltage levels before and during transmission.

Each adapter runs the CSMA/CD protocol without explicit coordination with the other adapters on the Ethernet. Within a specific adapter, the CSMA/CD protocol works as follows:

1. The adapter obtains a network-layer PDU from its parent node, prepares an Ethernet frame, and puts the frame in an adapter buffer.

2. If the adapter senses that the channel is idle (that is, there is no signal energy from the channel entering the adapter), it starts to transmit the frame. If the adapter senses that the channel is busy, it waits until it senses no signal energy (plus a few hundred microseconds) and then starts to transmit the frame.

3. While transmitting, the adapter monitors for the presence of signal energy coming from other adapters. If the adapter transmits the entire frame without detecting signal energy from other adapters, the adapter is done with the frame.

4. If the adapter detects signal energy from other adapters while transmitting, it stops transmitting its frame and instead transmits a 48-bit jam signal.

5. After aborting (that is, transmitting the jam signal), the adapter enters an **exponential backoff** phase. Specifically, when transmitting a given frame, after experiencing the nth collision in a row for this frame, the adapter chooses a value for K at random from $\{0,1,2, \ldots, 2^m - 1\}$ where $m: = \min(n,10)$. The adapter then waits $K \cdot 512$ bit times and then returns to Step 2.

A few comments about the CSMA/CD protocol are certainly in order. The purpose of the jam signal is to make sure that all other transmitting adapters become aware of the collision. Let's look at an example. Suppose adapter A begins to transmit a frame, and just before A's signal reaches adapter B, adapter B begins to transmit. So B will have transmitted only a few bits when it aborts its transmission. These few bits will indeed propagate to A, but they may not constitute enough energy for A to detect the collision. To make sure that A detects the collision (so that it to can also abort), B transmits the 48-bit jam signal.

Next consider the exponential backoff algorithm. The first thing to notice here is that a bit time (that is, the time to transmit a single bit) is very short; for a 10 Mbps Ethernet, a bit time is 0.1 microseconds. Now let's look at an example. Suppose that an adapter attempts for the first time to transmit a frame, and while transmitting it detects a collision. The adapter then chooses $K = 0$ with probability 0.5 and chooses $K = 1$ with probability 0.5. If the adapter chooses $K = 0$, then it immediately jumps to Step 2 after transmitting the jam signal. If the adapter chooses $K = 1$, it waits 51.2 microseconds before returning to Step 2. After a second collision, K is chosen with equal probability from $\{0,1,2,3\}$. After three collisions, K is chosen with equal probability from $\{0,1,2,3,4,5,6,7\}$. After ten or more collisions, K is chosen with equal probability from $\{0,1,2, \ldots, 1023\}$. Thus the size of the sets from which K is chosen grows exponentially with the number of collisions (until $n = 10$); it is for this reason that Ethernet's backoff algorithm is referred to as "exponential backoff."

The Ethernet standard imposes limits on the distance between any two nodes. These limits ensure that if adapter A chooses a lower value of K than all the other adapters involved in a collision, then adapter A will be able to transmit its frame without experiencing a new collision. We will explore this property in more detail in the homework problems.

Why use exponential backoff? Why not, for example, select K from {0,1,2,3,4,5,6,7} after every collision? The reason is that when an adapter experiences its first collision, it has no idea how many adapters are involved in the collision. If there are only a small number of colliding adapters, it makes sense to choose K from a small set of small values. On the other hand, if many adapters are involved in the collision, it makes sense to choose K from a larger, more dispersed set of values (why?). By increasing the size of the set after each collision, the adapter appropriately adapts to these different scenarios.

We also note here that each time an adapter prepares a new frame for transmission, it runs the CSMA/CD algorithm presented above. In particular, the adapter does not take into account any collisions that may have occurred in the recent past. So it is possible that an adapter with a new frame will be able to immediately sneak in a successful transmission while several other adapters are in the exponential backoff state.

Ethernet efficiency. When only one node has a frame to send (which is typically the case), the node can transmit at the full rate of the Ethernet technology (either 10 Mbps, 100 Mbps, or 1 Gbps). However, if many nodes have frames to transmit, the effective transmission rate of the channel can be much less. We define the **efficiency of Ethernet** to be the long-run fraction of time during which frames are being transmitted on the channel without collisions when there is a large number of active nodes, with each node having a large number of frames to send. In order to present a closed-form approximation of the efficiency of Ethernet, let t_{prop} denote the maximum time it takes signal energy to propagate between any two adapters. Let t_{trans} be the time to transmit a maximum size Ethernet frame (approximately 1.2 msecs for a 10 Mbps Ethernet). A derivation of the efficiency of Ethernet is beyond the scope of this book (see [Lam 1980] and [Bertsekas 1991]). Here we simply state the following approximation:

$$\text{efficiency} = \frac{1}{1 + 5t_{prop}/t_{trans}}.$$

We see from this formula that as t_{prop} approaches 0, the efficiency approaches 1. This is intuitive because if the propagation delay is zero, colliding nodes will abort immediately without wasting the channel. Also, as t_{trans} becomes very large, efficiency approaches 1. This is also intuitive because when a frame grabs the channel, it will hold on to the channel for a very long time; thus the channel will be doing productive work most of the time.

5.5.3 Ethernet Technologies

The most common Ethernet technologies today are 10Base2, which uses thin coaxial cable in a bus topology and has a transmission rate of 10 Mbps; 10BaseT, which uses twisted-pair copper wire in a star topology and has a transmission rate of 10 Mbps; 100BaseT, which typically uses twisted-pair copper wire in a star topology and has a transmission rate of 100 Mbps; and Gigabit Ethernet, which uses both fiber and twisted-pair copper wire and transmits at a rate of 1 Gbps. These Ethernet technologies are standardized by the IEEE 802.3 working groups. For this reason, Ethernet is often referred to as an 802.3 LAN.

Before discussing specific Ethernet technologies, we need to discuss **repeaters,** which are commonly used in LANs as well as in wide-area transport. A repeater is a physical-layer device that acts on individual bits rather than on packets. It has two or more interfaces. When a bit, representing a zero or a one, arrives from one interface, the repeater simply recreates the bit, boosts its energy strength, and transmits the bit onto all the other interfaces. Repeaters are commonly used in LANs in order to extend their geographical range. When used with Ethernet, it is important to keep in mind that repeaters do not implement carrier sensing or any other part of CSMA/CD; a repeater repeats an incoming bit on all outgoing interfaces even if there is signal energy on some of the interfaces.

10Base2 Ethernet. 10Base2 is a very popular Ethernet technology. If you look at how your computer (at work or at school) is connected to the network, it is very possible you will see a 10Base2 connection. The "10" in 10Base2 stands for "10 Mbps"; the "2" stands for "200 meters," which is the approximate maximum distance between any two nodes without repeaters between them. (The actual maximum distance is 185 meters.) A 10Base2 Ethernet is shown in Figure 5.26.

We see from Figure 5.26 that 10Base2 uses a bus topology; that is, nodes are connected (through their adapters) in a linear fashion. The physical medium used to connect the nodes is **thin coaxial cable,** which is similar to what is used in cable TV, but with a thinner and lighter cable. When an adapter transmits a frame, the frame passes through a "tee connector"; two copies of the frame leave the tee connector, one copy going in one direction and one copy in the other direction. As the frames travel towards the terminators, they leave a copy at every node they pass. (More precisely, as a bit passes in front of a node, part of the energy of the bit leaks into the adapter.) When the frame finally reaches a terminator, it gets absorbed by the terminator. Note when an adapter transmits a frame, the frame is received by every other adapter on the Ethernet. Thus, 10Base2 is indeed a broadcast technology.

Suppose you want to connect a dozen PCs in your office using 10Base2 Ethernet. To do this, you would need to purchase 12 Ethernet cards with thin Ethernet ports; 12 BNC trees, which are small metallic objects that attach to the adapters (less than one dollar each); a dozen or so thin coax segments, 5–20 meters each; and two "terminators," which you put at the two ends of the bus. The cost of the whole network, including adapters, is likely to be less than the cost of a

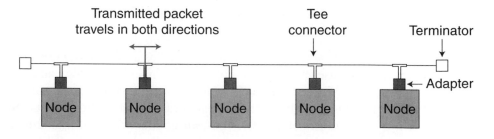

FIGURE 5.26   A 10Base2 Ethernet

single PC! Because 10Base2 is incredibly inexpensive, it is often referred to as "cheapnet."

Without a repeater, the maximum length of a 10Base2 bus is 185 meters. If the bus becomes any longer, then signal attenuation can cause the system to malfunction. Also, without a repeater, the maximum number of nodes is 30, as each node contributes to signal attenuation. Repeaters can be used to connect 10Base2 segments in a linear fashion, with each segment having up to 30 nodes and having a length up to 185 meters. Up to four repeaters can be included in a 10Base2 Ethernet, which creates up to five "segments." Thus a 10Base2 Ethernet bus can have a total length of 985 meters and support up to 150 nodes. Note that the CSMA/CD access protocol is completely oblivious to the repeaters; if any two of 150 nodes transmit at the same time, there will be a collision.

10BaseT and 100BaseT.   We discuss 10BaseT and100BaseT Ethernet together, as they are similar technologies. The most important difference between them is that 10BaseT transmits at 10 Mbps and 100BaseT Ethernet transmits at 100 Mbps. 100BaseT is also commonly called "fast Ethernet" and "100 Mbps Ethernet." 10BaseT and 100BaseT are also very popular Ethernet technologies; in fact, for new installations, 10BaseT and 100BaseT Ethernet are often today the technology of choice. Both 10BaseT and 100BaseT Ethernet use a star topology, as shown in Figure 5.27.

In the star topology there is a central device called a **hub** (also sometimes called a concentrator.) Each adapter on each node has a direct, point-to-point connection to the hub. This connection consists of two pairs of twisted-pair copper wire, one for transmitting and the other for receiving. At each end of the connection there is a connector that resembles the RJ-45 connector used for ordinary telephones. The "T" in 10BaseT and 100BaseT stands for "twisted pair." For both

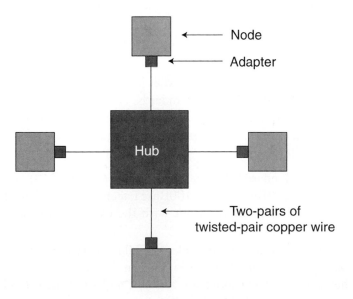

FIGURE 5.27   Star topology for 10BaseT and 100BaseT

10BaseT and 100BaseT, the maximum length of the connection between an adapter and the hub is 100 meters; the maximum length between any two nodes is 200 meters. As we will discuss in the next section, this maximum distance can be increased by using tiers of hubs, bridges, switches and fiber links.

In essence, a hub is a repeater: when it receives a bit from an adapter, it sends the bit to all the other adapters. In this manner, each adapter can (1) sense the channel to determine if it is idle, and (2) detect a collision while it is transmitting. But hubs are popular because they also provide network management features. For example, if an adapter malfunctions and continually sends Ethernet frames (a so-called "jabbering adapter"), then a 10Base2 Ethernet will become totally dysfunctional; none of the nodes will be able to communicate. But a 10BaseT network will continue to function, because the hub will detect the problem and internally disconnect the malfunctioning adapter. With this feature, the network administrator doesn't have to get out of bed and drive back to work in order to correct the problem for hackers who work late at night. Also, most hubs can gather information and report the information to a host that connects directly to the hub. This monitoring host provides a graphical interface that displays statistics and graphs, such as bandwidth usage, collision rates, average frame sizes, etc. Network administrators can use this information to not only debug and correct problems, but also to plan how the LAN should evolve in the future.

Many Ethernet adapters today are 10/100 Mbps adapters. This means that they can be used for both 10BaseT and 100BaseT Ethernets. 100BaseT, which typically uses category-5 twisted pair (a high-quality twisted pair with a lot of twists). Unlike the 10Base2 and 10BaseT, 100BaseT does not use Manchester encoding, but instead a more efficient encoding called 4B5B: every group of five clock periods is used to send 4 bits in order to provide enough transitions to allow clock synchronization.

We briefly mention at this point that both 10 Mbps and 100 Mbps Ethernet technologies can employ fiber links. A fiber link is often used to interconnect to hubs that are in different buildings on the same campus. Fiber is expensive because of cost of the cost of its connectors, but it has excellent noise immunity. The IEEE 802 standards permit a LAN to have a larger geographically reach when fiber is used to connect backbone nodes.

Gigabit Ethernet.   Gigabit Ethernet is an extension to the highly successful 10 Mbps and 100 Mbps Ethernet standards. Offering a raw data rate of 1,000 Mbps, Gigabit Ethernet maintains full compatibility with the huge installed base of Ethernet equipment. The standard for Gigabit Ethernet, referred to as IEEE 802.3z, does the following:

■ Uses the standard Ethernet frame format (Figure 5.19), and is backward compatible with 10BaseT and 100BaseT technologies. This allows for easy integration of Gigabit Ethernet with the existing installed base of Ethernet equipment.

■ Allows for point-to-point links as well as shared broadcast channels. Point-to-point links use switches (see Section 5.6) where as broadcast channels use hubs, as described above for 10BaseT and 100 BaseT. In Gigabit Ethernet jargon, hubs are called "buffered distributors."

- Uses CSMA/CD for shared broadcast channels. In order to have acceptable efficiency, the maximum distance between nodes must be severely restricted.

- Allows for full-duplex operation at 1,000 Mbps in both directions for point-to-point channels.

Like 10BaseT and 100BaseT, Gigabit Ethernet has a star topology with a hub or switch at its center. (Ethernet switches will be discussed in Section 5.6.) Gigabit Ethernet often serves as a backbone for interconnecting multiple 10 Mbps and 100 Mbps Ethernet LANs. Initially operating over optical fiber, Gigabit Ethernet will be able to use Category 5 UTP cabling.

The Gigabit Ethernet Alliance is an open forum whose purpose is to promote industry cooperation in the development of Gigabit Ethernet. Their Web site is rich source of information on Gigabit Ethernet [Alliance 1999]. The Interoperability Lab at the University of New Hampshire also maintains a nice page on Gigabit Ethernet [Interoperability 1999].

5.6   HUBS, BRIDGES, AND SWITCHES

Institutions—including companies, universities, and high schools—typically consist of many departments, with each department having and managing its own Ethernet LAN. Naturally, an institution will want its departments to interconnect their departmental LAN segments. In this section, we consider a number of different approaches in which LANs can be connected together. We'll cover three approaches—hubs, bridges, and switches—in the following subsections. All three of these approaches are in widespread use today.

5.6.1   Hubs

The simplest way to interconnect LANs is to use a hub. A hub is a simple device that takes an input (that is, a frame's bits) and retransmits the input on the hub's outgoing ports. Hubs are essentially repeaters, operating on bits. They are thus physical-layer devices. When a bit comes into a hub interface, the hub simply broadcasts the bit on all the other interfaces.

Figure 5.28 shows how three academic departments in a university might interconnect their LANs. In this figure, each of the three departments has a 10BaseT Ethernet that provides network access to the faculty, staff and students of the departments. Each host in a department has a point-to-point connection to the departmental hub. A fourth hub, called a **backbone hub,** has point-to-point connections to the departmental hubs, interconnecting the LANs of the three departments. The design shown in Figure 5.28 is a **multi-tier hub design** because the hubs are arranged in a hierarchy. It is also possible to create multi-tier designs with more than two tiers—for example, one tier for the departments, one tier for the schools within the university (for example, engineering school, business

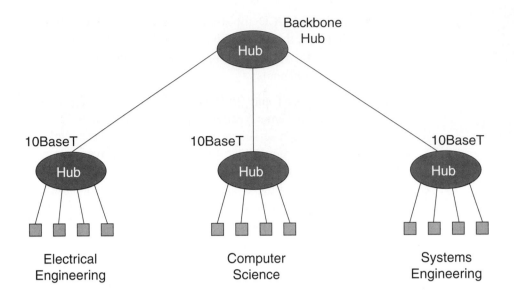

FIGURE 5.28 Three departmental Ethernets interconnected with a hub

school, etc.) and one tier at the highest university level. Multiple tiers can also be created out of 10Base2 (bus topology Ethernets) with repeaters.

In a multi-tier design, we refer to the entire interconnected network as a LAN, and we refer to each of the departmental portions of the LAN (that is, the departmental hub and the hosts that connect to the hub) as a **LAN segment.** It is important to note that all of the LAN segments in Figure 5.28 belong to the same **collision domain,** that is, whenever two or more nodes on the LAN segments transmit at the same time, there will be a collision and all of the transmitting nodes will enter exponential backoff.

Interconnecting departmental LANs with a backbone hub has many benefits. First and foremost, it provides inter-departmental communication to the hosts in the various departments. Second, it extends the maximum distance between any pair of nodes on the LAN. For example, with 10BaseT the maximum distance between a node and its hub is 100 meters; therefore, in a single LAN segment the maximum distance between any pair of nodes is 200 meters. By interconnecting the hubs, this maximum distance can be extended, since the distance between directly-connected hubs can also be 100 meters when using twisted pair (and more when using fiber). A third benefit is that the multi-tier design provides a degree of graceful degradation. Specifically, if any one of the departmental hubs starts to malfunction, the backbone hub can detect the problem and disconnect the departmental hub from the LAN; in this manner, the remaining departments can continue to operate and communicate while the faulty departmental hub gets repaired.

Although a backbone hub is a useful interconnection device, it has three serious limitations that hinder its deployment. First, and perhaps more important, when departmental LANs are interconnected with a hub (or a repeater), then the independent collision domains of the departments are transformed into one large and common collision domain. Let us explore this issue in the context of Figure 5.28. Before interconnecting the three departments, each departmental LAN had a maximum throughput of 10 Mbps, so that maximum aggregate throughput of the three LANs was 30 Mbps. But once the three LANs are interconnected with a hub, all of the hosts in the three departments belong to the same collision domain, and the maximum aggregate throughput is reduced to 10 Mbps.

A second limitation is that if the various departments use different Ethernet technologies, then it may not be possible to interconnect the departmental hubs with a backbone hub. For example, if some departments use 10BaseT and the remaining departments use 100BaseT, then it is impossible to interconnect all the departments without some frame buffering at the interconnection point; since hubs are essentially repeaters and do not buffer frames, they cannot interconnect LAN segments operating at different rates.

A third limitation is that each of the Ethernet technologies (10Base2, 10BaseT, 100BaseT, etc.) has restrictions on the maximum number of nodes that can be in a collision domain, the maximum distance between two hosts in a collision domain, and the maximum number of tiers that can be present in a multi-tier design. These restrictions constrain both the total number of hosts that connect to a multi-tier LAN as well as geographical reach of the multi-tier LAN.

5.6.2   Bridges

In contrast to hubs, which are physical-level devices, bridges operate on Ethernet frames and thus are layer-2 devices. In fact, bridges are full-fledged packet switches that forward and filter frames using the LAN destination addresses. When a frame comes into a bridge interface, the bridge does not just copy the frame onto all of the other interfaces. Instead, the bridge examines the destination address of the frame and attempts to forward the frame on the interface that leads to the destination.

Figure 5.29 shows how the three academic departments of our previous example might be interconnected with a bridge. The three numbers next to the bridge are the interface numbers for the three bridge interfaces. When the departments are interconnected by a bridge, as in Figure 5.29, we again refer to the entire interconnected network as a LAN, and we again refer to each of the departmental portions of the network as LAN segments. But in contrast to the multi-tier hub design in Figure 5.28, each LAN segment is now an isolated collision domain.

Bridges can overcome many of the problems that plague hubs. First, bridges permit inter-departmental communication while preserving isolated collision domains for each of the departments. Second, bridges can interconnect different LAN technologies, including 10 Mbps and 100 Mbps Ethernets. Third, there is no limit to how big a LAN can be when bridges are used to interconnect LAN segments: in theory, using bridges, it is possible to build a LAN that spans the entire globe.

Bridge forwarding and filtering.   **Filtering** is the ability to determine whether a frame should be forwarded to some interface or should just be dropped. When the frame should be forwarded, **forwarding** is the ability to determine which of

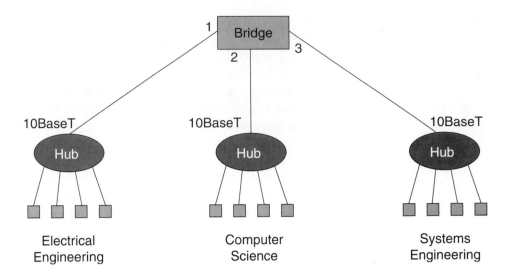

FIGURE 5.29 Three departmental LANs interconnected with a bridge

the interfaces the frame should be directed to. Bridge filtering and forwarding are done with a **bridge table.** For each node on the LAN, the bridge table contains (1) the LAN address of the node, (2) the bridge interface that leads towards the node, (3) and the time at which the entry for the node was placed in the table. An example bridge table for the LAN in Figure 5.29 is shown in Figure 5.30. This description of frame forwarding may sound similar to our discussion of datagram forwarding in Chapter 4. We note here that the addressees used by bridges are physical addresses (not network addresses). We will also see shortly that a bridge table is constructed in a very different manner than routing tables.

To understand how bridge filtering and forwarding works, suppose a frame with destination address DD-DD-DD-DD-DD-DD arrives to the bridge on interface *x*. The bridge indexes its table with the LAN address DD-DD-DD-DD-DD-DD and finds the corresponding interface *y*.

- If *x* equals *y*, then the frame is coming from a LAN segment that contains adapter DD-DD-DD-DD-DD-DD. There being no need to forward the frame to any of the other interfaces, the bridge performs the filtering function by discarding the frame.

Address	Interface	Time
62-FE-F7-11-89-A3	1	9:32
7C-BA-B2-B4-91-10	3	9:36
.....	.....	.....

FIGURE 5.30 Portion of a bridge table for the LAN in Figure 5.29

■ If x does not equal y, then the frame needs to be routed to the LAN segment attached to interface y. The bridge performs its forwarding function by putting the frame in an output buffer that precedes interface y.

These simple rules allow a bridge to preserve separate collision domains for each of the different LAN segments connected to its interfaces. The rules also allow the nodes on different LAN segments to communicate.

Let's walk through these rules for the network in Figures 5.29 and its bridge table in Figure 5.30. Suppose that a frame with destination address `62-FE-F7-11-89-A3` arrives to the bridge from interface 1. The bridge examines its table and sees that the destination is on the LAN segment connected to interface 1 (that is, the Electrical Engineering LAN). This means that the frame has already been broadcast on the LAN segment that contains the destination. The bridge therefore filters (that is, discards) the frame. Now suppose a frame with the same destination address arrives from interface 2. The bridge again examines its table and sees that the destination is the direction of interface 1; it therefore forwards the frame to the output buffer preceding interface 1. It should be clear from this example that as long as the bridge table is complete and accurate, the bridge isolates the departmental collision domains while permitting the departments to communicate.

Recall that when a hub (or a repeater) forwards a frame onto a link, it just sends the bits onto the link without bothering to sense whether another transmission is currently taking place on the link. In contrast, when a bridge wants to forward a frame onto a link, it runs the CSMA/CD algorithm discussed in Section 5.3. In particular, the bridge refrains from transmitting if it senses that some other node on the LAN segment is transmitting; furthermore, the bridge uses exponential backoff when one of its transmissions results in a collision. Thus bridge interfaces behave very much like node adapters. But technically speaking, they are *not* node adapters because neither a bridge nor its interfaces have LAN addresses. Recall that a node adapter always inserts its LAN address into the source address of every frame it transmits. This statement is true for router adapters as well as host adapters. A bridge, on the other hand, does not change the source address of the frame.

One significant feature of bridges is that they can be used to combine Ethernet segments using different Ethernet technologies. For example, if in Figure 5.29, Electrical Engineering has a 10Base2 Ethernet, Computer Science has a 100BaseT Ethernet, and Systems Engineering has a 10BaseT Ethernet, then a bridge can be purchased that can interconnect the three LANs. With Gigabit Ethernet bridges, it is possible to have an additional 1 Gbps connection to a router, which in turn connects to a larger university network. As we mentioned earlier, this feature of being able to interconnect different link rates is not available with hubs.

Also, when bridges are used as interconnection devices, there is no theoretical limit to the geographical reach of a LAN. In theory, we can build a LAN that spans the globe by interconnecting hubs in a long, linear topology, with each pair of neighboring hubs interconnected by a bridge. Because in this design each of the hubs has its own collision domain, there is no limit on how long the LAN can be. We shall see shortly, however, that it is undesirable to build very large networks exclusively using bridges as interconnection devices—large networks need routers as well.

Self-learning.   A bridge has the property of building its table automatically, dynamically, and autonomously—without any intervention from a network administrator or from a configuration protocol. In other words, bridges are **self-learning.** This is accomplished as follows.

1. The bridge table is initially empty.

2. When a frame arrives on one of the interfaces and the frame's destination address is not in the table, then the bridge forwards copies of the frame to the output buffers of all of the other interfaces. (At each of these other interfaces, the frame accesses the LAN segment using CSMA/CD.)

3. For each frame received, the bridge stores in its table (1) the LAN address in the frame's *source address field,* (2) the interface from which the frame arrived, (3) the current time. In this manner the bridge records in its table the LAN segment on which the sending node resides. If every node in the LAN eventually sends a frame, then every node will eventually get recorded in the table.

4. When a frame arrives on one of the interfaces and the frame's destination address is in the table, then the bridge forwards the frame to the appropriate interface.

5. The bridge deletes an address in the table if no frames are received with that address as the source address after a period of time (the *aging time*). In this manner, if a PC is replaced by another PC (with a different adapter), the LAN address of the original PC will eventually be purged from the bridge table.

Let's walk through the self-learning property for the network in Figures 5.29 and its corresponding bridge table in Figure 5.30. Suppose at time 9:39 a frame with source address 01-12-23-34-45-56 arrives from interface 2. Suppose that this address is not in the bridge table. Then the bridge appends a new entry in the table, as shown in Figure 5.31.

Continuing with this same example, suppose that the aging time for this bridge is 60 minutes and no frames with source address 62-FE-F7-11-89-A3 arrive to the bridge between 9:32 and 10:32. Then at time 10:32, the bridge removes this address from its table.

Bridges are **plug and play devices** because they require absolutely no intervention from a network administrator or user. When a network administrator wants to

Address	Interface	Time
01-12-23-34-45-56	2	9:39
62-FE-F7-11-89-A3	1	9:32
7C-BA-B2-B4-91-10	3	9:36
.....	.....	.....

FIGURE 5.31 Bridge learns about the location of the adapter with address 01-12-23-34-45-56

install a bridge, it does no more than connect the LAN segments to the bridge inter-faces. The administrator does not have to configure the bridge tables at the time of installation or when a host is removed from one of the LAN segments. Because bridges are plug and play, they are also referred to as **transparent bridges.**

Spanning tree.   One of the problems with a pure hierarchical design for inter-connected LAN segments is that if a hub or a bridge near the top of the hierarchy fails, then much (if not all) of the interconnected LAN will go down. For this rea-son it is desirable to build networks with multiple paths between LAN segments. An example of such a network is shown in Figure 5.32.

Multiple redundant paths between LAN segments (such as departmental LANs) can greatly improve fault tolerance. But, unfortunately, multiple paths have a serious side effect—frames cycle and multiply within the interconnected LAN, thereby crashing the entire network [Perlman 1999]. To see this, suppose that the bridge tables in Figure 5.32 are empty, and a host in Electrical Engineer-ing sends a frame to a host in Computer Science. When the frame arrives to the Electrical Engineering hub, the hub will generate two copies of the frame and send one copy to each of the two bridges. When a bridge receives the frame, it will generate two copies, send one copy to the Computer Science hub and the other copy to the Systems Engineering hub. Since both bridges do this, there will be four identical frames in the LAN. This multiplying of copies will continue indefi-nitely since the bridges do not know where the destination host resides. (To route the frame to the destination host in Computer Science, the destination host has to first generate a frame so that its address can be recorded in the bridge tables.) The number of copies of the original frame grows exponentially fast, crashing the entire network.

To prevent the cycling and multiplying of frames, bridges use a spanning tree protocol [Perlman 1999]. In the **spanning tree protocol,** bridges communicate

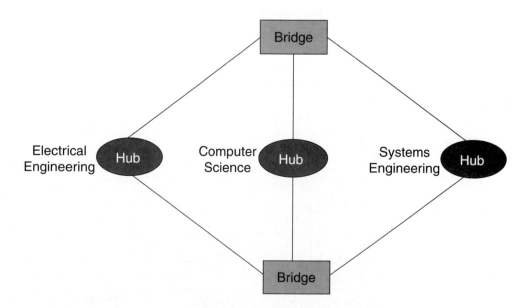

FIGURE 5.32   Interconnected LAN segments with redundant paths

with each other over the LANs in order to determine a spanning tree, that is, a subset of the original topology that has no loops. Once the bridges determine a spanning tree, the bridges disconnect appropriate interfaces in order to create the spanning tree out of the original topology. For example, in Figure 5.32, a spanning tree is created by having the top bridge disconnect its interface to Electrical Engineering and the bottom bridge disconnect its interface to Systems Engineering. With the interfaces disconnected and the loops removed, frames will no longer cycle and multiply. If, at some later time, one of links in the spanning tree fails, the bridges can reconnect the interfaces, run the spanning tree algorithm again, and determine a new set of interfaces that should be disconnected.

Bridges versus routers. As we learned in Chapter 4, routers are store-and-forward packet switches that forward packets using IP addresses. Although a bridge is also a store-and-forward packet switch, it is fundamentally different from a router in that it forwards packets using LAN addresses. Whereas a router is layer-3 packet switch, a bridge is a layer-2 packet switch.

Even though bridges and routers are fundamentally different, network administrators must often choose between them when installing an interconnection device. For example, for the network in Figure 5.29, the network administrator could have just as easily used a router instead of a bridge. Indeed, a router would have also kept the three collision domains separate while permitting interdepartmental communication. Given that both bridges and routers are candidates for interconnection devices, what are the pros and cons of the two approaches?

First consider the pros and cons of bridges. As mentioned above, bridges are plug and play, a property that is cherished by all the over-worked network administrators of the world. Bridges can also have relatively high packet filtering and forwarding rates—as shown in Figure 5.33, bridges only have to process packets up through layer 2, whereas routers have to process frames up through layer 3. On the other hand, the spanning tree protocol restricts the effective topology of a bridged network to a spanning tree. This means that all frames must flow along the spanning tree, even when there are more direct (but disconnected) paths between source and destination. The spanning tree restriction also concentrates the traffic on the spanning tree links when it could have otherwise been spread through all the links of the original topology. Furthermore, bridges do not offer any protection against broadcast storms—if one host goes haywire and transmits

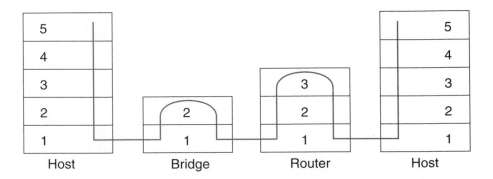

FIGURE 5.33 Packet processing and bridges, routers, and hosts

an endless stream of Ethernet broadcast packets, the bridges will forward all of the packets and the entire network will collapse.

Now consider the pros and cons of routers. Because IP addressing is hierarchical (and not flat as is LAN addressing), packets do not normally cycle through routers even when the network has redundant paths. (Actually, packets can cycle when router tables are misconfigured; but as we learned in Chapter 4, IP uses a special datagram header field to limit the cycling.) Thus, packets are not restricted to a spanning tree and can use the best path between source and destination. Because routers do not have the spanning tree restriction, routers have allowed the Internet to be built with a rich topology which includes, for example, multiple active links between Europe and North America. Another feature of routers is that they provide firewall protection against layer-2 broadcast storms. Perhaps the most significant drawback of routers is that they are not plug and play—they and the hosts that connect to them need their IP addresses to be configured. Also, routers often have a larger per-packet processing time than bridges, because they have to process up through the layer-3 fields. Finally, there are two different ways to pronounce the word "router," either as "rootor" or as "rowter," and people waste a lot of time arguing over the proper pronunciation [Perlman 1999].

Given that both bridges and routers have their pros and cons, when should an institutional network (for example, university campus network or a corporate campus network) use bridges, and when should it use routers? Typically, small networks consisting of a few hundred hosts have a few LAN segments. Bridges suffice for these small networks, as they localize traffic and increase aggregate throughput without requiring any configuration of IP addresses. But larger networks consisting of thousands of hosts typically include routers within the network (in addition to bridges). The routers provide a more robust isolation of traffic, control broadcast storms, and use more "intelligent" routes among the hosts in the network.

Connecting LAN segments with backbones.   Consider once again the problem of interconnecting the Ethernets in the three departments in Figure 5.29 with bridges. An alternative design is shown in Figure 5.34. This alternative design uses two two-interface bridges (that is, bridges with two interfaces), with one bridge connecting Electrical Engineering to Computer Science, and the other bridge connecting Computer Science to Systems Engineering. Although two-interface bridges are very popular due to their low cost and simplicity, the design in Figure 5.34 is *not recommended* for two reasons. First, if the Computer Science hub were to fail, then

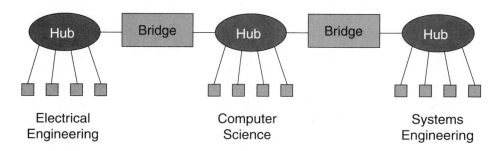

FIGURE 5.34   An example of an institutional LAN *without* a backbone

Electrical Engineering and Systems Engineering would no longer be able to communicate. Second, and more important, all the inter-departmental traffic between Electrical and Systems Engineering has to pass through Computer Science, which may overly burden the Computer Science LAN segment.

One important principle when designing an interconnected LAN is that the various LAN segments should be interconnected with a backbone. A **backbone** is a network that has direct connections to all the LAN segments. When a LAN has a backbone, then each pair of LAN segments can communicate without passing through a third-party LAN segment. The design shown in Figure 5.29 uses a three-interface bridge for a backbone. In the homework problems at the end of this chapter, we shall explore how to design backbone networks with two-interface bridges.

5.6.3   Switches

Up until the mid 1990s, three types of LAN interconnection devices were essentially available: hubs (and their cousins, repeaters), bridges, and routers. More recently yet another interconnection device became widely available, namely, Ethernet switches. Ethernet switches, often trumpeted by network equipment manufacturers with great fanfare, are in essence high-performance multi-interface bridges. As do bridges, they forward and filter frames using LAN destination addresses, and they automatically build routing tables using the source addresses in the traversing frames. The most important difference between a bridge and switch is that bridges usually have a small number of interfaces (that is, 2–4), whereas switches may have dozens of interfaces. A large number of interfaces generates a high aggregate forwarding rate through the switch fabric, therefore necessitating a high-performance design (especially for 100 Mbps and 1 Gbps interfaces).

Switches can be purchased with various combinations of 10 Mbps, 100 Mbps and 1 Gbps interfaces. For example, you can purchase switches with four 100 Mbps interfaces and twenty 10 Mbps interfaces; or switches with four 100 Mbps interfaces and one 1 Gbps interface. Of course, the more interfaces and the higher transmission rates of the various interfaces, the more you pay. Many switches also operate in a **full-duplex mode;** that is, they can send and receive frames at the same time over the same interface. With a full duplex switch (and corresponding full duplex Ethernet adapters in the hosts), host A can send a file to host B while that host B simultaneously sends to host A.

One of the advantages of having a switch with a large number of interfaces is that it facilitates direct connections between hosts and the switch. When a host has a full-duplex direct connection to a switch, it can transmit (and receive) frames at the full transmission rate of its adapter; in particular, the host adapter always senses an idle channel and never experiences a collision. When a host has a direct connection to a switch (rather than a shared LAN connection), the host is said to have **dedicated access.** In Figure 5.35, an Ethernet switch provides dedicated access to six hosts. This dedicated access allows A to send a file to A′ while that B is sending a file to B′ and C is sending a file to C′. If each host has a 10 Mbps adapter card, then the aggregate throughput during the three simultaneous file transfers is 30 Mbps. If A and A′ have 100 Mbps adapters and the remaining hosts have 10 Mbps adapters, then the aggregate throughput during the three simultaneous file transfers is 120 Mbps.

Figure 5.36 shows how an institution with several departments and several critical servers might deploy a combination of hubs, Ethernet switches, and routers. In

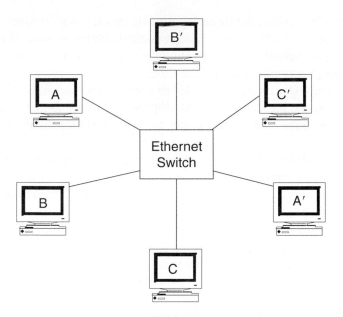

FIGURE 5.35   An Ethernet switch providing dedicated Ethernet access to six hosts

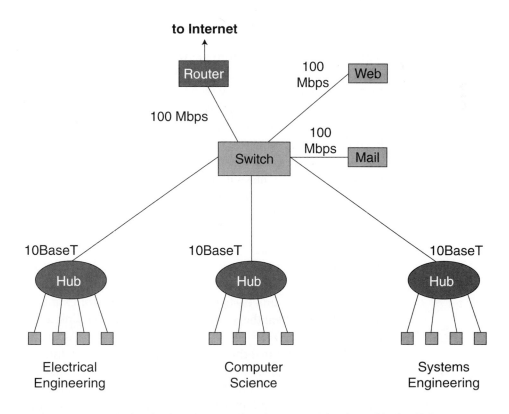

FIGURE 5.36   An institutional network using a combination of hubs, Ethernet switches, and a router

Figure 5.36, each of the three departments has its own 10 Mbps Ethernet segment with its own hub. Because each departmental hub has a connection to the switch, all intra-departmental traffic is confined to the Ethernet segment of the department (assuming the routing tables in the Ethernet switch are complete). The Web and mail servers each have dedicated 100 Mbps access to the switch. Finally, a router, leading to the Internet, has dedicated 100 Mbps access to the switch. Note that this switch has at least three 10 Mbps interfaces and three 100 Mbps interfaces.

Cut-through switching. In addition to large numbers of interfaces, support for multitudes of physical media types and transmission rates, and enticing network management features, Ethernet switch manufacturers often tout that their switches use **cut-through switching** rather than store-and-forward packet switching, used by routers and bridges. The difference between store-and-forward and cut-through switching is subtle. To understand this difference consider a packet that is being forwarded through a packet switch (that is, a router, a bridge, or an Ethernet switch). The packet arrives to the switch on a *inbound link* and leaves the switch on a *outbound link*. When the packet arrives, there may or may not be other packets in the outbound link's output buffer. When there are packets in the output buffer, there is absolutely no difference between store-and-forward and cut-through switching. The two switching techniques only differ when the output buffer is empty.

Recall from Chapter 1, when a packet is forwarded through a store-and-forward packet switch, the packet is first gathered and stored in its entirety before the switch begins to transmit it on the outbound link. In the case when the output buffer becomes empty before the whole packet has arrived to the switch, this gathering generates a store-and-forward delay at the switch, a delay which contributes to the total end-to-end delay (see Chapter 1). An upper bound on this delay is L/R, where L is the length of the packet and R is transmission rate of the *inbound* link. Note that a packet only incurs a store-and-forward delay if the output buffer becomes empty before the entire packet arrives to the switch.

With cut-through switching, if the buffer becomes empty before the entire packct has arrived, the switch can start to transmit the front of the packet while the back of the packet continues to arrive. Of course, before transmitting the packet on the outbound link, the portion of the packet that contains the destination address must first arrive. (This small delay is inevitable for all types of switching, as the switch must determine the appropriate outbound link.) In summary, with cut-through switching, a packet does not have to be fully "stored" before it is forwarded; instead the packet is forwarded through the switch when the output link is free. If the output link is shared with other hosts (for example, the output link connects to a hub), then the switch must also sense the link as idle before it can "cut-through" a packet.

To shed some insight on the difference between store-and-forward and cut-through switching, let us recall the caravan analogy introduced in Section 1.6. In this analogy, there is a highway with occasional toll booths, with each toll booth having a single attendant. On the highway there is a caravan of 10 cars traveling together, each at the same constant speed. The cars in the caravan are the only cars on the highway. Each toll booth services the cars at a constant rate, so that when the cars leave the toll booth they are equally spaced apart. As before, we can think

Table 5.1 Comparison of the typical features of popular interconnection devices

	hubs	bridges	routers	Ethernet switches
traffic isolation	*no*	*yes*	*yes*	*yes*
plug and play	*yes*	*yes*	*no*	*yes*
optimal routing	*no*	*no*	*yes*	*no*
cut-through	*yes*	*no*	*no*	*yes*

of the caravan as being a packet, each car in the caravan as being a bit, and the toll booth service rate as the transmission rate of a link. Consider now what the cars in the caravan do when they arrive to a toll booth. If each car proceeds directly to the toll booth upon arrival, then the toll booth is a "cut-through toll booth." If, on the other hand, each car waits at the entrance until all the remaining cars in the caravan arrive, then the toll booth is a "store-and-forward toll booth." The store-and-forward toll booth clearly delays the caravan more than the cut-through toll booth.

A cut-through switch can reduce a packet's end-to-end delay, but by how much? As we mentioned above, the maximum store-and-forward delay is L/R, where L is the packet size and R is the rate of the inbound link. The maximum delay is approximately 1.2 msec for 10 Mbps Ethernet and 0.12 msec for 100 Mbps Ethernet (corresponding to a maximum size Ethernet packet). Thus, a cut-through switch only reduces the delay by 0.12 to 0.2 msec, and this reduction only occurs when the outbound link is lightly loaded. How significant is this delay? Probably not very much in most practical applications, so you may want to think about selling the family house before investing in the cut-through feature.

We have learned in this section that hubs, bridges, routers, and switches can all be used as an interconnection device for hosts and LAN segments. Table 5.1 provides a summary of the features of each of these interconnection devices. The Cisco Web site provides numerous comparisons of the different interconnection technologies [Cisco LAN Switches 1999].

5.7 IEEE 802.11 LANs

In Section 5.5, we examined the dominant wired LAN protocol—Ethernet. In the previous section we examined how LAN segments can be connected together via hubs, bridges, and switches to form larger LANs. In this section we examine a LAN standard (belonging to the same IEEE 802 family as Ethernet) that is being increasingly deployed for untethered (wireless) LAN communication. The IEEE 802.11 standard [Brenner 1997, Crow 1997, IEEE 802.11 1999] defines the physical layer and media access control (MAC) layer for a wireless local area network. The standard defines three different physical layers for the 802.11 wireless LAN, each operating in a different frequency range and at rates of 1 Mbps and 2 Mbps.

In this section we focus on the architecture of 802.11 LANs and their media access protocols. We'll see that although it belongs to the same standard family as Ethernet, it has a significantly different architecture and media access protocol.

5.7.1 802.11 LAN Architecture

Figure 5.37 illustrates the principal components of the 802.11 wireless LAN architecture. The fundamental building block of the 802.11 architecture is the cell, known as the **basic service set (BSS)** in 802.11 parlance. A BSS typically contains one or more wireless stations and a central base station, known as an **access point (AP)** in 802.11 terminology. The stations, which may be either fixed or mobile, and the central base station communicate among themselves using the IEEE 802.11 wireless MAC protocol. Multiple APs may be connected together (for example, using a wired Ethernet or another wireless channel) to form a so-called **distribution system (DS).** The DS appears to upper level protocols (for example, IP) as a single 802 network, in much the same way that a bridged, wired 802.3 Ethernet network appears as a single 802 network to the upper layer protocols.

Figure 5.38 shows that IEEE 802.11 stations can also group themselves together to form an **ad hoc network**—a network with no central control and with no connections to the "outside world." Here, the network is formed "on the fly," simply because there happens to be mobile devices that have found themselves in proximity to each other, that have a need to communication, and that find no pre-existing network infrastructure (for example, a pre-existing 802.11 BSS with an AP) in the location. An ad hoc network might be formed, for example, when people with laptops meet together (for example, in a conference room, a train, or a car) and want to exchange data in the absence of a centralized

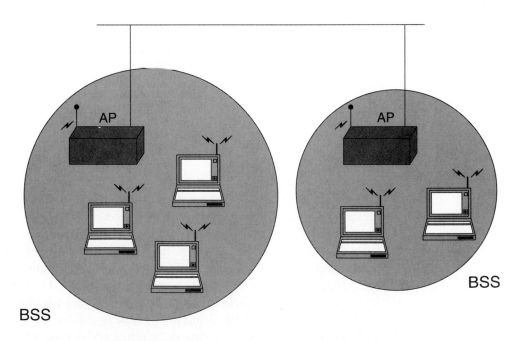

FIGURE 5.37 IEEE 802.11 LAN architecture

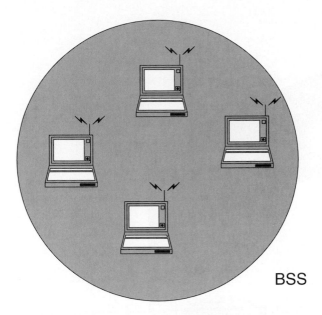

BSS

FIGURE 5.38   An IEEE 802.11 *ad hoc* network

AP. There has been a tremendous recent increase in interest in *ad hoc* networking, as communicating portable devices continue to proliferate. Within the IETF, activity in ad hoc networking is centered around the mobile ad hoc networks (manet) working group.

5.7.2   802.11 media access protocols

Just as in a wired 802.3 Ethernet network, stations in an IEEE 802.11 wireless LAN must coordinate their access and use of the shared communication media (in this case the radio frequency). Once again, this is the job of the Media Access Control (MAC) protocol. The IEEE 802.11 MAC protocol is a carrier sense multiple access protocol with collision avoidance (**CSMA/CA**). Recall from our study of Ethernet in Section 5.5 that a CSMA protocol first senses the channel to determine if the channel is "busy" with the transmission of a frame from some other station. In the 802.11 specification, the physical layer monitors the energy level on the radio frequency to determine whether or not another station is transmitting and provides this carrier sensing information to the MAC protocol. If the channel is sensed idle for an amount of time equal to or greater than the Distributed Inter Frame Space (DIFS), a station is then allowed to transmit. As with any random access protocol, this frame will be successfully received at the destination station if no other station's transmission has interfered with the frame's transmission.

When a receiving station has correctly and completely received a frame for which it was the addressed recipient, it waits a short period of time (known as the Short Inter Frame Spacing—SIFS) and then sends an explicit acknowledgment frame back to the sender. This data link layer acknowledgment lets the sender know that the receiver has indeed correctly received the sender's data frame. We will see shortly that this explicit acknowledgment is needed because, unlike the

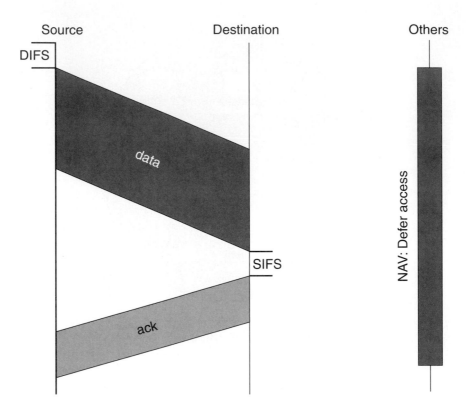

FIGURE 5.39   Data transmission and acknowledgment in IEEE 802.11

case of wired Ethernet, a wireless sender can not itself determine whether or not its frame transmission was successfully received at the destination. The transmission of a frame by a sending station and its subsequent acknowledgment by the destination station is shown in Figure 5.39.

Figure 5.39 illustrates the case when thc sender senses the channel to be idle. What happens if the sender senses the channel busy? In this case, the station performs a backoff procedure that is similar to that of Ethernet. More specifically, a station that senses the channel busy will defer its access until the channel is later sensed idle. Once the channel is sensed idle for an amount of time equal to DIFS, the station then computes an *additional* random backoff time and counts down this time as the channel is sensed idle. When the random backoff timer reaches zero, the station transmits its frame. As in the case of Ethernet, the random backoff timer serves to avoid having multiple stations immediately begin transmission (and thus collide) after a DIFS idle period. As in the case of Ethernet, the interval over which the backoff timer randomizes is doubled each time a transmitted frame experiences a collision.

We noted above that unlike the 802.3 Ethernet protocol, the wireless 802.11 MAC protocol does *not* implement collision detection. There are a couple of reasons for this:

- The ability to detect collisions requires the ability to both send (one's own signal) and receive (to determine if another station's transmissions is interfering with one's own transmission) at the same time. This can be costly.

- More importantly, even if one had collision detection and sensed no collision when sending, a collision could still occur at the receiver.

This situation results from the particular characteristics of the wireless channel. Suppose that station A is transmitting to station B. Suppose also that station C is transmitting to station B. With the so-called **hidden terminal problem,** physical obstructions in the environment (for example a mountain) may prevent A and C from hearing each others transmissions, even though A's and C's transmissions are indeed interfering at the destination, B. This is shown in Figure 5.40(a). A second scenario that results in undetectable collisions at the receiver results from the **fading** of a signal's strength as propagates through the wireless medium. Figure 5.40(b) illustrates the case where A and C are placed such that their signal strengths are not strong enough for them to detect each others' transmissions, and yet their transmissions are strong enough to have interfered with each other at station B.

Given these difficulties with detecting collisions at a wireless receiver, the designers of IEEE 802.11 developed an access protocol which aimed to avoid collisions (hence the name CSMA/CA), rather than detect and recover from collisions (CSMA/CD). First, the IEEE 802.11 frame contains a duration field in which the sending station explicitly indicates the length of time that its frame will be transmitting on the channel. This value allows other stations to determine the minimum amount of time (the so-called network allocation vector, NAV) for which they should defer their access, as shown in Figure 5.39.

The IEEE 802.11 protocol can also use a short Request To Send (RTS) control frame and a short Clear To Send (CTS) frame to *reserve* access to the channel. When a sender wants to send a frame, it can first send a RTS frame to the receiver, indicating the duration of the data packet and the ACK packet. A receiver that receives an RTS frame responds with a CTS frame, giving the sender explicit permission to send. All other stations hearing the RTS or CTS then know about the pending data transmission and can avoid interfering with those transmissions. The RTS, CTS, DATA, and ACK frames are shown in Figure 5.41. An IEEE 802.11

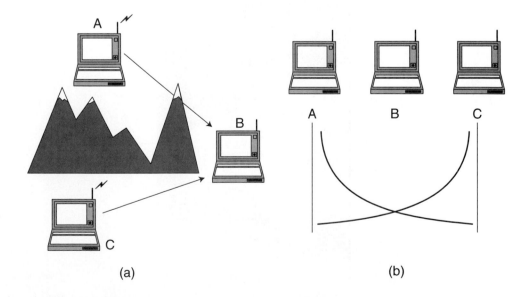

(a)   (b)

FIGURE 5.40   Hidden terminal problem (a) and fading (b)

sender can operate either using the RTS/CTS control frames, as shown in Figure 5.41, or can simply send its data without first using the RTS control frame, as shown in Figure 5.39.

The use of the RTS and CTS frames helps avoid collisions in three important ways:

▪ Because the receiver's transmitted CTS frame will be heard by all stations within the receiver's vicinity, the CTS frame helps avoid both the hidden station problem and the fading problem.

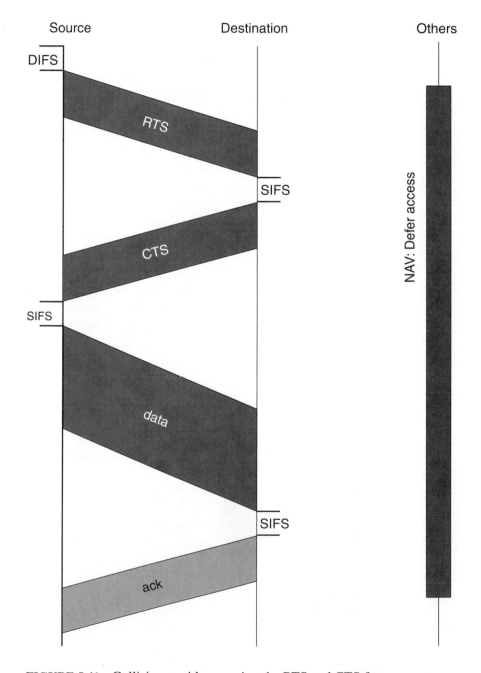

FIGURE 5.41   Collision avoidance using the RTS and CTS frames

- Because the RTS and CTS frames are short, a collision involving an RTS or CTS frame will only last for the duration of the whole RTS or CTS frame. Note that when the RTS and CTS frames are correctly transmitted, there should be no collisions involving the subsequent DATA and ACK frames.

In our discussion above, we have only highlighted some of the key aspects of the 802.11 protocol. Additional protocol capabilities such as time synchronization, power management, joining and leaving a network (that is, roaming stations) are covered in the full IEEE 802.11 standard. See [Brenner 1997, Crow 1997, IEEE 802.11 1999] for details.

5.8   PPP: THE POINT-TO-POINT PROTOCOL

Most of our discussion of data link protocols thus far has focused on protocols for broadcast channels. In this section we cover a data link protocol for point-to-point links—PPP, the Point-to-Point protocol. Because PPP is typically the protocol of choice for a dialup link from residential hosts, it is undoubtedly one of the most widely-deployed data link protocols today. The other important data link protocol in use today is the HDLC (High Level Data Link Control) protocol; see [Spragins 1991] for a discussion of HDLC. Our discussion here of the simpler PPP protocol will allow us to explore many of the most important features of point-to-point data link protocol.

As its name implies, the Point-to-Point Protocol (PPP) [RFC 1661, RFC 2153] is a data link layer protocol that operates over a **point-to-point link**—a link connecting two communicating link-level peers, one on each end of the link. The point-to-point link over which PPP operates might be a serial dialup telephone line (for example, a 56K modem connection), a SONET/SDH link, an X.25 connection, or over an ISDN circuit. An noted above, PPP has become the protocol of choice for connecting home users to their ISP's over a dialup connection.

Before diving into the details of PPP, it is instructive to examine the original requirements that the IETF placed on the design of PPP [RFC 1547]:

- *Packet framing.* The PPP protocol data link layer sender must be able to take a network-level packet and frame (*a.k.a.* encapsulate) it within the PPP data link layer frame such that the receiver will be able to identify the start and end of both the data link frame, and the network layer packet within the frame.

- *Transparency.* The PPP protocol must not place any constraints on data appearing on the network layer packet (headers or data). Thus, for example, the PPP protocol can not forbid the use of certain bit patterns in the network layer packet. We'll return to this issue shortly in our discussion of byte stuffing.

- *Multiple network layer protocols.* The PPP protocol must be able to support multiple network layer protocols (for example, IP and DECnet) running over the *same* physical link at the *same* time. Just as the IP protocol is required to multiplex different transport level protocols (for example, TCP and UDP) over a single end-to-end connection, so too must PPP be able to multiplex different network layer protocols over a single point-to-point connection. This requirement means that at a minimum, PPP will likely require a "protocol type" field or some similar mechanism so the receiving side PPP can demultiplex a received frame up to the appropriate network layer protocol.

- *Multiple types of links.* In addition to being able to carry multiple higher level protocols, PPP must also be able to operate over a wide variety of link types, including links that are either serial (transmitting a bit at a time in a given direction) or parallel (transmitting bits in parallel), synchronous (transmitting a clock signal along with the data bits) or asynchronous, low speed or high speed, electrical or optical.

- *Error detection.* A PPP receiver must be able to detect bit errors in the received frame.

- *Connection liveness.* PPP must be able to detect a failure at the link level (for example, the inability to transfer data from the sending side of the link to the receiving side of this link) and signal this error condition to the network layer.

- *Network Layer Address Negotiation.* PPP must provide a mechanism for the communicating network layers (for example, IP) to learn or configure each other's network layer address.

- *Simplicity.* PPP was required to meet a number of additional requirements beyond the seven listed above. On top of all of these requirements, first and foremost among all of the PPP requirements is that of "simplicity." RFC 1547 states "the watchword for a point-to-point protocol should be simplicity." A tall order indeed given all of the other requirements placed on the design of PPP! More than 50 RFC's now define the various aspects of this "simple" protocol.

While it may appear that many requirements were placed on the design of PPP, the situation could actually have been much more difficult! The design specifications for PPP also explicitly note protocol functionality that PPP was *not* required to implement:

- *Error correction.* PPP is required to detect bit errors but is *not* required to correct them.

- *Flow control.* A PPP receiver is expected to be able to receive frames at the full rate of the underlying physical layer. If a higher layer can not receive packets at this full rate, it is then up to the higher layer to drop packets or throttle the sender at the higher layer. That is, rather than having the PPP sender throttle its own transmission rate, it is the responsibility of a higher level protocol to throttle the rate at which packets are delivered to PPP for sending.

- *Sequencing.* PPP is *not* required to deliver frames to the link receiver in the same order in which they were sent by the link sender. It is interesting to note that while this flexibility is compatible with the IP service model (which allows IP packets to be delivered end-to-end in any order), other network layer protocols which operate over PPP do require sequenced end-to-end packet delivery.

- *Multipoint links.* PPP need only operate over links that have a single sender and a single receiver. Other link layer protocols (for example, HDLC) can accommodate multiple receivers (for example, an Ethernet-like scenario) on a link.

Having now considered the design goals (and non-goals) for PPP, let us see how the design of PPP met these goals.

5.8.1   PPP Data Framing

Figure 5.42 shows a PPP data frame using HDLC-like framing [RFC 1662]. The PPP frame contains the following fields:

- *Flag field.* Every PPP frame begins and ends with a 1 byte flag field with a value of `01111110`.

- *Address field.* The only possible value for this field is `11111111`.

- *Control Field.* The only possible value of this field is `00000011`. Because both the address and control fields can currently take only a fixed value, one wonders why the fields are even defined in the first place. The PPP specification [RFC 1662] states that other values "may be defined at a later time," although none have been defined to date. Because these fields take fixed values, PPP allows the sender to simply not send the address and control bytes, thus saving two bytes of overhead in the PPP frame.

- *Protocol.* The protocol field tells the PPP receiver the upper layer protocol to which the received encapsulated data (that is, the contents of the PPP frame's info field) belongs. On receipt of a PPP frame, the PPP receiver will check the frame for correctness and then pass the encapsulated data on to the appropriate protocol. [RFC 1700] defines the 16-bit protocol codes used by PPP. Of interest to us is the IP protocol (that is, the data encapsulated in the PPP frame is an IP datagram) which has a value of 21 hexadecimal, other network layer protocols such as Appletalk (29) and DECnet (27), the PPP link control protocol (c021 hexadecimal) that we discuss in detail in the following section, and the IP Control Protocol (8021) which is called by PPP when a link is first activated in order to configure the IP-level connection between the two routers on each end of the link (see below).

- *Information.* This field contains the encapsulate packet (data) that is being sent by an upper layer protocol (for example, IP) over the PPP link. The default maximum length of the information field is 1500 bytes, although this can be changed when the link is first configured, as discussed below.

- *Checksum.* The checksum field is used to detect bit errors in a transmitted frame. It uses either a two or four byte HDLC-standard cyclic redundancy code.

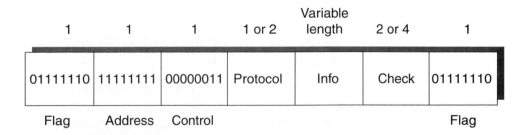

FIGURE 5.42   PPP data frame format

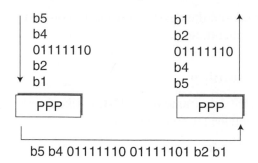

b5 b4 01111110 01111101 b2 b1

FIGURE 5.43 Byte stuffing

Byte stuffing. Before closing our discussion of PPP framing, let us consider a problem that arises when any protocol uses a specific bit pattern (flag field) to delineate the beginning or end of the frame: what happens if the flag pattern itself occurs elsewhere in the packet? For example, what happens if the flag field value of 01111110 appears in the information field? Will the receiver incorrectly detect the end of the PPP frame?

One way to solve this problem would be for PPP to forbid the upper layer protocol from sending data containing the flag field bit pattern. The PPP requirement of transparency discussed above obviates this possibility. An alternate solution, and the one taken in PPP and many other protocols, is to use a technique known as **byte stuffing.**

PPP defines a special control escape byte, 01111101. If the flag sequence, 01111110 appears anywhere in the frame, except in the flag field, PPP precedes that instance of the flag pattern with the control escape byte. That is, it "stuffs" (adds) a control escape byte into the transmitted data stream, before the 01111110, to indicate that the following 011111110 is *not* a flag value but is, in fact, actual data. A receiver that sees a 01111110 preceded by a 01111101 will, of course, remove the stuffed control escape to reconstruct the original data. Similarly, if the control escape byte bit pattern itself appears as actual data, it too must be preceded by a stuffed control escape byte. Thus, when the receiver see a single control escape byte by itself in the data stream, it knows that the byte was stuffed into the data stream. A pair of control escape bytes occurring back-to-back means that one instance of the control escape byte appears in the original data being sent. Figure 5.43 illustrates PPP byte stuffing. (Actually, PPP also XORs the data byte being escaped with 20 hexadecimal, a detail we omit here for simplicity.)

5.8.2 PPP Link Control Protocol (LCP) and Network Control Protocols

Thus far, we have seen how PPP frames the data being sent over the point-to-point link. But how does the link get initialized when a host or router on one end of the PPP link is first turned on? The initialization, maintenance, error reporting, and shutdown of a PPP link is accomplished using PPP's Link Control Protocol (LCP) and family of PPP network control protocols.

Before any data is exchanged over a PPP link, the two peers (one at each end of the PPP link) must first perform a considerable amount of work to configure the link, in much the same way that a TCP sender and receiver must perform a three-way handshake (see Section 3.4) to set the parameters of the TCP connection before TCP data segments are transmitted. Figure 5.44 illustrates the state transition diagram for the LCP protocol for configuring, maintaining, and terminating the PPP link.

The PPP link always begins and ends in the dead state. When an event such as a carrier detection or network administrator intervention indicates that a physical layer is present and ready to be used, PPP enters the link establishment state. In this state, one end of the link sends its desired link configuration options using an LCP `configure-request` frame (a PPP frame with the protocol field set to LCP and the PPP information field containing the specific configuration request). The other side then responds with a `configure-ack` frame (all options acceptable), a `configure-nak` frame (all options understood but not acceptable) or a `configure-reject` frame (options not recognizable or not acceptable for negotiation). LCP configuration options include a maximum frame size for the link, the specification of an authentication protocol (if any) to be used, and an option to skip the use of the address and control fields in the PPP frames.

Once the link has been established, link options negotiated, and the authentication (if any) performed, the two sides of the PPP link then exchange network-layer-specific network control packets with each other. If IP is running over the PPP link, the IP Control Protocol [RFC 1332] is used to configure the IP protocol modules at each end of the PPP link. IPCP packets are carried within a PPP frame (with a protocol field value of 8021), just as LCP packets are carried in a PPP frame. IPCP allows the two IP modules to exchange or configure their IP addresses and negotiate whether or not IP packets will be set in compressed form. Similar network control protocols are defined for other network layer protocols,

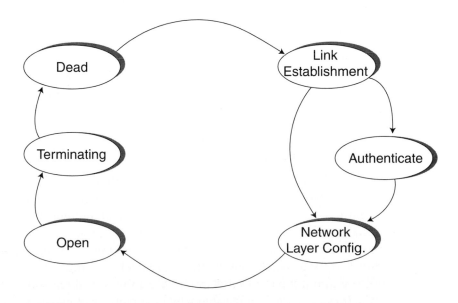

FIGURE 5.44   PPP Link Control Protocol

such as DECnet [RFC 1762] and AppleTalk [RFC 1378]. Once the network layer has been configured, PPP may then begin sending network-layer datagrams—the link is in the opened state and data has begun to flow across the PPP link. The LCP echo-request packet and echo-reply packet can be exchanged between the two PPP endpoints in order to check the status of the link.

The PPP link remains configured for communication until an LCP terminate-request packet is sent. If a terminate-request LCP packet is sent by one end of the PPP link and replied to with a terminate-ack LCP packet, the link then enters the dead state.

In summary, PPP is a data link layer protocol by which two communicating link-level peers, one on each end of a point-to-point link, exchange PPP frames containing network layer datagrams. The principal components of PPP are:

- *Framing.* A method for encapsulating data in a PPP frame, identifying the beginning and end of the frame, and detecting errors in the frame.
- *Link Control Protocol.* A protocol for initializing, maintaining, and taking down the PPP link.
- *Network control protocols.* A family of protocols, one for each upper layer network protocol, that allows the network layer modules to configure themselves before network-level datagrams begin flowing across the PPP link.

5.9   ATM

In Section 1.10 we briefly introduced ATM. In this section we cover ATM in more detail and discuss ATM's current role in the Internet. But before we begin, we list a few useful references. A nice tutorial on ATM is given in [LeBoudec 1992]. IP-over-ATM is discussed in detail in [Kercheval 1998].

Recall that ATM was standardized in 1990 by two standards bodies, the ATM Forum [ATM Forum] and the International Telecommunications Union [ITU]. Paralleling the development of the ATM standards, major companies throughout the world made significant investments in ATM research and development. These investments lead to a myriad of high-performing ATM technologies, including ATM switches that have throughputs of terabits per second. Because Internet backbone networks need to distribute traffic at very high (and exponentially growing) rates, many backbone ISPs currently make extensive use of ATM.

5.9.1   IP over ATM

Figure 5.45 shows such an ATM backbone with four entry/exit points for Internet IP traffic. Note that each entry/exit point is a router. An ATM backbone can span an entire continent and may have tens or even hundreds of ATM switches. Most ATM backbones have a permanent Virtual Channel (VC) between each pair of entry/exit points. (Recall that ATM uses the jargon "virtual channel" for "virtual circuit.") By using permanent VCs, ATM cells are routed from entry point to exit point without having to dynamically establish and tear-down VCs. Permanent VCs, however, are only feasible when the number of entry/exit points is relatively small. For n entry points, $n(n-1)$ permanent VCs are necessary.

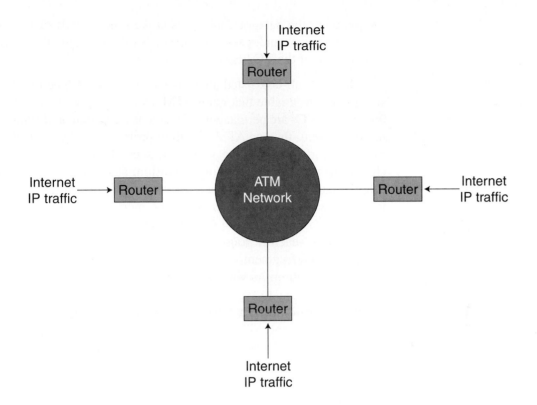

FIGURE 5.45   ATM network in the core of an Internet backbone

Each router interface that connects to the ATM network will have two addresses. The router interface will have an IP address, as usual, and the router will have an ATM address, which is essentially a LAN address (see Section 5.4).

Consider now an IP datagram that is to be moved across the backbone in Figure 5.45. Let us refer to the router at which the datagram enters the ATM network as the "entry router" and the router at which the datagram leaves the network as the "exit router." The entry router does the following:

1. Examines the destination address of the datagram.
2. Indexes its routing table and determines the IP address of the exit router (that is, the next router in the datagram's route).
3. To get the datagram to the exit router, the entry router views ATM as just another link-layer protocol. In particular, the entry router indexes an ATM ARP table with the IP address of the exit router and determines the ATM address of the exit router.
4. IP in the entry router then passes down to the link layer (that is, ATM) the datagram along with the ATM address of the exit router.

After these four steps have been completed, the job of moving the datagram to the exit router is out of the hands of IP and in the hands of ATM. ATM must now move the datagram to the ATM destination address obtained in Step 3 above. This task has two sub-tasks:

▪ Determine the VCI for the VC that leads to the ATM destination address.

- Segment the datagram into cells at the sending side of the VC (that is, at the entry router), and reassemble the cells into the original datagram at the receiving side of the VC (that is, at the exit router).

The first sub-task listed above is straightforward. The interface at the sending side maintains a table that maps ATM addresses to VCIs. Because we are assuming that the VCs are permanent, this table is up-to-date and static. (If the VCs were not permanent, then an ATM signaling protocol would be needed to dynamically establish and tear down the VCs.) The second task merits careful consideration. One approach is to use IP fragmentation, as discussed in Section 4.4. With IP fragmentation, the sending router would first fragment the original datagram into fragments, with each fragment being no more than 48 bytes, so that the fragment could fit into the payload of the ATM cell. But this fragmentation approach has a big problem—each IP fragment typically has 20 bytes of header, so that an ATM cell carrying a fragment would have 25 bytes of "overhead" and only 28 bytes of useful information. As we shall see in Section 5.8, the ATM standard provides a more efficient way to segment and reassemble a datagram.

Recall from Section 1.10 that ATM has three layers: the physical layer, the ATM layer, and the ATM adaptation layer. We now provide a brief introduction into these layers. We will then return to the issue just raised: How does ATM efficiently segment and reassemble IP datagrams that are sent across an ATM backbone?

5.9.2 ATM Physical Layer

The physical layer is concerned with sending an ATM cell over a single physical link. As shown in Table 5.2, the physical layer has two sublayers: the Physical Medium Dependent (PMD) Sublayer and the Transmission Convergence (TC) Sublayer.

The Physical Medium Dependent (PMD) Sublayer.   The PMD sublayer is at the very bottom of the ATM protocol stack. As the name implies, the PMD sublayer depends on the physical medium of the link; in particular, the sublayer is specified differently for different physical media (fiber, copper, etc.). As shown in the above chart, it specifies the medium itself. It is also responsible for generating

Table 5.2   The two sublayers of the physical layer, and their responsibilities

Sublayer	Responsibilities
Transmission Convergence (TC) Sublayer	Idle Cell Insertion Cell Delineation Transmission Frame Adaptation
Physical Medium Dependent (PMD) Sublayer	Physical Medium Bit voltages and timings Frame structure

and delineating bits. There are two classes of PMD sublayers: PMD sublayers which have a transmission frame structure (for example, T1, T3, SONET, or SDH) and PMD sublayers which do not have a transmission frame structure. If the PMD has a frame structure, then it is responsible for generating and delineating frames. (The terminology "frames" in this section is not to be confused with link-layer frames used in the earlier sections of this chapter. The transmission frame is a physical-layer mechanism for organizing the bits sent on a link.) The PMD sublayer does not recognize cells. Some possible PMD sublayers include:

1. SONET/SDH (Synchronous Optical Network/Synchronous Digital Hierarchy) over single-mode fiber. Like T1 and T3, SONET and SDH have frame structures which establish bit synchronization between the transmitter and receiver at the two ends of the link. There are several standardized rates, including:

    OC-1: 51.84 Mbps

    OC-3: 155.52 Mbps

    OC-12: 622.08 Mbps

2. T1/T3 frames over fiber, microwave, and copper.

3. Cell based with no frames. In this case, the clock at receiver is derived from a transmitted signal.

Transmission Convergence (TC) sublayer.   The ATM layer is specified independently of the physical layer; it has no concept of SONET, T1, or physical media. A sublayer is therefore needed (1) at the sending side of the link to accept ATM cells from the ATM layer and put the cells' bits on the physical medium, and (2) at the receiving side of the link to group bits arriving from the physical medium into cells and pass the cells to the ATM layer. These are the jobs of the TC sublayer, which sits on top of the PMD sublayer and just below the ATM layer. We note that the TC sublayer is also physical medium dependent—if we change the physical medium or the underlying frame structure, then we must also change the TC sublayer.

On the transmit side, the TC sublayer places ATM cells into the bit and transmission frame structure of the PMD sublayer. On the receive side, it extracts ATM cells from the bit and transmission frame structure of the PMD sublayer. It also performs header error correction (HEC). More specifically, the TC sublayer has the following tasks:

▪ At the transmit side, the TC sublayer generates the HEC byte for each ATM cell that is to be transmitted. At the receive side, the TC sublayer uses the HEC byte to correct all one-bit errors in the header and some multiple-bit errors in the header, reducing the possibility of incorrect routing of cells. (The HEC is created by dividing the first 32 bits of the header by the polynomial $x^8 + x^2 + x + 1$ and then taking the 8-bit remainder.)

▪ At the receive side, the TC sublayer delineates cells. If the PMD Sublayer is cell based with no frames, then this is typically done by running the HEC on all contiguous sets of 40 bits (that is, 5 bytes). When a match occurs, a cell is delineated. Upon matching four consecutive cells, cell synchronization is declared and subsequent cells are passed to the ATM layer.

■ If the PMD sublayer is cell based with no frames, the sublayer sends an idle cell when ATM layer has not provided a cell, thereby generating a continuous stream of cells. The receiving TC sublayer does not pass idle cells to the ATM layer. Idle cells are marked in the PT field in the ATM header.

5.9.3 ATM Layer

When IP runs over ATM, the ATM cell plays the role of the link-layer frame. The ATM layer defines the structure of the ATM cell and the meaning of the fields within this structure. The first 5 five bytes of the cell constitute the ATM header; the remaining 48 bytes constitute the ATM payload. Figure 5.46 shows the structure of the ATM header.

The fields in the ATM cell are as follows:

■ *VCI (Virtual Channel Identifier).* Indicates the VC to which the cell belongs. As with most network technologies that use virtual circuits, a cell's VCI is translated from link to link (see Section 1.3).

■ *PT (Payload Type).* Indicates the type of payload the cell contains. There are several data payload types, several maintenance payload types, and an idle cell payload type. (Recall that idle cells are sometimes needed by the physical layer for synchronization.)

■ *CLP (Cell Loss Priority) bit.* Can be set by the source (entry router in Figure 5.42) to differentiate between high-priority traffic and low priority traffic. If congestion occurs and an ATM switch must discard cells, the switch can use this bit to first discard low-priority traffic.

■ *Header Error Checksum (HEC) byte.* A checksum across the header, as described in Section 5.8. Recall that the TC sublayer (of the physical layer) calculates the HEC byte at the transmitter and the checks the header at the receiver.

Virtual Channels. Before a source can begin to send cells to a destination, the ATM network must first establish a virtual channel (VC) from source to destination. A virtual channel is nothing more than a VC, as described in Section 1.4. Each VC is a path consisting of a sequence of links between source and destination. On each of the links the VC has a Virtual Circuit Identifier (VCI). Whenever a VC is established or torn-down, VC translation tables must be updated (see Section 1.4). As we mentioned above, ATM backbones in the Internet often use permanent VCs, which obviates the need for dynamic VC establishment and tear-down.

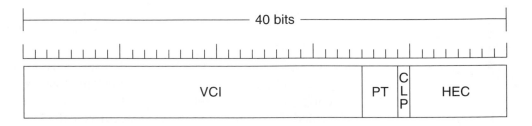

FIGURE 5.46 The format of the ATM cell header

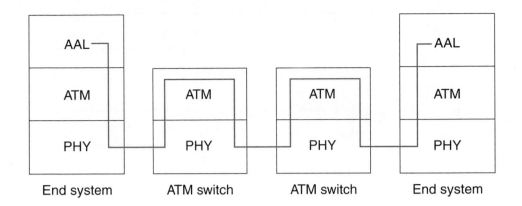

FIGURE 5.47   The AAL layer is present only at the edges of the ATM network

5.9.4   ATM Adaptation Layer

The purpose of the AAL is to allow existing protocols (for example, IP) and applications (for example, constant-bit-rate video) to run on top of ATM. As shown in Figure 5.47, AAL is implemented in the ATM end systems (for example, entry end exit routers in an Internet backbone), not in the intermediate ATM switches. In this respect, the AAL layer is analogous to the transport layer in the Internet protocol stack.

   The AAL sublayer has its own header fields. As shown in Figure 5.48, these fields occupy a small portion of the payload in the ATM cell.

   The ITU and the ATM Forum have standardized several AALs. Some of the most important AALs include:

   AAL 1: For Constant Bit Rate (CBR) services and circuit emulation.

   AAL 2: For Variable Bit Rate (VBR) services.

   AAL 5: For data (for example, IP datagrams)

AAL structure.   AAL has two sublayers: the Segmentation And Reassembly (SAR) sublayer and the Convergence Sublayer (CS). As shown in Figure 5.49, the SAR sits just above the ATM layer; the CS sublayer sits between the user application and the SAR sublayer.

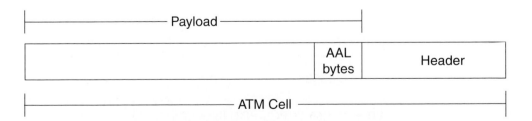

FIGURE 5.48   The AAL fields within the ATM payload

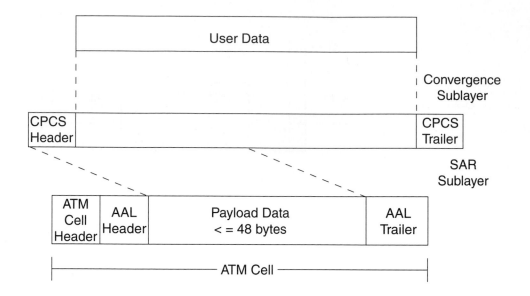

FIGURE 5.49   The sublayers of the AAL

The user data (for example, an IP datagram) is first encapsulated in a Common Part Convergence Sublayer (CPCS) PDU in the Convergence Sublayer. This PDU can have CPCS header and CPSC trailer. Typically the CPCS-PDU is much too large to fit into the payload of an ATM cell; thus the CPCS-PDU has to be segmented at the ATM source and reassembled at the ATM destination. The SAR sublayer segments the CPCS-PDU and adds AAL header and trailer bits to form the payloads of the ATM cells. Depending on the AAL types, the AAL and CPCS header and trailers could be empty.

AAL 5 (Simple and Efficient Adaptation Layer—SEAL).   AAL5 is a low-overhead AAL that is used to transport IP datagrams over ATM networks. With AAL5, the AAL header and trailer are empty; thus, all 48 bytes of the ATM payload are used to carry segments of the CPCS-PDU. An IP datagram occupies the CPCS-PDU payload, which can be from 1 to 65,535 bytes. The AAL5 CPCS-PDU is shown in Figure 5.50.

The PAD ensures that the CPCS-PDU is an integer multiple of 48 bytes. The length field identifies the size of the CPCS-PDU payload, so that the PAD can be removed at the receiver. The CRC is the same one that is used by Ethernet, Token Ring and FDDI.

CPCS-PDU payload	PAD	Length	CRC
0-65535	0-47	2	4

FIGURE 5.50   CPCS-PDU for AAL5

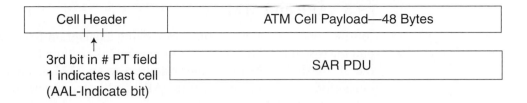

FIGURE 5.51 The `AAL_indicate` bit is used to reassemble IP datagrams from ATM cells

At the ATM source, the AAL5 SAR chops the CPCS-PDU into 48-byte segments. As shown in Figure 5.51, a bit in the PT field of the ATM cell header, which is normally 0, is set to 1 for the last cell of the CPCS-PDU. At the ATM destination, the ATM layer directs cells with a specific VCI to a SAR-sublayer buffer. The ATM cell headers are removed, and the AAL-indicate bit is used to delineate the CPCS-PDUs. Once the CPCS-PDU is delineated, it is passed to the AAL convergence sublayer. At the convergence sublayer, the length field is used to extract the CPCS-PDU payload (for example, an IP datagram), which is passed to the higher layer.

Moving a datagram through an Internet backbone. Let us now return to the problem of moving a datagram from an entry router to an exit router in Figure 5.45. Recall that IP in the entry router passes the datagram down to ATM along with the ATM address of the exit router. ATM in the entry router indexes an ATM table to determine the VCI for the VC that leads to the ATM destination address. AAL5 then creates ATM cells out of the IP datagram:

- The datagram is encapsulated in a CPCS-PDU using the format in Figure 5.51.
- The CPCS-PDU is chopped up into 48-byte chunks. Each chunk is placed in the payload field of an ATM cell.
- All of the cells except for the last cell have the third bit of the PT field set to zero. The last cell has the bit set to one.

AAL5 then passes the cells to the ATM layer. ATM sets the VCI and CLP fields and passes each cell to the TC sublayer. For each cell, the TC sublayer calculates the HEC and inserts it in the HEC field. The TC sublayer then inserts the bits of the cells into the PMD sublayer.

The ATM network then moves each cell across the network to the ATM destination address. At each ATM switch between ATM source and ATM destination, the ATM cell is processed by the ATM physical and ATM layers, but not by the AAL layer. At each switch the VCI is typically translated (see Section 1.4) and the HEC is recalculated. When the cells arrive at the ATM destination address, they are directed to an AAL buffer that has been put aside for the particular VC. The CPCS-PDU is reconstructed using the `AAL_indicate` bit to determine which cell is the last cell of the CPCS-PDU. Finally, the IP datagram is extracted out of the CPCS-PDU and is passed up the protocol stack to the IP layer.

5.9.5   ARP and ATM

Consider once again the problem of moving a datagram from entry router to exit router across the ATM network in Figure 5.42. Recall that ARP has the important role of translating the exit router's address to an ATM destination address. This translation is straightforward if the ARP table is complete and accurate. But as with Ethernet, ATM ARP tables are auto-configured and may not be complete. As with Ethernet, if the desired mapping is not in the table, an ARP protocol must contact the exit router and obtain the mapping. However, there is a fundamental difference here between Ethernet and ATM—Ethernet is a broadcast technology and ATM is a switched technology. What this means is that ATM cannot simply send ARP request message when a broadcast packet. ATM must work harder to get the mapping. There are two generic approaches that can be used: broadcast ARP request messages and ARP server.

Broadcast ARP request messages.   In this approach, the entry router constructs an ARP request message, converts the message to cells, and sends the cells into the ATM network. These cells are sent by the source along a special VC reserved for ARP request messages. The switches broadcast all cells received on this special VC. The exit router receives the ARP request message and sends the entry router an ARP response message (which is not broadcasted). The entry router then updates its ARP table. This approach can place a significant amount of overhead ARP broadcast traffic into the network.

ARP server.   In this approach, ARP server is attached directly to one of the ATM switches in the network, and permanent VCs exist between each router and the ARP server. All of these permanent VCs use the same VCI on all links from the routers to the ARP server. There are also permanent VCs from the ARP server to each router; each of these VCs have different VCIs out of the ARP server. The ARP server contains an up-to-date ARP table that maps IP addresses to ATM addresses. Using some registration protocol, all routers must register themselves with the ARP server. This approach eliminates the broadcast ARP traffic. However it requires an ARP server, which can swamped with ARP request messages.

An important reference for running ARP over ATM is [RFC 1577], which discusses IP and ARP over ATM. [RFC 1932] also provides a good overview of IP over ATM.

5.10   X.25 AND FRAME RELAY

In this section we discuss two end-to-end wide-area-networking (WAN) technologies, namely X.25 and Frame Relay. Introduced in the early 1980s and popular in Europe up through the mid 1990s, X.25 is arguably the first public packet-switching technology. Frame relay, a successor to X.25, is another public packet-switching technology which has been popular in North America throughout the 1990s.

Given that X.25 and Frame Relay are end-to-end WAN technologies, you may be wondering why we are discussing them in a chapter that is devoted to the data-link layer? We have chosen to discuss these technologies in this chapter for the same reason we chose to discuss ATM in this chapter—all of these technologies are often employed today to carry IP datagrams from one IP router to another. Thus, from the perspective of IP (which is also an end-to-end WAN technology), X.25, Frame Relay, and ATM are link layer technologies. Because IP is one of the protocols being highlighted in this book, we have put X.25, Frame Relay, and ATM where IP believes these technologies belong, namely, in the link layer.

Although X.25 still exists throughout Europe and in certain niche markets in North America, the X.25 networks are on the verge of extinction throughout the world. They were designed almost twenty years ago for a technological context that is very different from today's. Frame Relay had great appeal to corporate customers throughout the 1990s, but it is increasingly fighting fierce competition from the public Internet. In fact, due to this competition, Frame Relay may become a minor player in the mid 2000s. Even though X.25 is on its way out (if not already completely gone), and Frame Relay may disappear as well a few years down the road, we have chosen to cover these technologies in this book because of their immense historical importance.

5.10.1 A Few Words About X.25

The X.25 protocol suite was designed in the late 1970s. To understand the motivation behind the design, we need to understand the technological context of that ancient era. Although the Apple II personal computer was making a big hit at this time [Nerds], PCs and workstations were not widespread and didn't have much networking support. Instead, most people were using inexpensive "dumb terminals" to access distant mainframes over computer networks. These dumb terminals had minimal intelligence and storage (no disks); what appeared on their screens was completely controlled by the mainframe at the other end of the network. In order to widely support dumb terminals, the designers of X.25 decided to "put the intelligence in the network." This philosophy, as we now know, is very different from the Internet philosophy, which puts intelligence in the end systems and assumes little about the network.

One way the designers put intelligence in the X.25 network was by employing virtual circuits in X.25 networks. Recall from Chapter 1 that virtual-circuit networks require the packet switches to maintain state information. In particular, the switch must maintain a table that maps inbound interface/VC-number to outbound interface/VC-number. Moreover, complex signaling protocols are needed to establish VCs and tear them down. As we learned in Chapter 4, the IP protocol is connectionless and, thus, does not use VCs. When a node wants to send an IP packet into the network, it just stamps the datagram with a destination address and injects it into the network; it does not first request the network to establish a virtual circuit between itself and the destination.

Another important part of the technological context of the late 1970s and early 1980s concerns the physical links. In those days, almost all of the wired links were noisy, error-prone copper links. Fiber-optic links were only being researched in the laboratory at that time. Bit error rates over long-haul copper links were *many* orders of magnitude higher than they are now over fiber links. Because of the high error rates, it made sense to design the X.25 protocol with error recovery on a hop-by-hop basis. In particular, whenever an X.25 switch sends a packet, it keeps a copy of the packet until the next switch (in the packet's route) returns an acknowledgment. Thus each switch, when receiving a packet, performs error checking, and if the packet is error-free, it sends an acknowledgment to the previous switch. Hop-by-hop error recovery significantly reduces link transmission rates, but it is consistent with the technological context of the era—high link error rates and dumb terminals. The X.25 design also calls for flow-control on a hop-by-hop basis. Recall, that the TCP transport protocol performs error recovery and flow control on an end-to-end basis, and thereby does not require the links to perform these tasks.

5.10.2 Frame Relay

Frame Relay, designed in the late 1980s and widely deployed in the 1990s, is in many ways a second-generation X.25. Like X.25, it uses virtual circuits. However, because the fiber-based systems of the 1990s had much lower bit error rates than the copper-based systems of the 1980s, Frame Relay was naturally designed for much lower error rates. The essence of Frame Relay is a VC-based packet-switching service with no error recovery and no flow control. Whenever a Frame Relay switch detects an error in a packet, its only possible course of action is to discard the data. This results in a network with lower processing overheads and higher transmission rates than X.25, but requires intelligent end systems for data integrity. In most cases today, the Frame Relay network is owned by a public network service provider (for example, AT&T, Sprint, or Bell Atlantic) and its use is contracted on a multi-year basis to corporate customers. Frame Relay is extensively used today to allow LANs on different corporate campuses to send data to each other at reasonably high speeds. As shown in Figure 5.52, often Frame Relay interconnects these LANs through IP routers, with each IP router in a different corporate campus. Frame Relay offers a corporation an alternative to sending its inter-campus IP traffic over the public Internet, for which the corporation may have reliability and security concerns.

Frame Relay networks can use either switched VCs (SVCs) or Permanent Virtual Circuits (PVC's). For router interconnection, a PVC is often permanently established between each pair of routers. $N(N - 1)/2$ PVC's are necessary to

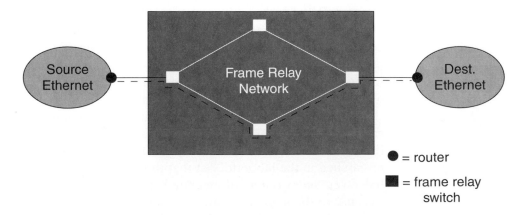

FIGURE 5.52 Public Frame Relay network interconnected two Ethernets through routers located on the Ethernets. The dotted line represents a virtual circuit.

interconnect *N* routers. Throughout our discussion we shall assume that the frame relay network uses PVCs (which is the more common case).

Sending an IP datagram from Ethernet to Frame Relay to Ethernet. Consider the transmission of an IP datagram between two end systems on two Ethernets interconnected by a Frame Relay network. Let us walk through the steps in the context of Figure 5.52. When an Ethernet frame arrives to the source router, the router's Ethernet card strips off the Ethernet fields and passes the IP datagram to the network layer. The network layer passes the IP datagram to the Frame Relay interface card. This card encapsulates the IP datagram in the Frame Relay packet, as shown in Figure 5.53. It also calculates the CRC (2 bytes) and inserts the resulting value in the CRC field. The link layer field (2 bytes) includes a 10-bit virtual circuit number field. The interface card obtains the VC number from a table that associates IP network numbers to VC numbers. The interface card then transmits the packet.

The interface card transmits the Frame Relay packet onto a leased line, typically obtained from local telephone company (for example, Bell Atlantic). The leased line connects the router to a nearby Frame Relay switch, owned by the Frame Relay service provider (for example, Sprint). The switch examines the FCS field. If the frame has an error, the switch discards the frame; unlike X.25, frame relay does not bother to retransmit packets on a hop-by-hop basis. If there is no error in the frame, the switch uses the frame's VC number to route the frame to the next switch (or to the destination router). The destination router removes the frame relay fields and then delivers the datagram over Ethernet to the destination host. If TCP segments are lost or arrive out of sequence, then TCP in the communicating hosts (intelligent end systems) correct the problem. For more details about how an IP datagram is sent across an IP network, see [RFC 2427].

Committed Information Rate (CIR). Frame Relay makes use of an innovative mechanism referred to as the **committed information rate (CIR).** Every frame relay VC has a committed information rate. We will define the CIR rigorously

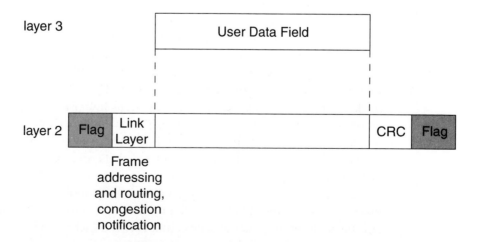

FIGURE 5.53 Encapsulating user data (for example, an IP datagram) into a Frame Relay frame

below, but roughly, the CIR is a *commitment* on the part of the Frame Relay network to dedicate to the VC a specified transmission rate determined by the CIR. The CIR service, introduced by Frame Relay in the early 1990s, is in many ways a forerunner to the Internet's differentiated service (see Chapter 6). As we shall shortly see, Frame Relay provides the CIR service by marking packets.

In Frame Relay networks, Frame Relay packets can belong to one of two priority levels—either high priority or low priority. Packets are assigned priorities by *marking* a special bit in the packet header—the so-called Discard Eligibility (DE) bit—to either 0 for high priority and 1 for low priority. If a frame is a high-priority frame, then the Frame Relay network should deliver the packet to the destination under all but the most desperate network conditions, including periods of congestion and backbone link failures. However, for low priority packets, the Frame Relay network is permitted to discard the frame under congested conditions. Under particularly draconian conditions, the network can even discard high-priority packets. Congestion is typically measured by the state of output buffers in Frame Relay switches. When an output buffer in a Frame Relay switch is about to overflow, the switch will first discard the low priority packets, that is, the packets in the buffer with the DE bit set to 0.

The actions that a Frame Relay switch takes on the marked packets should be clear, but we haven't said anything about how packets get marked. This is where the CIR comes in. To explain this, we need to introduce a little frame-relay jargon, which we do in the context of Figure 5.45. The **access rate** is the rate of the access link, that is, the rate of the link from the source router to the "edge" Frame Relay switch. This rate is often 64 Kbps but integer multiples of 64 Kbps up to 1.544 Mbps are also common. Denote R for the access rate. As we learned in Chapter 1, each packet sent over the link of rate R is transmitted at rate R bps. The edge switch is responsible for marking packets that arrive from the source router. To perform the marking, the edge switch examines the arrival times of packets from the source router over short, fixed intervals of time, called the **measurement interval,** denoted by T_c. Most frame-relay service providers use a T_c value that falls somewhere between 100 msecs and 1 sec.

Now we can precisely describe the CIR. Each VC that emanates from the source router (there may be many, possibly destined to different LANs) is assigned a **committed information rate (CIR),** which is in units of bits/sec. The CIR is never greater than R, the access rate. Customers pay for a specific CIR; the higher the CIR, the more the customer pays to the Frame Relay service provider. If the VC generates packets at a rate that is less than the CIR, than all of the VCs packets will be marked as high-priority packets (DE = 0). However, if the rate at which the VC generates packets exceeds the CIR, then the fraction of the VC's packets that exceed the rate will be marked as low priority packets. More specifically, over each measurement interval T_c, for the first $CIR \cdot T_c$ bits the VC sends, the edge switch marks the corresponding packets as high-priority packets ($DE = 0$). The edge switch marks all additional packets sent over this interval as low priority packets (DE = 1).

To get a feel for what is going on here, let us look at an example. Let us suppose that the Frame Relay service provider uses a measurement interval of $T_c = 500$ msec. Suppose that the access link is $R = 64$ Kbps and that the CIR assigned to a particular VC is 32 Kbps. Also suppose, for simplicity, that each Frame Relay packet consists of exactly $L = 4,000$ bits. This means that every 500 msec the VC can send CIR $\cdot$ $T_c/L = 4$ packets as high-priority packets. All additional packets sent within the 500 msec interval are marked as low priority packets. Note that up to 4 low-priority packets can be sent in over each 500 msec interval (in addition to 4 high-priority packets). Because the frame relay network "almost" guarantees that all of the high-priority packets will be delivered to the destination frame-relay node, the VC is essentially guaranteed of a throughput of at least 32 Kbps. Frame Relay does not, however, make any guarantees about the end-to-end delays of either the high- or low-priority packets.

Increasing the measurement interval T_c increases the potential burstiness of the high-priority packets emitted from the source router. In the previous example, if $T_c = 0.5$ sec, up to four high-priority packets can be emitted back-to-back; for $T_c = 1$ sec, up to eight high-priority packets can be emitted back-to-back. When the frame relay network uses a smaller value of T_c, it forces the stream of high priority packets to be smoother (less bursty); but a large value of T_c gives the VC more flexibility. In any case, for every choice of T_c, the long-run average rate of bits emitted as high-priority bits never exceeds the CIR of the VC.

We must keep in mind that many PVCs may emanate from the source router and travel over the access link. It is interesting to note that the sum of the CIRs for all these VCs is permitted to exceed the access rate, R. This is referred to as *overbooking*. Because overbooking is permitted, an access link may transmit high-priority packets at a corresponding bit rate that exceeds the CIR (even though each individual VC sends priority packets at a rate that does not exceed the CIR).

We conclude this section by mentioning that the Frame Relay Forum [FRForum] maintains a number or relevant specifications. An excellent introductory course for frame relay is made available on the Hill Associates Web site [Hill]. Walter Goralski has also written a readable yet in depth book about frame relay [Goralski 1999].

SUMMARY

In this chapter, we've examined the data link layer—its services, the principles underlying its operation, and a number of important specific protocols that use these principles in implementing data link services.

We saw that the basic service of the data link layer is to move a network-layer datagram from one node (router or host) to an adjacent node. We saw that all data link protocols operate by encapsulating a network-layer datagram within a link-layer frame before transmitting the frame over the "link" to the adjacent node. Beyond this common framing function, however, we learned that different data link protocols can provide very different link access, delivery (reliability, error detection/correction), flow control, and transmission (for example, full-duplex versus half-duplex) services. These differences are due in part to the wide variety of link types over which data link protocols must operate. A simple point-to-point link has a single sender and receiver communicating over a single "wire." A multiple access link is shared among many senders and receivers; consequently, the data link protocol for a multiple access channel has a protocol (its multiple access protocol) for coordinating link access. In the cases of ATM, X.25, and frame relay, we saw that the "link" connecting two adjacent nodes (for example, two IP routers that are adjacent in an IP sense—that they are next-hop IP routers toward some destination), may actually be a *network* in and of itself. In one sense, the idea of a network being considered as a "link" should not seem odd. A telephone "link" connecting a home modem/computer to a remote modem/router, for example, is actually a path through a sophisticated and complex telephone *network*.

Among the principles underlying data link communication, we examined error detection and correction techniques, multiple access protocols, link-layer addressing, and the construction of extended local area networks via hubs, bridges, and switches. In the case of error detection/correction, we examined how it is possible to add additional bits to a frame's header that are used to detect, and in some cases correct, bit-flip errors that might occur when the frame is transmitted over the link. We covered simple parity and checksumming schemes, as well as the more robust cyclic redundancy check. We then moved on to the topic of multiple access protocols. We identified and studied three broad approaches for coordinating access to a broadcast channel: channel partitioning approaches (TDM, FDM, CDMA), random access approaches (the ALOHA protocols, and CSMA protocols), and taking-turns approaches (polling and token passing). We saw that a consequence of having multiple nodes share a single broadcast channel was the need to provide node addresses at the data link level. We learned that physical addresses were quite different from network-layer addresses, and that in the case of the Internet, a special protocol (ARP—the address resolution protocol) is used to translate between these two forms of addressing. We then examined how nodes sharing a broadcast channel form a local area network (LAN), and how multiple LANs can be connected together to form larger LANs—all *without* the intervention of network-layer routing to interconnect these local nodes. Finally, we covered a number of specific data link layer protocols in detail—Ethernet, the wireless IEEE 802.11 protocol, and the Point-to-Point protocol, PPP. As discussed in Sections 5.9 and 5.10, ATM, X.25, and Frame Relay can also be used to connect two network-layer routers. For example, in the IP-over-ATM scenario, two adjacent IP routers can be connected to each other by a virtual circuit through an ATM network. In such circumstances, a network that is based on one network architecture (for example, ATM, or Frame Relay) can serve as a single logical link between two neighboring nodes (for example, IP routers) in another network architecture.

Having covered the data link layer, *our journey down the protocol stack is now over*! Certainly, the physical layer lies below the data link layer, but the details of the physical layer is a topic probably best left for another course (for example, in communication theory, rather than computer networking). We have, however, touched upon several aspects of the physical layer in this chapter (for example, our brief discussions of Manchester encoding in Section 5.5 and of signal fading in Section 5.7) and in Chapter 1 (our discussion of physical media in Section 1.5).

Although our journey down the protocol stack is over, our study of computer networking is not yet over. In the following three chapters we cover multimedia networking, network security, and network management. These three topics do not fit conveniently into any one layer; indeed, each topic crosscuts many layers. Understanding these topics (sometimes billed as "advanced topics" in some networking texts) thus requires a firm foundation in all layers of the protocol stack— a foundation that is now complete with our completed study of the data link layer!

HOMEWORK PROBLEMS AND QUESTIONS

Chapter 5

Review Questions

Sections 5.1–5.3

1. If all the links in the Internet were to provide the reliable-delivery service, would the TCP reliable-delivery service be completely redundant? Why or why not?

2. What are some of the possible services that a link-layer protocol can offer to the network layer? Which of these link-layer services have corresponding services in IP? In TCP?

3. Suppose the information content of a packet is the bit pattern `1010101010101011` and an even parity scheme is being used. What would be the value of the checksum field in a single parity scheme?

4. Suppose two nodes start to transmit at the same time a packet of length L over a broadcast channel of rate R. Denote the propagation delay between the two nodes as t_{prop}. Will there be a collision if $t_{prop} < L/R$? Why or why not?

5. In Section 5.2.1, we listed four desirable characteristics of a broadcast channel. Slotted ALOHA has which of these characteristics? Token passing has which of these characteristics?

6. What are human cocktail analogies for polling and token passing protocols?

7. Why would the token-ring protocol be inefficient if the LAN has a very large perimeter?

8. How big is the LAN address space? The IPv4 address space? The IPv6 address space?

9. Suppose nodes A, B, and C each attach to the same broadcast LAN (through their adapters). If A sends thousands of frames to B with each frame addressed to the LAN address of B, will C's adapter process these frames? If so, will C's adapter pass the IP datagrams in these frames to C (that is, the adapter's parent node)? How will your answers change if A sends frames with the LAN broadcast address?

10. Why is an ARP query sent within a broadcast frame? Why is an ARP response sent within a frame with a specific LAN address?

11. For the network in Figure 5.12, the router has two ARP modules, each with its own ARP table. Is it possible that the same LAN address appears in both tables?

12. Compare the frame structures for 10BaseT, 100BaseT, and Gigabit Ethernet. How do they differ?

13. Suppose a 10 Mbps adapter sends into a channel an infinite stream of 1s using Manchester encoding. The signal emerging from the adapter will have how many transitions per second?

14. After the 5th collision, what is the probability that the value of K that a node chooses is 4? The result $K = 4$ corresponds to a delay of how many seconds on a 10 Mbps Ethernet?

Section 5.6

15. In the IEEE 802.11 specification, the length of the SIFS period must be shorter than the DIFS period. Why?

16. Suppose the IEEE 802.11 RTS and CTS frames were as long as the standard DATA and ACK frames. Would there be any advantage to using the CTS and RTS frames? Why?

Section 5.9

17. Does the TC sublayer distinguish between different VCs at either the transmitter or receiver?

18. Why is it important for the TC Sublayer in the transmitter to provide a continuous stream of cells when the PMD Sublayer is cell based?

19. Does the TC sublayer at the transmitter fill in any of the fields in the ATM header? Which ones?

PROBLEMS

1. Suppose the information content of a packet is the bit pattern `1010101010101011` and an even parity scheme is being used. What would the value of the checksum field be for the case of a two-dimensional parity scheme? Your answer should be such that a minimum length checksum field is used.

2. Give an example (other than the one in Figure 5.6!) showing that two-dimensional parity checks can correct and detect a single bit error. Show by counterexample that a double bit error cannot always be corrected. Show by example that some double bit errors can be detected.

3. Suppose the information portion of a packet (D in Figure 5.4) contains 10 bytes consisting of the 8-bit unsigned binary representation of the integers 0 through 9. Compute the Internet checksum for this data.

4. Consider the 4-bit generator, G shown in Figure 5.8, and suppose that D has the value `10101010`. What is the value of R?

5. Consider the single sender CDMA example in Figure 5.12. What would be the sender's output (for the two data bits shown) if the sender's CDMA code were $(1, -1, 1, -1, 1, -1, 1, -1)$?

6. Consider sender 2 in Figure 5.13. What is the sender's output to the channel (before it is added to the signal from sender 1), $Z_{i,m}^2$?

7. Suppose that the receiver in Figure 5.13 wanted to receive the data being sent by sender 2. Show (by calculation), that the receiver is indeed able to recover sender 2's data from the aggregate channel signal by using sender 2's code.

8. In Section 5.3, we provided an outline of the derivation of the efficiency of slotted ALOHA. In this problem we'll complete the derivation.

   a. Recall that when there are N active nodes the efficiency of slotted ALOHA is $Np(1 - p)^{N-1}$. Find the value of p that maximizes this expression.

b. Using the value of p found in part (a), find the efficiency of slotted ALOHA by letting N approach infinity. *Hint:* $(1 - 1/N)^N$ approaches $1/e$ as N approaches infinity.

9. Show that the maximum efficiency of pure ALOHA is $1/(2e)$. *Note:* This problem is easy if you have completed the problem above!

10. Graph the efficiency of slotted ALOHA and pure ALOHA as a function of p for $N = 100$.

11. Consider a broadcast channel with N nodes and a transmission rate of R bps. Suppose the broadcast channel uses polling (with an additional polling node) for multiple access. Suppose the amount of time from when a node completes transmission until the subsequent node is permitted to transmit (that is, the polling delay) is t_{poll}. Suppose that within a polling round, a given node is allowed to transmit at most Q bits. What is the maximum throughput of the broadcast channel?

12. Consider three LANs interconnected by two routers, as shown in the diagram below.

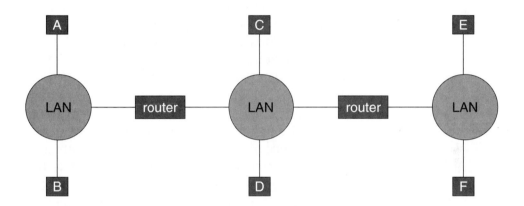

a. Redraw the diagram to include adapters.

b. Assign IP addresses to all of the interfaces. For LAN 1 use addresses of the form `111.111.111.xxx`; for LAN 2 uses addresses of the form `122.222.222.xxx`; and for LAN 3 use addresses of the form `133.333.333.xxx`.

c. Assign LAN addresses to all of the adapters.

d. Consider sending an IP datagram from host A to host F. Suppose all of the ARP tables are up-to-date. Enumerate all the steps as done for the single-router example in Section 5.3.2.

e. Repeat (d), now assuming that the ARP table in the sending host is empty (and the other tables are up-to-date).

13. Recall that with the CSMA/CD protocol, the adapter waits $K \cdot 512$ bit times after a collision, where K is drawn randomly. For $K = 100$, how long does the adapter wait until returning to Step 2 for a 10 Mbps Ethernet? For a 100 Mbps Ethernet?

14. Suppose nodes A and B are on the same 10 Mbps Ethernet segment, and the propagation delay between the two nodes is 225 bit times. Suppose node A

begins transmitting a frame, and before it finishes, station B begins transmitting a frame. Can A finish transmitting before it detects that B has transmitted? Why or why not? If the answer is yes, then A incorrectly believes that its frame was successfully transmitted without a collision.

Hint: Suppose at time $t = 0$ bit times, A begins transmitting a frame. In the worst case, A transmits a minimum size frame of $512 + 64$ bit times. So A would finish transmitting the frame at $t = 512 + 64$ bit times. Thus, the answer is no, if B's signal reaches A before bit time t=512+64 bits. In the worst case, when does B's signal reach A?

15. Suppose nodes A and B are on the same 10 Mbps Ethernet segment, and the propagation delay between the two nodes is 225 bit times. Suppose A and B send frames at the same time, the frames collide, and then A and B choose different values of K in the CSMA/CD algorithm. Assuming no other nodes are active, can the retransmissions from A and B collide? For our purposes, it suffices to work out the following example. Suppose A and B begin transmission at $t = 0$ bit times. They both detect collisions at $t = 225$ bit times. They finish transmitting a jam signal at $t = 225 + 48 = 273$ bit times. Suppose $K_A = 0$ and $K_B = 1$. At what time does B schedule its retransmission? At what time does A begin transmission? (*Note:* the nodes must wait for an idle channel after returning to Step 2— see protocol.) At what time does A's signal reach B? Does B refrain from transmitting at its scheduled time?

16. Consider a 100Mbps 100BT Ethernet. In order to have an efficiency of 0.50, what should be the maximum distance between a node and the hub? Assume a frame length of 64 bytes and that there are no repeaters. Does this maximum distance also ensure that a transmitting node A will be able to detect whether any other node transmitted while A was transmitting? Why or why not? How does your maximum distance compare to the actual 100 Mbps standard?

17. In this problem you will derive the efficiency of a CSMA/CD-like multiple access protocol. In this protocol, time is slotted and all adapters are synchronized to the slots. Unlike slotted ALOHA, however, the length of a slot (in seconds) is much less than a frame time (the time to transmit a frame). Let S be the length of a slot. Suppose all frames are of constant length $L = k R S$, where R is the transmission rate of the channel and k is a large integer. Suppose there are N nodes, each with an infinite number of frames to send. We also assume that $t_{prop} < S$, so that all nodes can detect a collision before the end of a slot time. The protocol is as follows:

If, for a given slot, no node has possession of the channel, all nodes contend for the channel; in particular, each node transmits in the slot with probability p. If exactly one node transmits in the slot, that node takes possession of the channel for the subsequent $k - 1$ slots and transmits its entire frame.

If some node has possession of the channel, all other nodes refrain from transmitting until the node that possesses the channel has finished transmitting its frame. Once this node has transmitted its frame, all nodes contend for the channel.

Note that the channel alternates between two states: the "productive state," which lasts exactly k slots, and the non-productive state, which lasts for a random number of slots. Clearly, the channel efficiency is the ratio of $k/(k + x)$, where x is the expected number of consecutive unproductive slots.

a. For fixed N and p, determine the efficiency of this protocol.

b. For fixed N, determine the p that maximizes the efficiency.

c. Using the p (which is a function of N) found in part b, determine the efficiency as N approaches infinity.

d. Show that this efficiency approaches 1 as the frame length becomes large.

18. Suppose two nodes, A and B, are attached to opposite ends of a 900 m cable, and that they each have one frame of 1,000 bits (including all headers and preambles) to send to each other. Both nodes attempt to transmit at time $t = 0$. Suppose there are four repeaters between A and B, each inserting a 20-bit delay. Assume the transmission rate is 10 Mbps, and CSMA/CD with backoff intervals of multiples of 512 bits is used. After the first collision, A draws $K = 0$ and B draws $K = 1$ in the exponential backoff protocol. Ignore the jam signal.

a. What is the one-way propagation delay (including repeater delays) between A and B in seconds. Assume that the signal propagation speed is $2 \cdot 10^8$ m/sec.

b. At what time (in seconds) is A's packet completely delivered at B.

c. Now suppose that only A has a packet to send and that the repeaters are replaced with bridges. Suppose that each bridge has a 20-bit processing delay in addition to a store-and-forward delay. At what time, in seconds, is A's packet delivered at B?

19. You are to design a LAN for the campus layout shown below.

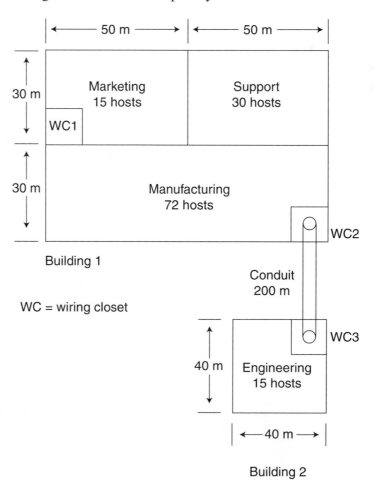

Building 1

WC = wiring closet

Building 2

You may use the following equipment:

Equipment	Cost
Thin Coax	$1 per meter
UTP	$1 per meter
Fiber Optic Cable—pair	$2 per meter
NIC—thin coax ports	$70
NIC—UTP port	$70
2-Port Repeater	$800
Multiport Repeater (8 thin coax ports)	$1,500
Multiport Fiber Repeater (6 Fiber ports)	$2,000
2-Port Bridge (any combo of thin coax, UTP, fiber)	$2,200
Hub—36 UTP ports	$4,000
Hub—6 fiber ports, 24 UTP ports	$6,000
Pentium File Server—w/NOS (max. 30 users)	$9,000
Bridges always include interface cards	

You must respect the following design requirements:

- Each department must have access to the resources of all other departments.
- The traffic generated by users of one department cannot affect another department's LAN unless accessing a resource on that other department's LAN.
- A file server can support only 30 users.
- File servers may not be shared by multiple departments.
- All repeaters, bridges, and hubs must reside in the wiring closets (WCs).

a. You are required to use thin coax (no UTP) and, if deemed necessary, fiber optics. Provide a diagram for your design. Also provide a list of the equipment you use (with quantities) and the total cost of the LAN.

b. Repeat (a), but use UTP (no thin coax) and, if deemed necessary, fiber optics.

20. Suppose a frame-relay VC generates packets of fixed length L. Let R, T_c, and *CIR* denote the access rate, the measurement interval and the committed information rate, respectively.

a. As a function of these variables, determine how many high-priority packets the VC can send in a measurement interval.

b. As a function of these variables, determine how many low-priority packets the VC can send in a measurement interval.

For part (b) assume that in each measurement interval, the VC first generates the maximum number of high-priority packets permitted and then generates low-priority packets.

21. In Figure 5.45, suppose the source Ethernet includes a Web server that is very busy serving requests from clients in the destination Ethernet. Each HTTP response message is carried in one or more IP datagrams. When the IP datagrams arrive to the frame relay interface, each datagram is encapsulated in a Frame Relay frame. Suppose that each Web object is of size O and each frame-relay packet is of size L. Suppose that the Web server begins to serve one object at the beginning of each measurement interval. Ignoring all packet overheads (at the application, transport, IP, and frame-relay layers!), determine the maximum size of O (as a function of T_c, *CIR*, and L) such that each object is entirely carried by high-priority Frame Relay packets.

DISCUSSION QUESTIONS

You are encouraged to surf the Web in answering the following questions.

1. Roughly, what is the current price range of a 10 Mbps Ethernet adapter? Of a 10/100 Mbps adapter? Of a Gigabit Ethernet adapter?

2. Hubs and switches are often priced in terms of number of interfaces (also called ports in LAN jargon). Roughly, what is the current per-interface price range for a 10 Mbps hub? For a 100 Mbps hub? For a switch consisting of only 10 Mbps interfaces? For a switch consisting of only 100 Mbps interfaces?

3. Many of the functions of an adapter can be performed in software that runs on the node's CPU. What are the advantages and disadvantages of moving this functionality from the adapter to the node?

4. Use the Web to find the protocol numbers used in an Ethernet frame for IP and ARP.

5. Is some form of ARP protocol necessary for IP over frame relay? Why or why not?

Chapter 6 | Multimedia Networking

6.1 MULTIMEDIA NETWORKING APPLICATIONS

Back in Chapter 2 we examined the Web, file transfer, and electronic mail in some detail. The data carried by these networking applications is, for the most part, static content such as text and images. When static content is sent from one host to another, it is desirable for the content to arrive at the destination as soon as possible. Nevertheless, moderately long end-to-end delays, up to tens of seconds, are often tolerated for static content.

In this chapter we consider networking applications whose data contains audio and video content. We shall refer to networking applications as **multimedia networking applications.** (Some authors refer to these applications as **continuous-media** applications.) Multimedia networking applications are typically *highly* sensitive to delay; depending on the particular multimedia networking application, packets that incur more than an x second delay—where x can range from 100 msecs to five seconds—are useless. On the other hand, multimedia networking applications are typically **loss tolerant;** occasional loss only causes occasional glitches in the audio/video playback, and often these losses can be partially or fully concealed. Thus, in terms of service requirements, multimedia applications are diametrically opposite of static-content applications: Multimedia applications are delay sensitive and loss tolerant whereas the static-content applications are delay tolerant and loss intolerant.

6.1.1 Examples of Multimedia Applications

The Internet carries a large variety of exciting multimedia applications. In the following sections, we define three classes of multimedia applications.

Streaming stored audio and video. In this class of applications, clients request on-demand compressed audio or video files, which are stored on servers. For audio, these files can contain a professor's lectures, rock songs, symphonies, archives of famous radio broadcasts, and historical archival recordings. For video, these files can contain video of professors' lectures, full-length movies, prerecorded television shows, documentaries, video archives of historical events, video recordings of sporting events, cartoons, and music video clips. At any time, a client machine can request an audio/video file from a server. In most of the existing stored audio/video applications, after a delay of a few seconds the client begins to playback the audio file *while* it continues to receive the file from the server. The feature of playing back audio or video while the file is being received is called **streaming.** Many of the existing products also provide for **user interactivity,** for example, pause/resume and temporal jumps to the future and past of the audio file. The delay from when a user makes a request (for example, request to hear an audio file or skip two-minutes forward) until the action manifests itself at the user host (for example, user begins to hear audio file) should be on the order of 1 to 10 seconds for acceptable responsiveness. Requirements for packet delay and jitter are not as stringent as those for real-time applications such as Internet telephony and real-time video conferencing (see below). There are many streaming products for stored audio/video, including RealPlayer from RealNetworks and NetShow from Microsoft.

One to many streaming of real-time audio and video.   This class of applications is similar to ordinary broadcast of radio and television, except the transmission takes place over the Internet. These applications allow a user to receive a radio or television transmission emitted from any corner of the world. (For example, one of the authors of this book often listens to his favorite Philadelphia radio stations from his home in France.) Microsoft provides an Internet radio station guide.

Typically, there are many users who are simultaneously receiving the same real-time audio/video program. This class of applications is non-interactive; a client cannot control a server's transmission schedule. As with streaming of stored multimedia, requirements for packet delay and jitter are not as stringent as those for Internet telephony and real-time video conferencing. Delays up to tens of seconds from when the user clicks on a link until audio/video playback begins can be tolerated. Distribution of the real-time audio/video to many receivers is efficiently done with multicast; however, as of this writing, most of the one-to-many audio/video transmissions in the Internet are done with separate unicast streams to each of the receivers.

Real-time interactive audio and video.   This class of applications allows people to use audio/video to communicate with each other in real time. Real-time interactive audio is often referred to as **Internet phone,** since, from the user's perspective, it is similar to traditional circuit-switched telephone service. Internet phone can potentially provide PBX, local, and long-distance telephone service at very low cost. It can also facilitate computer-telephone integration (CTI), group real-time communication, directory services, caller identification, caller filtering, etc. There are many Internet telephone products currently available. With real-time interactive video, also called video conferencing, individuals communicate visually as well as orally. During a group meeting, a user can open a window for each participant the user is interested in seeing. There are also many real-time interactive video products currently available for the Internet, including Microsoft's Netmeeting. Note that in a real-time interactive audio/video application, a user can speak or move at anytime. The delay from when a user speaks or moves until the action is manifested at the receiving hosts should be less than a few hundred milliseconds. For voice, delays smaller than 150 milliseconds are not perceived by a human listener, delays between 150 and 400 milliseconds can be acceptable, and delays exceeding 400 milliseconds result in frustrating if not completely unintelligible voice conversations.

One-to-many real-time audio and video is not interactive—a user cannot pause or rewind a transmission that hundreds of others listen to. Although streaming stored audio/video allows for interactive actions such as pause and rewind, it is not real time, since the content has already been gathered and stored on hard disks. Finally, real-time interactive audio/video is interactive in the sense that participants can orally and visually respond to each other in real time.

6.1.2   Hurdles for Multimedia in the Internet

IP, the Internet's network-layer protocol, provides a **best-effort service** to all the datagrams it carries. In other words, the Internet makes its best effort to move each datagram from sender to receiver as quickly as possible. However, the best-effort service does not make any promises whatsoever about the end-to-end delay for an individual packet. Nor does the service make any promises about the variation of packet delay within a packet stream. As we learned in Chapter 3, because TCP and UDP run over IP, neither of these protocols can make any delay guarantees to invoking applications. Due to the lack of any special effort to deliver packets in a timely manner, it is an extremely challenging problem to develop successful multimedia networking applications for the Internet. To date, multimedia over the Internet has achieved significant but limited success. For example, streaming stored audio/video with user-interactivity delays of five-to-ten seconds is now commonplace in the Internet. But during peak traffic periods, performance may be unsatisfactory, particularly when intervening links are congested links (such as congested transoceanic links).

Internet phone and real-time interactive video has, to date, been less successful than streaming stored audio/video. Indeed, real-time interactive voice and video impose rigid constraints on packet delay and packet jitter. **Packet jitter** is the variability of packet delays within the same packet stream. Real-time voice and video can work well in regions where bandwidth is plentiful, and hence delay and jitter are minimal. But quality can deteriorate to unacceptable levels as soon as the real-time voice or video packet stream hits a moderately congested link.

The design of multimedia applications would certainly be more straightforward if there were some sort of first-class and second-class Internet services, whereby first-class packets are limited in number and always get priorities in router queues. Such a first-class service could be satisfactory for delay-sensitive applications. But to date, the Internet has mostly taken an egalitarian approach to packet scheduling in router queues. All packets receive equal service; no packets, including delay-sensitive audio and video packets, get any priorities in the router queues. No matter how much money you have or how important you are, you must join the end of the line and wait your turn!

So for the time being we have to live with the best effort service. No matter how important or how rich we are, our packets have to wait their turn in router queues. But given this constraint, we can make several design decisions and employ a few tricks to improve the user-perceived quality of a multimedia networking application. For example, we can send the audio and video over UDP, and thereby circumvent TCP's low throughput when TCP enters its slow-start phase. We can delay playback at the receiver by 100 msecs or more in order to diminish the effects of network-induced jitter. We can timestamp packets at the sender so that the receiver knows when the packets should be played back. For stored audio/video we can prefetch data during playback when client storage and extra bandwidth is available. We can even send redundant information in order to mitigate the effects of network-induced packet loss. We shall investigate many of these techniques in this chapter.

6.1.3 How Should the Internet Evolve to Better Support Multimedia?

Today there is a tremendous—and sometimes ferocious—debate about how the Internet should evolve in order to better accommodate multimedia traffic with its rigid timing constraints. At one extreme, some researchers argue that it isn't necessary to make any fundamental changes to the best-effort service and the underlying Internet protocols. Instead, according to these extremists, it is only necessary to add more bandwidth to the links (along with network caching for stored information and multicast support for one-to-many real-time streaming). Opponents to this viewpoint argue that additional bandwidth can be costly, and as soon as it is put in place it will be eaten up by new bandwidth-hungry applications (for example, high-definition video on demand).

At the other extreme, some researchers argue that fundamental changes should be made to the Internet so that applications can explicitly reserve end-to-end bandwidth. These researchers feel, for example, that if a user wants to make an Internet phone call from host A to host B, then the user's Internet phone application should be able to explicitly reserve bandwidth in each link along a route from host A to host B. But allowing applications to make reservations and requiring the network to honor the reservations requires some big changes. First we need a protocol that, on the behalf of applications, reserves bandwidth from the senders to their receivers. Second, we need to modify scheduling policies in the router queues so that bandwidth reservations can be honored. With these new scheduling policies, all packets no longer get equal treatment; instead, those that reserve (and pay) more get more. Third, in order to honor reservations, the applications need to give the network a description of the traffic that they intend to send into the network. The network must then police each application's traffic to make sure that it abides to the description. Finally, the network must have a means of determining whether it has sufficient available bandwidth to support any new reservation request. These mechanisms, when combined, require new and complex software in the hosts and routers as well as new types of services.

There is a camp between the two extremes—the so-called differentiated services camp. This camp wants to make relatively small changes at the network and transport layers, and introduce simple pricing and policing schemes at the edge of the network (that is, at the interface between the user and the user's ISP). The idea is to introduce a small number of classes (possibly just two classes), assign each datagram to one of the classes, give datagrams different levels of service according to their class in the router queues, and charge users to reflect the class of packets that they are emitting into the network. A simple example of a differentiated-services Internet is as follows. By toggling a single bit in the datagram header, all IP datagrams are labeled as either first-class or second-class datagrams. In each router queue, each arriving first-class datagram jumps in front of all the second-class datagrams; in this manner, second-class datagrams do not interfere with first-class datagrams—it is as if the first-class packets have their own network! The network edge counts the number of first-class datagrams each user sends into the network each week. When a user subscribes to an Internet service, the user can opt for a "platinum service" whereby the user is permitted to send a large but limited number of first-class datagrams into the network each week; first-class datagrams in excess of the limit are converted to second-class datagrams at the network edge. A user can also opt for a "low-budget" service, whereby all of his datagrams are second-class datagrams. Of course, the user pays a higher subscription rate for the platinum service than for the low-budget service. Finally, the network is dimensioned and the first-class service is priced so that "almost always" first-class datagrams experience insignificant delays at all router queues. In this manner, sources of audio/video can subscribe to the first-class service, and thereby receive "almost always" satisfactory service. We will cover differentiated services in Section 6.9.

6.1.4   Audio and Video Compression

Before audio and video can be transmitted over a computer network, it has to be digitized and compressed. The need for digitization is obvious: Computer networks transmit bits, so all transmitted information must be represented as a sequence of bits. Compression is important because uncompressed audio and video consumes a tremendous amount of storage and bandwidth; removing the inherent redundancies in digitized audio and video signals can reduce by orders of magnitude the amount of data that needs to be stored and transmitted. As an example, a single image consisting of 1024 pixels $\times$ 1024 pixels with each pixel encoded into 24 bits requires 3 MB of storage without compression. It would take seven minutes to send this image over a 64 Kbps link. If the image is compressed at a modest 10:1 compression ratio, the storage requirement is reduced to 300 KB and the transmission time drops to under six seconds.

The fields of audio and video compression are vast. They have been active areas of research for more than 50 years, and there are now literally hundreds of popular techniques and standards for both audio and video compression. Most universities offer entire courses on audio and video compression, and often offer a separate course on audio compression and a separate course on video compression. Furthermore, electrical engineering and computer science departments often offer independent courses on the subject, with each department approaching the subject from a different angle. We therefore provide here a brief and high-level introduction to the subject.

Audio compression in the Internet.   A continuously-varying analog audio signal (which could emanate from speech or music) is normally converted to a digital signal as follows:

1. The analog audio signal is first sampled at some fixed rate, for example, at 8,000 samples per second. The value of each sample is an arbitrary real number.

2. Each of the samples is then "rounded" to one of a finite number of values. This operation is referred to as "quantization." The number of finite values—called quantization values—is typically a power of 2, for example, 256 quantization values.

3. Each of the quantization values is represented by a fixed number of bits. For example if there are 256 quantization values, then each value—and hence each sample—is represented by 1 byte. Each of the samples is converted to its bit representation. The bit representations of all the samples are concatenated together to form the digital representation of the signal.

As an example, if an analog audio signal is sampled at 8,000 samples per second, each sample is quantized and represented by 8 bits, then the resulting digital signal will have a rate of 64,000 bits per second. This digital signal can then be converted back—that is, decoded—to an analog signal for playback. However, the decoded analog signal is typically different from the original audio signal. By increasing the sampling rate and the number of quantization values, the decoded signal can approximate (and even be exactly equal to) the original analog signal. Thus, there is a clear tradeoff between the quality of the decoded signal and the storage and bandwidth requirements of the digital signal.

The basic encoding technique that we just described is called **Pulse Code Modulation (PCM).** Speech encoding often uses PCM, with a sampling rate of 8000 samples per second and 8 bits per sample, giving a rate of 64 Kbps. The audio Compact Disk (CD) also uses PCM, without a sampling rate of 44,100 samples per second with 16 bits per sample; this gives a rate of 705.6 Kbps for mono and 1.411 Mbps for stereo.

A bit rate of 1.411 Mbps for stereo music exceeds most access rates, and even 64 Kbps for speech exceeds the access rate for a dial-up modem user. For these reasons, PCM encoded speech and music is rarely used in the Internet. Instead compression techniques are used to reduce the bit rates of the stream. Popular compression techniques for speech include **GSM** (13 Kbps), **G.729** (8 Kbps) and **G.723** (both 6.4 and 5.3 Kbps), and also a large number of proprietary techniques, including those used by RealNetworks. A popular compression technique for near CD-quality stereo music is **MPEG layer 3,** more commonly known as **MP3.** MP3 compresses the bit rate for music to 128 or 112 Kbps, and produces very little sound degradation. An MP3 file can be broken up into pieces, and each piece is still playable. This headerless file format allows MP3 music files to be streamed across the Internet (assuming the playback bit rate and speed of the Internet connection are compatible). The MP3 compression standard is complex; it uses psychoacoustic masking, redundancy reduction. and bit reservoir buffering.

Video compression in the Internet. A video is a sequence images, with each image typically being displayed at a constant rate, for example at 24 or 30 images per second. An uncompressed, digitally encoded image consists of an array of pixels, with each pixel encoded into a number of bits to represent luminance and color. There are two types of redundancy in video, both of which can be exploited for compression. Spatial redundancy is the redundancy within a given image. For example, an image that consists of mostly white space can be efficiently compressed. Temporal redundancy reflects repetition from image to subsequent image. If, for example, an image and the subsequent image are exactly the same, there is no reason to re-encode the subsequent image; it is more efficient to simply indicate during encoding that the subsequent image is exactly the same.

The MPEG compression standards are among the most popular compression techniques. These include **MPEG 1** for CD-ROM quality video (1.5 Mbps), **MPEG 2** for high-quality **DVD** video (3–6 Mbps), and **MPEG 4** for object-oriented video compression. The MPEG standard draws heavily from the JPEG standard for image compression. The **H.261** video compression standards are also very popular in the Internet, as well as numerous proprietary standards.

Readers interested in learning more about audio and video encoding are encouraged to see [Rao 1996] and [Solari 1997].

6.2   STREAMING STORED AUDIO AND VIDEO

In recent years, audio/video streaming has become a popular class of applications and a major consumer of network bandwidth. We expect this trend to continue for several reasons. First, the cost of disk storage is decreasing at phenomenal rates, even faster than processing and bandwidth costs. Cheap storage will lead to an exponential increase in the amount of stored/audio video in the Internet. Second, improvements in Internet infrastructure, such as high-speed residential access (that is, cable modems and ADSL, as discussed in Chapter 1), network caching of video (see Section 2.2), and new QoS-oriented Internet protocols (see Sections 6.5–6.9) will greatly facilitate the distribution of stored audio and video. And third, there is an enormous pent-up demand for high-quality video streaming, an application that combines two existing killer communication technologies—television and the on-demand Web.

In audio/video streaming, clients request compressed audio/video files, which are resident on servers. As we shall discuss in this section, the servers can be "ordinary" Web servers, or can be special streaming servers tailored for the audio/video streaming application. The files on the servers can contain any type of audio/video content, including a professor's lectures, rock songs, movies, television shows, recorded sporting events, etc. Upon client request, the server directs an audio/video file to the client by sending the file into a socket. (Sockets are discussed in Sections 2.6–2.7.) Both TCP and UDP socket connections are used in practice. Before sending the audio/video file into the network, the file is segmented, and the segments are typically encapsulated with special headers appropriate for audio/video traffic. **Real-Time Protocol (RTP),** discussed in Section 6.4, is a public-domain standard for encapsulating the segments. Once the client begins to receive the requested audio/video file, the client begins to render the file (typically) within a few seconds. Most of the existing products also provide for user interactivity, for example, pause/resume and temporal jumps to the future and past of the audio/video file. User interactivity also requires a protocol for client/server interaction. **Real Time Streaming Protocol (RTSP),** discussed at the end of this section, is a public-domain protocol for providing user interactivity.

Audio/video streaming is often requested by users through a Web client (that is, browser). But because audio/video playout is not integrated directly in today's Web clients, a separate **helper application** is required for playing out the audio/video. The helper application is often called a **media player,** the most popular of which are currently RealNetworks' Real Players and the Microsoft Windows Media Player. The media player performs several functions, including:

- *Decompression.* Audio/video is almost always compressed to save disk storage and network bandwidth. A media player has to decompress the audio/video on the fly during playout.
- *Jitter-removal.* Packet jitter is the variability of packet delays within the same packet stream. Packet jitter, if not suppressed, can easily lead to unintelligible audio and video. As we shall examine in some detail in Section 6.3, packet jitter can often be limited by buffering audio/video for a few seconds at the client before playback.
- *Error correction.* Due to unpredictable congestion in the Internet, a fraction of packets in the packet stream can be lost. If this fraction becomes too large, user-perceived audio/video quality becomes unacceptable. To this end, many streaming systems attempt to recover from losses by either (1) reconstructing lost packets through the transmission of redundant packets, (2) by having the client explicitly request retransmissions of lost packets, (3) or both.
- *Graphical user interface with control knobs.* This is the actual interface that the user interacts with. It typically includes volume controls, pause/resume buttons, sliders for making temporal jumps in the audio/video stream, etc.

Plug-ins may be used to embed the user interface of the media player within the window of the Web browser. For such embeddings, the browser reserves screen space on the current Web page, and it is up to the media player to manage the screen space. But either appearing in a separate window or within the browser window (as a plug-in), the media player is a program that is being executed separately from the browser.

6.2.1   Accessing Audio and Video from a Web Server

The stored audio/video can either reside on a Web server, which delivers the audio/video to the client over HTTP, or on an audio/video streaming server, which delivers the audio/video over non-HTTP protocols (protocols that can be either proprietary or in the public domain). In this subsection, we examine the delivery of audio/video from a Web server; in the next subsection, we examine the delivery from a streaming server.

Consider first the case of audio streaming. When an audio file resides on a Web server, the audio file is an ordinary object in the server's file system, just as are HTML and JPEG files. When a user wants to hear the audio file, the user's host establishes a TCP connection with the Web server and sends an HTTP request for the object (see Section 2.2). Upon receiving a request, the Web server bundles the audio file in an HTTP response message and sends the response message back into the TCP connection. The case of video can be a little more tricky, because the audio and video parts of the "video" may be stored in two different files, that is, they may be two different objects in the Web server's file system. In this case, two separate HTTP requests are sent to the server (over two separate TCP connections for HTTP/1.0), and the audio and video files arrive at the client in parallel. It is up to the client to manage the synchronization of the two streams. It is also possible that the audio and video are interleaved in the same file, so that only one object has to be sent to the client. To keep the discussion simple, for the case of "video" we assume that the audio and video is contained in one file for the remainder of this section.

A naive architecture for audio/video streaming is shown in Figure 6.1. In this architecture:

1. The browser process establishes a TCP connection with the Web server and requests the audio/video file with an HTTP request message.
2. The Web server sends to the browser the audio/video file in an HTTP response message.
3. The `content-type` header line in the HTTP response message indicates a specific audio/video encoding. The client browser examines the `content-type` of the response message, launches the associated media player, and passes the file to the media player.
4. The media player then renders the audio/video file.

Although this approach is very simple, it has a major drawback: The media player (that is, the helper application) must interact with the server through the intermediary of a Web browser. This can lead to many problems. In particular, when the browser is an intermediary, the entire object must be downloaded before the browser passes the object to a helper application. The resulting initial delay is typically unacceptable for audio/video clips of moderate length. For this reason,

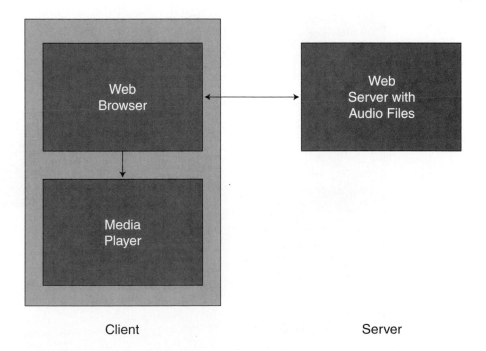

FIGURE 6.1   A naive implementation for audio streaming

audio/video streaming implementations typically have the server send the audio/video file directly to the media player process. In other words, a direct socket connection is made between the server process and the media player process. As shown in Figure 6.2, this is typically done by making use of a **meta file,** which is a file that provides information (for example, URL, type of encoding) about the audio/video file that is to be streamed.

A direct TCP connection between the server and the media player is obtained as follows:

1. The user clicks on a hyperlink for an audio/video file.
2. The hyperlink does not point directly to the audio/video file, but instead to a meta file. The meta file contains the URL of the actual audio/video file. The HTTP response message that encapsulates the meta file includes a `content-type` header line that indicates the specific audio/video application.
3. The client browser examines the `content-type` header line of the response message, launches the associated media player, and passes the entire body of the response message (that is, the meta file) to the media player.
4. The media player sets up a TCP connection directly with the HTTP server. The media player sends an HTTP request message for the audio/video file into the TCP connection.
5. The audio/video file is sent within an HTTP response message to the media player. The media player streams out the audio/video file.

The importance of the intermediate step of acquiring the meta file is clear. When the browser sees the `content-type` for the file, it can launch the appropriate media player, and thereby have the media player directly contact the server.

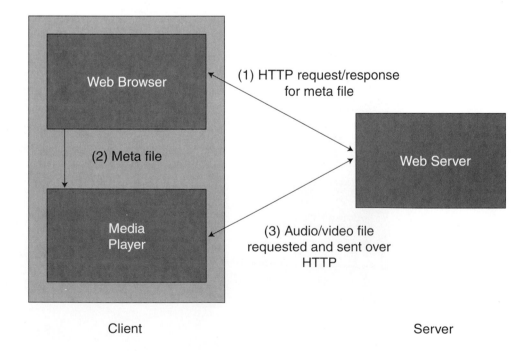

FIGURE 6.2 Web server sends audio/video directly to the media player

We have just learned how a meta file can allow a media player to dialogue directly with a Web server housing an audio/video. Yet many companies that sell products for audio/video streaming do not recommend the architecture we just described. This is because the architecture has the media player communicate with the server over HTTP and hence also over TCP. HTTP is often considered insufficiently rich to allow for satisfactory user interaction with the server; in particular, HTTP does not easily allow a user (through the media server) to send pause/resume, fast-forward, and temporal jump commands to the server. TCP is often considered inappropriate for audio/video streaming, particularly when users are behind slow modem links. This is because, upon packet loss, the TCP sender rate almost comes to a halt, which can result in extended periods of time during which the media player is starved. Nevertheless, audio and video is often streamed from Web servers over TCP with satisfactory results.

6.2.2   Sending Multimedia from a Streaming Server to a Helper Application

In order to get around HTTP and/or TCP, the audio/video can be stored on and sent from a streaming server to the media player. This streaming server could be a proprietary streaming server, such as those marketed by RealNetworks and Microsoft, or could be a public-domain streaming server. With a streaming server, the audio/video can be sent over UDP (rather than TCP) using application-layer protocols that may be better tailored to audio/video streaming than is HTTP.

This architecture requires two servers, as shown in Figure 6.3. One server, the HTTP server, serves Web pages (including meta files). The second server, the **streaming server,** serves the audio/video files. The two servers can run on the same end system or on two distinct end systems. (If the Web server is very busy serving Web pages, it may be advantageous to put the streaming server on its own

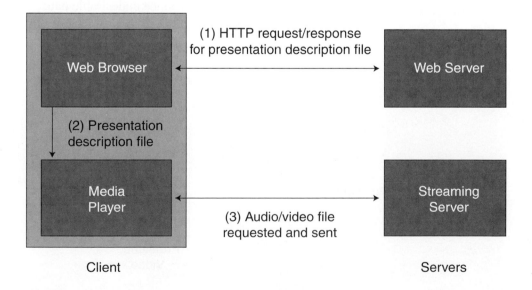

FIGURE 6.3   Streaming from a streaming server to a media player

machine.) The steps for this architecture are similar to those described in the previous architecture. However, now the media player requests the file from a streaming server rather than from a Web server, and now the media player and streaming server can interact using their own protocols. These protocols can allow for rich user interaction with the audio/video stream. Furthermore, the audio/video file can be sent to the media player over UDP instead of TCP.

In the architecture of Figure 6.3, there are many options for delivering the audio/video from the streaming server to the media player. A partial list of the options is given below:

1. The audio/video is sent over UDP at a constant rate equal to the drain rate at the receiver (which is the encoded rate of the audio/video). For example, if the audio is compressed using GSM at a rate of 13 Kbps, then the server clocks out the compressed audio file at 13 Kbps. As soon as the client receives compressed audio/video from the network, it decompresses the audio/video and plays it back.

2. This is the same as option 1, but the media player delays playout for 2–5 seconds in order to eliminate network induced jitter. The client accomplishes this task by placing the compressed media that it receives from the network into a **client buffer,** as shown in Figure 6.4. Once the client has "prefetched" a few seconds of the media, it begins to drain the buffer. For this, and the previous option, the drain rate d is equal to the fill rate $x(t)$, except when there is packet loss, in which case $x(t)$ is momentarily less than d.

3. The audio is sent over TCP and the media player delays play out for 2–5 seconds. The server passes data to the TCP socket at a constant rate equal to the receiver drain rate d. TCP retransmits lost packets, and thereby possibly improves sound quality. But the fill rate $x(t)$ now fluctuates with time due to TCP slow start and window flow control, even when there is no packet loss. If there is no packet loss, the average fill rate should be approximately equal to the drain rate d. Furthermore, after packet loss, TCP congestion control may reduce the instantaneous rate to less than d for long periods of time. This can empty the client buffer and introduce undesirable pauses into the output of the audio/video stream at the client.

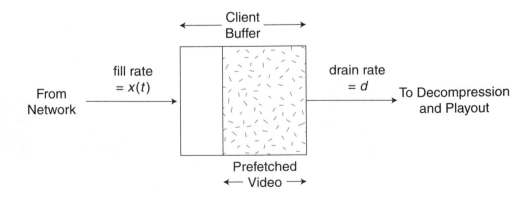

FIGURE 6.4   Client buffer being filled at rate $x(t)$ and drained at rate d

4. This is the same as option 3, but now the media player uses a large client buffer—large enough to hold most, if not all, of the audio/video file (possibly within disk storage). The server pushes the audio/video file into its TCP socket as quickly as it can; the client reads from its TCP socket as quickly as it can, and places the decompressed audio/video into the large client buffer. In this case, TCP makes use of all the instantaneous bandwidth available to the connection, so that at times $x(t)$ can be much larger than d. When the instantaneous bandwidth drops below the drain rate, the receiver does not experience loss as long as the client buffer is nonempty.

6.2.3   Real Time Streaming Protocol (RTSP)

Audio, video, and SMIL presentations are often referred to as continuous media. (SMIL stands for Synchronized Multimedia Integration Language; it is a document language standard, as is HTML. As its name suggests, SMIL defines how continuous media objects, as well as static objects, are synchronized in a presentation that unravels over time. An in-depth discussion of SMIL is beyond the scope of this book.) Users typically want to *control* the playback of continuous media by pausing playback, repositioning playback to a future or past point of time, visual fast-forwarding playback, visual rewinding playback, etc. This functionality is similar to what a user has with a VCR when watching a video cassette or with a CD player when listening to CD music. To allow a user to control playback, the media player and server need a protocol for exchanging playback control information. RTSP, defined in [RFC 2326], is such a protocol.

But before getting into the details of RTSP, let us indicate what RTSP does not do:

- RTSP does not define compression schemes for audio and video.
- RTSP does not define how audio and video is encapsulated in packets for transmission over a network; encapsulation for streaming media can be provided by RTP or by a proprietary protocol. (RTP is discussed in Section 6.4) For example, RealMedia's G2 server and player use RTSP to send control information to each other. But the media stream itself can be encapsulated RTP packets or with some proprietary RealNetworks scheme.
- RTSP does not restrict how the streamed media is transported; it can be transported over UDP or TCP.
- RTSP does not restrict how the media player buffers the audio/video. The audio/video can be played out as soon as it begins to arrive at the client, it can be played out after a delay of a few seconds, or it can be downloaded in its entirety before playout.

So if RTSP doesn't do any of the above, what does RTSP do? RTSP is a protocol that allows a media player to control the transmission of a media stream. As mentioned above, control actions include pause/resume, repositioning of playback, fast forward and rewind. RTSP is a so-called **out-of-band protocol.** In particular, the RTSP messages are sent out-of-band, whereas the media stream, whose packet structure is not defined by RTSP, is considered "in-band." The RTSP messages use different port numbers than the media stream. RTSP uses port number 554. (If the RTSP messages were to use the same port numbers as the media stream, then RTSP messages would be said to be "interleaved" with the media stream.) The RTSP specification [RFC 2326] permits RTSP messages to be sent over either TCP or UDP.

Recall from Section 2.3, that File Transfer Protocol (FTP) also uses the out-of-band notion. In particular, FTP uses two client/server pairs of sockets, each pair with its own port number: one client/server socket pair supports a TCP connection that transports control information; the other client/server socket pair supports a TCP connection that actually transports the file. The control TCP connection is the so-called out-of-band channel whereas the TCP connection that transports the file is the so-called data channel. The out-of-band channel is used for sending remote directory changes, remote file deletion, remote file renaming, file download requests, etc. The in-band channel transports the file itself. The RTSP channel is in many ways similar to FTP's control channel.

Let us now walk through a simple RTSP example, which is illustrated in Figure 6.5. The Web browser first requests a presentation description file from a Web server. The presentation description file can have references to several continuous-media files as well as directives for synchronization of the continuous-media files. Each reference to a continuous-media file begins with the URL method, `rtsp://`. Below we provide a sample presentation file, which has been adapted from a paper by [Schulzrinne 1997]. In this presentation, an audio and video stream are played in parallel and in lip sync (as part of the same "group"). For the audio

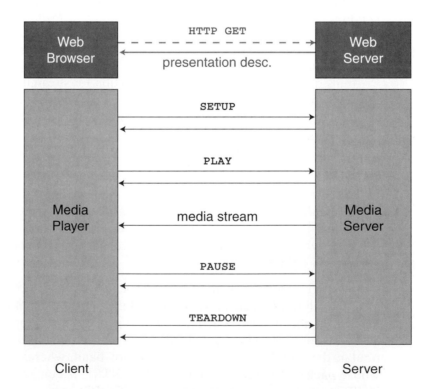

FIGURE 6.5 Interaction between client and server using RTSP

stream, the media player can choose ("switch") between two audio recordings, a low fidelity recording and a high fidelity recording.

```
<title>Twister</title>
<session>
   <group language=en lipsync>
          <switch>
              <track type=audio
                    e="PCMU/8000/1"
                    src = "rtsp://audio.example.com/twister/audio.en/lofi">
              <track type=audio
                    e="DVI4/16000/2" pt="90 DVI4/8000/1"
                    src="rtsp://audio.example.com/twister/audio.en/hifi">
          </switch>
        <track type="video/jpeg"
                    src="rtsp://video.example.com/twister/video">
   </group>
</session>
```

The Web server encapsulates the presentation description file in an HTTP response message and sends the message to the browser. When the browser receives the HTTP response message, the browser invokes a media player (that is, the helper application) based on the content-type field of the message. The presentation description file includes references to media streams, using the URL method rtsp://, as shown in the above sample. As shown in Figure 6.5, the player and the server then send each other a series of RTSP messages. The player sends an RTSP SETUP request, and the server sends an RTSP SETUP response. The player sends an RTSP PLAY request, say, for low fidelity audio, and the server sends an RTSP PLAY response. At this point, the streaming server pumps the low fidelity audio into its own in-band channel. Later, the media player sends an RTSP PAUSE request, and the server responds with an RTSP PAUSE response. When the user is finished, the media player sends an RTSP TEARDOWN request, and the server responds with an RTSP TEARDOWN response.

Each RTSP session has a session identifier, which is chosen by the server. The client initiates the session with the SETUP request, and the server responds to the request with an identifier. The client repeats the session identifier for each request, until the client closes the session with the TEARDOWN request. The following is a simplified example of an RTSP session:

```
C: SETUP rtsp://audio.example.com/twister/audio RTSP/1.0
   Transport: rtp/udp; compression; port=3056; mode=PLAY
S: RTSP/1.0 200 1 OK
   Session 4231
C: PLAY rtsp://audio.example.com/twister/audio.en/lofi
     RTSP/1.0
   Session: 4231
   Range: npt=0-
C: PAUSE rtsp://audio.example.com/twister/audio.en/
     lofi RTSP/1.0
   Session: 4231
```

```
         Range: npt=37
```
C: `TEARDOWN rtsp://audio.example.com/twister/audio.en/`
`lofi RTSP/1.0 Session: 4231`

S: `200 3 OK`

Notice that in this example, the player chose not to play back the complete presentation, but instead only the low fidelity portion of the presentation. The RTSP protocol is actually capable of doing much more than described in this brief introduction. In particular, RTSP has facilities that allow clients to stream towards the server (for example, for recording). RTSP has been adapted by RealNetworks, currently the industry leader in audio/video streaming. RealNetworks makes available a Web page on RTSP [RealNetworks].

6.3 MAKING THE BEST OF THE BEST-EFFORT SERVICE: AN INTERNET PHONE EXAMPLE

The Internet's network layer protocol, IP, provides a **best-effort service.** That is to say that the Internet makes its best effort to move each datagram from source to destination as quickly as possible. However, the best-effort service does not make any promises whatsoever on the extent of the end-to-end delay for an individual packet, or on the extent of packet jitter and packet loss within the packet stream.

Real-time interactive multimedia applications, such as Internet phone and real-time video conferencing, are acutely sensitive to packet delay, jitter, and loss. Fortunately, designers of these applications can introduce several useful mechanisms that can preserve good audio and video quality as long as delay, jitter, and loss are not excessive. In this section, we examine some of these mechanisms. To keep the discussion concrete, we discuss these mechanisms in the context of an **Internet phone application,** described in the paragraph below. The situation is similar for real-time video conferencing applications [Bolot 1994].

The speaker in our Internet phone application generates an audio signal consisting of alternating talk spurts and silent periods. In order to conserve bandwidth, our Internet phone application only generates packets during talk spurts. During a talk spurt the sender generates bytes at a rate of 8 Kbytes per second, and every 20 milliseconds the sender gathers bytes into chunks. Thus, the number of bytes in a chunk is (20 msecs) · (8 Kbytes/sec) = 160 bytes. A special header is attached to each chunk, the contents of which is discussed below. The chunk, along with its header, are encapsulated in a UDP segment, and then the UDP datagram is sent into the socket interface. Thus, during a talk spurt, a UDP segment is sent every 20 msec.

If each packet makes it to the receiver (that is, no loss) and has a small constant end-to-end delay, then packets arrive at the receiver periodically every 20 msec during a talk spurt. In these ideal conditions, the receiver can simply play back each chunk as soon as it arrives. But, unfortunately, some packets can be lost and most packets will not have a fixed end-to-end delay, in even a lightly congested Internet. For this reason, the receiver must take more care in (1) determining when to play back a chunk, and (2) determining what to do with a missing chunk.

6.3.1   The Limitations of a Best-Effort Service

We mentioned that the best-effort service can lead to packet loss, excessive end-to-end delay, and delay jitter. Let's examine these issues in more detail.

Packet loss.   Consider one of the UDP datagrams generated by our Internet phone application. The UDP segment is encapsulated in an IP datagram, and the IP datagram makes its way through the network towards the receiver. As the datagram wanders through the network, it passes through buffers (that is, queues) in the routers in order to access outbound links. It is possible that one or more of the buffers in the route from sender to receiver is full and cannot admit the IP datagram. In this case, the IP datagram is discarded and becomes a **lost packet.** It never arrives at the receiving application.

Loss could be eliminated by sending the packets over TCP rather than over UDP. Recall that TCP retransmits packets that do not arrive at the destination. However, retransmission mechanisms are generally not acceptable for interactive real-time audio applications, such as Internet phone, because they increase end-to-end delay [Bolot 1996]. Furthermore, due to TCP congestion control, after packet loss the transmission rate at the sender can be reduced to a rate that is lower than the drain rate at the receiver. This can have a severe impact on voice intelligibility at the receiver. For these reasons, almost all existing Internet phone applications run over UDP and do not bother to retransmit lost packets.

But losing packets is not necessarily as grave as one might think. Indeed, packet loss rates between 1% and 20% can be tolerated, depending on how the voice is encoded and transmitted, and on how the loss is concealed at the receiver. For example, Forward Error Correction (FEC) can help conceal packet loss. As we shall see below, with FEC redundant information is transmitted along with the original information so that some of the lost original data can be recovered from the redundant information. Nevertheless, if one or more of the links between sender and receiver is severely congested, and packet loss exceeds 10–20%, then there is really nothing that can be done to achieve acceptable sound quality. The best-effort service has its limitations.

End-to-end delay.   **End-to-end delay** is the accumulation of processing and queuing delays in routers, propagation delays, and end-system processing delays. For highly interactive audio applications, like Internet phone, end-to-end delays smaller than 150 milliseconds are not perceived by a human listener; delays between 150 and 400 milliseconds can be acceptable but not ideal; and delays exceeding 400 milliseconds result in unintelligible voice conversations. The receiver in an Internet phone application will typically disregard any packets that are delayed more than a certain threshold, for example, more than 400 milliseconds. Thus, packets that are delayed by more than the threshold are effectively lost.

Delay jitter.   One of the components of end-to-end delay is the random queuing delays in the routers. Because of these random queuing delays within the network, the time from when a packet is generated at the source until it is received at the receiver can fluctuate from packet to packet. This phenomenon is called **jitter.**

As an example, consider two consecutive packets within a talk spurt in our Internet phone application. The sender sends the second packet 20 msec after sending the first packet. But at the receiver, the spacing between these packets can become greater than 20 msec. To see this, suppose the first packet arrives at a nearly empty queue at a router, but just before the second packet arrives at the queue a large number of packets from other sources arrive to the same queue. Because the second packet suffers a large queuing delay, the first and second packets become spaced apart by more than 20 msecs. (In fact, the spacing between two consecutive packets can become one second or more.) The spacing between consecutive packets can also become less than 20 msecs. To see this, again consider two consecutive packets within a talk spurt. Suppose the first packet joins the end of a queue with a large number of packets, and the second packet arrives at the queue before packets from other sources arrive at the queue. Thus, our two packets find themselves right behind each other in the queue. If the time it takes to transmit a packet on the router's inbound link is less than 20 msecs, then the first and second packets become spaced apart by less than 20 msecs.

The situation is analogous to driving cars on roads. Suppose you and your friend are each driving in your own cars from San Diego to Phoenix. Suppose you and your friend have similar driving styles, and that you both drive at 100 km/hour, traffic permitting. Finally, suppose your friend starts out one hour before you. Then, depending on intervening traffic, you may arrive at Phoenix more or less than one hour after your friend.

If the receiver ignores the presence of jitter, and plays out chunks as soon as they arrive, then the resulting audio quality can easily become unintelligible at the receiver. Fortunately, jitter can be often be removed by using **sequence numbers,** **timestamps,** and a **playout delay,** as we discuss below.

6.3.2 Removing Jitter at the Receiver for Audio

For a voice application such as Internet phone or audio-on-demand, the receiver should attempt to provide synchronous playout of voice chunks in the presence of random network jitter. This is typically done by combining the following three mechanisms:

- Appending a **sequence number** to each chunk. The sender increments the sequence number by one for each of the packet it generates.
- Appending a **timestamp** on each chunk. The sender stamps each chunk with time at which the chunk was generated.
- **Delaying playout** of chunks at the receiver. The playout delay of the received audio chunks must be long enough so that most of the packets are received before their scheduled playout times. This playout delay can be either fixed throughout the duration of the conference, or it may vary adaptively during the conference's lifetime. Packets that do not arrive before their scheduled playout times are considered lost and forgotten; as mentioned above, the receiver may use some form of speech interpolation to attempt to conceal the loss.

The sequence number and timestamp occupy fields in the header of the audio chunk. A standardized format for the header of the audio chunks is described in the next section.

We now discuss how these three mechanisms, when combined, can alleviate or even eliminate the effects of jitter. We examine two playback strategies: fixed playout delay and adaptive playout delay.

Fixed playout delay. With the fixed delay strategy, the receiver attempts to playout each chunk exactly q msecs after the chunk is generated. So if a chunk is timestamped at time t, the receiver plays out the chunk at time $t + q$, assuming the chunk has arrived by the scheduled playout time $t + q$. Packets that arrive after their scheduled playout times are discarded and considered lost.

Note that sequence numbers are not necessary for this fixed delay strategy. Also note that even in the presence of occasional packet loss, we can continue to operate the fixed delay strategy.

What is a good choice for q? Internet telephone can support delays up to about 400 msecs, although a more satisfying interactive experience is achieved with smaller values of q. On the other hand, if q is made much smaller than 400 msecs, then many packets may miss their scheduled playback times due to the network-induced delay jitter. Roughly speaking, if large variations in end-to-end delay are typical, it is preferable to use a large q; on the other hand, if delay is small and variations in delay are also small, it is preferable to use a small q, perhaps less than 150 msecs.

The tradeoff between the playback delay and packet loss is illustrated in Figure 6.6. The figure shows the times at which packets are generated and played out for a single talkspurt. Two distinct initial playout delays are considered. As shown by the left-most staircase, the sender generates packets at regular intervals—specifically, every 20 msec. The first packet in this talkspurt is received at time r. As shown in the figure, the arrivals of subsequent packets are not evenly spaced due to the network jitter.

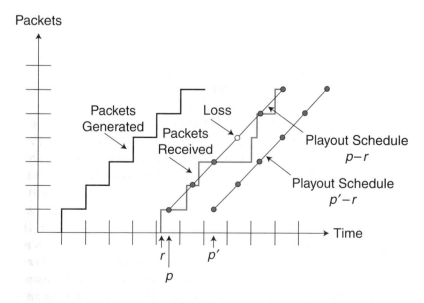

FIGURE 6.6 Packet loss for different fixed playout delays

For the first playout schedule, the fixed initial playout delay is set to $p - r$. With this schedule, the fourth packet does not arrive by its scheduled playout time, and the receiver considers it lost. For the second playout schedule, the fixed initial playout delay is set to $p' - r$. For this schedule, all of the packets arrive before their scheduled playout times, and there is therefore no loss.

Adaptive playout delay. The above example demonstrates an important delay-loss tradeoff that arises when designing a playout strategy with fixed playout delays. By making the initial playout delay large, most packets will make their deadlines and there will therefore be negligible loss; however, for interactive services such as Internet phone, long delays can become bothersome if not intolerable. Ideally, we would like the playout delay to be minimized subject to the constraint that the loss be below a few percent.

The natural way to deal with this tradeoff is to estimate the network delay and the variance of the network delay, and to accordingly adjust the playout delay at the beginning of each talkspurt. This adaptive adjustment of the playout delays at the beginning of the talkspurts will cause the sender's silent periods to be compressed and elongated; however, compression and elongation of silence by a small amount is not noticeable in speech.

Following the paper [Ramjee 1994], we now describe a generic algorithm that the receiver can use to adaptively adjust its playout delays. To this end, let

t_i = timestamp of the ith packet = the time packet was generated by sender

r_i = the time packet i is received by receiver

p_i = the time packet i is played at receiver

The end-to-end network delay of the ith packet is $r_i - t_i$. Due to network jitter, this delay will vary from packet to packet. Let d_i denote an estimate of the *average* network delay upon reception of the ith packet. This estimate is constructed from the timestamps as follows:

$$d_i = (1 - u)\, d_{i-1} + u\, (r_i - t_i)$$

where u is a fixed constant (for example, $u = 0.01$). Thus d_i is a smoothed average of the observed network delays $r_1 - t_1, \ldots, r_i - t_i$. The estimate places more weight on the recently observed network delays than on the observed network delays of the distant past. This form of estimate should not be completely unfamiliar; a similar idea is used to estimate round-trip times, as discussed in Chapter 3. Let v_i denote an estimate of the average deviation of the delay from the estimated average delay. This estimate is also constructed from the timestamps:

$$v_i = (1 - u)\, v_{i-1} + u\, |\, r_i - t_i - d_i\, |.$$

The estimates d_i and v_i are calculated for every packet received, although they are only used to determine the playout point for the first packet in any talkspurt.

Once having calculated these estimates, the receiver employs the following algorithm for the playout of packets. If packet i is the first packet of a talkspurt, its playout time, p_i, is computed as:

$$p_i = t_i + d_i + Kv_i,$$

where K is a positive constant (for example, $K = 4$). The purpose of the Kv_i term is to set the playout time far enough into the future so that only a small fraction of the arriving packets in the talkspurt will be lost due to late arrivals. The playout point for any subsequent packet in a talkspurt is computed as an offset from the point in time when the first packet in the talkspurt was played out. In particular, let

$$q_i = p_i - t_i,$$

be the length of time from when the first packet in the talkspurt is generated until it is played out. If packet j also belongs to this talkspurt, it is played out at time

$$p_j = t_j + q_i.$$

The algorithm just described makes perfect sense assuming that the receiver can tell whether a packet is the first packet in the talkspurt. If there is no packet loss, then the receiver can determine whether packet i is the first packet of the talkspurt by comparing the timestamp of the ith packet with the timestamp of the $(i - 1)$st packet. Indeed, if $t_i - t_{i-1} > 20$ msec, then the receiver knows that ith packet starts a new talkspurt. But now suppose there is occasional packet loss. In this case two successive packets received at the destination may have timestamps that differ by more than 20 msec when the two packets belong to the same talkspurt. So here is where the sequence numbers becomes useful. The receiver can use the sequence numbers to determine whether the > 20 msec difference in timestamps is due to a new talkspurt or to lost packets.

6.3.3   Recovering from Packet Loss

We have discussed in some detail how an Internet phone application can deal with packet jitter. We now briefly describe a few schemes that attempt to preserve acceptable audio quality in the presence of packet loss. Such schemes are called **loss recovery schemes.** Here we define packet loss in a broad sense: a packet is lost if either it never arrives at the receiver or if it arrives after its scheduled playout time. Our Internet phone example will again serve as a context for describing the loss recovery schemes.

As mentioned at the beginning of this section, retransmitting lost packets is not appropriate in an interactive real-time application such as Internet phone. Indeed, retransmitting a packet that missed its playout deadline serves absolutely no purpose. And retransmitting a packet that overflowed a router queue cannot normally be accomplished quickly enough. Because retransmissions are inappropriate, Internet phone applications often use some type of loss anticipation scheme. Two types of loss-anticipation schemes are **forward error correction (FEC)** and **interleaving.**

Forward Error Correction (FEC).   The basic idea of FEC is to add redundant information to the original packet stream. For the cost of marginally increasing the transmission rate of the audio of the stream, the redundant information can be used to reconstruct "approximations" or exact versions of some of the lost packets. Following [Bolot 1996] and [Perkins 1998], we now outline two FEC mechanisms. The first mechanism sends a redundant encoded chunk after every n chunks. The redundant chunk is obtained by exclusive OR-ing the n original chunks [Shacham 1990]. In this manner if any one packet of the group of $n + 1$ packets is lost, the receiver can fully reconstruct the lost packet. But if two or more packets in a group are lost, their receiver cannot reconstruct the lost packets. By keeping $n + 1$, the group size, small, a large fraction of the lost packets can be recovered when loss is not excessive. However, the smaller the group size, the greater the relative increase of the transmission rate of the audio stream. In particular, the transmission rate increases by a factor of $1/n$; for example, if $n = 3$, then the transmission rate increases by 33%. Furthermore, this simple scheme increases the playout delay because the receiver must receive the entire group of packets before it can playout a group. (During a talkspurt, the receiver schedules periodic playback of the chunks based on the worst-case scenario—namely, the first packet in a group is lost within some group. This requires the receiver to delay playback of each packet for the time it takes to receive an entire group.)

The second FEC mechanism is to send a lower quality audio stream as the redundant information. For example, the sender creates a nominal audio stream and a corresponding low-bit rate audio stream. (The nominal stream could be a PCM encoding at 64 Kbps and the lower-quality stream could be a GSM encoding at 13 Kbps.) The low-bit rate stream is referred to as the redundant stream. As shown in Figure 6.7, the sender constructs the nth packet by taking the nth chunk from the nominal stream and appending to it the $(n - 1)$st chunk from the redundant stream. In this manner, whenever there is nonconsecutive packet loss, the receiver can conceal the loss by playing out the low-bit-rate encoded chunk that arrives with the subsequent packet. Of course, low-bit-rate chunks give lower quality than the nominal chunks but a stream of mostly high-quality chunks, occasional low-quality chunks, and no missing chunks gives good overall audio quality. Note that in this scheme, the receiver only has to receive two packets before playback, so that the increased playout delay is small. Furthermore, if the low-bit-rate encoding is much less than the nominal encoding, then the marginal increase in the transmission rate is small.

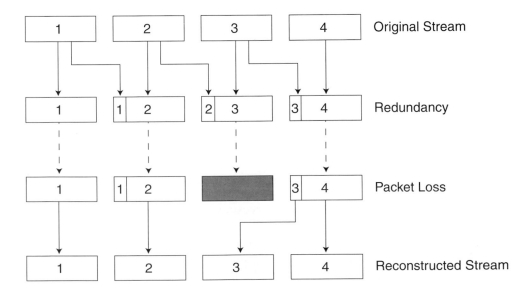

FIGURE 6.7 Piggybacking lower-quality redundant information

In order to cope with nonconsecutive loss, a simple variation can be employed. Instead of appending just the $(n - 1)$st low-bit-rate chunk to the nth nominal chunk, the sender can append the $(n - 1)$st and $(n - 2)$nd low-bit-rate chunk, or append the $(n - 1)$st and $(n - 3)$rd low-bit-rate chunk, etc. By appending more low-bit-rate chunks to each nominal chunk, the audio quality at the receiver becomes acceptable for a wider variety of harsh best-effort environments. On the other hand, the additional chunks increase the transmission bandwidth and the playout delay.

Free Phone [Freephone 1999] and RAT [RAT 1999] are well-documented Internet phone applications that use FEC. They can transmit lower-quality audio streams along with the nominal audio stream, as described above.

Interleaving.   As an alternative to redundant transmission, an Internet phone application can send interleaved audio. As shown in Figure 6.8, the sender resequences units of audio data before transmission, so that originally adjacent units are separated by a certain distance in the transmitted stream. Interleaving reduces the effect of packet losses. If, for example, units are 5 msec in length and chunks are 20 ms (that is, 4 units per chunk), then the first chunk could contain units 1, 5, 9, 13; the second chunk could contain units 2, 6, 10, 14; and so on. Figure 6.8 shows that the loss of a single packet from an interleaved stream results in multiple small gaps in the reconstructed stream, as opposed to the single large gap which would occur in a noninterleaved stream.

Interleaving can significantly improve the perceived quality of an audio stream [Perkins 1998]. The obvious disadvantage of interleaving is that it increases latency. This limits its use for interactive applications such as Internet phone, although it can perform well for streaming stored audio. The major advantage of interleaving is that it does not increase the bandwidth requirements of a stream.

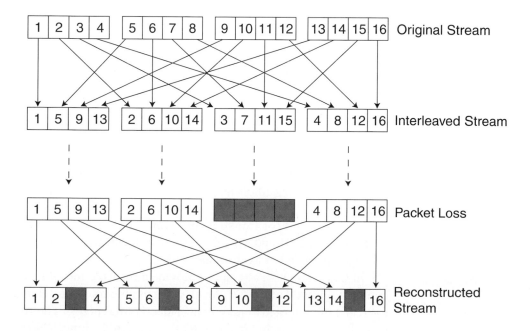

FIGURE 6.8   Sending interleaved audio

Receiver-based repair of damaged audio streams. Receiver-based recovery schemes attempt to produce a replacement for a lost packet that is similar to the original. As discussed in [Perkins 1998], this is possible since audio signals, and in particular speech, exhibit large amounts of short-term self similarity. As such, these techniques work for relatively small loss rates (less than 15%), and for small packets (4–40 msec). When the loss length approaches the length of a phoneme (5–100 msec) these techniques breakdown, since whole phonemes may be missed by the listener.

A simple form of receiver-based recovery is packet repetition. Packet repetition replaces lost packets with copies of the packets that arrived immediately before the loss. It has low computational complexity and performs reasonably well. Another form of receiver-based recovery is interpolation, which uses audio before and after the loss to interpolate a suitable packet to cover the loss. It performs somewhat better than packet repetition, but is significantly more computationally intensive [Perkins 1998].

6.3.4 Streaming Stored Audio and Video

We conclude this section with a few words about streaming stored audio and video. Streaming stored audio/video can also use sequence numbers, timestamps, and playout delay to alleviate or even eliminate the effects of network jitter. However, there is an important difference between real-time interactive audio/video and streaming stored audio/video. Specifically, streaming of stored audio/video can tolerate significantly larger delays. Indeed, when a user requests an audio/video clip, the user may find it acceptable to wait five seconds or more before playback begins. And most users can tolerate similar delays after interactive actions such as a temporal jump to the future. This greater tolerance for delay gives the application developer greater flexibility when designing stored media applications.

6.4 RTP

In the previous section we learned that the sender side of a multimedia application appends header fields to the audio/video chunks before passing the chunks to the transport layer. These header fields include sequence numbers and timestamps. Since most multimedia networking applications can make use of sequence numbers and timestamps, it is convenient to have a standardized packet structure that includes fields for audio/video data, sequence number, and timestamp, as well as other potentially useful fields. RTP, defined in [RFC 1889], is such a standard. RTP can be used for transporting common formats such as WAV or GSM for sound and MPEG1 and MPEG2 for video. It can also be used for transporting proprietary sound and video formats.

In this section we attempt to provide a readable introduction to RTP and to its companion protocol, RTCP. We also discuss the role of RTP in the H.323 standard for real-time interactive audio and video conferencing. The reader is encouraged to visit Henning Schulzrinne's RTP site [Schulzrinne 1999], which provides a wealth of information on the subject. Also, readers may want to visit the Free Phone site [Freephone 1999], which describes an Internet phone application that uses RTP.

6.4.1   RTP Basics

RTP typically runs on top of UDP. Specifically, audio or video chunks of data, generated by the sending side of a multimedia application, are encapsulated in RTP packets, and each RTP packet is in turn encapsulated in a UDP segment. Because RTP provides services (timestamps, sequence numbers, etc.) to the multimedia application, RTP can be viewed as a **sublayer of the transport layer,** as shown in Figure 6.9.

From the application developer's perspective, however, RTP is not part of the transport layer but instead part of the application layer. This is because the developer must integrate RTP into the application. Specifically, for the sender side of the application, the developer must write code into the application which creates the RTP encapsulating packets. The application then sends the RTP packets into a UDP socket interface. Similarly, at the receiver side of the application, the RTP packets enter the application through a UDP socket interface. The developer therefore must write code into the application that extracts the media chunks from the RTP packets. This is illustrated in Figure 6.10.

As an example, consider using RTP to transport voice. Suppose the voice source is PCM encoded (that is, sampled, quantized, and digitized) at 64 Kbps. Further suppose that the application collects the encoded data in 20 msec chunks, that is, 160 bytes in a chunk. The application precedes each chunk of the audio data with an **RTP header,** which includes the type of audio encoding, a sequence number, and a timestamp. The audio chunk along with the RTP header form the

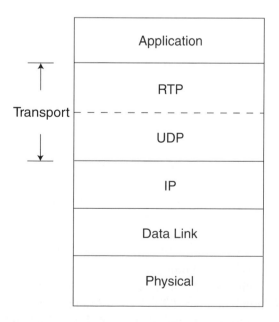

FIGURE 6.9   RTP can be viewed as a sublayer of the transport layer.

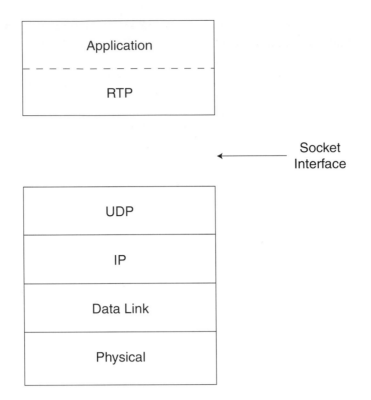

FIGURE 6.10 From a developer's perspective, RTP is part of the application layer

RTP packet. The RTP packet is then sent into the UDP socket interface, where it is encapsulated in a UDP packet. At the receiver side, the application receives the RTP packet from its socket interface. The application extracts the audio chunk from the RTP packet, and uses the header fields of the RTP packet to properly decode and playback the audio chunk.

If an application incorporates RTP—instead of a proprietary scheme to provide payload type, sequence numbers, or timestamps—then the application will more easily interoperate with other networking applications. For example, if two different companies develop Internet phone software and they both incorporate RTP into their product, there may be some hope that a user using one of the Internet phone products will be able to communicate with a user using the other Internet phone product. At the end of this section we shall see that RTP has been incorporated into an important part of an Internet telephony standard.

It should be emphasized that RTP in itself does not provide any mechanism to ensure timely delivery of data or provide other quality of service guarantees; it does not even guarantee delivery of packets or prevent out-of-order delivery of packets. Indeed, RTP encapsulation is only seen at the end systems—it is not seen by intermediate routers. Routers do not distinguish between IP datagrams that carry RTP packets and IP datagrams that don't.

RTP allows each source (for example, a camera or a microphone) to be assigned its own independent RTP stream of packets. For example, for a video-conference between two participants, four RTP streams could be opened—two streams for transmitting the audio (one in each direction) and two streams for the video (again, one in each direction). However, many popular encoding techniques—including MPEG1 and MPEG2—bundle the audio and video into a single stream during the encoding process. When the audio and video are bundled by the encoder, then only one RTP stream is generated in each direction.

RTP packets are not limited to unicast applications. They can also be sent over one-to-many and many-to-many multicast trees. For a many-to-many multicast session, all of the senders and sources in the session typically send their RTP streams into the same multicast tree with the same multicast address. RTP multicast streams belonging together, such as audio and video streams emanating from multiple senders in a videoconference application, belong to an **RTP session.**

6.4.2   RTP Packet Header Fields

As shown in Figure 6.11, the four principle packet header fields are the payload type, sequence number, timestamp, and the source identifier.

Payload Type field.   The Payload Type field in the RTP packet is seven bits long. Thus 2^7 or 128 different payload types can be supported by RTP. For an audio stream, the payload type field is used to indicate the type of audio encoding (for example, PCM, adaptive delta modulation, linear predictive encoding) that is being used. If a sender decides to change the encoding in the middle of a session, the sender can inform the receiver of the change through this Payload Type field. The sender may want to change the encoding in order to increase the audio quality or to decrease the RTP stream bit rate. Table 6.1 lists some of the audio payload types currently supported by RTP.

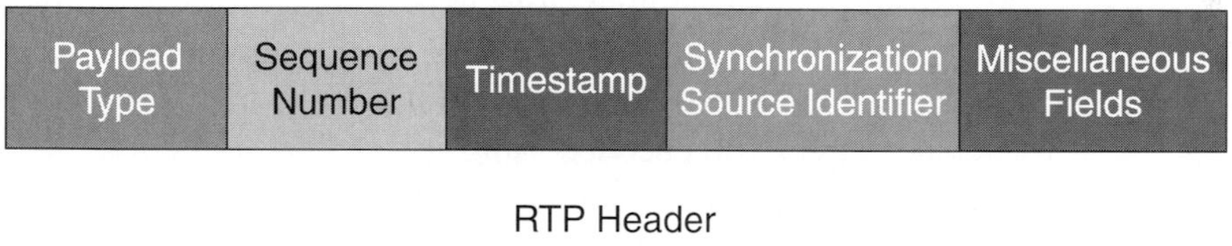

| Payload Type | Sequence Number | Timestamp | Synchronization Source Identifier | Miscellaneous Fields |

RTP Header

FIGURE 6.11   RTP header fields

Table 6.1   Some audio payload types supported by RTP

Payload Type Number	Audio Format	Sampling Rate	Throughput
0	PCM mu-law	8 KHz	64 Kbps
1	1016	8 KHz	4.8 Kbps
3	GSM	8 KHz	13 Kbps
7	LPC	8 KHz	2.4 Kbps
9	G.722	8 KHz	48-64 Kbps
14	MPEG Audio	90 KHz	—
15	G.728	8 KHz	16 Kbps

Table 6.2   Some video payload types supported by RTP

Payload Type Number	Video Format
26	Motion JPEG
31	H.261
32	MPEG1 video
33	MPEG2 video

For a video stream the payload type can be used to indicate the type of video encoding (for example, motion JPEG, MPEG1, MPEG2, H.231). Again, the sender can change video encoding on-the-fly during a session. Table 6.2 lists some of the video payload types currently supported by RTP.

Sequence Number field.   The Sequence Number field is 16-bits long. The sequence number increments by one for each RTP packet sent, and may be used by the receiver to detect packet loss and to restore packet sequence. For example, if the receiver side of the application receives a stream of RTP packets with a gap between sequence numbers 86 and 89, then the receiver knows that packets 87 and 88 were lost. The receiver can then attempt to conceal the lost data.

Timestamp field.   The Timestamp Field is 32 bytes long. It reflects the sampling instant of the first byte in the RTP data packet. As we saw in the previous section, the receiver can use the timestamps in order to remove packet jitter introduced in the network and to provide synchronous playout at the receiver. The timestamp is derived from a sampling clock at the sender. As an example, for audio, the timestamp clock increments by one for each sampling period (for example, each 125 usecs for an 8 kHz sampling clock); if the audio application generates chunks consisting of 160 encoded samples, then the timestamp increases by 160 for each RTP packet when the source is active. The timestamp clock continues to increase at a constant rate even if the source is inactive.

Synchronization Source Identifier (SSRC).   The SSRC field is 32 bits long. It identifies the source of the RTP stream. Typically, each stream in a RTP session has a distinct SSRC. The SSRC is not the IP address of the sender, but instead a number that the source assigns randomly when the new stream is started. The probability that two streams get assigned the same SSRC is very small.

6.4.3   RTP Control Protocol (RTCP)

[RFC 1889] also specifies RTCP, a protocol that a multimedia networking application can use in conjunction with RTP. The use of RTCP is particularly attractive when the networking application multicasts audio or video to multiple receivers from one or more senders. As shown in Figure 6.12, RTCP packets are transmitted by each participant in an RTP session to all other participants in the session. The RTCP packets are distributed to all the participants using IP multicast. For an RTP session typically there is a single multicast address and all RTP and RTCP packets belonging to the session use the multicast address. RTP and RTCP packets are distinguished from each other through the use of distinct port numbers.

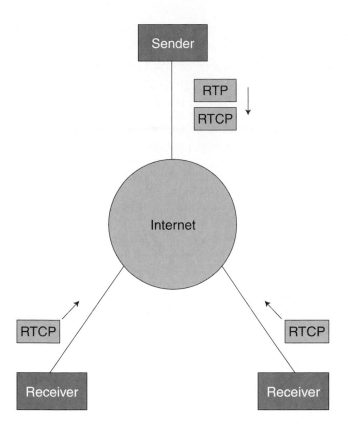

FIGURE 6.12   Both senders and receivers send RTCP messages.

RTCP packets do not encapsulate chunks of audio or video. Instead, RTCP packets are sent periodically and contain sender and/or receiver reports that announce statistics that can be useful to the application. These statistics include number of packets sent, number of packets lost, and interarrival jitter. The RTP specification [RFC 1889] does not dictate what the application should do with this feedback information. It is up to the application developer to decide what it wants to do with the feedback information. Senders can use the feedback information, for example, to modify their transmission rates. The feedback information can also be used for diagnostic purposes; for example, receivers can determine whether problems are local, regional, or global.

RTCP packet types.   For each RTP stream that a receiver receives as part of a session, the receiver generates a reception report. The receiver aggregates its reception reports into a single RTCP packet. The packet is then sent into the multicast tree that connects together all the participants in the session. The reception report includes several fields, the most important of which are listed below.

- The SSRC of the RTP stream for which the reception report is being generated.
- The fraction of packets lost within the RTP stream. Each receiver calculates the number of RTP packets lost divided by the number of RTP packets sent as part of the stream. If a sender receives reception reports indicating that the receivers are receiving only a small fraction of the sender's transmitted

packets, the sender can switch to a lower encoding rate, thereby decreasing the congestion in the network, which may improve the reception rate.

▪ The last sequence number received in the stream of RTP packets.

▪ The interarrival jitter, which is calculated as the average interarrival time between successive packets in the RTP stream.

For each RTP stream that a sender is transmitting, the sender creates and transmits RTCP sender report packets. These packets include information about the RTP stream, including:

▪ The SSRC of the RTP stream.

▪ The timestamp and wall clock time of the most recently generated RTP packet in the stream.

▪ The number of packets sent in the stream.

▪ The number of bytes sent in the stream.

The sender reports can be used to synchronize different media streams within an RTP session. For example, consider a videoconferencing application for which each sender generates two independent RTP streams, one for video and one for audio. The timestamps in these RTP packets are tied to the video and audio sampling clocks, and are not tied to the *wall clock time* (that is, to real time). Each RTCP sender report contains, for the most recently generated packet in the associated RTP stream, the timestamp of the RTP packet and the wall clock time for when the packet was created. Thus the RTCP sender report packets associate the sampling clock to the real-time clock. Receivers can use this association in the RTCP sender reports to synchronize the playout of audio and video.

For each RTP stream that a sender is transmitting, the sender also creates and transmits source description packets. These packets contain information about the source, such as e-mail address of the sender, the sender's name, and the application that generates the RTP stream. It also includes the SSRC of the associated RTP stream. These packets provide a mapping between the source identifier (that is, the SSRC) and the user/host name.

RTCP packets are stackable, that is, receiver reception reports, sender reports, and source descriptors can be concatenated into a single packet. The resulting packet is then encapsulated into a UDP segment and forwarded into the multicast tree.

RTCP bandwidth scaling. The astute reader will have observed that RTCP has a potential scaling problem. Consider for example an RTP session that consists of one sender and a large number of receivers. If each of the receivers periodically generate RTCP packets, then the aggregate transmission rate of RTCP packets can greatly exceed the rate of RTP packets sent by the sender. Observe that the amount of traffic sent into the multicast tree does not change as the number of receivers increases, whereas the amount of RTCP traffic grows linearly with the number of receivers. To solve this scaling problem, RTCP modifies the rate at which a participant sends RTCP packets into the multicast tree as a function of the number of participants in the session. Observe that, because each participant sends control packets to everyone else, each participant can keep track of the total number of participants in the session.

RTCP attempts to limit its traffic to 5% of the session bandwidth. For example, suppose there is one sender, which is sending video at a rate of 2 Mbps. Then RTCP attempts to limit its traffic to 5% of 2 Mbps, or 100 Kbps, as follows. The protocol gives 75% of this rate, or 75 Kbps, to the receivers; it gives the remaining 25% of the rate, or 25 Kbps, to the sender. The 75 Kbps devoted to the receivers is equally shared among the receivers. Thus, if there are R receivers, then each receiver gets to send RTCP traffic at a rate of 75/R Kbps and the sender gets to send RTCP traffic at a rate of 25 Kbps. A participant (a sender or receiver) determines the RTCP packet transmission period by dynamically calculating the average RTCP packet size (across the entire session) and dividing the average RTCP packet size by its allocated rate. In summary, the period for transmitting RTCP packets for a sender is

$$T = \frac{\text{number of senders}}{.25 \cdot .05 \cdot \text{session bandwidth}}(\text{avg. RTCP packet size})$$

And the period for transmitting RTCP packets for a receiver is

$$T = \frac{\text{number of receivers}}{.75 \cdot .05 \cdot \text{session bandwidth}}(\text{avg. RTCP packet size})$$

6.4.4 H.323

H.323 is a standard for real-time audio and video conferencing among end systems on the Internet. As shown in Figure 6.13, it also covers how end systems attached to the Internet communicate with telephones attached to ordinary circuit-switched telephone networks. In principle, if manufacturers of Internet telephony and video conferencing all conform to H.323, then all their products should be

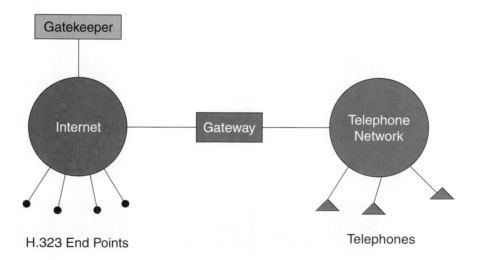

FIGURE 6.13 H.323 end systems attached to the Internet can communicate with telephones attached to a circuit-switched telephone network

able to interoperate, and should be able to communicate with ordinary telephones. We discuss H.323 in this section, as it provides an application context for RTP. Indeed, we shall see below that RTP is an integral part of the H.323 standard.

H.323 **end points** (terminals) can be stand-alone devices (for example, Web phones and Web TVs) or applications in a PC (for example, Internet phone or video conferencing software). H.323 equipment also includes **gateways** and **gate-keepers.** Gateways permit communication among H.323 end points and ordinary telephones in a circuit-switched telephone network. Gatekeepers, which are optional, provide address translation, authorization, bandwidth management, accounting, and billing. We will discuss gatekeepers in more detail at the end of this section.

The H.323 is an umbrella specification that includes:

- A specification for how endpoints negotiate common audio/video encodings. Because H.323 supports a variety of audio and video encoding standards, a protocol is needed to allow the communicating endpoints to agree on a common encoding.

- A specification for how audio and video chunks are encapsulated and sent over network. As you may have guessed, this is where RTP comes into the picture.

- A specification for how endpoints communicate with their respective gate-keepers.

- A specification for how Internet phones communicate through a gateway with ordinary phones in the public circuit-switched telephone network.

Figure 6.14 shows the H.323 protocol architecture.

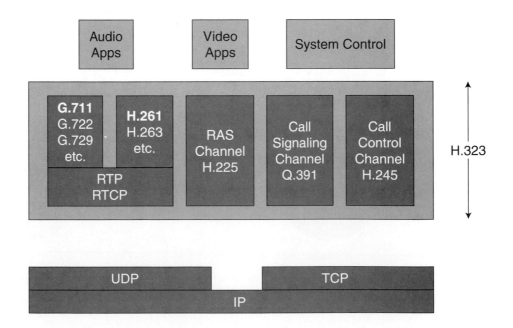

FIGURE 6.14   H.323 protocol architecture

Minimally, each H.323 endpoint *must* support the G.711 speech compression standard. G.711 uses PCM to generate digitized speech at either 56 Kbps or 64 Kbps. Although H.323 requires every endpoint to be voice capable (through G.711), video capabilities are optional. Because video support is optional, manufacturers of terminals can sell simpler speech terminals as well as more complex terminals that support both audio and video.

As shown in Figure 6.14, H.323 also requires that all H.323 end points use the following protocols:

- *RTP.* The sending side of an endpoint encapsulates all media chunks within RTP packets. The sending side then passes the RTP packets to UDP.
- *H.245.* An "out-of-band" control protocol for controlling media between H.323 endpoints. This protocol is used to negotiate a common audio or video compression standard that will be employed by all the participating endpoints in a session.
- *Q.931.* A signaling protocol for establishing and terminating calls. This protocol provides traditional telephone functionality (for example, dial tones and ringing) to H.323 endpoints and equipment.
- *RAS (Registration/Admission/Status) channel protocol.* A protocol that allows end points to communicate with a gatekeeper (if a gatekeeper is present).

Audio and video compression.   The H.323 standard supports a specific set of audio and video compression techniques. Let's first consider audio. As we just mentioned, all H.323 end points must support the G.711 speech encoding standard. Because of this requirement, two H.323 end points will always be able to default to G.711 and communicate. But H.323 allows terminals to support a variety of other speech compression standards, including G.723.1, G.722, G.728, and G.729. Many of these standards compress speech to rates that will pass through 28.8 Kbps dial-up modems. For example, G.723.1 compresses speech to either 5.3 Kbps or 6.3 Kbps, with sound quality that is comparable to G.711.

As we mentioned earlier, video capabilities for an H.323 endpoint are optional. However, if an endpoint does supports video, then it must (at the very least) support the QCIF H.261 (176x144 pixels) video standard. A video-capable endpoint may optionally support other H.261 schemes, including CIF, 4CIF, 16CIF, and the H.263 standard. As the H.323 standard evolves, it will likely support a longer list of audio and video compression schemes.

H.323 channels.   When an end point participates in an H.323 session, it maintains several channels, as shown in Figure 6.15. Examining Figure 6.15, we see that an end point can support many simultaneous RTP media channels. For each media type, there will typically be one send media channel and one receive media channel; thus, if audio and video are sent in separate RTP streams, there will typically be four media channels. Accompanying the RTP media channels, there is one RTCP media control channel, as discussed in Section 6.4.3. All of the RTP and RTCP channels run over UDP. In addition to the RTP/RTCP channels, two other channels are required: the call control channel and the call signaling channel. The H.245 call control channel is a TCP connection that carries H.245 control messages. Its principle tasks are (1) opening and closing media

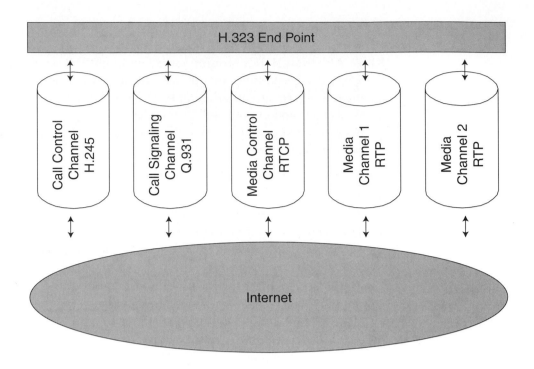

FIGURE 6.15 H.323 channels

channels, and (2) capability exchange, that is, before sending media, endpoints agree on an encoding algorithm. H.245, being a control protocol for real-time interactive applications, is analogous to RTSP, which is a control protocol for streaming of stored multimedia. Finally, the Q.931 call signaling channel provides classical telephone functionality, such as dial tone and ringing.

Gatekeepers. The gatekeeper is an optional H.323 device. Each gatekeeper is responsible for an H.323 zone. A typical deployment scenario is shown in Figure 6.16. In this deployment scenario, the H.323 terminals and the gatekeeper are all attached to the same LAN, and the H.323 zone is the LAN itself. If a zone has a gatekeeper, then all H.323 terminals in the zone are required to communicate with it using the RAS protocol, which runs over TCP. Address translation is one of the more important gatekeeper services. Each terminal can have an alias address, such as the name of the person at the terminal, the e-mail address of the person at the terminal, etc. The gateway translates these alias addresses to IP addresses. This address translation service is similar to the DNS service, covered in Section 2.5. Another gatekeeper service is bandwidth management: The gatekeeper can limit the number of simultaneous real-time conferences in order to save some bandwidth for other applications running over the LAN. Optionally, H.323 calls can be routed through gatekeeper, which is useful for billing.

The H.323 terminal must register itself with the gatekeeper in its zone. When the H.323 application is invoked at the terminal, the terminal uses RAS to send its IP address and alias (provided by user) to the gatekeeper. If the gatekeeper is present in a zone, each terminal in the zone must contact the gatekeeper to ask

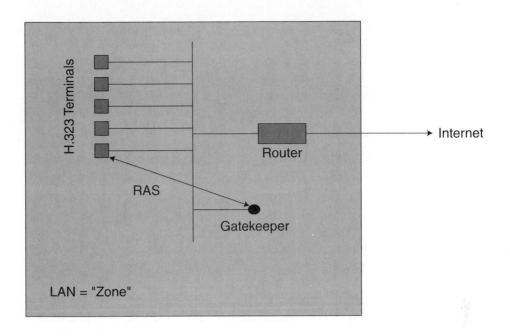

FIGURE 6.16   H.323 terminals and gatekeeper on the same LAN

permission to make a call. Once it has permission, the terminal can send the gate-keeper an e-mail address, alias string, or phone extension for the terminal it wants to call, which may be in another zone. If necessary, a gatekeeper will poll other gatekeepers in other zones to resolve an IP address.

    An excellent tutorial on H.323 is provided by [WebProForum 1999]. The reader is also encouraged to see [Rosenberg 1999] for an alternative architecture to H.323 for providing telephone service in the Internet.

6.5   BEYOND BEST-EFFORT

In previous sections we learned how sequence numbers, timestamps, FEC, RTP, and RTCP can be used by multimedia applications in today's Internet. But are these techniques alone enough to support reliable and robust multimedia applications, for example, an IP telephony service that is equivalent to a service in today's telephone network? Before answering this question, let us first recall that today's Internet provides a best-effort service to all of its applications, that is, does not make any promises about the Quality of Service (QoS) an application will receive. An application will receive whatever level of performance (for example, end-to-end packet delay and loss) that the network is able to provide at that moment. Recall also that today's public Internet does not allow delay-sensitive multimedia applications to request any special treatment. All packets are treated equal at the routers, including delay-sensitive audio and video packets. Given that all packets are treated equally, all that's required to ruin the quality of an on-going IP telephone call is enough interfering traffic (that is, network congestion) to noticeably increase the delay and loss seen by an IP telephone call.

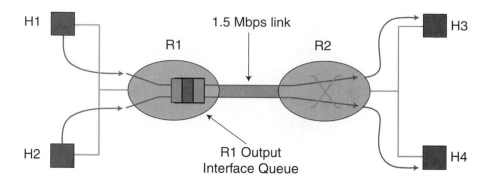

FIGURE 6.17 A simple network with two applications

In this section, we will identify *new* architectural components that can be added to the Internet architecture to shield an application from such congestion and thus make high-quality networked multimedia applications a reality. Many of the issues that we will discuss in this, and the remaining sections of this chapter, are currently under active discussion in the IETF diffserv, intserv, and rsvp working groups.

Figure 6.17 shows a simple network scenario that illustrates the most important architectural components that have been proposed for the Internet in order to provide explicit support for the QoS needs of multimedia applications. Suppose that two application packet flows originate on hosts H1 and H2 on one LAN and are destined for hosts H3 and H4 on another LAN. The routers on the two LANs are connected by a 1.5 Mbps link. Let us assume the LAN speeds are significantly higher than 1.5 Mbps, and focus on the output queue of router R1; it is here that packet delay and packet loss will occur if the aggregate sending rate of the H1 and H2 exceeds 1.5 Mbps. Let us now consider several scenarios, each of which will provide us with important insight into the underlying principles for providing QoS guarantees to multimedia applications.

6.5.1 Scenario 1: A 1 Mbps Audio Application and an FTP Transfer

Scenario 1 is illustrated in Figure 6.18. Here, a 1 Mbps audio application (for example, a CD-quality audio call) shares the 1.5 Mbps link between R1 and R2 with an FTP application that is transferring a file from H2 to H4. In the best-effort Internet, the audio and FTP packets are mixed in the output queue at R1 and (typically) transmitted in a first-in-first-out (FIFO) order. In this scenario, a burst of packets from the FTP source could potentially fill up the queue, causing IP audio packets to be excessively delayed or lost due to buffer overflow at R1. How should we solve this potential problem? Given that the FTP application does not have time constraints, our intuition might be to give strict priority to audio packets at R1. Under a strict priority scheduling discipline, an audio packet in the R1 output buffer would always be transmitted before any FTP packet in the R1 output buffer.

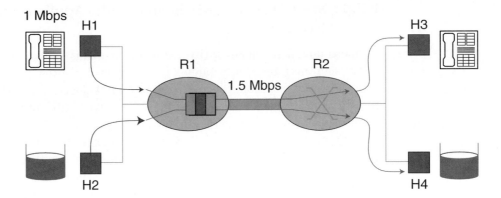

FIGURE 6.18   Competing audio and ftp applications

The link from R1 to R2 would look like a dedicated link of 1.5 Mbps to the audio traffic, with FTP traffic only using the R1-to-R2 link when no audio traffic is queued.

In order for R1 to distinguish between the audio and FTP packets in its queue, each packet must be marked as belonging to one of these two "classes" of traffic. Recall from Section 4.7, that this was the original goal of the Type-of-Service (ToS) field in IPv4. As obvious as this might seem, this then is our first principle underlying the provision of quality of service guarantees:

> **Principle 1:** Packet marking allows a router to distinguish among packets belonging to different classes of traffic.

6.5.2   Scenario 2: A 1 Mbps Audio Application and a High Priority FTP Transfer

Our second scenario is only slightly different from scenario 1. Suppose now that the FTP user has purchased "platinum service" (that is, high priced) Internet access from its ISP, while the audio user has purchased cheap, low-budget Internet service that costs only a minuscule fraction of platinum service. Should the cheap user's audio packets be given priority over FTP packets in this case? Arguably not. In this case, it would seem more reasonable to distinguish packets on the basis of the sender's IP address. More generally, we see that it is necessary for a router to *classify* packets according to some criteria. This then calls for a slight modification to principle 1:

> **Principle 1 (modified):** Packet classification allows a router to distinguish among packets belonging to different classes of traffic.

Explicit packet marking is one way in which packets may be distinguished. However, the marking carried by a packet does not, by itself, mandate that the packet will receive a given quality of service. Marking is but one *mechanism* for distinguishing packets. The manner in which a router distinguishes among packets by treating them differently is a *policy* decision.

6.5.3   Scenario 3: A Misbehaving Audio Application and an FTP Transfer

Suppose now that somehow (by use of mechanisms that we will study in subsequent sections), the router knows it should give priority to packets from the 1 Mbps audio application. Since the outgoing link speed is 1.5 Mbps, even though the FTP packets receive lower priority, they will still, on average, receive 0.5 Mbps of transmission service. But what happens if the audio application starts sending packets at a rate of 1.5 Mbps or higher (either maliciously or due to an error in the application)? In this case, the FTP packets will starve, that is, will not receive any service on the R1-to-R2 link. Similar problems would occur if multiple applications (for example, multiple audio calls), all with the same priority, were sharing a link's bandwidth; one non-compliant flow could degrade and ruin the performance of the other flows. Ideally, one wants a degree of *isolation* among flows, in order to protect one flow from another misbehaving flow. This, then, is a second underlying principle the provision of QoS guarantees.

> **Principle 2:** It is desirable to provide a degree of isolation among traffic flows, so that one flow is not adversely affected by another misbehaving flow.

In the following section, we will examine several specific mechanisms for providing this isolation among flows. We note here that two broad approaches can be taken. First, it is possible to "police" traffic flows, as shown in Figure 6.19. If a traffic flow must meet certain criteria (for example, that the audio flow not exceed a peak rate of 1 Mbps), then a policing mechanism can be put into place to ensure that this criteria is indeed observed. If the policed application misbehaves, the policing mechanism will take some action (for example, drop or delay packets that are in violation of the criteria) so that the traffic actually entering the network conforms to the criteria. The leaky bucket mechanism that we examine in the following section is perhaps the most widely used policing mechanism. In Figure 6.19, the packet classification and marking mechanism (Principle 1) and the policing mechanism (Principle 2) are co-located at the "edge" of the network, either in the end system, or at an edge router.

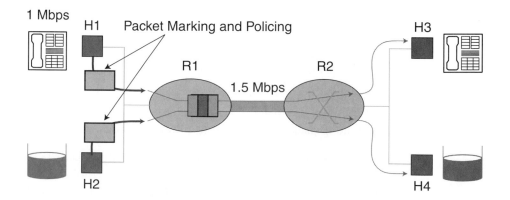

FIGURE 6.19   Policing (and marking) the audio and FTP traffic flows

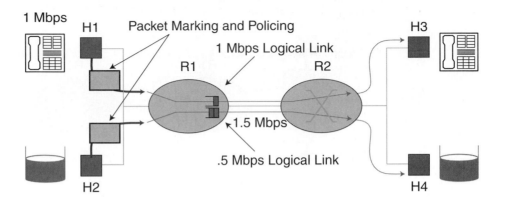

FIGURE 6.20   Logical isolation of audio and FTP application flows

An alternate approach for providing isolation among traffic flows is for the link-level packet scheduling mechanism to explicitly allocate a fixed amount of link bandwidth to each application flow. For example, the audio flow could be allocated 1Mbps at R1, and the ftp flow could be allocated 0.5 Mbps. In this case, the audio and FTP flows see a logical link with capacity 1.0 and 0.5 Mbps, respectively, as shown in Figure 6.20.

With strict enforcement of the link-level allocation of bandwidth, a flow can only use the amount of bandwidth that has been allocated; in particular, it cannot utilize bandwidth that is not currently being used by the other applications. For example, if the audio flow goes silent (for example, if the speaker pauses and generates no audio packets), the FTP flow would still not be able to transmit more than 0.5 Mbps over the R1-to-R2 link, even though the audio flow's 1 Mbps bandwidth allocation is not being used at that moment. It is therefore desirable to use bandwidth as efficiently as possible, allowing one flow to use another flow's unused bandwidth at any given point in time. This is the third principle underlying the provision of quality of service:

> **Principle 3:** While providing isolation among flows, it is desirable to use resources (for example, link bandwidth and buffers) as efficiently as possible.

6.5.4   Scenario 4: Two 1 Mbps Audio Applications over an Overloaded 1.5 Mbps Link

In our final scenario, two 1-Mbps audio connections transmit their packets over the 1.5 Mbps link, as shown in Figure 6.21. The combined data rate of the two flows (2 Mbps) exceeds the link capacity. Even with classification and marking (principle 1), isolation of flows (principle 2), and sharing of unused bandwidth (principle 3), of which there is none, this is clearly a losing proposition. There is simply not enough bandwidth to accommodate the applications' needs. If the two applications equally share the bandwidth, each would only receive 0.75 Mbps. Looked at another way, each application would lose 25% of its transmitted packets. This is such an unacceptably low quality of service that the application is

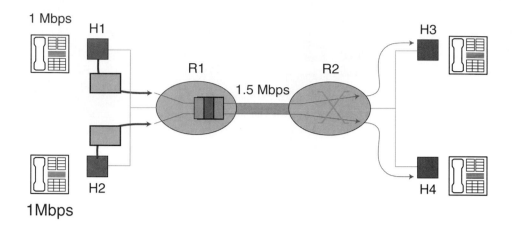

FIGURE 6.21   Two competing audio applications overloading the R1-to-R2 link

completely unusable; there's no need even to transmit any audio packets in the first place.

For a flow that needs a minimum quality of service in order to be considered "usable," the network should either allow the flow to use the network (*if* the network can provide the required QoS) or else *block* the flow from using the network. The telephone network is an example of a network that performs such call blocking—if the required resources (an end-to-end circuit, in the case of the telephone network) cannot be allocated to the call, the call is blocked (prevented from entering the network) and a busy signal is returned to the user. In our example above, there is no gain in allowing a flow into the network if it will not receive a sufficient QoS to be considered "usable." Indeed, there is a *cost* to admitting a flow that does not receive its needed QoS, as network resources are being used to support a flow that provides no utility to the end user.

Implicit with the need to provide a guaranteed QoS to a flow is the need for the flow to declare its QoS requirements. This process of having a flow declare its QoS requirement, and then having the network either accept the flow (at the required QoS) or block the flow (because the resources needed to meet the declared QoS requirements cannot be provided) is referred to as the call admission process. The need for call admission is the fourth underlying principle in the provision of QoS guarantees:

> **Principle 4:** A call admission process is needed in which flows declare their QoS requirements and are then either admitted to the network (at the required QoS) or blocked from the network (if the required QoS cannot be provided by the network).

In our discussion above, we have identified four basic principles in providing QoS guarantees for multimedia applications. These principles are summarized in Figure 6.22. In the following section, we consider various *mechanisms* for implementing these principles. In the sections following that, we examine proposed Internet service models for providing QoS guarantees.

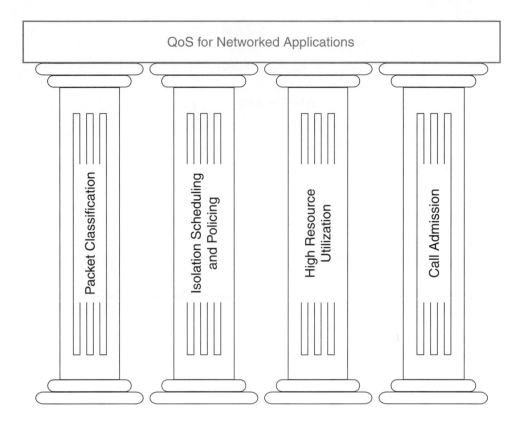

FIGURE 6.22   Four principles of providing QoS support

6.6   SCHEDULING AND POLICING MECHANISMS

In the previous section, we identified the important underlying principles in providing quality of service (QoS) guarantees to networked multimedia applications. In this section, we will examine various mechanisms that are used to provide these QoS guarantees. In the following section, we will examine how these mechanisms can be combined to provide various forms of Quality of Service in the Internet.

6.6.1   Scheduling Mechanisms

Recall from our discussion in Section 1.6 and Section 4.8, that packets belonging to various network flows are multiplexed together and queued for transmission at the output buffers associated with a link. The manner in which queued packets are selected for transmission on the link is known as the **link scheduling discipline.** We saw in the previous section, that the link scheduling discipline plays an important role in providing QoS guarantees. Let us now consider several of the most important link scheduling disciplines in more detail.

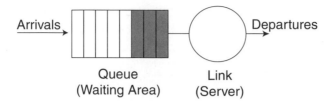

FIGURE 6.23 FIFO queuing abstraction

First-In-First-Out (FIFO). Figure 6.23 shows the queuing model abstractions for the First-in-First-Out (FIFO) link scheduling discipline. Packets arriving at the link output queue are queued for transmission if the link is currently busy transmitting another packet. If there is not sufficient buffering space to hold the arriving packet, the queue's **packet discarding policy** then determines whether the packet will be dropped ("lost") or whether other packets will be removed from the queue to make space for the arriving packet. In our discussion below we will ignore packet discard. When a packet is completely transmitted over the outgoing link (that is, receives service) it is removed from the queue.

The FIFO scheduling discipline (also known as First-Come-First-Served—FCFS) selects packets for link transmission in the same order in which they arrived at the output link queue. We're all familiar with FIFO queuing from bus stops (particularly in England, where queuing seems to have been perfected) or other service centers, where arriving customers join the back of the single waiting line, remain in order, and are then served when they reach the front of the line.

Figure 6.24 shows an example of the FIFO queue in operation. Packet arrivals are indicated by numbered arrows above the upper timeline, with the number indicating the order in which the packet arrived. Individual packet departures are

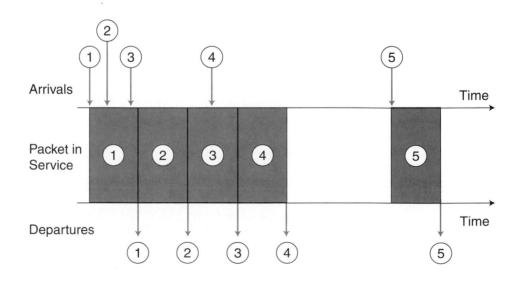

FIGURE 6.24 The FIFO queue in operation

shown below the lower timeline. The time that a packet spends in service (being transmitted) is indicated by the shaded rectangle between the two timelines. Because of the FIFO discipline, packets leave in the same order in which they arrived. Note that after the departure of packet 4, the link remains idle (since packets 1 through 4 have been transmitted and removed from the queue) until the arrival of packet 5.

Priority queuing.   Under **priority queuing,** packets arriving at the output link are classified into one of two or more priority classes at the output queue, as shown in Figure 6.25. As discussed in the previous section, a packet's priority class may depend on an explicit marking that it carries in its packet header (for example, the value of the Type of Service (ToS) bits in an IPv4 packet), its source or destination IP address, its destination port number, or other criteria. Each priority class typically has its own waiting area (queue). When choosing a packet to transmit, the priority queuing discipline will transmit a packet from the highest priority class that has a non-empty queue (that is, has packets waiting for transmission). The choice among packets *in the same priority class* is typically done in a FIFO manner.

Figure 6.26 illustrates the operation of a priority queue with two priority classes. Packets 1, 3, and 4 belong to the high priority class and packets 2 and 5 belong to the low priority class. Packet 1 arrives and, finding the link idle, begins transmission. During the transmission of packet 1, packets 2 and 3 arrive and are queued in the low and high priority queues, respectively. After the transmission of packet 1, packet 3 (a high priority packet) is selected for transmission over packet 2 (which, even though it arrived earlier, is a low priority packet). At the end of the transmission of packet 3, packet 2 then begins transmission. Packet 4 (a high priority packet) arrives during the transmission of packet 3 (a low priority packet). Under a so-called non-preemptive priority queuing discipline, the transmission of a packet is not interrupted once it has begun. In this case, packet 4 queues for transmission and begins being transmitted after the transmission of packet 2 is completed.

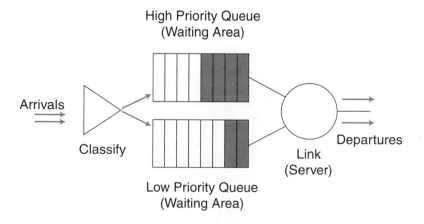

FIGURE 6.25   Priority queuing model

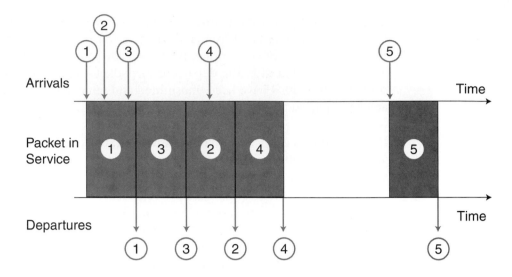

FIGURE 6.26 Operation of the priority queue

Round robin and Weighted Fair Queuing (WFQ). Under the **round robin queuing discipline,** packets are again sorted into classes, as with priority queuing. However, rather than there being a strict priority of service among classes, a round robin scheduler alternates service among the classes. In the simplest form of round robin scheduling, a class 1 packet is transmitted, followed by a class 2 packet, followed by a class 1 packet, followed by a class 2 packet, etc. A so-called work-conserving queuing discipline will never allow the link to remain idle whenever there are packets (of any class) queued for transmission. A **work-conserving round robin discipline** that looks for a packet of a given class but finds none will immediately check the next class in the round robin sequence.

Figure 6.27 illustrates the operation of a two-class round robin queue. In this example, packets 1, 2, and 4 belong to class one, and packets 3 and 5 belong to the

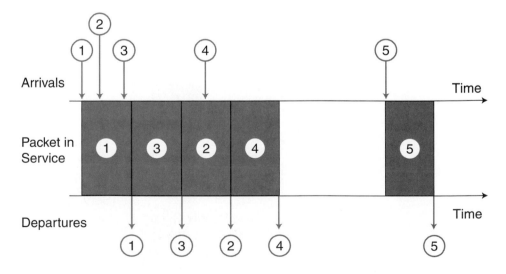

FIGURE 6.27 Operation of the two-class round robin queue

second class. Packet 1 begins transmission immediately upon arrival at the output queue. Packets 2 and 3 arrive during the transmission of packet 1 and thus queue for transmission. After the transmission of packet 1, the link scheduler looks for a class-two packet and thus transmits packet 3. After the transmission of packet 3, the scheduler looks for a class-one packet and thus transmits packet 2. After the transmission of packet 2, packet 4 is the only queued packet; it is thus transmitted immediately after packet 2.

A generalized abstraction of round robin queuing that has found considerable use in QoS architectures is the so-called **Weighted Fair Queuing (WFQ) discipline** [Demers 1990, Parekh 1993]. WFQ is illustrated in Figure 6.28. Arriving packets are again classified and queued in the appropriate per-class waiting area. As in round robin scheduling, a WFQ scheduler will again serve classes in a circular manner—first serving class 1, then serving class 2, then serving class 3, and then (assuming there are three classes) repeating the service pattern. WFQ is also a work-conserving queuing discipline and thus will immediately move on to the next class in the service sequence upon finding an empty class queue.

WFQ differs from round robin in that each class may receive a *differential* amount of service in any interval of time. Specifically, each class, i, is assigned a weight, w_i. Under WFQ, during any interval of time during which there are class i packets to send, class i will then be guaranteed to receive a fraction of service equal to $w_i/(\Sigma w_j)$, where the sum in the denominator is taken over all classes that also have packets queued for transmission. In the worst case, even if all classes have queued packets, class i will still be guaranteed to receive a fraction $w_i/(\Sigma w_j)$ of the bandwidth. Thus, for a link with transmission rate R, class i will always achieve a throughput of at least $R \cdot w_i/(\Sigma w_j)$. Our description of WFQ has been an idealized one, as we have not considered the fact that packets are discrete units of data and a packet's transmission will not be interrupted to begin transmission of another packet; [Demers 1990] and [Parekh 1993] discuss this packetization issue. As we will see in the following sections, WFQ plays a central role in QoS architectures. It is also widely available in today's router products [Cisco QoS 1997]. (Intranets that use WFQ-capable routers can therefore provide QoS to their internal flows.)

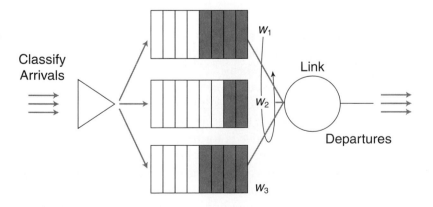

FIGURE 6.28 Weighted Fair Queuing (WFQ)

6.6.2 Policing: The Leaky Bucket

In Section 6.5, we also identified **policing,** the regulation of the rate at which a flow is allowed to inject packets into the network, as one of the cornerstones of any QoS architecture. But what aspects of a flow's packet rate should be policed? We can identify three important policing criteria, each differing from the other according to the time scale over which the packet flow is policed:

- *Average rate.* The network may wish to limit the long-term average rate (packets per time interval) at which a flow's packets can be sent into the network. A crucial issue here is the interval of time over which the average rate will be policed. A flow whose average rate is limited to 100 packets per second is more constrained than a source that is limited to 6000 packets per minute, even though both have the same average rate over a long enough interval of time. For example, the latter constraint would allow a flow to send 1000 packets in a given second-long interval of time (subject to the constraint that the rate be less that 6000 packets over a minute-long interval containing these 1000 packets), while the former constraint would disallow this sending behavior.

- *Peak rate.* While the average rate-constraint limits the amount of traffic that can be sent into the network over a relatively long period of time, a peak-rate constraint limits the maximum number of packets that can be sent over a shorter period of time. Using our example above, the network may police a flow at an average rate of 6000 packets per minute, while limiting the flow's peak rate to 1500 packets per second.

- *Burst size.* The network may also wish to limit the maximum number of packets (the "burst" of packets) that can be sent into the network over an extremely short interval of time. In the limit, as the interval length approaches zero, the burst size limits the number of packets that can be instantaneously sent into the network. While it is physically impossible to instantaneously send multiple packets into the network (after all, every link has a physical transmission rate that cannot be exceeded!), the abstraction of a maximum burst size is a useful one.

The leaky bucket (also called a token bucket) mechanism is an abstraction that can be used to characterize these policing limits. As shown in Figure 6.29, a leaky bucket consists of a bucket that can hold up to b tokens. Tokens are added to this bucket as follows. New tokens, which may potentially be added to the bucket, are always being generated at a rate of r tokens per second. (We assume here for simplicity that the unit of time is a second.) If the bucket is filled with less that b tokens when a token is generated, the newly generated token is added to the bucket; otherwise the newly generated token is ignored, and the token bucket remains full with b tokens.

Let us now consider how the leaky bucket can be used to police a packet flow. Suppose before a packet is transmitted into the network, it must first remove a token from the token bucket. If the token bucket is empty, the packet must wait for a token. (An alternative is for the packet to be dropped, although we will not consider that option here.) Let us now consider how this behavior polices a traffic flow. Because there can be at most b tokens in the bucket, the maximum burst size for a leaky-bucket-policed flow is b packets. Furthermore, because the token generation rate is r, the maximum number of packets that can enter the network of *any* interval of time of length t is $rt + b$. Thus, the token generation rate, r, serves

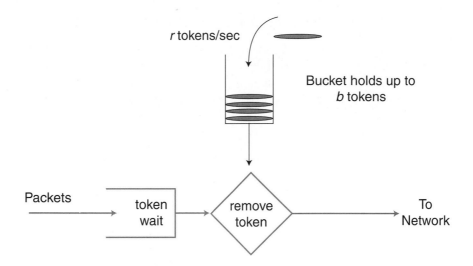

FIGURE 6.29 The Leaky Bucket Policer

to limit the long term average rate at which the packet can enter the network. It is also possible to use leaky buckets (specifically, two leaky buckets in series) to police a flow's peak rate in addition to the long-term average rate; see the homework problems at the end of this chapter.

Leaky Bucket + Weighted Fair Queuing provides Provable Maximum Delay in a Queue.   In Sections 6.7 and 6.8 we will examine the so-called `intserv` and `diffserv` approaches for providing Quality of Service in the Internet. We will see that both leaky bucket policing and WFQ scheduling will play an important role. Let us thus close this section by considering a router's output that multiplexes n flows, each policed by a leaky bucket with parameters b_i and r_i, $i = 1, \ldots,$ n, using WFQ scheduling. We assume that each flow is treated as a separate class by the WFQ scheduler, as shown in Figure 6.30.

Recall from our discussion of WFQ that each flow is guaranteed to receive a share of the link bandwidth equal to at least $R \cdot w_1/(\Sigma w_j)$, where R is the transmission rate of the link in packets/sec. What then is the maximum delay that a packet will experience while waiting for service in the WFQ (that is, after passing through the leaky bucket)? Let us focus on flow 1. Suppose that flow 1's token bucket is initially full. A burst of b_1 packets then arrives to the leaky bucket policer for flow 1. These packets remove all of the tokens (without wait) from the leaky bucket and then join the WFQ waiting area for flow 1. Since these b_1 packets are served at a rate of at least $R \cdot w_1/(\Sigma w_j)$ packet/sec., the last of these packets will then have a maximum delay, d_{max}, until its transmission is completed, where

$$d_{max} = \frac{b_1}{C \cdot w_1/\Sigma w_j}$$

The justification of this formula is that if there are b_1 packets in the queue and packets are being serviced (removed) from the queue at a rate of at least $C \cdot w_i/(\Sigma w_j)$ packets per second, then the amount of time until the last bit of the last packet is transmitted cannot be more than $b_1/(C \cdot w_i/(\Sigma w_j))$. A homework problem

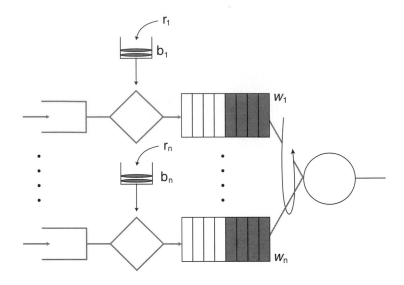

FIGURE 6.30 *n* multiplexed leaky bucket flows with WFQ scheduling

asks you to prove that as long as $r_1 < C \cdot w_i/(\Sigma w_j)$, then d_{max} is indeed the maximum delay that any packet in flow 1 will ever experience in the WFQ queue.

6.7 INTEGRATED SERVICES

In the previous sections, we identified both the principles and the mechanisms used to provide Quality of Service in the Internet. In this section, we consider how these ideas are exploited in a particular architecture for providing quality of service in the Internet—the so-called intserv (Integrated Services) Internet architecture. Intserv is a framework developed within the IETF to provide individualized quality of service guarantees to individual application sessions. Two key features lie at the heart of intserv architecture:

- *Reserved Resources.* A router is required to know what amounts of its resources (buffers, link bandwidth) are already reserved for on-going sessions.
- *Call Setup.* A session requiring QoS guarantees must first be able to reserve sufficient resources at each network router on its source-to-destination path to ensure that its end-to-end QoS requirement is met. This call setup (also known as call admission) process requires the participation of each router on the path. Each router must determine the local resources required by the session, consider the amounts of its resources that are already committed to other on-going sessions, and determine whether it has sufficient resources to satisfy the per-hop QoS requirement of the session at this router without violating local QoS guarantees made to an already admitted session.

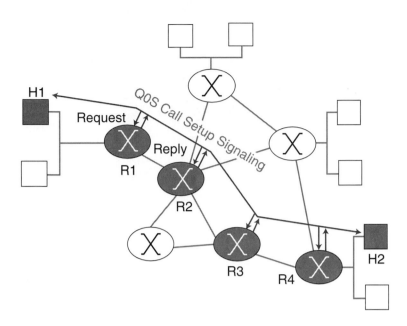

FIGURE 6.31   The call setup process

Figure 6.31 depicts the call setup process. Let us now consider the steps involved in call admission in more detail:

1. *Traffic characterization and specification of the desired QoS.* In order for a router to determine whether or not its resources are sufficient to meet the QoS requirements of a session, that session must first declare its QoS requirement, as well as characterize the traffic that it will be sending into the network, and for which it requires a QoS guarantee. In the Intserv architecture, the so-called Rspec (R for reserved) defines the specific QoS being requested by a connection; the so-called Tspec (T for traffic) characterizes the traffic the sender will be sending into the network, or the receiver will be receiving from the network. The specific form of the Rspec and Tspec will vary, depending on the service requested, as discussed below. The Tspec and Rspec are defined in part in [RFC 2210] and [RFC 2215].

2. *Signaling for call setup.* A session's Tspec and Rspec must be carried to the routers at which resources will be reserved for the session. In the Internet, the RSVP protocol, which is discussed in detail in the next section, is currently the signaling protocol of choice. [RFC 2210] describes the use of the RSVP resource reservation protocol with the Intserv architecture.

3. *Per-element call admission.* Once a router receives the Tspec and Rspec for a session requesting a QoS guarantee, it can determine whether or not it can admit the call. This call admission decision will depend on the traffic specification, the requested type of service, and the existing resource commitments already made by the router to on-going sessions. Per-element call admission is shown in Figure 6.32.

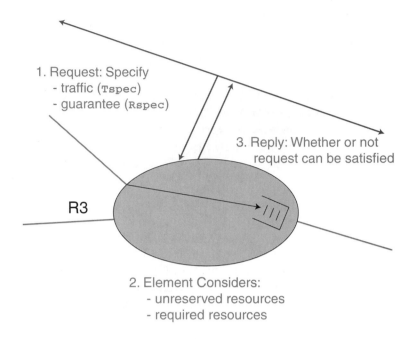

1. Request: Specify
   - traffic (Tspec)
   - guarantee (Rspec)

3. Reply: Whether or not
   request can be satisfied

R3

2. Element Considers:
   - unreserved resources
   - required resources

FIGURE 6.32   Per-element call behavior

The Intserv architecture defines two major classes of service: Guaranteed Service and Controlled-Load service. We will see shortly that each provides a very different form of a quality of service guarantee.

6.7.1   Guaranteed Quality of Service

The Guaranteed Service definition, defined in [RFC 2212] provides firm (mathematically provable) bounds on the queuing delays that a packet will experience in a router. While the details behind Guaranteed Service are rather complicated, the basic idea is really quite simple. To a first approximation, a source's traffic characterization is given by a leaky bucket (see Section 6.6) with parameters (r,b) and the requested service is characterized by a transmission rate, R, at which packets will be transmitted. In essence, a session requesting Guaranteed Service is requiring that the bits in its packet be guaranteed a forwarding rate of R bits/sec. Given that traffic is specified using a leaky bucket characterization, and a guaranteed rate of R is being requested, it is also possible to bound the maximum queuing delay at the router. Recall that with a leaky bucket traffic characterization, the amount of traffic (in bits) generated over any interval of length t is bounded by $rt + b$. Recall also from Section 6.6, that when a leaky bucket source is fed into a queue which guarantees that queued traffic will be serviced at least at a rate of R bits per second, then the maximum queuing delay experienced by any packet will be bounded by b/R, as long as R is greater than r. The actual delay bound guaranteed under the Guaranteed Service definition is slightly more complicated, due to packetization effects (the simple b/R bound assumes that data is in the form of a fluid-like flow rather than discrete packets), the fact that the traffic arrival process is subject to the peak rate limitation of the input link (the simple b/R bound assumes that a burst of b bits can arrive in zero time), and possible additional variations in a packet's transmission time.

6.7.2 Control Load Network Service

A session receiving Controlled-Load service will receive "a quality of service closely approximating the QoS that same flow would receive from an unloaded network element" [RFC 2211]. In other words, the session may assume that a "very high percentage" of its packets will successfully pass through the router without being dropped and will experience a queuing delay in the router that is close to zero. Interestingly, Control Load service makes no quantitative guarantees about performance—it does not specify what constitutes a "very high percentage" of packets nor what quality of service closely approximates that of an unloaded network element.

The Controlled Load service targets real-time multimedia applications that have been developed for today's Internet. These applications perform quite well when the network is unloaded, but rapidly degrade in performance as the network becomes more loaded.

6.8 RSVP

As we learned in the previous section, in order for a network to provide QoS guarantees, there must be a signaling protocol that allows applications running in hosts to reserve resources in the Internet. RSVP [RFC 2205, Zhang 1993], is such a signaling protocol for the Internet.

When people talk about *resources* in the Internet context, they usually mean link bandwidth and router buffers. To keep the discussion concrete and focused, however, we shall assume that the word *resource* is synonymous with *bandwidth*. For our pedagogic purposes, RSVP stands for Bandwidth Reservation Protocol.

6.8.1 The Essence of RSVP

The RSVP protocol allows applications to reserve bandwidth for their data flows. It is used by a host, on the behalf of an application data flow, to request a specific amount of bandwidth from the network. RSVP is also used by the routers to forward bandwidth reservation requests. To implement RSVP, RSVP software must be present in the receivers, senders, and routers. The two principle characteristics of RSVP are:

1. It provides **reservations for bandwidth in multicast trees** (unicast is handled as a special case).
2. It is **receiver-oriented,** that is, the receiver of a data flow initiates and maintains the resource reservation used for that flow.

These two characteristics are illustrated in Figure 6.33. The diagram shows a multicast tree with data flowing from the top of the tree to six hosts. Although data originates from the sender, the reservation messages originate from the receivers.

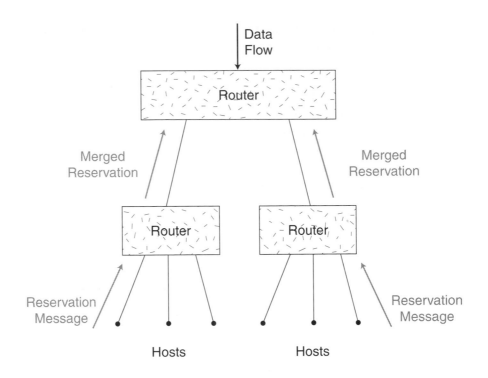

FIGURE 6.33 RSVP: multicast- and receiver-oriented

When a router forwards a reservation message upstream towards the sender, the router may merge the reservation message with other reservation messages arriving from downstream.

Before discussing RSVP in greater detail, we need to recall the notion of a **session.** As with RTP, a session can consist of multiple multicast data flows. Each sender in a session is the source of one or more data flows; for example, a sender might be the source of a video data flow and an audio data flow. Each data flow in a session has the same multicast address. To keep the discussion concrete, we assume that routers and hosts identify the session to which a packet belongs by the packet's multicast address. This assumption is somewhat restrictive; the actual RSVP specification allows for more general methods to identify a session. Within a session, the data flow to which a packet belongs also needs to be identified. This could be done, for example, with the flow identifier field in IPv6.

What RSVP is not. We emphasize that the RSVP standard [RFC 2205] does not specify how the network provides the reserved bandwidth to the data flows. It is merely a protocol that allows the applications to reserve the necessary link bandwidth. Once the reservations are in place, it is up to the routers in the Internet to actually provide the reserved bandwidth to the data flows. This provisioning is done with the scheduling mechanisms (priority scheduling, weighted fair queuing, etc.) discussed in Section 6.6.

It is also important to understand that RSVP is not a routing protocol—it does not determine the links in which the reservations are to be made. Instead it depends on an underlying routing protocol (unicast or multicast) to determine the routes for the flows. Once the routes are in place, RSVP can reserve bandwidth in the links along these routes. (We shall see shortly that when a route changes, RSVP re-reserves resources.) And once the reservations are in place, the routers' packet schedulers can actually provide the reserved bandwidth to the data flows. Thus, RSVP is only one piece—albeit an important piece—in the QoS guarantee puzzle.

RSVP is sometimes referred to as a *signaling protocol*. By this it is meant that RSVP is a protocol that allows hosts to establish and tear down reservations for data flows. The term "signaling protocol" comes from the jargon of the circuit-switched telephony community.

Heterogeneous Receivers.   Some receivers can receive a flow at 28.8 Kbps, others at 128 Kbps, and yet others at 10 Mbps or higher. This heterogeneity of the receivers poses an interesting question. If a sender is multicasting a video to a group of heterogeneous receivers, should the sender encode the video for low quality at 28.8 Kbps, for medium quality at 128 Kbps, or for high quality at 10 Mbps? If the video is encoded at 10 Mbps, then only the users with 10 Mbps access will be able to watch the video. On the other hand, if the video is encoded at 28.8 Kbps, then the 10 Mbps users will have to see a low-quality image when they know they can see something much better.

To resolve this dilemma it is often suggested that video and audio be encoded in layers. For example, a video might be encoded into two layers: a base layer and an enhancement layer. The base layer could have a rate of 20 Kbps whereas the enhancement layer could have a rate of 100 Kbps; in this manner receivers with 28.8 Kbps access could receive the low-quality base-layer image, and receivers with 128 Kbps could receive both layers to construct a high-quality image.

We note that the sender does not have to know the receiving rates of all the receivers. It only needs to know the maximum rate of all its receivers. The sender encodes the video or audio into multiple layers and sends all the layers up to the maximum rate into multicast tree. The receivers pick out the layers that are appropriate for their receiving rates. In order to not excessively waste bandwidth in the network's links, the heterogeneous receivers must communicate to the network the rates they can handle. We shall see that RSVP gives foremost attention to the issue of reserving resources for heterogeneous receivers.

6.8.2   A Few Simple Examples

Let us first describe RSVP in the context of a concrete one-to-many multicast example. Suppose there is a source that is transmitting into the Internet the video of a major sporting event. This session has been assigned a multicast address, and the source stamps all of its outgoing packets with this multicast address. Also suppose that an underlying multicast routing protocol has established a multicast tree from the sender to four receivers as shown below; the numbers next to the receivers are the rates at which the receivers want to receive data. Let us also assume that the video is layered and encoded to accommodate this heterogeneity of receiver rates.

Crudely speaking, RSVP operates as follows for this example. Each receiver sends a reservation message upstream into the multicast tree. This reservation message specifies the rate at which the receiver would like to receive the data from the source. When the reservation message reaches a router, the router adjusts its packet scheduler to accommodate the reservation. It then sends a reservation upstream. The amount of bandwidth reserved upstream from the router depends on the bandwidths reserved downstream. In the example in Figure 6.34, receivers R1, R2, R3, and R4 reserve 20 Kbps, 120 Kbps, 3 Mbps, and 3 Mbps, respectively. Thus router D's downstream receivers request a maximum of 3 Mbps. For this one-to-many transmission, Router D sends a reservation message to Router B requesting that Router B reserve 3 Mbps on the link between the two routers. Note that only 3 Mbps are reserved and not 3+3=6 Mbps; this is because receivers R3 and R4 are watching the same sporting event, so their reservations may be merged. Similarly, Router C requests that Router B reserve 100 Kbps on the link between routers B and C; the layered encoding ensures that receiver R1's 20 Kbps stream is included in the 100 Mbps stream. Once Router B receives the reservation message from its downstream routers and passes the reservations to its schedulers, it sends a new reservation message to its upstream router, Router A. This message reserves 3 Mbps of bandwidth on the link from Router A to Router B, which is again the maximum of the downstream reservations.

We see from this first example that RSVP is **receiver-oriented,** that is, the receiver of a data flow initiates and maintains the resource reservation used for that flow. Note that each router receives a reservation message from each of its downstream links in the multicast tree and sends only one reservation message into its upstream link.

As another example, suppose that four persons are participating in a video conference, as shown in Figure 6.35. Each person has three windows open on her computer to look at the other three persons. Suppose that the underlying routing protocol has established the multicast tree among the four hosts as shown in the diagram below. Finally, suppose each person wants to see each of the videos at 3 Mbps. Then on each of the links in this multicast tree, RSVP would reserve 9 Mbps in one direction and 3 Mbps in the other direction. Note that RSVP does

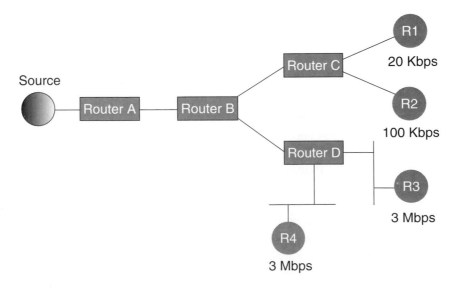

FIGURE 6.34   An RSVP example

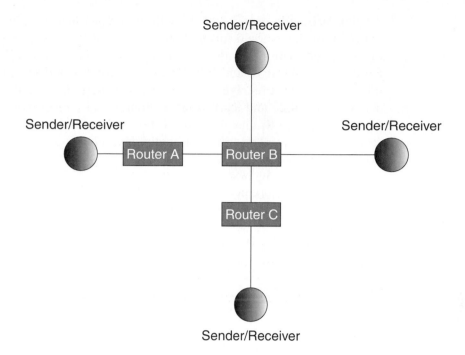

FIGURE 6.35 An RSVP video conference example

not merge reservations in this example, as each person wants to receive three distinct streams.

Now consider an audio conference among the same four persons over the same multicast tree. Suppose b bps are needed for an isolated audio stream. Because in an audio conference it is rare that more than two persons speak at the same time, it is not necessary to reserve $3 \cdot b$ bps into each receiver; $2 \cdot b$ should suffice. Thus, in this last application we can conserve bandwidth by merging reservations.

Call admission.   Just as the manager of a restaurant should not accept reservations for more tables than the restaurant has, the amount of bandwidth on a link that a router reserves should not exceed the link's capacity. Thus whenever a router receives a new reservation message, it must first determine if its downstream links on the multicast tree can accommodate the reservation. This *admission test* is performed whenever a router receives a reservation message. If the admission test fails, the router rejects the reservation and returns an error message to the appropriate receiver(s).

RSVP does not define the admission test; but it assumes that the routers perform such a test and that RSVP can interact with the test.

6.8.3   Path Messages

So far we have only discussed the RSVP reservation messages, which originate at the receivers and flow upstream towards the senders. *Path messages* are another important RSVP message type; they originate at the senders and flow downstream towards the receivers.

The principle purpose of the path messages is to let the routers know on which links they should forward the reservation messages. Specifically, a path message sent within the multicast tree from a Router A to a Router B contains Router A's unicast IP address. Router B puts this address in a `path-state` table, and when it receives a reservation message from a downstream node it accesses the table and learns that it should send a reservation message up the multicast tree to Router A. In the future some routing protocols may supply reverse path forwarding information directly, replacing the reverse-routing function of the path state.

Along with some other information, the path messages also contain a *sender* `Tspec`, which defines the traffic characteristics of the data stream that the sender will generate (see Section 6.7). This `Tspec` can be used to prevent over-reservation.

6.8.4 Reservation Styles

Through its *reservation style,* a reservation message specifies whether merging of reservations from the same session is permissible. A reservation style also specifies from which senders in a session the receiver desires to receive data. Recall that a router can identify the sender of a datagram from the datagram's source IP address.

There are currently three reservation styles defined: *wildcard-filter style, fixed-filter style;* and *shared-explicit style.*

- *Wildcard-Filter Style.* When a receiver uses the wildcard-filter style in its reservation message, it is telling the network that it wants to receive all flows from all upstream senders in the session and that its bandwidth reservation is to be shared among the senders.

- *Fixed-Filter Style.* When a receiver uses the fixed-filter style in its reservation message, it specifies a list of senders from which it wants to receive a data flow along with a bandwidth reservation for each of these senders. These reservations are distinct, that is, they are not to be shared.

- *Shared-Explicit Style.* When a receiver uses the shared-explicit style in its reservation message, it specifies a list of senders from which it wants to receive a data flow along with a single bandwidth reservation. This reservation is to be shared among all the senders in the list.

Shared reservations, created by the wildcard filter and the shared-explicit styles, are appropriate for a multicast session whose sources are unlikely to transmit simultaneously. Packetized audio is an example of an application suitable for shared reservations; because a limited number of people talk at once, each receiver might issue a wildcard-filter or a shared-explicit reservation request for twice the bandwidth required for one sender (to allow for over speaking). On the other hand, the fixed-filter reservation, which creates distinct reservations for the flows from different senders, is appropriate for video teleconferencing.

Examples of reservation styles. Following the Internet RFC, we now give examples for the three reservation styles. In Figure 6.36, a router has two incoming interfaces, labeled A and B, and two outgoing interfaces, labeled C and D. The many-to-many multicast session has three senders—S1, S2, and S3—and three

FIGURE 6.36   Sample scenario for RSVP reservation styles

receivers—R1, R2, and R3. Figure 6.36 also shows that interface D is connected to a LAN.

Suppose first that all of the receivers use the *wildcard-filter reservation*. As shown in the Figure 6.37, receivers R1, R2, and R3 want to reserve 4*b*, 3*b*, and 2*b*, respectively, where *b* is a given bit rate. Then the router reserves 4b on interface C and 3*b* on interface D. Because of the wildcard-filter reservation, the two reservations from R2 and R3 are merged for interface D: the larger of the two reservations is used rather than the sum of reservations. The router then sends a reservation message upstream to interface A and another to interface B; each of these reservation message requests is 4*b*, which is the larger of 3*b* and 4*b*.

Now suppose that all of the receivers use the *fixed-filter reservation*. As shown in Figure 6.38, receiver R1 wants to reserve 4b for source S1 and 5b for source S2; also shown in the figure are the reservation requests from R2 and R3. Because of the fixed-filter style, the router reserves two disjoint chunks of bandwidth on

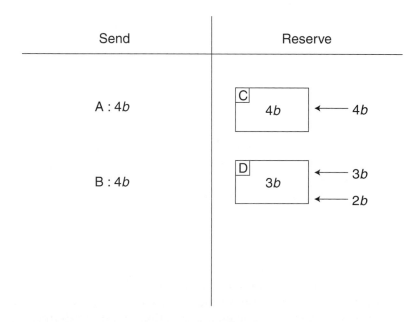

FIGURE 6.37   Wildcard filter reservations

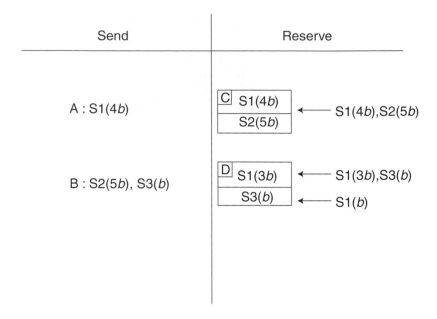

FIGURE 6.38 Fixed filter reservations

interface C: one chunk of $4b$ for S1 and another chunk of $5b$ for S2. Similarly, the router reserves two disjoint chunks of bandwidth on interface D: one chunk of $3b$ for S1 (the maximum of b and $3b$) and one chunk of b for S3. On interface A, the router sends a message with a reservation for S1 of $4b$ (the maximum of $3b$ and $4b$). On interface B, the router sends a message with a reservation of $5b$ for S2 and b for S3.

Finally suppose that each of the receivers use the *shared-explicit reservation.* As shown in Figure 6.39, receiver R1 desires a pipe of $1b$ which is to be shared between sources S1 and S2, receiver R2 desires a pipe of $3b$ to be shared between sources S1 and S3, and receiver R3 wants a pipe of $2b$ for source S2. Because of the shared-explicit style, the reservations from R2 and R3 are merged for interface D: only one pipe is reserved on interface D, although it is reserved at the maximum of the reservation rates. RSVP will reserve on interface B a pipe of $3b$ to be shared by S2 and S3; note that $3b$ is the maximum of the downstream reservations for S2 and S3.

In each of the above examples the three receivers used the same reservation style. Because receivers make independent decisions, the receivers participating in a session could use different styles. RSVP does not permit, however, reservations of different styles to be merged.

6.8.5 Soft State

The reservations in the routers and hosts are maintained with **soft states.** By this it is meant that each reservation for bandwidth stored in a router has an associated timer. If a reservation's timer expires, then the reservation is removed. If a receiver desires to maintain a reservation, it must periodically refresh the reservation by sending reservation messages. A receiver can also change its reservation

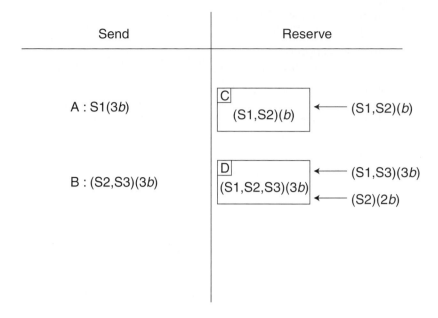

FIGURE 6.39   Shared-explicit reservations

(for example, the amount of bandwidth or the senders it wants to receive from) by adjusting its reservation in its stream of refresh messages.

The senders must also refresh the path state by periodically sending path messages. When a route changes, the next path message initializes the path state on the new route, and future reservation messages will establish reservation state in the route. The state on the old segments of the route will time out.

Soft state, whereby the state is maintained with refresh messages, is used by many other protocols in data networking. For example, as we learned in Chapter 5, in the routing tables in transparent bridges, the entries are refreshed by data packets that arrive to the bridge; entries that are not refreshed are timed-out. A protocol that takes explicit actions to modify or release state is called a **hard-state** protocol. An example of a hard-state protocol is TCP, whereby the connection does not timeout if it stops being used; instead, one side of the connection must explicitly destroy the connection.

6.8.6   Transport of Reservation Messages

RSVP messages are sent hop-by-hop directly over IP. Thus the RSVP message is placed in the information field of the IP datagram; the protocol number in the IP datagram is set to 46. Because IP is unreliable, RSVP messages are not acknowledged upon arrival. If an RSVP path or reservation message is lost, a replacement refresh message should arrive soon.

An RSVP reservation message that originates in a host will have the host's IP address in the source address field of the encapsulating IP datagram. It will have the IP address of the first router along the reserve-path in the multicast tree in the destination address in the encapsulating IP datagram. When the IP datagram arrives at the first router, the router strips off the IP fields and passes the reservation message to the router's RSVP module. The RSVP module examines the messages multicast address (that is, session identifier) and style type, examines its current state, and then acts appropriately; for example, the RSVP module may merge the reservation with a reservation originating from another interface and then send a new reservation message to the next router upstream in the multicast tree.

Insufficient resource. Because a reservation request that fails an admission test may embody a number of requests merged together, a reservation error must be reported to all the concerned receivers. These reservation errors are reported within **ResvError messages.** The receivers can then reduce the amount of resource that they request and try reserving again. The RSVP standard provides mechanisms to allow the backtracking of the reservations when insufficient resources are available; unfortunately, these mechanisms add significant complexity to the RSVP protocol. Furthermore, RSVP suffers from the so-called **killer-reservation problem,** whereby a receiver requests a large reservation over and over again, each time getting its reservation rejected due to lack of sufficient resources. Because this large reservation may have been merged with smaller reservations downstream, the large reservation may be excluding smaller reservations from being established. To solve this thorny problem, RSVP uses the `ResvError` messages to establish additional state in routers, called **blockade state.** Blockade state in a router modifies the merging procedure to omit the offending reservation from the merge, allowing a smaller request to be forwarded and established. The blockade state adds yet further complexity to the RSVP protocol and its implementation.

6.9 DIFFERENTIATED SERVICES

In the previous section we saw how RSVP reserves *per-flow* resources at routers within the network. The ability to request and reserve per-flow resources, in turn, makes it possible for the Intserv framework to provide quality of service guarantees to individual flows. As work on Intserv and RSVP proceeded, however, researchers involved with these efforts (for example, [Zhang 1998]) have begun to uncover some of the difficulties associated with the Intserv model and per-flow reservation of resources:

■ *Scalability.* The per-flow resource reservation in RSVP implies the need for a router to process resource reservations and to maintain per-flow state for *each* flow passing though the router. With recent measurements [Thompson 1997] suggesting that even for an OC-3 speed link, approximately 256,000 source-destination pairs might be seen in one minute in a backbone router, per-flow reservation processing represents a considerable overhead in large networks.

■ *Flexible service models.* The Intserv framework provides for a small number of pre-specified service classes. This particular set of service classes does not allow for more qualitative or relative definitions of service distinctions (for example, "Service class A will received preferred treatment over service class B."). These more qualitative definitions might better fit our intuitive notion of service distinction (for example, first class versus coach class in air travel; "platinum" versus "gold" versus "standard" credit cards).

- *Better-than-best-effort service to applications, without the need for host RSVP signaling.* Few hosts in today's Internet are able to generate RSVP signaling or express the Rspec and Tspec in the detail needed by the Intserv model.

These considerations have led to the recent so-called "diffserv" (Differentiated Services) activity [Diffserv 1999] within the Internet Engineering Task Force. The diffserv working group is developing an architecture for providing *scalable* and *flexible* service differentiation—that is, the ability to handle different "classes" of traffic in different ways within the Internet. The need for *scalability* arises from the fact that hundreds of thousands of simultaneous source-destination traffic flows may be present at a backbone router of the Internet. We will see shortly that this need is met by placing only simple functionality within the network core, with more complex control operations being implemented toward the "edge" of the network. The need for *flexibility* arises from the fact that new service classes may arise and old service classes may become obsolete. The differentiated services architecture is flexible in the sense that it does *not* define specific services or service classes (for example, as is the case with Intserv). Instead, the differentiated services architecture provides the functional components, that is, the "pieces" of a network architecture, with which such services can be built. Let us now examine these components in detail.

6.9.1 Differentiated Services: A Simple Scenario

To set the framework for defining the architectural components of the differentiated service model, let us begin with the simple network shown in Figure 6.40. In the following, we describe one possible use of the diffserv components. Many other possible variations are possible, as described in [RFC 2475]. Our goal here

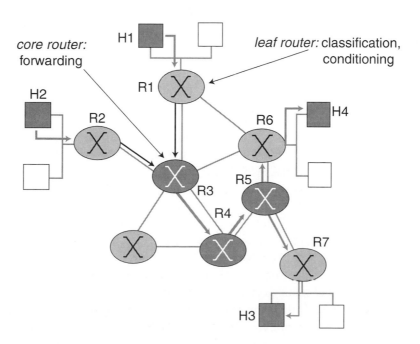

FIGURE 6.40 A simple diffserv network example

is to provide an introduction to the key aspects of differentiated services, rather than to describe the architectural model in exhaustive detail.

The differentiated services architecture consists of two sets of functional elements:

■ *Edge functions: packet classification and traffic conditioning.* At the incoming "edge" of the network (that is, at either a differentiated services-capable host that generates traffic or at the first DS-capable router that the traffic passes through), arriving packets are marked. More specifically, the Differentiated Service (DS) field of the packet header is set to some value. For example, in Figure 6.40, packets being sent from H1 to H3 might be marked at R1, while packets being sent from H2 to H4 might be marked at R2. The mark that a packet receives identifies the class of traffic to which it belongs. Different classes of traffic will then receive different service within the core network. The RFC defining the differentiated service architecture [RFC 2475] uses the term "**behavior aggregate**" rather than "class of traffic." After being marked, a packet may then be immediately forwarded into the network, delayed for some time before being forwarded, or may be discarded. We will see shortly that many factors can influence how a packet is to be marked, and whether it is to be forwarded immediately, delayed, or dropped.

■ *Core function: forwarding.* When a DS-marked packet arrives at a DS-capable router, the packet is forwarded onto its next hop according to the so-called **per-hop behavior** associated with that packet's class. The per-hop behavior influences how a router's buffers and link bandwidth are shared among the competing classes of traffic. A crucial tenet of the DS architecture is that a router's per-hop behavior will be based *only* on packet markings, that is, the class of traffic to which a packet belongs. Thus, if packets being sent from H1 to H3 in Figure 6.31 receive the same marking as packets from H2 to H4, then the network routers treat these packets as a aggregate, without distinguishing whether the packets originated at H1 or H2. For example, R3 would not distinguish between packets from H1 and H2 when forwarding these packets on to R4. Thus, the differentiated service architecture obviates the need to keep router state for individual source-destination pairs—an important consideration in meeting the scalability requirement discussed at the beginning of this section.

An analogy might prove useful here. At many large-scale social events (for example, a large public reception, a large dance club or discothèque, a concert, a football game), people entering the event receive a "pass" of one type or another. There are VIP passes for Very Important People; there are over-18 passes for people who are eighteen years old or older (for example, if alcoholic drinks are to be served); there are backstage passes at concerts; there are press passes for reporters; there is an ordinary pass (sometimes simply the lack of a special pass) for the Ordinary Person. These passes are typically distributed on entry to the event, that is, at the "edge" of the event. It is here at the edge where computationally intensive operations such as paying for entry, checking for the appropriate type of invitation, and matching an invitation against a piece of identification, are performed. Furthermore, there may be a limit on the number of people of a given type that are allowed into an event. If there is such a limit, people may have to wait before entering the event. Once inside the event, one's pass allows one to receive differentiated service at many locations around the event—a VIP is provided with free drinks, a better table, free food, entry to exclusive rooms, and fawning service. Conversely, an Ordinary Person is excluded from certain areas, pays for drinks, and receives only basic service. In both cases, the service received within the event depends solely on the type of one's pass. Moreover, all people within a class are treated alike.

6.9.2 Traffic Classification and Conditioning

In the differentiated services architecture, a packet's mark is carried within the so-called Differentiated Services (DS) field in the IPv4 or IPv6 packet header. The definition of the DS field is intended to supersede the earlier definitions of the IPv4 Type-of-Service field (see Section 4.4) and the IPv6 Traffic Class Field (see Section 4.7). The structure of this 8-bit field is shown below in Figure 6.41.

The 6-bit Differentiated Service Code Point (DSCP) subfield determines the so-called per-hop behavior (see Section 6.8.4) that the packet will receive within the network. The 2-bit CU subfield of the DS field is currently unused. Restrictions are placed on the use of half of the DSCP values in order to preserve backward compatibility with the IPv4 ToS field use; see [RFC 2474] for details. For our purposes here, we need only note that a packet's mark, its "code point" in the DS terminology, is carried in the 8-bit DS field.

As noted above, a packet is marked (more specifically, its DS field value is set) at the edge of the network. This can either happen at a DS-capable host or at the first point at which the packet encounters a DS-capable router. For our discussion here, we will assume marking occurs at an edge router that is directly connected to a sender, as shown in Figure 6.42.

Figure 6.42 provides a logical view of the classification and marking function within the edge router. Packets arriving to the edge router are first "classified." The classifier selects packets based on the values of one or more packet header fields (for example, source address, destination address, source port, destination port, protocol ID) and steers the packet to the appropriate marking function. The DS field value is then set accordingly at the marker. Once packets are marked, they are then forwarded along their route to the destination. At each subsequent DS-capable router, these marked packets then receive the service associated with the packets' marks. Even this simple marking scheme can be used to support different classes of service within the Internet. For example, all packets coming from a certain set of source IP addresses (for example, those IP addresses that have paid for an expensive priority service within their ISP) could be marked on entry to the

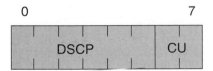

FIGURE 6.41 Structure of the DS field in IVv4 and IPv6 header

FIGURE 6.42 Simple packet classification and marking

ISP, and then receive a specific forwarding service (for example, a higher priority forwarding) at all subsequent DS-capable routers. A question not addressed by the diffserv working group is how the classifier obtains the "rules" for such classification. This could be done manually, that is, the network administrator could load a table of source addresses that are to be marked in a given way into the edge routers, or this could be done under the control of some yet-to-be-specified signaling protocol.

In Figure 6.42, all packets meeting a given header condition receive the same marking, regardless of the packet arrival rate. In some scenarios, it might also be desirable to limit the rate at which packets bearing a given marking are injected into the network. For example, an end-user might negotiate a contract with its ISP to receive high priority service, but at the same time agree to limit the maximum rate at which it would send packets into the network. That is, the end user agrees that its packet sending rate would be within some declared **traffic profile.** The traffic profile might contain a limit on the peak rate, as well as the burstiness of the packet flow, as we saw in Section 6.6 with the leaky bucket mechanism. As long as the user sends packets into the network in a way that conforms to the negotiated traffic profile, the packets receive their priority marking. On the other hand, if the traffic profile is violated, the out-of-profile packets might be marked differently, might be shaped (for example delayed so that a maximum rate constraint would be observed), or might be dropped at the network edge. The role of the **metering function,** shown in Figure 6.43, is to compare the incoming packet flow with the negotiated traffic profile and to determine whether a packet is within the negotiated traffic profile. The actual decision about whether to immediately re-mark, forward, delay, or drop a packet is *not* specified in the diffserv architecture. The diffserv architecture only provides the framework for performing packet marking and shaping/dropping; it

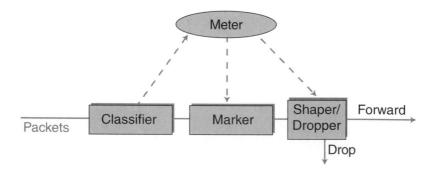

FIGURE 6.43 Logical view of packet classification and traffic conditioning at the edge router

docs *not* mandate any specific policy for what marking and conditioning (shaping or dropping) is actually to be done. The hope, of course, is that the diffserv architectural components are together flexible enough to accommodate a wide and constant evolving set of services to end users.

6.9.3   Per-Hops Behavior

So far, we have focused on the edge functions in the differentiated services architecture. The second key component of the DS architecture involves the per hop behavior (that is, packet forwarding function) performed by DS-capable routers. The per-hop behavior (PHB) is rather cryptically, but carefully, defined as "a description of the externally observable forwarding behavior of a DS node applied to a particular DS behavior aggregate." [RFC 2475]. Digging a little deeper into this definition, we can see several important considerations embedded within:

- A PHB can result in different classes of traffic (that is, traffic with different DS field values) receiving different performance (that is, different externally observable forwarding behavior).

- While a PHB defines differences in performance (behavior) among classes, it does not mandate any particular mechanism for achieving these behaviors. As long as the externally observable performance criteria are met, any implementation mechanism and any buffer/bandwidth allocation policy can be used. For example, a PHB would not require that a particular packet queuing discipline, for example, a priority queue versus a weighted-fair-queuing queue versus a first-come-first-served queue, be used to achieve a particular behavior. The PHB is the "end," to which resource allocation and implementation mechanisms are the "means."

- Differences in performance must be observable, and hence measurable.

An example of a simple PHB is one that guarantees that a given class of marked packets receive at least $x\%$ of the outgoing link bandwidth over some interval of time. Another per-hop behavior might specify that one class of traffic will always receive strict priority over another class of traffic—that is, if a high priority packet and a low priority packet are present in a router's queue at the same time, the high priority packet will always leave first. Note that while a priority queuing discipline might be a natural choice for implementing this second PHB, any queuing discipline that implements the required observable behavior is acceptable.

Currently, two PHB's are under active discussion within the diffserv working group: an Expedited Forwarding (EF) PHB [RFC 2598] and an Assured Forwarding (AF) PHB [RFC 2597]:

- The **Expedited Forwarding** PHB specifies that the departure rate of a class of traffic from a router must equal or exceed a configured rate. That is, during any interval of time, the class of traffic can be guaranteed to receive enough bandwidth so that the output rate of the traffic equals or exceeds this minimum configured rate. Note that the EF per hop behavior implies some form of isolation among traffic classes, as this guarantee is made *independently* of the traffic intensity of any other classes that are arriving to a router. Thus, even if the other classes of traffic are overwhelming router and link resources, enough of those resources must still be made available to the class to ensure that it receives its minimum rate guarantee. EF thus provides a class with the simple *abstraction* of a link with a minimum guaranteed link bandwidth.

▪ The **Assured Forwarding** PHB is more complex. AF divides traffic into four classes, where each AF class is guaranteed to be provided with some minimum amount of bandwidth and buffering. Within each class, packets are further partitioned into one of three "drop preference" categories. When congestion occurs within an AF class, a router can then discard (drop) packets based on their drop preference values. See [RFC 2597] for details. By varying the amount of resources allocated to each class, an ISP can provide different levels of performance to the different AF traffic classes.

The AF PHB could be used as a building block to provide different levels of service to the end systems, for example, an Olympic-like gold, silver, and bronze classes of service. But what would be required to do so? If gold service is indeed going to be "better" (and presumably more expensive!) than silver service, then the ISP must ensure that gold packets receive lower delay and/or loss than silver packets. Recall, however, that a minimum amount of bandwidth and buffering are to be allocated to *each* class. What would happen if gold service was allocated x% of a link's bandwidth and silver service was allocated $x/2$% of the link's bandwidth, but the traffic intensity of gold packets was 100 times higher than that of silver packets? In this case, it is likely that silver packets would receive *better* performance than the gold packets! (An outcome that leaves the silver service buyers happy, but the high-spending gold service buyers extremely unhappy!) Clearly, when creating a service out of a PHB, more than just the PHB itself will come into play. In this example, the dimensioning of resources—determining how much resources will be allocated to each class of service—must be done hand-in-hand with knowledge about the traffic demands of the various classes of traffic.

6.9.4 A Beginning

The differentiated services architecture is still in the early stages of its development and is rapidly evolving. RFCs 2474 and 2475 [RFC 2474], [RFC 2475] define the fundamental framework of the `diffserv` architecture but themselves are likely to evolve as well. The AF and EF PHBs discussed above have yet to enter the RFC standards track. The ways in which PHBs, edge functionality, and traffic profiles can be combined to provide an end-to-end service, such as a virtual leased line service [RFC 2638] or an Olympic-like gold/silver/bronze service [RFC 2597], are still under investigation. In our discussion above, we have assumed that the `DS` architecture is deployed within a single administrative domain. The (typical) case where an end-to-end service must be fashioned from a connection that crosses several administrative domains, and through non-`DS` capable routers, pose additional challenges beyond those described above.

SUMMARY

Multimedia networking is perhaps the most exciting development in the Internet today. People throughout the world are spending less time in front their radios and televisions and are instead turning to the Internet to receive audio and video emissions, both live and prerecorded. As high-speed access penetrates more residences, this trend will continue—couch potatoes throughout the world will access their favorite video programs through the Internet rather then through the traditional microwave and satellite channels. In addition to audio and video distribution, the Internet is also being used to transport phone calls. In fact, over the next ten years the Internet may render the traditional circuit-switched telephone system obsolete in many countries. The Internet will not only provide phone service for less money, but will also provide numerous value-added services, such as video conferencing, online directory services, and voice messaging services.

In Section 6.1 we classified multimedia applications into three categories: streaming stored audio and video; one-to-many transmission of real-time audio and video; and real-time interactive audio and video. We emphasized that multimedia applications are delay sensitive and loss tolerant, which is very different from static-content applications, which are delay tolerant and loss intolerant. We also discussed some of the hurdles that today's best-effort Internet places before multimedia applications. We surveyed several proposals to overcome these hurdles, including simply improving the existing networking infrastructure (by adding more bandwidth, more network caches, and deploying multicast), adding functionality to the Internet so that applications can reserve end-to-end resources (and so that the network can honor these reservations), and finally, introducing service classes to provide service differentiation.

In Sections 6.2–6.4 we examined architectures and mechanisms for multimedia networking in a best-effort network. In Section 6.2 we surveyed several architectures for streaming stored audio and video. We discussed user interaction—such as pause/resume, repositioning, and visual fast forward—and provided an introduction to RTSP, a protocol that provides client-server interaction to streaming applications. In Section 6.3 we examined how interactive real-time applications can be designed to run over a best-effort network. We saw how a combination of client buffers, packet sequence numbers, and timestamps can greatly alleviate the effects of network induced jitter. We also studied how forward error correction and packet interleaving can improve user perceived performance when a fraction of the packets are lost or are significantly delayed. In Section 6.4 we explored media chunk encapsulation, and we investigated in some detail one of the more important standards for media encapsulation, namely, RTP. We also looked at how RTP fits into the emerging H.323 architecture for interactive real-time conferencing.

Sections 6.5–6.9 looked at how the Internet can evolve to provide guaranteed QoS to its applications. In Section 6.5 we identified several principles for providing QoS to multimedia applications. These principles include packet marking and classification, isolation of packet flows, efficient use of resources, and call admission. In Section 6.6 we surveyed a variety of scheduling policies and policing mechanisms that can provide the foundation of a QoS networking architecture. The scheduling policies include priority scheduling, round-robin scheduling, and weighted-fair queuing. We then explored the leaky bucket as a policing mechanism, and showed how the leaky bucket and weighted-fair queuing can be combined to bound the maximum delay a packet experiences at the output queue of a router.

In Sections 6.7–6.9 we showed how these principles and mechanisms have led to the definitions of new standards for providing QoS in the Internet. The first class of these standards is the so-called intserv standard, which includes two services—the guaranteed QoS service and the controlled load service. The guaranteed QoS service provides hard, mathematical provable guarantees on the delay of each of the individual packets in a flow. The control-load service does not provide any hard guarantees, but instead ensures that most of an application's packets will pass through a seemingly uncongested Internet. The intserv architecture requires a signaling protocol for reserving bandwidth and buffer resources within the network. In Section 6.8 we examined in some detail an Internet signaling protocol for reservations, namely, RSVP. We indicated that one of the drawbacks of RSVP (and hence the Intserv architecture) is the need for routers to maintain per-flow state, which may not scale. We concluded the chapter in Section 6.9 by outlining a recent and promising proposal for providing QoS in the Internet, namely, the diffserv architecture. The diffserv architecture does not require routers to maintain per-flow state; it instead classifies packets into a small number of aggregate classes, to which routers provide per-hop behavior. The diffserv architecture is still in its infancy, but because the architecture requires relatively minor changes to the existing Internet protocols and infrastructure, it could be deployed relatively quickly.

Now that we have finished our study of multimedia networking, it is time to move on to another exciting topic in networking, namely, network security. Recent advances in multimedia networking may displace the distribution of audio and video information to the Internet; as we shall see in the next chapter, recent advances in network security may displace the majority of economic transactions to the Internet.

HOMEWORK PROBLEMS AND QUESTIONS

Chapter 6

Review Questions

Sections 6.1–6.2

1. What is meant by interactivity for streaming stored audio/video? What is meant by interactivity for real-time interactive audio/video?

2. Three "camps" were discussed for evolving the Internet so that it better supports multimedia applications. Briefly summarize the views of each camp. In which camp do you belong?

3. Figures 6.2, 6.3, and 6.4 present three schemes for streaming stored media. What are the advantages and disadvantages of each scheme?

Sections 6.3–6.4

4. What is the difference between end-to-end delay and delay jitter? What are the causes of delay jitter?

5. Why is a packet that is received after its scheduled playout time considered lost?

6. Section 6.3 describes two FEC schemes. Briefly summarize them. Both schemes increase the transmission of the stream by adding overhead. Does interleaving also increase the transmission rate?

7. How are different RTP streams in different sessions identified by a receiver? How are different streams from within the same session identified? How are RTP and RTPC packets (as part of the same session) distinguished?

8. Three RTCP packet types are described in Section 6.4. Briefly summarize the information contained in each of these packet types.

9. In Figure 6.15, which of the H.323 channels run over TCP and which over UDP? Why?

Sections 6.5–6.9

10. In Section 6.6, we discussed non-preemptive priority queuing. What would be preemptive priority queuing? Does preemptive priority queuing make sense for computer networks?

11. Give an example of scheduling discipline that is *not* work conserving.

12. Guaranteed Service provides an application no loss and firm bounds on delay. Referring back to Figure 2.2, are there any applications that require both no loss and firm bounds on delay?

13. What are some of the difficulties associated with the Intserv model and per-flow reservation of resources?

PROBLEMS

1. Surf the Web and find three products for streaming stored audio and/or video. For each product, determine: (a) whether meta files are used; (b) whether the audio/video is sent over UDP or TCP; (c) whether RTP is used; and (d) whether RTSP is used.

2. Write a poem, a short story, a description of a recent vacation, or any other piece that takes 2-5 minutes to recite. Recite and record your piece. Convert your recording to one of the RealNetworks audio formats using one of the RealNetworks free encoders. Upload the file to the same server that holds your personal homepage. Also upload the corresponding meta file to the server. Finally, create a link from your homepage to the meta file.

3. Consider the client buffer shown in Figure 6.4. Suppose that the streaming system uses the fourth option, that is, the server pushes the media into the socket as quickly as possible. Suppose the available TCP bandwidth >> d most of the time. Also suppose that the client buffer can only hold about one third of the media. Describe how $x(t)$ and the contents of the client buffer will evolve over time.

4. Are the TCP receive buffer and the media player's client buffer the same thing? If not, how do they interact?

5. In the Internet phone example in Section 6.3, let h be the total number of header bytes added to each chunk, including UDP and IP header.

   a. Assuming an IP datagram is emitted every 20 msec, find the transmission in bits per second for the datagrams generated by one side of this application.

6. Consider the procedure described in Section 6.3 for estimating average delay d_i. Suppose that $u = 0.1$. Let $r_1 - t_1$ be the most recent sample delay, let $r_2 - t_2$ be the next most recent sample delay, etc.

   a. For a given audio application suppose four packets have arrived at the receiver with sample delays $r_4 - t_4$, $r_3 - t_3$, $r_2 - t_2$, $r_1 - t_1$. Express the estimate of delay d in terms of the four samples.

   b. Generalize your formula for n sample delays.

   c. For the formula in part (b) let n approach infinity and give the resulting formula. Comment on why this averaging procedure is called an exponential moving average.

7. Repeat the above question for the estimate of average delay deviation.

8. Compare the procedure described in Section 6.3 for estimating average delay with the procedure in Section 3.5 for estimating round-trip time. What do the procedures have in common? How are they different?

9. Consider the adaptive playout strategy described in Section 6.3.

   a. How can two successive packets received at the destination have time-stamps that differ by more than 20 msecs when the two packets belong to the same talkspurt?

   b. How can the receiver use sequence numbers to determine whether a packet is the first packet in a talkspurt? Be specific.

10. Recall the two FEC schemes for Internet phone described in Section 6.3. Suppose that the first scheme generates a redundant chunk for every four original chunks. Suppose the second scheme uses a low-bit-rate encoding whose transmission rate is 25% of the transmission rate of the nominal stream.

    a. How much additional bandwidth does each scheme require? How much playback delay does each scheme add?

    b. How do the two schemes perform if at most one packet is lost in every group of five packets? Which scheme will have better audio quality?

    c. How do the two schemes perform if at most one packet is lost in every group of two packets? Which scheme will have better audio quality?

11. How is the interarrival time jitter calculated in the RTCP reception report? Hint: Read the RTP RFC.

12. Suppose in an RTP session there are S senders and R receivers. Use the formulas at the end of Section 6.4 to show that RTCP limits its traffic to 5% of the session bandwidth.

13. a. How is RSTP similar to HTTP? Does RSTP have methods? Can HTTP be used to request a stream?

    b. How is RSTP different from HTTP? For example, is HTTP in-band or out-of-band? Does RTSP require state information about the client (consider the pause/resume function)?

14. What are the current Microsoft products for audio/video real-time conferencing. Do these products use any of the protocols discussed in this chapter (for example, RTP or RTSP)?

15. Suppose that the WFQ scheduling policy is applied to a buffer that supports three classes, and suppose the weights are 0.5, 0.25, and 0.25 for the three classes.

a. Suppose that each class has a large number of packets in the buffer. In what sequence might the three classes be served in to achieve the WFQ weights? (For round-robin scheduling, a natural sequence is 123123123 . . .).

b. Suppose that classes 1 and 2 have a large number of packets in the buffer, and there are no class 2 packets in the buffer. In what sequence might the three classes be served in to achieve the WFQ weights?

16. Consider the leaky bucket policer (discussed in Section 6.6) that polices the average rate and burst size of a packet flow. We now want to police the peak rate, p, as well. Show how the output of this leaky bucket policer can be fed into a second leaky bucket policer so that the two leaky buckets in series police the average rate, peak rate, and burst size. Be sure to give the bucket size and token generation rate for the second policer.

17. A packet flow is said to conform to a leaky bucket specification (r,b) with burst size b and average rate r if the number of packets that arrive to the leaky bucket is less than $rt + b$ packets in every interval of time of length t for all t. Will a packet flow that conforms to a leaky bucket specification (r,b) ever have to wait at a leaky bucket policer with parameters r and b? Justify your answer.

18. Show that as long as $r_1 < R * w_1/(\Sigma w_j)$, then d_{max} is indeed the maximum delay that any packet in flow 1 will ever experience in the WFQ queue.

DISCUSSION QUESTIONS

1. How can a host use RTCP feedback information to determine whether problems are local, regional, or global?

2. Do you think it is better to stream stored audio/video on top of TCP or UDP?

3. In RSVP, are reservation styles relevant for one-to-many multicast sessions?

4. Write a one-page report on prospects for Internet phone in the market place.

5. Can the problem of providing QoS guarantees be solved simply by "throwing enough bandwidth" at the problem, that is, by upgrading all link capacities so that bandwidth limitations are no longer a concern?

6. An interesting emerging market is using Internet phone and a company's high-speed LAN to replace the same company's PBX (private branch exchange). Write a one-page report on this issue. Cover the following questions in your report:

a. What is a traditional PBX? Who uses them?

b. Consider a call between a user in the company and another user out of the company, who is connected to the traditional telephone network. What sort of technology is needed at the interface between the LAN and the traditional telephone network?

c. In addition to Internet phone software and the interface of question (b), what else is needed to replace the PBX?

7. Consider the four "pillars" of providing QoS support in Section 6.5. Describe the circumstances, if any, under which each of these pillars can be removed.

8. Use the Web to find three companies that manufacture H.323 gatekeepers. Describe their products.

Chapter 7 Security in Computer Networks

7.1 WHAT IS NETWORK SECURITY?

Let us introduce Alice  and Bob , two people who want to communicate "securely." This being a networking text, we should remark that Alice and Bob may be two routers that want to securely exchange routing tables, two hosts that want to establish a secure transport connection, or two e-mail applications that want to exchange secure e-mail—all case studies that we will consider later in this chapter. Alice and Bob are well-known fixtures in the security community, perhaps because their names are more fun than a generic entity named "A" that wants to securely communicate with a generic entity named "B." Illicit love affairs, wartime communication, and business transactions are the commonly cited human needs for secure communications; preferring the first to the latter two, we're happy to use Alice and Bob as our sender and receiver, and imagine them in this first scenario.

7.1.1 Secure Communication

We said that Alice and Bob want to communicate "securely," but what precisely does this mean? Certainly, Alice wants only Bob to be able to understand a message that she has sent, even though they are communicating over an "insecure" medium where an intruder (Trudy, the intruder) may intercept, read, and perform computations on whatever is transmitted from Alice to Bob. Bob also wants to be sure that the message that he receives from Alice was indeed sent by Alice, and Alice wants to make sure that the person with whom she is communicating is indeed Bob. Alice and Bob also want to make sure that the contents of Alice's message have not been altered in transit. Given these considerations, we can identify the following desirable properties of **secure communication:**

- *Secrecy.* Only the sender and intended receiver should be able to understand the contents of the transmitted message. Because eavesdroppers may intercept the message, this necessarily requires that the message be somehow **encrypted** (data disguised) so that an intercepted message cannot be

decrypted (understood) by an interceptor. This aspect of secrecy is probably the most commonly perceived meaning of the term "secure communication." Note, however, that this is not only a restricted definition of secure communication (we list additional aspects of secure communication below), but a rather restricted definition of secrecy as well. For example, Alice might also want the mere fact that she is communicating with Bob (or the timing or frequency of her communications) to be a secret! We will study cryptographic techniques for encrypting and decrypting data in Section 7.2.

- *Authentication.* Both the sender and receiver need to confirm the identity of other party involved in the communication—to confirm that the other party is indeed who or what they claim to be. Face-to-face human communication solves this problem easily by visual recognition. When communicating entities exchange messages over a medium where they cannot "see" the other party, authentication is not so simple. Why, for instance, should you believe that a received e-mail containing a text string saying that the e-mail came from a friend of yours indeed came from that friend? If someone calls on the phone claiming to be your bank and asking for your account number, secret Personal Identification Number (PIN), and account balances for verification purposes, would you give that information out over the phone? Hopefully not. We will examine authentication techniques in Section 7.3, including several that, perhaps surprisingly, also rely on the cryptographic techniques we study in Section 7.2.

- *Message Integrity.* Even if the sender and receiver are able to authenticate each other, they also want to ensure that the content of their communication is not altered, either maliciously or by accident, in transmission. Extensions to the checksumming techniques that we encountered in reliable transport and data link protocols will also be studied in Section 7.4; these techniques also rely on cryptographic concepts in Section 7.2.

Having established what we mean by secure communication, let us next consider exactly what is meant by an "insecure channel." What information does an intruder have access to, and what actions can be taken on the transmitted data? Figure 7.1 illustrates the scenario.

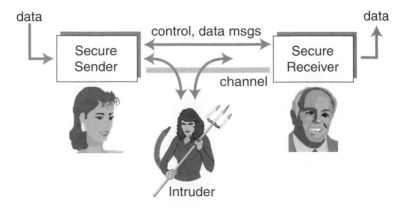

FIGURE 7.1 Sender, receiver, and intruder (Alice, Bob, and Trudy)

Alice, the sender, wants to send data to Bob, the receiver. In order to securely exchange data, while meeting the requirements of secrecy, authentication, and message integrity, Alice and Bob will exchange both control messages and data messages (in much the same way that TCP senders and receivers exchange both control segments and data segments). All, or some of these messages will typically be encrypted. A **passive intruder** can listen to and record the control and data messages on the channel; an **active intruder** can remove messages from the channel and/or add messages into the channel.

7.1.2 Network Security Considerations in the Internet

Before delving into the technical aspects of network security in the following sections, let's conclude our introduction by relating our fictitious characters—Alice, Bob, and Trudy—to "real world" scenarios in today's Internet.

Let's begin with Trudy, the network intruder. Can a "real world" network intruder really listen to and record network messages? Is it easy to do so? Can an intruder actively inject or remove messages from the network? The answer to all of these questions is an emphatic *yes*. A **packet sniffer** is a program running in a network-attached device that passively receives all data-link layer frames passing by the device's network interface. In a broadcast environment such as an Ethernet LAN, this means that the packet sniffer receives all frames being transmitted from or to all hosts on the LAN. Any host with an Ethernet card can easily serve as a packet sniffer, as the Ethernet NIC needs only be set to **promiscuous mode** to receive all passing Ethernet frames. These frames can then be passed on to application programs that extract application-level data. For example, in the Telnet scenario shown in Figure 7.2, the login password prompt sent from A to B, as well as the password entered at B are "sniffed" at host C. Packet sniffing is a double-edged sword—it can be invaluable to a network administrator for network monitoring and management (see Chapter 8) but also used by the unethical hacker. Packet-sniffing software is freely available at various WWW sites, and as a commercial product. Professors teaching a networking course have been known to assign lab exercises that involve writing a packet-sniffing and application-level data reconstruction program.

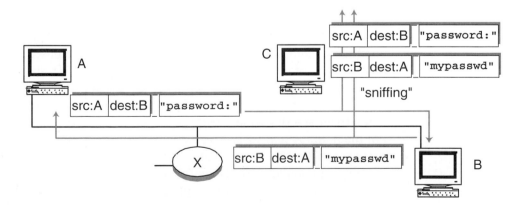

FIGURE 7.2 Packet sniffing

Any Internet-connected device (for example, a host) necessarily sends IP datagrams into the network. Recall from Chapter 4 that these datagrams carry the sender's IP address, as well as upper-layer data. A user with complete control over that device's software (in particular its operating system) can easily modify the device's protocols to place an arbitrary IP address into a datagram's Source Address field. This is known as **IP spoofing.** A user can thus craft an IP packet containing any payload (upper-layer) data it desires and make it appear as if that data was sent from an arbitrary IP host. Packet sniffing and IP spoofing are just two of the more common forms of security "attacks" on the Internet. These and other network attacks are discussed in the collection of essays [Denning 1997]. A summary of reported attacks is maintained at the CERT Coordination Center [CERT 1999].

Having established that there are indeed real bogeymen (*a.k.a.* "Trudy") loose in the Internet, what are the Internet equivalents of Alice and Bob, our two friends who need to communicate securely? Certainly, "Bob" and "Alice" might be human users at two end systems, for example, a real Alice and a real Bob who really *do* want to exchange secure e-mail. They might also be participants in an electronic commerce transaction, for example, a real Alice might want to securely transfer her credit card number to a WWW server to purchase an item online. Similarly, a real Alice might want to interact with her bank online. As noted in [RFC 1636], however, the parties needing secure communication might also themselves be part of the network infrastructure. Recall that the Domain Name System (DNS, see Section 2.5), or routing daemons that exchange routing tables (see Section 4.5) require secure communication between two parties. The same is true for network management applications, a topic we examine in Chapter 8. An intruder that could actively interfere with, control, or corrupt DNS lookups and updates, routing computations, or network management functions could wreak havoc in the Internet.

Having now established the framework, a few of the most important definitions, and the need for network security, let us next delve into cryptography, a topic of central importance to many aspects of network security.

7.2 PRINCIPLES OF CRYPTOGRAPHY

Although cryptography has a long history dating back to Julius Caesar (we will look at the so-called Caesar cipher shortly), modern cryptographic techniques, including many of those used in today's Internet, are based on advances made in past twenty years. Kahn's book, "The Codebreakers," [Kahn 1967] provides a fascinating look at this long history. A detailed (but entertaining and readable) technical discussion of cryptography, particularly from a network standpoint, is [Kaufman 1995]. [Diffie 1998] provides a compelling and up-to-date examination of the political and social (for example, privacy) issues that are now inextricably intertwined with cryptography. A complete discussion of cryptography itself requires a complete book [Kaufman 1995, Schneier 1996] and so we only touch on the essential aspects of cryptography, particularly as they are practiced in

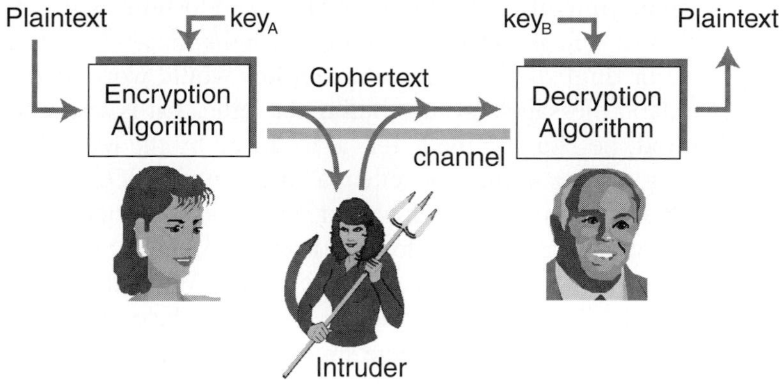

FIGURE 7.3 Cryptographic components

today's Internet. Two excellent on-line sites are [Kessler 1998] and the RSA Labs FAQ page [RSA FAQ 1999].

Cryptographic techniques allow a sender to disguise data so that an intruder can gain no information from the intercepted data. The receiver, of course, must be able to recover the original data from the disguised data. Figure 7.3 illustrates some of the important terminology.

Suppose now that Alice wants to send a message to Bob. Alice's message in its original form (for example, "`Bob, I love you. Alice`") is known as **plaintext,** or **cleartext.** Alice encrypts her plaintext message using an **encryption algorithm** so that the encrypted message, known as **ciphertext,** looks unintelligible to any intruder. Interestingly, in many modern cryptographic systems, including those used in the Internet, the encryption technique itself is *known*—published, standardized, and available to everyone (for example, [RFC 1321, RFC 2437, RFC 2420), even a potential intruder! Clearly, if everyone knows the method for encoding data, then there must be some bit of secret information that prevents an intruder from decrypting the transmitted data. This is where keys come in.

In Figure 7.3, Alice provides a **key,** K_A, a string of numbers or characters, as input to the encryption algorithm. The encryption algorithm takes the key and the plaintext as input and produces ciphertext as output. Similarly, Bob will provide a key, K_B, to the **decryption algorithm,** that takes the ciphertext and Bob's key as input and produces the original plaintext as output. In so-called **symmetric key systems,** Alice and Bob's keys are identical and are secret. In **public key systems,** the key that Alice uses is known to all (!), while Bob's key is secret. In the following two subsections, we consider symmetric key and public key systems in more detail.

7.2.1 Symmetric Key Cryptography

All cryptographic algorithms involve substituting one thing for another, for example, taking a piece of plaintext and computing and then substituting the appropriate ciphertext to create the encrypted message. Before studying a modern key-based cryptographic system, let us first "get our feet wet" by studying a very old simple symmetric key algorithm attributed to Julius Caesar, known as the Caesar cipher (a "cipher" is a method for encrypting data).

For English text, the **Caesar cipher** would work by taking each letter in the plaintext message and substituting the letter that is k letters later (allowing wraparound; i.e., having the letter 'a' followed by the letter 'z') in the alphabet. For example if $k = 4$, then the letter "a" in plaintext becomes "d" in ciphertext; "b" in plaintext becomes "e" in ciphertext, and so on. Here, the value of k serves as the key. As an example, the plaintext message "`bob, I love you. alice.`" becomes "`yly, f ilsb vlr. xifzb.`" in ciphertext. While the ciphertext does indeed look like gibberish, it wouldn't take long to break the code if you knew that the Caesar cipher was being used, as there are only twenty-five possible key values.

An improvement to the Caesar cipher is the so-called **monoalphabetic cipher** that also substitutes one letter in the alphabet with another letter in the alphabet. However, rather than substituting according to a regular pattern (for example, substitution with an offset of k for all letters), any letter can be substituted for any other letter, as long as each letter has a unique substitute letter and vice versa. The substitution rule in Figure 7.4 shows one possible rule for encoding plaintext.

The plaintext message "`bob, I love you. alice.`" becomes "`nkn, s gktc wky. mgsbc.`" Thus, as in the case of the Caesar cipher, this looks like gibberish. A monoalphabetic cipher would also appear to be better than the Caesar cipher in that there are 26! (on the order of 10^{26}) possible pairings of letters rather than twenty-five possible pairings. A brute force approach of trying all 10^{26} possible pairings would require far too much work to be a feasible way of breaking the encryption algorithm and decoding the message. However, by statistical analysis of the plaintext language, for example, knowing that the letters "e" and "t" are the most frequently occurring letters in typical text (accounting for 13% and 9% of letter occurrences), and knowing that particular two- and three-letter occurrences of letters appear quite often together (for example, "in," "it," "the," "ion," "ing," etc.) make it relatively easy to break this code. If the intruder has some knowledge about the possible contents of the message, then it is even easier to break the code. For example, if Trudy the intruder is Bob's wife and suspects Bob of having an affair with Alice, then she might suspect that the names "bob" and "alice" appear in the text. If Trudy knew for certain that those two names appeared in the ciphertext and had a copy of the example ciphertext message above, then she could immediately determine seven of the twenty-six letter pairings, requiring 10^9 fewer possibilities to be checked by a brute force method. Indeed, if Trudy suspected Bob of having an affair, she might well expect to find some other choice words in the message as well.

When considering how easy it might be for Trudy to break Bob and Alice's encryption scheme, one can distinguish three different scenarios, depending on what information the intruder has:

- *Ciphertext only attack.* In some cases, the intruder may only have access to the intercepted ciphertext, with no certain information about the contents of

Plaintext Letter:	a b c d e f g h i f k l m n o p q r s t u v w x y z
Ciphertext Letter:	m n b v c x z a s d f g h j k l p o i u y t r e w q

FIGURE 7.4 A monoalphabetic cipher

the plaintext message. We have seen how statistical analysis can help in a ciphertext-only attack on an encryption scheme.

■ *Known plaintext attack.* We saw above that if Trudy somehow knew for sure that "`bob`" and "`alice`" appeared in the ciphertext message then she could have determined the (plaintext, ciphertext) pairings for the letters `a`, `l`, `i`, `c`, `e`, `b`, and `o`. Trudy might also have been fortunate enough to have recorded all of the ciphertext transmissions and then found Bob's own decrypted version of one of transmissions scribbled on a piece of paper. When an intruder knows some of the (plaintext, ciphertext) pairings, we refer to this as a known plaintext attack on the encryption scheme.

■ *Chosen plaintext attack.* In a chosen plaintext attack, the intruder is able to choose the plaintext message and obtain its corresponding ciphertext form. For the simple encryption algorithms we've seen so far, if Trudy could get Alice to send the message, "`The quick fox jumps over the lazy brown dog`," she can completely break the encryption scheme. We'll see shortly that for more sophisticated encryption techniques, a chosen plaintext attack does not necessarily mean that the encryption technique can be broken.

Five hundred years ago, techniques improving on monoalphabetic encryption, known as **polyalphabetic encryption** were invented. These techniques, incorrectly attributed to Blaise de Vigenere [Kahn 1967], have come to be known as **Vigenere ciphers.** The idea behind Vigenere ciphers is to use multiple monoalphabetic ciphers, with a specific monoalphabetic cipher to encode a letter in a specific position in the plaintext message. Thus, the same letter, appearing in different positions in the plaintext message might be encoded differently. The Vigenere cipher shown in Figure 7.5 has two different Caesar ciphers (with $k = 6$ and $k = 20$), shown as rows in Figure 7.5. One might choose to use these two Caesar ciphers, C_1 and C_2, in the repeating pattern C_1, C_2, C_2, C_1, C_2. That is, the first letter of plaintext is to be encoded using C_1, the second and third using C_2, the fourth using C_1, and the fifth using C_2. The pattern then repeats, with the sixth letter being encoded using C_1, the seventh with C_2, and so on. The plaintext message "`bob, I love you. alice.`" is thus encrypted "`ghu, n etox dhz.`" Note that the first "`b`" in the plaintext message is encrypted using C_1, while the second "`b`" is encrypted using C_2. In this example, the encryption and decryption "key" is the knowledge of the two Caesar keys ($k = 4$, $k = 20$) and the pattern C_1, C_2, C_2, C_1, C_2.

Data Encryption Standard (DES). Let us now fast-forward to modern time and examine the **Data Encryption Standard (DES)** [NIST 1993], a symmetric key encryption standard published in 1977 and updated most recently in 1993 by

plaintext letter:	a b c d e f g h i f k l m n o p q r s t u v w x y z
$C_1(k = 6)$:	f g h i j k l m n o p q r s t u v w x y z a b c d e
$C_2(k = 20)$:	t u v w x y z a b c d e f g h i j k l m n o p q r s

FIGURE 7.5 A Vigenere cipher using two Caesar ciphers

the US National Bureau of Standards for commercial and nonclassified US government use. DES encodes plaintext in 64-bit chunks using a 64-bit key. Actually, 8 of these 64 bits are odd parity bits (there is one parity bit for each of the eight bytes), so the DES key is effectively 56 bits long. The National Institute of Standards (the successor to the National Bureau of Standards) states the goal of DES as follows: "The goal is to completely scramble the data and key so that every bit of the ciphertext depends on every bit of the data and every bit of the key . . . . With a good algorithm, there should be no correlation between the ciphertext and either the original data or key." [NIST 1999].

The basic operation of DES is illustrated in Figure 7.6. In our discussion we will overview DES operation, leaving the nitty-gritty bit-level details (there are *many*) to those wishing to consult [Kaufman 1995, Schneier 1995] (with [Schneier 1995] including a C implementation as well). The DES consists of two permutation steps (the first and last steps of the algorithm), in which all 64 bits are permuted, and 16 identical "rounds" of operation in between. The operation of each round is identical, taking the output of the previous round as input. During

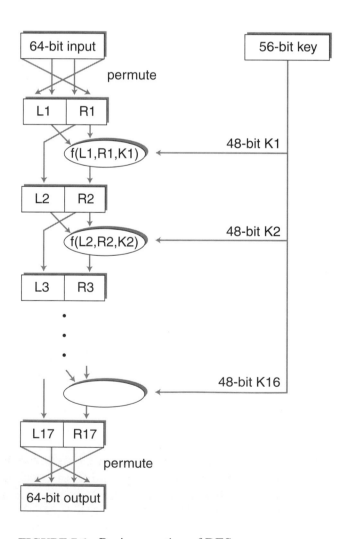

FIGURE 7.6   Basic operation of DES

each round, the rightmost 32 bits of the input are moved to the left 32 bits of the output. The entire 64-bit input to the *ith* round and the 48-bit key for the *ith* round (derived from the larger DES 56-bit key) are taken as input to a function that involves expansion of 4-bit input chunks into 6-bit chunks, exclusive OR-ing with the expanded 6-bit chunks of the 48-bit key *Ki*, a substitution operation and further exclusive OR-ing with the leftmost 32 bits of the input; see [Kaufman 1995, Schneier 1995] for details. The resulting 32-bit output of the function is then used as the rightmost 32 bits of the round's 64-bit output, as shown in Figure 7.6. Decryption works by reversing the algorithm's operations.

How well does DES work? How secure is it? No one can tell for sure, although recent speculation is that one could build a special purpose machine that exhaustively searched through the 56-bit key space for under a million dollars [Kaufman 1995]. In 1997, a network security company, RSA Data Security Inc, launched a DES Challenge contest to "crack" (decode) a short phrase it had encrypted using 56-bit DES. The unencoded phrase ("Strong cryptography makes the world a safer place.") was determined only 140 days later by a team that used volunteers throughout the Internet to systematically explore the key space. The team claimed the $10,000 prize after testing only a quarter of the key space—about 18 quadrillion keys [RSA 1997]. The most recent 1999 DES Challenge III was won in a record time of a little over twenty-two hours, with a network of volunteers and a special purpose computer that was built for less than $250,000 (nick-named "DES Cracker") and is documented on-line [EFF 1999].

If 56-bit DES is considered too insecure, one can simply run the 56-bit algorithm multiple times, taking the 64-bit output from one iteration of DES as the input to the next DES iteration, using a different encryption key each time. For example, so-called **triple-DES** (3DES), is a proposed US government standard [NIST 1999b] and has been proposed as the encryption standard for the Point-to-Point (PPP) protocol [RFC 2420] for the data-link layer (see Section 5.7). A detailed discussion of key lengths and the estimated time and budget needed to crack DES can be found in [Blaze 1996].

We should also note that our description above has only considered the encryption of a 64-bit quantity. When longer messages are encrypted, which is typically the case, DES is often used with a technique known as **cipher-block chaining,** in which the encrypted version of the *jth* 64-bit quantity of data is XOR'ed with the $(j + 1)$st unit of data before the $(j + 1)$st unit of data is encrypted.

7.2.2 Public Key Encryption

For more than 2000 years (since the time of the Caesar cipher and up to the 1970's), encrypted communication required that the two communicating parties share a common secret—the symmetric key used for encryption and decryption. One difficulty with this approach is that the two parties must somehow agree on the shared key; but to do so requires (presumably *secure*) communication! Perhaps the parties could first meet and agree on the key in person (for example, two of Caesar's centurions might meet at the Roman baths) and thereafter communicate with encryption. In a networked world, however, communicating parties may never meet and may never converse except over the network. Is it possible for two parties to communicate with encryption without having a shared secret key that is known in advance? In 1976, Diffie and Hellman [Diffie 1976] demonstrated an algorithm (known now as Diffie-Hellman Key

Exchange) to do just that—a radically different and marvelously elegant approach towards secure communication that has led to the development of today's public key cryptography systems. We will see shortly that public key cryptography systems also have several wonderful properties that make them useful not only for encryption, but for authentication and digital signatures as well. The ideas begun with [Diffie 1976] have evolved, with a significant milestone being [RSA 1978], into the public key systems in use today.

The use of public key cryptography is quite simple. Suppose Alice wants to communicate with Bob. As shown in Figure 7.7, rather than Bob and Alice sharing a single secret key (as in the case of symmetric key systems), Bob (the recipient of Alice's messages) instead has two keys—a **public key** that is available to *everyone* in the world (*including Trudy the intruder*) and a **private key** that is known only to Bob. In order to communicate with Bob, Alice first fetches Bob's public key. Alice then encrypts her message to Bob using Bob's public key and a known (for example, standardized) encryption algorithm. Bob receives Alice's encrypted message and uses his private key and a known (for example, standardized) decryption algorithm to decrypt Alice's message. In this manner, Alice can send a secret message to Bob without either of them having to have to distribute any secret keys!

Using the notation of Figure 7.7, for any message m, $d_B(e_B(m)) = m$, that is, applying Bob's public key, then Bob's private key to the message m gives back m. We will see shortly that we can interchange the public key and private key encryption and get the same result, that is, $e_B(d_B(m)) = d_B(e_B(m)) = m$.

The use of public key cryptography is thus conceptually simple. But two immediate worries may spring to mind. A first concern is that although an intruder intercepting Alice's encrypted message will only see gibberish, the intruder knows both the key (Bob's public key, which is available for all the world to see) and the algorithm that Alice used for encryption. Trudy can thus mount a chosen plaintext attack, using the known standardized encryption algorithm and Bob's publicly available encryption key to encode any message she chooses! Trudy might well try, for example, to encode messages, or parts of messages, that she

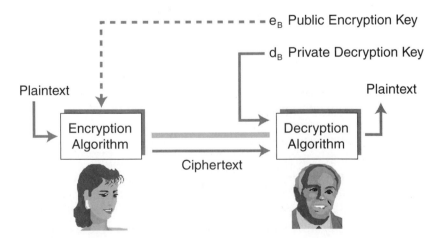

FIGURE 7.7   Public key cryptography

suspects that Alice might send. Clearly, if public key cryptography is to work, key selection and encryption/decryption must be done in such a way that it is impossible (or at least so hard as to be nearly impossible) for an intruder to either determine Bob's private key or somehow otherwise decrypt or guess Alice's message to Bob. A second concern is that since Bob's encryption key is public, anyone can send an encrypted message to Bob, including Alice or someone *claiming* to be Alice. In the case of a single shared secret key, the fact that the sender knows the secret key implicitly identifies the sender to the receiver. In the case of public key cryptography, however, this is no longer the case since anyone can send an encrypted message to Bob using Bob's publicly available key. Certificates, which we will study in Section 7.5, are needed to bind an entity (such as Bob) to a specific public key.

While there may be many algorithms and keys that have this property, the **RSA algorithm** (named after its founders, Ron Rivest, Adi Shamir, and Leonard Adleman) has become almost synonymous with public key cryptography. Let's first see how RSA works and then examine why it works. Suppose that Bob wants to receive encrypted messages, as shown in Figure 7.7. There are two inter-related components of RSA:

- choice of the public key and the private key
- the encryption and decryption algorithm

In order to choose the public and private keys, Bob must do the following:

1. Choose two large prime numbers, p and q. How large should p and q be? The larger the values, the more difficult it is to break RSA but the longer it takes to perform the encoding and decoding. RSA Laboratories recommends that the product of p and q be on the order of 768 bits for personal use and 1024 bits for corporate use [RSA Key 1999]. (Which leads one to wonder why corporate use is deemed so much more important than personal use!)

2. Compute $n = pq$ and $z = (p - 1)(q - 1)$.

3. Choose a number, e, less than n, which has no common factors (other than 1) with z. (In this case, e and z are said to be relatively prime). The letter 'e' is used since this value will be used in encryption.

4. Find a number, d, such that $ed - 1$ is exactly divisible (that is, with no remainder) by z. The letter 'd' is used because this value will be used in decryption. Put another way, given e, we choose d such that the integer remainder when ed is divided by z is 1. (The integer remainder when an integer x is divided by the integer n, is denoted $x \bmod n$).

5. The public key that Bob makes available to the world is the pair of numbers (n,e); his private key is the pair of numbers (n,d).

The encryption by Alice, and the decryption by Bob is done as follows:

1. Suppose Alice wants to send Bob a bit pattern, or number, m, such that $m < n$. To encode, Alice performs the exponentiation, m^e, and then computes the integer remainder when m^e is divided by n. Thus, the encrypted value, c, of the plaintext message, m, that Alice sends is:

$$c = m^e \bmod n$$

Table 7.1 Alice's RSA encryption, e = 5, n = 35

Plaintext Letter	m: numeric representation	m^e	ciphertext $c = m^e \bmod n$
l	12	248832	17
o	15	759375	15
v	22	5153632	22
e	5	3125	10

2. To decrypt the received ciphertext message, c, Bob computes

$$m = c^d \bmod n$$

which requires the use of his secret key (n,d).

As a simple example of RSA, suppose Bob chooses $p = 5$ and $q = 7$ (admittedly, these values are far too small to be secure). Then $n = 35$ and $z = 24$. Bob chooses $e = 5$, since 5 and 24 have no common factors. Finally, Bob chooses $d = 29$, since $5 * 29 - 1$ (that is, $ed - 1$) is exactly divisible by 24. Bob makes the two values, $n = 35$ and $e = 5$, public and keeps the value $d = 29$ secret. Observing these two public values, suppose Alice now wants to send the letters 'l' 'o' 'v' and 'e' to Bob. Interpreting each letter as a number between 1 and 26 (with 'a' being 1, and 'z' being 26), Alice and Bob perform the encryption and decryption shown in Tables 7.1 and 7.2, respectively:

Given that the "toy" example in Tables 7.1 and 7.2 has already produced some extremely large numbers, and given that we know that we saw earlier that p and q should each be several hundred bits long, several practical issues regarding RSA come to mind. How does one choose large prime numbers? How does one then choose e and d? How does one perform exponentiation with large numbers? A discussion of these important issues is beyond the scope of this book; see [Kaufman 1995] and the references therein for details.

We do note here that the exponentiation required by RSA is a rather time consuming process. RSA Data Security [RSA Fast 1999] says its software toolkit can encrypt/decrypt at a throughput of 21.6 Kbits per second with a 512-bit value for

Table 7.2 Bob's RSA decryption, d = 29, n = 35

Ciphertext c	c^d	$m = c^d \bmod n$	Plaintext Letter
17	4819685721067509150914118252223072000	12	l
15	127834039488589391112327575683594000	15	o
22	8.5164331908653770195619449972111e+38	22	v
10	100000000000000000000000000000	5	e

n and 7.4 Kbits per second with a 1024-bit value. DES is at least one hundred times faster in software and between 1,000 and 10,000 times faster in hardware. As a result, RSA is often used in practice in combination with DES. For example, if Alice wants to send Bob a large amount of encrypted data at high speed, she could do the following. First Alice chooses a DES key that will be used to encode the data itself; this key is sometimes referred to as a session key, K_S. Alice must inform Bob of the session key, since this is the shared secret key they will use for DES. Alice thus encrypts the session key value using Bob's public RSA key, that is, computes $c = (K_S)^e \bmod n$. Bob receives the RSA-encrypted session key, c, and decrypts to obtain the session key, K_S. Bob now knows the session key that Alice will use for her DES-encrypted data transfer.

Why does RSA work?   The RSA encryption/decryption above appears rather magical. Why should it be that by applying the encryption algorithm and then the decryption algorithm, one recovers the original message? In order to understand why RSA works, we'll need to perform arithmetic operations using so-called *modulo-n* arithmetic. In modular arithmetic, one performs the usual operations of addition, multiplication, and exponentiation. However, the result of each operation is replaced by the integer remainder that is left when the result is divided by n. We will take $n = pq$, where p and q are the large prime numbers used in the RSA algorithm.

Recall that under RSA encryption, a message (represented by an integer), m, is first exponentiated to the power e using *modulo-n* arithmetic to encrypt. Decryption is performed by raising this value to the power d, again using *modulo-n* arithmetic. The result of an encryption step, followed by a decryption step is thus $(m^e)^d$. Let's now see what we can say about this quantity. We have:

$$(m^e)^d \bmod n = m^{ed} \bmod n$$

Although we're trying to remove some of the "magic" about why RSA works, we'll need to use a rather magical result from number theory here. Specifically, we'll need the result that says if p and q are prime, and $n = pq$, then $x^y \bmod n$ is the same as $x^{(y \bmod (p-1)(q-1))} \bmod n$ [Kaufman 1995]. Applying this result, we have

$$(m^e)^d \bmod n = m^{(ed \bmod (p-1)(q-1))} \bmod n$$

But remember that we chose e and d such that $ed - 1$ is exactly divisible (that is, with no remainder) by $(p - 1)(q - 1)$, or equivalently that ed is divisible by $(p - 1)(q - 1)$ with a reminder of 1, and thus $ed \bmod (p - 1)(q - 1) = 1$. This gives us

$$(m^e)^d \bmod n = m^1 \bmod n = m$$

that is, that

$$(m^e)^d \bmod n = m.$$

This is the result we were hoping for! By first exponentiating to the power of e (that is, encrypting) and then exponentiating to the power of d (that is, decrypting), we obtain the original value, m. Even *more* remarkable is the fact that if we first exponentiate to the power of d and then exponentiate to the power of e, that is, we reverse the order of encryption and decryption, performing the decryption operation first and then applying the encryption operation, we also obtain the original value, m! (The proof for this result follows the exact same reasoning as above.) We will see shortly that this wonderful property of the RSA algorithm,

$$(m^e)^d \bmod n = m = (m^d)^e \bmod n$$

will be of great use.

The security of RSA relies on the fact that there are no known algorithms for quickly factoring a number, in this case the public value n, into the primes p and q. If one knew p and q, then given the public value e, one could then easily compute the secret key, d. On the other hand, it is not known whether or not there exist fast algorithms for factoring a number, and in this sense the security of RSA is not "guaranteed."

7.3 AUTHENTICATION: WHO ARE YOU?

Authentication is the process of proving one's identity to someone else. As humans, we authenticate each other in many ways: we recognize each other's faces when we meet, we recognize each other's voices on the telephone, we are authenticated by the customs official who checks us against the picture on our passport.

In this section we consider how one party can authenticate another party when the two are communicating over a network. We focus here on authenticating a "live" party, at the point in time when communication is actually occurring. We will see that this is a subtly different problem from proving that a message received at some point in the past (for example, that may have been archived) did indeed come from that claimed sender. This latter problem is referred to as the **digital signature** problem, which we explore in Section 7.4.

When performing authentication over the network, the communicating parties cannot rely on biometric information, such as a visual appearance or a voiceprint. Indeed, we will see in our later case studies that it is often network elements such as routers and client/server processes that must authenticate each other. Here, authentication must be done solely on the basis of messages and data exchanged as part of an **authentication protocol.** Typically, an authentication protocol would run *before* the two communicating parties run some other protocol (for example, a reliable data transfer protocol, a routing table exchange protocol, or an e-mail protocol). The authentication protocol first establishes the identities of the parties to each others' satisfaction; only after authentication do the parties get down to the work at hand.

As in the case of our development of a reliable data transfer (rdt) protocol, in Chapter 3, we will find it instructive here to develop various versions of an authentication protocol, which we will call **ap** ("authentication protocol"), and poke holes (that is, find security flaws) in each version as we proceed. Let's begin by assuming that Alice needs to authenticate herself to Bob.

FIGURE 7.8   Protocol *ap1.0* and a failure scenario

7.3.1   Authentication Protocol *ap1.0*

Perhaps the simplest authentication protocol we can imagine is one where Alice simply sends a message to Bob saying she is Alice. This protocol is shown in Figure 7.8. The flaw here is obvious—there is no way for Bob to actually know that the person sending the message, "I am Alice" is indeed Alice. For example, Trudy (the intruder) could just as well send such a message.

7.3.2   Authentication Protocol *ap2.0*

In the case that Alice has a well-known network address (for example, IP address) from which she always communicates, Bob could attempt to authenticate Alice by verifying that the source address on the IP datagram carrying the authentication message matches Alice's well-known address. If so, then Alice would be authenticated. This might stop a very network-naive intruder from impersonating Alice. But it wouldn't stop the determined student studying this book, or many others!

FIGURE 7.9   Protocol *ap2.0* and a failure scenario

Given that we have now studied both the network and data-link layers, we know that it is not that hard (for example, if one had access to the operating system code and could build one's own operating system kernel, as is the case with Linux and several other freely available operating systems) to create an IP datagram, put whatever IP source address we want (for example, including Alice's well-known IP address) into the IP datagram, and send the datagram over the link layer protocol to the first hop router. From then on, the incorrectly source-addressed datagram would be dutifully forwarded to Bob. This approach is a form of **IP spoofing,** a well-known security attack technique [CERT 1996]. IP spoofing can be avoided if a router is configured to refuse IP datagrams that do not have a given source address. For example, Trudy's first hop router could be configured to only forward datagrams containing Trudy's IP source address. However, this capability is not universally deployed or enforced. Bob would thus be foolish to assume that Trudy's network manager (who might be Trudy *herself*) had configured Trudy's first hop router to only forward appropriately addressed datagrams.

7.3.3   Authentication Protocol *ap3.0*

One classic approach to authentication is to use a secret password. We have PIN numbers to identify ourselves to automatic teller machines and login passwords for operating systems. The password is a shared secret between the authenticator and the person being authenticated. We saw in Section 2.2.4 that HTTP uses a password-based authentication scheme. Telnet and FTP use password authentication as well. In protocol *ap3.0,* Alice thus sends her secret password to Bob, as shown in Figure 7.10.

The security flaw here is clear. If Trudy eavesdrops on Alice's communication, then she can learn Alice's password. Lest you think this is unlikely, consider the fact that when one Telnets to another machine and logs in, the login password is sent unencrypted to the Telnet server. Someone connected to the Telnet client or server's LAN can possibly "sniff" (read and store) all packets transmitted on the LAN and thus steal the login password. In fact, this is a well-known approach for stealing passwords (see, for example, [Jimenez 1997]). Such a threat is obviously very real, so *ap3.0* clearly won't do.

FIGURE 7.10   Protocol *ap3.0* and a failure scenario

7.3.4 Authentication Protocol *ap3.1*

Having just studied the previous section on cryptography, our next idea for fixing *ap3.0* is naturally to use encryption. By encrypting the password, Trudy will not be able to learn Alice's password! If we assume that Alice and Bob share a symmetric secret key, K_{A-B}, then Alice can encrypt the password, send her identification message, "I am Alice," and her encrypted password to Bob. Bob then decrypts the password and, assuming the password is correct, authenticates Alice. Bob feels comfortable in authenticating Alice since not only does Alice know the password, but she also knows the shared secret key value needed to encrypt the password. Let's call this protocol *ap3.1*.

While it is true that *ap3.1* prevents Trudy from learning Alice's password, the use of cryptography here does not solve the authentication problem! Bob is again subject to a so-called **playback attack:** Trudy needs only eavesdrop on Alice's communication, record the encrypted version of the password, and then later play back the encrypted version of the password to Bob to pretend that she is Alice. The use of an encrypted password doesn't make the situation manifestly different from that in Figure 7.10.

7.3.5 Authentication Protocol *ap4.0*

The problem with *ap3.1* is that the same password is used over and over again. One way to solve this problem would be to use a different password each time. Alice and Bob could agree on a sequence of passwords (or on an algorithm for generating passwords) and use each password only once, in sequence. This idea is used in the S/KEY system [RFC 1760], adopting an approach due to Lamport [Lamport 1981] for generating a sequence of passwords.

Rather than just stop here with this solution, however, let us consider a more general approach for combating the playback attack. The failure scenario in Figure 7.10 resulted from the fact that Bob could not distinguish between the original authentication of Alice and the later playback of Alice's original authentication. That is, Bob could not tell if Alice was "live" (that is, was currently really on the other end of the connection) or whether the messages he was receiving were a recorded playback of a previous authentication of Alice. The very (*very*) observant reader will recall that the 3-way TCP handshake protocol needed to address the same problem—the server side of a TCP connection did not want to accept a connection if the received SYN segment was an old copy (retransmission) of a SYN segment from an earlier connection. How did the TCP server side solve the problem of determining if the client was really "live"? It chose an initial sequence number (which had not been used in a very long time), sent that number to the client, and then waited for the client to respond back with an ACK segment containing that number. We can adopt the same idea here for authentication purposes.

A **nonce** is a number that a protocol will only ever use once-in-a-lifetime. That is, once a protocol uses a nonce, it will never use that number again. Our *ap4.0* protocol uses a nonce as follows:

1. Alice sends the message, "I am Alice," to Bob.
2. Bob chooses a nonce, *R*, and sends it to Alice.

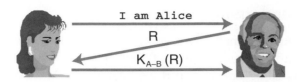

FIGURE 7.11 Protocol *ap 4.0:* no failure scenario

3. Alice encrypts the nonce using Alice and Bob's symmetric secret key, $K_{A\text{-}B}$, and sends the encrypted nonce, $K_{A\text{-}B}(R)$ back to Bob. As in protocol *ap3.1,* it is the fact that Alice knows $K_{A\text{-}B}$ and uses it to encrypt a value that lets Bob know that the message he receives was generated by Alice. The nonce is used to ensure that Alice is "live."

4. Bob decrypts the received message. If the decrypted nonce equals the nonce he sent Alice, then Alice is authenticated.

Protocol *ap4.0* is illustrated in Figure 7.11. By using the once-in-a-lifetime value, R, and then checking the returned value, $K_{A\text{-}B}(R)$, Bob can be sure that both Alice is who she says she is (since she knows the secret key value needed to encrypt R) and is "live" (since she has encrypted the nonce, R, that Bob just created).

7.3.6 Authentication Protocol *ap5.0*

The use of a nonce and symmetric key cryptography formed the basis of our successful authentication protocol, *ap4.0.* A natural question is whether we can use a nonce and public key cryptography (rather than symmetric key cryptography) to solve the authentication problem. The use of a public key approach would obviate a difficulty in any shared key system—worrying about how the two parties learn the secret shared key value in the first place. A protocol that uses public key cryptography in a manner analogous to the use of symmetric key cryptography in protocol *ap4.0* is protocol *ap5.0:*

1. Alice sends the message, "I am Alice," to Bob.

2. Bob chooses a nonce, R, and sends it to Alice. Once again, the nonce will be used to ensure that Alice is "live."

3. Alice uses her decryption algorithm with her private key, d_A, to the nonce and sends the resulting value $d_A(R)$ to Bob. Since only Alice knows her decryption key, no one except Alice can generate $d_A(R)$.

4. Bob applies Alice's public encryption algorithm, e_A to the received message, that is, Bob computes $e_A(d_A(R))$. Recall from our discussion of RSA public key cryptography in Section 7.2 that $e_A(d_A(R)) = R = d_A(e_A(R))$. Thus, Bob computes R and authenticates Alice.

The operation of protocol *ap5.0* is illustrated in Figure 7.12. Is protocol *ap5.0* as secure as protocol *ap4.0*? Both use nonces. Since *ap5.0* uses public key techniques, it requires that Bob retrieve Alice's public key. This leads to an interesting

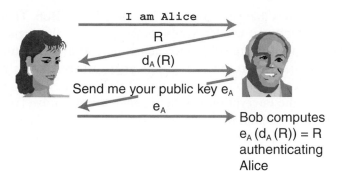

FIGURE 7.12   Protocol *ap5.0* working correctly

scenario, shown in Figure 7.13, in which Trudy may be able to impersonate Alice to Bob:

1. Trudy sends the message, "I am Alice," to Bob.
2. Bob chooses a nonce, R, and sends it to Alice, but the message is intercepted by Trudy.
3. Trudy applies her decryption algorithm with her private key, d_T, to the nonce and sends the resulting value, $d_T(R)$, to Bob. To Bob, $d_T(R)$ is just a bunch of bits and he doesn't know whether the bits represent $d_T(R)$ or $d_A(R)$.
4. Bob must now get Alice's public key in order to apply e_A to the value he just received. He sends a message to Alice asking her for e_A. Trudy intercepts this message as well, and replies back to Bob with e_T, that is Trudy's public key. Bob computes $e_T(d_T(R)) = R$, and thus authenticates Trudy as Alice!

From the above scenario, it is clear that protocol *ap5.0* is only as "secure" as is the distribution of public keys. There *are* secure ways of distributing public keys, a topic we will examine shortly in Section 7.5.

In the scenario in Figure 7.13, Bob and Alice might together eventually discover that something is amiss, as Bob will claim to have interacted with Alice,

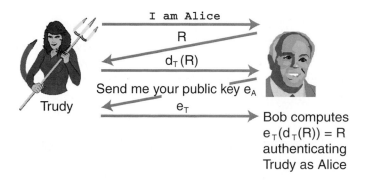

FIGURE 7.13   A security hole in protocol *ap5.0*

but Alice knows that she has never interacted with Bob. There is an even more insidious attack that would avoid this detection. In the scenario in Figure 7.14, both Alice and Bob are talking to each other, but by exploiting the same hole in the authentication protocol, Trudy is able to *transparently* interpose herself between Alice and Bob. In particular, if Bob begins sending encrypted data to Alice using the encryption key he receives from Trudy, Trudy can recover the plaintext of the communication from Bob to Alice. At the same time, Trudy can forward Bob's data to Alice (after re-encrypting data using Alice's real public key).

Bob is happy to be sending encrypted data, and Alice is happy to be receiving data encrypted using her own public key; both are unaware of Trudy's presence. Should Bob and Alice meet later and discuss their interaction, Alice will have received exactly what Bob sent, so nothing will be detected as being amiss. This is one example of the so-called **man-in-the-middle attack** (more appropriately here, a "woman-in-the-middle" attack). It is also sometimes known as a **bucket-brigade attack,** since Trudy's passing of data between Alice and Bob resembles the passing of buckets of water along a chain of people (a so-called "bucket brigade") who are putting out a fire using a remote source of water.

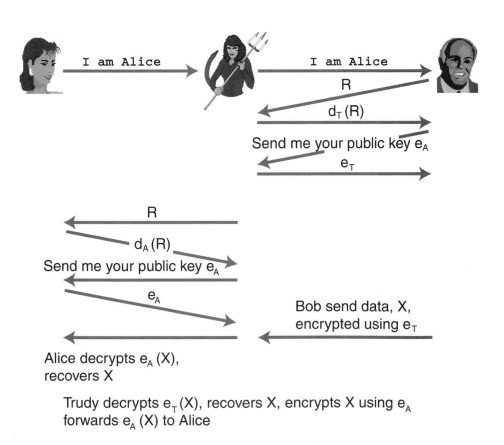

FIGURE 7.14 A "man-in-the-middle" attack

INTEGRITY

Think of the number of the times you've signed your name to a piece of paper during the last week. You sign checks, credit card statements, legal documents, and letters. Your signature attests to the fact that you (as opposed to someone else) have acknowledged and/or agreed with the document's contents. In a digital world, one often wants to indicate the owner or creator of a document, or to signify one's agreement with a document's content. A **digital signature** is a cryptographic technique for achieving these goals in a digital world.

Just as with human signatures, digital signing should be done in such a way that digital signatures are verifiable, nonforgible, and nonrepudiable. That is, it must be possible to "prove" that a document signed by an individual was indeed signed by that individual (the signature must be verifiable) and that *only* that individual could have signed the document (the signature cannot be forged, and a signer cannot later repudiate or deny having signed the document). This is easily accomplished with public key cryptography.

7.4.1 Generating Digital Signatures

Suppose that Bob wants to digitally sign a "document," m. Think of the document as a file or a message that Bob is going to sign and send. As shown in Figure 7.15, to sign this document, Bob simply uses his private decryption key, d_B, to compute $d_B(m)$. At first, it might seem odd that Bob is running a decryption algorithm over a document that hasn't been encrypted. But recall that "decryption" is nothing more than a mathematical operation (exponentiation to the power of d in RSA; see Section 7.2) and recall that Bob's goal is not to scramble or obscure the contents of the document, but rather to sign the document in a manner that is verifiable, nonforgible, and nonrepudiable. Bob has the document, m, and his digital signature of the document, $d_B(m)$.

Does the digital signature, $d_B(m)$, meet our requirements of being verifiable, nonforgible, and nonrepudiable? Suppose Alice has m and $d_B(m)$. She wants to

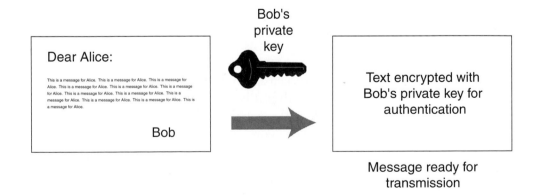

FIGURE 7.15 Creating a digital signature for a document

prove in court (being litigious) that Bob had indeed signed the document and was the only person who could have possibly signed the document. Alice takes Bob's public key, e_B, and applies it to the digital signature, $d_B(m)$, associated with the document, m. That is, she computes $e_B(d_B(m))$, and *voilà*, with a dramatic flurry, she produces m, which exactly matches the original document! Alice then argues that only Bob could have signed the document because:

- Whoever signed the message must have used the private encryption key, d_B, in computing the signature $d_B(m)$, such that $e_B(d_B(m)) = m$.
- The only person who could known the private key, d_B, is Bob. Recall from our discussion of RSA in Section 7.2 that knowing the public key, e_B, is of no help in learning the private key, d_B. Therefore, the only person who could know d_B is the person who generated the pair of keys, (e_B, d_B), in the first place, Bob.

It is also important to note that if the original document, m, is ever modified to some alternate form, m', the signature that Bob created for m will not be valid for m', since $e_B(d_B(m))$ does not equal m'.

Thus we see that public key cryptography techniques provide a simple and elegant way to digitally sign documents that is verifiable, nonforgible, and non-repudiable, and that protects against later modification of the document.

7.4.2 Message Digests

We have seen above that public key encryption technology can be used to create a digital signature. One concern with signing data by encryption, however, is that encryption and decryption are computationally expensive. When digitally signing a really important document, say a merger between two large multinational corporations or an agreement with a child to have him/her clean her room weekly, computational cost may not be important. However, many network devices and processes (for example, routers exchanging routing table information and e-mail user agents exchanging e-mail) routinely exchange data that may not need to be encrypted. Nonetheless, they do want to ensure that:

- The sender of the data is as claimed, that is, that the sender has signed the data and this signature can be checked
- The transmitted data has not been changed since the sender created and signed the data.

Given the overheads of encryption and decryption, signing data via complete encryption/decryption can be overkill. A more efficient approach using so-called message digests can accomplish these two goals without full message encryption.

A **message digest** is in many ways like a checksum. Message digest algorithms take a message, m, of arbitrary length and compute a fixed length "finger-print" of the data known as a message digest, $H(m)$. The message digest protects the data in the sense that if m is changed to m' (either maliciously or by accident) then $H(m)$, computed for the original data (and transmitted with that data), will not match the $H(m)$ computed over the changed data. While the message digest provides for data integrity, how does it help with signing the message m? The goal here is that rather than having Bob digitally sign (encrypt) the entire message by computing $d_B(m)$, he should be able to sign just the message digest by computing

$d_B(H(m))$. That is, having m and $d_B(H(m))$ together (note that m is not encrypted) should be "just as good as" having a signed complete message, $d_B(m)$; this means that m and $d_B(H(m))$ together should be nonforgible, verifiable, and nonrepudiable. Nonforgibility will require that the message digest algorithm that computes the message digest have some special properties, as we will see below.

Our definition of a message digest may seem quite similar to the definition of a checksum (for example, the Internet checksum, see Section 4.4) or a more powerful error detection code such as a cyclic redundancy check (see Section 5.1). Is it really any different? Checksums, cyclic redundancy checks, and message digests are all examples of so-called **hash functions.** As shown in Figure 7.16, a hash function takes an input, m, and computes a fixed-size string known as a hash. The Internet checksum, CRCs, and message digests all meet this definition. If signing a message digest is going to be "just as good as" signing the entire message, in particular if it is going to satisfy the nonforgibility requirement, then a message digest algorithm must have the following additional properties:

- Given a message digest value, x, it is computationally infeasible to find a message, y, such that $H(y) = x$.
- It is computationally infeasible to find any two messages x and y such that $H(x) = H(y)$.

Informally, these two properties mean that it is computationally infeasible for an intruder to substitute one message for another message that is protected by a message digest. That is, if $(m,H(m))$ are the message and message digest pair created by the sender, then an intruder cannot forge the contents of another message, y, that has the same message digest value as the original message. When Bob signs m by computing $d_B(H(m))$, we know that no other message can be substituted for m. Furthermore, Bob's digital signature of $H(m)$ uniquely identifies Bob as the verifiable, nonrepudiable signer of $H(m)$ (and as a consequence, m as well) as discussed above in Section 7.4.1.

In the context of Bob sending a message to Alice, Figure 7.17 provides a summary of the operational procedure of creating a digital signature. Bob puts his original long message through a hash function to create a message digest. He then encrypts the message digest with his own private key. The original message (in clear text) along with the digitally signed message digest (henceforth referred to as the digital signature) is then sent to Alice. Figure 7.18 provides a summary of

FIGURE 7.16 Hash functions are used to create message digests

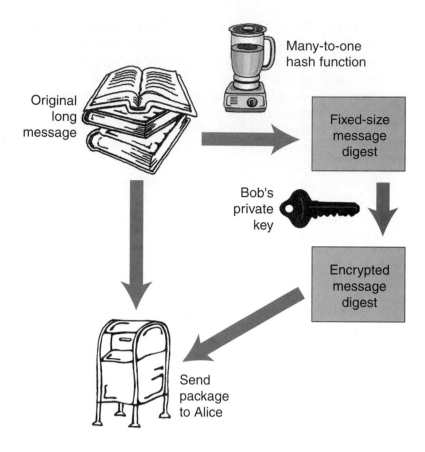

FIGURE 7.17   Sending a digitally signed message

the operational procedure of verifying message integrity. Alice applies the sender's public key to the message to recover the message digest. Alice also applies the hash function to the clear text message to obtain a second message digest. If the two message digests match, then the recipient can be sure about the integrity and author of the message.

7.4.3   Hash Function Algorithms

Let's convince ourselves that a simple checksum, such as the Internet checksum, would make a poor message digest algorithm. Rather than performing 1 complements arithmetic (as in the Internet checksum), let us compute a checksum by treating each character as a byte and adding the bytes together using 4-byte chunks at a time. Suppose Bob owes Alice $100.99 and sends an IOU to Alice consisting of the text string "IOU100.99BOB." The ASCII representation (in hexadecimal notation) for these letters is 49, 4F, 55, 31, 30, 30, 2E, 39, 39, 42, 4F, 42.

Figure 7.19 (top) shows that the 4-byte checksum for this message is B2 C1 D2 AC. A slightly different message (and a much more costly one for Bob) is shown in the bottom half of Figure 7.19. The message "IOU100.99BOB" and

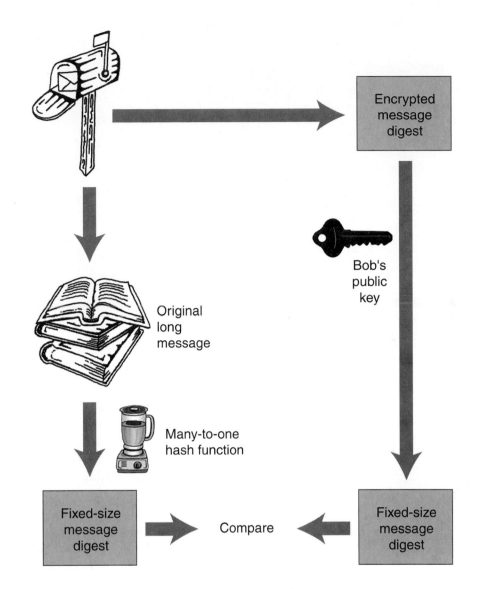

FIGURE 7.18   Verifying the integrity of a signed message

"`IOU900.19BOB`" have the *same* checksum. Thus, this simple checksum algorithm violates the two required requirements above. Given the original data, it is simple to find another set of data with the same checksum. Clearly, for security purposes. we are going to need a more powerful hash function than a checksum.

The MD5 message digest algorithm by Ron Rivest [RFC 1321] is in wide use today. It computes a 128-bit message digest in a four-step process consisting of a padding step (adding a one followed by enough zero's so that the length of the message satisfies certain conditions), an append step (appending a 64-bit representation of the message length before padding), an initialization of an accumulator, and a final looping step in which the message's 16-word blocks are processed (mangled) in four rounds of processing. It is not known whether MD5 actually

```
                         ASCII
   Message          Representation
   I  O  U  1        49   4F   55   31
   0  0  .  9        30   30   2E   39
   9  B  O  B        39   42   4F   42
                    ─────────────────
                     B2   C1   D2   AC     Checksum
```

```
                         ASCII
   Message          Representation
   I  O  U  9        49   4F   55   39
   0  0  .  1        30   30   2E   31
   9  B  O  B        39   42   4F   42
                    ─────────────────
                     B2   C1   D2   AC     Checksum
```

FIGURE 7.19   Initial message and fraudulent message have the same checksum!

satisfies the requirements listed above. The author of MD5 claims "It is conjectured that the difficulty of coming up with two messages having the same message digest is on the order of 2^{64} operations, and that the difficulty of coming up with any message having a given message digest is on the order of 2^{128} operations." No one has argued with this claim. For a description of MD5 (including a C source code implementation) see [RFC 1321].

The second major message digest algorithm in use today is SHA-1, the Secure Hash Algorithm [FIPS 1995]. This algorithm is based on principles similar to those used in the design of MD4 [RFC 1320], the predecessor to MD5. The Secure Hash Algorithm (SHA-1), a US federal standard, is required for use whenever a secure message digest algorithm is required for federal applications. It produces a 160-bit message digest.

7.5   KEY DISTRIBUTION AND CERTIFICATION

In Section 7.2 we saw that a drawback of symmetric key cryptography was the need for the two communicating parties to have agreed upon their secret key ahead of time. With public key cryptography, this *a priori* agreement on a secret value is not needed. However, as we discussed in Section 7.2, public key encryption has its own difficulties, in particular the problem of obtaining someone's true public key. Both of these problems—determining a shared key for symmetric key cryptography, and securely obtaining the public key for public key cryptography—can be solved using a **trusted intermediary.** For symmetric key cryptography, the trusted intermediary is called a **Key Distribution Center (KDC),** which is a single, trusted network entity with whom one has established a shared secret key. We will see that one can use the KDC to obtain the shared keys needed to communicate securely with *all* other network entities, avoiding some of the pitfalls we uncovered in Section 7.3. For public key cryptography, the trusted intermediary is called a **Certification Authority (CA).** A certification authority certifies that a public key belongs to a particular entity (a person or a network entity). For a certified public key, if one can safely trust the CA that certified the key, then one can be sure about to whom the public key belongs. Once a public key is certified, then it can be distributed from just about anywhere, including a public key server, a personal Web page, or a diskette.

7.5.1   The Key Distribution Center

Suppose once again that Bob and Alice want to communicate using symmetric key cryptography. They have never met (perhaps they just met in an online chat room) and thus have not established a shared secret key in advance. How can they now agree on a secret key, given that they can only communicate with each other over the network? A solution often adopted in practice is to use a trusted Key Distribution Center (KDC).

The KDC is a server that shares a different secret symmetric key with each registered user. This key might be manually installed at the server when a user first registers. The KDC knows the secret key of each user, and each user can communicate securely with the KDC using this key. Let's see how knowledge of this one key allows a user to securely obtain a key for communicating with any other registered user. Suppose that Alice and Bob are users of the KDC; they only know their individual key, $K_{A\text{-}KDC}$ and $K_{B\text{-}KDC}$, respectively, for communicating securely with the KDC. Alice takes the first step, and they proceed as illustrated in Figure 7.20.

1. Using $K_{A\text{-}KDC}$ to encrypt her communication with the KDC, Alice sends a message to the KDC saying she (*A*) wants to communicate with Bob (*B*). We denote this message, $K_{A\text{-}KDC}(A,B)$. As part of this exchange, Alice should authenticate the KDC (see Homework Problems), for example, using an authentication protocol (for example, our protocol *ap4.0)* and the shared key $K_{A\text{-}KDC}$.

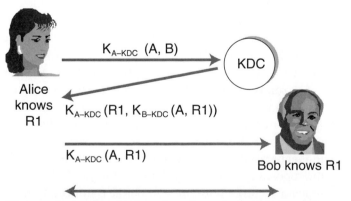

Alice, Bob communicate using shared session key R1

FIGURE 7.20   Setting up a one-time session key using a Key Distribution Center

2. The KDC, knowing $K_{A\text{-}KDC}$, decrypts $K_{A\text{-}KDC}(A,B)$. The KDC then authenticates Alice. The KDC then generates a random number, $R1$. This is the shared key value that Alice and Bob will use to perform symmetric encryption when they communicate with each other. This key is referred to as a **one-time session key** (see Section 7.5.4), as Alice and Bob will use this key for only this one session that they are currently setting up. The KDC now needs to inform Alice and Bob of the value of $R1$. The KDC thus sends back an encrypted message to Alice containing the following:

   ▪ $R1$, the one-time session key that Alice and Bob will use to communicate.
   ▪ A pair of values: A, and $R1$, encrypted by the KDC using Bob's key, $K_{B\text{-}KDC}$. We denote this $K_{B\text{-}KDC}(A,R1)$. It is important to note that KDC is sending Alice not only the value of $R1$ for her own use, but also an encrypted version of $R1$ and Alice's name, encrypted using Bob's key. Alice can't decrypt this pair of values in the message (she doesn't know Bob's encryption key), but then she doesn't really need to. We'll see shortly that Alice will simply forward this encrypted pair of values to Bob (who can decrypt them).

   These items are put into a message and encrypted using Alice's shared key. The message from the KDC to Alice is thus $K_{A\text{-}KDC}(R1,K_{B\text{-}KDC}(R1))$.

3. Alice receives the message from the KDC, verifies the nonce (if there is one), extracts $R1$ from the message and saves it. Alice now knows the one-time session key, $R1$. Alice also extracts $K_{B\text{-}KDC}(A,R1)$ and forwards this to Bob.

4. Bob decrypts the received message, $K_{B\text{-}KDC}(A,R1)$, using $K_{B\text{-}KDC}$ and extracts A and $R1$. Bob now knows the one-time session key, $R1$, and the person with whom he is sharing this key, A. Of course, he takes care to authenticate Alice using $R1$ before proceeding any further.

7.5.2 Kerberos

Kerberos [RFC 1510, Neuman 1994] is an authentication service developed at MIT that uses symmetric key encryption techniques and a Key Distribution Center. Although it is conceptually the same as the generic KDC we described in Section 7.5.1, its vocabulary is slightly different. Kerberos also contains several nice variations and extensions of the basic KDC mechanisms. Kerberos was designed to authenticate users accessing network servers and was initially targeted for use within a single administrative domain such as a campus or company. Thus, Kerberos is framed in the language of users who want to access network services (servers) using application-level network programs such as Telnet (for remote login) and NFS (for access to remote files), rather than human-to-human conversants who want to authenticate themselves to each other, as in our examples above. Nonetheless, the key (pun intended) underlying techniques remain the same.

The **Kerberos Authentication Server** (AS) plays the role of the KDC. The AS is the repository of not only the secret keys of all users (so that each user can communicate securely with the AS) but also information about which users have access privileges to which services on which network servers. When Alice wants to access a service on Bob (who we now think of as a server), the protocol closely follows our example in Figure 7.20:

1. Alice contacts the Kerberos AS, indicating that she wants to use Bob. All communication between Alice and the AS is encrypted using a secret key that is shared between Alice and the AS. In Kerberos, Alice first provides her name and password to her local host. Alice's local host and the AS then determine the one-time secret session key for encrypting communication between Alice and the AS.

2. The AS authenticates Alice, checks that she has access privileges to Bob, and generates a one-time symmetric session key, *R1*, for communication between Alice and Bob. The Authentication Server (in Kerberos parlance, now referred to as the Ticket Granting Server) sends Alice the value of *R1*, and also a **ticket** to Bob's services. The ticket contains Alice's name, the one-time session key, *R1*, and an expiration time, all encrypted using Bob's secret key (known only by Bob and the AS), as in Figure 7.20. Alice's ticket is valid only until its expiration time, and will be rejected by Bob if presented after that time. For Kerberos V4, the maximum lifetime of a ticket is about twenty-one hours. In Kerberos V5, the lifetime must expire before the end of year 9999, a definite Y10K problem!

3. Alice then sends her ticket to Bob. She also sends along an R1-encrypted timestamp that is used as a nonce. Bob decrypts the ticket using his secret key, obtains the session key, and decrypts the timestamp using the just-learned session key. Bob sends back the timestamp value plus one depending on the version of Kerberos.

The most recent version of Kerberos (V5) provides support for multiple Authentication Servers, delegation of access rights, and renewable tickets. [Kaufman 1995] [RFC 1510] provide ample details.

7.5.3 Public Key Certification

One of the principle features of public key encryption is that it is possible for two entities to exchange secret messages without having to exchange secret keys. For example, when Alice wants to send a secret message to Bob, she simply encrypts the message with Bob's public key and sends the encrypted message to Bob; she doesn't need to know Bob's secret (that is, private) key, nor does Bob need to know her secret key. Thus, public key cryptography obviates the need for KDC infrastructure, such as Kerberos.

Of course, with public key encryption, the communicating entities still have to exchange public keys. A user can make its public key publicly available in many ways, for example, by posting the key on the user's personal Web page, placing the key in a public key server, or by sending the key to a correspondent by e-mail. A Web commerce site can place its public key on its server in a manner such that browsers automatically download the public key when connecting to the site. Routers can place their public keys on public key servers, thereby allowing other network entities to retrieve them.

There is, however, a subtle, yet critical, problem with public key cryptography. To gain insight to this problem, let's consider an Internet commerce example.

Suppose that Alice is in the pizza delivery business and she accepts orders over the Internet. Bob, a pizza lover, sends Alice a plaintext message that includes his home address and the type of pizza he wants. In this message, Bob also includes a digital signature (that is, an encrypted message digest for the original plaintext message). As discussed in Section 7.4, Alice can obtain Bob's public key (from his personal Web page, a public key server, or from an e-mail message) and verify the digital signature. In this manner she makes sure that Bob indeed made the order and not some adolescent prankster.

This all sounds fine until clever Trudy comes along. As shown in Figure 7.21, Trudy decides to play a prank. Trudy sends a message to Alice in which she says she is Bob, gives Bob's home address, and orders a pizza. She also attaches a digital signature, but she attaches the signature by signing the message digest with her (that is, Trudy's) private key. Trudy also masquerades as Bob by sending Alice Trudy's public key but saying that it belongs to Bob. In this example, Alice will apply Trudy's public key (thinking that it is Bob's) to the digital signature and conclude that the plaintext message was indeed created by Bob. Bob will be very surprised when the delivery person brings to his home a pizza with everything on it!

We see from this example that in order for public key cryptography to be useful, entities (users, browsers, routers, etc.) need to know *for sure* that they have the public key of the entity with which they are communicating. For example, when Alice is communicating with Bob using public key cryptography, she needs to know for sure that the public key that is supposed to be Bob's is indeed Bob's.

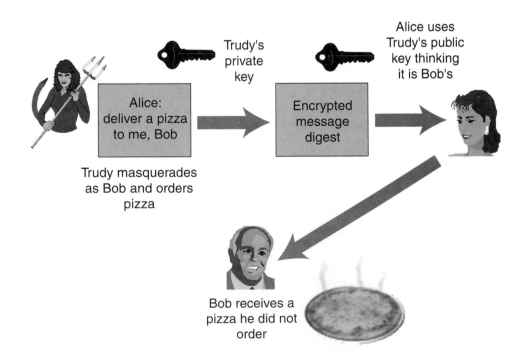

FIGURE 7.21   Trudy masquerades as Bob using public key cryptography

Binding a public key to a particular entity is typically done by a **certification authority** (CA), which validates identities and issues certificates. A CA has the following roles:

1. First to verify that an entity (a person, a router, etc) is who it says it is. There are no mandated procedures for how certification is done. When dealing with a CA, one must trust the CA to have performed a suitably rigorous identity verification. For example, if Trudy were able to walk into the Fly-by-Night Certificate Authority and simply announce "I am Alice" and receive keys associated with the identity of "Alice," then one shouldn't put much faith in public keys offered by the Fly-by-Night Certificate Authority. On the other hand, one might (or might not!) be more willing to trust a CA that is part of a federal—or state—sponsored program (for example, [Utah 1999]). One can trust the "identity" associated with a public key only to the extent that one can trust a CA and its identity-verification techniques. What a tangled web of trust we spin!

2. Once the CA verifies the identity of the entity, the CA creates a **certificate** that binds the public key of the identity to the identity. The certificate contains the public key and identifying information about the owner of the public key (for example a human name or an IP address). The certificate is digitally signed by the CA. These steps are shown in Figure 7.22.

Let us now see how certificates can be used to combat pizza-ordering pranksters, like Trudy, and other undesirables. When Alice receives Bob's order, she gets Bob's certificate, which may be on his Web page, in an e-mail message, or in

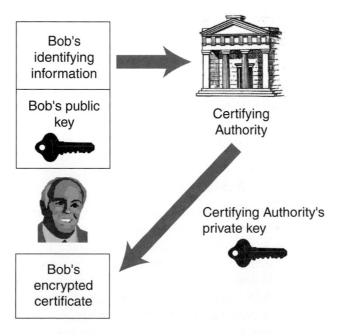

FIGURE 7.22   Bob obtains a certificate from the certification authority

Table 7.3 Selected fields in a X.509 and RFC 1422 public key certificate

Field Name	Description
Version	Version number of X.509 specification
Serial Number	CA-issued unique identifier for a certificate
Signature	Specifies the algorithm used by CA to "sign" this certificate
Issuer Name	Identity of CA issuing this certificate, in so-called Distinguished Name(DN) [RFC 1779] format
Validity Period	Start and end of period of validity for certificate
Subject Name	Identity of entity whose public key is associated with this certificate, in DN format
Subject Public Key	The subject's public key as well as an indication of the public key algorithm (and algorithm parameters) to be used with this key

a certificate server. Alice uses the CA's public key to verify that the public key in the certificate is indeed Bob's. If we assume that the public key of the CA itself is known to all (for example, it could be published in a trusted, public, and well-known place, such as *The New York Times,* so that it is known to all and cannot be spoofed), then Alice can be sure that she is indeed dealing with Bob. Figure 7.22 illustrates the steps involved in CA-mediated public key encryption.

Both the International Telecommunication Union (ITU) and the IETF have developed standards for Certification Authorities. ITU X.509 [ITU 1993] specifies an authentication service as well as a specific syntax for certificates. RFC 1422 [1422] describes CA-based key management for use with secure Internet e-mail. It is compatible with X.509 but goes beyond X.509 by establishing procedures and conventions for a key management architecture. Table 7.3 describes some of the important fields in a certificate.

With the recent boom in electronic commerce and the consequent widespread need for secure transactions, there has been increased interest in Certification Authorities. Among the companies providing CA services are Cybertrust [Cybertrust 1999], Verisign [Verisign 1999], and Netscape [Netscape Certificate 1999].

A certificate issued by the US Postal Service, as viewed through a Netscape browser, is shown in Figure 7.23.

7.5.4 One-Time Session Keys

We have seen above that a **one-time session key** is generated by a KDC for use in symmetric key encryption of a single session between two parties. By using the one-time session keys from the KDC, a user is freed from having to establish *a priori* its own shared key for each and every network entity with whom it wishes to communicate. Instead, a user need only have one shared secret key for communicating with the KDC, and will receive one-time session keys from the KDC for all of its communication with other network entities.

One-time session keys are also used in public key cryptography. Recall from our discussion in Section 7.2.2, that a public key encryption technique such as RSA is orders of magnitude more computationally expensive than a symmetric

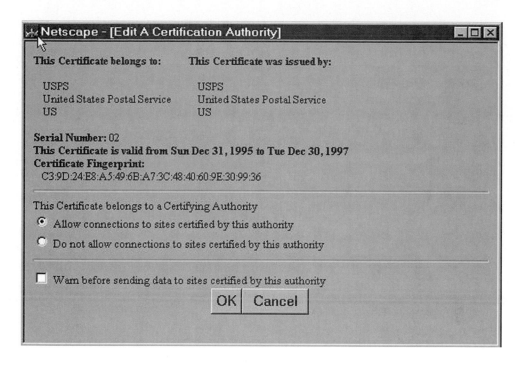

FIGURE 7.23   A US Postal Service issued certificate

key system such as DES. Thus, public key systems are often used for authentication purposes. Once two parties have authenticated each other, they then use public-key-encrypted communication to agree on a shared one-time symmetric session key. This symmetric session key is then used to encrypt the remainder of the communication using a more efficient symmetric encryption technique, such as DES.

7.6   SECURE E-MAIL

In previous sections we examined several fundamental issues in network security, including symmetric key and public key encryption, authentication, key distribution, message integrity, and digital signatures. We are now going to examine how these tools are being used to provide security in the Internet. Interestingly, it is possible to provide security services in any of the top four layers of the Internet protocol stack [Molva 1999]. When security is provided for a specific application-layer protocol, then the application using the protocol will enjoy one or more security services, such as secrecy, authentication, or integrity. When security is provided for a transport-layer protocol, then all applications that use that protocol enjoy the security services of the transport protocol. When security is provided at the network layer on a host-to-host basis, then all transport-layer segments (and hence all application-layer data) enjoy the security services of the network layer. When security is provided on a link basis, then all IP datagrams traveling over the link receive security services of the link.

In this and the following two sections we examine how the security tools are being used in the application, transport, and network layers. Being consistent with the general structure of this book, we begin at the top of the protocol stack and discuss security at the application-layer. Our approach here is to use a specific application, namely, e-mail, as a case study for application-layer security. We then move down the protocol stack. In Section 7.7 we examine the SSL protocol, which provides security at the transport layer for TCP. And in Section 7.8, we will consider IPsec, which provides security at the network layer.

You might be wondering why security functionality is being provided at more than one layer in the Internet? Wouldn't it suffice to simply provide the security functionality at the network layer, and be done with it? There are two answers to this question. First, although security at the network layer can offer "blanket coverage" by encrypting all the data in the datagrams (that is, all the transport-layer segments) and by authenticating all the source IP addresses, it can't provide user-level security. For example, a commerce site cannot rely on IP-layer security to authenticate a customer who is purchasing goods at the commerce site. Thus, there is a need for security functionality at higher layers as well as blanket coverage at lower layers. Second, in the Internet it is generally easier to deploy new services, including security services, at the higher layers of the protocol stack. While waiting for security to be broadly deployed at the network layer, which is probably still many years in the future, many application developers "just do it" and introduce security functionality into to their favorite applications. A classic example is PGP, which provides secure e-mail (discussed later in this section). Requiring only client and server application code, PGP was one of the first security technologies to be broadly used in the Internet. Similarly, transport-layer security with SSL was broadly introduced into the Internet, as it too only required new code in the end systems. However, IP-layer security—so-called IPsec—is taking much longer to broadly deploy, as it requires significant changes in the routers in the network core.

7.6.1 Principles of Secure E-Mail

In this section we use many of the tools introduced in the previous section to create a high-level design of a secure e-mail system. We create this high-level design in an incremental manner, at each step introducing new security services. When designing a secure e-mail system, let us keep in mind the racy example introduced in Section 7.1—the illicit love affair between Alice and Bob. In the context of e-mail, Alice wants to send an e-mail message to Bob, and Trudy wants to intrude.

Before plowing ahead and designing a secure e-mail system for Alice and Bob, we should first consider which security features would be most desirable for them. First and foremost is *secrecy*. As discussed in Section 7.1, neither Alice nor Bob wants Trudy to read Alice's e-mail message. The second feature that Alice and Bob would most likely want to see in the secure e-mail system is *sender authentication*. In particular, when Bob receives the message from Alice, "I don't love you anymore. I never want to see you again. Formerly yours, Alice," Bob would naturally want to be sure that the message came from Alice and not from Trudy. Another feature that the two lovers would appreciate is *message integrity,* that is, assurance that the message Alice sends is not modified while en route to Bob. Finally, the e-mail system should provide *receiver authentication,* that is, Alice wants to make sure that she is indeed sending the letter to Bob and not to someone else (for example, Trudy) who is impersonating Bob.

So let's begin by addressing the foremost concern of Alice and Bob, namely, secrecy. The most straightforward way to provide secrecy is for Alice to encrypt the message with symmetric key technology (such as DES) and for Bob to decrypt the message upon message receipt. As discussed in Section 7.2, if the symmetric key is long enough, and if only Alice and Bob have the key, then it is extremely difficult for anyone else (including Trudy) to read the message. Although this approach is straightforward, it has a fundamental problem as we discussed in Section 7.2—it is difficult to distribute a symmetric key so that only Alice and Bob have copies of it. So we naturally consider an alternative tool, namely, public key cryptography (using, for example, RSA). In the public-key approach, Bob makes his public key publicly available (for example, in a public-key server or on his personal Web page), Alice encrypts her message with Bob's public key, and sends the encrypted message to Bob's e-mail address. (The encrypted message is encapsulated with MIME headers and sent over ordinary SMTP, as discussed in Section 2.4.) When Bob receives the message, he simply decrypts it with his private key. Assuming that Alice knows for sure that the public key is Bob's public key (and that the key is long enough), then this approach is an excellent means to provide the desired secrecy. One problem, however, is that public-key encryption is relatively inefficient, particularly for long messages. (Long e-mail messages are now commonplace in the Internet, due to the increasing use of attachments, images, audio, and video.)

To overcome the efficiency problem, let's make use of a session key (discussed in Section 7.5). In particular, (1) Alice selects a symmetric key, K_S, at random, (2) encrypts her message, m, with the symmetric key, K_S, (3) encrypts the symmetric key with Bob's public key, e_B, (4) concatenates the encrypted message and the encrypted symmetric key to form a "package," and (5) sends the package to Bob's e-mail address. The steps are illustrated in Figure 7.24. (In this and the subsequent figures, the "+" represents concatenation and the "-" represents deconcatenation.) When Bob receives the package, he (1) uses his private key d_B to obtain the symmetric key, K_s, and (2) uses the symmetric key K_s to decrypt the message m.

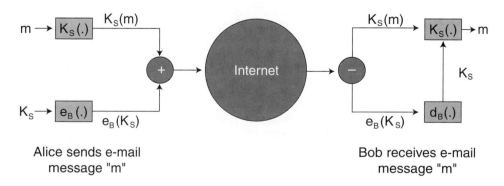

Alice sends e-mail
message "m"

Bob receives e-mail
message "m"

FIGURE 7.24 Alice uses a symmetric session key, K_S, to send a secret e-mail to Bob

Having designed a secure e-mail system that provides secrecy, let's now design another system that provides both sender authentication and integrity. We shall suppose, for the moment, that Alice and Bob are no longer concerned with secrecy (they want to share their feelings with everyone!), and are only concerned about sender authentication and message integrity. To accomplish this task, we use digital signatures and message digests, as described in Section 7.4. Specifically, (1) Alice applies a hash function, H (for example, MD5), to her message m to obtain a message digest, (2) encrypts the result of the hash function with her private key, d_A, to create a digital signature, (3) concatenates the original (unencrypted message) with the signature to create a package, (4) and sends the package to Bob's e-mail address. When Bob receives the package, (1) he applies Alice's public key, e_A, to the electronic signature and (2) compares the result of this operation to his own hash, H, of the message. The steps are illustrated in Figure 7.25. As discussed in Section 7.5, if the two results are the same, Bob can be pretty confident that the message came from Alice and is unaltered.

Now let's consider designing an e-mail system that provides secrecy, sender authentication, *and* message integrity. This can be done by combining the procedures in Figure 7.24 and 7.25. Alice first creates a preliminary package, exactly as in Figure 7.25, which consists of her original message along with a digitally signed hash of the message. She then treats this preliminary package as a message in itself, and sends this new message through the sender steps in Figure 7.24, creating a new package that is sent to Bob. The steps applied by Alice are shown in Figure 7.26. When Bob receives the package, he first applies his side of Figure 7.21 and then his side of Figure 7.25. It should be clear that this design achieves the goal of providing secrecy, sender authentication, and message integrity. Note in this scheme that Alice applies public key encryption twice: once with her own private key and once with Bob's public key. Similarly, Bob applies public key encryption twice—once with his private key and once with Alice's public key.

The secure e-mail design outlined in Figure 7.26 probably provides satisfactory security for most e-mail users for most occasions. But there is still one important issue that remains to be addressed. The design in Figure 7.26 requires Alice to obtain Bob's public key, and requires Bob to obtain Alice's public key. The distribution of these public keys is a nontrivial problem. For example, Trudy might

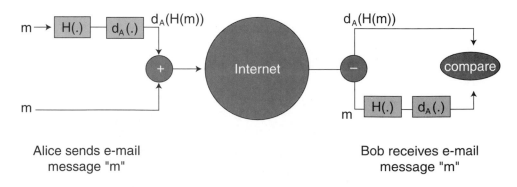

Alice sends e-mail
message "m"

Bob receives e-mail
message "m"

FIGURE 7.25 Using hash functions and digital signatures to provide sender authentication and message integrity

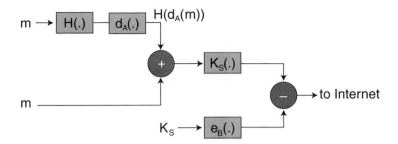

FIGURE 7.26 Alice uses symmetric-key cryptography, public-key cryptography, a hash function, and a digital signature to provide secrecy, sender authentication, and message integrity

masquerade as Bob and give Alice her own public key while saying that it is Bob's public key. As we learned in Section 7.5, a popular approach for securely distributing public keys is to *certify* the public keys.

7.6.2   PGP

Originally written by Phil Zimmerman in 1991, pretty good privacy (PGP) is an e-mail encryption scheme that has become a de-facto standard, with thousands of users all over the globe. Versions of PGP are available in the public domain; for example, you can find the PGP software for your favorite platform as well as lots of interesting reading at the International PGP Home Page [PGPI 1999]. (A particularly interesting essay by the author of PGP is [Zimmerman 1999].) PGP is also commercially available [Network Associates 1999], and is also available as a plug-in for many e-mail user agents, including Microsoft's Exchange and Outlook, and Qualcomm's Eudora.

The PGP design is, in essence, the same as the design shown in Figure 7.26. Depending on the version, the PGP software uses MD5 or SHA for calculating the message digest; CAST, Triple-DES, or IDEA for symmetric key encryption; and RSA for the public key encryption. In addition, PGP provides data compression.

When PGP is installed, the software creates a public key pair for the user. The public key can be posted on the user's Web site or placed in a public key server. The private key is protected by the use of a password. The password has to be entered every time the user accesses the private key. PGP gives the user the option of digitally signing the message, encrypting the message, or both digitally signing and encrypting. Figure 7.27 shows a PGP signed message. This message appears after the MIME header. The encoded data in the message is $d_A(H(m))$, that is, the digitally signed message digest. As we discussed above, in order for Bob to verify the integrity of the message, he needs to have access to Alice's public key.

Figure 7.28 shows a PGP secret message. This message also appears after the MIME header. Of course, the plaintext message is not included within the secret e-mail message. When a sender (such as Alice) wants both secrecy and integrity,

```
-----BEGIN PGP SIGNED MESSAGE-----
Hash: SHA1

Bob:

My husband is out of town tonight.

Passionately yours, Alice

-----BEGIN PGP SIGNATURE-----
Version: PGP for Personal Privacy 5.0
Charset: noconv
yhHJRHhGJGhgg/12EpJ+lo8gE4vB3mqJhFEvZP9t6n7G6m5Gw2
-----END PGP SIGNATURE-----
```

FIGURE 7.27   A PGP signed message

the PGP would contain a message like that of Figure 7.28 contained within the message of Figure 7.27.

PGP also provides a mechanism for public key certification, but the mechanism is quite different from the more conventional certification authority. PGP public keys are certified by a web of trust. Alice can certify any key/user name pair for which she believes the pair really belongs together. In addition, PGP permits Alice to say that she trusts another user to vouch for the authenticity of more keys. Some PGP users sign each other's keys by holding *key signing parties*. Users physically gather, exchange floppy disks containing public keys, and certify each other's keys by signing them with their private keys. PGP public keys are also distributed by *PGP public key servers* on the Internet. When a user submits a public key to such a server, the server stores a copy of the key, sends a copy of the key to all the other public-key servers, and serves the key to anyone who requests it. Although key signing parties and PGP public key servers actually exist, by far the most common way for users to distribute their public keys is by posting them on their personal Web pages. Of course, keys on personal Web pages are not certified by anyone, but they are easy to access.

```
-----BEGIN PGP MESSAGE-----
Version: PGP for Personal Privacy 5.0

u2R4d+/jKmn8Bc5+hgDsqAewsDfrGdszX68liKm5F6Gc4sDfcXyt

RfdSlOjuHgbcfDssWe7/K=lKhnMikLo0+l/BvcX4t==Ujk9PbcD4

Thdf2awQfgHbnmKlok8iy6gThlp
-----END PGP MESSAGE
```

FIGURE 7.28   A secret PGP message

7.7   INTERNET COMMERCE

In the previous section, we considered the application-layer use (in secure e-mail) of the various security technologies that we studied earlier in this chapter: encryption, authentication, key distribution, message integrity, and digital signatures. In this section, we'll continue our case study of various security mechanisms by dropping down a layer in the protocol stack and covering secure sockets and a secure transport layer. We'll take Internet commerce as a motivating application, since business and financial transactions are an important driver for Internet security.

We define **Internet commerce** to be the purchasing of "goods" over the Internet. Here we consider goods in a very broad sense to include books, CDs, hardware, software, airline tickets, stocks and bonds, consulting services, etc. In the 1990s many schemes were designed for Internet commerce, some providing minimal levels of security and others providing a high-level of security along with customer anonymity (similar to the anonymity provided by ordinary person-to-person cash transactions [Loshin 1997].) In the late 1990s, however, there was a major shake out, as only a few of these schemes were widely implemented in Web browsers and servers. As of this writing, two schemes have taken hold: SSL, which is currently used by the vast majority of Internet transactions; and SET, which is to expected to fiercely compete with SSL in the upcoming years.

Internet commerce, whether with SSL or SET, makes extensive use of the existing payment card (credit and debit) infrastructure that consumers, merchants, and financial institutions have used for many years. There are three major players in this infrastructure: the customer who is purchasing a product, the merchant who is selling the product, and the merchant's bank, which authorizes the purchase. We shall see in our discussion below that Internet commerce with SSL provides security for communication between the first two of these three players (that is, the customer and the merchant), whereas SET provides security for communication among all three players.

7.7.1   Internet Commerce Using SSL

Let us walk through a typical Internet commerce scenario. Bob is surfing the Web and arrives at the Alice Incorporated site which is selling some durable good. The Alice Incorporated site displays a form in which Bob is supposed to enter the quantity desired, his address, and his payment card number. Bob enters this information, clicks on "submit," and then expects to receive (say, from, ordinary mail) the good; he also expects to receive a charge for the good in his next payment card statement. This all sounds good, but if no security measures are taken—such as encryption or authentication—Bob could be in for a few surprises:

- An intruder could intercept the order and obtain Bob's payment card information. The intruder could then make purchases at Bob's expense.
- The site could display Alice Incorporated's famous logo, but actually be a site maintained by Trudy, who is masquerading as Alice Incorporated. Trudy could take Bob's money and run. Or Trudy could make her own purchases and have them billed to Bob's account.

Many other surprises are possible, and we will discuss a few of these in the next subsection. But the two problems listed above are two of the most serious problems. Internet commerce using the SSL protocol can address both these problems.

Secure sockets layer (SSL), originally developed by Netscape, is a protocol designed to provide data encryption and authentication between a Web client and a Web server. The protocol begins with a handshake phase that negotiates an encryption algorithm (for example, DES or IDEA) and keys, and authenticates the server to the client. Optionally, the client can also be authenticated to the server. Once the handshake is complete and the transmission of application data begins, all data is encrypted using session keys negotiated during the handshake phase. SSL is widely used in Internet commerce, being implemented in almost all popular browsers and Web servers. Furthermore, it is also the basis of the Transport Layer Security (TLS) protocol [RFC 2246].

SSL and TLS are not limited to the Web application; for example, they can similarly be used for authentication and data encryption for IMAP mail access. SSL can be viewed as a layer that sits between the application layer and the transport layer. On the sending side, SSL receives from the application raw application data (such as an HTTP or IMAP message), encrypts the data, and directs the encrypted data to a TCP socket. On the receiving side, SSL reads from the TCP socket, decrypts the data, and directs the data to the application. Although SSL can be used with many Internet applications, we shall discuss it in the context of the Web, where it is principally being used today for Internet commerce.

SSL provides the following features:

- *SSL server authentication,* allowing a user to confirm a server's identity. An SSL-enabled browser maintains a list of trusted certifying authorities (CAs) along with the public keys of the CAs. When the browser wants to do business with an SSL-enabled Web server, the browser obtains from the server a certificate containing the server's public key. The certificate is issued (that is, digitally signed) by a certificate authority (CA) listed in the client's list of trusted CAs. This feature allows the browser to authenticate the server before the user submits a payment card number. In the context of the earlier example, this server authentication enables Bob to verify that he is indeed sending his payment card number to Alice Incorporated, and not to someone else who might be masquerading as Alice Incorporated.

- *An encrypted SSL session,* in which all information sent between browser and server is encrypted by the sending software (browser or Web server) and decrypted by the receiving software (browser or Web server). This confidentially may be important to both the customer and the merchant. Also, SSL provides a mechanism for detecting tampering of the information by an intruder.

- *SSL client authentication,* allowing a server to confirm a user's identity. Analogous to server authentication, client authentication makes use of client certificates, which have also been issued by CAs. This authentication is important if the server, for example, is a bank sending confidential financial information to a customer and wants to check the recipient's identity. Client authentication, although supported by SSL, is optional. To keep our discussion focused, we will henceforth ignore it.

How SSL works.   A user, say Bob, surfs the Web and clicks on a link that takes him to a secure page housed by Alice's SSL-enabled server. The protocol part of the URL for this page is "https" rather than the ordinary "http." The browser and server then run the SSL handshake protocol, which (1) authenticates the server and (2) generates a shared symmetric key. Both of these tasks make use of the

RSA public-key technology. The main flow of events in the handshake phase is shown in Figure 7.29. During this phase, Alice sends Bob her certificate, from which Bob obtains Alice's public key. Bob then creates a random symmetric key, encrypts it with Alice's public key, and sends the encrypted key to Alice. Bob and Alice now share a symmetric session key. Once this handshake protocol is complete, all data sent between the browser and server (over TCP connections) is encrypted using the symmetric session key.

Having given a high-level overview of SSL, let's take a closer look at some of the more important details. The SSL handshake performs the following steps:

1. The browser sends the server the browser's SSL version number and cryptography preferences. The browser sends its cryptography preferences because the browser and server negotiate which symmetric key algorithm they are going to use.

2. The server sends the browser the server's SSL version number, cryptography preferences, and its certificate. Recall that the certificate includes the server's RSA public key and is certified by some CA, that is, the certificate has been encrypted by a CA's private key.

3. The browser has an entrusted list of CAs and a public key for each CA on the list. When the browser receives the certificate from the server, it checks to see if the CA is on the list. If not, the user is warned of the problem and informed that an encrypted and authenticated connection can not be established. If the

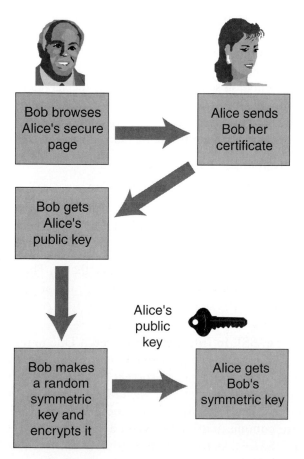

FIGURE 7.29   High-level overview of the handshake phase of SSL

CA is on the list, the browser uses the CA's public key to decrypt the certificate and obtain the server's public key.

4. The browser generates a symmetric session key, encrypts it with the server's public key, and sends the encrypted session key to the server.

5. The browser sends a message to the server informing it that future messages from the client will be encrypted with the session key. It then sends a separate (encrypted) message indicating that the browser portion of the handshake is finished.

6. The server sends a message to the browser informing it that future messages from the server will be encrypted with the session key. It then sends a separate (encrypted) message indicating that the server portion of the handshake is finished.

7. The SSL handshake is now complete, and the SSL session has begun. The browser and the server use the session keys to encrypt and decrypt the data they send to each other and to validate its integrity.

The SSL handshake actually has many more steps than listed above. You can find more information about SSL at Netscape's Security Developer Central [Netscape Security 1999]. In addition to payment card purchases, we point out here that SSL can (and is) be used for other financial transactions including online banking and stock trading.

SSL in action.   We recommend that you visit a secure Web site, such as a Quebec maple syrup site (http://www.jam.ca/syrup). When you enter a secure section of such a site, SSL will perform the handshake protocol. Assuming that the server's certificate checks out, the browser will notify you, for example by displaying a special icon. All information sent between you and the server will now be encrypted. Your browser should let you actually see the certificate for the merchant. (For example, with Internet Explorer, go to `File`, `Properties`, `Certificates`.) In April 1999, the maple syrup site's certificate included the following information:

Company: Netfarmers Enterprises Inc.

Certification Authority: Thawte Certification

Public Key (in hexadecimal):
       88:79:85:D5:D0:7D:60:39:10:51:31:EC:17:DE:E7:80

If your browser lets you do secure transactions with the merchant, then you should also be able to see the certificate for CA, that is, Thawte Certification. (For example, with Internet Explorer, go to `View`, `Internet Options`, `Content`, `Certificate Authorities`.)

The limitations of SSL in Internet commerce.   Due to its simplicity and early development, SSL is widely implemented in browsers, servers, and Internet commerce products. These SSL-enabled servers and browsers provide a popular platform for payment card transactions. Nevertheless, we should keep in mind that SSL was not specifically tailored for payment card transactions, but instead for generic secure communication between a client and server. Because of this generic design, SSL lacks many features that the payment-card industry would like to see in an Internet commerce protocol.

Consider once again what happens when Bob makes a purchase from Alice Incorporated over SSL. The signed certificate that Bob receives from Alice assures Bob that he is really dealing with Alice Incorporated, and that Alice Incorporated is a *bona fide* company. However, the generic certificate does not indicate whether Alice Incorporated is authorized to accept payment-card purchases nor if the company is a reliable merchant. This opens the door for merchant fraud. And there is a similar problem for client authorization. Even if SSL client authentication is used, the client certificate does not tie Bob to a specific authorized payment card; thus, Alice Incorporated has no assurance about whether Bob is authorized to make a payment-card purchase. This opens the door to all kinds of fraud, including purchases with stolen credit cards and customer repudiation of purchased goods [Abbott 1999].

Of course, this kind of fraud is already rampant in mail order and telephone order (MOTO) purchases. With MOTO transactions, the law dictates that the merchant accepts liability for fraudulent transactions. Thus, if a customer makes a MOTO purchase with a payment card and claims to have never made the purchase, then the merchant is liable, that is, the merchant is legally bound to return the money to the customer (unless the merchant can prove that the customer actually ordered and received the goods). Similarly, if a MOTO purchase is made with a stolen payment card, the merchant is again liable. On the other hand, with physically-present transactions, the merchant's bank accepts the liability; as you might expect, it is more difficult for a customer to repudiate a physically-present purchase that involves a hand-written signature or a PIN.

SSL purchases are similar to MOTO purchases, and naturally the merchant is liable for a fraudulent SSL purchase. It would be preferable, of course, to use a protocol that provides superior authentication of the customer and of the merchant, something that is as good or better than a physically-present transaction. Authentication involving payment-card authorization would reduce fraud and merchant liability.

7.7.2   Internet Commerce Using SET

SET (Secure Electronic Transactions) is a protocol specifically designed to secure payment-card transactions over the Internet. It was originally developed by Visa International and MasterCard International in February 1996 with participation from leading technology companies around the world. SET Secure Electronic Transaction LLC (commonly referred to as SETCo) was established in December 1997 as a legal entity to manage and promote the global adoption of SET [SETCo 1999]. Some of the principle characteristics of SET include:

- SET is designed to encrypt specific kinds of payment-related messages; it cannot be used to encrypt arbitrary data (such as text and images) as can SSL.
- The SET protocol involves all three players mentioned at the beginning of this section, namely, the customer, the merchant, and *the merchant's bank*. All sensitive information sent between the three parties is encrypted.
- SET requires all three players to have certificates. The customer's and merchant's certificates are issued by their banks, thereby assuring that these players are permitted to make and receive payment-card purchases. The customer certificate provides merchants with assurance that transactions will not be

fraudulently charged back. It is an electronic representation of the customer's payment card. It contains information about the account, the issuing financial institution, and other cryptographic information. The merchant certificate assures the consumer that *that* merchant is authorized to accept payment-card purchases. It contains information about the merchant, the merchant's bank, and the financial institution issuing the certificate.

▪ SET specifies the legal meaning of the certificates held by each party and the apportionment of liabilities connected with a transaction [Abbott 1999].

▪ In a SET transaction, the customer's payment-card number is passed to the merchant's bank without the merchant ever seeing the number in plain text. This feature prevents fraudulent or careless merchants from stealing or accidentally leaking the payment-card number.

A SET transaction uses three software components:

▪ *Browser wallet.* The browser wallet application is integrated with the browser and provides the customer with storage and management of payment cards and certificates while shopping. It responds to SET messages from the merchant, prompting the customer to select a payment card for payment.

▪ *Merchant server.* The merchant server is the merchandizing and fulfillment engine for merchants selling on the Web. For payments, it processes cardholder transactions and communicates with the merchant's bank for approval and subsequent payment capture.

▪ *Acquirer gateway.* The acquirer gateway is the software component at the merchant's bank. It processes the merchant's payment card transaction for authorization and payment.

In what follows, we give a highly simplified overview of the SET protocol. In reality, the protocol is substantially more complex.

Steps in making a purchase. Suppose Bob wants to purchase a good over the Internet from Alice Incorporated.

1. Bob indicates to Alice that he is interested in making a credit card purchase.
2. Alice sends the customer an invoice and a unique transaction identifier.
3. Alice sends Bob the merchant's certificate which includes the merchant's public key. Alice also sends the certificate for her bank, which includes the bank's public key. Both of these certificates are encrypted with the private key of a certifying authority.
4. Bob uses the certifying authority's public key to decrypt the two certificates. Bob now has Alice's public key and the bank's public key.
5. Bob generates two packages of information: the **order information** (OI) package and the **purchase instructions** (PI) package. The OI, destined for Alice, contains the transaction identifier and brand of card being used; it does not include Bob's card number. The PI, destined for Alice's bank, contains the transaction identifier, the card number, and the purchase amount agreed to by Bob. The OI and PI are *dual encrypted:* the OI is encrypted with Alice's public key; the PI is encrypted with Alice's bank's public key. (We are bending the truth here in order to see the big picture. In reality, the OI and PI are

encrypted with a customer-merchant session key and a customer-bank session key.) Bob sends the `OI` and the `PI` to Alice.

6. Alice generates an authorization request for the card payment request, which includes the transaction identifier.

7. Alice sends to her bank a message encrypted with the bank's public key. (Actually, a session key is used.) This message includes the authorization request, the `PI` package received from Bob, and Alice's certificate.

8. Alice's bank receives the message and unravels it. The bank checks for tampering. It also makes sure that the transaction identifier in the authorization request matches the one in Bob's `PI` package.

9. Alice's bank then sends a request for payment authorization to Bob's payment-card bank through traditional bank-card channels—just as Alice's bank would request authorization for any normal payment-card transaction.

10. Once Bob's bank authorizes the payment, Alice's bank sends a response to Alice, which is (of course) encrypted. The response includes the transaction identifier.

11. If the transaction is approved, Alice sends her own response message to Bob. This message serves as a receipt and informs Bob that the payment was accepted and that the goods will be delivered.

One of the key features of SET is the nonexposure of the credit number to the merchant. This feature is provided in Step 5, in which the customer encrypts the credit card number with the bank's key. Encrypting the number with the bank's key prevents the merchant from seeing the credit card. Note that the SET protocol closely parallels the steps taken in a standard payment-card transaction. To handle all the SET tasks, the customer will have a so-called digital wallet that runs the client-side of the SET protocol and stores customer payment-card information (card number, expiration date, etc.). Readers interested in learning more about SET are encouraged to see the SETCo page [SETCo 1999] or the SET documentation at the MasterCard site [MasterCard 1999]. There are also several good books on SET [Merkow 1998] [Loeb 1998].

7.8   NETWORK LAYER SECURITY: IPSEC

The IP Security protocol, more commonly known as IPsec, is a suite of protocols that provides security at the network layer. IPsec is a rather complex animal, and different parts of it are described in more than a dozen RFCs. In this section, we will discuss IPsec in a specific context, namely, in the context that *all* hosts in the Internet support IPsec. Although this context is many years away, the context will simplify the discussion and help us understand the key features of IPsec. Two key RFCs are [RFC 2401], which describes the overall IP security architecture and [RFC 2411], which provides an overview of the IPsec protocol suite and the documents describing it. A nice introduction to IPsec is given in [Kessler 1998].

Before getting into the specifics of IPsec, let us step back and consider what it means to provide security at the network layer. Consider first what it means to provide **network layer secrecy.** The network layer would provide secrecy if all the data carried by all IP datagrams were encrypted. This means that whenever a host wants to send a datagram, it encrypts the data field of the datagram before shipping it out into the network. In principle, the encryption could be done with symmetric key encryption, public key encryption, or with session keys that are negotiated using public key encryption. The data field could be a TCP segment, a UDP segment, an ICMP message, etc. If such a network-layer service were in place, all data sent by hosts—including e-mail, Web pages, control, and management messages (such as ICMP and SNMP)—would be hidden from any third party that is "wire tapping" the network. (However, the data could be snooped at the source or destination hosts.) Thus, such a service would provide a certain "blanket coverage" for all Internet traffic, thereby giving all of us a certain sense of security.

In addition to secrecy, one might want the network layer to also provide **source authentication.** When a destination host receives an IP datagram with a particular IP source address, it authenticates the source by making sure that the IP datagram was indeed generated by the host with that IP source address. Such a service prevents attackers from spoofing IP addresses.

In the IPsec protocol suite there are two principal protocols: the **Authentication Header (AH) protocol** and the **Encapsulation Security Payload (ESP) protocol.** When a source host sends secure datagrams to a destination host, it does so with either the AH protocol or with the ESP protocol. The AH protocol provides source authentication and data integrity but does not provide secrecy. The ESP protocol provides data integrity and secrecy. Providing more services, the ESP protocol is naturally more complicated and requires more processing than the AH protocol. We will discuss both of these protocols below.

For both the AH and the ESP protocols, before sending secured datagrams from a source host to a destination host, the source and network hosts handshake and create a network layer logical connection. This logical channel is called a **security agreement (SA).** Thus, IPsec transforms the traditional connectionless network layer of the Internet to a layer with logical connections! The logical connection defined by an SA is a simplex connection, that is, it is unidirectional. If both hosts want to send secure datagrams to each other, then two SAs (that is, logical connections) need to be established, one in each direction. An SA is uniquely identified by a 3-tuple consisting of:

- a security protocol (AH or ESP) identifier
- the source IP address for the simplex connection
- a 32-bit connection identifier called the Security Parameter Index (SPI).

For a given SA (that is, a given logical connection from source host to destination host), each IPsec datagram will have a special field for the SPI. All of the datagrams in the SA will use the same SPI value in this field.

7.8.1 Authentication Header (AH) Protocol

As mentioned above, the AH protocol provides source host identification and data integrity but not secrecy. When a particular source host wants to send one or more datagrams to a particular destination, it first establishes an SA with the destination. After having established the SA, the source can send secure datagrams to the destination host. The secure datagrams include the AH header, which is inserted between the original IP datagram data (for example, a TCP or UDP segment) and the IP header, as shown in Figure 7.30. Thus the AH header augments the original data field, and this augmented data field is encapsulated as a standard IP datagram. For the protocol field in the IP header, the value 51 is used to indicate that the datagram includes an AH header. When the destination host receives the IP datagram, it takes note of the 51 in the protocol field, and processes the datagram using the AH protocol. (Recall that the protocol field in the IP datagram is traditionally used to distinguish between UDP, TCP, ICMP, etc.) Intermediate routers process the datagrams just as they always have—they examine the destination IP address and route the datagrams accordingly.

The AH header includes several fields, including:

- *Next Header* field, which has the role that the protocol field has for an ordinary datagram. It indicates if the data following the AH header is a TCP segment, UDP segment, ICMP segment, etc. (Recall that the protocol field in the datagram is now being used to indicate the AH protocol, so it can no longer be used to indicate the transport-layer protocol.)
- *Security Parameter Index (SPI)* field, an arbitrary 32-bit value that, in combination with the destination IP address and the security protocol, uniquely identifies the SA for the datagram.
- *Sequence Number* field, a 32-bit field containing a sequence number for each datagram. It is initially set to 0 at the establishment of an SA. The AH protocol uses the sequence numbers to prevent playback and man-in-the-middle attacks (see Section 7.3).
- *Authentication Data* field, a variable-length field containing a signed message digest (that is, a digital signature) for this packet. The message digest is calculated over the original IP datagram, thereby providing source host authentication and IP datagram integrity. The digital signature is computed using the authentication algorithm specified by the SA, such as DES, MD5, or SHA.

When the destination host receives an IP datagram with an AH header, it determines the SA for the packet and then authenticates the integrity of the datagram by processing the authentication data field. The IPsec authentication scheme (for both the AH and ESP protocols) uses a scheme called HMAC, which is an encrypted message digest described in [RFC 2104]. HMAC uses a shared secret key between two parties rather than public key methods for message authentication. Further details about the AH protocol can be found in [RFC 2402].

Protocol = 51

FIGURE 7.30   Position of the AH header in the IP datagram

7.8.2 The ESP Protocol

The ESP protocol provides network-layer secrecy as well as source host authentication. Once again, it all begins with a source host establishing an SA with a destination host. Then the source host can send secured datagrams to the destination host. As shown in Figure 7.31, a secured datagram is created by surrounding the original IP datagram data with header and trailer fields, and then inserting this encapsulated data into the data field of an IP datagram. For the protocol field in the header of the IP datagram, the value 50 is used to indicate that the datagram includes an ESP header and trailer. When the destination host receives the IP datagram, it takes note of the 50 in the protocol field, and processes the datagram using the ESP protocol. As shown in Figure 7.31, the original IP datagram data along with the ESP Trailer field are encrypted. Secrecy is provided with DES-CBC encryption [RFC 2405]. The ESP header consists of a 32-bit field for the SPI and 32-bit field for the sequence number, which have exactly the same role as in the AH protocol. The trailer includes the Next Header field, which also has exactly the same role. Note that because the Next Header field is encrypted along with the original data, an intruder will not be able to determine the transport protocol that is being used. Following the trailer there is the Authentication Data field, which again serves the same role as in the AH protocol. Further details about the AH protocol can be found in [RFC 2406].

7.8.3 SA and Key Management

For successful deployment of IPsec, a scalable and automated SA and key management scheme is necessary. Several protocols have been defined for these tasks, including:

- The Internet Key Exchange (IKE) algorithm [RFC 2409] is the default key management protocol for IPsec.
- The Internet Security Association and Key Management Protocol (ISKMP) defines procedures for establishing and tearing down SAs [RFC 2407] [RFC 2408]. ISKMP's security association is completely separate from IKE key exchange.

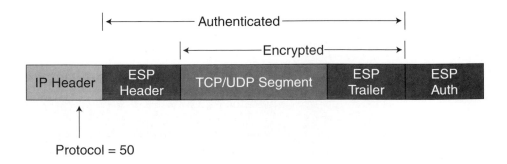

FIGURE 7.31 The ESP fields in the IP datagram

This wraps up our summary of IPsec. We have discussed IPsec in the context of IPv4 and the "transport mode." IPsec also defines a "tunnel mode," in which routers introduce the security functionality rather than the hosts. Finally, IPsec describes encryption procedures for IPv6 as well as IPv4.

SUMMARY

In this chapter, we've examined the various mechanisms that our secret lovers, Bob and Alice, can use to communicate "securely." We've seen that Bob and Alice are interested in secrecy (so that they alone are able to understand the contents of a transmitted message), authentication (so that they are sure that they are talking with each other), and message integrity (so that they are sure that their messages are not altered in transit). Of course, the need for secure communication is not confined to secret lovers. Indeed, we saw in Section 7.1 that security is needed at various layers in a network architecture to protect against "bad guys" who may sniff packets, remove packets from the network, or inject falsely addressed packets into the network.

The first part of this chapter presented various principles underlying secure communication. We covered cryptographic techniques for coding and decoding data in Section 7.2, including both symmetric key cryptography and public key cryptography. DES and RSA were examined as specific case studies of these two major classes of cryptographic techniques in use in today's networks. In Section 7.3 we turned our attention to authentication, and developed a series of increasingly sophisticated authentication protocols to ensure that a conversant is indeed who he/she claims to be, and is "live." We saw that both symmetric key cryptography and public key cryptography can play an important role not only in disguising data (encryption/decryption), but also in performing authentication. Techniques for "signing" a digital document in a manner that is verifiable, nonforgible, and nonrepudiable were covered in Section 7.4. Once again, the application of cryptographic techniques proved essential. We examined both digital signatures and message digests—a shorthand way of signing a digital document. In Section 7.5 we examined key distribution protocols. We saw that for symmetric key encryption, a key distribution center—a single trusted network entity—can be used to distribute a shared symmetric key among communicating parties. For public key encryption, a certification authority distributes certificates to validate public keys.

Armed with the techniques covered in Sections 7.2 through 7.5, Bob and Alice can communicate securely (one can only hope that they are networking students who have learned this material and can thus avoid having their tryst uncovered by Trudy!). In the second part of this chapter we thus turned our attention to the use of various security techniques in networks. In Section 7.6, we used e-mail as a case study for application-layer security, designing an e-mail system that provided secrecy, sender authentication, and message integrity. We also examined the use of PGP as a public-key e-mail encryption scheme. Our case studies continued as we headed down the protocol stack and examined the secure sockets layer (SSL) and secure electronic transactions, the two primary protocols in use today for secure electronic commerce. Both are based on public key techniques. Finally, in Section 7.8 we examined a suite of security protocols for the IP layer of the

Internet—the so-called IPsec protocols. These can be used to provide secrecy, authentication, and message integrity between two communication IP devices.

HOMEWORK PROBLEMS AND QUESTIONS

Review Questions

1. What are the differences between message secrecy and message integrity? Can you have one without the other? Justify your answer.

2. What is the difference between an active and a passive intruder?

3. What is an important difference between a symmetric key system and a public key system?

4. Suppose that an intruder has an encrypted message as well as the decrypted version of that message. Can the intruder mount a cipher-text only attack, a known-plaintext, or a chosen-plaintext attack?

5. Suppose N people want to communicate with each of the $N-1$ other people using symmetric key encryption. All communication between any two people, i and j, is visible to all other people, and no other person should be able to decode their communication. How many keys are required in the system as a whole? Now suppose that public key encryption is used. How many keys are required in this case?

6. What is the purpose of a nonce in an authentication protocol?

7. What does it mean to say that a nonce is a once-in-a-lifetime value? In whose lifetime?

8. What is the man-in-the-middle attack? Can this attack occur when symmetric keys are used?

9. What does it mean for a signed document to be verifiable, nonforgible, and nonrepudiable?

10. In what way does a message digest provide a better message integrity check than a checksum such as the Internet checksum?

11. In what way does a message digest provide a "better" digital signature than using a public key digital signature?

12. Is the message associated with a message digest encrypted? Since either "yes" or "no" are acceptable answers here, you should explain your answer.

13. What is a key distribution center? What is a certification authority?

14. Summarize the key differences in the services provided by the Authentication Header protocol and the Encapsulation Security Payload (ESP) protocol in IPsec.

PROBLEMS

1. Using the monoalphabetic cipher in Figure 7.4. Encode the message "This is an easy problem." Decode the message "rmij'u uamu xyj."

2. Show that Eve's known plaintext attack in which she knows the (ciphertext, plaintext) translation pairs for seven letters reduces the number of possible substitutions to be checked in the example in Section 7.2.1 by approximately 10^9.

3. Consider the Vigenere system shown in Figure 7.5. Will a chosen plaintext attack that is able to get the plaintext encoding of the message, "The quick fox jumps over the lazy brown dog" be sufficient to decode all messages? Why?

4. Using RSA, choose $p = 3$ and $q = 11$, and encode the phrase "hello." Apply the decryption algorithm, to the encrypted version to recover the original plaintext message.

5. In the man-in-the-middle attack in Figure 7.14, Alice has not authenticated Bob. If Alice were to require Bob to authenticate himself using *ap5.0,* would the man-in-the-middle attack be avoided? Explain your reasoning.

6. The Internet BGP routing protocol uses the MD5 message digest rather than public key encryption to sign BGP messages. Why do you think MD5 was chosen over public key encryption?

7. Compute a third message, different from the two messages in Figure 7.19, that has the same checksum as the messages in Figure 7.19.

8. Augment the KDC protocol shown in Figure 7.20 to include the necessary authentication messages. Be sure to show the use of nonces and indicate which key values are used to encrypt which messages.

9. In the protocol and discussion of Figure 7.20, why doesn't Alice have to explicitly authenticate Bob?

10. In the protocol in Figure 7.20, Alice did not include her own identity in the message to the CA. Anyone could thus spoof a message from Alice to the CA. Does this compromise the integrity of the CA's public key distribution? Justify your answer.

11. Why is there no explicit authentication in the protocol in Figure 7.20? Is authentication needed? Why?

12. Consider the KDC and the CA servers. Suppose a KDC goes down. What is the impact on the ability of parties to communicate securely, that is, who can, and cannot, communicate? Justify your answer. Suppose now that a CA goes down. What is the impact of this failure?

DISCUSSION QUESTIONS

1. Suppose that an intruder could both insert and remove DNS messages into the network. Give three scenarios showing the problems that such an intruder could cause.

2. No one has formally "proven" that 3-DES or RSA are "secure." Given this, what evidence do we have that they are indeed secure?

3. If IPsec provides security at the network layer, why is it that security mechanisms are still needed at layers above IP?

4. Go to the International PGP homepage (http://www.pgpi.org/). What version of PGP are you legally allowed to download, given the country you are in?

Chapter 8 | Network Management

8.1 WHAT IS NETWORK MANAGEMENT?

Having made our way through the first seven chapters of this text, we're now well aware that a network consists of *many* complex, interacting pieces of hardware and software—from the links, bridges, routers, hosts, and other devices that comprise the physical components of the network to the many protocols (in both hardware and software) that control and coordinate these devices. When hundreds or thousands of such components are cobbled together by an organization to form a network, it is not surprising that components will occasionally malfunction, that network elements will be misconfigured, that network resources will be overutilized, or that network components will simply "break" (for example, a cable will be cut, a can of soda will be spilled on top of a router). The network administrator, whose job it is to keep the network "up and running," must be able to respond to (and better yet, avoid) such mishaps. With potentially thousands of network components spread out over a wide area, the network administrator in a network operations center (NOC) clearly needs tools to help monitor, manage, and control the network. In this chapter, we'll examine the architecture, protocols, and information base used by a network administrator in this task.

Before diving in to network management itself, let's first consider a few illustrative "real-world" non-networking scenarios in which a complex system with many interacting components must be monitored, managed, and controlled by an administrator. Electrical power-generation plants (at least as portrayed in the popular media in such movies as the *China Syndrome*) have a control room where dials, gauges, and lights monitor the status (temperature, pressure, flow) of remote valves, pipes, vessels, and other plant components. These devices allow the operator to monitor the plant's many components, and may alert the operator (the famous flashing red warning light) when trouble is imminent. Actions are taken by the plant operator to control these components. Similarly, an airplane cockpit is instrumented to allow a pilot to monitor and control the many components that make up an airplane. In these two examples, the "administrator" *monitors* remote devices and *analyzes* their data to ensure that they are operational and operating within prescribed limits (for example, that a core meltdown of a nuclear power plant is not imminent, or that the plane is not about to run out of fuel), *reactively controls* the system by making adjustments in response to the changes within the system or its environment, and *proactively manages* the system (for example, by detecting trends or anomalous behavior, allowing action to be taken before serious problems arise). In a similar sense, the network administrator will actively monitor, manage, and control the system with which she/he is entrusted.

In the early days of networking, when computer networks were research artifacts rather than a critical infrastructure used by millions of people a day, "network management" was an unheard of thing. If one encountered a network problem, one might run a few pings to locate the source of the problem and then modify system settings, reboot hardware or software, or call a remote colleague to do so. (A very readable discussion of the first major "crash" of the ARPAnet on October 27, 1980, long before network management tools were available, and the efforts taken to recover from and understand the crash is [RFC 789]). As the public Internet and private intranets have grown from small networks into a large global infrastructure, the need to more systematically manage the huge number of hardware and software components within these networks has grown more important as well.

In order to motivate our study of network management, let's begin with a simple example. Figure 8.1 illustrates a small network consisting of three routers, and a number of hosts and servers. Even in such a simple network, there are many sce-

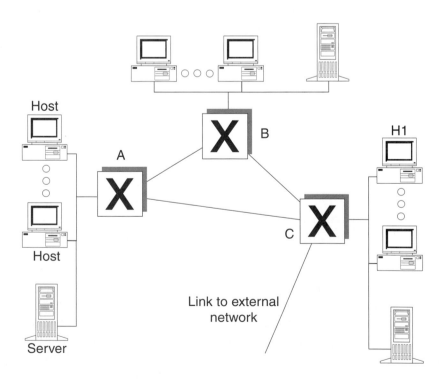

FIGURE 8.1 A simple scenario illustrating the uses of network management

narios in which a network administrator might benefit tremendously from having appropriate network management tools:

- *Failure of an interface card* at a host (for example, H1) or a router (for example, A). With appropriate network management tools, a network entity (for example router A) may report to the network administrator that one of its interfaces has gone down (which is certainly preferable than a phone call to the NOC from an irate user who says the network connection is down). A network administrator who actively monitors and analyzes network traffic may be able to *really* impress the would-be irate user by actually detecting problems in the interface ahead of time and replacing the interface card before it fails. This could be done, for example, if the administrator noted an increase in checksum errors in frames being sent by the soon-to-die interface.

- *Monitoring traffic to aid in resource deployment.* A network administrator might monitor source-to-destination traffic patterns and notice, for example, that by switching servers between LAN segments, the amount of traffic that crosses multiple LANs could be significantly decreased. Imagine the happiness all around (especially in higher administration) when better performance is achieved with no new equipment costs. Similarly, by monitoring link utilization, a network administrator might determine that a LAN segment, or the external link to the outside world is overloaded and a higher-bandwidth link should thus be provisioned (alas, at an increased cost). The network administrator might also want to be notified automatically when congestion levels on a link exceed a given threshold value in order to address a provisioning problem before it becomes serious.

- *Detecting rapid changes in routing tables.* Route flapping—frequent changes in the routing tables—may indicate instabilities in the routing or a misconfigured router. Certainly, the network administrator who has improperly configured a router would prefer to discover the error his/herself, before the network goes down.

- *Monitoring for SLAs.* With the advent of **Service Level Agreements (SLA)**—contracts that define specific performance metrics and acceptable levels of network provider performance with respect to these metrics—interest in traffic monitoring has increased significantly over the past few years [Larsen 1997]. UUnet and AT&T are just two of the many network providers that guarantee SLAs [UUNet 1999, AT&T SLA 1998] to their customers. These SLAs include service availability (outage), latency, throughput, and outage notification requirements. Clearly, if performance criteria are to be part of a service agreement between a network provider and its users, then measuring and managing performance will be of great importance to the network administrator.

- *Intrusion detection.* A network administrator may want to be notified when network traffic arrives from, or is destined to, a suspicious source (for example, host or port number). Similarly, a network administrator may want to detect (and in many cases filter) the existence of certain types of traffic (for example, source-routed packets, or a large number of SYN packets directed to a given host) that are known to be characteristic of certain attacks.

The ISO, the organization that gave us the well-known seven-layer ISO reference model (see Chapter 1), has also created a network management model that is useful for placing the above anecdotal scenarios in a more structured framework. Five areas of network management are defined:

- *Performance management.* The goal of performance management is to quantify, measure, report, analyze, and control the performance (for example, utilization, throughput) of different network components. These components include individual devices (for example, links, routers, and hosts) as well as end-end abstractions such as a path through the network. We will see shortly that protocol standards such as the Simple Network Management Protocol (SNMP) [RFC 2570] play a central role in performance management.

- *Fault management.* The goal of fault management is to log, detect, and respond to fault conditions in the network. The line between fault management and performance management is rather blurred. We can think of fault management as the immediate handling of transient network failures (for example, link, host, or router hardware or software outages), while performance management takes the longer term view of providing acceptable levels of performance in the face of varying traffic demands and (hopefully rare) network device failures. As with performance management, the SNMP protocol plays a central role in fault management of IP networks.

- *Configuration management.* Configuration management allows a network manager to track which devices are on the managed network and the hardware and software configurations of these devices.

- *Accounting management.* Accounting management allows the network manager to specify, log, and control user and device access to network resources. Usage quotas, usage-based charging, and the allocation of resource-access privileges all fall under accounting management.

- *Security management.* The goal of security management is to control access to network resources according to some well-defined policy. The key distribution centers and certificate authorities that we studied in Section 7.5 are components of security management. The use of firewalls to monitor and control external access points to one's network, a topic we will study in Section 8.4, is another crucial component.

In this chapter, we'll cover only the rudiments of network management. Our focus will be purposefully narrow—we'll examine only the *infrastructure* for network management—the overall architecture, network management protocols, and information base through which a network administrator "keeps the network up and running." We'll *not* cover the decision-making processes of the network administrator, who must plan, analyze, and respond to the management information that is conveyed to the NOC. In this area, topics such as fault identification and management [Katzela 1995, Mehdi 1997], proactive anomaly detection [Thottan 1998], alarm correlation [Jakobson 1993], and more come into consideration. Nor will we cover the broader topic of service management [Saydam 1996]—the provisioning of resources such as bandwidth, server capacity, and the other computational/communication resources needed to meet the mission-specific service requirements of an enterprise. In this latter area, standards such as TMN [Glitho 1995, Sidor 1998] and TINA [Hamada 1997] are larger, more encompassing (and arguably much more cumbersome) standards that address this larger issue. TINA, for example, is described as "a set of common goals, principles, and concepts that cover the management of services, resources, and parts of the Distributed Processing Environment" [Hamada 1997]. Clearly, all of these topics are enough for a separate text and would take us a bit far afield from the more technical aspects of computer networking. So, as noted above, our more modest goal here will be to cover the important "nuts and bolts" of the infrastructure through which the network administrator keeps the bits flowing smoothly.

An often-asked question is "What is network management?". Our discussion above has motivated the need for, and illustrated a few of the uses of, network management. We'll conclude this section with a single-sentence (albeit a rather long, run-on sentence) definition of network management from [Saydam 1996]:

> "Network management includes the deployment, integration, and coordination of the hardware, software, and human elements to monitor, test, poll, configure, analyze, evaluate, and control the network and element resources to meet the real-time, operational performance, and Quality of Service requirements at a reasonable cost."

It's a mouthful, but it's a good workable definition. In the following sections, we'll add some meat to this rather bare-bones definition of network management.

8.2   THE INFRASTRUCTURE FOR NETWORK MANAGEMENT

We've seen in the previous section that network management requires the ability to "monitor, test, poll, configure, . . . and control" the hardware and software and components in a network. Because the network devices are distributed, this will minimally require that the network administrator be able to gather data (for example, for monitoring purposes) from a remote entity and be able to affect changes (for example, control) at that remote entity. A human analogy will prove useful here for understanding the infrastructure needed for network management.

Imagine that you're the head of a large organization that has branch offices around the world. It's your job to make sure that the pieces of your organization are operating smoothly. How would you do so? At a minimum, you'll periodically gather data from your branch offices in the form of reports and various quantitative measures of activity, productivity, and budget. You'll occasionally (but not always) be explicitly notified when there's a problem in one of the branch offices; the branch manager who wants to climb the corporate ladder (perhaps to get your job) may send you unsolicited reports indicating how smoothly things are running at his/her branch. You'll sift through the reports you receive, hoping to find smooth operations everywhere, but no doubt finding problems in need of your attention. You might initiate a one-on-one dialogue with one of your problem branch offices, gather more data in order to understand the problem, and then pass down an executive order ("Make this change!") to the branch office manager.

Implicit in this very common human scenario is an infrastructure for controlling the organization—the boss (you), the remotes sites being controlled (the branch offices), your remote agents (the branch office managers), communication protocols (for transmitting standard reports and data, and for one-on-one dialogues), and data (the report contents and the quantitative measures of activity, productivity, and budget). Each of these components in human organizational management has an exact counterpart in network management.

The architecture of a network management system is conceptually identical to this simple human organizational analogy. The network management field has its own specific terminology for the various components of a network management architecture, and so we adopt that terminology here. As shown in Figure 8.2, there are three principle components of a network management architecture: a managing entity (the boss in our above analogy—you), the managed devices (the branch office), and a network management protocol.

The **managing entity** is an application, typically with a human in the loop, running in a centralized network management station in the network operations center (NOC). The managing entity is the central locus of activity for network management; it controls the collection, processing, analysis, and/or display of network management information. It is here that actions are initiated to control network behavior and here that the human network administrator interacts with the network devices.

A **managed device** is a piece of network equipment (including its software) that resides on a managed network. This is the branch office in our human analogy. A managed device might be a host, router, bridge, hub, printer, or modem device. Within a managed device, there may be several so-called **managed objects.** These managed objects are the actual pieces of hardware within the managed device (for example, a network interface card), and the sets of configuration parameters for the pieces of hardware and software (for example, an intradomain routing protocol such as RIP). In our human analogy, the managed objects might be the departments within the branch office. These managed objects have pieces of information associated with them that are collected into a **management information base (MIB);** we'll see that the values of these pieces of information are

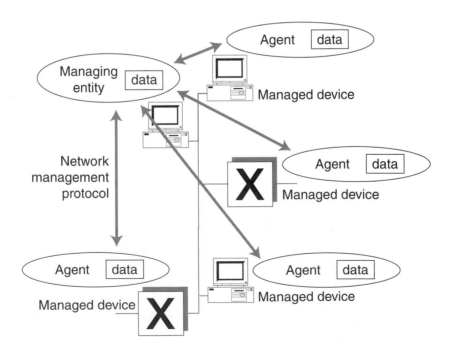

FIGURE 8.2   Principal components of a network management architecture

available to (and in many cases able to be set by) the managing entity. In our human analogy, the MIB corresponds to quantitative data (measures of activity, productivity, and budget, with the latter being setable by the managing entity!) exchanged between the branch office and the main office. We'll study MIBs in detail in Section 8.3. Finally, also resident in each managed device is a **network management agent,** a process running in the managed device that communicates with the managing entity, taking local actions on the managed device under the command and control of the managing entity. The network management agent is the branch manager in our human analogy.

The third piece of a network management architecture is the **network management protocol.** The protocol runs between the managing entity and the managed devices, allowing the managing entity to query the status of managed devices and indirectly take actions at these devices via its agents. Agents can use the network management protocol to inform the managing entity of exceptional events (for example, component failures or violation of performance thresholds).

Although the infrastructure for network management is conceptually simple, one can often get bogged down with the network-management-speak vocabulary of "managing entity," "managed device," "managing agent," and "management information base." Hopefully, keeping the human organizational analogy and its obvious parallels with network management in mind will be of help as we continue through this chapter.

Our discussion of network management architecture above has been generic, and broadly applied to a number of the network management standards and efforts that have been proposed over the years. Network management standards began maturing in the late 1980s, with OSI **CMISE/CMIP (the Common Management Service Element/Common Management Information Protocol)** [Piscatello 1993, Stallings 1993, Glitho 1998] and the Internet **SNMP (Simple Network Management Protocol)** [Stallings 1993, RFC 2570, Stallings 1999, Rose 1996] emerging as the two most important standards. Both are designed to be independent of vendor-specific products or networks. Because SNMP was quickly designed and deployed at a time when the need for network management was becoming painfully clear, SNMP found widespread use and acceptance. Today, SNMP has emerged as the most widely used and deployed network management framework. We cover SNMP in detail in the following section.

8.3

THE INTERNET NETWORK MANAGEMENT FRAMEWORK

Contrary to what the name SNMP (Simple Network Management Protocol) might suggest, network management in the Internet is much more than just a protocol for moving management data between a management entity and its agents, and has grown to be more complex than the word "simple" might suggest. The current Internet Standard Management Framework traces it roots back to the Simple Gateway Monitoring Protocol, SGMP [RFC 1028] that was designed by a group of university network researchers, users, and managers; their experience with SGMP allowed them to design, implement, and deploy SNMP in just a few months [Lynch 1993]—a far cry from today's rather drawn out standardization process. Since then, SNMP has evolved from SNMPv1 through SNMPv2 to the most recent version, SNMPv3 [RFC 2570], released in April 1999.

When describing any framework for network management, certain questions must inevitably be addressed:

- What (from a semantic viewpoint) is being monitored? And what form of control can be exercised by the network administrator?
- What is the specific form of the information that will be reported and/or exchanged?
- What is the protocol for communication protocol for exchanging this information?

Recall our human organizational analogy from the previous section. The boss and the branch managers will need to agree on the measures of activity, productivity, and budget used to report the branch office's status. Similarly, they'll need to agree on the actions the boss can take (for example, cut the budget, order the branch manager to change some aspect of the office's operation). At a lower level of detail, they'll need to agree on the form in which this data is reported (for example, In what currency (dollars, euros?) will the budget be reported? In what units will productivity be measured?). While these are trivial details, they must be agreed upon, nonetheless. Finally, the manner in which information is conveyed between the main office and the branch offices (that is, their communication protocol) must be specified.

The Internet Network Management Framework exactly addresses the questions posed above. The framework consists of four parts:

- Definitions of *network management objects* known as MIB objects. In the Internet network management framework, management information is represented as a collection of managed objects that together form a virtual information store, known as the Management Information Base (MIB). An MIB object might be a counter, such as the number of IP datagrams discarded at a router due to errors in an IP datagram header or the number of carrier sense errors in an Ethernet interface; descriptive information such as the version of the software running on a DNS server; status information such as whether a particular device is functioning correctly or not; or protocol-specific information such as a routing path to a destination. MIB objects thus define the management information maintained by a managed node. Related MIB objects are gathered into so-called **MIB modules.** In our human organization analogy, the MIB defines the information conveyed between the branch office and the main office.
- A *data definition language,* known as SMI (Structure of Management Information) that defines the data types, an object model, and rules for writing and revising management information. MIB objects are specified in this data definition language. In our human organizational analogy, the SMI is used to define the details of the *format* of the information to be exchanged.
- A *protocol, SNMP,* for conveying information and commands between a managing entity and an agent executing on behalf of that entity within a managed network device.
- *Security and administration capabilities.* The addition of these capabilities represents the major enhancement in SNMPv3 over SNMPv2.

The Internet network management architecture is thus modular by design, with a protocol-independent data definition language and MIB, and an MIB-independent protocol. Interestingly, this modular architecture was first put in place to ease the transition from an SNMP-based network management to a network management framework being developed by the International Organization for Standardization (ISO), the competing network management architecture when SNMP was first conceived—a transition that never occurred. Over time, however, SNMP's design modularity has allowed it to evolve through three major revisions, with each of the four major parts of SNMP discussed above evolving independently. Clearly, the right decision about modularity was made, if even for the wrong reason!

In the following four sections, we cover the four major components of the Internet network management framework in more detail.

8.3.1   Structure of Management Information: SMI

The **Structure of Management Information, SMI,** (a rather oddly named component of the network management framework whose name gives no hint of its functionality) is the language used to define the management information residing in a managed network entity. Such a definition language is needed to ensure that the syntax and semantics of the defined network management data are well-defined and unambiguous. Note that the SMI does not define a specific instance of the data in a managed network entity, but rather the language in which such information is specified. The documents describing the SMI for SNMPv3 (which rather confusingly, is called SMIv2) are [RFC 2578, RFC 2579, RFC 2580]. Let us examine the SMI in a bottom-up manner, starting with the base data types in the SMI. We'll then look at how managed objects are described in SMI, and then how related managed objects are grouped into modules.

SMI base data types.   [RFC 2578] specifies the basic data types in the SMI MIB module-definition language. Although the SMI is based on the ASN.1 (Abstract Syntax Notation One) [ISO 1987, ISO X.680] object definition language (see Section 8.4) developed by the ISO in the 1980s, enough SMI-specific data types have been added that SMI should be considered a data definition language in its own right. The eleven basic data types defined in RFC 2578 are shown in Table 8.1. In addition to these scalar objects, it is also possible to impose a tabular structure on an ordered collection of MIB objects using the SEQUENCE OF construct; see [RFC 2578] for details. Most of the data types in Table 8.1 will be familiar (or self-explanatory) to most readers. The one data type we will discuss in more detail shortly is the OBJECT IDENTIFIER data type, which is used to name an object.

SMI higher-level constructs.   In addition to the basic data types, the SMI data definition language also provides higher-level language constructs:

The OBJECT-TYPE construct is used to specify the data type, status, and semantics of a managed object. Collectively, these managed objects contain the management data that lie at the heart of network management. There are nearly 10,000 defined objects in various Internet RFC's [RFC 2570]. The OBJECT-TYPE construct has four clauses. The SYNTAX clause of an OBJECT-TYPE definition specifies the basic data type associated with the object. The MAX-ACCESS clause specifies whether the managed object can be read, be written, be created, or have its value included in a notification. The STATUS clause indicates whether

Table 8.1   Basic data types of the SMI

Data type	Description
INTEGER	32 bit integer, as defined in ASN.1, with a value between -2^{31} and $2^{31}-1$ inclusive, or a value from a list of possible named constant values
Integer32	32 bit integer with a value between [ms]2^{31} and $2^{31}-1$ inclusive
Unsigned32	Unsigned 32 bit integer in the range 0 to $2^{23}-1$ inclusive
OCTET STRING	ASN.1-format byte string representing arbitrary binary or textual data, up to 65535 bytes long
OBJECT IDENTIFIER	ASN.1-format administratively assigned (structured name); see Section 8.3
IPaddress	32-bit Internet address, in network byte order
Counter32	32-bit counter that increases from 0 to $2^{32}-1$ and then wraps around to 0.
Counter64	64-bit counter
Gauge32	32-bit integer that will not count above $2^{31}-2$ nor decrease beyond 0 when increased or decreased
TimeTicks	time, measured in 1/100ths of seconds since some event
Opaque	uninterpreted ASN.1 string, needed for backward compatibility

object definition is current and valid, obsolete (in which case it should not be implemented, as its definition is included for historical purposes only) or deprecated (obsolete, but implementable for interoperability with older implementations). The DESCRIPTION clause contains a human-readable textual definition of the object; this "documents" the purpose of the managed object and should provide all the semantic information needed to implement the managed object.

As an example of the OBJECT-TYPE construct, consider the `ipInDelivers` object type definition from [RFC 2011]. This object defines a 32-bit counter that keeps track of the number of IP datagrams that were received at the managed node and were successfully delivered to an upper layer protocol. The final line of this definition is concerned with the name of this object, a topic we will consider in the following section.

```
ipInDelivers OBJECT-TYPE
    SYNTAX       Counter32
    MAX-ACCESS   read-only
    STATUS       current
    DESCRIPTION
            "The total number of input datagrams
            successfully delivered to IP user-protocols
            (including ICMP)."
    ::= { ip 9 }
```

The MODULE-IDENTITY construct allows related objects to be grouped together within a "module." For example, [RFC 2011] specifies the MIB module that defines managed objects (including `ipInDelivers`) for managing implementations of the Internet Protocol (IP) and its associated Internet Control Message Protocol (ICMP). [RFC 2012] specifies the MIB module for TCP and [RFC 2013] specifies the MIB module for UDP. [RFC 2021] defines the MIB module for RMON remote monitoring. In addition to containing the OBJECT-TYPE definitions of the managed objects within the module, the MODULE-IDENTITY construct contains clauses to document contact information of the author of the module, the date of the last update, a revision history, and a textual description of the module. As an example, consider the module definition for management of the IP protocol:

```
ipMIB MODULE-IDENTITY
    LAST-UPDATED "9411010000Z"
    ORGANIZATION "IETF SNMPv2 Working Group"
    CONTACT-INFO
            "       Keith McCloghrie

            Postal: Cisco Systems, Inc.
                    170 West Tasman Drive
                    San Jose, CA 95134-1706
                    US

            Phone:  +1 408 526 5260
            E-mail: kzm@cisco.com"

    DESCRIPTION
            "The MIB module for managing IP and ICMP
            implementations, but excluding their management
            of IP routes."
    REVISION "9103310000Z"
    DESCRIPTION
            "The initial revision of this MIB module was part
            of MIB-II."
    ::= { mib-2 48}
```

The NOTIFICATION-TYPE construct is used to specify information regarding "SNMPv2-Trap" and "InformationRequest" messages generated by an agent, or a managing entity; see Section 8.3.3. This information includes a textual DESCRIPTION of when such messages are to be sent, as well as list of values to be included in the message generated; see [RFC 2578] for details.

The MODULE-COMPLIANCE construct defines the set managed objects within a module that an agent must implement.

The AGENT-CAPABILITIES construct specifies the capabilities of agents with respect to object and event notification definitions.

8.3.2 Management Information Base: MIB

As noted above, the **Management Information Base, MIB,** can be thought of as a virtual information store, holding managed objects whose values collectively reflect the current "state" of the network. These values may be queried and/or set by a managing entity by sending SNMP messages to the agent that is executing in a managed node on behalf of the managing entity. Managed objects are specified using the OBJECT-TYPE SMI construct discussed above and gathered into **MIB modules** using the MODULE-IDENTITY construct.

The IETF has been busy standardizing the MIB modules (that is, the management information) associated with routers, hosts, and other network equipment. This includes basic identification data about a particular piece of hardware, and management information about the device's network interfaces and protocols. As of the release of SNMPv3 (mid-1999), there were nearly 100 standards-based MIB modules and an even larger number of vendor-specific (private) MIB modules. With all of these standards, the IETF needed a way to identify and name the standardized modules, as well as the specific managed objects within a module. Rather than start from scratch, the IETF adopted a standardized object identification (naming) framework that had already been put in place by the International Organization for Standardization (ISO). As is the case with many standards bodies, the ISO had "grand plans" for their standardized object identification framework—to identify every possible standardized object (for example, data format, protocol, or piece of information) in any network, regardless of the network standards organization (for example, Internet IETF, ISO, IEEE, or ANSI), equipment manufacturer, or network owner. A lofty goal indeed! The object identification framework adopted by ISO is part of the ASN.1 (Abstract Syntax Notation One) [ISO 1987, ISO X.680] object definition language (see Section 8.4). Standardized MIB modules have their own cozy corner in the all encompassing naming framework, as discussed below.

As shown in Figure 8.3, objects are named in the ISO naming framework in a hierarchical manner. Note that each branch point in the tree has both a name and a number (shown in parentheses); any point in the tree is thus identifiable by the sequence of names or numbers that specify the path from the root to that point in the identifier tree. A fun, but incomplete and unofficial, WWW-based utility for traversing part of the object identifier tree (using branch information contributed by volunteers) is http://www.alvestrand.no/harald/objectid/top.html.

At the top of the hierarchy are the International Organization for Standardization (ISO) and the Telecommunication Standardization Sector of the International Telecommunication Union (ITU-T), the two main standards organizations dealing with ASN.1, as well as a branch for joint efforts by these two organizations. Under the ISO branch of the tree, we find entries for all ISO standards (1.0) and for standards issued by standards bodies of various ISO-member countries (1.2). Although not shown in Figure 8.3, under (ISO ISO-Member-Body, a.k.a. 1.2) we would find USA (1.2.840), under which we would find a number of IEEE, ANSI, and company-specific standards. These include RSA (1.2.840.11359) and Microsoft (1.2.840.113556), under which we find the Microsoft File Formats (1.2.840.112556.4) for various Microsoft products, such as Word (1.2.840.11356.4.2). But we are interested here in networking (*not* Microsoft Word files), so let us turn our attention to the branch labeled 1.3, the standards issued by bodies recognized by the ISO. These include the U.S. Department of Defense (6) (under which we will find the Internet standards), the Open Software Foundation (22), the airline association SITA (69) and NATO-identified bodies (57), as well as many other organizations.

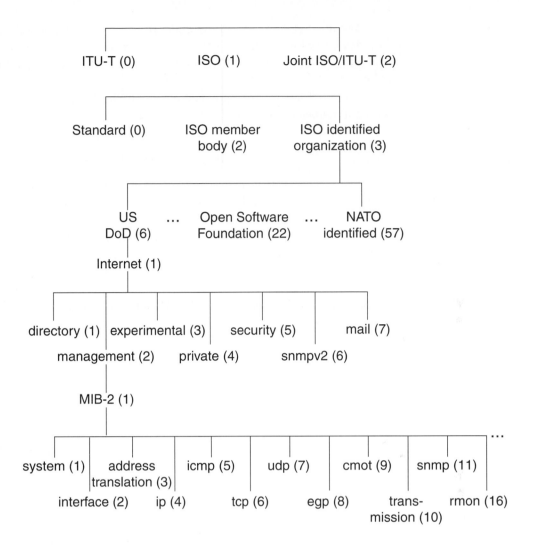

FIGURE 8.3   ASN.1 Object identifier tree

Under the `Internet` branch of the tree (1.3.6.1), there are seven categories. Under the `private` (1.3.6.1.4) branch, we will find a list [IANA 1999b] of the names and private enterprise codes of more than 4000 private companies that have registered with the Internet Assigned Numbers Authority (IANA) [IANA 1999]. Under the `management` (1.3.6.1.2) and `MIB-2` branch (1.3.6.1.2.1) of the object identifier tree, we find the definitions of the standardized MIB modules.

Standardized MIB modules.   The lowest level of the tree in Figure 8.3 shows some of the important hardware-oriented MIB modules (`system` and `inter-face`) as well as modules associated with some of the most important Internet protocols. [RFC 2400] lists all of the standardized MIB modules. While MIB-related RFC's make for rather tedious and dry reading, it is instructive (that is, like eating vegetables, it is "good for you") to consider a few MIB module definitions to get a flavor for the type of information in a module.

The managed objects falling under `system` contain general information about the device being managed; all managed devices must support the system MIB objects. Table 8.2 defines the objects in the system group, as defined in [RFC 1213].

Table 8.3 defines the managed objects in the MIB module for the UDP protocol at a managed entity.

8.3.3 SNMP Protocol Operations and Transport Mappings

The Simple Network Management Protocol Version 2 (SNMPv2) [RFC 1905] is used to convey MIB information that has been specified in the SMI among managing entities and agents executing on behalf of managing entities. The most common usage of SNMP is in a **request-response mode** in which an SNMPv2 managing entity sends a request to an SNMPv2 agent, who receives the request, performs some action, and sends a reply to the request. Typically, a request will be used to query (retrieve) or modify (set) MIB object values associated with a managed device. A second common usage of SNMP is for an agent to send an unsolicited message, known as a **trap message,** to a managing entity. Trap messages are used to notify a managing entity of an exceptional situation that has resulted in changes to MIB object values. We saw earlier in Section 8.1 that the network administrator might want to receive a trap message, for example, when an interface goes down, congestion reaches a predefined level on a link, or some other noteworthy event

Table 8.2   Managed objects in the MIB-2 system group

Object Identifier	Name	Type	Description (from RFC 1213)
1.3.6.1.2.1.1.1	sysDescr	OCTET STRING	"full name and version identification of the system's hardware type, software operating-system, and networking software"
1.3.6.1.2.1.1.2	sysObjectID	OBJECT IDENTIFIER	Vendor assigned object ID that "provides an easy and unambiguous means for determining 'what kind of box' is being managed."
1.3.6.1.2.1.1.3	sysUpTime	TimeTicks	"The time (in hundredths of a second) since the network management portion of the system was last re-initialized."
1.3.6.1.2.1.1.4	sysContact	OCTET STRING	"The contact person for this managed node, together with information on how to contact this person."
1.3.6.1.2.1.1.5	sysName	OCTET STRING	"An administratively assigned name for this managed node. By convention, this is the node's fully qualified domain name"
1.3.6.1.2.1.1.6	sysLocation	OCTET STRING	"The physical location of this node."
1.3.6.1.2.1.1.7	sysServices	Integer32	A coded value that indicates the set of services available at this node: physical (for example, a repeater), datalinkl/subnet (for example, bridge), Internet (for example, IP gateway), end-end (for example, host), applications.

Table 8.3   Managed objects in the MIB-2 udp module

Object Identifier	Name	Type	Description (from RFC 2013)
1.3.6.1.2.1.7.1	udpInDatagrams	Counter32	"total number of UDP datagrams delivered to UDP users"
1.3.6.1.2.1.7.2	udpNoPorts	Counter32	"total number of received UDP datagrams for which there was no application at the destination port"
1.3.6.1.2.1.7.3	udpInErrors	Counter32	"number of received UDP datagrams that could not be delivered for reasons other than the lack of an application at the destination port"
1.3.6.1.2.1.7.4	udpOutDatagrams	Counter32	"total number of UDP datagrams sent from this entity"
1.3.6.1.2.1.7.5	udpTable	SEQUENCE of UdpEntry	a sequence of UdpEntry objects, one for each port that is currently open by an application, giving the IP address and the port number used by application

occurs. Note that there are a number of important tradeoffs between polling (request-response interaction) and trapping; see the homework problems.

SNMPv2 defines seven types of messages, known generically as Protocol Data Units—PDUs, as shown in Table 8.4. The format of the PDU is shown in Figure 8.4. The `GetRequest`, `GetNextRequest`, and `GetBulkRequest` PDUs are all sent from a managing entity to an agent to request the value of one or more MIB objects at the agent's managed device. The object identifiers of the MIB

Table 8.4   SNMPv2 PDU types

SNMPv2 PDU Type	sender-receiver	Description
`GetRequest`	manager-to-agent	get value of one or more MIB object instances
`GetNextRequest`	manager-to-agent	get value of next MIB object instance in list or table
`GetBulkRequest`	manager-to-agent	get values in large block of data, for example values in a large table
`InformRequest`	manager-to-manager	inform remote managing entity of MIB values remote to its access
`SetRequest`	manager-to-agent	set value of one or more MIB object instances
`Response`	agent-to-manager or manager-to-manager	generated in response to `GetRequest`, `GetNextRequest`, `GetBulkRequest`, `SetRequestPDU`, or `InformRequest`
SNMPv2-Trap	agent-to-manager	inform manager of an exceptional event

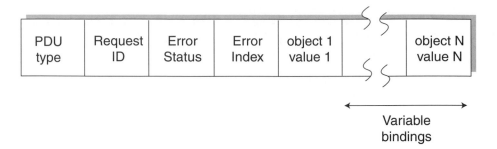

PDU type	Request ID	Error Status	Error Index	object 1 value 1		object N value N

FIGURE 8.4   SNMP PDU format

objects whose values are being requested are specified in the variable binding portion of the PDU. `GetRequest`, `GetNextRequest`, and `GetBulkRequest` differ in the granularity of their data requests. `GetRequest` can request an arbitrary set of MIB values; multiple `GetNextRequests` can be used to sequence through a list or table of MIB objects; `GetBulkRequest` allows a large block of data to be returned, avoiding the overhead incurred if multiple `GetRequest` or `GetNext-Request` messages were to be sent. In all three cases, the agent responds with a `Response` PDU containing the object identifiers and their associated values.

The `SetRequest` PDU is used by a managing entity to set the value of one or more MIB objects in a managed device. An agent replies with a `Response` PDU with the 'noError' Error Status to confirm that the value has indeed been set.

The `InformRequest` PDU is used by a managing entity to notify another managing entity of MIB information that is remote to the receiving entity. The receiving entity replies with a `Response` PDU with the 'noError' Error Status to acknowledge receipt of the `InformRequest` PDU.

Given the request-response nature of SNMPv2, it is worth noting here that although SNMP PDUs can be carried via many different transport protocols, the SNMP PDU is typically carried in the payload of a UDP datagram. Indeed, [RFC 1906] states that UDP is "the preferred transport mapping." Since UDP is an unreliable transport protocol, there is no guarantee that a request, or its response will be received at the intended destination. The Request ID field of the PDU is used by the managing entity to number its requests to an agent; an agent's response takes its Request ID from that of the received request. Thus, the Request ID field can be used by the managing entity to detect lost requests or replies. It is up to the managing entity to decide whether to retransmit a request if no corresponding response is received after a given amount of time. In particular, the SNMP standard does not mandate any particular procedure for retransmission, or even if retransmission is to be done in the first place. It only requires that the managing entity "needs to act responsibly in respect to the frequency and duration of retransmissions." This, of course, leads one to wonder how a "responsible" protocol should behave!

The final type of SNMPv2 PDU is the trap message. Trap message are generated asynchronously, that is, *not* in response to a received request but rather in response to an event for which the managing entity requires notification. [RFC

1907] defines well-known trap types that include a cold or warm start by a device, a link going up or down, the loss of a neighbor, or an authentication failure event. A received trap request has no required response from a managing entity.

8.3.4 Security and Administration.

The designers of SNMPv3 have said that "SNMPv3 can be thought of as SNMPv2 with additional security and administration capabilities" [RFC 2570]. Certainly, there are changes in SNMPv3 over SNMPv2, but nowhere are those changes more evident than in the area of administration and security.

As SNMP has matured through three versions, its functionality has grown but so too, alas, has the number of SNMP-related standards documents. This is evidenced by the fact that there is even now an RFC [RFC 2571] that " describes an architecture for describing SNMP Management Frameworks"! While the notion of an "architecture" for "describing a framework" might be a bit much to wrap one's mind around, the goal of RFC 2571 is an admirable one—to introduce a common language for describing the functionality and actions taken by an SNMPv3 agent or managing entity. The architecture of an SNMPv3 entity is straightforward, and a tour through the architecture will serve to solidify our understanding of SNMP.

The so-called **SNMP applications** consist of a command generator, notification receiver, and proxy forwarder (all of which are typically found in a managing entity); a command responder and notification originator (both of which are typically found in an agent); and the possibility of other applications. The command generator generates the `GetRequest`, `GetNextRequest`, `GetBulkRequest`, and `SetRequest` PDUs that we examined in Section 8.3.3 and handles the received responses to these PDUs. The command responder executes in an agent and receives, processes, and replies (using the `Response` message) to received `GetRequest`, `GetNextRequest`, `GetBulkRequest`, and `SetRequest` PDUs. The notification originator application in an agent generates `Trap` PDUs; these PDUs are eventually received and processed in a notification receiver application at a managing entity. The proxy forwarder application forwards request, notification, and response PDUs.

A PDU sent by an SNMP application next passes through the SNMP "engine" before it is sent via the appropriate transport protocol. Figure 8.5 shows how a PDU generated by the command generator application first enters the dispatch module, where the SNMP version is determined. The PDU is then processed in the message processing system, where the PDU is wrapped in a message header containing the SNMP version number, a message ID and message size information. If encryption or authentication is needed, then the appropriate header fields for this information are included as well; see [RFC 2571] for details. Finally, the SNMP message (the application-generated PDU plus the message header information) is passed to the appropriate transport protocol. The preferred transport protocol for carrying SNMP messages is UDP (that is, SNMP messages are carried as the payload in a UDP datagram), and the preferred port number for the SNMP is port 161.

We have seen above that SNMP messages are used to not just monitor, but also to control (for example, through the `SetRequest` command) network elements.

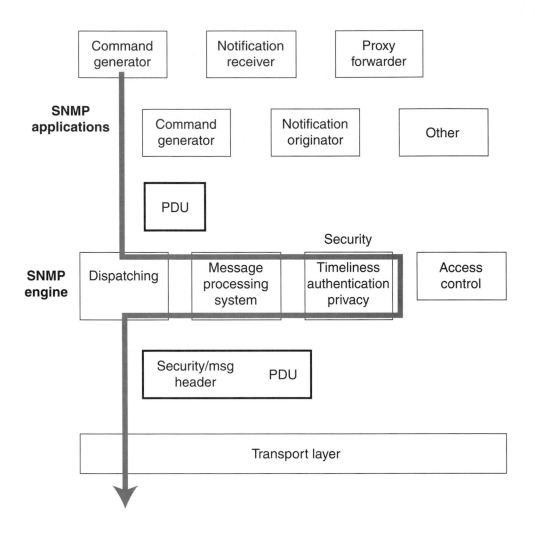

FIGURE 8.5   SNMPv3 engine and applications

Clearly, an intruder that could intercept SNMP messages and/or generate its own SNMP packets into the management infrastructure could wreak havoc in the network. Thus, it is crucial that SNMP messages be transmitted securely. Surprisingly, it is only in the most recent version of SNMP that security has received the attention that it deserves. SNMPv3 provides for encryption, authentication, protection against playback attacks (see Sections 7.2 and 7.3), and access control. SNMPv3 security is known as **user-based security** [RFC 2574] in that there is the traditional concept of a user, identified by a user name, with which security information such as a password, key value, or access privileges are associated.

- *Encryption.* SNMP PDUs can be encrypted using the Data Encryption Standard (DES) in cipher block chaining mode; see Section 7.2 for a discussion of DES. Note that since DES is a shared key system, the secret key of the user encrypting data must be known at the receiving entity that must decrypt the data.

- *Authentication.* SNMP combines the use of a hash function, such as the MD5 algorithm that we studied in Section 7.4, with a secret key value to provide both authentication and protection against tampering. The approach, known as HMAC (Hashed Message Authentication Codes) [RFC 2104] is conceptually simple. Suppose the sender has an SNMP PDU, m, that it wants to send to the receiver. This PDU may have already been encrypted. Suppose also that both the sender and receiver know a shared secret key, K, which need not be the same key used for encryption. The sender will send m to the receiver. However, rather than sending along a simple Message Integrity Code (MIC), $MIC(m)$, that has been computed over m (see Section 7.4.2) to protect against tampering, the sender appends the shared secret key to m and computes a MIC, $MIC(m,K)$ over the combined PDU and key. The value $MIC(m,K)$ (but not the secret key!) is then transmitted along with m. When the receiver receives m, it appends the secret key K and computes $MIC(m,K)$. If this computed value matches the transmitted value of $MIC(m,K)$, then the receiver knows not only that the message has not been tampered with, but also that the message was sent by someone who knows the value of K, that is, by a trusted, and now authenticated, sender. In operation, HMAC actually performs the append-and-hash operation twice, using a slightly modified key value each time; see [RFC 2104] for details.

■ *Protection against playback.* Recall from our discussion in Chapter 7 that nonces can be used to guard against playback attacks. SNMPv3 adopts a related approach. In the SNMP scenario, the message receiver wants to insure that a received message is not a replay of some earlier message. In order to assure this, the receiver requires that the sender include a value in each message that is based on a counter in the *receiver.* This counter, which functions as a nonce, reflects the amount of time since the last reboot of the receiver's network management software and the total number of reboots since the receiver's network management software was last configured. As long as the counter in a received message is within some margin of error from the receiver's actual value, the message is accepted as a non-replay message, at which point is may be authenticated and/or decrypted. See [RFC 2574] for details.

■ *Access control.* SNMPv3 provides a view based access control [RFC 2575] that controls which network management information can be queried and/or set by which users. An SNMP entity retains information about access rights and policies in a Local Configuration Datastore (LCD). Portions of the LCD are themselves accessible as managed objects, defined in the View-based Access Control Model Configuration MIB [RFC 2575], and thus can be managed and manipulated remotely via SNMP.

8.4   ASN.1

In this book we have covered a number of interesting topics in computer networking. This section on ASN.1, however, may not make the top-10 list of interesting topics. Like vegetables, knowledge about ASN.1 and the broader issue of presentation services is something that is "good for you." ASN.1 is an ISO-originated standard that is used in a number of Internet related protocols, particularly in the area of network management. For example, we saw in Section 8.2 that MIB variables in SNMP were inextricably tied to ASN.1. So while the material on ASN.1 in this section may be rather dry, the reader will hopefully take it on faith that the material *is* important.

In order to motivate our discussion here, consider the following thought experiment. Suppose one could reliably copy data from one computer's memory directly into another remote computer's memory. If one could do this, would the communication problem be "solved"? The answer to the question depends on one's definition of "the communication problem." Certainly, a perfect memory-to-memory copy would exactly communicate the bits and bytes from one machine to another. But does such an exact copy of the bits and bytes mean that when software running on the receiving computer accesses this data, it will see the same values that were stored into the sending computer's memory? The answer to this question is "not necessarily"! The crux of the problem is that different computer architectures, different operating systems, and compilers have different conventions for storing and representing data. If data is to be communicated and stored among multiple computers (as it is in every communication network!), this problem of data representation must clearly solved.

As an example of this problem, consider the simple C code fragment below. How might this structure be laid out in memory?

```
struct {
  char code;
  int x;
  } test;
  test.x = 259;
  text.c = 'a';
```

The left side of Figure 8.6 shows a possible layout of this data on one hypothetical architecture: there is a single byte of memory containing the character 'a', followed by a 16-bit word containing the integer value 259, stored with the most significant byte first. The layout in memory on another computer is shown in the right half of Figure 8.6. The character 'a' is followed by the integer value stored with the least significant byte stored first and with the 16-bit integer aligned to start on a 16-bit word boundary. Certainly, if one were to perform a

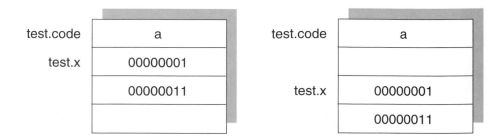

FIGURE 8.6 Two different data layouts on two different architectures

verbatim copy between these two computers' memories and use the same structure definition to access the stored values, one would see very different results on the two computers!

The problem of different architectures having a different internal data format is a real and pervasive problem. The particular problem of integer storage in different formats in different architectures is so common that it has a name. "Big-endian" order for storing integers has the most significant bytes of the integer stored first (at the lowest storage address). "Little-endian" order stores the least significant bytes first. Sun SPARC and Motorola processors are big-endian, while Intel and DEC Alpha processors are little-endian. As an aside, the terms "big-endian" and "little-endian" come from the book, "Gulliver's Travels" by Jonathan Smith, in which two groups of people dogmatically insist on doing a simple thing in two different ways (hopefully, the analogy to the computer architecture community is clear). One group in the land of Lilliput insists on breaking their eggs at the larger end ("the big-endians"), while other insists on breaking them at the smaller end. The difference was the cause of great civil strife and rebellion.

Given that different computers store and represent data in different ways, how should networking protocols deal with this? For example, if an SNMP agent is about to send a `Response` message containing the integer count of the number of received UDP datagrams, how should it represent the integer value to be sent to the managing entity—in big-endian or little-endian order? One option would be for the agent to send the bytes of the integer in the same order in which they would be stored in the managing entity. Another option would be for the agent to send in its own storage order and have the receiving entity reorder the bytes, as needed. Either option would require the sender or receiver to learn the other's format for integer representation.

A third option is to have a machine-, OS-, language-independent method for describing integers and other data types (that is, a data description language) and rules that state the manner in which each of the data types are to be transmitted over the network. When data of a given type is received, it is received in a known format and can then be stored in whatever machine-specific format is required. Both the SMI that we studied in Section 8.3 and ASN.1 adopt this third option. In ISO parlance, these two standards describe a **presentation service**—the service of transmitting and translating information from one machine-specific format to another. Figure 8.7 illustrates a real-world presentation problem; neither receiver understands the essential idea being communicated—that the speaker likes something. As shown in Figure 8.8, a presentation service can solve this problem by translating the idea into a commonly understood (by the presentation service), person-independent language, sending that information to the receiver, and then translating into a language understood by the receiver.

Table 8.5 shows a few of the ASN.1 defined data types. Recall that we encountered the INTEGER, OCTET STRING, and OBJECT IDENTIFIER data types in our earlier study of the SMI. Since our goal here is (mercifully) not to provide a complete introduction to ASN.1, we refer the reader to the standards or to the printed and on-line book [Larmouth 1996] for a description of ASN.1 types and constructors such as SEQUENCE and SET that allow for the definition of more structures.

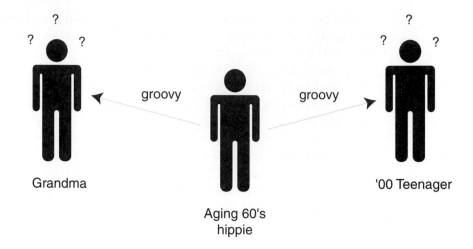

FIGURE 8.7   The presentation problem

In addition to providing a data description language, ASN.1 also provides **Basic Encoding Rules (BER)** that specify how instances of objects that have been defined using the ASN.1 data description language are to be sent over the network. The BER adopts a so-called **TLV (Type, Length, Value) approach** to encoding data for transmission. For each data item to be sent, the data type, the length of the data item, and then the actual value of the data item are sent, in that order. With this simple convention, the received data is essentially self identifying.

Figure 8.9 shows how the two data items in a simple example would be sent. In this example, the sender wants to send the character string 'smith' followed by the value 259 decimal (which equals 00000001 00000011 in binary, or a byte value of 1 followed by a byte value of 3) assuming big-endian order. The first byte

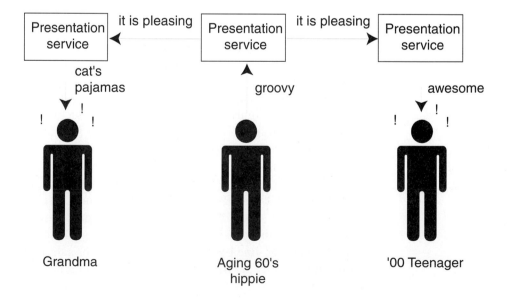

FIGURE 8.8   The presentation problem solved

Table 8.5   Selected ASN.1 data types

Tag	Type	Description
1	BOOLEAN	value is "true" or "false"
2	INTEGER	can be arbitrarily large
3	BITSTRING	list of one or more bits
4	OCTET STRING	list of one or more bytes
5	NULL	no value
6	OBJECT IDENTIFIER	name, in the ASN.1 standard naming tree, see Section 8.2.2
9	REAL	floating point

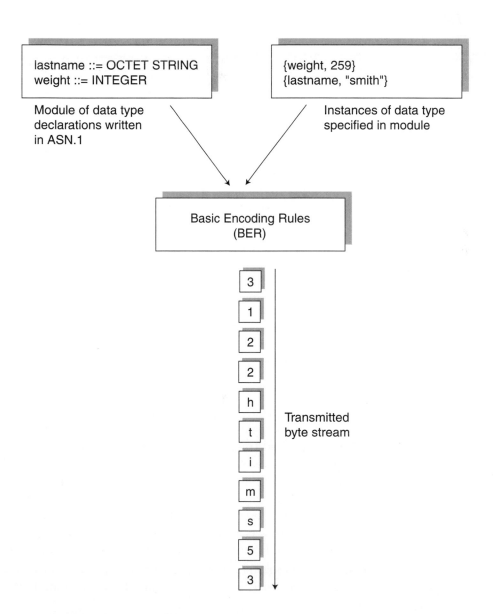

FIGURE 8.9   BER encoding example

in the transmitted stream has the value 3, indicating that the type of the following data item is an OCTET STRING; this is the 'T' in the TLV encoding. The second byte in the stream contains the length of the OCTET STRING, in this case 5. The third byte in the transmitted stream begins the OCTET STRING of length five; it contains the ASCII representation of the letter 's'. The T, L, and V values of the next data item are 2 (the INTEGER type tag value), 2 (that is, an integer of length 2 bytes), and the two-byte big-endian representation of the value 259 decimal.

In our discussion above, we have only touched on a small and simple subset of ASN.1. Resources for learning more about ASN.1 include the ASN.1 standards document [ISO 1987, ISOX.680], Philipp Hoschka's ASN.1 homepage [Hoschka 1997], and [Larmouth 1996].

8.5   FIREWALLS

In motivating the need for security in Chapter 7, we noted that the Internet is not a very "safe" place—ne'er-do-wells are "out there" breaking into networks at an alarming rate. (For a summary of reported attacks, see the CERT Coordination Center [CERT 1999]. For a discussion of nearly 300 known attacks that firewalls, the topic we consider here, are designed to thwart, see [Newman 1998].) As a result, network administrators must not only be concerned with keeping the bits flowing smoothly through their network, but also with securing their network infrastructure from outside threats.

We've seen that SNMPv3 provides authentication, encryption, and access control in order to secure network management functions. While this is important (certainly, the network administrator does not want others to gain access to network management functionality), it is only a small part of the network administrator's security concerns. In addition to monitoring and controlling the components of one's network, a network administrator also wants to exclude unwanted traffic (that is, intruders) from the managed network. This is where firewalls come in. A **firewall** is a combination of hardware and software that isolates an organization's internal network from the Internet at large, allowing specific connections to pass and blocking others. Organizations employ firewalls for one or more of the following reasons:

- *To prevent intruders from interfering with the daily operation of the internal network.* An organization's competitor—or just some Internet prankster looking for a good time—can wreak havoc on an unsecured network. In the denial-of-service attack, an intruder monopolizes a critical network resource, bringing the internal network (at its network administrator) to its knees. An example of a denial of service attack is so-called **SYN flooding,** in which the attacker sends forged TCP connection-establishment segments to a particular host. The host sets aside buffer space for each connection, and within minutes there is no TCP buffer space left for "honest" TCP connections.
- *To prevent intruders from deleting or modifying information stored within the internal network.* For example, an attacker can attempt to meddle with an

organization's public presence on a Web server—a successful attack may be seen by thousands of people in a matter of minutes. Attackers may also be able to obtain customer purchase card information from Web servers that provide Internet commerce (see Section 7.7).

- *To prevent intruders from obtaining secret information.* Most organizations have secret information that is stored on computers. This information includes trade secrets, product development plans, marketing strategies, personal employee records, and financial analysis.

The simplest firewall consists of a packet filter. More sophisticated firewalls consist of combinations of packet filters and application gateways.

8.5.1   Packet Filtering

An organization typically has a router that connects its internal network to its ISP (and hence to the Internet). All traffic leaving and entering the internal network passes through this router. Most router manufacturers provide options for filtering; when these options are turned on, the router becomes a filter in addition to a router. As the name implies, a **filter** lets some datagrams pass through the router and filters out other datagrams. Filtering decisions are typically based on:

- The IP address the data is (supposedly) coming from.
- IP destination address.
- TCP or UDP source and destination port.
- ICMP message type.
- Connection initialization datagrams using the TCP ACK bit.

As a simple example, a filter can be set to block all UDP segments and all Telnet connections. Such a configuration prevents outsiders from logging onto internal hosts using Telnet, insiders from logging onto external hosts using Telnet, and "weird" UDP traffic from entering or leaving the internal network. The router filters the UDP traffic by blocking all datagrams whose IP protocol field is set to 17 (corresponding to UDP); it filters all Telnet connections by blocking all TCP segments (each encapsulated in a datagram) whose source or destination port number is 23 (corresponding to Telnet). Filtering of UDP traffic is a popular policy for corporations—causing much chagrin to leading audio and video streaming vendors, whose products stream over UDP in the default mode. Filtering Telnet connections is also popular, as it prevents outside intruders from logging onto internal machines.

A filtering policy can also be based on the combination of addresses and port numbers. For example, the router can forward all Telnet packets (port 23) except those going to and coming from a list of specific IP addresses. This policy permits Telnet connections to and from hosts on the list. It is highly recommended to reject all datagrams that have internal source IP addresses—that is, packets that claim to be coming from internal hosts but are actually coming in from the outside. These packets are often part of address spoofing attacks, whereby the attacker is pretending to be coming from an internal machine. Unfortunately, basing the policy on external addresses provides no protection from an external host claiming to be a different external host.

Table 8.6   Header fields for inbound and outbound Telnet connections

Connection Origination	Packet Direction	Source IP Address	Destination IP Address	Source Port	Destination Port
Internal	Outbound	Internal	External	p	23
Internal	Inbound	External	Internal	23	p
External	Inbound	External	Internal	q	23
External	Outbound	Internal	External	23	q

Filtering can also be based on whether or not the TCP ACK bit is set. This trick is quite useful if an organization wants to let its internal clients connect to external servers, but wants to prevent external clients from connecting to internal servers. Recall from Section 3.4 that the first segment in every TCP connection has the ACK bit set to 0 whereas all the other segments in the connection have the ACK bit set to 1. Thus, if an organization wants to prevent external clients from initiating connections to internal servers, it simply filters all incoming segments with the ACK bit set to 0. This policy kills all TCP connections originating from the outside, but permits connections originating internally.

Now suppose an organization doesn't want to block all connections originating from outside; instead it just wants to block only the Telnet connections originating from outside. How can filtering accomplish this task? To see how filters handle this, let's look at how the fields are set for Telnet connections originating internally and Telnet connections originating externally (Table 8.6):

The p and q in the above table are the port numbers (> 1023) assigned to the client machines (see Section 3.1). From this table we see that the filter can block Telnet connections originating from outside by blocking inbound packets (external source address and internal destination address) with destination port 23; or by blocking outbound packets (internal source address and external destination address) with source port 23.

8.5.2   Application Gateways

Filters allow an organization to perform coarse-grain filtering on IP and TCP/UDP headers, including IP addresses, port numbers, and acknowledgment bits. We saw that filtering based on a combination of IP addresses and port numbers can allow internal clients to Telnet outside while preventing external clients from Telneting inside. But what if an organization wants to provide the Telnet service to a restricted set of internal users? Such a task is beyond the capabilities of a filter. Indeed, information about the identity of the internal users is not included in the IP/TCP/UDP headers, but is instead in the application-layer data.

In order to have a finer level security, firewalls must combine packet filters with application gateways. Application gateways look beyond the IP/TCP/UDP headers and actually make policy decisions based on application data. An **application gateway** is an application-specific server through which all application data (inbound and outbound) must pass. Multiple application gateways can run on the same host, but each gateway is a separate server with its own processes.

To get some insight into application gateways, let us design a firewall that allows only a restricted set of internal users to Telnet outside and prevents all external clients from Telneting inside. Such a policy can be accomplished by implementing a combination of a packet filter (in a router) and a Telnet application gateway, as shown in Figure 8.10. The filter is configured to block all Telnet connections except those that originate form the IP address of the application gateway. Such a filter configuration forces all outbound Telnet connections to pass through the application gateway. When a internal user wants to Telnet to the outside world, it first sets up a Telnet session with the gateway. The gateway prompts the user for its user id and password; when the user supplies this information, the gateway checks to see if the user has permission to Telnet to the outside world. If not, the gateway terminates the Telnet session. If the user has permission, then the gateway (1) prompts the user for the hostname of the external host to which the user wants to connect, (2) sets up a Telnet session between the gateway and the external host, (3) relays to the external host all data arriving from the user, and relays to the user all data arriving from the external host. Thus the Telnet application gateway not only performs user authorization but also acts as a Telnet server and a Telnet client. Note that the filter will permit step (2) because the application gateway initiates the Telnet connection.

Internal networks often have multiple application gateways, for example, gateways for Telnet, HTTP, FTP, and e-mail. In fact, an organization's mail server (see Section 2.4) and Web cache (see Section 2.9) are application gateways.

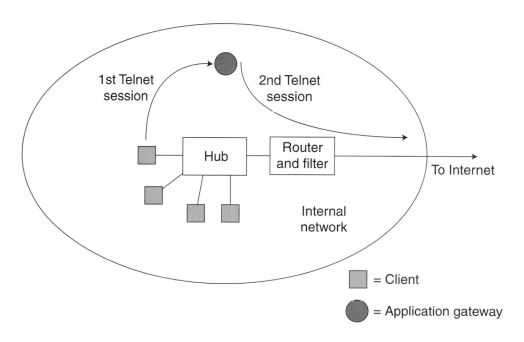

FIGURE 8.10   Firewall consisting of an application gateway and a filter

Application gateways do not come without their disadvantages. First, you need a different application gateway for each application, which requires installing and configuring a new server for each application. Second, either:

- the client software must know how to contact the gateway instead of the external server when the user makes a request, and must know how to tell the gateway what external server to connect to,
- or the user must explicitly connect to the external server through the gateway.

We conclude this section by mentioning that firewalls are by no means a panacea for all security problems. They introduce a tradeoff between the degree of communication with the outside world and level of security. Because filters can't stop spoofing of IP addresses and port numbers, filters often use an all or nothing policy (for example, banning all UDP traffic). Gateways can have software bugs, allowing attackers to penetrate them. Also, firewalls are even less effective if the internal users have wireless communication with the external world. For these reasons and others, firewalls remain controversial, with many security experts and network administrators being reluctant to use them.

SUMMARY

Our study of network management, and indeed of all of networking, is now complete!

In this final chapter on network management, we began by motivating the need for providing appropriate tools for the network administrator—the person whose job it is to keep the network "up and running"—for monitoring, testing, polling, configuring, analyzing, evaluating, and controlling the operation of the network. Our analogies with the management of complex systems such as power plants, airplanes, and human organization helped motivate this need. We saw that the architecture of network management systems revolve around five key components—(1) a network manager, (2) a set of managed remote (from the network manager) devices, (3) the management information bases (MIBs) at these devices, containing data about the device's status and operation, (4) remote agents that report MIB information and take action under the control of the network manager, and (5) a protocol for communicating between the network manager and the remote devices.

We then delved into the details of the Internet Network Management Framework, and the SNMP protocol in particular. We saw how SNMP instantiates the five key components of a network management architecture, and spent considerable time examining MIB objects, the SMI—the data definition language for specifying MIB's, and the SNMP protocol itself. Noting that the SMI and ASN.1 are inextricably tied together, and that ASN.1 plays a key role in the presentation layer in the ISO/OSI seven layer reference model, we then briefly examined ASN.1. Perhaps more important than the details of ASN.1 itself, was the noted need to provide for translation between machine-specific data formats in a network. While the ISO/OSI reference model explicitly acknowledges the important of this service by the existence of the presentation layer, we noted that this layer is absent in the Internet protocol stack. Finally, we concluded this chapter with a discussion of firewalls—a topic that falls within the realms of both security and network management. We saw how packet filtering and application-level gateways can be used to provide the network with some level of protection against unwanted intruders, perhaps allowing the network manager to sleep better at night, knowing the network is relatively safe from these intruders.

It is also worth noting that there are many topics in network management that we chose *not* to cover—topics such as fault identification and management, proactive anomaly detection, alarm correlation, and the larger issues of service management (for example, as opposed to network management). While important, these topics would form a text in their own right, and we refer the reader to the references noted in Section 8.1.

HOMEWORK PROBLEMS AND QUESTIONS

Chapter 8

Review Questions

1. Why would a network manager benefit from having network management tools? Describe five scenarios.

2. What are the five areas of network management defined by the ISO?

3. What is the difference between network management and service management?

4. Define the following terms: managing entity, managed device, management agent, MIB, network management protocol.

5. What is the role of the SMI in network management?

6. What is the purpose of the ASN.1 Object Identifier tree?

7. What is an important difference between a request-response message and a trap message in SNMP?

8. What are the seven message types used in SNMP?

9. What is meant by an "SNMP engine"?

10. What is the role of ASN.1 in the ISO/OSI reference model's presentation layer?

11. Does the Internet have a presentation layer? If not, how are concerns about differences in machine architectures, for example, the different representation of integers on different machines, addressed?

12. What is meant by TLV encoding?

13. What is the difference between using a filter, and using an application-level gateway approach in a firewall?

PROBLEMS

1. Consider the two ways in which communication occurs between a managing entity and a managed device: request-response mode and trapping. What are the pros and cons of these two approaches, in terms of (1) overhead, (2) notification time when exceptional events occur, and (3) robustness with respect to lost messages between the managing entity and the device?

2. In Section 8.3 we saw that it was preferable to transport SNMP messages in unreliable UDP datagrams. Why do you think the designers of SNMP chose UDP rather than TCP as the transport protocol of choice for SNMP?

3. What is the ASN.1 object identifier for the ICMP protocol (see Figure 8.3)?

4. Consider Figure 8.9. What would be the BER encoding of `{weight, 271}` `{lastname, "Jackson"}`?

DISCUSSION QUESTIONS

1. In addition to analogies to a power plant and an airplane cockpit, what is another analogy of a complex distributed system that needs to be controlled?

2. Consider the motivating scenario in Figure 8.1. What other activities do you think a network administrator might want to monitor? Why?

3. Read [RFC 789]. How might the ARPAnet crash of 1980 have been avoided (or its recovery simplified) if the ARPAnet's managers had today's network management tools?

References

A URL for the reference is provided wherever possible. Unfortunately, URLs can become out of date. Please consult the online version of this book for an up-to-date bibliography (and note that the hyperlinks in the on-line version of this book will take you directly to the URL).

[**@Home 1998**] @Home, "Frequently Asked Questions," http://www.home.com/support/ie/faq/faq.html

[**3Com 1999**] 3Com Corporation, "Network Interface Cards," http://www.3com.com/products/nics.html

[**Abbott 1999**] S. Abbott, "The Debate for Secure E-Commerce," *Performance Computing,* Feb. 1999, http://www.performancecomputing.com/features/9902f1.shtml

[**Abitz 1993**] P. Albitz and C. Liu, *DNS and BIND,* O'Reilly & Associates, Petaluma, CA, 1993.

[**Abramson 1970**] N. Abramson, "The Aloha System—Another Alternative for Computer Communications," *Proceedings of Fall Joint Computer Conference, AFIPS Conference,* p. 37, 1970.

[**Abramson 1985**] N. Abramson, "Development of the Alohanet," *IEEE Transactions on Information Theory,* Vol. IT-31, No. 3 (Mar. 1985), pp. 119–123.

[**ADSL 1998**] ADSL Forum, "ADSL Tutorial," http://www.adsl.com/adsl_tutorial.html

[**Ahn 1995**] J. S. Ahn, P. B. Danzig, Z. Liu, and Y. Yan, "Experience with TCP Vegas: Emulation and Experiment", *Proceedings of ACM SIGCOMM '95* (Boston, Aug. 1995), pp. 185–195. http://www.acm.org/sigcomm/sigcomm95/papers/ahn.html

[**Alliance 1999**] Gigabit Ethernet Alliance, http://www.gigabit-ethernet.org/

[**Almanac 1998**] Computer Industry Almanac, http://www.c-i-a.com/

[**ARIN 1996**] ARIN, "IP allocation report," ftp://rs.arin.net/netinfo/ip_network_allocations

[Ash 1998] G. R. Ash, *Dynamic Routing in Telecommunications Networks,* McGraw Hill, NY, NY, 1998.

[AT&T Apps 1998] AT&T, "Killer Apps," http://www.att.com/technology/forstudents/brainspin/networks/killerapps.html

[AT&T Bandwidth 1999] AT&T, "Bandwidth: The Need for Speed," http://www.att.com/technology/forstudents/brainspin/networks/bandwidth/game.html

[AT&T Optics 1999] AT&T, "What are fiber optics?," http://www.att.com/technology/forstudents/brainspin/fiberoptics/

[AT&T SLA 1999] AT&T, "AT&T raises the bar on data networking guarantees," http://www.att.com/press/0198/980127.bsc.html

[ATM Forum] The ATM Forum Web site, http://www.atmforum.com/

[ATM Forum 1996] ATM Forum, "Traffic Management 4.0," ATM Forum document af-tm-0056.0000. ftp://ftp.atmforum.com/pub/approved-specs/af-tm-0056.000.pdf

[ATM Forum 1997] ATM Forum. "Technical Specifications: Approved ATM Forum Specifications." http://www.atmforum.com/atmforum/specs/approved.html

[Baran 1964] P. Baran, "On Distributed Communication Networks," *IEEE Transactions on Communication Systems,* Mar. 1964. Rand Corporation Technical report with the same title (Memorandum RM-3420-PR, 1964). http://www.rand.org/publications/RM/RM3420/

[Berners-Lee 1989] T. Berners-Lee, CERN, "Information Management: A Proposal," Mar. 1989, May 1990. http://www.w3.org/History/1989/proposal.html

[Bertsekas 1991] D. Bertsekas and R. Gallagher, *Data Networks, 2nd Ed.,* Prentice Hall, Englewood Cliffs, NJ, 1991.

[Biersack 1992] E. W. Biersack, "Performance evaluation of forward error correction in ATM networks", *Proc. 1992 ACM Sigcomm Conference* (Baltimore, MD 1992), pp. 248–257.

[BIND] Internet Software Consortium page on BIND, http://www.isc.org/bind.html

[Blaze 1996] M. Blaze, W. Diffie, R. Rivest, B. Schneier, T. Shimomura, E. Thompson, and M. Weiner, "Minimal Key Lengths for Symmetric Ciphers to Provide Adequate Commercial Security," http://www.counterpane.com/keylength.html

[Bochman 84] G. V. Bochmann and C. A. Sunshine, "Formal methods in communication protocol design," *IEEE Transactions on Communications,* Vol. COM-28, No. 4 (Apr. 1980), pp. 624–631.

[Boggs 1988] D. Boggs, J. Mogul, and C. Kent, "Measured capacity of an Ethernet: myths and reality," *Proc ACM Sigcomm 1988* (Stanford, California), pp. 222–234

[Bolot 1994] J-C. Bolot and T. Turletti, "A rate control scheme for packet video in the Internet," *Proceedings of IEEE Infocom,* 1994, pp. 1216–1223.

[Bolot 1996] J-C. Bolot and Andreas Vega-Garcia, "Control Mechanisms for Packet Audio in the Internet," *Proceedings of IEEE Infocom,* 1996, pp. 232–239.

[Bradner 1996] S. Bradner, A. Mankin, *IPng: Internet Protocol Next Generation,* Addison Wesley, Reading, MA, 1996.

[Brakmo 1995] L. Brakmo and L. Peterson, "TCP Vegas: End to End Congestion Avoidance on a Global Internet," *IEEE Journal of Selected Areas in Communications,* Vol. 13, No. 8, pp. 1465–1480, Oct. 1995. ftp://ftp.cs.arizona.edu/xkernel/Papers/jsac.ps

[Brassil 1994] J. T. Brassil, A. K. Choudhury, N. F. Maxemchuk, "The Manhattan Street Network: A High Performance, Highly Reliable Metropolitan Area Network," *Computer Networks and ISDN Systems,* Mar. 1994.

[Brenner 1997] P. Brenner, "A Technical Tutorial on the IEEE802.11 Protocol," Breezecom Wireless Communications. http://sss-mag.com/pdf/802_11tut.pdf

[Brodnik 1997] A. Brodnik, S. Carlsson, M. Degemark, S. Pink, "Small Forwarding Tables for Fast Routing Lookups," *Proc. 1997 ACM Sigcomm Conference.* (Cannes, France), Oct. 1997, pp. 3–15. http://www.acm.org/sigs/sigcomm/sigcomm97/papers/p192.html

[Bush 1945] V. Bush, "As We May Think," *The Atlantic Monthly,* July 1945. http://www.theatlantic.com/unbound/flashbks/computer/bushf.htm

[Byers 1998] J. Byers, M. Luby, M. Mitzenmacher, A Rege, "A digital fountain approach to reliable distribution of bulk data," *Proc. 1998 ACM Sigcomm Conference* (Vancouver, 1998), pp. 56–67

[Cable 1998] Cable Data News, "Overview of Cable Modem Technology and Services," 1998. http://www.cabledatacomnews.com/cmic/cmic1.html

[Cain 1999] B. Cain, S. Deering, A. Thyagarajan, "Internet Group Management Protocol, Version 3," work in progress, Aug. 1999. http://info.internet.isi.edu:80/0/in-drafts/files/draft-ietf-idmr-igmp-v3-01.txt

[Casner 1992] Casner, S., Deering, S., "First IETF Internet Audiocast," *ACM SIGCOMM Computer Communications Review,* Vol. 22, No. 3 (July 1992), pp. 92–97. ftp://venera.isi.edu/pub/ietf-audiocast-article.ps

[Cerf 1974] V. Cerf and R. Kahn, "A Protocol for Packet Network Interconnection," *IEEE Transactions on Communications Technology,* Vol. COM-22, No. 5, pp. 627–641.

[Cert 1996] CERT, "Advisory CA-96.21: TCP SYN Flooding and IP Spoofing Attacks," http://www.cert.org/advisories/index.html

[Cert 1999] CERT, "CERT Summaries," http://www.cert.org/summaries/

[Chapman 1995] D. E. Chapman and E. D. Zwicky, *Building Internet Firewalls,* O'Reilly and Associates, Sebastopol, CA, 1995.

[Checkpoint 1999] Checkpoint Software Technologies Ltd. homepage, http://www.checkpoint.com

[Cheswick 1994] W. R. Cheswick and S. M. Bellovin, *Firewalls and Internet Security,* Addison Wesley, Reading, MA, 1994.

[Chiu 1989] D. Chiu and R. Jain, "Analysis of the Increase and Decrease Algorithms for Congestion Avoidance in Computer Networks," *Computer Networks and ISDN Systems,* Vol. 17, No. 1, pp. 1–14.

[Cisco 8500 1999] Cisco Systems Inc., "Catalyst 8500 Campus Switch Router Architecture," http://www.cisco.com/warp/public/cc/cisco/mkt/switch/cat/8500/tech/8510_wp.htm, 1999.

[Cisco 12000 1998] Cisco Systems, "Cisco 12000 Series Gigabit Switch Routers," http://www.cisco.com/warp/public/767/dspages/infoblast/infoblast/733/12000/12000_ov.htm, 1998.

[Cisco Addressing 1999] Cisco Systems Inc., "ATM Signaling and Addressing," July 1999. http://www.cisco.com/univercd/cc/td/doc/product/atm/c8540/wa5/12_0/12_3/net_tech/sig_addr.htm#12122

[Cisco Congestion 1999] Cisco Systems Inc., "Congestion Management Overview," http://www.cisco.com/univercd/cc/td/doc/product/software/ios120/12cgcr/qos_c/qcpart2/qcconman.htm

[Cisco IGRP 1997] Cisco Systems Inc, "Enhanced IGRP," http://www.cisco.com/univercd/cc/td/doc/cisintwk/ito_doc/en_igrp.htm

[Cisco LAN 1998] Cisco Systems Inc., "Designing Switched LAN Internetworks," http://www.cisco.com/univercd/cc/td/doc/cisintwk/idg4/nd2012.htm

[Cisco LAN Switches 1999] Cisco Systems Inc, "Lan Switches," http://www.cisco.com/warp/public/cc/cisco/mkt/switch/index.shtml

[Cisco QoS 1997] Cisco Systems Inc, "Advanced QoS Services for the Intelligent Internet." http://www.cisco.com/warp/public/732/net_enabled/qos_wp.htm

[Cisco Queue 1995] Cisco Systems Inc., "Interface Queue Management," http://www.cisco.com/warp/public/614/16.html

[Cisco Switches 1999] Cisco Systems Inc, "Next Generation ClearChannel Architecture for Catalyst 1900/2820 Ethernet Switches," http://www.cisco.com/warp/public/cc/cisco/mkt/switch/cat/c1928/tech/nwgen_wp.htm, 1999.

[Claffy 1998] K. Claffy, G. Miller, and K. Thompson, "The Nature of the Beast: Recent Traffic Measurements from the Internet Backbone," CAIDA Web site, http://www.caida.org/Papers/Inet98/index.html, 1998.

[Corman 1990] T. Corman, C. Leiserson, R. Rivest, *Introduction to Algorithms,* The MIT Press, Cambridge, Massachusetts, 1990.

[Crow 1997] B. Crow, I. Widjaja, J. Kim, P. Sakai, "IEEE 802.11 Wireless Local Area Networks," *IEEE Communications Magazine,* Sept. 1997, pp. 116–126.

[Crowcroft 1995] J. Crowcroft, Z. Wang, A. Smith, J. Adams, "A Comparison of the IETF and ATM Service Models," *IEEE Communications Magazine,* Nov./Dec. 1995, pp. 12–16. ftp://cs.ucl.ac.uk/darpa/atm-ietf.ps.Z

[Cybertrust 1999] Cybertrust Solutions homepage, http://www.cybertrust.com

[Daigle 1991] J. N. Daigle, *Queuing Theory for Telecommunications,* Addison-Wesley, Reading, MA, 1991.

[DEC 1990] Digital Equipment Corporation, "In Memoriam: J. C. R. Licklider 1915–1990," SRC Research Report 61, Aug. 1990. http://gatekeeper.dec.com/pub/DEC/SRC/research-reports/abstracts/src-rr-061.html

[Denning 1997] D. Denning (Editor), P. Denning (Preface), *Internet Besieged: Countering Cyberspace Scofflaws,* Addison-Wesley, Reading, MA, 1997.

[Deering 1991] S. Deering, "Multicast Routing in a Datagram Network," PhD thesis, Dept. of Computer Science, Stanford University, 1991.

[Deering 1996] S. Deering, D. Estrin, D. Faranacci, V. Jacobson, C. Liu, L. Wei, "The PIM Architecture for Wide Area Multicasting," *IEEE/ACM Transactions on Networking,* Vol. 4, No. 2, Apr. 1996.

[Demers 1990] A. Demers, S. Keshav, and S. Shenker, "Analysis and Simulation of a Fair Queuing Algorithm," *Internetworking: Research and Experience,* Vol. 1, No. 1, pp. 3–26, 1990.

[Diffie 1976] W. Diffie and M. E. Hellman, "New Directions in Cryptography," *IEEE Transactions on Information Theory,* IT-22: 644–654, 1976.

[Diffie 1998] W. Diffie and S. Landau, *Privacy on the Line, The Politics of Wiretapping and Encryption,* MIT Press, Cambridge MA, 1998.

[Diffserv 1999] The IETF Differentiated Services Working Group homepage, http://www.ietf.org/html.charters/diffserv-charter.html

[DNSNet] DNSNet page on DNS resources, http://www.dns.net/dnsrd/docs/

[Dodge 1999] M. Dodge, "An Atlas of Cyberspaces," http://www.cybergeography.org/atlas/isp_maps.html

[Doeringer 1996] W. Doeringer, G. Karjoth, M. Nassehi, "Routing on Longest Matching Prefixes," *IEEE/ACM Transactions on Networking,* Vol. 4, No. 1, pp. 86–97, Feb. 1996.

[EFF 1999] Electronic Frontier Foundation, "Cracking DES," http://www.eff.org/DEScracker/

[Estrin 1997] D. Estrin, M. Handley, A. Helmy, P. Huang, D. Thaler, "A Dynamic Bootstrap Mechanism for Rendezvous-based Multicast Routing," Technical Report, Department of Computer Science, USC. 1997. http://netweb.usc.edu/estrin

[Estrin 1998a] Deborah Estrin, David Meyer, David Thaler, "Border Gateway Multicast Protocol (BGMP): Protocol Specification," work in progress.

[Estrin 1998b] Deborah Estrin, V. Jacobson, D. Farinacci, L. Wei, Steve Deering, Mark Handley, David Thaler, Ching-Gung Liu, Puneet Sharma, A. Helmy, "Protocol Independent Multicast-Sparse Mode (PIM-SM): Motivation and Architecture," work in progress.

[Fall 1996] K. Fall, S. Floyd, "Simulation-based Comparisons of Tahoe, Reno and SACK TCP," *ACM Computer Communication Review,* Vol. 26, No. 3, pp. 5–21, July 1996. ftp://ftp.ee.lbl.gov/papers/sacks.ps.Z

[Feldmeier 1988] D. Feldmeier, "Improving Gateway Performance with a Routing Table Cache," *Proc. 1988 IEEE Infocom Conference* (New Orleans LA, Mar. 1988).

[Feldmeier 1995] D. Feldmeier, "Fast Software Implementation of Error Detection Codes," *IEEE/ACM Transactions on Networking,* Vol. 3., No. 6 (Dec. 1995), pp. 640–652.

[FIPS-46-1] US National Bureau of Standards, "Data Encryption Standard", Federal Information Processing Standard (FIPS) Publication 46-1, Jan. 1988.

[FIPS 1995] Federal Information Processing Standard, "Secure Hash Standard", FIPS Publication 180-1. http://www.itl.nist.gov/fipspubs/fip180-1.htm

[Fletcher 1982] J. G. Fletcher, "An Arithmetic Checksum for Serial Transmissions", *IEEE Transactions on Communications,* Vol. 30, No. 1 (Jan. 1982), pp. 247–253.

[Floyd 1991] S. Floyd, "Connections with Multiple Congested Gateways in Packet-Switched Networks, Part 1: One-Way Traffic," *ACM Computer Communications Review,* Vol. 21, No. 5, pp. 30–47, Oct. 1991. http://www-nrg.ee.lbl.gov/papers/gates1.pdf

[Floyd TCP 1994] S. Floyd, "TCP and Explicit Congestion Notification," *ACM Computer Communication Review,* Vol. 24, No. 5, pp. 10–23, Oct. 1994. ftp://ftp.ee.lbl.gov/papers/tcp_ecn.4.ps.Z

[Floyd Synchronization 1994] S. Floyd, V. Jacobson, "Synchronization of Periodic Routing Messages," *IEEE/ACM Transactions on Networking,* Vol. 2, No. 2, pp. 122–136, Apr. 1994. ftp://ftp.ee.lbl.gov/papers/synch_94.ps.Z

[Floyd 1997] S. Floyd, V. Jacobson, C. Liu, S. McCanne, and L. Zhang, "A Reliable Multicast Framework for Light-weight Sessions and Application Level Framing," *IEEE/ACM Transactions on Networking,* Dec. 1997, Vol. 5, No. 6, pp. 784–803.

[Fraser 1983] A. G. Fraser, "Towards a Universal Data Transport System," *IEEE Journal on Selected Areas in Communications,* SAC-1(5):803–816.

[Fraser 1993] A. G. Fraser (1993). "Early Experiments with Asynchronous Time Division Networks," *IEEE Network Magazine,* 7(1):12–27.

[Freephone 1999] "Freephone: Why use the Plain Old Telephone when you can get so much better on the Internet?" http://www-sop.inria.fr/rodeo/fphone/

[FRForum] Frame Relay Forum, http://www.frforum.com

[Fritz 1997] J. Fritz, "Demystifying ATM Addressing," *Byte Magazine,* Dec. 1997. http://www.byte.com/art/9712/sec4/art3.htm

[Frost 1994] J. Frost, "BSD Sockets: A Quick and Dirty Primer," http://world.std.com/~jimf/papers/sockets/sockets.html

[Garber 1999] L. Garber, "Steve Deering on IP Next Generation," *IEEE Computer,* pp. 11–13, Apr. 1999.

[Garcia-Luna 1993] J. J. Garcia-Lunes-Aceves, "Loop-free routing using diffusing computations," *IEEE/ACM Transactions on Networking,* Vol. 1, No. 1, pp. 130–141.

[Garey 1978] M. R. Garey, R. L. Graham, and D. S. Johnson, "The complexity of computing Steiner minimal trees," *SIAM Journal on Applied Mathematics,* Vol. 34, pp. 477–495, 1978.

[Garrett 1996] M. Garett, "A Service Architecture for ATM: From Applications to Scheduling," *IEEE Network Magazine,* pp. 6–14, May/June 1996.

[Gauthier 1999] L. Gauthier, C. Diot, and J. Kurose, "End-to-end Transmission Control Mechanisms for Multiparty Interactive Applications on the Internet," *Proceedings of IEEE Infocom 99,* Apr. 1999. ftp://ftp.sprintlabs.com/diot/infocom99-mimiaze.zip

[Gay 1997] V. Gay and B. Dervella, "MHEGAM—A Multimedia Messaging System," *IEEE Multimedia Magazine,* pp. 22–29, Oct.–Dec. 1997.

[Giacopelli 1990] J. Giacopelli, M. Littlewood, W. D. Sincoskie "Sunshine: A high performance self-routing broadband packet switch architecture," *1990 International Switching Symposium.*

[GigaAdapter] Data Communications, "Lan Gear," http://www.data.com/hot_products/lan_gear/alteon.html

[Gilligan 1996] R. Gilligan and R. Callon, "IPv6 Transition Mechanisms Overview," in *IPng: Internet Protocol Next Generation* (S. Bradner, A. Mankin, ed), Addison Wesley, Reading, MA, 1996.

[Girard 1990] A. Girard, *Routing and Dimensioning in Circuit-Switched Networks,* Addison Wesley, Reading, MA, 1990.

[Glitho 1995] R. Glitho and S. Hayes (eds.), special issue on Telecommunications Management Network, *IEEE Communications Magazine,* Vol. 33, No. 3 (Mar. 1995).

[Glitho 1998] R. Glitho, "Contrasting OSI Systems Management to SNMP and TMN," *Journal of Network and Systems Management,* Vol. 6, No. 2 (June 1998), pp. 113–131.

[Goodman 1997] D. Goodman (Chair), *The Evolution of Untethered Communications,* National Academy Press, Washington DC, Dec. 1997. http://www.nap.edu/readingroom/books/evolution/index.html

[Goralski 1999] W. Goralski, *Frame Relay for High-Speed Networks,* John Wiley, New York, 1999.

[Greenberg 1997] I. Greenberg, "The Future of the Living Room." http://www.cnet.com/Content/Features/Dlife/Living/index.html

[Gupta 1998] P. Gupta, S. Lin, N. McKeown. "Routing lookups in hardware at memory access speeds," *Proc. IEEE Infocom 1998,* pp. 1241–1248.

[GutmannLinks 1999] P. Gutman, "Security Resource Link Farm," http://www.cs.auckland.ac.nz/~pgut001/links.html

[GutmannTutorial 1999] P. Gutmann, "Godzilla Crypto Tutorial," http://www.cs.auckland.ac.nz/~pgut001/tutorial/index.html

[Hakimi 1971] S. L. Hakimi, "Steiner's problem in graphs and its implications," *Networks,* Vol. 1, pp. 113–133, 1971.

[Halabi 1997] B. Halabi, *Internet Routing Architectures,* Cisco Systems Publishing, Indianapolis, 1997.

[Hamada 1997] T. Hamada, H. Kamata, S. Hogg, "An Overview of the TINA Management Architecture," *Journal of Network and Systems Management,* Vol. 5. No. 4 (Dec. 1997). pp. 411–435.

[Haynal 1999] R. Haynal, "Internet Backbones," http://navigators.com/isp.html

[Heidemann 1997] J. Heidemann, K. Obraczka, and J. Touch, "Modeling the Performance of HTTP over Several Transport Protocols," *IEEE/ACM Transactions on Networking,* Vol. 5, No. 5, pp. 616–630, Oct. 1997.

[Hess 1998] C. Hess, D. Lin and K. Nahrstedt, "VistaMail: An Integrated Multimedia Mailing System," *IEEE Multimedia Magazine,* pp. 13–23, Oct.–Dec. 1988.

[Hill] Hill Associates Web site, http://www.hill.com

[Hobbes 1999] R. H. Zakon, "Hobbes Internet Timeline," Version 4.2, 1999. http://www.isoc.org/guest/zakon/Internet/History/HIT.html

[Hoe 1996] J. C. Hoe, "Improving the Start-up Behavior of a Congestion Control Scheme for TCP," *Proceedings of ACM SIGCOMM '96,* Stanford, Aug. 1996, pp. 270–280. http://www.acm.org/sigcomm/sigcomm96/papers/hoe.html

[Holbrook 1999] H. Holbrook, D. Cheriton, "IP Multicast Channels: EXPRESS Support for Large-Scale Single-Source Applications," *Proceedings of ACM Sigcomm '99* (Boston, MA, Aug. 1999). http://www.acm.org/sigs/sigcomm/sigcomm99/papers/session2-3.html

[Hoschka 1997] P. Hoschka, "ASN.1 homepage," http://www-sop.inria.fr/rodeo/personnel/hoschka/asn1.html

[Huffaker 1998] B. Huffaker, J. Jung, D. Wessels, and K. Claffy, "Visualization of the Growth and Topology of the NLANR Caching Hierarchy," http://squid.nlanr.net/Squid/, http://www.caida.org/Tools/Plankton/Paper/plankton.html, 1998.

[Hughes 1998] L. Hughes, *Internet E-mail: Protocols, Standards and Implementation,* Artech House, Norwood, MA, 1998.

[Huitema 1995] C. Huiteman, *Routing in the Internet,* Prentice Hall, Englewood Cliffs, New Jersey, 1995.

[Huitema 1997] C. Huitema, *IPv6: The New Internet Protocol,* Prentice Hall, Englewood Cliffs, NJ, 1997.

[IANA 1999] Internet Assigned Number Authority homepage, http://www.iana.org/

[IANA 1999b] Internet Assigned Number Authority, "Private Enterprise Numbers," ftp://ftp.isi.edu/in-notes/iana/assignments/enterprise-numbers

[IDMR 1998] IETF Interdomain Multicast Routing working group, homepage: http://www.ietf.org/html.charters/idmr-charter.html

[IEEE 802.5 1998] IEEE, "Token Ring Access Method (ISO/IEC 8802-5: 1998 and 8802-5: 1998/Amd 1)," 1998. See the 802.5 standards page at http://www.8025.org/802.5/documents/

[IEEE 802.3 1998] IEEE, "Carrier sense multiple access with collision detection (CSMA/CD) access method and physical layer specifications," 1998. See the IEEE 802.3 publication catalog at http://standards.ieee.org/catalog/IEEE802.3.html

[IEEE 802.11 1999] IEEE P802.11, Working Group for Wireless Local Area Networks. http://grouper.ieee.org/groups/802/11/main.html

[IMAP 1999] The IMAP Connection, http://www.imap.org/

[Interoperability 1999] Interoperability Lab Gigabit Ethernet Page, http://www.iol.unh.edu/training/ge.html

[IP Multicast Initiative 1998] IP Multicast Initiative, "IP Multicast Buyers Guide," http://www.ipmulticast.com/ipmi_dir/dc_indexes/protocols/0.html

[Iren 1999] S. Iren, P. Amer, P. Conrad, "The Transport Layer: Tutorial and Survey," *ACM Computing Surveys,* June 1999.

[ISO 1987] International Organization for Standardization, "Information processing systems—Open Systems Interconnection—Specification of Abstract Syntax Notation One (ASN.1)," International Standard 8824 (Dec. 1987).

[ISO X.680] International Organization for Standardization, "X.680: ITU-T Recommendation X.680 (1997) | ISO/IEC 8824-1:1998, Information Technology—Abstract Syntax Notation One (ASN.1): Specification of Basic Notation."

[ITU] The ITU Web site, http://www.itu.ch/

[ITU 1993] International Telecommunication Union, "Recommendation X.509 (11/93) The Directory: Authentication Framework."

[ITU 1997] International Telecommunications Union, "Recommendation E.164/ I.331—The international public telecommunication numbering plan," May 1997. http://www.itu.int/itudoc/itu-t/rec/e/s_e164.html

[Jacobson 1988] V. Jacobson, "Congestion Avoidance and Control," *Proceedings of the ACM, Sigcomm 1988 Conference,* pp. 314–329, Aug. 1988. ftp:// ftp.ee.lbl.gov/papers/congavoid.ps.Z

[Jain 1989] R. Jain, "A Delay-Based Approach for Congestion Avoidance in Interconnected Heterogeneous Computer Networks," *ACM Computer Communications Review,* Vol. 19, No. 5, pp. 56–71, 1989.

[Jain 1994] R. Jain, *FDDI Handbook: High-Speed Networking Using Fiber and Other Media,* Addison-Wesley, Reading, MA, 1994.

[Jain 1996] R. Jain. S. Kalyanaraman, S. Fahmy, R. Goyal, and S. Kim, "Tutorial Paper on ABR Source Behavior," *ATM Forum*/96-1270, Oct. 1996. http:// www.cis.ohio-state.edu/~jain/atmf/a96-1270.htm

[Jakobson 1993] G. Jacobson and M. Weissman, "Alarm Correlation," *IEEE Network Magazine,* 1993, pp. 52–59.

[Jimenez 1997] D. Jimenez, "Outside Hackers Infiltrate MIT Network, Compromise Security," *The Tech,* Vol. 117, No. 49 (Oct. 1997), pp. 1. http://www-tech.mit.edu/V117/N49/hackers.49n.html

[Kahn 1967] D. Kahn, *The Codebreakers, the Story of Secret Writing,* The Macmillan Company, 1967.

[Kapoor 1997] H. Kapoor, "CoreBuilder 5000 SwitchModule Architecture," http://www.3com.com/technology/tech_net/white_papers/500645.html, 1997.

[Karol 1987] M. Karol, M. Hluchyj, A. Morgan, "Input Versus Output Queuing on a Space-Division Packet Switch," *IEEE Transactions on Communications,* Vol. COM-35, No. 12, pp. 1347–1356, Dec. 1987.

[Katzela 1995] I. Katzela, and M. Schwartz. "Schemes for Fault Identification in Communication Networks," *IEEE/ACM Transactions on Networking,* Vol. 3, No. 6 (Dec. 1995), pp. 753–764.

[Kaufman 1995] C. Kaufman, R. Perlman, M. Speciner, *Network Security, Private Communication in a Public World,* Prentice Hall, Englewood Cliffs, NJ, 1995.

[Kegel 1999] Dan Kegel's ISDN Page, http://alumni.caltech.edu/~dank/isdn/

[Kercheval 1998] B. Kercheval, *TCP/IP Over ATM,* Prentice Hall, Englewood Cliffs, New Jersey, 1998.

[Keshav 1998] S. Keshav, R. Sharma, "Issues and Trends in Router Design," *IEEE Communications Magazine,* Vol. 36, No. 5, pp. 144–151, May 1998.

[Kessler 1998] G. C. Kessler, "An Overview of Cryptography," May 1998, Hill Associates, http://www.hill.com/library/staffpubs/crypto.html

[Kleinrock 1961] L. Kleinrock, "Information Flow in Large Communication Networks," RLE Quarterly Progress Report, July 1961.

[Kleinrock 1964] L. Kleinrock, *1964 Communication Nets: Stochastic Message Flow and Delay,* McGraw-Hill, NY, NY, 1964; later re-issued by Dover Books.

[Kleinrock 1975] L. Kleinrock, *Queuing Systems, Vol. 1,* John Wiley, New York, 1975.

[Kleinrock 1975b] L. Kleinrock and F. A. Tobagi, "Packet Switching in Radio Channels: Part I—Carrier Sense Multiple-Access Modes and Their Throughput-Delay Characteristics," *IEEE Transactions on Communications,* Vol. COM-23, No. 12, pp. 1400–1416, Dec. 1975.

[Kleinrock 1976] L. Kleinrock, *Queuing Systems, Vol. 2,* John Wiley, New York, 1976.

[Kleinrock 1998] L. Kleinrock, "The Birth of the Internet," http://millenium.cs.ucla.edu/LK/Inet/birth.html

[Kou 1981] L. Kou, G. Markowsky, and L. Berman, "A Fast Algorithm for Steiner Trees," *Acta Informatica,* Vol. 15, pp. 141–145, 1981.

[Kumar 1998] K. Kumar, P. Radoslavov, D. Thaler, C. Alaettinoglu, D. Estrin, M. Handley. "The MASC/BGMP Architecture for Inter-Domain Multicast Routing," *Proc. ACM Sigcomm 98,* Sept. 1998, Vancouver, Canada.

[Kurose 1996] J. F. Kurose, Unix Network Programming. http://www-aml.cs.umass.edu/~amldemo/courseware/intro.html

[Lakshman 1995] T. V. Lakshman and U. Madhow, "Performance Analysis of Window-Based Flow Control Using TCP/IP: The Effect of High Bandwidth-Delay Products and Random Loss," *IFIP Transactions C-26,* High Performance Networking V, pp. 135–150, North Holland, 1994.

[Lam 1980] S. Lam, "A Carrier Sense Multiple Access Protocol for Local Networks," *Computer Networks,* Vol. 4, pp. 21–32, 1980.

[Lamport 1981] L. Lamport, "Password Authentication with Insecure Communication", *Communications of the ACM,* Vol. 24, No. 11 (Nov. 1981), pp. 770–772.

[LaPolla 1997] S. LaPolla, "IP Multicast makes headway among ISPs," *PC Week On-Line,* http://www.zdnet.com/pcweek/news/1006/06isp.html

[Larsen 1997] A. Larsen, "Guaranteed Service: Monitoring Tools," *Data Communications,* June 1997, pp. 85–94.

[Larmouth 1996] J. Larmouth, *Understanding OSI,* International Thomson Computer Press 1996. Chapter 8 of this book deals with ASN.1 and is available online at http://www.salford.ac.uk/iti/books/osi/all.html#head8

[Leboudec 1992] Jean-Yves LeBoudec, "ATM: A Tutorial," *Computer Networks and ISDN Systems,* Vol. 24, 1992, pp. 279–309.

[Leiner 1998] B. Leiner, V. Cerf, D. Clark, R. Kahn, L. Kleinrock, D. Lynch, J. Postel, L. Roberts, and S. Woolf, "A Brief History of the Internet," http://www.isoc.org/internet/history/brief.html

[List 1999] "The List: The Definitive ISP Buyer's Guide," http://thelist.internet.com/

[Loeb 1998] L. Loeb, *Secure Electronic Transactions: Introduction and Technical Reference,"* Artech House, New York, 1998.

[Loshin 1997] P. Loshin, P. Murphy, *Electronic Commerce: On-Line Ordering and Digital Money,* Charles River Media, Aug. 1997.

[Luotonen 1998] A. Luotonen, *Web Proxy Servers,* Prentice Hall, Englewood Cliffs, New Jersey, 1998.

[Lynch 1993] D. Lynch, M. Rose, *Internet System Handbook,* Addison Wesley, Reading, MA, 1993.

[Macedonia 1994] Macedonia, M. R., Brutzman, D. P., "MBone Provides Audio and Video Across the Internet," *IEEE Computer Magazine,* Vol. 27, No. 4, pp. 30–36, Apr. 1994.

[Mathis 1996] M. Mathis, J. Mahdavi, "Forward Acknowledgment: Refining TCP Congestion Control", *Proceedings of ACM SIGCOMM'96,* Aug. 1996, Stanford, CA. http://www.psc.edu/networking/papers/papers.html

[Mahdavi] J. Mahdavi and S. Floyd, "The TCP-Friendly Website," http://www.psc.edu/networking/tcp_friendly.html

[Mahdavi 1997] J. Mahdavi and S. Floyd, "TCP-Friendly Unicast Rate-Based Flow Control," unpublished note, Jan. 1997. http://www.psc.edu/networking/papers/tcp_friendly.html

[MasterCard 1999] MasterCard Web site, "SET Secure Electronic Transaction," http://www.mastercard.com/shoponline/set/

[McAuley 1994] A. McAuley, "Weighted Sum Codes for Error Detection and Their Comparison with Existing Codes," *IEEE/ACM Transactions on Networking,* Vol. 2, No. 1 (Feb. 1994), pp. 16–22.

[McKeown 1997a] N. McKeown, M. Izzard, A. Mekkittikul, W. Ellersick, M. Horowitz, "The Tiny Tera: A Packet Switch Core," *IEEE Micro Magazine,* Jan.–Feb. 1997. http://tiny-tera.stanford.edu/~nickm/papers/HOTI_96.ps

[McKeown 1997b] N. McKeown, "A Fast Switched Backplane for a Gigabit Switched Router," *Business Communications Review,* Vol. 27, No. 12. http://www.bcr.com/bcrmag/12/mckeown.htm

[Metcalfe 1976] R. M. Metcalfe and D. R. Boggs. "Ethernet: Distributed Packet Switching for Local Computer Networks," *Communications of the Association for Computing Machinery,* Vol. 19, No. 7, July 1976.

[McKusik 1996] Marshall Kirk McKusick, Keith Bostic, Michael Karels, and John Quarterman, *The Design and Implementation of the 4.4BSD Operating System,* Addison-Wesley, Reading, MA, 1996.

[Mehdi 1997] D. Mehdi and D. Tipper (eds.), Special Issue: Fault Management in Communication Networks, *Journal of Network and Systems Management,* Vol. 5. No. 2 (June 1997).

[Merkow 1998] M. Merkow, K. Wheeler, and J. Breithaupt, *Building SET Applications for Secure Transactions,* John Wiley and Sons, New York, 1998.

[Microsoft Routing 1998] Microsoft Corp., "Microsoft Routing and Remote Access Service for Windows NT Server 4.0," http://www.microsoft.com/ntserver/basics/communications/basics/remoteaccess/routing/default.asp

[Molle 1987] M. L. Molle, K. Sohraby, and A. N. Venetsanopoulos, "Space-Time Models of Asynchronous CSMA Protocols for Local Area Networks," *IEEE Journal on Selected Areas in Communications,* Vol. 5, No. 6, pp. 956–968, 1987.

[Molva 1999] R. Molva, "Internet Security Architecture," *Computer Networks and ISDN Systems,* 1999.

[mrouted 1996] "mrouted," v3.8 of DVMRP routing software for various workstation routing platforms, ftp://parcftp.xerox.com/pub/net-research/ipmulti

[Mills 1998] S. Mills, "TV set-tops set to take off," CNET News.com, Oct. 1998. http://news.cnet.com/news/0-1006-200-334433.html

[NAS 1995] National Academy of Sciences, *The Unpredictable Certainty: Information Infrastructure Through 2000,* National Academy of Sciences Press, 1995. http://www.nap.edu/readingroom/books/unpredictable/chap4.html

[Nerds] Triumph of the Nerds, Web site for PBS television special, http://www.pbs.org/nerds

[Netcraft] The Netcraft Web Server Survey, Netcraft Web Site, http://www.netcraft.com/Survey/

[NetscapePK 1998] Netscape Communications Corp., "Introduction to Public-Key Cryptography," http://developer.netscape.com/docs/manuals/security/pkin/contents.htm

[Netscape Certificate 1999] Netscape Communications Corp., "Netscape Certificate Server FAQ," http://sitesearch.netscape.com/certificate/v1.0/faq/index.html

[Netscape Security 1999] Nescape Communications Corp., Security Developer Central, http://developer.netscape.com/tech/security/

[Network 1996] Network Wizards, "Internet Domain Survey", July 1996, http://www.nw.com/zone/WWW-9607/report.html

[Network 1999] Network Wizards, "Internet Domain Survey," Jan. 1999, http://www.isc.org/ds/

[Network Associates 1999] Network Associates, http://www.nai.com/default_pgp.asp

[Neuman 1994] B. Neuman and T. Tso, "Kerberos: An Authentication Service for Computer Networks," *IEEE Communication Magazine,* Vol. 32, No. 9 (Sept. 1994), pp. 33–38.

[Neumann 1997] R. Neumann, "Internet Routing Black Hole," *The Risks Digest: Forum on Risks to the Public in Computers and Related Systems,* Vol. 19, No. 12 (May 1997). http://catless.ncl.ac.uk/Risks/19.12.html#subj1.1

[Newman 1998] D. Newman, H. Holzbar, M. Carter, "Firewalls: Tough Enough," *Data Communications Magazine,* Apr. 1998. http://www.data.com/lab_tests/ntfirewalls.html

[Nielsen 1997] H. F. Nielsen, J. Gettys, A. Baird-Smith, E. Prud'hommeaux, H. W. Lie, and C. Lilley, "Network Performance Effects of HTTP/1.1, CSS1, and PNG," *W3C Document,* 1997 (also appears in *Proc. ACM SIGCOMM' 97,* Cannes, France, pp. 155–166). http://www.w3.org/Protocols/HTTP/Performance/Pipeline

[NIST 1993] National Institute of Standards and Technology, "Federal Information. Data Encryption Standard," Processing Standards Publication 46-2, 1993. http://www.itl.nist.gov/fipspubs/fip46-2.htm

[NIST 1999] National Institute of Standards and Technology, "Data Encryption Standard Fact Sheet," http://csrc.nist.gov/cryptval/des/des.txt

[NIST 1999b] National Institute of Standards and Technology, "Draft Federal Information Processing Standard (FIPS) 46-3, Data Encryption Standard (DES), and Request for Comments," http://csrc.nist.gov/cryptval/des/fr990115.htm

[NLANR] A Distributed Testbed for National Information Provisioning, http://ircache.nlanr.net/

[Nonnenmacher 1998] J. Nonnenmacher, E. Biersak, D. Towsley, "Parity-Based Loss Recovery for Reliable Multicast Transmission," *IEEE/ACM Transactions on Networking,* Vol. 6, No. 4 (Aug. 1998), pp. 349–361.

[Pacific Bell 1998] Pacific Bell, "ISDN Users Guide," http://www.pacbell.com/products/business/fastrak/networking/isdn/info/isdn-guide/index.html

[Padhye 1999] J. Padhye and J. Kurose, "An Empirical Study of Client Interactions with a Continuous-Media Courseware Server," *IEEE Internet Computing,* Apr. 1999. ftp://gaia.cs.umass.edu/pub/Padh97:Empirical.ps.gz

[Parekh 1993] A. Parekh and R. Gallager, "A generalized processor sharing approach to flow control in integrated services networks: the single-node case," *IEEE/ACM Transactions on Networking,* Vol. 1, No. 3 (June 1993), pp. 344–357.

[Partridge 1998] C. Partridge, et al. "A Fifty Gigabit per second IP Router," *IEEE/ACM Transactions on Networking,* Vol. 6, No. 3, pp. 237–248, Jun. 1998.

[Perkins 1994] A. Perkins, "Networking with Bob Metcalfe," *The Red Herring Magazine,* Nov. 1994. http://www.herring.com/mag/issue15/bob.html

[Perkins 1998] C. Perkins, O. Hodson and V. Hardman, "A Survey of Packet Loss Recovery Techniques for Streaming Audio," *IEEE Network Magazine,* Sept./Oct. 1998, pp. 40–47.

[Perlman 1999] R. Perlman, *Interconnections: Bridges, Routers, Switches, and Internetworking Protocols,* 2nd ed., Addison-Wesley Professional Computing Series, Reading, MA, 1999.

[PGPI 1999] The International PGP Home Page, http://www.pgpi.org

[Pickholtz 1982] R. Pickholtz, D. Schilling, L. Milstein, "Theory of Spread Spectrum Communication—a Tutorial," *IEEE Transactions on Communications,* Col. COM-30, No. 5 (May 1982), pp. 855–884.

[Piscatello 1993] D. Piscatello and A. Lyman Chapin, *Open Systems Networking,* Addison Wesley, Reading, MA, 1993.

[Punks 1999] Cypherpunks Web Page, ftp://ftp.csua.berkeley.edu/pub/cypher-punks/Home.html

[Quebec 1999] Quebec Maple Syrup homepage, http://www.jam.ca/syrup/

[Ramakrishnan 1990] K. K. Ramakrishnan and Raj Jain, "A Binary Feedback Scheme for Congestion Avoidance in Computer Networks," *ACM Transactions on Computer Systems,* Vol. 8, No. 2, pp. 158–181, May 1990.

[Raman 1999] S. Raman, S. McCanne, "A Model, Analysis, and Protocol Framework for Soft State-based Communication," *Proceedings of ACM Sigcomm '99* (Boston, MA, Aug. 1999). http://www.acm.org/sigs/sigcomm/sigcomm99/papers/session1-2.html

[Ramjee 1994] R. Ramjee, J. Kurose, D. Towsley, and H. Schulzrinne, "Adaptive Playout Mechanisms for Packetized Audio Applications in Wide-Area Networks," *Proceeding IEEE Infocom 94.* ftp://gaia.cs.umass.edu/pib/Ramj94:Adaptive.ps.Z

[Rao 1996] K. R. Rao and J. J. Hwang, *Techniques and Standards for Image, Video and Audio Coding,* Prentice Hall, Englewood Cliffs, NJ, 1996.

[RAT 1999] Robust Audio Tool, http://www-mice.cs.ucl.ac.uk/multimedia/projects/rat/

[RealNetworks] RTSP Resource Center, http://www.real.com/devzone/library/fireprot/rtsp/

[RFC 001] S. Crocker, "Host Software," RFC 001 (the *very first* RFC!).

[RFC 768] J. Postel, " Datagram Protocol," RFC 768, Aug. 1980. http://info.internet.isi.edu/in-notes/rfc/files/rfc768.txt

[RFC 789] E. Rosen, "Vulnerabilities of Network Control Protocols," RFC 789. http://info.internet.isi.edu/in-notes/rfc/files/rfc789.txt

[RFC 791] J. Postel, "Internet Protocol: DARPA Internet Program Protocol Specification," RFC 791, Sept. 1981. http://info.internet.isi.edu/in-notes/rfc/files/rfc791.txt

[RFC 792] J. Postel, "Internet Control Message Protocol," RFC 792, Sep-01-1981. http://info.internet.isi.edu/in-notes/rfc/files/rfc792.txt

[RFC 793] J. Postel, "Transmission Control Protocol," RFC 793, Sept. 1981. http://info.internet.isi.edu/in-notes/rfc/files/rfc793.txt

[RFC 801] J. Postel, "NCP/TCP Transition Plan," RFC 801 Nov. 1981. http://info.internet.isi.edu/in-notes/rfc/files/rfc801.txt

[RFC 821] J. B. Postel, "Simple Mail Transfer Protocol," RFC 821, Aug. 1982. http://info.internet.isi.edu/in-notes/rfc/files/rfc821.txt

[RFC 822] D. H. Crocker, "Standard for the Format of ARPA Internet Text Messages," RFC 822, Aug. 1982. http://info.internet.isi.edu/in-notes/rfc/files/rfc822.txt

[RFC 826] D. C. Plummer, "An Ethernet Address Resolution Protocol," RFC 826, Nov. 1982. http://info.internet.isi.edu/in-notes/rfc/files/rfc826.txt

[RFC 833] P. V. Mockapetris, "Domain names: Implementation specification," RFC 833, Nov. 1, 1983. http://info.internet.isi.edu/in-notes/rfc/files/rfc833.txt

[RFC 854] J. Postel and J. Reynolds, "TELNET Protocol Specification," RFC 854. May 1993. http://info.internet.isi.edu/in-notes/rfc/files/rfc854.txt

[RFC 904] D. Mills, "Exterior Gateway Protocol Formal Specification," RFC 904, Apr. 1984. http://info.internet.isi.edu/in-notes/rfc/files/rfc904.txt

[RFC 950] J. Mogul, J. Postel, "Internet Standard Subnetting Procedure," RFC 950, Aug. 1985. http://info.internet.isi.edu/in-notes/rfc/files/rfc950.txt

[RFC 959] J. Postel and J. Reynolds, "File Transfer Protocol (FTP)," RFC 959, Oct. 1985. http://info.internet.isi.edu/in-notes/rfc/files/rfc959.txt

[RFC 977] B. Kantor and P. Lapsley, "Network News Transfer Protocol," RFC 977, Feb. 1986. http://info.internet.isi.edu/in-notes/rfc/files/rfc977.txt

[RFC 1028] J. Davin, J. Casem, M. Fedor, M. Schoffstall, "A Simple Gateway Monitoring Protocol," RFC 1028, ftp://ftp.isi.edu/in-notes/rfc1028.txt.

[RFC 1034] P. V. Mockapetris, "Domain Names—Concepts and Facilities," RFC 1034, Nov. 1, 1987. http://info.internet.isi.edu/in-notes/rfc/files/rfc1034.txt

[RFC 1035] P. Mockapetris, "Domain Names—Implementation and Specification," RFC 1035, Nov. 1987. http://info.internet.isi.edu/in-notes/rfc/files/rfc1035.txt

[RFC 1058] C. L. Hendrick, "Routing Information Protocol," RFC 1058, June 1988. http://info.internet.isi.edu/in-notes/rfc/files/rfc1058.txt

[RFC 1071] R. Braden, D. Borman, and C. Partridge, "Computing The Internet Checksum," RFC 1071, Sept. 1988. http://info.internet.isi.edu/in-notes/rfc/files/rfc1071.txt

[RFC 1075] D. Waitzman, S. Deering, C. Partridge, "Distance Vector Multicast Routing Protocol," RFC 1075, Nov. 1988. http://info.internet.isi.edu/in-notes/rfc/files/rfc1075.txt. The version of DVMRP in use today is considerably enhanced over the RFC1075 spec. A more up-to-date "work-in-progress" defines a version 3 of DVMRP: T. Pusateri, "Distance Vector Multicast Routing Protocol," work-in-progress, draft-ietf-idmr-v3-09.txt.

[RFC 1112] S. Deering, "Host Extension for IP Multicasting," RFC 1112, Aug. 1989. http://info.internet.isi.edu/in-notes/rfc/files/rfc1112.txt

[RFC 1122] R. Braden, "Requirements for Internet Hosts—Communication Layers," RFC 1122, Oct. 1989. http://info.internet.isi.edu/in-notes/rfc/files/rfc1122.txt

[RFC 1180] T. Socolofsky and C. Kale, "A TCP/IP Tutorial," RFC 1180, Jan. 1991. http://info.internet.isi.edu/in-notes/rfc/files/rfc1180.txt

[RFC 1213] K. McCloghrie, M. T. Rose, "Management Information Base for Network Management of TCP/IP-based internets: MIB-II," RFC 1213, Mar. 1991. http://info.internet.isi.edu/in-notes/rfc/files/rfc1213.txt

[RFC 1256] S. Deering, "ICMP Router Discovery Messages," RFC 1256, Sept. 1991. http://info.internet.isi.edu/in-notes/rfc/files/rfc1256.txt

[RFC 1320] R. Rivest, "The MD4 Message-Digest Algorithm," RFC 1320, Apr. 1992. http://info.internet.isi.edu/in-notes/rfc/files/rfc1320.txt

[RFC 1321] R. Rivest, "The MD5 Message-Digest Algorithm," RFC 1321, Apr. 1992. http://info.internet.isi.edu/in-notes/rfc/files/rfc1321.txt

[RFC 1323] V. Jacobson, S. Braden, and D. Borman, "TCP Extensions for High Performance," RFC 1323, May 1992. http://info.internet.isi.edu/in-notes/rfc/files/rfc1323.txt

[RFC 1332] G. McGregor, "The PPP Internet Protocol Control Protocol (IPCP)," RFC 1332, May 1992. http://info.internet.isi.edu/in-notes/rfc/files/rfc1332.txt

[RFC 1378] B. Parker, "The PPP AppleTalk Control Protocol (ATCP)," RFC 1378, Nov. 1992. http://info.internet.isi.edu/in-notes/rfc/files/rfc1378.txt

[RFC 1422] S. Kent, "Privacy Enhancement for Internet Electronic Mail: Part II: Certificate-Based Key Management", RFC 1422, Feb. 1993. http://info.internet.isi.edu/in-notes/rfc/files/rfc1422.txt

[RFC 1510] J. Kohl, C. Neuman, "The Kerberos Network Authentication Service (V5)," RFC 1510, Sept. 1993. http://info.internet.isi.edu/in-notes/rfc/files/rfc1510.txt

[RFC 1542] W. Wimer, "Clarifications and Extensions for the Bootstrap Protocol," RFC 1542, Oct. 1993. http://info.internet.isi.edu/in-notes/rfc/files/rfc1542.txt

[RFC 1547] D. Perkins, "Requirements for an Internet Standard Point-to-Point Protocol," RFC 1547, Dec. 1993. http://info.internet.isi.edu/in-notes/rfc/files/rfc1547.txt

[RFC 1577] M. Laubach, "Classical IP and ARP over ATM," RFC 1577, Jan. 1994. http://info.internet.isi.edu/in-notes/rfc/files/rfc1577.txt

[RFC 1584] J. Moy, "Multicast Extensions to OSPF," RFC 1584, Mar. 1994. http://info.internet.isi.edu/in-notes/rfc/files/rfc1584.txt

[RFC 1633] R. Braden, D. Clark, S. Shenker, "Integrated Services in the Internet Architecture: an Overview," RFC 1633, June 1994. http://info.internet.isi.edu/in-notes/rfc/files/rfc1633.txt

[RFC 1636] R. Braden, D. Clark, S. Crocker, C. Huitema, "Report of IAB Workshop on Security in the Internet Architecture," RFC 1636, Nov. 1994. http://info.internet.isi.edu/in-notes/rfc/files/rfc1633.txt

[RFC 1661] W. Simpson (ed.), "The Point-to-Point Protocol (PPP)," RFC 1661, July 1994. http://info.internet.isi.edu/in-notes/rfc/files/rfc1661.txt

[RFC 1662] W. Simpson (ed.), "PPP in HDLC-like framing," RFC 1662, July 1994. http://info.internet.isi.edu/in-notes/rfc/files/rfc1662.txt

[RFC 1700] J. Reynolds and J. Postel, "Assigned Numbers," RFC 1700, Oct. 1994. http://info.internet.isi.edu/in-notes/rfc/files/rfc1700.txt

[RFC 1723] G. Malkin, "RIP Version 2—Carrying Additional Information," RFC 1723, Nov. 1994. http://info.internet.isi.edu/in-notes/rfc/files/rfc1723.txt

[RFC 1730] M. Crispin, "Internet Message Access Protocol—Version 4," RFC 1730, Dec. 1994. http://info.internet.isi.edu/in-notes/rfc/files/rfc1730.txt

[RFC 1752] S. Bradner, A. Mankin, "The Recommendations for the IP Next Generation Protocol," RFC 1752, Jan. 1995. http://info.internet.isi.edu/in-notes/rfc/files/rfc1752.txt

[RFC 1760] N. Haller, "The S/KEY One-Time Password System," RFC 1760, Feb. 1995. http://info.internet.isi.edu/in-notes/rfc/files/rfc1760.txt

[RFC 1762] S. Senum, "The PPP DECnet Phase IV Control Protocol (DNCP)," RFC 1762, Mar. 1995. http://info.internet.isi.edu/in-notes/rfc/files/rfc1762.txt

[RFC 1771] Y. Rekhter and T. Li, "A Border Gateway Protocol 4 (BGP-4)," RFC 1771, Mar. 1995. http://info.internet.isi.edu/in-notes/rfc/files/rfc1771.txt

[RFC 1772] Y. Rekhter and P. Gross, "Application of the Border Gateway Protocol in the Internet," RFC 1772, Mar. 1995. http://info.internet.isi.edu/in-notes/rfc/files/rfc1772.txt

[RFC 1773] P. Traina, "Experience with the BGP-4 protocol," RFC 1773, Mar. 1995. http://info.internet.isi.edu/in-notes/rfc/files/rfc1773.txt

[RFC 1779] S. Kille, "A String Representation of Distinguished Names," RFC 1779, Mar. 1995. http://info.internet.isi.edu/in-notes/rfc/files/rfc1779.txt

[RFC 1810] J. Touch, "Report on MD5 Performance," RFC 1810, June 1995. http://info.internet.isi.edu/in-notes/rfc/files/rfc1810.txt

[RFC 1884] R. Hinden, S. Deering, "IP Version 6: addressing architecture," RFC 1884, Dec. 1995. http://info.internet.isi.edu/in-notes/rfc/files/rfc1884.txt

[RFC 1889] H. Schulzrinne, S. Casner, R. Frederick, and V. Jacobson, "RTP: A Transport Protocol for Real-Time Applications," RFC 1889, 1996. http://info.internet.isi.edu/in-notes/rfc/files/rfc1889.txt

[RFC 1905] J. Case, K. McCloghrie, M. Rose, S. Waldbusser, "Protocol Operations for Version 2 of the Simple Network Management Protocol (SNMPv2)," RFC 1905, Jan. 1996. http://info.internet.isi.edu/in-notes/rfc/files/rfc1905.txt

[RFC 1906] J. Case, K. McCloghrie, M. Rose, S. Waldbusser, "Transport Mappings for Version 2 of the Simple Network Management Protocol (SNMPv2)," RFC 1906, Jan. 1996. http://info.internet.isi.edu/in-notes/rfc/files/rfc1906.txt

[RFC 1907] J. Case, K. McCloghrie, M. Rose, and S. Waldbusser, "Management Information Base for Version 2 of the Simple Network Management Protocol (SNMPv2)", RFC 1907, Jan. 1996. http://info.internet.isi.edu/in-notes/rfc/files/rfc1907.txt

[RFC 1911] G. Vaudreuil, "Voice Profile for Internet Mail," RFC 1911, Feb. 1996. http://info.internet.isi.edu/in-notes/rfc/files/rfc1911.txt

[RFC 1932] R. Cole, S. Shur, and C. Villamizar," IP over ATM: A Framework Document," RFC 1932, Apr. 1996. http://info.internet.isi.edu/in-notes/rfc/files/rfc1932.txt

[RFC 1939] J. Myers and M. Rose, "Post Office Protocol—Version 3," RFC 1939, May 1996. http://info.internet.isi.edu/in-notes/rfc/files/rfc1939.txt

[RFC 1945] T. Berners-Lee, R. Fielding, and H. Frystyk, "Hypertext Transfer Protocol—HTTP/1.0," RFC 1945, May 1996. http://info.internet.isi.edu/in-notes/rfc/files/rfc1945.txt

[RFC 1993] R. Gilligan, E. Nordmark, "Transition Mechanisms for IPv6 Hosts and Routers," RFC 1993, Apr. 1996. http://info.internet.isi.edu/in-notes/rfc/files/rfc1993.txt

[RFC 2001] W. Stevens, "TCP Slow Start, Congestion Avoidance, Fast Retransmit, and Fast Recovery Algorithms," RFC 2001, Jan. 1997. http://info.internet.isi.edu/in-notes/rfc/files/rfc2001.txt. See also [RFC 2581].

[RFC 2002] C. Perkins, "IP Mobility Support," RFC 2002, 1996. http://info.internet.isi.edu/in-notes/rfc/files/rfc2002.txt

[RFC 2003] C. Perkins, "IP Encapsulation within IP," RFC 2003, Oct. 1996. http://info.internet.isi.edu/in-notes/rfc/files/rfc2003.txt

[RFC 2011] K. McCloghrie, "SNMPv2 Management Information Base for the Internet Protocol using SMIv2," RFC 2011, Nov. 1996. http://info.internet.isi.edu/in-notes/rfc/files/rfc2011.txt

[RFC 2012] K. McCloghrie, "SNMPv2 Management Information Base for the Transmission Control Protocol using SMIv2," RFC 2012, Nov. 1996. http://info.internet.isi.edu/in-notes/rfc/files/rfc2012.txt

[RFC 2013] K. McCloghrie, "SNMPv2 Management Information Base for the User Datagram Protocol using SMIv2," RFC 2013, Nov. 1996. http://info.internet.isi.edu/in-notes/rfc/files/rfc2013.txt

[RFC 2018] M. Mathis, J. Mahdavi, S. Floyd, and A. Romanow, "TCP Selective Acknowledgment Options," RFC 2018, Oct. 1996. http://info.internet.isi.edu/in-notes/rfc/files/rfc2018.txt

[RFC 2021] S. Waldbusser, "Remote Network Monitoring Management Information Base Version 2 using SMIv2," RFC 2021, Jan. 1997. http://info.internet.isi.edu/in-notes/rfc/files/rfc2021.txt

[RFC 2045] N. Borenstein and N. Freed, "Multipurpose Internet Mail Extensions (MIME) Part One: Format of Internet Message Bodies," RFC 2045, Nov. 1996. http://info.internet.isi.edu/in-notes/rfc/files/rfc2045.txt

[RFC 2046] N. Borenstein and N. Freed, "Multipurpose Internet Mail Extensions (MIME) Part Two: Media Types," RFC 2046, Nov. 1996. http://info.internet.isi.edu/in-notes/rfc/files/rfc2046.txt

[RFC 2048] N. Freed, J. Klensin, and J. Postel "Multipurpose Internet Mail Extensions (MIME) Part Four: Registration Procedures," RFC 2048, Nov. 1996. http://info.internet.isi.edu/in-notes/rfc/files/rfc2048.txt

[RFC 2050] K. Hubbard, M. Kosters, D. Conrad, D. Karrenberg, J. Postel, "Internet Registry IP Allocation Guidelines," RFC 2050, Nov. 1996. http://info.internet.isi.edu/in-notes/rfc/files/rfc2050.txt

[RFC 2068] R. Fielding, J. Gettys, J. Mogul, H. Frystyk, and T. Berners-Lee, "Hypertext Transfer Protocol—HTTP/1.1," RFC 2068, Jan. 1997. http://info.internet.isi.edu/in-notes/rfc/files/rfc2068.txt

[RFC 2104] H. Krawczyk, M. Bellare, R. Canetti, "HMAC: Keyed-Hashing for Message Authentication," RFC 2104, Feb. 1997. http://info.internet.isi.edu/in-notes/rfc/files/rfc2104.txt

[RFC 2109] D. Kristol and L. Montulli, "HTTP State Management Mechanism," RFC 2109, Feb. 1997. http://info.internet.isi.edu/in-notes/rfc/files/rfc2109.txt

[RFC 2131] R. Droms, "Dynamic Host Configuration Protocol," RFC 2131, Mar. 1997. http://info.internet.isi.edu/in-notes/rfc/files/rfc2131.txt

[RFC 2136] P. Vixie, S. Thomson, Y. Rekhter, and J. Bound, "Dynamic Updates in the Domain Name System," RFC 2136, Apr. 1997. http://info.internet.isi.edu/in-notes/rfc/files/rfc2136.txt

[RFC 2153] W. Simpson, "PPP Vendor Extensions," RFC 2153, May 1997. http://info.internet.isi.edu/in-notes/rfc/files/rfc2153.txt

[RFC 2178] J. Moy, "Open Shortest Path First Version 2," RFC 2178, July 1997. http://info.internet.isi.edu/in-notes/rfc/files/rfc2178.txt

[RFC 2186] K. Claffy and D. Wessels, "Internet Caching Protocol (ICP), version 2," RFC 2186, Sept. 1997. http://info.internet.isi.edu/in-notes/rfc/files/rfc2186.txt

[RFC 2189] A. Ballardie, "Core Based Trees (CBT version 2) Multicast Routing: Protocol Specification," RFC 2189, Sept. 1997. http://info.internet.isi.edu/in-notes/rfc/files/rfc2189.txt

[RFC 2201] A. Ballardie, "Core Based Trees (CBT) Multicast Routing Architecture," RFC 2201, Sept. 1997. http://info.internet.isi.edu/in-notes/rfc/files/rfc2201.txt

[RFC 2205] R. Braden, Ed., L. Zhang, S. Berson, S. Herzog, S. Jamin, "Resource ReSerVation Protocol (RSVP)—Version 1 Functional Specification," RFC 2205, Sept. 1997. http://info.internet.isi.edu/in-notes/rfc/files/rfc2205.txt

[RFC 2210] J. Wroclawski, "The Use of RSVP with IETF Integrated Services," RFC 2210, Sept. 1997. http://info.internet.isi.edu/in-notes/rfc/files/rfc2210.txt

[RFC 2211] J. Wroclawski, "Specification of the Controlled-Load Network Element Service," RFC 2211, Sept. 1997. http://info.internet.isi.edu/in-notes/rfc/files/rfc2211.txt

[RFC 2212] S. Shenker, C. Partridge, R. Guerin, "Specification of Guaranteed Quality of Service," RFC 2212, Sept. 1997. http://info.internet.isi.edu/in-notes/rfc/files/rfc2212.txt

[RFC 2215] S. Shenker, J. Wroclawski, "General Characterization Parameters for Integrated Service Network Elements," RFC 2215, Sept. 1997. http://info.internet.isi.edu/in-notes/rfc/files/rfc2215.txt

[RFC 2236] R. Fenner, "Internet Group Management Protocol, Version 2," RFC 2236, Nov. 1997. http://info.internet.isi.edu/in-notes/rfc/files/rfc2236.txt

[RFC 2246] T. Dierks and C. Allen, "The TLS Protocol," RFC 2246, Jan. 1998. http://info.internet.isi.edu/in-notes/rfc/files/rfc2246.txt

[RFC 2326] H. Schulzrinne, A. Rao, R. Lanphier, "Real Time Streaming Protocol (RTSP)", RFC 2326, Apr. 1998. http://info.internet.isi.edu/in-notes/rfc/files/rfc2326.txt

[RFC 2362] D. Estrin, D. Farinacci, A. Helmy, D. Thaler, S. Deering, M. Handley, V. Jacobson, C. Liu, P. Sharma, L. Wei, "Protocol Independent Multicast-Sparse Mode (PIM-SM): Protocol Specification," RFC 2362, June 1998. http://info.internet.isi.edu/in-notes/rfc/files/rfc2362.txt

[RFC 2400] J. Postel, J. Reynolds, "Internet Official Protocol Standards," RFC 2400, Oct. 1998. http://info.internet.isi.edu/in-notes/rfc/files/rfc2400.txt

[RFC 2401] S. Kent and R. Atkinson, "Security Architecture for the Internet Protocol," RFC 2401, Nov. 1998. http://info.internet.isi.edu/in-notes/rfc/files/rfc2401.txt

[RFC 2402] S. Kent and R. Atkinson, "IP Authentication Header," RFC 2402, Nov. 1998. http://info.internet.isi.edu/in-notes/rfc/files/rfc2402.txt

[RFC 2405] C. Madson and N. Doraswamy, "The ESP DES-CBC Cipher Algorithm with Explicit IV," RFC 2405, Nov. 1998. http://info.internet.isi.edu/in-notes/rfc/files/rfc2405.txt

[RFC 2406] S. Kent and R. Atkinson, "IP Authentication Header," RFC 2406, Nov. 1998. http://info.internet.isi.edu/in-notes/rfc/files/rfc2406.txt

[RFC 2407] D. Piper, "The Internet IP Security Domain of Interpretation for ISAKMP," RFC 2407, Nov. 1998. http://info.internet.isi.edu/in-notes/rfc/files/rfc2407.txt

[RFC 2408] D. Maughan, M. Schertler, M. Schneider and J. Turner, "Internet Security Association and Key Management Protocol (ISAKMP)," RFC 2408, Nov. 1998. http://info.internet.isi.edu/in-notes/rfc/files/rfc2408.txt

[RFC 2409] D. Harkins and D. Carrel, "The Internet Key Exchange (IKE)," RFC 2409, Nov. 1998. http://info.internet.isi.edu/in-notes/rfc/files/rfc2409.txt

[RFC 2411] R. Thayer, N. Doraswamy, and R. Glenn, "IP Security Document Road Map," RFC 2411, Nov. 1998. http://info.internet.isi.edu/in-notes/rfc/files/rfc2411.txt

[RFC 2420] H. Kummert, "The PPP Triple-DES Encryption Protocol (3DESE)," RFC 2420, Sept. 1998. http://info.internet.isi.edu/in-notes/rfc/files/rfc2420.txt

[RFC 2437] B. Kaliski, J. Staddon, "PKCS #1: RSA Cryptography Specifications, Version 2," RFC 2437, Oct. 1998. http://info.internet.isi.edu/in-notes/rfc/files/rfc2437.txt

[RFC 2427] C. Brown and A. Malis, "Multiprotocol Interconnect over Frame Relay," RFC 2427, Sept. 1998. http://info.internet.isi.edu/in-notes/rfc/files/rfc2427.txt

[RFC 2460] S. Deering and R. Hinden, "Internet Protocol, Version 6 (IPv6) Specification," RFC 2460, Dec. 1998. http://info.internet.isi.edu/in-notes/rfc/files/rfc2460.txt

[RFC 2463] A. Conta, S. Deering, "Internet Control Message Protocol (ICMPv6) for the Internet Protocol Version 6 (IPv6)," RFC 2463, Dec. 1998. http://info.internet.isi.edu/in-notes/rfc/files/rfc2463.txt

[RFC 2474] K. Nicols, S. Blake, F. Baker, D. Black, "Definition of the Differentiated Services Field (DS Field) in the IPv4 and IPv6 Headers", RFC 2474, Dec. 1998. http://info.internet.isi.edu/in-notes/rfc/files/rfc2474.txt

[RFC 2475] S. Blake, D. Black, M. Carlson, E. Davies, Z. Wang, W. Weiss, "An Architecture for Differentiated Services", RFC 2475, Dec. 1998. http://info.internet.isi.edu/in-notes/rfc/files/rfc2475.txt

[RFC 2481] K. K. Ramakrishnan and S. Floyd, "A Proposal to Add Explicit Congestion Notification (ECN) to IP," RFC 2481, Jan. 1999. http://info.internet.isi.edu/in-notes/rfc/files/rfc2481.txt

[RFC 2570] J. Case, R. Mundy, D. Partain, B. Stewart, "Introduction to Version 3 of the Internet-standard Network Management Framework," RFC 2570, May 1999. http://info.internet.isi.edu/in-notes/rfc/files/rfc2570.txt

[RFC 2571] B. Wijnen, D. Harrington, R. Presuhn, "An Architecture for Describing SNMP Management Frameworks," RFC 2571, Apr. 1999. http://info.internet.isi.edu/in-notes/rfc/files/rfc2571.txt

[RFC 2574] U. Blumenthal, B. Wijnen, "User-based Security Model (USM) for version 3 of the Simple Network Management Protocol (SNMPv3), " RFC 2574, Apr. 1999. http://info.internet.isi.edu/in-notes/rfc/files/rfc2574.txt

[RFC 2575] B. Wijnen, R. Presuhn, K. McCloghrie, "View-based Access Control Model (VACM) for the Simple Network Management Protocol (SNMP)," RFC 2575, Apr. 1999. http://info.internet.isi.edu/in-notes/rfc/files/rfc2575.txt

[RFC 2578] K. McCloghrie, D. Perkins, J. Schoenwaelder, "Structure of Management Information Version 2 (SMIv2)," RFC 2578, Apr. 1999. http://info.internet.isi.edu/in-notes/rfc/files/rfc2578.txt

[RFC 2579] K. McCloghrie, D. Perkins, J. Schoenwaelder, "Textual Conventions for SMIv2," RFC 2579, Apr. 1999. http://info.internet.isi.edu/in-notes/rfc/files/rfc2579.txt

[RFC 2580] K. McCloghrie, D. Perkins, J. Schoenwaelder, "Conformance Statements for SMIv2," RFC 2580, Apr. 1999. http://info.internet.isi.edu/in-notes/rfc/files/rfc2580.txt

[RFC 2581] M. Allman, V. Paxson, W. Stevens, " TCP Congestion Control," RFC 2581, Apr. 1999. http://info.internet.isi.edu/in-notes/rfc/files/rfc2581.txt

[RFC 2597] J. Heinanen, F. Baker, W. Weiss, J. Wroclawski, "Assured Forwarding PHB Group," RFC 2597, June 1999. http://info.internet.isi.edu/in-notes/rfc/files/rfc2597.txt

[RFC 2598] V. Jacobson, K. Nichols, K. Poduri, "An Expedited Forwarding PHB," RFC 2598, June 1999. http://info.internet.isi.edu/in-notes/rfc/files/rfc2598.txt

[RFC 2638] K. Nichols, V. Jacobson, L. Zhang, "A Two-bit Differentiated Services Architecture for the Internet," RFC 2638, July 1999. http://info.internet.isi.edu/in-notes/rfc/files/rfc2638.txt

[Roberts 1967] L. Roberts, and T. Merril "Toward a Cooperative Network of Time-Shared Computers," *AFIPS Fall Conference,* Oct. 1966.

[Rom 1990] R. Rom and M. Sidi, *Multiple Access Protocols: Performance and Analysis,* Springer-Verlag, New York, 1990.

[Rose 1996] M. Rose, *The Simple Book: An Introduction to Internet Management, Revised Second Edition,* Prentice Hall, Englewood Cliffs, NJ, 1996.

[Rosenberg 1999] J. Rosenberg and Henning Schulzrinne, "The IETF Internet telephony architecture and protocols," *IEEE Network Magazine,* Vol. 13, pp.18–23, May/June 1999.

[Ross 1995] K. W. Ross, *Multiservice Loss Models for Broadband Telecommunication Networks,* Springer, Berlin, 1995.

[Ross 1997] K. W. Ross, "Hash-Routing for Collections of Shared Web Caches," *IEEE Network Magazine,* Nov.–Dec. 1997.

[Ross 1998] K. W. Ross, Distribution of Stored Information in the Web, An Online Tutorial, http://www.eurecom.fr/~ross/CacheTutorial/DistTutorial.html, 1998.

[RSA 1978] R. L. Rivest, A. Shamir, and L. M. Adleman, "A method for obtaining digital signatures and public-key cryptosystems," *Communications of the ACM,* 21(2): 120–126, Feb. 1978.

[RSA 1997] RSA Data Security Inc, "DES RSA Challenge Cracked: Government encryption standard DES takes a fall," http://www.rsa.com/des/

[RSA Key 1999] RSA Laboratories, "How large a key should be used in RSA?" http://www.rsa.com/rsalabs/faq/html/3-1-5.html

[RSA FAQ 1999] RSA Laboratories, "RSA Labs FAQ," http://www.rsa.com/rsalabs/faq/index.html

[RSA Fast 1999] RSA Laboratories, "How fast is RSA," http://www.rsa.com/rsalabs/faq/html/3-1-2.html

[Rubenstein 1998] D. Rubenstein, J. Kurose, D. Towsley "Real-Time Reliable Multicast Using Proactive Forward Error Correction," *Proceedings of NOSSDAV '98* (Cambridge, UK, July 1998). http://gaia.cs.umass.edu/pub/Rubenst98:proact.ps.gz

[Saydam 1996] T. Saydam and T. Magedanz, "From Networks and Network Management into Service and Service Management," *Journal of Networks and System Management,* Vol. 4, No. 4 (Dec. 1996), pp. 345–348.

[Schneier 1995] B. Schneier, *Applied Cryptography: Protocols, Algorithms, and Source Code in C,* John Wiley and Sons, 1995.

[Schulzrinne 1997] H. Schulzrinne, "A Comprehensive Multimedia Control Architecture for the Internet," *NOSSDAV'97 (Network and Operating System Support for Digital Audio and Video),* St. Louis, Missouri; May 19, 1997. http://www.cs.columbia.edu/~hgs/papers/Schu9705_Comprehensive.ps.gz

[Schulzrinne 1999] Henning Schulzrinne's RTP site, http://www.cs.columbia.edu/~hgs/rtp/, 1999.

[Schurmann 1996] G. Schurmann, "Multimedia Mail," *Multimedia Systems,* ACM Press, pp. 281–295, Oct. 1996.

[Schwartz 1980] M. Schwartz, *Information, Transmission, Modulation, and Noise,* McGraw Hill, NY, NY 1980.

[Schwartz 1982] M. Schwartz, "Performance Analysis of the SNA Virtual Route Pacing Control," *IEEE Transactions on Communications,* Vol. COM-30, No. 1, pp. 172–184, Jan. 1982.

[Shacham 1990] N. Shacham, P. McKenney, "Packet Recovery in High-Speed Networks Using Coding and Buffer Management," *Proc. IEEE Infocom Conference* (San Francisco, 1990), pp. 124–131.

[Shenker 1990] S. Shenker, L. Zhang, and D. D. Clark, "Some Observations on the Dynamics of a Congestion Control Algorithm," *ACM Computer Communications Review,* Vol. 20, No. 4, pp. 30–39, Oct. 1990.

[Semeria 1997] C. Semeria and T. Maufer, "Introduction to IP Multicast Routing," WWW http://www.3com.com/nsc/501303.html.

[Setco 1999] SETCo LLC Website, http://www.setco.org/

[Sharma 1997] Puneet Sharma, Deborah Estrin, Sally Floyd, Van Jacobson, "Scalable Timers for Soft State Protocols," *Proc. IEEE Infocom97 Conference,* Apr. 1997 (Kobe, Japan).

[Sidor 1998] D. Sidor, "TMN Standards: Satisfying Today's Needs While Preparing for Tomorrow," *IEEE Communications Magazine,* Vol. 36, No. 3 (Mar. 1998), pp. 54–64.

[Singh 1999] S. Singh, *The Code Book: The Evolution of Secrecy from Mary, Queen of Scots to Quantum Cryptography,* Doubleday Press, 1999.

[Solari 1997] S. J. Solari, *Digital Video and Audio Compression,* McGraw Hill, NY, NY, 1997.

[Solensky 1996] F. Solensky, "IPv4 Address Lifetime Expectations," *in IPng: Internet Protocol Next Generation* (S. Bradner, A. Mankin, ed), Addison-Wesley, Reading, MA, 1996.

[Spragins 1991] J. D. Spragins, *Telecommunications Protocols and Design,* Addison-Wesley, Reading, MA, 1991.

[Spurgeon 1999] C. Spurgeon, "Charles Spurgeon's Ethernet Web Site," http://wwwhost.ots.utexas.edu/ethernet/ethernet-home.html

[Squid] Squid Web Proxy Cache, http://squid.nlanr.net/Squid/

[Stallings 1993] W. Stallings, *SNMP, SNMP v2, and CMIP The Practical Guide to Network Management Standards,* Addison-Wesley, Reading, MA, 1993.

[Stallings 1999] W. Stallings, *SNMP, SNMPv2, SNMPv3, and RMON 1 and 2,* Addison-Wesley, Reading, MA, 1999.

[Stevens 1990] W. R. Stevens, *Unix Network Programming,* Prentice-Hall, Englewood Cliffs, NJ.

[Stevens 1994] W. R. Stevens, *TCP/IP Illustrated, Vol. 1: The Protocols,* Addison-Wesley, Reading, MA, 1994.

[Strayer 1992] W. T. Strayer, B. Dempsey, A. Weaver, *XTP: The Xpress Transfer Protocol,* Addison-Wesley, Reading, MA, 1992.

[Sunshine 1978] C. Sunshine and Y. K. Dalal, "Connection Management in Transport Protocols," *Computer Networks,* North-Holland, Amsterdam, 1978.

[Talpade 95] Talpade, R., Ammar, M. H., "Single Connection Emulation (SCE): An Architecture for Providing a Reliable Multicast Transport Service," *Proceedings of the IEEE International Conference on Distributed Computing Systems,* Vancouver, BC, Canada, June 1995. ftp://ftp.cc.gatech.edu/pub/coc/tech_reports/1994/GIT-CC-94-47.ps.Z

[Thaler 1997] D. Thaler and C. Ravishankar, "Distributed Center-Location Algorithms," *IEEE Journal on Selected Areas in Communications,* Vol. 15, No. 3, pp. 291–303, Apr. 1997.

[Thinplanet] Thinplanet homepage, http://www.thinplanet.com/

[Thomson 1997] K. Thomson, G. Miller, R. Wilder, "Wide Area Traffic Patterns and Characteristics," *IEEE Network Magazine,* Dec. 1997.

[Thottan 1998] M. Thottan and C. Ji, "Proactive Anomaly Detection Using Distributed Intelligent Agents," *IEEE Network Magazine,* Vol. 12, No. 5 (Sept./Oct. 1998), pp. 21–28.

[Tobagi 1990] F. Tobagi, "Fast Packet Switch Architectures for Broadband Integrated Networks," *Proc. of the IEEE,* Vol. 78, No. 1, pp. 133–167.

[Turner 1986] J. Turner, "New Directions in Communications (or Which Way to the Information Age?)," *Proceedings of the Zürich Seminar on Digital Communication,* pp. 25–32, Mar. 1986.

[Turner 1988] J. S. Turner "Design of a Broadcast packet switching network," *IEEE Transactions on Communications,* pp. 734–743, June 1988.

[Turner 1999] D. A. Turner and K. W. Ross, "Continuous-Media Internet E-Mail: Infrastructure Inadequacies and Solutions," http://www.eurecom.fr/~ross/MMNetLab.htm

[Utah 1999] State of Utah Department of Commerce, "Utah Digital Signature Program," http://www.commerce.state.ut.us/digsig/dsmain.htm

[UUnet 1999] UUnet, "Service Level Agreement," http://www.uk.uu.net/support/sla/

[Valloppillil 1997] V. Valloppillil and K. W. Ross, "Cache Array Routing Protocol," Internet Draft, <draft-vinod-carp-v1-03.txt>, June 1997

[Verisign 1999] Verisign home page, http://www.verisign.com/

[Viterbi 1995] A. Viterbi, *CDMA: Principles of Spread Spectrum Communication,* Addison-Wesley, Reading, MA, 1995).

[W3C 1995] The World Wide Web Consortium, "A Little History of the World Wide Web," 1995. http://www.w3.org/History.html

[Wakeman 1992] Ian Wakeman, Jon Crowcroft, Zheng Wang, and Dejan Sirovica, "Layering Considered Harmful," *IEEE Network,* Jan. 1992, p. 7.

[Waldvogel 1997] M. Waldvogel et al., "Scalable High Speed IP Routing Lookup," *Proc. 1997 ACM SIGCOMM Conference* (Cannes, France, Sept. 1997). http://www.acm.org/sigs/sigcomm/sigcomm97/papers/p182.html

[Wall 1980] D. Wall, "Mechanisms for Broadcast and Selective Broadcast," PhD dissertation, Stanford U., June 1980.

[Waung 1998] W. Waung, "Wireless Mobile Data Networking The CDPD Approach," Wireless Data Forum, 1998. http://www2.wirelessdata.org/public/whatis/whatis.html

[Waxman 1988] B. M. Waxman, "Routing of multipoint connections," *IEEE Journal on Selected Areas in Communications,* Vol. 6, No. 9, pp. 1617–1622, Dec. 1988.

[Web ProForum 1999] Web ProForum, "Tutorial on H.323," 1999, http://www.webproforum.com/h323/index.html

[Wei 1993] L. Wei and D. Estrin, "A comparison of multicast trees and algorithms," TR USC-CD-93-560, Dept. Computer Science, University of California, Sept. 1993.

[Wireless 1998] Wireless Data Forum, "CDPD System Specification Release 1.1," 1998. http://www2.wirelessdata.org/public/specification/index.html

[Wood 1999] L. Wood, "Lloyds Satellites Constellations," http://www.ee.surrey.ac.uk/Personal/L.Wood/constellations/iridium.html

[Yahoo-MIME 1999] Yahoo MIME WWW page, http://dir.yahoo.com/ Computers_and_Internet/Multimedia/MIME/

[Yeager 1996] N. J. Yeager and R. E. McGrath, *Web Server Technology,* Morgan Kaufmann Publishers, San Francisco, 1996.

[Zegura 1997] E. Zegura, K. Calvert, M. Donahoo, "A Quantitative Comparison of Graph-based Models for Internet Topology," *IEEE/ACM Transactions on Networking,* Vol. 5, No. 6, Dec. 1997. http://www.cc.gatech.edu/fac/ Ellen.Zegura/papers/ton-model.ps.gz. See also http://www.cc.gatech.edu/ projects/gtim for a software package that generates networks with realistic structure.

[Zhang 1991] L. Zhang, S. Shenker, and D. D. Clark, "Observations on the Dynamics of a Congestion Control Algorithm: The Effects of Two Way Traffic," *Proc. ACM SIGCOMM '91,* Zürich, 1991. http://www1.acm.org/pubs/ citations/proceedings/comm/115992/p133-zhang/

[Zhang 1993] L. Zhang, S. Deering, D. Estrin, S. Shenker, D. Zappala, "RSVP: A New Resource Reservation Protocol," *IEEE Network Magazine,* Vol. 7, No. 9 (Sept. 1993), pp. 8–18.

[Zhang 1998] L. Zhang, R. Yavatkar, Fred Baker, Peter Ford, Kathleen Nichols, M. Speer, Y. Bernet, "A Framework for Use of RSVP with Diff-serv Networks", <draft-ietf-diffserv-rsvp-01.txt>, 11/20/1998. Work in progress.

[Ziff-Davis 1998] Ziff-Davis Publishing, "Ted Nelson: Hypertext pioneer," 1998. http://www.zdnet.com/zdtv/screensavers_story/0,3656,2127396-2102293,00.html

[Zimmerman 1999] P. Zimmerman, "Why do you need PGP?" http:// www.pgpi.org/doc/whypgp/en/

Index